IMPORTANT!
DO NOT DISCARD!

P9-APL-750

WHAT'S INSIDE:
An innovative approach to teaching and learning
Principles of Management

Student Tested, Faculty Approved

Portable Review & Prep Tools

CHUCK WILLIAMS | MGMT 2008 Edition

CONGRATULATIONS!

This is your access to the MGMT website
(www.mgmt4me.com) where you'll find:

- Cell phone downloads
- Interactive quizzes
- Interactive Self-Assessments
- Videos
- Flashcards
- Games

TEAR OUT CARD MISSING?

Access to this web site is only available with the purchase of new textbooks. If the tear-out portion of this card is missing or if the access code has already been used, you will not have access. *Access codes can be used only once and are not transferable.*

HOW TO REGISTER YOUR ACCESS CODE:

1. Launch a web browser and go to **www.mgmt4me.com** and click on the "student" link

2. Click on the "register" button to enter your access code

3. Enter your access code *exactly* as it appears below and follow the online prompts to create an account.

4. Record your User ID and password below and store this card in a secure location for future visits.

ACCESS CODE:

PP8XW43P3FC7H4

DURATION: 1 SEMESTER

EMAIL: **PASSWORD:**

NOTE: The duration of your access to the multimedia learning tools begins as soon as registration is complete.
For technical support, visit our web site at **academic.cengage.com/support**

JDuffy2 @eastern.Edu

Emergencies:
JDuffy@CRCHealth.com
267-229-2776

AN INNOVATIVE APPROACH TO TEACHING AND LEARNING

www.mgmt4me.com

ONLINE DELIVERY

STUDENTS ACCESS COURSE MATERIALS WHEN AND WHERE THEY CAN LEARN BEST.

M G M T

MGMT 2008 Edition
Chuck Williams
University of the Pacific

President:
Eduardo Moura

VP/Editorial Director:
Jack W. Calhoun

VP/Director of Marketing:
Bill Hendee

Editor-In-Chief:
Melissa Acuña

Director:
Neil Marquardt

Executive Editor:
Joe Sabatino

Executive Marketing Manager:
Kimberly Kanakes

Marketing Manager:
Clint Kernan

Developmental Editor:
Jamie Bryant, B-books

Production Director:
Amy McGuire, B-books

Editorial Assistant:
Ruth Belanger

Sr. Marketing Coordinator:
Sarah Rose

Marketing Communications Manager:
Jim Overly

Manager, Editorial Media:
John Barans

Technology Project Editor:
Kristen Meere

Sr. Manufacturing Coordinator:
Doug Wilke

Production House:
B-books

Printer:
Quebecor World
Dubuque, Iowa

Sr. Art Director:
Tippy McIntosh

Internal & Cover Designer:
Ke Design

Photography Manager:
Deanna Ettinger

Photo Researcher:
Susan van Etten

Library of Congress Control Number:
2007935608

For more information about our products, contact us at:

Cengage Learning
Customer & Sales Support
1-800-354-9706

South-Western
5191 Natorp Boulevard
Mason, OH 45040
USA

MGMT ENTER
Brief Contents

INTRODUCTION TO MANAGEMENT 2

4 Ethics and Social Responsibility 60

② PLANNING 78

5 Planning and Decision Making 78

6 Organizational Strategy 96

7 Innovation and Change 116

8 Global Management 134

3

ORGANIZING 154

9 Designing Adaptive Organizations 154

10 Managing Teams 174

4

LEADING 234

15 Managing Communication 274

CONTROLLING 292

16 Control 292

17 Managing Information 310

18 Managing Service and Manufacturing Operations 328

MANAGEMENT

What Is Management?

Management issues are fundamental to any organization: How do we plan to get things done, organize the company to be efficient and effective, lead and motivate employees, and put in place controls to make sure our plans are followed and our goals are met? Good management is basic to starting a business, growing a business, and maintaining a business once it has achieved some measure of success.

So think about this: Mistake #1. A high-level bank manager reduces a marketing manager to tears by angrily criticizing her in front of others for a mistake that wasn't hers.[1] Mistake #2. Guidant waited for three years, forty-five device failures, and two patient deaths before recalling 50,000 defective heart defibrillators, 77 percent of which were already implanted in patients.[2]

Ah, bad managers and bad management. Is it any wonder that companies pay management consultants nearly $150 billion a year for advice on basic management issues, such as how to lead people effectively, organize the company efficiently, and manage large-scale projects and processes?[3] This textbook will help you understand some of the basic issues that management consultants help companies resolve (and it won't cost you billions of dollars).

 After reading the next two sections, you should be able to

1 describe what management is.

2 explain the four functions of management.

Learning Outcomes

1 describe what management is.

2 explain the four functions of management.

3 describe different kinds of managers.

4 explain the major roles and subroles that managers perform in their jobs.

5 explain what companies look for in managers.

6 discuss the top mistakes that managers make in their jobs.

7 describe the transition that employees go through when they are promoted to management.

8 explain how and why companies can create competitive advantage through people.

©Getty Images News

1 Management Is . . .

Many of today's managers got their start welding on the factory floor, clearing dishes off tables, helping customers fit a suit, or wiping up a spill in aisle 3. Similarly, lots of you will start at the bottom and work your way up. There's no better way to get to know your competition, your customers, and your business. But whether you begin your career at the entry level or as a supervisor, your job is not to do the work, but to help others do theirs. **Management** is getting work done through others. Pat Carrigan, a former elementary school principal who became a manager at a General Motors' car parts plant, says, "I've never made a part in my life, and I don't really have any plans to make one. That's not my job. My job is to create an environment where people who do make them can make them right, can make them right the first time, can make them at a competitive cost, and can do so with some sense of responsibility and pride in what they're doing. I don't have to know how to make a part to do any of those things."[4]

Pat Carrigan's description of managerial responsibilities suggests that managers also have to be concerned with efficiency and effectiveness in the work process. **Efficiency** is getting work done with a minimum of effort, expense, or waste.

> **Management** getting work done through others
>
> **Efficiency** getting work done with a minimum of effort, expense, or waste

For example, United Parcel Service, which delivers over 3.5 billion packages a year, has started saving 14 million gallons of fuel per year by using a completely computerized route and load planning system that shows truck loaders where to put packages on the delivery truck (to maximize the number of packages per truck), determines how many packages and stops a driver has and what routes should be taken (to minimize travel time, distances, and fuel costs), and tells drivers exactly where your package is on the truck when they stop in front of your house (to minimize search time at each stop).[5]

By itself, efficiency is not enough to ensure success. Managers must also strive for **effectiveness**, which is accomplishing tasks that help fulfill organizational objectives, such as customer service and satisfaction.

2 Management Functions

Henri Fayol, who was a managing director (CEO) of a large steel company in the early 1900s, was one of the founders of the field of management. You'll learn more about Fayol and management's other key contributors when you read about the history of management in Chapter 2. Based on his 20 years of experience as a CEO, Fayol argued that "the success of an enterprise generally depends much more on the administrative ability of its

perform these management functions well are more successful. For example, the more time that CEOs spend planning, the more profitable their companies are.[9] Over a 25-year period, AT&T found that employees with better planning and decision-making skills were more likely to be promoted into management jobs, to

> EBay succeeds because of CEO Meg Whitman's capabilities as a manager and not because of her ability to write computer code.

leaders than on their technical ability."[6] In other words, eBay, the world's largest online auction company, succeeds because of CEO Meg Whitman's capabilities as a manager and not because of her ability to write computer code.

According to Fayol, to be successful, managers need to perform five managerial functions: planning, organizing, coordinating, commanding, and controlling.[7] Today, though, most management textbooks have dropped the coordinating function and refer to Fayol's commanding function as "leading." Consequently, Fayol's management functions are known today as planning, organizing, leading, and controlling. Studies indicate that managers who

be successful as managers, and to be promoted into upper levels of management.[10]

The evidence is clear. Managers serve their companies well when they plan, organize, lead, and control. (That's why this book is organized around the functions of management.)

Now let's take a closer look at each of the management functions: 2.1 planning, 2.2 organizing, 2.3 leading, and 2.4 controlling.

2.1 Planning

Planning is determining organizational goals and a means for achieving them. As you'll learn in Chapter 5, planning is one of the best ways to improve performance. It encourages people to work harder, to work hard for extended periods, to engage in behaviors directly related to goal accomplishment, and to think of better ways to do their jobs. But most importantly,

Effectiveness accomplishing tasks that help fulfill organizational objectives

Planning (management functions) determining organizational goals and a means for achieving them companies that plan have larger profits and faster growth than companies that don't plan.

For example, the question, "What business are we in?" is at the heart of strategic planning, which you'll learn about in Chapter 6. If you can answer the question, "What business are you in?" in two sentences or less, chances are you have a very clear plan for your business.

Exxon Mobil CEO Rex Tillerson knows precisely what business his company is in—and not in—and he'll tell you so.[11] Same for Google. Even though the company makes money selling search-based Internet advertising, Google says that it is not in the advertising business, but in the business of organizing the world's information.[12] Even Google's $1.65 billion purchase of YouTube adheres to the business Google is in by helping users access and organize video content. *You'll learn more about planning in Chapter 5 on planning and decision making, Chapter 6 on organizational strategy, Chapter 7 on innovation and change, and Chapter 8 on global management.*

2.2 Organizing

Organizing is deciding where decisions will be made, who will do what jobs and tasks, and who will work for whom in the company. Go to Yahoo!'s home page and take a look at the vast number of topics, news, mail, messenger, shopping (from autos and finance to Hot Jobs, music, and real estate), small business, and featured services (downloads, mobile, voice, and per-

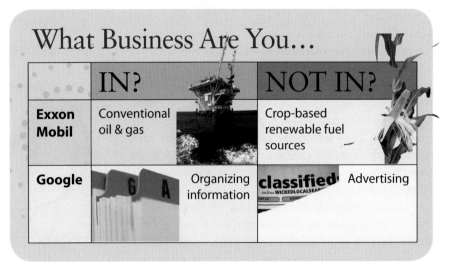

What Business Are You...

	IN?	NOT IN?
Exxon Mobil	Conventional oil & gas	Crop-based renewable fuel sources
Google	Organizing information	Advertising

group supports the entire organization by creating technological capabilities and platforms. Yahoo! CEO Terry Semel says, "We believe having a more customer-focused organization, supported by robust technology, will speed the development of leading-edge experiences for our most valuable audience segments."[13]

You'll learn more about organizing in Chapter 9 on designing organizations, Chapter 10 on managing teams, Chapter 11 on managing human resources, and Chapter 12 on managing individuals and a diverse work force.

2.3 Leading

Our third management function, **leading,** involves inspiring and motivating workers to work hard to achieve organizational goals. When Anne Mulcahy became Xerox's CEO, the company was on the brink of bankruptcy—it was $17.1 billion in debt and had only $154 million in cash. In addition, three years of steeply declining revenues and increasing losses had dropped the

Not all managerial jobs are the same.

sonal websites). How would you organize this vast array of topics and activities? Yahoo! does it with two customer groups, audience and advertiser/publisher, and one technology group. The audience group has responsibility for Yahoo!'s products in search, media, communities, and communications. The advertising/publishing group helps large advertisers and agencies, small- and medium-sized businesses, local advertisers, resellers, and publishers connect with their target customers across the Internet. Finally, the technology

company's stock price from $64 a share to just $4.43. Mulcahy admits that the responsibility of turning the company around frightened her: "Nothing spooked me as much as waking up in the middle of the night and thinking about 96,000 people and

Organizing deciding where decisions will be made, who will do what jobs and tasks, and who will work for whom

Leading inspiring and motivating workers to work hard to achieve organizational goals retirees and what would happen if this thing went south."[14] Still, she took the job.

Mulcahy, who traveled to two and sometimes three cities a day to talk to Xerox managers and employees, implored them to "save each dollar as if it were your own." And at each stop, she reminded them, "Remember, by my calculations, there are [she fills in the number] selling days left in the quarter."[15] Mulcahy said, "One of the things I care most about at Xerox is the morale and motivation at the company. I think it is absolutely critical to being able to deliver results. People have to feel engaged, motivated and feel they are making a contribution to something that is important. I spend the vast majority of my time with customers and employees, and there is nothing more important for any of us to do as leaders than communicate and engage with our two most important constituencies."[16]

Today, as a result of Mulcahy's leadership and the hard work of dedicated Xerox employees, Xerox is back on its feet, having returned to profitability and financial stability.[17] *You'll learn more about leading in Chapter 13 on motivation, Chapter 14 on leadership, and Chapter 15 on managing communication.*

2.4 Controlling

The last function of management, **controlling,** is monitoring progress toward goal achievement and taking corrective action when progress isn't being made. The basic control process involves setting standards to achieve goals, comparing actual performance to those standards, and then making changes to return performance to those standards.

Needing to cut costs (the standard) to restore profitability (the goal), Continental Airlines started giving passengers small cups of their soft drinks instead of an entire can (one corrective action, among many). Company spokesperson Rahsaan Johnson defended the move, saying, "Flight attendants have been telling us that the trash bags they carry were so heavy because of all the [wasted] liquid. We were pouring almost half away."[18] Although Continental will still give entire soft drink cans to customers who request them, serving smaller drinks saves the company $100,000 a year in costs.

You'll learn more about the control function in Chapter 16 on control, Chapter 17 on managing information, and Chapter 18 on managing service and manufacturing operations.

Controlling monitoring progress toward goal achievement and taking corrective action when needed

Top managers executives responsible for the overall direction of the organization

What Do Managers Do?

Not all managerial jobs are the same. The demands and requirements placed on the CEO of Sony are significantly different from those placed on the manager of your local Wendy's restaurant.

After reading the next two sections, you should be able to

3 describe different kinds of managers.

4 explain the major roles and subroles that managers perform in their jobs.

3 Kinds of Managers

As shown in Exhibit 1.1, there are four kinds of managers, each with different jobs and responsibilities: **3.1 top managers, 3.2 middle managers, 3.3 first-line managers,** and **3.4 team leaders.**

3.1 Top Managers

Top managers hold positions like chief executive officer (CEO), chief operating officer (COO), chief financial officer (CFO), and chief information officer (CIO), and are responsible for the overall direction of the organization. Top managers have the following responsibilities.[19] First, they are responsible for creating a context for change. In fact, the CEOs of Walt Disney, Fannie Mae, Boeing, Morgan Stanley, American International Group, Merck, and Pfizer were all fired within a year's time precisely because they had not moved fast enough to bring about significant changes in their companies. Indeed, in both Europe and the United States, 35 percent of all CEOs are eventually fired because of their failure to successfully change their companies.[20] Creating a context for change includes forming a long-range vision or mission for the company.

Once that vision or mission is set, then the second responsibility of top managers is to develop employees' commitment to and ownership of the company's performance. That is, top managers are responsible for getting employee buy-in. Third, top managers are responsible for creating a positive organizational culture through lan-

Exhibit 1.1

What the Four Kinds of Managers Do

Jobs	Responsibilities
TOP Managers CEO CIO COO Vice President CFO Corporate Heads	 change commitment culture environment
Middle Managers General Manager Plant Manager Regional Manager Divisional Manager	 resources objectives coordination subunit performance strategy implementation
First-Line Managers Office Manager Shift Supervisor Department Manager	 nonmanagerial worker supervision teaching and training scheduling facilitation
Team Leaders Team Leader Team Contact Group Facilitator	 facilitation external relationships internal relationships

guage and action. Top managers impart company values, strategies, and lessons through what they do and say to others, both inside and outside the company. Above all, no matter what they communicate, it's critical for CEOs to send and reinforce clear, consistent messages.[21] A former *Fortune* 500 CEO said, "I tried to [use] exactly the same words every time so that I didn't produce a lot of, 'Last time you said this, this time you said that.' You've got to say the same thing over and over and over."[22]

Finally, top managers are responsible for monitoring their business environments. This means that top managers must closely monitor customer needs, competitors' moves, and long-term business, economic, and social trends.

3.2 Middle Managers

Middle managers hold positions like plant manager, regional manager, or divisional manager. They are re-sponsible for setting objectives consistent with top management's goals and for planning and implementing subunit strategies for achieving those objectives.[23] One specific middle management responsibility is to plan and allocate resources to meet objectives. Another major responsibility is to coordinate and link groups, departments, and divisions within a company. After a hurricane destroyed five miles of railroad tracks outside New Orleans, Jeff McCracken, a chief engineer at Norfolk Southern, consulted with three bridge companies, and managed a team of 100 employees and dozens of engineers who, by sleeping in campers and working around the clock, rebuilt the tracks in less than a week. McCracken said, "It was a

Middle managers managers responsible for setting objectives consistent with top management's goals and for planning and implementing subunit strategies for achieving these objectives

Feats of Daring Duet

Trusting that his 61,000 employees could dramatically increase product innovation at Whirlpool appliances, CEO David Whitman told them to come up with new ideas, tell their bosses about their ideas, and, if their bosses wouldn't listen, bring their new product ideas directly to him. Employees flocked to an in-house Web site featuring a course on innovation and a list of all the new suggestions and ideas, racking up 300,000 "hits" on the site each month. Today, revenue from innovative products has quadrupled. And instead of cutting prices to maintain sales, Whirlpool's prices are now rising 5 percent per year because customers are willing to pay more for its innovative products, such as the Duet washer and dryer.[24]

colossal job that took more than 400 moves with heavy equipment." But, McCracken was happiest about "working with people from all parts of the company—and getting the job done without anyone getting hurt."[25]

A third responsibility of middle management is to monitor and manage the performance of the subunits and individual managers who report to them. Graeme Betts is the manager of the Southwest region for Lloyds Pharmacy in England. While Betts works with people at all levels, from healthcare assistants to board directors, he spends most of his time with the nine area managers who report to him. He monitors and manages the performance of his area managers and, in turn, the store managers who report to them.[26]

Finally, middle managers are also responsible for implementing the changes or strategies generated by top managers. Wal-Mart's strategy reflects its advertising slogan, "Always Low Prices." When Wal-Mart began selling groceries in its new 200,000-square-foot supercenters, it made purchasing manager Brian Wilson responsible for buy-

First-line managers managers who train and supervise the performance of nonmanagerial employees who are directly responsible for producing the company's products or services

ing perishable goods more cheaply than Wal-Mart's competitors. When small produce suppliers had trouble meeting Wal-Mart's needs, Wilson worked closely with them and connected them to RetailLink, Wal-Mart's computer network, "which allows our suppliers immediate access to all information needed to help run the business." Over time, these steps helped the produce suppliers lower costs and deliver the enormous quantities of fresh fruits and vegetables that Wal-Mart's supercenters need.[27] They also helped Wal-Mart become the world's largest grocer.[28]

3.3 First-Line Managers

First-line managers hold positions like office manager, shift supervisor, or department manager. The primary responsibility of first-line managers is to manage the performance of entry-level employees, who are directly responsible for producing a company's goods and services. Thus, first-line managers are the only managers who don't supervise other managers. First-line managers have the following responsibilities.

First-line managers encourage, monitor, and reward the performance of their workers. They also teach entry-level employees how to do their jobs. Damian Mogavero's company, Avero LLC, helps restaurants analyze sales data for each member of a restaurant's wait staff. Restaurant managers who use these data, says Mogavero, will often take their top-selling server to lunch each week as a reward. The best managers, however, will also take their poorest-selling servers out to lunch to talk about what they can do to improve their performance.[29]

First-line managers also make detailed schedules and operating plans based on middle management's intermediate-range plans. In fact, in contrast to the long-term plans of top managers (three to five years out) and the intermediate plans of middle managers (6 to 18 months out), first-line managers engage in plans and actions that typically produce results within two weeks.[30] For example, consider the typical convenience store manager (e.g., 7-Eleven) who starts the day by driving past competitors' stores to inspect their gasoline prices and then checks the outside of his or her store for anything that might need maintenance, such as burned-out lights or signs, or restocking, like windshield washer fluid and paper towels. Then comes an inside check, where the manager determines what needs to be done for that day (Are there enough coffee and donuts for breakfast or enough sandwiches for lunch?). Once the day is planned, the manager turns to weekend orders. After accounting for the weather (hot or cold) and the sales trends at the same time last year, the manager makes sure the store will have enough beer, soft drinks, and Sunday papers on hand. Finally, the manager looks 7 to 10 days ahead for hiring needs. Because of strict hiring procedures (basic math tests, drug tests, and background checks), it can take that long to hire new employees. Said one convenience store manager, "I have to continually interview, even if I am fully staffed."[31]

3.4 Team Leaders

The fourth kind of manager is a team leader. This relatively new kind of management job developed as companies shifted to self-managing teams, which, by definition, have no formal supervisor. In traditional management hierarchies, first-line managers are responsible for the performance of nonmanagerial employees and have the authority to hire and fire workers, make job assignments, and control resources. Team leaders play a very different role because in this new structure, teams now perform nearly all of the functions performed by first-line managers under traditional hierarchies.[32] Instead of directing individuals' work, **team leaders** facilitate team activities toward goal accomplishment. Team leaders who fail to understand this key difference often struggle in their roles. A team leader at Texas Instruments said, "I didn't buy into teams, partly because there was no clear plan on what I was supposed to do. . . . I never let the operators [team members] do any scheduling or any ordering of parts because that was mine. I figured as long as I had that, I had a job."[33]

Team leaders fulfill the following responsibilities.[34] First, team leaders are responsible for facilitating team performance. This doesn't mean team leaders are responsible for team performance. They aren't. The team is. Team leaders help their team members plan and schedule work, learn to solve problems, and work effectively with each other. Management consultant Franklin Jonath says, "The idea is for the team leader to be at the service of the group. It should be clear that the team members own the outcome. The leader is there to bring intellectual, emotional, and spiritual resources to the team. Through his or her actions, the leader should be able to show the others how to think about the work that they're doing in the context of their lives."[35]

Second, team leaders are responsible for managing external relationships. Team leaders act as the bridge or liaison between their teams and other teams, departments, and divisions in a company. For example, if a member of Team A complains about the quality of Team B's work, Team A's leader needs to initiate a meeting with Team B's leader. Together, these team leaders are responsible for getting members of both teams to work together to solve the problem. If it's done right, the problem is solved without involving company management or blaming members of the other team.[36]

Team leaders managers responsible for facilitating team activities toward goal accomplishment

Even first-line managers perform the four functions of management.

©Getty Images News

Third, team leaders are responsible for internal team relationships. Getting along with others is much more important in team structures because team members can't get work done without the help of their teammates. You will learn more about teams in Chapter 10.

4 Managerial Roles

So far, we have described managerial work by focusing on the functions of management and by examining the four kinds of managerial jobs. Although those are valid and accurate ways of categorizing managerial work, if you followed managers around as they performed their jobs, you probably would not use the terms *planning, organizing, leading,* and *controlling* to describe what they do.

In fact, that's exactly the conclusion that management researcher Henry Mintzberg came to when he observed five American CEOs. Mintzberg spent a week "shadowing" each of the CEOs and analyzing their mail, their conversations, and their actions. Mintzberg concluded that managers fulfill three major roles while performing their jobs[37]:

- interpersonal roles
- informational roles
- decisional roles

In other words, managers talk to people, gather and give information, and make decisions. Furthermore, as shown in Exhibit 1.2, these three major roles can be subdivided into 10 subroles. *Let's examine each major role— **4.1 interpersonal**, **4.2 informational**, and **4.3 decisional** roles—and their 10 subroles.*

Figurehead role the interpersonal role managers play when they perform ceremonial duties

Leader role the interpersonal role managers play when they motivate and encourage workers to accomplish organizational objectives

Liaison role the interpersonal role managers play when they deal with people outside their units

4.1 Interpersonal Roles

More than anything else, management jobs are people-intensive. Estimates vary with the level of management, but most managers spend between two-thirds and four-fifths of their time in face-to-face communication with others.[38] If you're a loner, or if you consider dealing with

people a pain, then you may not be cut out for management work. In fulfilling the interpersonal role of management, managers perform three subroles: figurehead, leader, and liaison.

In the **figurehead role,** managers perform ceremonial duties like greeting company visitors, speaking at the opening of a new facility, or representing the company at a community luncheon to support local charities. In the **leader role,** managers motivate and encourage workers to accomplish organizational objectives. At J.M. Smucker, managers regularly thank employees with celebratory lunches and gift certificates. Tonie Williams, director of marketing for peanut butter, says she's been thanked more in her two years at Smucker than she was in her nine years at Nestlé, Kraft, and Procter & Gamble combined.[39] Smucker's has been on *Fortune* magazine's annual list of the top 100 places to work in the United States since the list began.[40]

In the **liaison role,** managers deal with people outside their units. Studies consistently indicate that man-

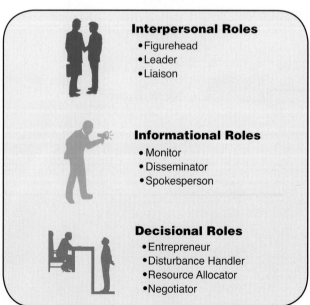

Exhibit 1.2

Mintzberg's Managerial Roles

Interpersonal Roles
- Figurehead
- Leader
- Liaison

Informational Roles
- Monitor
- Disseminator
- Spokesperson

Decisional Roles
- Entrepreneur
- Disturbance Handler
- Resource Allocator
- Negotiator

agers spend as much time with "outsiders" as they do with their own subordinates and their own bosses.[41]

4.2 Informational Roles

Not only do managers spend most of their time in face-to-face contact with others, but they spend much of it obtaining and sharing information. Indeed, Mintzberg found that the managers in his study spent 40 percent of their time giving and getting information from others. In this regard, management can be viewed as processing information, gathering information by scanning the business environment and listening to others in face-to-face conversations, and then sharing that information with people inside and outside the company. Mintzberg described three informational subroles: monitor, disseminator, and spokesperson.

In the **monitor role,** managers scan their environment for information, actively contact others for information, and, because of their personal contacts, receive a great deal of unsolicited information. Besides receiving firsthand information, managers monitor their environment by reading local newspapers and the *Wall Street Journal* to keep track of customers, competitors, and technological changes that may affect their businesses. Now, managers can also take advantage of electronic monitoring and distribution services that track the news wires (Associated Press, Reuters, and so on) for stories related to their businesses.

Because of their numerous personal contacts and their access to subordinates, managers are often hubs for the distribution of critical information. In the **disseminator role,** managers share the information they have collected with their subordinates and others in the company. Although there will never be a complete substitute for face-to-face dissemination of information, the primary methods of communication in large companies are email and voice mail. John Chambers, Cisco's CEO, says that 90 percent of his communication with employees is through email and voice mail. Says Chambers, "If you don't have the ability to interface with customers, employees, and suppliers, you can't manage your business."[42]

In contrast to the disseminator role, in which managers distribute information to employees inside the company, in the **spokesperson role,** managers share information with people outside their departments and companies. One of the most common ways CEOs serve as spokespeople for their companies is at annual meetings with company shareholders or the board of directors. For example, at a Microsoft annual shareholder meeting, CEO Steve Ballmer told investors that Microsoft intended to offer its own Internet search service and that, although

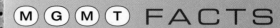

MGMT FACTS

Connect to Your Business

These services deliver customized electronic newspapers that include only stories on topics the managers specify:

√ Business Wire (http://www.businesswire.com) offers services such as IndustryTrak, which monitors and distributes daily news headlines from major industries (e.g., automotive, banking and financial, health, high tech).

√ CyberAlert (http://www.cyberalert.com) keeps round-the-clock track of news stories in categories chosen by each subscriber.

√ FNS NewsClips Online (http://www.news-clips.com) provides subscribers daily electronic news clips from more than 5,000 online news sites.[43]

Microsoft was late to the search engine business, "We will catch up, and we will surpass" Google and Yahoo in the Internet search and advertising business.[44]

4.3 Decisional Roles

Mintzberg found that obtaining and sharing information is not an end in itself. Obtaining and sharing information with people inside and outside the company is useful to managers because it helps them make good decisions. According to Mintzberg, managers engage in four decisional subroles: entrepreneur, disturbance handler, resource allocator, and negotiator.

In the **entrepreneur role,** managers adapt themselves, their subordinates, and their units to change. Veterans Affairs (VA) hospitals had long had a reputation for red tape, inefficiency, and second class medical treatment, but today they rank as some of the best in the country. Fifteen years ago, the VA's leadership instituted a culture of accountability and change aimed at

Monitor role the informational role managers play when they scan their environment for information

Disseminator role the informational role managers play when they share information with others in their departments or companies

Spokesperson role the informational role managers play when they share information with people outside their departments or companies

Entrepreneur role the decisional role managers play when they adapt themselves, their subordinates, and their units to change improving its entire system. Doctors, nurses, staffers, and administrators met regularly to review possible improvements. After a VA nurse noticed that rental car companies used hand-held barcode scanners to check in returned cars, she suggested using barcodes on patients' ID bracelets and their bottled medicines. Today, the VA's barcode scanners are tied to an electronic records system that prevents nurses from handing out the wrong medicines and automatically alerts the hospital pharmacy to possibly harmful drug interactions or dangerous patient allergies.[45]

In the **disturbance handler role,** managers respond to pressures and problems so severe that they demand immediate attention and action. Managers often play the role of disturbance handler when the board of a failing company hires a new CEO, who is charged with turning the company around. After Ford Motor Company's market share shrank from 25 to 16 percent and the company lost $7 billion in nine months, Alan Mulally came from Boeing to become Ford's new CEO. Mulally quickly ar-

they will get. For instance, E-Trade Financial, which is known for its online stock trading accounts, increased its marketing budget by $46 million to make potential customers more aware of its additional banking, loan, and mortgage services.[47] At E-Trade, top managers acted as resource allocators by changing budgets.

In the **negotiator role,** managers negotiate schedules, projects, goals, outcomes, resources, and employee raises. When Sprint bought Nextel (another cell phone company), the Federal Communications Commission required it to buy new radios for police and firefighters because its cell phone tower transmissions were interfering with emergency service communications in hundreds of locations. Sprint Nextel, which will spend $2.8 billion to fix the problem, has, for instance, been negotiating with law-enforcement agencies in Maryland and Washington to replace 35,000 radios. It took Sprint a year to negotiate a $609,000 deal with the city of Fairfax, Virginia, just to develop plans to replace its

... MANAGERS DECIDE WHO WILL GET WHAT RESOURCES AND HOW MUCH OF EACH RESOURCE THEY WILL GET.

ranged $23.5 billion in financing to cover the losses. He plans to cut costs by reducing the number of cars Ford produces, standardizing the use of shared parts across Ford vehicles, and laying off half of Ford's 82,000 factory workers. Mulally said, "I've seen this movie before [at Boeing]. Some very good and loyal people are going to leave this company between now and next summer, and that's going to be tough on everyone. [But,] As demoralizing as a slide down may be, the ride back up is infinitely more exhilarating."[46]

In the **resource allocator role,** managers decide who will get what resources and how much of each resource

Disturbance handler role the decisional role managers play when they respond to severe problems that demand immediate action

Resource allocator role the decisional role managers play when they decide who gets what resources

Negotiator role the decisional role managers play when they negotiate schedules, projects, goals, outcomes, resources, and employee raises

Resource Allocation

Cadillac Style

©Susan Van Etten

Hoping to revive sales of its luxury cars, top managers at General Motors acted as resource allocators by redirecting long-term investment of $4 billion to the company's Cadillac brand. Put in perspective, that means that executives invested nearly 10 percent of GM's total capital budget in a division that accounts for only 4 percent of GM sales.[48]

radios.[49] Negotiating, as you can see from Sprint's dilemma, is a key to success and a basic part of managerial work.

What Does It Take to Be a Manager?

I didn't have the slightest idea what my job was. I walked in giggling and laughing because I had been promoted and had no idea what principles or style to be guided by. After the first day, I felt like I had run into a brick wall. (Sales Representative #1)

Suddenly, I found myself saying, boy, I can't be responsible for getting all that revenue. I don't have the time. Suddenly you've got to go from [taking care of] yourself and say now I'm the manager, and what does a manager do? It takes a while thinking about it for it to really hit you . . . a manager gets things done through other people. That's a very, very hard transition to make.[50] (Sales Representative #2)

The statements above come from two star sales representatives, who, on the basis of their superior performance, were promoted to the position of sales manager. As their comments indicate, at first they did not feel confident about their ability to do their jobs as managers. Like most new managers, these sales managers suddenly realized that the knowledge, skills, and abilities that led to success early in their careers (and were probably responsible for their promotion into the ranks of management) would not necessarily help them succeed as managers. As sales representatives, they were responsible only for managing their own performance. But as sales managers, they were now directly responsible for supervising all of the sales representatives in their sales territories. Furthermore, they were now directly accountable for whether those sales representatives achieved their sales goals.

If performance in nonmanagerial jobs doesn't necessarily prepare you for a managerial job, then what does it take to be a manager?

After reading the next three sections, you should be able to

5 explain what companies look for in managers.

6 discuss the top mistakes that managers make in their jobs.

7 describe the transition that employees go through when they are promoted to management.

5 What Companies Look for in Managers

When companies look for employees who would be good managers, they look for individuals who have technical skills, human skills, conceptual skills, and the motivation to manage.[51] Exhibit 1.3 shows the relative importance of these four skills to the jobs of team leaders, first-line managers, middle managers, and top managers.

Technical skills are the ability to apply the specialized procedures, techniques, and knowledge required to get the job done. For the sales managers described above, technical skills are the ability to find new sales prospects, develop accurate sales pitches based on customer needs, and close the sale. For a nurse supervisor, technical skills include being able to insert an IV or operate a crash cart if a patient goes into cardiac arrest.

Technical skills are most important for team leaders and lower-level managers because they supervise the workers who produce products or serve customers. Team leaders and first-line managers need technical knowledge and skills to train new employees and help employees

> **Technical skills** the ability to apply the specialized procedures, techniques, and knowledge required to get the job done

Exhibit 1.3
Management Skills

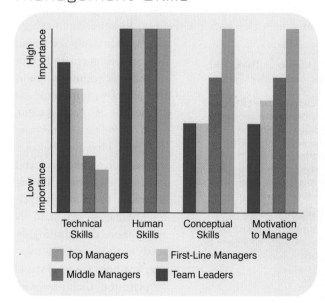

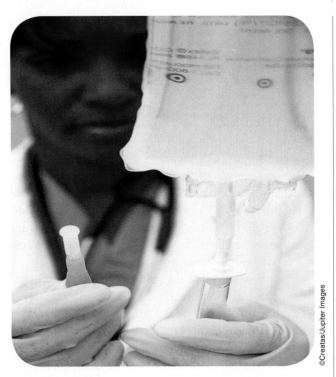
©Creatas/Jupiter Images

solve problems. Technical knowledge and skills are also needed to troubleshoot problems that employees can't handle. Technical skills become less important as managers rise through the managerial ranks, but they are still important.

people, but that percentage increases to 63 percent for middle managers and 78 percent for top managers.[52]

Conceptual skills are the ability to see the organization as a whole, to understand how the different parts of the company affect each other, and to recognize how the company fits into or is affected by its external environment, such as the local community, social and economic forces, customers, and the competition. Good managers have to be able to recognize, understand, and reconcile multiple complex problems and perspectives. In other words, managers have to be smart! In fact, intelligence makes so much difference for managerial performance that managers with above-average intelligence typically outperform managers of average intelligence by approximately 48 percent.[53] Clearly, companies need to be careful to promote smart workers into management. Conceptual skills increase in importance as managers rise through the management hierarchy.

Good management involves much more than intelligence, however. For example, making the department genius a manager can be disastrous if that genius lacks technical skills, human skills, or one other factor known as the motivation to manage. **Motivation to manage** is an assessment of how motivated employees are to interact with superiors, participate in competitive situations, behave assertively toward others, tell others what to do, reward

> Good management involves **much more** than intelligence.

Human skills can be summarized as the ability to work well with others. Managers with people skills work effectively within groups, encourage others to express their thoughts and feelings, are sensitive to others' needs and viewpoints, and are good listeners and communicators. Human skills are equally important at all levels of management, from first-line supervisors to CEOs. However, because lower-level managers spend much of their time solving technical problems, upper-level managers may actually spend more time dealing directly with people. On average, first-line managers spend 57 percent of their time with

Human skills the ability to work well with others

Conceptual skills the ability to see the organization as a whole, understand how the different parts affect each other, and recognize how the company fits into or is affected by its environment

Motivation to manage an assessment of how enthusiastic employees are about managing the work of others

good behavior and punish poor behavior, perform actions that are highly visible to others, and handle and organize administrative tasks. Managers typically have a stronger motivation to manage than their subordinates, and managers at higher levels usually have a stronger motivation to manage than managers at lower levels. Furthermore, managers with a stronger motivation to manage are promoted faster, are rated as better managers by their employees, and earn more money than managers with a weak motivation to manage.[54]

6 Mistakes Managers Make

Another way to understand what it takes to be a manager is to look at the mistakes managers make. In other words, we can learn just as much from what managers shouldn't do as from what they should do.

Several studies of U.S. and British managers have compared "arrivers," or managers who made it all the way to the top of their companies, with "derailers," managers who were successful early in their careers but were knocked off the fast track by the time they reached the middle to upper levels of management.[55] The researchers found that there were only a few differences between arrivers and derailers. For the most part, both groups were talented and both groups had weaknesses. But what distinguished derailers from arrivers was that derailers possessed two or more "fatal flaws" with respect to the way that they managed people! Although arrivers were by no means perfect, they usually had no more than one fatal flaw or had found ways to minimize the effects of their flaws on the people with whom they worked.

The number one mistake made by derailers was that they were insensitive to others by virtue of their abrasive, intimidating, and bullying management style. The authors of one study described a manager who walked into his subordinate's office and interrupted a meeting by saying, "I need to see you." When the subordinate tried to explain that he was not available because he was in the middle of a meeting, the manager barked, "I don't give a damn. I said I wanted to see you now."[56] Not surprisingly, only 25 percent of derailers were rated by others as being good with people, compared to 75 percent of arrivers.

The second mistake was that derailers were often cold, aloof, or arrogant. Although

Top Ten Mistakes That Managers Make

1. Insensitive to others: abrasive, intimidating, bullying style.
2. Cold, aloof, arrogant.
3. Betrayal of trust.
4. Overly ambitious: thinking of next job, playing politics.
5. Specific performance problems with the business.
6. Overmanaging: unable to delegate or build a team.
7. Unable to staff effectively.
8. Unable to think strategically.
9. Unable to adapt to boss with different style.
10. Overdependent on advocate or mentor.

Source: M. W. McCall, Jr. & M. M. Lombardo, "What Makes a Top Executive?" *Psychology Today*, February 1983, 26–31.

this sounds like insensitivity to others, it has more to do with derailed managers being so smart, so expert in their areas of knowledge, that they treated others with contempt because they weren't experts, too. For example, AT&T called in an industrial psychologist to counsel its vice president of human resources because she had been blamed for ruffling too many feathers at the company.[57] Interviews with the vice president's coworkers and subordinates revealed that they thought she was brilliant, was "smarter and faster than other people," "generates a lot of ideas," and "loves to deal with complex issues." Unfortunately, these smarts were accompanied by a cold, aloof, and arrogant management style. The people she worked with complained that she does "too much too fast," treats coworkers with "disdain," "impairs teamwork," "doesn't always show her warm side," and has "burned too many bridges."

The third and fourth mistakes made by the derailers, betraying a trust and being overly ambitious, reflect a lack of concern for coworkers and subordinates. Betraying a trust doesn't mean being dishonest. Instead, it means making others look bad by not doing what you said you would do when you said you would do it.

©InspireStock/Jupiter Images

> Managers who always have their **eye on their next job** rarely establish more than superficial relationships with peers and coworkers.

That mistake, in itself, is not fatal because managers and their workers aren't machines. Tasks go undone in every company every single business day. There's always too much to do and not enough time, people, money, or resources to do it. The fatal betrayal of trust is failing to inform others when things will not be done on time. This failure to admit mistakes, quickly inform others of the mistakes, take responsibility for the mistakes, and then fix them without blaming others distinguished the behavior of derailers from arrivers.

The fourth mistake, as mentioned above, was being overly political and ambitious. Managers who always have their eye on their next job rarely establish more than superficial relationships with peers and coworkers. In their haste to gain credit for successes that would be noticed by upper management, they make the fatal mistake of treating people as though they don't matter. An employee with an overly ambitious boss described him this way: "He gave me a new definition of shared risk: If something I did was successful, he took the credit. If it wasn't, I got the blame."[58]

The fatal mistakes of being unable to delegate, build a team, and staff effectively indicate that many derailed managers were unable to make the most basic transition to managerial work: to quit being hands-on doers and start getting work done through others. Two things go wrong when managers make these mistakes. First, when managers meddle in decisions that their subordinates should be making—when they can't stop being doers—they alienate the people who work for them. According to Richard Kilburg of Johns Hopkins University,

when managers interfere with workers' decisions, "You . . . have a tendency to lose your most creative people. They're able to say, 'Screw this. I'm not staying here.'"[59] Second, because they are trying to do their subordinates' jobs in addition to their own, managers who fail to delegate will not have enough time to do anything well.

7 The Transition to Management: The First Year

In her book *Becoming a Manager: Mastery of a New Identity,* Harvard Business School professor Linda Hill followed the development of 19 people in their first year as managers. Her study found that becoming a manager produced a profound psychological transition that changed the way these managers viewed themselves and others. As shown in Exhibit 1.4, the evolution of the managers' thoughts, expectations, and realities over the course of their first year in management reveals the magnitude of the changes they experienced.

Initially, the managers in Hill's study believed that their job was to exercise formal authority and to manage tasks—basically being the boss, telling others what to do, making decisions, and getting things done. In fact, most of the new managers were attracted to management positions because they wanted to be "in charge." Surprisingly, the new managers did not believe that their job was to manage people. The only aspects of people management mentioned by the new managers were hiring and firing.

Exhibit 1.4
Stages in the Transition to Management

MANAGERS' INITIAL EXPECTATIONS			AFTER SIX MONTHS AS A MANAGER			AFTER A YEAR AS A MANAGER					
JAN	FEB	MAR	APR	MAY	JUN	JUL	AUG	SEP	OCT	NOV	DEC

MANAGERS' INITIAL EXPECTATIONS	AFTER SIX MONTHS AS A MANAGER	AFTER A YEAR AS A MANAGER
◉ Be the boss	◉ Initial expectations were wrong	◉ No longer "doer"
◉ Formal authority	◉ Fast pace	◉ Communication, listening, & positive reinforcement
◉ Manage tasks	◉ Heavy workload	◉ Learning to adapt to and control stress
◉ Job is not managing people	◉ Job is to be problem-solver and troubleshooter for subordinates	◉ Job is people development

After six months, most of the new managers had concluded that their initial expectations about managerial work were wrong. Management wasn't being "the boss." It wasn't just about making decisions and telling others what to do. The first surprise was the fast pace and heavy workload involved in being a manager. Said one manager, "This job is much harder than you think. It is 40 to 50 percent more work than being a producer! Who would have ever guessed?" The pace of managerial work was startling, too. Another manager said, "You have eight or nine people looking for your time . . . coming into and out of your office all day long." A somewhat frustrated manager declared that management was "a job that never ended . . . a job you couldn't get your hands around."

Informal descriptions like this are consistent with studies indicating that the average first-line manager spends no more than two minutes on a task before being interrupted by a request from a subordinate, a phone call, or an email. The pace is somewhat less hurried for top managers, who spend an average of approximately nine minutes on a task before having to switch to another. In practice, this means that supervisors may perform 30 different tasks per hour, while top managers perform seven different tasks per hour, with each task typically different from the one that preceded it. A manager described this frenetic level of activity by saying, "The only time you are in control is when you shut your door, and then I feel I am not doing the job I'm supposed to be doing, which is being with the people."

The other major surprise after six months on the job was that the managers' expectations about what they should do as managers were very different from their subordinates' expectations. Initially, the managers defined their jobs as helping their subordinates perform their jobs well. For the managers, who still defined themselves as doers rather than managers, assisting their subordinates meant going out on sales calls or handling customer complaints. But when the managers "assisted" in this way, their subordinates were resentful and viewed their help as interference. The subordinates wanted their managers to help them by solving problems that they couldn't solve. Once the managers realized this distinction, they embraced their role as problem-solver and

Top managers spend an average of 9 minutes on a given task before having to switch to another.

troubleshooter. Thus, they could help without interfering with their subordinates' jobs.

After a year on the job, most of the managers thought of themselves as managers and no longer as doers. In making the transition, they finally realized that people management was the most important part of their jobs. One manager summarized the lesson that had taken him a year to learn by saying, "As many demands as managers have on their time, I think their primary responsibility is people development. Not production, but people development." Another indication of how much their views had changed was that most of the managers now regretted the rather heavy-handed approach they had used in their early attempts to manage their subordinates. "I wasn't good at managing . . . , so I was bossy like a first-grade teacher." "Now I see that I started out as a drill sergeant. I was inflexible, just a lot of how-to's." By the end of the year, most of the managers had abandoned their authoritarian approach for one based on communication, listening, and positive reinforcement.

Finally, after beginning their year as managers in frustration, the managers came to feel comfortable with their subordinates, with the demands of their jobs, and with their emerging managerial styles. While being

managers had made them acutely aware of their limitations and their need to develop as people, it also provided them with an unexpected reward of coaching and developing the people who worked for them. One manager said, "I realize now that when I accepted the position of branch manager that it is truly an exciting vocation. It is truly awesome, even at this level; it can be terribly challenging and terribly exciting."

Why Management Matters

If you walk down the aisle of the business section in your local bookstore, you'll find hundreds of books that explain precisely what companies need to do to be successful. Unfortunately, the best-selling business books tend to be faddish, changing dramatically every few years. One thing that hasn't changed, though, is the importance of good people and good management: Companies can't succeed for long without them.

After reading this section, you should be able to

8 explain how and why companies can create competitive advantage through people.

8 Competitive Advantage through People

In his books *Competitive Advantage through People* and *The Human Equation: Building Profits by Putting People First,* Stanford University business professor Jeffrey Pfeffer contends that what separates top-performing companies from their competitors is the

way they treat their work forces—in other words, their management.[60]

Pfeffer found that managers in top-performing companies used ideas like employment security, selective hiring, self-managed teams and decentralization, high pay contingent on company performance, extensive training, reduced status distinctions (between managers and employees), and extensive sharing of financial information to achieve financial performance that, on average, was 40 percent higher than that of other companies. These ideas, which are explained in detail in Exhibit 1.5, help organizations develop workforces that are smarter, better trained, more motivated, and more committed than their competitors' workforces. And, as indicated by the phenomenal growth and return on investment earned by these companies, smarter, better trained, and more committed workforces provide superior products and service to customers, who keep buying and, by telling others about their positive experiences, bring in new customers.

Pfeffer also argues that companies that invest in their people will create long-lasting competitive advantages that are difficult for other companies to duplicate. Indeed, other studies clearly demonstrate that sound management practices can produce substantial advantages in four critical areas of organizational performance: sales revenues, profits, stock market returns, and customer satisfaction.

In terms of sales revenues and profits, a study of nearly 1,000 U.S. firms found that companies that use *just some* of the ideas shown in Exhibit 1.5 had $27,044 more sales per employee and $3,814 more profit per employee than companies that didn't.[61] For a 100-person company, these differences amount to $2.7 million more in sales and nearly $400,000 more in annual profit! For a 1,000-person company, the difference grows to $27 million more in sales and $4 million more in annual profit!

Another study investigating the effect of investing in people on company sales found that poorly performing companies that adopted management techniques as simple as setting performance expectations and coaching, reviewing, and rewarding employee performance were able to improve their average return on investment from

Exhibit 1.5

Competitive Advantage through People: Management Practices

1. **Employment Security**—Employment security is the ultimate form of commitment that companies can make to their workers. Employees can innovate and increase company productivity without fearing the loss of their jobs.

2. **Selective Hiring**—If employees are the basis for a company's competitive advantage, and those employees have employment security, then the company needs to aggressively recruit and selectively screen applicants in order to hire the most talented employees available.

3. **Self-Managed Teams and Decentralization**—Self-managed teams are responsible for their own hiring, purchasing, job assignments, and production. Self-managed teams can often produce enormous increases in productivity through increased employee commitment and creativity. Decentralization allows employees who are closest to (and most knowledgeable about) problems, production, and customers to make timely decisions. Decentralization increases employee satisfaction and commitment.

4. **High Wages Contingent on Organizational Performance**—High wages are needed to attract and retain talented workers and to indicate that the organization values its workers. Employees, like company founders, shareholders, and managers, need to share in the financial rewards when the company is successful. Why? Because employees who have a financial stake in their companies are more likely to take a long-run view of the business and think like business owners.

5. **Training and Skill Development**—Like a high-tech company that spends millions of dollars to upgrade computers or research and development labs, a company whose competitive advantage is based on its people must invest in the training and skill development of its people.

6. **Reduction of Status Differences**—These are fancy words that indicate that the company treats everyone, no matter what the job, as equal. There are no reserved parking spaces. Everyone eats in the same cafeteria and has similar benefits. The result: Much improved communication as employees focus on problems and solutions rather than on how they are less valued than managers.

7. **Sharing Information**—If employees are to make decisions that are good for the long-run health and success of the company, they need to be given information about costs, finances, productivity, development times, and strategies that was previously known only by company managers.

Source: J. Pfeffer, *The Human Equation: Building Profits by Putting People First* (Boston: Harvard Business School Press, 1996).

5.1 percent to 19.7 percent and increase sales by $94,000 per employee![62] So, in addition to significantly improving the profitability of healthy companies, sound management practices can turn around failing companies.

To determine the effect of investing in people on stock market performance, researchers matched companies on *Fortune* magazine's list of "100 Best Companies to Work for in America" with companies that were similar in industry, size, and—this is key—operating performance. In other words, both sets of companies were equally good performers; the key difference was how well they treated their employees. For both sets of companies, the researchers found that employee attitudes such as job satisfaction changed little from year to year. The people who worked for the "100 Best" companies were consistently much more satisfied with their jobs and employers year after year than were employees in the matched companies. More importantly, those stable differences in employee attitudes were strongly related to differences in stock market performance. Over a three-year period, an investment in the "100 Best Companies to Work for" would have resulted in an 82 percent cumulative stock return compared to just 37 percent for the matched companies.[63] This difference is remarkable given that both sets of companies were equally good performers at the beginning of the period.

Finally, research also indicates that managers have an important effect on customer satisfaction. Many people find this surprising. They don't understand how managers, who are largely responsible for what goes on inside the company, can affect what goes on outside the company. They wonder how managers, who often interact with customers under negative conditions (when customers are angry or dissatisfied), can actually improve customer satisfaction. It turns out that managers influence customer satisfaction through employee satisfaction. When employees are satisfied with their jobs, their bosses, and the companies they work for, they provide much better service to customers.[64] In turn, customers are more satisfied, too. You will learn more about the service-profit chain in Chapter 18 on managing service and manufacturing operations.

In 2007, Fortune ranked Google as America's Best Company to Work for. One of the perks at the Goggleplex: Free—and good—food at the cafeteria. And that includes a company sushi chef.

By the Numbers

3.5 billion packages shipped by UPS in a single year

$100,000 amount of money Continental saves a year by not giving passengers a full can of soda.

4 kinds of managers, kinds of skills it takes to be a manager

35% of CEOs eventually fired in a year

30 number of tasks a supervisor does in an hour

75% of arrivers ranked as good with people

3 number of major roles managers perform

Test coming up? Now what?

With MGMT you have a multitude of study aids at your fingertips. After reading the chapters, check out these ideas for further help:

Chapter in Review cards include all learning outcomes, definitions, and visual summaries for each chapter.

Online printable flash cards give you three additional ways to check your comprehension of key management concepts.

Other great ways to help you study include **interactive management games, podcasts, audio downloads, online tutorial quizzes with feedback,** and **cell phone quizzes**.

You can find it all at **www.mgmt4me.com**

THOMSON
SOUTH-WESTERN

HISTORY OF MANAGEMENT

In the Beginning

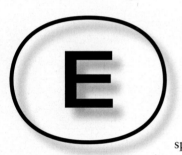

Each day, managers are asked to solve challenging problems and are given only a limited amount of time, people, or resources. Yet it's still their responsibility to get things done on time and within budget. Tell today's managers to "reward workers for improved production or performance," "set specific goals to increase motivation," or "innovate to create and sustain a competitive advantage," and they'll respond, "Duh! Who doesn't know that?" A mere 125 years ago, however, business ideas and practices were so different that today's widely accepted management ideas would have been as "self-evident" as space travel, cell phones, and the Internet. In fact, 125 years ago, management wasn't yet a field of study, and there were no management jobs and no management careers. So, if there were no managers 125 years ago, but you can't walk down the hall today without bumping into one, where did management come from?

After reading the next section, you should be able to

1 explain the origins of management.

1 The Origins of Management

Although we can find the seeds of many of today's management ideas throughout history, not until the last two centuries did systematic changes in the nature of work and organizations create a compelling need for managers.

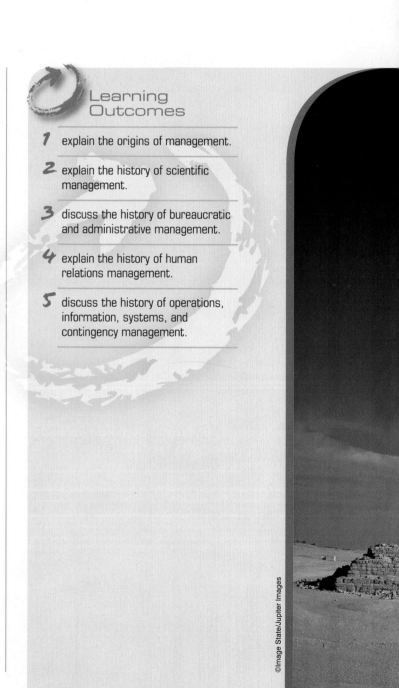

Learning
Outcomes

1 explain the origins of management.

2 explain the history of scientific management.

3 discuss the history of bureaucratic and administrative management.

4 explain the history of human relations management.

5 discuss the history of operations, information, systems, and contingency management.

©Image State/Jupiter Images

*Let's begin our discussion of the origins of management by learning about **1.1 management ideas and practice throughout history** and **1.2 why we need managers today**.*

1.1 Management Ideas and Practice throughout History

Examples of management thought and practice can be found throughout history.[1] For example, the Egyptians recognized the need for planning, organizing, and controlling; for submitting written requests; and for consulting staff for advice before making decisions. The practical problems they encountered while building the great pyramids no doubt led to the development of these management ideas. The enormity of the task they faced is evident in the pyramid of King Cheops, which contains 2.3 million blocks of stone. Each block had to be quarried, cut to precise size and shape, cured (hardened in the sun), transported by boat for two to three days, moved onto the construction site, numbered to identify where it would be placed, and then shaped and smoothed so that it would fit perfectly into place. It took 20,000 workers 23 years to complete this pyramid; more than 8,000 were needed just to quarry the stones and transport them. A typical "quarry expedition" might include 100 army officers, 50 government and religious officials, and 200 members of the king's court to lead the expedition; 130 stone masons to cut the stones; and 5,000 soldiers, 800 barbarians, and 2,000 bond servants to transport the stones on and off the ships.[2]

It took 20,000 workers 23 years to complete this pyramid; more than 8,000 were needed just to quarry the stones and transport them.

Exhibit 2.1

Management Ideas and Practice throughout History

Time	Individual or Group	Planning	Organizing	Leading	Controlling	Contributions to Management Thought and Practice
5000 B.C.	Sumerians				√	Record keeping.
4000 B.C. to 2000 B.C.	Egyptians	√	√		√	Recognized the need for planning, organizing, and controlling when building the pyramids. Submitted requests in writing. Made decisions after consulting staff for advice.
1800 B.C.	Hammurabi				√	Established controls by using witnesses (to vouch for what was said or done) and writing to document transactions.
600 B.C.	Nebuchadnezzar	√	√			Wage incentives and production control.
500 B.C.	Sun Tzu	√		√		Strategy; identifying and attacking opponent's weaknesses.
400 B.C.	Xenophon	√	√	√	√	Recognized management as a separate art.
400 B.C.	Cyrus		√	√	√	Human relations and motion study.
175	Cato		√			Job descriptions.
284	Diocletian		√			Delegation of authority.
900	Alfarabi			√		Listed leadership traits.
1100	Ghazali			√		Listed managerial traits.
1418	Barbarigo		√			Different organizational forms/structures.
1436	Venetians				√	Numbering, standardization, and interchangeability of parts.
1500	Sir Thomas More			√		Critical of poor management and leadership.
1525	Machiavelli	√	√			Cohesiveness, power, and leadership in organizations.

Source: C. S. George, Jr., *The History of Management Thought* (Englewood Cliffs, NJ: Prentice Hall, 1972).

Exhibit 2.1 shows how other management ideas and practices throughout history relate to the management functions in the textbook.

1.2 Why We Need Managers Today

Working from 8 A.M. to 5 P.M., coffee breaks, lunch hours, crushing rush hour traffic, and punching a time clock are things we associate with today's working world.

But for most of humankind's history, people didn't commute to work. Work usually occurred in homes or on farms. As recently as 1870, two-thirds of Americans earned their living from agriculture. Even most of those who didn't earn their living from agriculture didn't commute to work. Blacksmiths, furniture makers, leather-goods makers, and other skilled tradesmen or craftsmen, who formed trade guilds (the historical predecessors of labor unions) in England as early as 1093, typically worked out of shops in or next to their homes.[3] Likewise, until the late 1800s, cottage workers worked with each other out of small homes that were often built in a semicircle. A family in each cottage would complete a different production step, with work passed from one cottage to the next until production was complete. With small, self-organized work groups, and no commute, no bosses, and no common building, there wasn't a strong need for management.

During the Industrial Revolution (1750–1900), however, jobs and organizations changed dramatically.[4] First, thanks to the availability of power (steam engines and later electricity), low-paid, unskilled laborers running machines began to replace high-paid, skilled artisans who made entire goods by themselves by hand. This new mass production system was based on a division of labor: each worker, interacting with machines, performed separate, highly specialized tasks that were

For most of **humankind's history,** people didn't commute to work.

but a small part of all the steps required to make manufactured goods. While workers focused on their singular tasks, managers were needed to effectively coordinate the different parts of the production system and optimize its overall performance. Productivity skyrocketed at companies that understood this. For example, at Ford Motor Company, the time required to assemble a car dropped from 12.5 man hours to just 93 minutes.[5]

Second, instead of being performed in fields, homes, or small shops, jobs occurred in large, formal organizations where hundreds, if not thousands, of people worked under one roof.[6] In 1849, for example, with just 123 workers, Chicago Harvester (the predecessor of International Harvester) ran the largest factory in the United States. Yet, by 1913, Henry Ford employed 12,000 employees in his Highland Park, Michigan, factory alone. With individual factories employing so many workers under one roof, companies now had a strong need for disciplinary rules (to impose order and structure). For the first time, they needed managers who knew how to organize large groups, work with employees, and make good decisions.

Americans spend roughly 216 hours a year commuting to and from work. That's the equivalent of over 5 full-time work weeks.

©Robert Harding/Jupiter Images

http://factfinder.census.gov/servlet/STTable?_bm=y&-geo_id=01000US&-gr_name=ACS_2005_EST_G00_S0801&-ds_name=ACS_2005_EST_G00_&-redoLog=false

The Evolution of Management

Before 1880, business educators taught only basic bookkeeping and secretarial skills, and no one published books or articles about management.[7] Today, if you have a question about management, you can turn to dozens of academic journals, hundreds of business school and practitioner journals (such as *Harvard Business Review, Sloan Management Review,* and the *Academy of Management Executive*), and thousands of books and articles. In the next four sections, you will learn about other important contributors to the field of management and how their ideas shaped our current understanding of management theory and practice.

After reading the next four sections, which review the different schools of management thought, you should be able to

2 explain the history of scientific management.

3 discuss the history of bureaucratic and administrative management.

4 explain the history of human relations management.

5 discuss the history of operations, information, systems, and contingency management.

2 Scientific Management

Before scientific management, organizational decision making could best be described as "seat-of-the-pants." Decisions were made haphazardly without any systematic study, thought, or collection of information. If the "managers" hired by the company founder or owner decided that workers should work twice as fast, little or no thought was given to worker motivation. If workers resisted, "managers" often resorted to physical beatings to get workers to work faster, harder, or longer. With no incentives for "managers" to cooperate with workers and vice versa, managers and workers gamed the system trying to systematically take advantage of each other. Likewise, each worker did the same job in his or her own way with different methods and different tools. In short, there were no procedures to standardize operations, no standards by which to judge whether performance was good or bad, and no follow-up to determine if productivity or quality actually improved when changes were made.[8]

This all changed with the advent of **scientific management,** which thoroughly studied and tested different work methods to identify the best, most efficient ways to complete a job.

*Let's find out more about scientific management by learning about **2.1 Frederick W. Taylor, the father of scientific management; 2.2 Frank and Lillian Gilbreth and motion studies;** and **2.3 Henry Gantt and his Gantt charts.***

2.1 Father of Scientific Management: Frederick W. Taylor

Frederick W. Taylor (1856–1915), the "father of scientific management," began his career as a worker at Midvale Steel Company. He was later promoted to patternmaker, supervisor, and then chief engineer.

At Midvale, Taylor was deeply affected by his three-year struggle to get the men who worked for him to do, as he called it, "a fair day's work." Taylor explained that as soon as he became the boss, "the men who were working under me . . . knew that I was onto the whole game of **soldiering,** or deliberately restricting output [to one-third of what they were capable of producing]."[9]

Scientific management thoroughly studying and testing different work methods to identify the best, most efficient way to complete a job

Soldiering when workers deliberately slow their pace or restrict their work outputs

Rate buster a group member whose work pace is significantly faster than the normal pace in his or her group

When Taylor told his workers, "I am going to try to get a bigger output," the workers responded, "We warn you, Fred, if you try to bust any of these rates [a **rate buster** was someone who worked faster than the group] we will have you over the fence in six weeks."[10]

Over the next three years, Taylor tried everything he could think of to improve output. By doing the job himself, he showed workers that it was possible to produce more output. He hired new "intelligent" workers and trained them himself, hoping they would produce more. But they would not because of "very heavy social pressure" from the other workers. Pushed by Taylor, the workers began breaking their machines so that they couldn't produce. Taylor responded by fining them every time they broke a machine and for any violation of the rules, no matter how small, such as being late to work. Tensions became so severe that some of the workers threatened to shoot him. The remedy that Taylor eventually developed was scientific management.

The goal of scientific management was to use systematic study to find the "one best way" of doing each task. To do that, managers must follow the four principles shown in Exhibit 2.2.[11] First, "develop a science" for each element of work. Study it. Analyze it. Determine the "one best way" to do the work. For example, one of Taylor's controversial proposals at the time was to give rest breaks to factory workers doing physical labor. Today, we take breaks for granted, but in Taylor's day, factory workers were expected to work without stopping.[12] Through systematic experiments, he showed that frequent rest breaks greatly increased daily output.

Second, scientifically select, train, teach, and develop workers to help them reach their full potential. Before Taylor, supervisors often hired on the basis of favoritism and nepotism. Who you knew was often more important than what you could do. By contrast, Taylor instructed supervisors to hire "first class" workers on the basis of their aptitude to do a job well. For similar reasons, Taylor also recommended that companies train and develop their workers—a rare practice at the time.

Third, cooperate with employees to ensure implementation of the scientific principles. As Taylor knew from personal experience, more often than not workers and management viewed each other as enemies. Taylor said, "The majority of these men believe that the

Want Fries with That?

Don't think scientific management has much to do with today's work life? Think again: about the last time you were at the store and the clerk said, "Have a nice day." Service providers—particularly at restaurants—use scripts to ensure that employees are following the "one best way" of interacting with the customers. McDonald's uses a speech-only script (workers must say, "May I help you, ma'am?" instead of "Can I help someone?"). At Olive Garden, workers must greet the table within 30 seconds of arrival; take the drink order within 3 minutes; suggest five items while taking the order; and check back with the table 3 minutes after the food arrives.[13]

fundamental interests of employees and employers are necessarily antagonistic. Scientific management, on the contrary, has for its very foundation the firm conviction that the true interests of the two are one and the same; that prosperity for the employer cannot exist through a long term of years unless it is accompanied by prosperity for the employee and vice versa; and that it is possible to give the workman what he most wants—high wages—and the employer what he wants—a low labor cost—for his manufactures."[14]

The fourth principle of scientific management was to divide the work and the responsibility equally between management and workers. Prior to Taylor, workers alone were held responsible for productivity and performance. But, said Taylor, "Almost every act of the workman should be preceded by one or more preparatory acts of the management which enable him to do his work better and quicker than he otherwise could."[15]

Above all, Taylor felt these principles could be used to determine a "fair day's work," that is, what an average worker could produce at a reasonable pace, day in and day out. Once that was determined, it was man-

agement's responsibility to pay workers fairly for that "fair day's work." In essence, Taylor was trying to align management and employees so that what was good for employees was also good for management. In this way, he felt, workers and managers could avoid the conflicts that he had experienced at Midvale Steel. And one of the best ways, according to Taylor, to align management and employees was to use incentives to motivate workers. In particular, Taylor believed in piece-rate incentives in which work pay was directly tied to how much workers produced.

Although Taylor remains a controversial figure among some academics, nearly a century later it is inarguable that his key ideas have stood the test of time.[16] In fact, his ideas are so well accepted and widely used that we take most of them for granted. As eminent management scholar Edwin Locke says, "The point is not, as is often claimed, that he was 'right in the context of his time,' but is now outdated, but that *most of his insights are still valid today.*"[17]

2.2 Motion Studies: Frank and Lillian Gilbreth

The husband and wife team Frank and Lillian Gilbreth are best known for their use of motion studies to simplify work, but they also made significant contributions to industrial psychology. Like Frederick Taylor, their early experiences significantly shaped their interests and contributions to management.

Though admitted to MIT, Frank Gilbreth (1868–1924) began his career as an apprentice bricklayer. While learning the trade, he noticed the bricklayers using three different sets of motions—one to teach others how to lay bricks, a second to work at a slow pace,

Exhibit 2.2

Taylor's Four Principles of Scientific Management

First:	Develop a science for each element of a man's work, which replaces the old rule-of-thumb method.
Second:	Scientifically select and then train, teach, and develop the workman, whereas in the past he chose his own work and trained himself as best he could.
Third:	Heartily cooperate with the men so as to ensure all of the work being done is in accordance with the principles of the science that has been developed.
Fourth:	There is an almost equal division of the work and the responsibility between the management and the workmen. The management take over all the work for which they are better fitted than the workmen, while in the past almost all of the work and the greater part of the responsibility were thrown upon the men.

Source: F. W. Taylor, *The Principles of Scientific Management* (New York: Harper, 1911).

and a third to work at a fast pace.[18] Wondering which was best, he studied the various approaches and began eliminating unnecessary motions. For example, by designing a stand that could be raised to waist height, he eliminated the need to bend over to pick up each brick. By having lower-paid workers place all the bricks with their most attractive side up, bricklayers didn't waste time turning a brick over to find it. By mixing a more consistent mortar, bricklayers no longer had to tap each brick numerous times to put it in the right position. Together, Gilbreth's improvements raised productivity from 120 to 350 bricks per hour and from 1,000 bricks to 2,700 bricks per day.

As a result of his experience with bricklaying, Gilbreth and his wife Lillian developed a long-term interest in using motion study to simplify work, improve productivity, and reduce the level of effort required to safely perform a job. Indeed, Frank Gilbreth said, "The greatest waste in the world comes from needless, ill-directed, and ineffective motions."[19] The Gilbreths' motion study, however, is different from Frederick W. Taylor's time study.[20] Taylor developed time study to put an end to soldiering and to determine what could be considered a fair day's work. **Time study** worked by timing how long it took a "first-class man" to complete each part of his job. After allowing for rest periods, a standard time was established, and a worker's pay would increase or decrease depending on whether the worker exceeded or fell below that standard. By contrast, **motion study**, as we saw in Frank Gilbreth's analysis of bricklaying, broke each task or job into separate motions and then eliminated those that were unnecessary or

Time study timing how long it takes good workers to complete each part of their jobs

Motion study breaking each task or job into its separate motions and then eliminating those that are unnecessary or repetitive

repetitive. Because many motions were completed very quickly, the Gilbreths used motion-picture films, then a relatively new technology, to analyze jobs. Most film cameras, however, were hand-cranked and thus variable in their film speed, so Frank Gilbreth invented the micro chronometer, a large clock that could record time to 1/2,000th of a second. By placing the micro chronometer next to the worker in the camera's field of vision and attaching a flashing strobe light to the worker's hands to better identify the direction and sequence of key movements, the Gilbreths could use film to detect and precisely time even the slightest, fastest movements. Motion study typically yielded production increases of 25 to 300 percent.[21]

Lillian Gilbreth (1878–1972) was an important contributor to management as well. She was the first woman to receive a Ph.D. in management, as well as the first woman to become a member of the Society of Industrial Engineers and the American Society of Mechanical Engineers. When Frank died in 1924, she continued the work of their management consulting company (which they had shared for over a dozen years) on her own. Lillian, who was concerned with the human side of work, was one of the first contributors to industrial psychology, originating ways to improve office communication, incentive programs, job satisfaction, and management training. Her work also convinced the government to enact laws regarding workplace safety, ergonomics, and child labor.

©Michael Newman/Photo Edit Inc.

2.3 Charts: Henry Gantt

Henry Gantt (1861–1919) was first a protégé and then an associate of Frederick Taylor. Gantt is best known for the Gantt chart, but he also made significant contributions to management with respect to the training

and development of workers. As shown in Exhibit 2.3, a **Gantt chart,** which shows time in various units on the *x*-axis and tasks on the *y*-axis, visually indicates what tasks must be completed at which times in order to complete a project. For example, Exhibit 2.3 shows that to start construction on a new company headquarters by the week of November 18, the following tasks must be completed by the following dates: architectural firm selected by October 7, architectural planning done by November 4, permits obtained from the city by November 11, site preparation finished by November 18, and loans and financing finalized by November 18. Though simple and straightforward, Gantt charts were revolutionary in the era of "seat-of-the-pants" management because of the detailed planning information they provided to managers. Gantt said, "Such sheets show at a glance where the delays occur, and indicate what must have our attention in order to keep up the proper output." Today, the use of Gantt charts is so widespread that nearly all project management software and computer spreadsheets have the capability to create charts that track and visually display the progress being made on a project.

Finally, Gantt, along with Taylor, was one of the first to strongly recommend

Gantt chart a graphical chart that shows which tasks must be completed at which times in order to complete a project or task

Exhibit 2.3

Gantt Chart for Starting Construction on a New Headquarters

	Current Week				⋮					
Weeks		23 Sep to 30 Sep	30 Sep to 7 Oct	7 Oct to 14 Oct	14 Oct to 21 Oct	21 Oct to 28 Oct	28 Oct to 4 Nov	4 Nov to 11 Nov	11 Nov to 18 Nov	18 Nov to 25 Nov
Tasks										
Interview and select architectural firm		Architect by October 7								
Hold weekly planning meetings with architects					Weekly planning with architects by November 4					
Obtain permits and approval from city							Permits & approval by November 11			
Begin preparing site for construction								Site construction done by November 18		
Finalize loans and financing									Financing finalized by November 18	
Begin construction										Start building
Tasks										
Weeks		23 Sep to 30 Sep	30 Sep to 7 Oct	7 Oct to 14 Oct	14 Oct to 21 Oct	21 Oct to 28 Oct	28 Oct to 4 Nov	4 Nov to 11 Nov	11 Nov to 18 Nov	18 Nov to 25 Nov
	Current Week			⋮						

that companies train and develop their workers.[22] In his work with companies, he found that workers achieved their best performance levels if they were trained first. At the time, however, supervisors, fearing that they could lose their jobs to more knowledgeable workers, were reluctant to teach workers what they knew. Gantt overcame the supervisors' resistance by rewarding them with bonuses for properly training all of their workers. Thus, Gantt's approach to training was straightforward: "(1) a scientific investigation in detail of each piece of work, and the determination of the best method and the shortest time in which the work can be done. (2) A teacher capable of teaching the best method and the shortest time. (3) Reward for both teacher and pupil when the latter is successful."[23]

3 Bureaucratic and Administrative Management

The field of scientific management focused on improving the efficiency of manufacturing facilities and their workers. At about the same time, equally important ideas were developing in Europe. German sociologist Max Weber's ideas about bureaucratic management, which presented a new way to run entire organizations, were published in *The Theory of Economic and Social Organization* in 1922. Henri Fayol, an experienced French CEO, published his ideas about administrative management, including how and what managers should do in their jobs, in *General and Industrial Management* in 1916.

Let's find out more about Weber's and Fayol's contributions to management by learning about 3.1 bureaucratic management and 3.2 administrative management.

3.1 Bureaucratic Management: Max Weber

Today, when we hear the term *bureaucracy,* we think of inefficiency and red tape, incompetence and ineffectiveness, and rigid administrators blindly enforcing nonsensical rules. When German sociologist Max Weber (1864–1920) first proposed the idea of bureaucratic organizations, however, monarchies and patriarchies, not bureaucracies, were associated with these problems. In monarchies, where kings, queens, sultans, and emperors ruled, and patriarchies, where a council of elders, wise men, or male heads of extended families ruled, the top leaders typically achieved their positions by

Bureaucracy the exercise of control on the basis of knowledge, expertise, or experience

virtue of birthright. Likewise, promotion to prominent positions of authority was based on who you knew (politics), who you were (heredity), or traditions.

It was against this historical background that Weber proposed the then new idea of bureaucracy. According to Weber, **bureaucracy** is "the exercise of control on the basis of knowledge."[24] So, in a bureaucracy, rather than ruling by virtue of favoritism, or personal or family connections, people would lead by virtue of their rational-legal authority—in other words, their knowledge, expertise, or experience. Furthermore, the aim of bureaucracy is to achieve an organization's goals in the most efficient way possible.

Exhibit 2.4 shows the seven elements that, according to Weber, characterize bureaucracies. First, instead of hiring people because of their family or political connections or personal loyalty, they should be hired because their technical training or education qualifies them to do their jobs well. Second, along the same lines, promotion within the company would no longer be based on who you knew or who you were (heredity), but on your experience or achievements. And to further limit the influence of personal connections in the promotion process, managers, rather than organizational owners, should decide who gets promoted. Third, each position or job is part of a chain of command that clarifies who reports to whom throughout the organization. Those higher in the chain of command have the right, if they so choose, to give commands, take action, and make decisions concerning activities occurring anywhere below them in the chain. Fourth, to increase efficiency and effectiveness, tasks and responsibilities are separated and assigned to those best qualified to complete them. Fifth, an organization's rules and procedures should apply to all members, regardless of their position or status. Sixth, to ensure consistency and fairness over time and across different leaders, all rules, procedures, and decisions should be recorded in writing. Finally, to reduce favoritism, "professional" managers rather than company owners should manage or supervise the organization.

When viewed in historical context, Weber's ideas about bureaucracy represent a tremendous improvement. Fair-

Prisoners of Bureaucracy

Despite its advantages over monarchical and patriarchic organizational forms, even Weber recognized bureaucracy's limitations. He called it the "iron cage" and said, "Once fully established, bureaucracy is among those social structures which are the hardest to destroy."[25]

Exhibit 2.4

Elements of Bureaucratic Organizations

Qualification-based hiring:	Employees are hired on the basis of their technical training or educational background.
Merit-based promotion:	Promotion is based on experience or achievement. Managers, not organizational owners, decide who is promoted.
Chain of command:	Each job occurs within a hierarchy, the chain of command, in which each position reports and is accountable to a higher position. A grievance procedure and a right to appeal protect people in lower positions.
Division of labor:	Tasks, responsibilities, and authority are clearly divided and defined.
Impartial application of rules and procedures:	Rules and procedures apply to all members of the organization and will be applied in an impartial manner, regardless of one's position or status
Recorded in writing:	All administrative decisions, acts, rules, or procedure will be recorded in writing.
Managers separate from owners:	The owners of an organization should not manage or supervise the organization.

Source: M. Weber, *The Theory of Economic and Social Organization*, trans. A. Henderson & T. Parsons (New York: The Free Press, 1947), 329–334.

ness supplanted favoritism, the goal of efficiency replaced the goal of personal gain, and logical rules and procedures took the place of traditions or arbitrary decision making.

Today, however, after more than a century of experience we recognize that bureaucracy has limitations as well. In bureaucracies, managers are supposed to influence employee behavior by fairly rewarding or punishing employees for compliance or noncompliance with organizational policies, rules, and procedures. In reality, however, most employees would argue that bureaucratic managers emphasize punishment for noncompliance much more than rewards for compliance. Ironically, bureaucratic management was created to prevent just this type of managerial behavior.

3.2 Administrative Management: Henri Fayol

Though his work was not translated and widely recognized in the United States until 1949, Frenchman Henri Fayol (1841–1925) was as important a contributor to the field of management as Frederick Taylor. But, whereas Taylor's ideas changed companies from the shop floor up, Fayol's ideas, which were shaped by his experience as a managing director (CEO), generally changed companies from the board of directors down.[26] Fayol is best known for developing five functions of managers and 14 principles of management.

The most formative events in Fayol's business career came during his 20-plus years as the managing director (CEO) of Compagnie de Commentry-Fourchambault-Decazeville, commonly known as Comambault, a vertically integrated steel company that owned several coal and iron ore mines and employed 10,000 to 13,000 work-

ers. Fayol was initially hired by the board of directors to shut the "hopeless" steel company down. But, after "four months of reflection and study," he presented the board with a plan, backed by detailed facts and figures, to save the company.[27] With little to lose, the board agreed. Fayol then began the process of turning the company around by obtaining supplies of key resources, such as coal and iron ore; using research to develop new steel alloy products; carefully selecting key subordinates in research, purchasing, manufacturing, and sales and then delegating responsibility to them; and cutting costs by moving the company to a better location closer to key markets.[28] Looking back 10 years later, Fayol attributed his and the company's success to changes in management practices. He wrote, "When I assumed the responsibility for the restoration of Decazeville, I did not rely on my technical superiority. . . . I relied on my ability as an organizer [and my] skill in handling men."[29]

Based on his experience as a CEO, Fayol argued that "the success of an enterprise generally depends much more on the administrative ability of its leaders than on their technical ability."[30] And, as you learned in Chapter 1, Fayol argued that this means that if managers are to be successful, they need to perform five managerial functions or elements: planning, organizing, coordinating, commanding, and controlling.[31] Today, though, most management textbooks have dropped the coordinating function and now refer to Fayol's commanding function as "leading." Consequently, Fayol's management functions are widely known as planning (determining organizational goals and a means for achieving them), organizing (deciding where decisions will be made, who will do what jobs and tasks, and who will work for whom), leading (inspiring and

©Stone/Getty Images

motivating workers to work hard to achieve organizational goals), and controlling (monitoring progress toward goal achievement and taking corrective action when needed). In addition, according to Fayol, effective management is based on the 14 principles in Exhibit 2.5.

4 Human Relations Management

As we have seen, scientific management focused on improving efficiency; bureaucratic management focused on using knowledge, fairness, and logical rules and procedures; and administrative management focused on how and what managers should do in their jobs. In contrast, in the human relations approach to management, people were more than just extensions of machines; they were valuable organizational resources whose needs were important and whose efforts, motivation, and performance were affected by the work they did and their relationships with their bosses, coworkers, and work groups. In other words, efficiency alone is not enough. Organizational success also depends on treating workers well.

Integrative conflict resolution an approach to dealing with conflict in which both parties deal with the conflict by indicating their preferences and then working together to find an alternative that meets the needs of both

Let's find out more about human relations management by learning about 4.1 Mary Parker Follett's theories of constructive conflict; 4.2 Elton Mayo's Hawthorne Studies; and 4.3 Chester Barnard's theories of cooperation and acceptance of authority.

4.1 Constructive Conflict: Mary Parker Follett

Mary Parker Follett (1868–1933) was a social worker who, after 25 years of working with schools and nonprofit organizations, began lecturing and writing about management and working extensively as a consultant for business and government. Many of today's "new" management ideas can clearly be traced to her work.

Follett is known for developing ideas regarding constructive conflict, also called cognitive conflict, which is discussed in Chapter 5 on decision making and Chapter 10 on teams. Unlike most people, then and now, who view conflict as bad, Follett believed that conflict could be beneficial. She said that conflict is "the appearance of difference, difference of opinions, of interests. For that is what conflict means—difference." She went on to say, "As conflict—difference—is here in this world, as we cannot avoid it, we should, I think, use it to work for us. Instead of condemning it, we should set it to work for us. Thus we shall not be afraid of conflict, but shall recognize that there is a destructive way of dealing with such moments and a constructive way."[32]

Follett believed that the best way to deal with conflict was not "domination," where one side won and the other lost, nor compromise, where each side gave up some of what they wanted, but integration. Said Follett, "There is a way beginning now to be recognized at least, and even occasionally followed: when two desires are *integrated,* that means that a solution has been found in which both desires have found a place that neither side has had to sacrifice anything." So, rather than one side dominating the other or both sides compromising, the point of **integrative conflict resolution** is to have both parties indicate their preferences and then work together to find an alternative that meets the needs of both. According to Follett, "Integration involves invention, and the clever thing is to recognize this, and not to let one's thinking stay within the boundaries of two alternatives which are mutually exclusive." Indeed, Follett's ideas about the positive use of conflict and an integrative approach to conflict resolution predate accepted thinking in the negotiation and conflict resolution literature by six decades (see the best-selling book *Getting to Yes: Negotiating Agreement without Giving In* by Roger Fisher, William Ury, and Bruce Patton).

> Many of today's "new" management ideas can clearly be traced to **Follett's work.**

Exhibit 2.5

Fayol's 14 Principles of Management

1. **Division of work:**	Increase production by dividing work so that each worker completes smaller tasks or job elements.
2. **Authority and responsibility:**	A manager's authority, which is the "right to give orders," should be commensurate with the manager's responsibility. However, organizations should enact controls to prevent managers from abusing their authority.
3. **Discipline:**	Clearly defined rules and procedures are needed at all organizational levels to ensure order and proper behavior.
4. **Unity of command:**	To avoid confusion and conflict, each employee should report to and receive orders from just one boss.
5. **Unity of direction:**	One person and one plan should be used in deciding the activities to be used to accomplish each organizational objective.
6. **Subordination of individual interests to the general interest:**	Employees must put the organization's interests and goals before their own.
7. **Remuneration:**	Compensation should be fair and satisfactory to both the employees and the organization; that is, don't overpay or underpay employees.
8. **Centralization:**	Avoid too much centralization or decentralization. Strike a balance depending on the circumstances and employees involved.
9. **Scalar chain:**	From the top to the bottom of an organization, each position is part of a vertical chain of authority in which each worker reports to just one boss. For the sake of simplicity, communication outside normal work groups or departments should follow the vertical chain of authority.
10. **Order:**	To avoid conflicts and confusion, order can be obtained by having a place for everyone and having everyone in their place; in other words, there should be no overlapping responsibilities.
11. **Equity:**	Kind, fair, and just treatment for all will develop devotion and loyalty. This does not exclude discipline, if warranted, and consideration of the broader general interest of the organization.
12. **Stability of tenure of personnel:**	Low turnover, meaning a stable work force with high tenure, benefits an organization by improving performance, lowering costs, and giving employees, especially managers, time to learn their jobs.
13. **Initiative:**	Because it is a "great source of strength for business," managers should encourage the development of initiative, the ability to develop and implement a plan, in others.
14. **Esprit de corps:**	Develop a strong sense of morale and unity among workers that encourages coordination of efforts.

Sources: H. Fayol, *General and Industrial Management* (London: Pittman & Sons, 1949); M. Fells, "Fayol Stands the Test of Time," *Journal of Management History* 6 (2000): 345–360; C. Rodrigues, "Fayol's 14 Principles of Management Then and Now: A Framework for Managing Today's Organizations Effectively," *Management Decision* 39 (2001): 880–889.

Exhibit 2.6 on the next page summarizes, in Follett's own words, her contributions to management regarding power ("with" not "over" others), the giving of orders (discussing instructions and resentment), authority (flowing from job knowledge and experience, not position), leadership (that leaders make the team and that aggressive, dominating leaders may be harmful), coordination, and control (should be based on facts, information, and coordination). In the end, Follett's contributions added significantly to our understanding of the human, social, and psychological sides of management. Peter Parker, the former chairman of the London School of Economics, said about Follett: "People often puzzle about who is the father of management. I don't know who the father was, but I have no doubt about who was the mother."[33]

4.2 Hawthorne Studies: Elton Mayo

Australian-born Elton Mayo (1880–1948) is best known for his role in the famous Hawthorne Studies at the Western Electric Company.

The Hawthorne Studies were conducted in several stages between 1924 and 1932 at a Western Electric plant in Chicago. Although Mayo didn't join the studies until 1928, he played a significant role thereafter, writing about the results in his book, *The Human Problems*

Exhibit 2.6

Some of Mary Parker Follett's Key Contributions to Management

Constructive conflict	• "As conflict—difference—is here in this world, as we cannot avoid it, we should, I think, use it to work for us. Instead of condemning it, we should set it to work for us."
Power	• "Power might be defined as simply the ability to make things happen, to be a causal agent, to initiate change." • "It seems to me that whereas power usually means *power-over*, the power of some person or group over some other person or group, it is possible to develop the conception of *power-with*, a jointly developed power, a co-active, not a coercive power."
The giving of orders	• "Probably more industrial trouble has been caused by the manner in which orders have been given than in any other way." • "But even if instructions are properly framed, are not given in an overbearing manner, there are many people who react violently against anything that they feel is a command. It is often the command that is resented, not the thing commanded." • "An advantage of not exacting blind obedience, of discussing your instructions with your subordinates, is that if there is any resentment, any come-back, you get it out into the open, and when it is in the open you can deal with it."
Authority	• "Indeed there are many indications in the present reorganization of industry that we are beginning to rid ourselves of the over and under idea, that we are coming to a different conception of authority, many indications that there is an increasing tendency to let the job itself, rather than the position occupied in a hierarchy, dictate the kind and amount of authority." • "Authority should go with knowledge and experience, that is where obedience is due, no matter whether it is up the line or down."
Leadership	• "Of the greatest importance is the ability to grasp a total situation. . . . Out of a welter of facts, experience, desires, aims, the leader must find the unifying thread. He must see a whole, not a mere kaleidoscope of pieces. . . . The higher up you go, the more ability you have to have of this kind." • "The leader makes the team. This is pre-eminently the leadership quality—the ability to organize all the forces there are in an enterprise and make them serve a common purpose." • "[It is wrong to assume] that you cannot be a good leader unless you are aggressive, masterful, dominating. But I think not only that these characteristics are not the qualities essential to leadership but, on the contrary, that they often militate directly against leadership."
Coordination	• "One, which I consider a very important trend in business management is a system of cross-functioning between the different departments. . . . Each department is expected to get in touch with certain others." • "Many businesses are now organized in such a way that you do not have an ascending and descending ladder of authority. You have a degree of cross-functioning, of inter-relation of departments, which means a horizontal rather than a vertical authority." • "The most important thing to remember about unity is—that there is no such thing. There is only unifying. You cannot get unity and expect it to last a day—or five minutes. Every man in a business should be taking part in a certain process and that process is unifying."
Control	• "Control is coming more and more to mean fact-control rather than man-control." • "Central control is coming more and more to mean the co-relation of many controls rather than a superimposed control."

Source: Mary Parker Follett, *Mary Parker Follett—Prophet of Management: A Celebration of Writings from the 1920s*, ed. P. Graham (Boston: Harvard Business School Press, 1995).

of an Industrial Civilization.[34] The first stage of the Hawthorne Studies investigated the effects of lighting levels and incentives on employee productivity in the Relay Test Assembly Room, where workers took approximately a minute to put "together a coil, armature, contact springs, and insulators in a fixture and secure the parts by means of four machine screws."[35] Two groups of six experienced female workers, five to do the work and one to supply needed parts, were separated from the main part of the factory by a 10-foot partition and placed at a standard work bench with the necessary parts and tools. Over the next five years, the experimenters introduced various levels and combinations of lighting, financial incentives, and rest pauses (work breaks) to study the effect on productivity. Curiously, however, whether they increased or decreased the lighting, paid workers based on individual production or group production, or increased or decreased the number and length of rest pauses, production levels increased. The question, however, was why?

Mayo and his colleagues eventually concluded that two things accounted for the results. First, substantially more attention was paid to these workers than to workers in the rest of the plant. Mayo wrote, "Before every change of program [in the study], the group is consulted. Their comments are listened to and discussed; sometimes their objections are allowed to negate a suggestion. The group unquestionably develops a sense of participation in the critical determinations and becomes something of a social unit."[36]

The "Hawthorne Effect" cannot be understood, however, without giving equal importance to the "social units," which became intensely cohesive groups. (For years, the "Hawthorne Effect" has been *incorrectly* defined as increasing productivity by paying more attention to workers.[37]) Mayo said, "What actually happened was that six individuals became a team and the team gave itself wholeheartedly and spontaneously to cooperation in the experiment. The consequence was that they felt themselves to be participating freely and without afterthought, and were happy in the knowledge that they were working without coercion from above or limits from below."[38] Together, the increased attention from management and the development of a cohesive work group led to significantly higher levels of job satisfaction *and* productivity.

For the first time, human factors related to work were found to be more important than the physical conditions or design of the work. In short, workers' feelings and attitudes affected their work.

The next stage of the Hawthorne Studies was conducted in the Bank Wiring Room, where "the group consisted of nine wiremen, three solderers, and two inspectors. Each of these groups performed a specific task

Tough Jobs

During the early twentieth century, labor unrest, dissatisfaction, and protests (some of them violent) were widespread in the United States, Europe, and Asia. In 1919 alone, for example, more than four million American workers went on strike.[39] Working conditions contributed to the unrest. Millions of workers in large factories toiled at boring, repetitive, unsafe jobs for low pay. Employee turnover was high and absenteeism was rampant. With employee turnover approaching 380 percent in his automobile factories, Henry Ford had to double the daily wage of his manufacturing workers from $2.50, the going wage at the time, to $5.00 to keep enough workers at their jobs. It's not surprising that Mayo's ideas became popular during this period.

@Bettmann/CORBIS

and collaborated with the other two in completion of each unit of equipment. The task consisted of setting up the banks of terminals side-by-side on frames, wiring the corresponding terminals from bank to bank, soldering the connections, and inspecting with a test set for short circuits or breaks in the wire. One solderman serviced the work of the three wireman."[40] In contrast to the results from the Relay Test Assembly Room, where productivity increased no matter what the researchers did, productivity dropped in the Bank Wiring Room. Again, the question was why?

Interestingly, Mayo and his colleagues found that group effects were responsible. The difference was that the workers in the Bank Wiring Room had been an existing work group for some time and had already developed strong negative norms that governed their behavior. For instance, despite a group financial incentive for production, the group members decided that they would wire only 6,000 to 6,600 connections a day (depending on the kind of equipment they were wiring), well below the production goal of 7,300 connections that management had set for them. Individual workers who worked at a faster pace were socially ostracized from the group, or "binged," hit on the arm, until they slowed their work pace. Thus, the group's behavior was reminiscent of the soldiering that Frederick Taylor had observed.

In the end, the Hawthorne Studies demonstrated that the workplace was more complex than previously thought, that workers were not just extensions of machines, and that financial incentives weren't necessarily the most important motivator for workers. Thanks to Mayo and the Hawthorne Studies, managers better understood the effect that group social interactions and employee satisfaction and attitudes had on individual and group performance.

4.3 Cooperation and Acceptance of Authority: Chester Barnard

Like Henri Fayol, Chester Barnard (1886–1961) had experiences as a top executive that shaped his views of management. Barnard began his career in 1909 as an engineer and translator for AT&T, becoming a general manager at Pennsylvania Bell Telephone in 1922 and then president of New Jersey Bell in 1927.[41] Barnard's ideas, published in his classic book, *The Functions of the Executive,* influenced companies from the board of directors down. Barnard is best known for his ideas about cooperation and the acceptance of authority.

Organization a system of consciously coordinated activities or forces created by two or more people

In *The Functions of the Executive,* Barnard proposed a comprehensive theory of cooperation in formal organizations. In fact, he defines an **organization** as a "system of consciously coordinated activities or forces of two or more persons."[42] In other words, "organization" occurs whenever two people work together for some purpose. Thus, organization occurs when classmates work together to complete a class project, when Habitat for Humanity volunteers donate their time to build a house, and when managers work with subordinates to reduce costs, improve quality, or increase sales. Why did Barnard place so much emphasis on cooperation? Because, he said, it is the "abnormal, not the normal, condition." "Failure to cooperate, failure of cooperation, failure of organization, disorganization, disintegration, destruction of organization—and reorganization—are characteristic facts of human history."[43]

According to Barnard, the extent to which people willingly cooperate in an organization depends on how workers perceive executive authority and whether they're willing to accept it. According to Barnard, for many managerial requests or directives, there is a *zone of indifference,* in which acceptance of managerial authority is automatic. For example, if your boss asks you for a copy of the monthly inventory report, and compiling and writing that report is part of your job, you think nothing of the request and automatically send it. In general, people will not be indifferent to managerial directives or orders if they (1) are understood, (2) are consistent with the purpose of the organization, (3) are compatible with the people's personal interests, and (4) can actually be carried out by those people. Acceptance of managerial authority (i.e., cooperation) is not automatic, however. Ask people to do things contrary to the organization's purpose or to their own benefit and they'll put up a fight. So, while many people assume that managers have the authority to do whatever they want, Barnard, referring to the "fiction of superior authority," believed that workers ultimately grant managers their authority.

5 Operations, Information, Systems, and Contingency Management

In this last section, we review four other significant historical approaches to management that have influenced how today's managers produce goods and services on a daily basis, gather and manage the information they need to understand their businesses and make good decisions, understand how the different parts of the company work together as a whole, and recognize when and where particular management practices are likely to work.

To better understand these ideas, let's learn about **5.1 operations management; 5.2 information management; 5.3 systems management;** *and* **5.4 contingency management**.

5.1 Operations Management

In Chapter 18, you will learn about *operations management*, which involves managing the daily production of goods and services. In general, operations management uses a quantitative or mathematical approach to find ways to increase productivity, improve quality, and manage or reduce costly inventories. The most commonly used operations management tools and methods are quality control, forecasting techniques, capacity planning, productivity measurement and improvement, linear programming, scheduling systems, inventory systems, work measurement techniques (similar to the Gilbreths' motion studies), project management (similar to Gantt's charts), and cost-benefit analysis.[44]

Today, with those tools and techniques, we take it for granted that manufactured goods will be made with standardized, interchangeable parts; that the design of those parts will be based on specific, detailed plans; and that manufacturing companies will aggressively manage inventories to keep costs low and increase productivity. Surprisingly, these key elements of operations management have some rather strange origins: guns, geometry, and fire.

Since the 1500s, skilled craftsmen made the lock, stock, and barrel of a gun by hand. After each part was made, a skilled gun finisher assembled the parts into a complete gun. The gun finisher did not simply screw the different parts of a gun together, as is done today, however. Instead, each handmade part required extensive finishing and adjusting so that it would fit together with the other handmade gun parts. This was necessary because, even when made by the same skilled craftsman, no two parts were alike. Today, we would say that these parts were low quality because they varied so much from part to part.

All this changed in 1791, however, when the U.S. government, worried about a possible war with France, ordered 40,000 muskets from private gun contractors. Because each handmade musket was unique, if a part broke,

a replacement part had to be handcrafted. But one contractor, Eli Whitney, who is better known for his invention of the cotton gin, determined that if gun parts were made accurately enough, guns could be made with standardized, interchangeable parts. So he designed machine tools that allowed unskilled workers to make each gun part the same as the next. In 1801, he demonstrated the superiority of interchangeable parts to President-elect Thomas Jefferson by quickly and easily assembling complete muskets from randomly picked piles of musket parts.

Today, because of Whitney's ideas, most products are manufactured using standardized, interchangeable parts. But, even with this advance, manufacturers still faced the significant limitation that they could not produce a part unless they had seen or examined it firsthand. Thanks to Gaspard Monge, a Frenchman of modest beginnings, this soon changed.

Monge's greatest achievement was his book *Descriptive Geometry*. In it, he explained techniques for drawing three-dimensional objects on paper. For the first time, precise drawings permitted manufacturers to make standardized, interchangeable parts without first examining a prototype. Today, thanks to Monge, manufacturers rely on CAD (computer-aided design) and CAM (computer-aided manufacturing) to take three-dimensional designs straight from the computer to the factory floor.

Once standardized, interchangeable parts became the norm, and parts could be made from design drawings alone, manufacturers ran into a costly problem that they had never faced before: too much inventory. *Inventory* is the amount and number of raw materials, parts, and finished products that a company has in its possession. A solution to this problem was found in 1905 when the Oldsmobile Motor Works in Detroit burned down. After the Oldsmobile factory burned down, management rented a new production facility to get production up and running as quickly as possible. But because the new facility was much smaller, there was no room to store large stockpiles of inventory. Therefore, the company made do with what it called "hand-to-mouth inventories," in which each production station had only enough parts on hand to do a short production run. Since all of its parts suppliers were close by, Oldsmobile could place orders in the morning and receive them in the afternoon (even without telephones), just like today's computerized, just-in-time inventory systems. So, contrary to common belief, just-in-time inventory systems were not invented by Japanese manufacturers. Instead, they were invented out of necessity a century ago because of a fire.

5.2 Information Management

For most of recorded history, information has been costly, difficult to obtain, and slow to spread. Because of the immense labor and time it took to hand-copy information, books, manuscripts, and written documents of any kind were rare and extremely expensive. Word of Joan of Arc's death in 1431 took 18 months to travel from France across Europe to Constantinople (now Istanbul, Turkey).

Consequently, throughout history, organizations have pushed for and quickly adopted new information technologies that reduce the cost or increase the speed with which they can acquire, retrieve, or communicate information. The first "technologies" to truly revolutionize the business use of information were paper and the printing press. In the 14th century, water-powered machines were created to pulverize rags into pulp to make paper. Paper prices quickly dropped by 400 percent. Less than a half-century later, Johannes Gutenberg invented the printing press, which reduced the cost and time needed to copy written information by 99.8 percent. For instance, in 1483 in Florence, Italy, a scribe would charge one florin (an Italian unit of money) to hand-copy one document page. By contrast, a printer would set up and print 1,025 copies of the same document for just three florins.

What Gutenberg's printing press did for publishing, the manual typewriter did for daily communication. Before 1850, most business correspondence was written by hand and copied using the "letter press." With the ink still wet, the letter would be placed into a tissue paper "book." A hand press would then be used to squeeze the "book" and copy the still-wet ink onto the tissue paper. By the 1870s, manual typewriters made it cheaper, easier, and faster to produce and copy business correspondence. Of course, in the 1980s, slightly more than a century later, typewriters were replaced by personal computers and word processing software for identical reasons.

System a set of interrelated elements or parts that function as a whole

Subsystems smaller systems that operate within the context of a larger system

Synergy when two or more subsystems working together can produce more than they can working apart

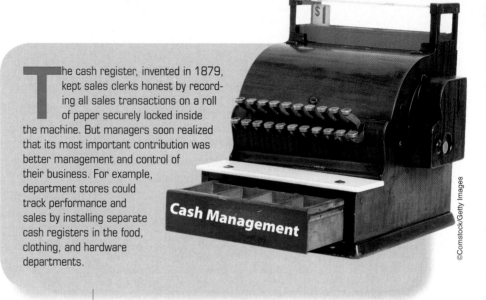

The cash register, invented in 1879, kept sales clerks honest by recording all sales transactions on a roll of paper securely locked inside the machine. But managers soon realized that its most important contribution was better management and control of their business. For example, department stores could track performance and sales by installing separate cash registers in the food, clothing, and hardware departments.

Cash Management

©Comstock/Getty Images

Finally, businesses have always looked for information technologies that would speed access to timely information. For instance, the Medici family, which opened banks throughout Europe in the early 1400s, used posting messengers to keep in contact with their more than 40 "branch" managers. The post messengers, who predated the U.S. Postal Service Pony Express by 400 years, could travel 90 miles per day, twice what average riders could cover, because the Medicis were willing to pay for the expense of providing them with fresh horses. This need for timely information also led companies to quickly adopt the telegraph in the 1860s, the telephone in the 1880s, and, of course, Internet technologies in the last decade.

5.3 Systems Management

Today's companies are much larger and more complex. They most likely manufacture, service, *and* finance what they sell. They also operate in complex, fast-changing, competitive, global environments that can quickly turn competitive advantages into competitive disadvantages.

How, then, can managers make sense of this complexity, both within and outside their organizations? One way to deal with organizational and environmental complexity is to take a systems view of organizations.[45] A **system** is a set of interrelated elements or parts that function as a whole. So, rather than viewing one part of an organization as separate from the other parts, a systems approach encourages managers to complicate their thinking by looking for connections between the different parts of the organization. Indeed, one of the more important ideas in the systems approach to management is that organizational systems are composed of parts or **subsystems,** which are simply smaller systems within larger systems. Subsystems and their connections matter in systems theory because of the possibility for managers to create synergy. **Synergy**

©Bridgeman Art Library/Getty Images

5.4 Contingency Management

Earlier you learned that the goal of scientific management was to use systematic study to find the "one best way" of doing each task and then use that "one best way" everywhere. The problem, as you may have gathered from reading about the various approaches to management, is that no one in management seems to agree on what that "one best way" is. Furthermore, more than 100 years of management research has shown that there are clear boundaries or limitations to most management theories and practices. No management ideas or practices are universal. Though they may work much of the time, none works all the time. But, then, how is a manager to decide what theory to use? Well, it depends on the situation. The **contingency approach** to management precisely states that there are no universal management theories and that the most effective management theory or idea depends on the kinds of problems or situations that managers or organizations are facing at a particular time.[47] In short, the "best way" depends on the situation.

occurs when two or more subsystems working together can produce more than they can working apart. In other words, synergy occurs when 1 + 1 = 3.

Exhibit 2.7 on the next page illustrates how the elements of systems management work together. Whereas **closed systems** can function without interacting with their environments, nearly all organizations should be viewed as **open systems** that interact with their environments and depend on them for survival. Therefore, rather than viewing what goes on within the organization as separate from what goes on outside it, the systems approach also encourages managers to look for connections between the different parts of the organization and the different parts of its environment.

A systems view of organizations offers several advantages. First, it forces managers to view their organizations as part of and subject to the competitive, economic, social, technological, and legal/regulatory forces in their environments.[46] Second, it also forces managers to be aware of how the environment affects specific parts of the organization. Third, because of the complexity and difficulty of trying to achieve synergies between different parts of the organization, the systems view encourages managers to focus on better communication and cooperation within the organization. Finally, survival also depends on making sure that the organization continues to satisfy critical environmental stakeholders, such as shareholders, employees, customers, suppliers, governments, and local communities.

> Synergy occurs when 1 + 1 = 3.

One of the practical implications of the contingency approach to management is that management is much harder than it looks. In fact, because of the clarity and obviousness of management theories (OK, most of them), students and workers often wrongly assume that if management would take just a few simple steps, then a company's problems would be quickly and easily solved. If this were true, few companies would have problems. A second implication of the contingency

Closed systems systems that can sustain themselves without interacting with their environments

Open systems systems that can sustain themselves only by interacting with their environments, on which they depend for their survival

Contingency approach holds that there are no universal management theories and that the most effective management theory or idea depends on the kinds of problems or situations that managers are facing at a particular time and place

Exhibit 2.7
Systems View of Organizations

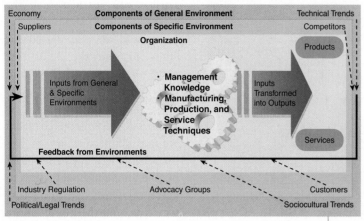

Components of General Environment — Economy, Technical Trends
Components of Specific Environment — Suppliers, Competitors
Organization
Products
Inputs from General & Specific Environments
- Management Knowledge
- Manufacturing, Production, and Service Techniques
Inputs Transformed into Outputs
Services
Feedback from Environments
Industry Regulation, Advocacy Groups, Customers
Political/Legal Trends, Sociocultural Trends

approach is that managers need to look for key contingencies that differentiate today's situation or problems from yesterday's situation or problems. Moreover, it means that managers need to spend more time analyzing problems, situations, and employees before taking action to fix them. Finally, it means that as you read this text and learn about management ideas and practices, you need to pay particular attention to qualifying phrases such as "usually," "in these situations," "for this to work," and "under these circumstances." Doing so will help you identify the key contingencies that will help you become a better manager.

Creating Synergy in the Toothpaste Aisle

When Procter & Gamble merged with Gillette, one of the much-anticipated synergies was the one to come from merging P & G's Crest (the world's No. 2 toothpaste) with Gillette's Oral-B (the world's No. 1 toothbrush). P & G hoped to leverage the expertise of both brands to create a presence that would overtake the world's leading toothpaste and overall oral care company: Colgate-Palmolive. Unfortunately, widely differing cultures of the two organizations kept many of the employees from connecting: P & G had a more rigid structure; Gillette was more informal. P & G preferred memos; Gillette was used to meetings. It seems that the engineers and scientists are the biggest beneficiaries of the new synergy. P & G's director of oral care research called the integration of the researchers "a big science love fest." The integrated research team is already trying to create an Oral-B toothbrush and Crest toothpaste that work best together.

Source: Ellen Byron, "Merger Challenge: Unite Toothbrush, Toothpaste," *Wall Street Journal*, 24 April 2007, A1.

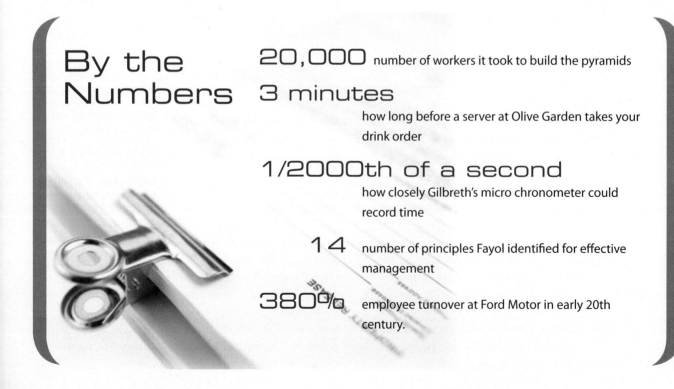

By the Numbers

20,000 number of workers it took to build the pyramids

3 minutes how long before a server at Olive Garden takes your drink order

1/2000th of a second how closely Gilbreth's micro chronometer could record time

14 number of principles Fayol identified for effective management

380% employee turnover at Ford Motor in early 20th century.

Listen Up!

MGMT was designed for students just like you – busy people who want choices, flexibility, and multiple learning options.

MGMT delivers concise, focused information in a fresh and contemporary format. And... *MGMT* gives you a variety of online learning materials designed with you in mind.

At **www.mgmt4me.com**, you'll find electronic resources such as **video podcasts, audio downloads,** and **cell phone quizzes** for each chapter. These resources will help supplement your understanding of core marketing concepts in a format that fits your busy lifestyle.

Visit **www.mgmt4me.com** to learn more about the multiple *MGMT* resources available to help you succeed!

ORGANIZATIONAL ENVIRONMENTS AND CULTURES

External Environments

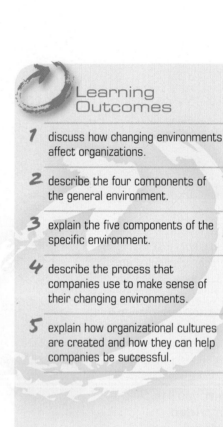

E **External environments** are the forces and events outside a company that have the potential to influence or affect it. Ask adults what their favorite afterschool snack was, and they're likely to tell you "milk and cookies." But today, overall cookie sales, including those of Oreos and Chips Ahoy, have dropped over 8 percent in the past five years.[1] Several trends in cookie companies' external environments are behind this decline. As part of the fight against obesity, parents and school systems are replacing cookies with healthier alternatives, such as fruits and vegetables. Trying to reverse the decline, Kraft Foods has developed the Vanilla Oreo, which has no unhealthy trans fats, and small, prewrapped 100-calorie packages of Oreos and Chips Ahoy "thin crisps."

This chapter examines the internal and external forces that affect business. We'll examine the two types of external organizational environments: the general environment that affects all organizations and the specific environment unique to each company. Then, we learn how managers make sense of their changing general and specific environments. The chapter finishes with a discussion of internal organizational environments by focusing on organizational culture. But first, let's see how the changes in external organizational environments affect the decisions and performance of a company.

Learning Outcomes

1 discuss how changing environments affect organizations.

2 describe the four components of the general environment.

3 explain the five components of the specific environment.

4 describe the process that companies use to make sense of their changing environments.

5 explain how organizational cultures are created and how they can help companies be successful.

External environments all events outside a company that have the potential to influence or affect it

©Food Pix/Jupiter Images

After reading the next four sections, you should be able to

1 discuss how changing environments affect organizations.

2 describe the four components of the general environment.

3 explain the five components of the specific environment.

4 describe the process that companies use to make sense of their changing environments.

1 Changing Environments

*Let's examine the three basic characteristics of changing external environments: **1.1 environmental change, 1.2 envi-**ronmental complexity, 1.3 resource scarcity**, and **1.4 the uncertainty that environmental change, complexity, and resource scarcity can create for organizational managers**.*

1.1 Environmental Change

Environmental change is the rate at which a company's general and specific environments change. In **stable environments,** the rate of environmental change is slow. For instance, except for more efficient ovens, bread is baked, wrapped, and delivered fresh to stores each day much as it was decades

> **Environmental change** the rate at which a company's general and specific environments change
>
> **Stable environment** an environment in which the rate of change is slow

As part of the fight against obesity, parents and school systems are replacing cookies with healthier alternatives, such as fruits and vegetables. Consequently, the Vista, California, school district stopped buying 28,000 chocolate chip cookies per month for its students. Can the cookie be saved?

ago. And although some new breads have become popular, the white and wheat breads that customers bought 20 years ago are still today's best sellers.

Just as baking companies have stable environments, EA Sports, whose best-selling products are sports games like Madden NFL (football) and Tiger Woods PGA Tour (golf), competes in one of the most dynamic external environments—video games. In **dynamic environments,** the rate of environmental change is fast. EA Sports' business environment is dynamic primarily because gaming technology changes so quickly. The company's first product was designed for the Atari 800, which was soon replaced by the more powerful Commodore 64, the Commodore Amiga, the 8-bit Nintendo, the 16-bit Sega Genesis, the 32-bit and 64-bit Segas, Nintendos, Sony PlayStations, desktop computers, and now the Sony PlayStation3, Nintendo's Gamecube and Wii, and Microsoft's Xbox 360. With development costs exceeding $10 million per game and marketing costs running as high as $15 million for some games, if EA Sports guesses wrong and develops games that prove to be unpopular or quickly become obsolete, it could join the dozens of game companies that have already closed their doors.[2]

Although you might think that a company's external environment would be *either* stable *or* dynamic, research suggests that companies often experience both. According to **punctuated equilibrium theory,** companies go through long, simple periods of stability (equilibrium) during which incremental changes occur, followed by short, complex periods of dynamic, fundamental change (revolutionary periods), finishing with a return to stability (new equilibrium).[3]

One example of punctuated equilibrium—the U.S. airline industry. Three times in the last 30 years, the U.S. airline industry has experienced revolutionary periods. The first, from mid-1979 to mid-1982, occurred immediately after airline deregulation in 1978. Prior to deregulation, the federal government controlled where airlines could fly, how much could be charged, when they could fly, and the number of flights they could have on a particular route. After deregulation, these choices were left to the airlines. The large financial losses during this period clearly indicate that the airlines had trouble adjusting to the intense competition that occurred after deregulation. By mid-1982, however, profits returned to the industry and held steady until mid-1989.

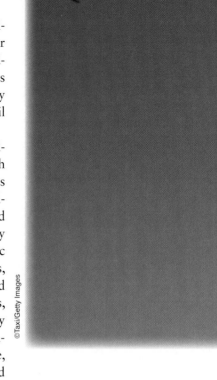

Then, after experiencing record growth and profits, U.S. airlines lost billions of dollars between 1989 and 1993 as the industry went through dramatic changes. Key expenses, including jet fuel and employee salaries, which had held steady for years, suddenly increased. Furthermore, revenues, which had grown steadily year after year, suddenly dropped because of dramatic changes in the airlines' customer base. Business travelers, who had typically paid full-priced fares, comprised more than half of all passengers during the 1980s. However, by the late 1980s, the largest customer base had changed to leisure travelers, who wanted the cheapest flights they could get.[4] With expenses suddenly up and revenues suddenly down, the airlines responded to these changes in their business environment by laying off 5 to 10 percent of their workers, canceling orders for new planes, and eliminating unprofitable routes. Starting in 1993 and lasting till 1998, these changes helped the airline industy to achieve profits far in excess of their historical levels. The industry began to stabilize, if not flourish, just as punctuated equilibrium theory predicts.[5]

The third revolutionary period for the U.S. airline industry began with the terrorist attacks of September 11, 2001, in which planes were used as missiles to bring down the World Trade Center towers and damage the Pentagon. The immediate effect was a 20 percent drop in scheduled flights, a 40 percent drop in passengers, and losses so large that the U.S. government approved a $15 billion bailout to keep the airlines in business. Heightened airport security also affected airports, the airlines themselves, and airline customers. Due to their financially weaker position, the airlines have now restructured operations to take advantage of the combined effect of increased passenger travel, a sharply reduced cost structure, and a 23 percent reduction in the fleet to move their businesses

©Taxi/Getty Images

Dynamic environment an environment in which the rate of change is fast

Punctuated equilibrium theory a theory that holds that companies go through long, simple periods of stability (equilibrium), followed by short periods of dynamic, fundamental change (revolution), and ending with a return to stability (new equilibrium)

back to profitability.[6] As a result, the airlines may be moving back to a more stable period of equilibrium.

1.2 Environmental Complexity

Environmental complexity is the number and the intensity of external factors in the environment that affect organizations. **Simple environments** have few environmental factors, whereas **complex environments** have many environmental factors. The dairy industry is an excellent example of a relatively simple external environment. Even accounting for decades-old advances in processing and automatic milking machines, milk is produced the same way today as it was 100 years ago. And while food manufacturers introduce dozens of new dairy-based products each year, U.S. milk production has grown a meager 1.25 percent per year over the last decade. In short, producing milk is a highly competitive but simple business that has experienced few changes.[7]

At the other end of the spectrum, few industries find themselves in more complex environments today than the recording industry. During its first century, the music industry was fairly simple: make recordings on records, 8-track tapes, cassette tapes, or compact discs, then sell those recordings to retailers who, in turn, sold them to consumers.

But things got much more complex after Napster created a peer-to-peer network that allowed users to easily (and usually illegally) share digital files with each other. Within a year, 30 percent of all PCs were running Napster, and the recording industry blamed illegal file sharing for sharp declines in CD sales. In an effort to create a legal downloading mechanism that would support the rights of the recording industry, Apple Computer developed iTunes.com where individual songs could be legally purchased and downloaded for 99 cents per song. Apple followed this up with the October 2001 release of its iPod, which uses an internal hard drive to store and play thousands of songs. More than one billion songs have been downloaded from iTunes since the inception of the iTunes/iPod model, clearly changing the way the recording industry distributes and profits from music.[8]

1.3 Resource Scarcity

The third characteristic of external environments is resource scarcity. **Resource scarcity** is the abundance or shortage of critical organizational resources in an organization's external environment.

For example, the primary reason that flat-screen, LCD (liquid crystal display) televisions with lifelike pictures are six times more expensive per inch than regular TVs, two times more expensive than rear projection TVs, and 25 percent more expensive than plasma TVs is that there aren't enough LCD screen factories to meet demand. As long as this condition persists, LCD TV prices will remain high. At $2 billion to $4 billion each, LCD factories are the scarce resource in this industry. LCD factories are expensive to build because, like computer chips, LCD flat screens must be made in superclean environments. Furthermore, the manufacturing process is complex and difficult to manage because the liquid crystal, which can be ruined by just one speck of dust, must be poured onto glass in a layer thinner than a sheet of paper.[9]

1.4 Uncertainty

As Exhibit 3.1 shows, environmental change, environmental complexity, and resource scarcity affect environmental **uncertainty,** which is how well managers can understand or predict the external changes and trends affecting their businesses. Starting at the left side of the figure, environmental uncertainty is lowest when

©murat Şen

Environmental complexity the number of external factors in the environment that affect organizations

Simple environment an environment with few environmental factors

Complex environment an environment with many environmental factors

Resource scarcity the abundance or shortage of critical organizational resources in an organization's external environment

Uncertainty extent to which managers can understand or predict which environmental changes and trends will affect their businesses

Exhibit 3.1

Environmental Change, Environmental Complexity, and Resource Scarcity

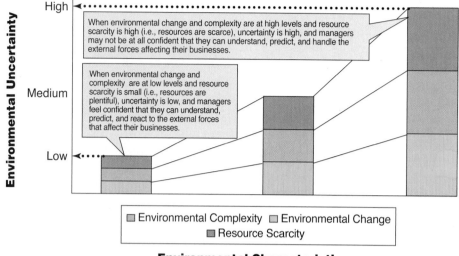

When environmental change and complexity are at high levels and resource scarcity is high (i.e., resources are scarce), uncertainty is high, and managers may not be at all confident that they can understand, predict, and handle the external forces affecting their businesses.

When environmental change and complexity are at low levels and resource scarcity is small (i.e., resources are plentiful), uncertainty is low, and managers feel confident that they can understand, predict, and react to the external forces that affect their businesses.

Environmental Uncertainty (vertical axis): High, Medium, Low

☐ Environmental Complexity   ☐ Environmental Change
☐ Resource Scarcity

Environmental Characteristics

environmental change and environmental complexity are at low levels and resource scarcity is small (i.e., resources are plentiful). In these environments, managers feel confident that they can understand, predict, and react to the external forces that affect their businesses. By contrast, the right side of the figure shows that environmental uncertainty is highest when environmental change and complexity are extensive and resource scarcity is a problem. In these environments, managers may not be confident that they can understand, predict, and handle the external forces affecting their businesses.

2 General Environment

As Exhibit 3.2 shows, two kinds of external environments influence organizations: the general environment and the specific environment. The **general environment** consists of the economy and the technological, sociocultural, and political/legal trends that indirectly affect *all* organizations. Changes in any sector of the general environment eventually affect most organizations. For example, when the Federal Reserve lowers its prime lending rate, most businesses benefit because banks and credit card com-

General environment
the economic, technological, sociocultural, and political trends that indirectly affect all organizations

Specific environment
the customers, competitors, suppliers, industry regulations, and advocacy groups that are unique to an industry and directly affect how a company does business

panies often lower the interest rates they charge for loans. Consumers can then borrow money more cheaply to buy homes, cars, refrigerators, and plasma or LCD large-screen TVs. By contrast, each organization also has a **specific environment** that is unique to that firm's industry and directly affects the way it conducts day-to-day business. For example, when the cost of coffee beans increased dramatically, Starbucks increased its prices, as did Kraft Foods, the maker of Maxwell House coffee.[10] But, only coffee-related businesses were affected. The specific environment, which will be discussed in detail in Section 3 of this chapter, includes customers, competitors, suppliers, industry regulation, and advocacy groups.

Let's take a closer look at the four components of the general environment: **2.1 the economy, and 2.2 the technological, 2.3 sociocultural, and 2.4 political/legal trends that indirectly affect all organizations**.

2.1 Economy

The current state of a country's economy affects virtually every organization doing business there. In general,

Exhibit 3.2

General and Specific Environments

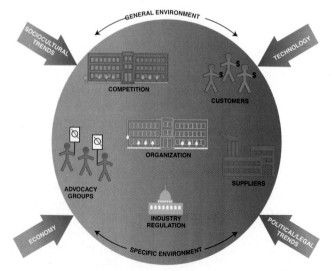

in a growing economy, more people are working and wages are growing, and therefore consumers have relatively more money to spend. More products are bought and sold in a growing economy than in a static or shrinking economy. Though an individual firm's sales will not necessarily increase, a growing economy does provide an environment favorable to business growth. In contrast, in a shrinking economy, consumers have less money to spend and relatively fewer products are bought and sold. Thus, a shrinking economy makes growth for individual businesses more difficult.

Because the economy influences basic business decisions, such as whether to hire more employees, expand production, or take out loans to purchase equipment, managers scan their economic environments for signs of significant change.

Some managers try to predict future economic activity by keeping track of business confidence. **Business confidence indices** show how confident actual managers are about future business growth. For example, the *Fortune* Business Confidence Index is a monthly survey of chief financial officers at large *Fortune* 1000 firms.[11] Another widely cited measure is the U.S. Chamber of Commerce Business Confidence Index, which asks 7,000 small business owners to express their optimism (or pessimism) about future business sales and prospects. Managers often prefer business confidence indices to economic statistics because they know that other managers make business decisions that are in line with their expectations concerning the economy's future. So if the *Fortune* or U.S. Chamber of Commerce business confidence indices are dropping, a manager might decide against hiring new employees, increasing production, or taking out additional loans to expand the business.

2.2 Technological Component

Technology is the knowledge, tools, and techniques used to transform inputs (raw materials, information, and so on) into outputs (products and services). For example, the inputs of authors, editors, and artists (knowledge) and the use of equipment like computers and printing presses (technology) transformed paper, ink, and glue (raw material) into this book (the finished product). In the case of a service company such as an airline, the technology consists of equipment, including airplanes, repair tools, computers, as well as the knowledge of mechanics, ticketers, and flight crews. The output is the service of transporting people from one place to another.

Changes in technology can help companies provide better products or produce their products more efficiently. For example, advances in surgical techniques and imaging equipment have made open-heart surgery much faster and safer in recent years. While technological changes can benefit a business, they can also threaten it. Companies must embrace new technology and find effective ways to use it to improve their products and services or decrease costs. If they don't, they will lose out to those companies that do.

2.3 Sociocultural Component

The sociocultural component of the general environment refers to the demographic characteristics, general behavior, attitudes, and beliefs of people in a particular society. Sociocultural changes and trends influence organizations in two important ways.

First, changes in demographic characteristics—such as the number of people with particular skills or the growth/decline in particular population segments (marital status, age, gender, ethnicity)—affect how companies staff their businesses. Married women with children are much more likely to work today than four decades ago. In 1960, only 18.6 percent of women with children under 6 years old and 39 percent of women with children between the ages of 6 and 17 worked. By 2004, those percentages had risen to 59.3 percent and 75.6 percent, respectively.

Second, sociocultural changes in behavior, attitudes, and beliefs also affect the demand for a business's products and services. Today, with traffic congestion creating longer commutes and both parents working longer hours, employees are much more likely to value products and services that allow them to recapture free time with their families. Circles, an

Business confidence indices indices that show managers' level of confidence about future business growth

Technology the knowledge, tools, and techniques used to transform input into output

Demographics: Percentage of Married Women (with Children) Who Work

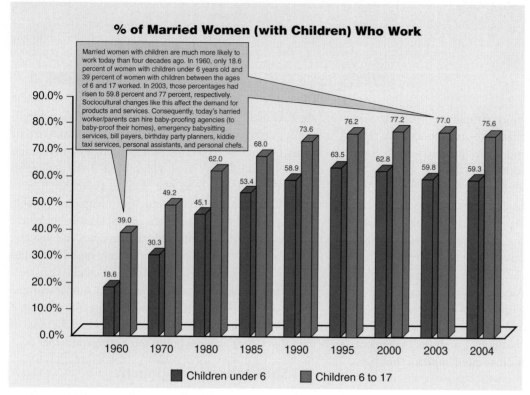

% of Married Women (with Children) Who Work

Married women with children are much more likely to work today than four decades ago. In 1960, only 18.6 percent of women with children under 6 years old and 39 percent of women with children between the ages of 6 and 17 worked. In 2003, those percentages had risen to 59.8 percent and 77 percent, respectively. Sociocultural changes like this affect the demand for products and services. Consequently, today's harried worker/parents can hire baby-proofing agencies (to baby-proof their homes), emergency babysitting services, bill payers, birthday party planners, kiddie taxi services, personal assistants, and personal chefs.

Children under 6 — Children 6 to 17

1960: 18.6, 39.0
1970: 30.3, 49.2
1980: 45.1, 62.0
1985: 53.4, 68.0
1990: 58.9, 73.6
1995: 63.5, 76.2
2000: 62.8, 77.2
2003: 59.8, 77.0
2004: 59.3, 75.6

Sources: U.S. Census Bureau, *Statistical Abstract of the United States, 1999, 2001,* and *2004–2005.* (Washington, D.C.: U.S. Government Printing Office, 1999, 2001, and 2004), "Employment Status of Women by Marital Status and Presence and Age of Children: 1960 to 1998," Table No. 631; "Employment Status of Women by Marital Status and Presence and Age of Children: 1970 to 2004," Table No. 586.

organization that provides employee concierge services, has over 300 employees helping over 250,000 client employees find more free time by planning their vacations, finding pet sitters, or running their errands.[12]

2.4 Political/Legal Component

The political/legal component of the general environment includes the legislation, regulations, and court decisions that govern and regulate business behavior. New laws and regulations continue to impose additional responsibilities on companies. Unfortunately, many managers are unaware of these new responsibilities. For example, under the 1991 Civil Rights Act (**http://www.eeoc.gov/policy/cra91.html**), if an employee is sexually harassed by anyone at work (a supervisor, a coworker, or even a customer), the company—not just the harasser—is potentially liable for damages, attorneys' fees, and back pay.[13] Under the Family and Medical Leave Act (**http://www.dol.gov/esa/whd/fmla**), employees who have been on the job one year are guaranteed 12 weeks of unpaid leave per year to tend to their own illnesses or to their elderly parents, a newborn baby, or a newly adopted child. Employees are guaranteed the same job, pay, and benefits when they return to work.[14]

Many managers are also unaware of the potential legal risks associated with traditional managerial decisions like recruiting, hiring, and firing employees. Increasingly, businesses and managers are being sued for negligent hiring and supervision, defamation, invasion of privacy, emotional distress, fraud, and misrepresentation during employee recruitment.[15] More than 24,000 suits for wrongful termination (unfairly firing employees) are filed each year.[16] In fact, wrongful termination lawsuits increased by 77 percent in the last decade and now account for 13 percent of all lawsuits against companies.[17] One in four employers will at some point be sued for wrongful termination. Employers lose 70 percent of these cases, and on average, the former employee is awarded $500,000 or more.[18]

Not everyone agrees that companies' legal risks are too severe. Indeed, many believe that the government should do more to regulate and restrict business behavior and that it should be easier for average citizens to sue dishonest or negligent corporations. From a managerial perspective, the best medicine against legal risk is prevention. As a manager, it is your responsibility to educate yourself about the laws, regulations, and potential lawsuits that could affect your business. Failure to do so may put you and your company at risk of sizable penalties, fines, or legal charges.

3 Specific Environment

As you just learned, changes in any sector of the general environment (economic, technological, sociocultural, and political/legal) eventually affect most organizations. By contrast, each organization also has a specific environment that is unique to that firm's industry and directly affects the way it conducts day-to-day business. For instance, if your customers decide to use another product, your main competitor cuts prices 10 percent, your best supplier can't deliver raw materials, federal regulators mandate reductions in pollutants in your industry, or environmental groups accuse your company of selling unsafe products, the impact from the specific environment on your business is immediate.

Let's examine how the **3.1 customer, 3.2 competitor, 3.3 supplier, 3.4 industry regulation,** *and* **3.5 advocacy group** *components of the specific environment affect businesses.*

Proactive monitoring of customers means identifying and addressing customer needs, trends, and issues *before* they occur. An example of proactive monitoring is the fast-food industry's use of multibranding, in which two or more food chains share space under the same roof. Multibranding brings in more customers by giving them more choice. Customer research suggested that people dining together might like to eat at different places at the same time. Families were a particular target of Yum! Brands, which often pairs its subsidiaries Taco Bell with KFC in one building, finds that sales are one-third higher in multibrand restaurants than in traditional single-brand restaurants.[21]

(Companies that **respond quickly** to customer letters of complaint are **viewed much more favorably** than companies that are slow to respond.)

3.1 Customer Component

Customers purchase products and services. Companies cannot exist without customer support. Therefore, monitoring customers' changing wants and needs is critical to business success. There are two basic strategies for monitoring customers: reactive and proactive.

Reactive customer monitoring is identifying and addressing customer trends and problems after they occur. One reactive strategy is to identify customer concerns by listening closely to customer complaints. This strategy involves not only listening to complaints but also responding to customer concerns. For example, companies that respond quickly to customer letters of complaint are viewed much more favorably than companies that are slow to respond or never respond.[19] In particular, studies have shown that when a company's follow-up letter thanks the customer for writing, offers a sincere, specific response to the complaint (not a form letter, but an explanation of how the problem will be handled), and contains a small gift, coupons, or a refund to make up for the problem, customers are much more likely to purchase products or services again from that company.[20]

©Getty Images News

3.2 Competitor Component

Competitors are companies in the same industry that sell similar products or services to customers. General Motors, Ford, Toyota, Honda, Nissan, Hyundai, Kia, and DaimlerChrysler all compete for automobile customers. NBC, ABC, CBS, and Fox (along with hundreds of cable channels) compete for TV viewers' attention. Often the difference between business success and failure comes down to whether your company is doing a better job of satisfying customer wants and needs than the competition. Consequently, companies need to keep close track of what their competitors are doing. To do this, managers perform a **competitive analysis,** which involves deciding who your competitors are, anticipating competitors' moves, and determining competitors' strengths and weaknesses.

Surprisingly, managers often do a poor job of identifying potential competitors because they tend to focus on only two or three well-known competitors with similar goals and resources.[22] Hoover, Dirt Devil, and, more recently, Oreck compete fiercely in the market for vacuum cleaners. Because these companies produced relatively similar vacuum cleaners, they paid attention to each other and competed mostly on price. When Dyson entered the market with its radically different vacuum that developed and maintained

Competitors companies in the same industry that sell similar products or services to customers

Competitive analysis a process for monitoring the competition that involves identifying competition, anticipating their moves, and determining their strengths and weaknesses significantly more suction power, the company garnered 20 percent market share within its first 12 months on the shelves.[23] Only then did Hoover and Dirt Devil design their own bagless vacuums.

Another mistake managers may make when analyzing the competition is to underestimate potential competitors' capabilities. When this happens, managers don't take the steps they should to continue to improve their products or services. The result can be significant decreases in both market share and profits. For nearly a decade, traditional phone companies ignored the threat to their business from VoIP (Voice over Internet Protocol), that is, the ability to make telephone calls over the Internet. Today, because phone companies were slow to respond, new VoIP competitors have slashed prices and are taking market share using high-speed Internet service. For example, Comcast, a cable TV provider that also offers high-speed Internet service, plans to roll out Internet phone service to 40 million U.S. homes over the next two years.[24] How much of a threat is Internet phone service? Jeff Pulver, CEO of Pulver.com, which owns the Internet phone company Free World Dialup, says, "Within the next 10 years, it's quite possible that 50 percent or more of voice traffic will take place off the traditional public telephone network and run on the Internet, wireless, or other systems."[25]

3.3 Supplier Component

Suppliers are companies that provide material, human, financial, and informational resources to other companies. A key factor influencing the impact and quality of the relationship between companies and their suppliers is how dependent they are on each other.[26] **Supplier dependence** is the degree to which a company relies on that supplier because of the importance of the supplier's product to the company and the difficulty of finding other sources for that product. Supplier dependence is very strong in the diamond business, given that De Beers Consolidated Mines provides 66 percent of the wholesale diamonds in the world and controls the supply, price, and quality of the best diamonds on the market. The company's 125 customers, or "sightholders," as they're known in the industry, are summoned to De Beers's London office 10 times a year and given a shoebox of diamonds that they are required to buy. If they refuse, they lose the opportunity to purchase any more diamonds.[27]

Buyer dependence is the degree to which a supplier relies on a buyer because of the importance of that buyer to the supplier's sales and the difficulty of finding other buyers for its products. For example, Superior Industries, which makes car wheels, gets 85 percent of its $840 million in annual sales from Ford and General Motors. When the two auto makers demanded that Superior match the low prices that Chinese wheel suppliers were offering, it had little choice. Superior's president, Steve Borick, says the ultimatum was presented very simply: "They said, 'This is the price we are getting [from Chinese suppliers], for this product. You either match that, or we'll take our business to them.'" He adds, "It's that black and white. Close the [cost] gap [of 20 to 40 percent] no matter how" you do it.[28]

As the De Beers and Superior Industries examples show, a high degree of buyer or seller dependence can lead to **opportunistic behavior,** in which one party benefits at the expense of the other. Though opportunistic behavior between buyers and suppliers will never be completely eliminated, many companies believe that both buyers and suppliers can benefit by improving the buyer-supplier relationship.[29] In contrast to opportunistic behavior, **relationship behavior** focuses on establishing a mutually beneficial, long-term relationship between buyers and suppliers.[30] Toyota is well known for developing positive long-term relationships with its key suppliers. Donald Esmond, who runs Toyota's U.S. division, says, "I think what they [i.e., suppliers] appreciate . . . is we don't go in and say, 'Reduce the costs by 6 percent; if you don't, somebody else is going to get the business.' We go in and say we want to come in and help you [figure out] where you can save costs so we can reduce our overall price. So it's a different approach."[31]

©Tetra Imags/Jupiter Images

Suppliers companies that provide material, human, financial, and informational resources to other companies

Supplier dependence the degree to which a company relies on a supplier because of the importance of the supplier's product to the company and the difficulty of finding other sources of that product

Buyer dependence the degree to which a supplier relies on a buyer because of the importance of that buyer to the supplier and the difficulty of finding other buyers for its products

Opportunistic behavior a transaction in which one party in the relationship benefits at the expense of the other

Relationship behavior mutually beneficial, long-term exchanges between buyers and suppliers

Shifting Power

Automakers have looked to suppliers to be "strategic partners," but what automakers really wanted was for suppliers to sell parts at prices that were attractive for the automaker and crippling for the supplier. Many (if not most) suppliers went along with that relationship, and many went bankrupt or out of business as a result. Suppliers who are still in business today are pushing back. When Michael Lord, the CEO of Bluewater Plastics, refused to sell parts at a too-low price, the purchasing manager of a Detroit automaker told him, "Obviously, you don't want to be strategic with us." Lord, however, was unfazed and confident the purchasing manager would call back. "I know we aren't the only ones pushing back—the supplier world is changing."

Source: J. McCracken and P. Glader, "New Detroit Woe: Makers of Parts Won't Cut Prices: Some Can't Afford to; Others Refuse, so Tactic of Auto Firms Withers," *Wall Street Journal*, 2 March 2007, A1, A15.

3.4 Industry Regulation Component

Whereas the political/legal component of the general environment affects all businesses, the **industry regulation** component consists of regulations and rules that govern the practices and procedures of specific industries, businesses, and professions. The auto industry is subject to CAFE (Corporate Average Fuel Economy) regulations that require cars and sports utility vehicles to average 27.5 and 22.5 miles, respectively, per gallon.[32]

Regulatory agencies affect businesses by creating and enforcing rules and regulations to protect consumers, workers, or society as a whole. The nearly 100 federal agencies and regulatory commissions can affect almost any kind of business. Overall, the number and cost of federal regulations has nearly tripled in the last 25 years. Today, for every $1 the federal government spends creating regulations, businesses spend $45 to comply with them.[33] In addition to federal regulations, businesses are also subject to state, county, and city regulations. Complying with all of these regulations costs businesses an estimated $189 billion per year or $1,700 per employee.[34] Surveys indicate that managers rank dealing with government regulation as one of the most demanding and frustrating parts of their jobs.[35]

3.5 Advocacy Groups

Advocacy groups are groups of concerned citizens who band together to try to influence the business practices of specific industries, businesses, and professions. The members of a group generally share the same point of view on a particular issue. For example, environmental advocacy groups might try to get manufacturers to reduce smokestack pollution emissions. Unlike the industry regulation component of the specific environment, advocacy groups cannot force organizations to change their practices. Nevertheless, they can use a number of techniques to try to influence companies, such as public communications, media advocacy, web pages, blogs, and product boycotts.

The **public communications** approach relies on *voluntary* participation by the news media and the advertising industry to send out an advocacy group's message. For example, a public service campaign to encourage people to quit smoking ran the following ads in newspapers and magazines throughout Europe: a photo showing the foot of a young person with a toe tag (indicating the person was dead), with the caption "Smokers die younger."[36]

Media advocacy is much more aggressive than the public communications approach. A **media advocacy** approach typically involves framing the group's concerns as public issues (affecting everyone); exposing questionable, exploitative, or unethical practices; and creating controversy that is likely to receive extensive news coverage. PETA (People for the Ethical Treatment of Animals), which has offices in the United States, England, Italy, and Germany, uses controversial publicity stunts and advertisements to try to change the behavior of large organizations, fashion designers, medical researchers, and anyone else it believes is hurting or mistreating animals. In one of its latest protests, PETA distributed 2,000 blood-covered, knife-holding, "evil Colonel Sanders" bobblehead dolls to news organizations and KFC restaurants. PETA spokesman Joe Hinkle says, "We'd like them to stop breeding and drugging chickens so that they grow so big that they actually cripple under their own bulk." KFC issued this response: "PETA has disparaged our brand and misrepresented the

Industry regulation regulations and rules that govern the business practices and procedures of specific industries, businesses, and professions

Advocacy groups groups of concerned citizens who band together to try to influence the business practices of specific industries, businesses, and professions

Public communications an advocacy group tactic that relies on voluntary participation by the news media and the advertising industry to get the advocacy group's message out

Media advocacy an advocacy group tactic that involves framing issues as public issues; exposing questionable, exploitative, or unethical practices; and forcing media coverage by buying media time or creating controversy that is likely to receive extensive news coverage truth about our responsible industry-leading animal welfare standards. KFC is committed to the humane treatment of chickens."[37]

A **product boycott** is a tactic in which an advocacy group actively tries to persuade consumers not to purchase a company's product or service. One example of this is the Rainforest Action Network (RAN), whose members have chained themselves to wood piles at select Home Depot stores to get the company to stop selling old-growth lumber.[38]

4 Making Sense of Changing Environments

In Chapter 1, you learned that managers are responsible for making sense of their business environments. As our discussions of the general and specific environments have indicated, however, making sense of busi-

Product boycott an advocacy group tactic that involves protesting a company's actions by convincing consumers not to purchase its product or service

©Maxppp/Jeff Moore/Landov

ness environments is not an easy task. Because external environments can be dynamic, confusing, and complex, managers use a three-step process to make sense of the changes in their external environments:

4.1 environmental scanning, 4.2 interpreting environmental factors, and *4.3 acting on threats and opportunities*

4.1 Environmental Scanning

Environmental scanning is searching the environment for important events or issues that might affect an organization. Managers scan the environment to stay up to date on important factors in their industry. For example, with one out of every four new car buyers purchasing highly profitable sports utility vehicles (SUVs), auto executives hadn't paid much attention to environmental groups' complaints about SUVs' extremely poor gas mileage. Now, however, market research is showing that current SUV owners are unhappy with their vehicles' poor gas mileage. In addition, the rapid rise in retail gas prices and increasingly strong disapproval of SUVs by younger car buyers have resulted in large unsold inventories of SUVs.[39]

Managers also scan their environments to reduce uncertainty. Faced with the responsibility of developing the marketing campaigns that sell their companies' most important products, the chief marketing officers (CMOs)

of the world's best organizations willingly pay $50,000 a year to join the "Marketing 50," an exclusive group of CMOs who meet several times a year to exchange ideas and pick each others' brains. Michael Linton, Best Buy's CMO, believes the "Marketing 50" is fantastic for finding out what other companies and CMOs are doing (i.e., reducing uncertainty). He says, "It's impossible for any one company to know about every new tool, so hearing what is working for others helps."[40]

Organizational strategies also affect environmental scanning. In other words, managers pay close attention to trends and events that are directly related to their company's ability to compete in the marketplace.[41] Microsoft used to take software hackers to court to prosecute them for the damage caused by their efforts. However, since Chairman Bill Gates declared that security is Microsoft's top priority, the company is actively try-

Operators Are Standing By

Ever wonder how so many people can vote on *American Idol* at the same time? AT&T has a whole division dedicated to identifying mass-calling events. Specialists keep on top of what's going on in the world that could cause a spike in phone traffic. They patrol the Internet, TV networks, and newspapers. They subscribe to the email newsletters of every major league sports team and regularly visit Ticketmaster.com and other ticket vendors. They know when concert tickets for popular bands go on sale, when major public appearances by dignitaries are scheduled, and when *American Idol* is asking viewers to call in. The goal of all this monitoring is to ensure that AT&T can manage call volumes without a disruption in service, which on a daily basis amounts to over 380 million calls.

Source: D. Searcey, "Grandmother Guards U.S. Phone Network from 'Idol' Threat," *Wall Street Journal,* 27 April 2007, A1.

ing to engage the services of friendly hackers. Though companies like Microsoft long considered hackers to be the enemy, they are now a source of competitive advantage. From Microsoft's perspective, teaming up with the hacker community to solve software problems prior to release simply makes good business sense. Microsoft security-program manager Steven Toulouse

> Managers pay **close attention** to **trends** and **events** that are directly related to their company's **ability to compete.**

stated that with the assistance of the so-called researchers, "we have discovered things during the development of these products that we might not have discovered otherwise."[42]

Finally, environmental scanning is important because it contributes to organizational performance. Environmental scanning helps managers detect environmental changes and problems before they become organizational crises.[43] Furthermore, companies whose CEOs do more environmental scanning have higher profits.[44] CEOs in better-performing firms scan their firm's environments more frequently and scan more key factors in their environments in more depth and detail than do CEOs in poorer-performing firms.[45]

Environmental scanning searching the environment for important events or issues that might affect an organization

According to money.cnn.com, consumers snapped up 500,000 iPhones during the first weekend the $600 cell phones were on the market.

4.2 Interpreting Environmental Factors

After scanning, managers determine what environmental events and issues mean to the organization. Typically, managers view environmental events and issues as either threats or opportunities. When managers interpret environmental events as threats, they take steps to protect the company from further harm. For example, now that Internet phone service (VoIP) has emerged as a threat, traditional phone companies have re- sponded by announcing billion-dollar plans to expand their fiber-optic networks so that they can offer phone (using VoIP), Internet service, and TV packages, just like those the cable and satellite companies offer.[46]

By contrast, when managers interpret environmental events as opportunities, they consider strategic alternatives for taking advantage of those events to improve company performance. The market for high-end "smart" phones, full-featured mobile phones that also function as a handheld personal computer, is growing 2 percent per year. These phones retail for between $500 and $20,000, generate high profit margins, and, as luxury goods, are insulated from fluctuations in consumer buying. Because of the opportunities in this market, Apple developed the iPhone, a $500 high-end "smart" phone featuring a wider screen and camera, the ability to use email, surf the Web, communicate with Bluetooth devices, use faster Wi-Fi networks, and, of course, download and play iTunes music. Apple hopes to sell 10 million iPhones within the first 18 months on the market, which will account for only a modest 1 percent of global handset sales but roughly half the U.S. demand for smart phones.[47]

Cognitive maps graphic depictions of how managers believe environmental factors relate to possible organizational actions

Internal environment the events and trends inside an organization that affect management, employees, and organizational culture

4.3 Acting on Threats and Opportunities

After scanning for information on environmental events and issues, and interpreting them as threats or opportunities, managers have to decide how to respond to these environmental factors. Deciding what to do under conditions of uncertainty is always difficult. Managers can never be completely confident that they have all the information they need or that they correctly understand the information they have.

Because it is impossible to comprehend all the factors and changes, managers often rely on simplified models of external environments called "cognitive maps." **Cognitive maps** summarize the perceived relationships between environmental factors and possible organizational actions. For example, the cognitive map shown in Exhibit 3.3 represents a small clothing store owner's interpretation of her business environment. The map shows three kinds of variables. The first variables, shown as rectangles, are environmental factors, such as a Wal-Mart or a large mall 20 minutes away. The second variables, shown in ovals, are potential actions that the store owner might take, such as a low-cost strategy; a good value, good service strategy; or a large selection of the latest fashions strategy. The third variables, shown as trapezoids, are company strengths, such as low employee turnover, and weaknesses, such as small size.

The plus and minus signs on the map indicate whether the manager believes there is a positive or negative relationship between variables. For example, the manager believes that a low-cost strategy won't work because Wal-Mart and Target are nearby. Offering a large selection of the latest fashions would not work either—not with the small size of the store and that large nearby mall. However, the manager believes that a good value, good service strategy would lead to success and profits because of the store's low employee turnover, good knowledge of customers, reasonable selection of clothes at reasonable prices, and good location.

Internal Environments

E

External environments are *external* trends and events that have the potential to affect companies. By contrast, the **internal environment** consists of the trends and events *within*

Exhibit 3.3
Cognitive Maps

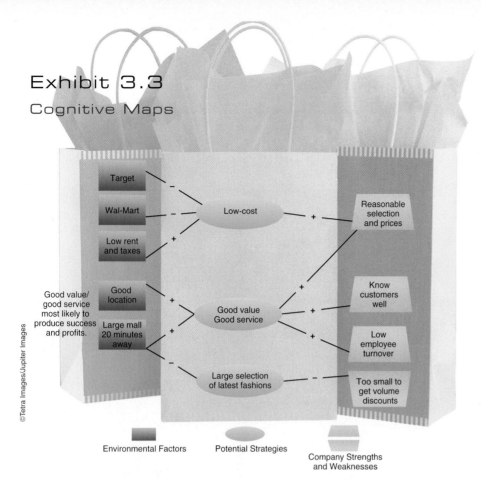

Target — Wal-Mart — Low rent and taxes → Low-cost

Good value/ good service most likely to produce success and profits.

Good location — Large mall 20 minutes away → Good value Good service

Large selection of latest fashions

Low-cost + → Reasonable selection and prices

Good value Good service + → Know customers well

+ → Low employee turnover

− − → Too small to get volume discounts

- Environmental Factors
- Potential Strategies
- Company Strengths and Weaknesses

5 Organizational Cultures: Creation, Success, and Change

*Let's take a closer look at **5.1 how organizational cultures are created and maintained, 5.2 the characteristics of successful organizational cultures,** and **5.3 how companies can accomplish the difficult task of changing organizational cultures.***

5.1 Creation and Maintenance of Organizational Cultures

A primary source of organizational culture is the company founder. Founders like Bill Gates (Microsoft) create organizations in their own images and imprint them with their beliefs, attitudes, and values. Microsoft employees share founder Bill Gates's determination to stay ahead of software competitors. Says a Microsoft vice president, "No matter how good your product, you are only 18 months away from failure."[49]

Though company founders are instrumental in the creation of organizational cultures, eventually founders retire, die, or choose to leave their companies. When the founders are gone, how are their values, attitudes, and beliefs sustained in the organizational culture? Answer: stories and heroes.

Organizational members tell **organizational stories** to make sense of organizational events and changes and to emphasize culturally consistent assumptions, decisions, and actions.[50] At Wal-Mart, stories abound about founder Sam Walton's thriftiness as he strove to make Wal-Mart the low-cost retailer that it is today.

In those days, we would go on buying trips with Sam, and we'd all stay, as much as we could, in one room or two. I remember one time in Chicago when we stayed eight of us to a room. And the room wasn't very big to begin with. You might say

an organization that affect the management, employees, and organizational culture. Internal environments are important because they affect what people think, feel, and do at work. The internal environment at SAS, the leading provider of statistical software, is unlike that of most software companies. Instead of expecting employees to work 12- to 14-hour days, SAS has a seven-hour workday and closes its offices at 6 P.M. every evening. Employees receive unlimited sick days each year. To encourage employees to spend time with their families, there's an on-site day-care facility, the company cafeteria has plenty of highchairs and baby seats. Given SAS's internal environment, it shouldn't surprise you to learn that almost no one quits. In a typical software company, 25 percent of the work force quits each year to take another job. At SAS, only 4 percent leave.[48]

The key component in internal environments is **organizational culture,** which is the set of key values, beliefs, and attitudes shared by organizational members.

After reading the next section, you should be able to

5 explain how organizational cultures are created and how they can help companies be successful.

> **Organizational culture** the values, beliefs, and attitudes shared by organizational members
>
> **Organizational stories** stories told by organizational members to make sense of organizational events and changes and to emphasize culturally consistent assumptions, decisions, and actions

we were on a pretty restricted budget. (Gary Reinboth, one of Wal-Mart's first store managers)[51]

Today, Sam Walton's thriftiness still permeates Wal-Mart. Everyone, including top executives and the CEO, flies coach rather than business or first class. When employees travel on business, it's still the norm to share rooms (though two to a room, not eight!) at relatively inexpensive motels like Motel 6 and Super 8 instead of Holiday Inns. Likewise, for business travel, Wal-Mart will reimburse only up to $15 per meal, which is half to one-third the reimbursement rate at similar-sized companies (remember, Wal-Mart is one of the largest companies in the world).

A second way in which organizational culture is sustained is by recognizing and celebrating heroes. By definition, **organizational heroes** are organizational people admired for their qualities and achievements within the organization. Bowa Builders is a full-service construction company in Virginia. When it was renovating a large auto dealership, its carpet subcontractor mistakenly scheduled the new carpet to be delivered two weeks *after* it was to be installed. Rather than allow construction to be delayed, a Bowa employee kept the project on schedule by immediately reordering the carpet, flying to the carpet manufacturer's factory, renting a truck, and then driving the carpet back to the auto dealership, all within 48 hours of learning about the problem. CEO and company cofounder Larry Weinberg says this story is told and retold within Bowa Builders as an example of heroic customer service. Moreover, the car dealership was so delighted with this extraordinary service that it has referred $10 million to $12 million in new business to Bowa Builders.[52]

5.2 Successful Organizational Cultures

Preliminary research shows that organizational culture is related to organizational success. Cultures based on adaptability, involvement, a clear vision, and consistency can help companies achieve higher sales growth, return on assets, profits, quality, and employee satisfaction.[53]

Adaptability is the ability to notice and respond

Organizational heroes
people celebrated for their qualities and achievements within an organization

Bowa Builders has no shortage of organizational heroes, in part because management supports employees' efforts to go to extraordinary lengths to please customers. Every Friday, managers bring lunch to workers on the job site.

to changes in the organization's environment. Cultures need to reinforce important values and behaviors, but a culture becomes dysfunctional if it prevents change.

In cultures that promote higher levels of *employee involvement* in decision making, employees feel a greater sense of ownership and responsibility. Employee involvement has been a hallmark of Genencor since its creation as a joint venture between Genentech and Corning in 1982. Genencor designs its human resources programs by regularly polling employees about which benefits they enjoy and which they would like the company to offer. Most dramatically, when Genencor built its headquarters, it gave its employees a say in the design. Scientists requested that the labs be placed along the building's exterior so they could receive natural light. "I've worked in labs without windows," says staff scientist Fiona Harding, "and seeing the sun makes the time spent in the lab much more pleasant." CEO Jean-Jacques Bienaime believes that these employee-driven design features lead to a more stimulating workplace. "If you want employees to be productive, you have to create a nurturing environment and let them be creative," he says.[54]

Company vision is the business's purpose or reason for existing. In organizational cultures with a clear company vision, the organization's strategic purpose and direction are apparent to everyone in the company. When managers are uncertain about their business environments, the vision helps guide the discussions, decisions, and behavior of the people in the company. At F. H. Faulding & Company (a subsidiary of Mayne Group Limited), an Australia-based provider of health-care products and services doing business in 70 countries, the vision is "delivering innovative and valued solutions in health care."[55] This vision lets employees know why the company is in business (to deliver health-care solutions) and the values that really matter (innovative and valued solutions).[56] Commenting on the value of Faulding's vision statement, Donna Martin, the senior vice president of human resources, says, "A vision has to be more than a set of target revenue or profit numbers to meet. It has to be elevating, inspiring, with a strong emphasis on the future. A vision has to be a compelling and crystal-clear statement about where the organization is heading."[57]

Finally, in **consistent organizational cultures,** the company actively defines and teaches organizational values, beliefs, and attitudes. Consistent organizational cultures are also called *strong cultures* because the core beliefs are widely shared and strongly held. Indeed, everyone who has ever worked at McDonald's has been taught its four core values: quality, service, cleanliness, and value.[58] Studies show that companies with consistent or strong corporate cultures will outperform those with inconsistent or weak cultures most of the time.[59] Why? The reason is that when core beliefs are widely shared and strongly held, it is easy for everyone to figure out what to do or not do to achieve organizational goals.

Having a consistent or strong organizational culture doesn't guarantee good company performance. When core beliefs are widely shared and strongly held, it is very difficult to bring about needed change. Consequently, companies with strong cultures tend to perform poorly when they need to adapt to dramatic changes in their external environments. Their consistency sometimes prevents them from adapting to those changes.[60] Indeed, McDonald's saw its sales and profits decline over the last decade as customer eating patterns began changing. To turn around performance, McDonald's developed hospitality and multilingual computer training programs; expanded its menu to include more healthful and snack-oriented selections. Over 5,000 McDonald's restaurants were remodeled in a three-year period and now feature warmer lighting, upbeat music, flat screen TVs, and Wi-

Fi networks. And the company's promotional message "I'm lovin' it" went from being derided by advertising executives to one of the most recognizable jingles in any market. Only a few years into the plan, McDonald's achieved 32 consecutive months of positive sales (its longest streak in 25 years), reached record annual revenues of more than $20 billion, and tripled the cash dividend paid to stockholders.[61]

5.3 Changing Organizational Cultures

As shown in Exhibit 3.4, organizational cultures exist on three levels.[62] First, on the surface level are the reflections of an organization's culture that can be seen and observed, such as symbolic artifacts (e.g., dress codes and office layouts), and workers' and managers' behaviors. Next, just below the surface, are the values and beliefs expressed by people in the company. You can't see these values and beliefs, but they become clear if you listen carefully to what people say and to how decisions are made or explained. Finally, unconsciously held assumptions and beliefs about the company are buried deep below the surface. These are the unwritten views and rules that are so strongly held and so widely shared that they are rarely discussed or even thought about unless someone attempts to change them or unknowingly violates them. Changing such assumptions and beliefs can be very difficult. Instead, managers should focus on the parts of the organizational culture they can control; these include observable surface-level items, such as workers' behaviors and symbolic artifacts, and expressed values and beliefs, which can be influenced through employee selection. Let's see how these can be used to change organizational cultures.

One way of changing a corporate culture is to use behavioral addition or behavioral substitution to establish new patterns of behavior among managers and employees. **Behavioral addition** is the process of having managers and employees perform a new behavior, while **behavioral substitution** is having managers and employees perform a

Company vision a business's purpose or reason for existing

Consistent organizational cultures when a company actively defines and teaches organizational values, beliefs, and attitudes

Behavioral addition the process of having managers and employees perform new behaviors that are central to and symbolic of the new organizational culture that a company wants to create

Behavioral substitution the process of having managers and employees perform new behaviors central to the "new" organizational culture in place of behaviors that were central to the "old" organizational culture

Exhibit 3.4

Three Levels of Organizational Culture

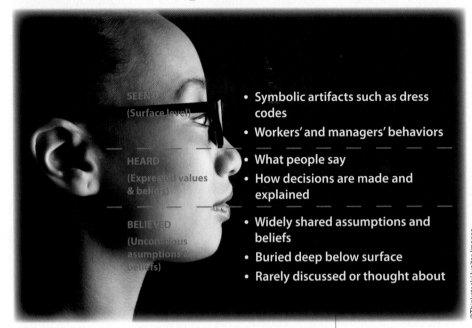

SEEN
(Surface level)

- Symbolic artifacts such as dress codes
- Workers' and managers' behaviors

HEARD
(Expressed values & beliefs)

- What people say
- How decisions are made and explained

BELIEVED
(Unconscious assumptions & beliefs)

- Widely shared assumptions and beliefs
- Buried deep below surface
- Rarely discussed or thought about

©Thinkstock/Jupiter Images

new behavior in place of another behavior. The key in both instances is to choose behaviors that are central to and symbolic of the "old" culture you're changing and the "new" culture that you want to create. When Mike Ullman became JCPenney's CEO, he thought the company's culture was stuck in the nineteenth century, when it was started: Employees called each other Mr. and Mrs., casual attire was unacceptable (even on Fridays), and any elaborate decoration of office cubicles was reported to a team of "office police" charged with enforcing corporate décor guidelines. Ullman quickly determined that the company's stringent code of conduct was, among other things, keeping it from recruiting the talent it needed. Mike Theilmann, the human resources officer, drafted a list of what he called "quick hits," small changes that would have a big impact on the culture. The first of Theilmann's initiatives was a campaign titled "Just Call Me Mike," which he hoped would cure employees of the entrenched practice of calling executives and managers "Mr." and "Mrs." Three JCPenney officers are named Mike, along with nearly 400 other employees at headquarters. Theilmann created posters containing photos of the three execu-

Visible artifacts visible signs of an organization's culture, such as the office design and layout, company dress code, and company benefits and perks, like stock options, personal parking spaces, or the private company dining room

tive Mikes along with a list of all the advantages of being on a first-name basis. Top of the list? "First names create a friendly place to shop and work."[63]

Another way in which managers can begin to change corporate culture is to change the **visible artifacts** of their old culture, such as the office design and layout, company dress code, and recipients (or nonrecipients) of company benefits and perks like stock options, personal parking spaces, or the private company dining room. To help anchor the internal culture change at JCPenney, Ullman declared that suitable work attire was business casual, and sold or donated most of the 300 pieces in the company's art collection. (He replaced them with pictures of Penney's employees and other company-oriented art.) Most strikingly, Ullman updated founder James Cash Penney's code of conduct and replaced it with one that allows all employees—not just management—to receive the company's traditional Honor, Confidence, Service, Cooperation award for employee loyalty.[64]

Cultures can also be changed by hiring and selecting people with values and beliefs consistent with the company's desired culture. *Selection* is the process of gathering information about job applicants to decide who should be offered a job. As discussed in Chapter 11 on human resources, most selection instruments measure whether job applicants have the knowledge, skills, and abilities needed to succeed in their jobs. Today, however, companies are increasingly testing job applicants to determine how they fit with the company's desired culture (i.e., values and beliefs). At Bristol-Myers Squibb, people who didn't fit the culture tended to leave. According to Ben Dowell, who runs Bristol-Myers Squibb's Center for Leadership Development, "What came through was, those who left were uncomfortable in our culture or violated some core area of our value system."[65] A key step in hiring people who have values consistent with the desired culture is to define and describe that culture. Bristol-Myers Squibb hired an organizational psychologist who spent four months interviewing senior managers. He concluded that the company had a team-driven culture that focused on research and development, which meant that it valued self-motivated, intellectually curious people.

Corporate cultures are very difficult to change. Consequently, there is no guarantee that any one approach—changing visible cultural artifacts, using behavioral substitution, or hiring people with values consistent with a company's desired culture—will change a company's organizational culture. The best results are obtained by combining these methods. Together, these are some of the best tools managers have for changing culture because they send the clear message to managers and employees that "the accepted way of doing things" has changed.

©Associated Press/©Photodisc/Getty Images

By the Numbers

2   types of external environments

99¢   price of a song on iTunes

75.6%   of U.S. women with children ages 6 to 17 who work

24,000   approximate number of lawsuits filed for wrongful termination each year

380 million   daily calls on AT&T network

3   levels of organizational culture

ETHICS AND SOCIAL RESPONSIBILITY

Today, it's not enough for companies to make a profit. We also expect managers to make a profit by "doing the right things." Unfortunately, one of the "real-world" aspects of "doing the right thing" is that no matter what managers decide to do, someone or some group will be unhappy with the outcome. Managers don't have the luxury of choosing theoretically optimal, win-win solutions that are obviously desirable to everyone involved. In practice, solutions to ethics and social responsibility problems aren't optimal. Often, managers must be satisfied with a solution that just "makes do" or "does the least harm." Crystal-clear rights and wrongs rarely reveal themselves to managers charged with "doing the right thing." The business world is much messier than that.

What Is Ethical and Unethical Workplace Behavior?

Ethics is the set of moral principles or values that defines right and wrong for a person or group. Unfortunately, numerous studies have consistently produced distressing results about the state of ethics in today's business world. A Society for Human Resources Management survey found that only 27 percent of employees felt that their organization's leadership was ethical.[1] In a

Ethics the set of moral principles or values that defines right and wrong for a person or group

©Paul Hardy/CORBIS

Learning Outcomes

1 identify common kinds of workplace deviance.

2 describe the U.S. Sentencing Commission Guidelines for Organizations and explain how they both encourage ethical behavior and punish unethical behavior by businesses.

3 describe what influences ethical decision making.

4 explain what practical steps managers can take to improve ethical decision making.

5 explain to whom organizations are socially responsible.

6 explain for what organizations are socially responsible.

7 explain how organizations can choose to respond to societal demands for social responsibility.

8 explain whether social responsibility hurts or helps an organization's economic performance.

study of 1,324 randomly selected workers, managers, and executives across multiple industries, 48 percent of the respondents admitted to actually committing an unethical or illegal act in the past year, including cheating on an expense account, discriminating against coworkers, forging signatures, paying or accepting kickbacks, and "looking the other way" when environmental laws were broken.[2]

Other studies, however, also contain good news. When people believe their work environment is ethical, they are six times more likely to stay with that company than if they believe they work in an unethical environment.[3] According to Dwight Reighard, the chief people officer at HomeBanc Mortgage Corp. in Atlanta,

"people want to work for leaders they trust."[4] In short, much needs to be done to make workplaces more ethical, but—and this is very important—most managers and employees want this to happen.

 After reading the next two sections, you should be able to

1   identify common kinds of workplace deviance.

2   describe the U.S. Sentencing Commission Guidelines for Organizations and explain how they both encourage ethical behavior and punish unethical behavior by businesses.

If you found a wallet containing $100, would you return it with the money? Informal studies typically show that 57 to 80 percent of people would and that women and people in small towns are more likely to return the wallet with the money.[5]

1 Workplace Deviance

Ethical behavior follows accepted principles of right and wrong. However, depending on which study you look at, one-third to three-quarters of all employees admit that they have stolen from their employers, committed computer fraud, embezzled funds, vandalized company property, sabotaged company projects, faked injuries to receive workers' compensation benefits or insurance, or been "sick" from work when they weren't really sick. Experts estimate that unethical behaviors like these, which researchers call "workplace deviance," may cost companies as much as $660 billion a year, or roughly 6 percent of their revenues.[6]

More specifically, **workplace deviance** is unethical behavior that violates organizational norms about right and wrong. As Exhibit 4.1 shows, workplace deviance can be categorized by how deviant the behavior is, from minor to serious, and by the target of the deviant behavior, either the organization or particular people in the workplace.[7] One kind of workplace deviance, called **production deviance,** hurts the quality and quantity of work produced. Examples include leaving early, taking excessively long work breaks, intentionally working more slowly, or wasting resources.

Property deviance is unethical behavior aimed at company property or products. Examples include sabotaging, stealing, or damaging equipment or products and overcharging for services and then pocketing the difference. Fifty-eight percent of office workers acknowledge taking company property for personal use, according to a survey conducted for Lawyers.com.[8] Property deviance also includes the sabotage of company property, such as using "software bombs" to destroy company programs and data.[9]

The theft of company merchandise by employees, called **employee shrinkage,** is another common form of property deviance. Employee shrinkage, which costs U.S. retailers more than $15.8 billion a year and

Ethical behavior
behavior that conforms to a society's accepted principles of right and wrong

Workplace deviance
unethical behavior that violates organizational norms about right and wrong

Production deviance
unethical behavior that hurts the quality and quantity of work produced

Property deviance
unethical behavior aimed at the organization's property or products

Employee shrinkage
employee theft of company merchandise

Political deviance using one's influence to harm others in the company

Personal aggression
hostile or aggressive behavior toward others

Exhibit 4.1

Types of Workplace Deviance

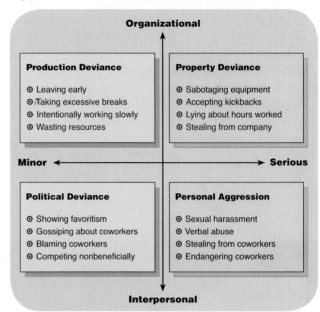

Source: Republished with permission of Academy of Management, P.O .Box 3020, Briar Cliff Manor, NY, 10510-8020. "A Typology of Deviant Workplace Behaviors," (Figure), S. L. Robinson & R. J. Bennett. *Academy of Management Journal*, 1995, Vol. 38. Reproduced by permission of the publisher via Copyright Clearance Center, Inc.

typically reduces store profits by 2 to 3 percent, takes many forms.[10] "Sweethearting" occurs when employees discount or don't ring up merchandise their family or friends bring to the cash register. In "dumpster diving," employees unload trucks, stash merchandise in a dumpster, and then retrieve it after work.[11]

Whereas production and property deviance harm companies, political deviance and personal aggression are unethical behaviors that hurt particular people within companies. **Political deviance** is using one's influence to harm others in the company. Examples include making decisions based on favoritism rather than performance, spreading rumors about coworkers, or blaming others for mistakes they didn't make. **Personal aggression** is hostile or aggressive behavior toward others. Examples include sexual harassment, verbal abuse, stealing from coworkers, or personally threatening coworkers. One of the fastest-growing kinds of personal aggression is workplace violence. More than 2 million Americans are victims of some form of workplace violence each year. According to a Bureau of Labor Statistics (BLS) survey of 7.4 million U.S. companies, 5.4 percent of all employees experienced an incident of workplace violence each year.[12] Between 650 and 1,000 people are actually killed at work each year.[13]

2 U.S. Sentencing Commission Guidelines for Organizations

Historically, if management was unaware of an employee's unethical activities, the company could not be held responsible. Since 1991, however, when the U.S. Sentencing Commission Guidelines for Organizations were established, companies can be prosecuted and punished *even if management didn't know about the unethical behavior.* Moreover, penalties can be substantial, with maximum fines approaching $300 million![14] An amendment made in 2004 outlines much stricter ethics training requirements and emphasizes creating a legal and ethical company culture.[15]

Let's examine **2.1 to whom the guidelines apply and what they cover** and **2.2 how, according to the guidelines, an organization can be punished for the unethical behavior of its managers and employees.**

2.1 Who, What, and Why

Nearly all businesses, nonprofits, partnerships, labor unions, unincorporated organizations and associations, incorporated organizations, and even pension funds, trusts, and joint stock companies are covered by the U.S. Sentencing Commission's guidelines. If your organization can be characterized as a business (remember, nonprofits count, too), then it is subject to the guidelines.[16]

The guidelines cover offenses defined by federal laws, such as invasion of privacy, price fixing, fraud, customs violations, antitrust violations, civil rights violations, theft, money laundering, conflicts of interest, embezzlement, dealing in stolen goods, copyright infringements, extortion, and more. It's not enough merely to stay "within the law," however. The purpose of the guidelines is not just to punish companies *after* they or their employees break the law, but rather to encourage companies to take proactive steps, such as ethics training, that will discourage or prevent white-collar crime *before* it happens. The guidelines also give companies an incentive to cooperate with and disclose illegal activities to federal authorities.[17]

2.2 Determining the Punishment

The guidelines impose smaller fines on companies that take proactive steps to encourage ethical behavior or

Life Imitates . . . Tony Soprano

If you think workplace violence is really only an issue for jobs like police officer, taxi driver, and convenient store clerk, consider this: Chris Albrecht resigned his position as the head of HBO after being arrested for assault in Las Vegas. He had previously been involved with a female subordinate, who received a settlement of $400,000 from Time Warner (HBO's parent company) for allegedly kicking and shoving her. Albrecht was a key figure in developing the popular programs *Sex in the City* and *The Sopranos.*

Source: B. Steinberg, "Incidents Bring Down HBO Chief," *Wall Street Journal,* 10 May 2007, B1, B2.

©Rob Kim/Landov

Exhibit 4.2

Offense Levels, Base Fines, Culpability Scores, and Possible Total Fines under the U.S. Sentencing Commission Guidelines for Organizations

Culpability Scores

Offense Level	Base Fine	0.05	0.5	1.0	2.0	3.0	4.0
6 or less	$ 5,000	$ 250	$ 2,500	$ 5,000	$ 10,000	$ 15,000	$ 20,000
7	7,500	375	3,750	7,500	15,000	22,500	30,000
8	10,000	500	5,000	10,000	20,000	30,000	40,000
9	15,000	750	7,500	15,000	30,000	45,000	60,000
10	20,000	1,000	10,000	20,000	40,000	60,000	80,000
11	30,000	1,500	15,000	30,000	60,000	90,000	120,000
12	40,000	2,000	20,000	40,000	80,000	120,000	160,000
13	60,000	3,000	30,000	60,000	120,000	180,000	240,000
14	85,000	4,250	42,500	85,000	170,000	255,000	340,000
15	125,000	6,250	62,500	125,000	250,000	375,000	500,000
16	175,000	8,750	87,500	175,000	350,000	525,000	700,000
17	250,000	12,500	125,000	250,000	500,000	750,000	1,000,000
18	350,000	17,500	175,000	350,000	700,000	1,050,000	1,400,000
19	500,000	25,000	250,000	500,000	1,000,000	1,500,000	2,000,000
20	650,000	32,500	325,000	650,000	1,300,000	1,950,000	2,600,000
21	910,000	45,500	455,000	910,000	1,820,000	2,730,000	3,640,000
22	1,200,000	60,000	600,000	1,200,000	2,400,000	3,600,000	4,800,000
23	1,600,000	80,000	800,000	1,600,000	3,200,000	4,800,000	6,400,000
24	2,100,000	105,000	1,050,000	2,100,000	4,200,000	6,300,000	8,400,000
25	2,800,000	140,000	1,400,000	2,800,000	5,600,000	8,400,000	11,200,000
26	3,700,000	185,000	1,850,000	3,700,000	7,400,000	11,100,000	14,800,000
27	4,800,000	240,000	2,400,000	4,800,000	9,600,000	14,400,000	19,200,000
28	6,300,000	315,000	3,150,000	6,300,000	12,600,000	18,900,000	25,200,000
29	8,100,000	405,000	4,050,000	8,100,000	16,200,000	24,300,000	32,400,000
30	10,500,000	525,000	5,250,000	10,500,000	21,000,000	31,500,000	42,000,000
31	13,500,000	675,000	6,750,000	13,500,000	27,000,000	40,500,000	54,000,000
32	17,500,000	875,000	8,750,000	17,500,000	35,000,000	52,500,000	70,000,000
33	22,000,000	1,100,000	11,000,000	22,000,000	44,000,000	66,000,000	88,000,000
34	28,500,000	1,425,000	14,250,000	28,500,000	57,000,000	85,500,000	114,000,000
35	36,000,000	1,800,000	18,000,000	36,000,000	72,000,000	108,000,000	144,000,000
36	45,500,000	2,275,000	22,750,000	45,500,000	91,000,000	136,500,000	182,000,000
37	57,500,000	2,875,000	28,750,000	57,500,000	115,000,000	172,500,000	230,000,000
38 or more	72,500,000	3,625,000	36,250,000	72,500,000	145,000,000	217,500,000	290,000,000

Source: "Chapter Eight—Part C—Fines," 2004 Federal Sentencing Guidelines, [Online] available at http://www.ussc.gov/2004guid/8c2_4.htm, 27 January 2005.

voluntarily disclose illegal activities to federal authorities. Essentially, the law uses a carrot-and-stick approach. The stick is the threat of heavy fines that can total millions of dollars. The carrot is a greatly reduced fine, but only if the company has started an effective compliance program (discussed below) to encourage ethical behavior *before* the illegal activity occurs.[18] The method used to determine a company's punishment illustrates the importance of establishing a compliance program.

The first step is to compute the *base fine* by determining what *level of offense* has occurred. The level of the offense (i.e., its seriousness) varies depending on the kind of crime, the loss incurred by the victims, and how much planning went into the crime. For example, simple fraud is a level 6 offense (there are 38 levels in all). But if the victims of that fraud lost more than $5 million, that level 6 offense becomes a level 22 offense. Moreover, anything beyond minimal planning to commit the fraud results in an increase of two levels to a level 24 offense. How much difference would this make to the company? As Exhibit 4.2 shows, crimes at or below level 6 incur a base fine of $5,000, whereas the base fine for level 24 is $2.1 million. So the difference is $2.095 million! The base fine for level 38, the top-level offense, is a hefty $72.5 million.

After assessing a *base fine,* the judge computes a culpability score, which is a way of assigning blame to

Exhibit 4.3

Compliance Program Steps for the U.S. Sentencing Guidelines for Organizations

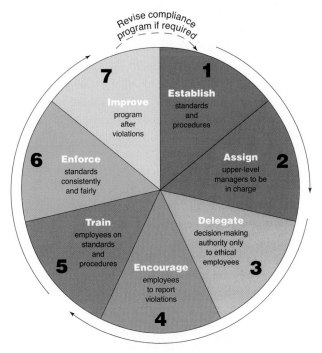

Revise compliance program if required

7 Improve program after violations

1 Establish standards and procedures

2 Assign upper-level managers to be in charge

3 Delegate decision-making authority only to ethical employees

4 Encourage employees to report violations

5 Train employees on standards and procedures

6 Enforce standards consistently and fairly

Source: D. R. Dalton, M. B. Metzger, & J. W. Hill, "The 'New' U.S. Sentencing Commission Guidelines: A Wake-up Call for Corporate America," *Academy of Management Executive* 8 (1994): 7–16.

the company. The culpability score can range from a minimum of 0.05 to a maximum of 4.0. The greater the corporate responsibility in conducting, encouraging, or sanctioning illegal or unethical activity, the higher the culpability score. A company that already has a compliance program and voluntarily reports the offense to authorities will incur a culpability score of 0.05. By contrast, a company whose management secretly plans, approves, and participates in illegal or unethical activity will receive the maximum score of 4.0.

The culpability score is critical because the total fine is computed by multiplying the base fine by the culpability score. Going back to our level 24 fraud offense, the left point of the upper arrow in Exhibit 4.2 shows that a company with a compliance program that turns itself in will be fined only $105,000 ($2,100,000 × 0.05). In contrast, a company that secretly planned, approved, and participated in illegal activity will be fined $8.4 million ($2,100,000 × 4.0), as shown by the right point of the upper arrow. The difference is even greater for level 38 offenses. As shown by the left point of the bottom arrow, a company with a compliance program and a 0.05 culpability score is fined only $3.625 million, whereas a company with the maximum 4.0 culpability score is fined a

whopping $290 million, as indicated by the right point of the bottom arrow. These differences clearly show the importance of having a compliance program in place. Over the last decade, 1,494 companies have been charged under the U.S. Sentencing Guidelines. Seventy-six percent of those charged were fined, with the average fine exceeding $2 million. Company fines are on average 20 times larger now than before the implementation of the guidelines in 1991.[19]

Fortunately, for companies that want to avoid paying these stiff fines, the U.S. Sentencing Guidelines clearly spell out the seven necessary components of an effective compliance program.[20] Exhibit 4.3 lists those components. Caremark International, a managed-care service provider in Delaware, pleaded guilty to criminal charges related to its physician contracts and improper patient referrals. When it was then sued by shareholders for negligence and poor management, the Delaware court dismissed the case, ruling that the company's ethics compliance program, built on the components described in Exhibit 4.3, was a "good-faith attempt" to monitor employees and that the company did not knowingly allow illegal and unethical behavior to occur. The court went on to rule that a compliance program based on the U.S. Sentencing Guidelines was enough to shield the company from liability.[21]

How Do You Make Ethical Decisions?

O

On a cold morning in the midst of a winter storm, schools were closed, and most people had decided to stay home from work. Nevertheless, Richard Addessi had already showered, shaved, and dressed for the office. He kissed his wife Joan goodbye, but before he could get to his car, he fell dead on the garage floor of a sudden heart attack. Addessi was four months short of his 30-year anniversary with the company. Having begun work at IBM at the age of 18, he was just 48 years old.[22]

You're the vice president in charge of benefits at IBM. Given that he was only four months short of full retirement, do you award full retirement benefits to Richard Addessi's wife and daughters? If the answer is yes, they will receive his full retirement benefits of $1,800 a month and free lifetime medical coverage. If you say no, his widow and two daughters will receive only $340 a month. They will also have to pay $473 a month just to continue their current medical coverage. As the VP in charge of benefits at IBM, what would be the ethical thing for you to do?

After reading the next two sections, you should be able to

3 describe what influences ethical decision making.

4 explain what practical steps managers can take to improve ethical decision making.

3 Influences on Ethical Decision Making

So, what did IBM decide to do? Since Richard Addessi had not completed 30 full years with the company, IBM officials felt they had no choice but to give Joan

are easily solved, many do not have clearly right or wrong answers.

The ethical answers that managers choose depend on **3.1 the ethical intensity of the decision, 3.2 the moral development of the manager,** *and* **3.3 the ethical principles used to solve the problem.**

3.1 Ethical Intensity of the Decision

Managers don't treat all ethical decisions the same. The manager who has to decide whether to deny or extend full benefits to Joan Addessi and her family is going to treat that decision much more seriously than the decision of how to deal with an assistant who has been taking computer paper home for personal use. These decisions differ in their **ethical intensity,** or the degree of concern people have about an ethical issue. When addressing an issue of high ethical intensity, managers are more aware of the impact their decision will have on others. They are more likely to view the decision as an ethical or moral decision rather than as an economic decision. They are also more likely to worry about doing the "right thing."

ALTHOUGH SOME **ETHICAL ISSUES** ARE EASILY SOLVED, MANY DO NOT HAVE CLEARLY **RIGHT** OR **WRONG** ANSWERS.

Addessi and her two daughters the smaller, partial retirement benefits. Do you think IBM's decision was ethical? Probably many of you don't. You wonder how the company could be so heartless as to deny Richard Addessi's family the full benefits to which you believe they were entitled. Yet others might argue that IBM did the ethical thing by strictly following the rules laid out in its pension benefit plan. After all, being fair means applying the rules to everyone. Although some ethical issues

Ethical intensity the degree of concern people have about an ethical issue

Magnitude of consequences the total harm or benefit derived from an ethical decision

Social consensus agreement on whether behavior is bad or good

Probability of effect the chance that something will happen and then harm others

Ethical intensity depends on six factors[23]:

- magnitude of consequences
- social consensus
- probability of effect
- temporal immediacy
- proximity of effect
- concentration of effect.

Magnitude of consequences is the total harm or benefit derived from an ethical decision. The more people who are harmed or the greater the harm to those people, the larger the consequences. **Social consensus** is agreement on whether behavior is bad or good. **Probability of effect** is the chance that something will happen and then result in harm to others. If we combine these factors, we can see the effect they can have on ethical intensity. For example, if there is *clear agreement* (social consensus) that a managerial decision or action is *certain* (probabil-

Exhibit 4.4

Kohlberg's Stages of Moral Development

Stage 1	Stage 2	Stage 3	Stage 4	Stage 5	Stage 6
Punishment and Obedience	Instrumental Exchange	Good Boy, Nice Girl	Law and Order	Social Contract	Universal Principle
Preconventional		Conventional		Postconventional	
Selfish		Societal Expectations		Internalized Principles	

Source: W. Davidson III & D. Worrell, "Influencing Managers to Change Unpopular Corporate Behavior through Boycotts and Divestitures," *Business & Society* 34 (1995): 171–196.

ity of effect) to have *large negative consequences* (magnitude of consequences) in some way, then people will be highly concerned about that managerial decision or action, and ethical intensity will be high.

Temporal immediacy is the time between an act and the consequences the act produces. Temporal immediacy is stronger if a manager has to lay off workers next week as opposed to three months from now. **Proximity of effect** is the social, psychological, cultural, or physical distance of a decision maker from those affected by his or her decisions. Thus, proximity of effect is greater for the manager who works with employees who are to be laid off than it is for a manager who works where no layoffs will occur. Finally, whereas the magnitude of consequences is the total effect across all people, **concentration of effect** is how much an act affects the average person. Temporarily laying off 100 employees for 10 months without pay is a greater concentration of effect than temporarily laying off 1,000 employees for 1 month.

Which of these six factors has the most impact? Studies indicate that managers are much more likely to view decisions as ethical decisions when the magnitude of consequences (total harm) is high and there is a social consensus (agreement) that a behavior or action is bad.[24]

3.2 Moral Development

A friend of yours has given you the latest version of Microsoft Office. She stuffed the software disks in your backpack with a note saying that you should install it on your computer and get it back to her in a couple of days. You're tempted. No one would find out. Even if someone does, Microsoft probably isn't going to come after you. Microsoft goes after the big fish—companies that illegally copy and distribute software to their workers. What would you do?[25]

In part, according to psychologist Lawrence Kohlberg, your decision will be based on your level of moral development. Kohlberg identified three phases of moral development, with two stages in each phase (see Exhibit 4.4).[26] At the **preconventional level of moral development,** people decide based on selfish reasons. For example, if you are in Stage 1, the punishment and obedience stage, your primary concern will be to avoid trouble for yourself. So, you won't copy the software because you are afraid of being caught and punished. Yet, in Stage 2, the instrumental exchange stage, you worry less about punishment and more about doing things that directly advance your wants and needs. So, you copy the software.

People at the **conventional level of moral development** make decisions that conform to societal expectations. In other words, they look to others for guidance on ethical issues. In Stage 3, the good boy, nice girl stage, you normally do what the other "good boys" and "nice girls" are doing. If everyone else is illegally copying software, you will, too. But if they aren't, you won't either. In the law and order stage, Stage 4, you again look for external guidance and do whatever the law permits, so you won't copy the software.

People at the **postconventional level of moral development** always use internalized ethical principles to solve ethical dilemmas. In Stage 5, the social contract stage, you will refuse to copy the software because, as a whole, society is better off

---

Temporal immediacy the time between an act and the consequences the act produces

Proximity of effect the social, psychological, cultural, or physical distance between a decision maker and those affected by his or her decisions

Concentration of effect the total harm or benefit that an act produces on the average person

Preconventional level of moral development the first level of moral development in which people make decisions based on selfish reasons

Conventional level of moral development the second level of moral development in which people make decisions that conform to societal expectations

Postconventional level of moral development the third level of moral development in which people make decisions based on internalized principles

Legal File Sharing

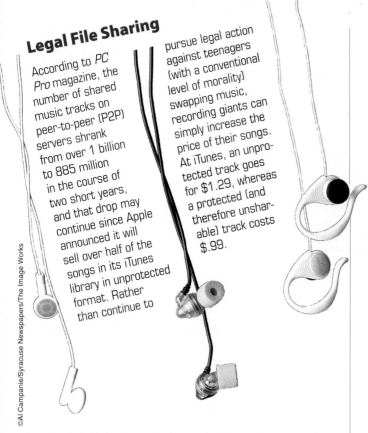

According to *PC Pro* magazine, the number of shared music tracks on peer-to-peer (P2P) servers shrank from over 1 billion to 885 million in the course of two short years, and that drop may continue since Apple announced it will sell over half of the songs in its iTunes library in unprotected format. Rather than continue to pursue legal action against teenagers (with a conventional level of morality) swapping music, recording giants can simply increase the price of their songs. At iTunes, an unprotected track goes for $1.29, whereas a protected (and therefore unsharable) track costs $.99.

Source: S. Aughton, "File Sharing Not to Blame for Music Industry's Decline," *PC Pro*, 25 August 2006, http://www.pcpro.co.uk; M. Himowitz, "Apple and EMI: Music Is the Winner," *Baltimore Sun*, 8 April 2007, http://www.technewsworld.com/story/56753.html.

when the rights of others—in this case, the rights of software authors and manufacturers—are not violated. In Stage 6, the universal principle stage, you might or

might not copy the software, depending on your principles of right and wrong. Moreover, you will stick to your principles even if your decision conflicts with the law (Stage 4) or what others believe is best for society (Stage 5). For example, those with socialist or communist beliefs would probably choose to copy the software because they believe goods and services should be owned by society rather than by individuals and corporations.

Kohlberg believed that as people became more edu-

cated and mature, they would progress sequentially from earlier stages to later stages. But only 20 percent of adults ever reach the postconventional stage of moral development where internal principles guide their decisions. By contrast, most adults are in the conventional stage of moral development in which they look outside themselves to others for guidance on ethical issues. This means that most people in the workplace look to and need leadership when it comes to ethical decision making.[27]

3.3 Principles of Ethical Decision Making

Besides an issue's ethical intensity and a manager's level of moral maturity, the particular ethical principles that managers use will also affect how they solve ethical dilemmas. Unfortunately, there is no one "ideal principle" to use in making ethical business decisions.

According to professor LaRue Hosmer, a number of different ethical principles can be used to make business decisions: long-term self-interest, personal virtue, religious injunctions, government requirements, utilitarian benefits, individual rights, and distributive justice.[28] All of these ethical principles encourage managers and employees to take others' interests into account when making ethical decisions. At the same time, however, these principles can lead to very different ethical actions, as we can see

by using these principles to decide whether to award full benefits to Joan Addessi and her children.

According to the **principle of long-term self-interest,** you should never take any action that is not in your or your organization's long-term self-interest. Although this sounds as if the principle promotes selfishness, it doesn't. What we do to maximize our long-term interests (save more, spend less, exercise every day, watch what we eat) is often very different from what we do to maximize short-term interests (max out our credit cards, be couch potatoes, eat whatever we want). At any given time, IBM has nearly 1,000 employees who are just months away from retirement. Thus, because of the costs involved, it serves IBM's long-term interest to

> (Only 20 percent of adults ever **reach the postconventional stage** of moral development.)

Principle of long-term self-interest an ethical principle that holds that you should never take any action that is not in your or your organization's long-term self-interest

Personal virtue?

©Reportage/Getty Images

pay full benefits only after employees have put in their 30 years.

The **principle of personal virtue** holds that you should never do anything that is not honest, open, and truthful and that you would not be glad to see reported in the newspapers or on TV. Using the principle of personal virtue, IBM should have quietly awarded Joan Addessi her husband's full benefits. Had it done so, it could have avoided the publication of an embarrassing *Wall Street Journal* article on this topic.

The **principle of religious injunctions** holds that you should never take an action that is unkind or that harms a sense of community, such as the positive feelings that come from working together to accomplish a commonly accepted goal. Using this principle, IBM would have been concerned foremost with compassion and kindness. Thus, it would have awarded full benefits to Joan Addessi.

According to the **principle of government requirements,** the law represents the minimal moral standards of society, so you should never take any action that violates the law. Using this principle, IBM would deny full benefits to Joan Addessi because her husband did not work for the company for 30 years. Indeed, an IBM spokesperson stated that making exceptions would violate the federal Employee Retirement Income Security Act of 1974.

The **principle of utilitarian benefits** states that you should never take an action that does not result in greater good for society. In short, you should do whatever creates the greatest good for the greatest number. At first, this principle seems to suggest that IBM should award full benefits to Joan Addessi. If IBM did this with any regularity, however, the costs would be enormous, profits would shrink, and IBM woud have to cut its stock dividend, harming countless shareholders, many of whom rely on IBM dividends for retirement income.

In this case, the principle does not lead to a clear choice.

The **principle of individual rights** holds that you should never take an action that infringes on others' agreed-upon rights. Using this principle, IBM would deny Joan Addessi full benefits. If it carefully followed the rules specified in its pension plan and granted Mrs. Addessi due process, meaning the right to appeal the decision, then IBM would not be violating her rights. In fact, it could be argued that providing full benefits to Mrs. Addessi would violate the rights of employees who had to wait 30 years to receive full benefits.

Finally, under the **principle of distributive justice,** you should never take any action that harms the least fortunate among us in some way. This principle is designed to protect the poor, the uneducated, and the unemployed. Although Joan Addessi could probably find a job, after 20 years as a stay-at-home mom, it's unlikely that she could easily find one that would support her and her daughters in the manner to which they are accustomed. Using the principle of distributive justice, IBM would award her full benefits.

As mentioned at the beginning of this chapter, one of the "real-world" aspects of ethical decisions is that no matter *what* you decide, someone or some group will be unhappy. This corollary is also true: No matter *how* you decide, someone or some group will be unhappy. Consequently, although all of these ethical

Principle of personal virtue an ethical principle that holds that you should never do anything that is not honest, open, and truthful and that you would not be glad to see reported in the newspapers or on TV

Principle of religious injunctions an ethical principle that holds that you should never take any action that is not kind and that does not build a sense of community

Principle of government requirements an ethical principle that holds that you should never take any action that violates the law, for the law represents the minimal moral standard

Principle of utilitarian benefits an ethical principle that holds that you should never take any action that does not result in greater good for society

Principle of individual rights an ethical principle that holds that you should never take any action that infringes on others' agreed-upon rights

Principle of distributive justice an ethical principle that holds that you should never take any action that harms the least fortunate among us: the poor, the uneducated, the unemployed principles encourage managers to balance others' needs against their own, they can also lead to very different ethical actions. So even when managers strive to be ethical, there are often no clear answers when it comes to doing "the" right thing.

4 Practical Steps to Ethical Decision Making

Managers can encourage more ethical decision making in their organizations by **4.1 carefully selecting and hiring ethical employees, 4.2 establishing a specific code of ethics, 4.3 training employees to make ethical decisions,** *and* **4.4 creating an ethical climate.**

4.1 Selecting and Hiring Ethical Employees

As an employer, you can increase your chances of hiring an honest person by giving job applicants integrity tests. **Overt integrity tests** estimate job applicants' honesty by directly asking them what they think or feel about theft or about punishment of unethical behaviors.[29] For example, an employer might ask an applicant, "Don't most people steal from their companies?" Surprisingly, unethical people will usually answer "yes" to such questions, because they believe that the world is basically dishonest and that dishonest behavior is normal.[30]

Personality-based integrity tests indirectly estimate job applicants' honesty by measuring psychological traits such as dependability and conscientiousness. For example, prison inmates serving time for white-collar crimes (counterfeiting, embezzlement, and fraud) scored much lower than a comparison group of middle-level managers on scales measuring reliability, dependability, honesty, conscientiousness, and abiding by rules.[31] These results show that companies can selectively hire and promote people who will be more ethical.[32]

4.2 Codes of Ethics

Today, almost all large corporations have similar ethics codes in place. Still, two things must happen if those codes are to encourage ethical decision making and behavior.[33] First, a company must communicate its code inside and outside the company. An example of a well-communicated code of ethics can be found at

Overt integrity test a written test that estimates job applicants' honesty by directly asking them what they think or feel about theft or about punishment of unethical behaviors

Personality-based integrity test a written test that indirectly estimates job applicants' honesty by measuring psychological traits, such as dependability and conscientiousness

Driving on the Right Side

After an internal bribery probe revealed that key officials made "improper payments" in Africa, Asia, and Eastern Europe to meet revenue targets, DaimlerChrysler dismissed several employees. In response, the company has established a "corporate compliance department" charged with examining its business practices to ensure compliance with anticorruption laws and the company's own ethics standards. It has also set up a "sales-practices hotline" that employees can call when they have questions and to report "questionable activities."

Source: S. Power and C. Rauwald, "Daimler Audit Sparks Scrutiny as Executives Are Suspended: Disclosures about Bus Unit Prompt New Questions Tied to Internal Controls," *Wall Street Journal*, 14 November 2006, A17.

©Iconica/Getty Images

Home Depot's Web site at http://www.homedepot.com/governance/ethics. With the click of a computer mouse, anyone inside or outside the company can obtain detailed information about the company's specific ethical business practices

Second, in addition to having an ethics code with general guidelines like "do unto others as you would have others do unto you," management must also develop practical ethical standards and procedures specific to the company's line of business. Visitors to Nortel's Web site at http://www.nortel.com/corporate/community/ethics/guide.html can instantly access references to very specific ethical standards on topics ranging from bribes and kickbacks to expense vouchers and illegal copying of software. For example, one of Nortel's ethical guidelines is "We do not accept or offer any form of bribe, kickback, improper or illegal inducement—even where the practice is widely considered a way of doing business."[34]

Specific codes of ethics such as this make it much easier for employees to decide what to do when they want to do the "right thing."

4.3 Ethics Training

The first objective of ethics training is to develop employees' awareness of ethics.[35] This means helping employees recognize which issues are ethical issues and then avoid rationalizing unethical behavior by thinking, "This isn't really illegal or immoral" or "No one will ever find out." Several companies have created board games to improve awareness of ethical issues.[36] Defense contractor Lockheed Martin has created "The Ethics Challenge," which every employee, including the CEO, must play at least once a year. Lockheed workers sit around a table, roll dice, and then move their tokens

ahead when they answer ethics questions correctly. Here's a sample question from the game:

A kickback may be in the form of:

A. *Cash*

B. *Gift to a family member*

C. *Donation to a charity at your request*

D. *All of these (the correct answer)*

The second objective for ethics training programs is to achieve credibility with employees. Some companies have hurt the credibility of their ethics programs by having outside instructors and consultants conduct the classes.[37] Employees often complain that outside instructors and consultants are teaching theory that has nothing to do with their jobs and the "real world." This is why Boeing has a vice president of ethics who employs 55 people to teach Boeing's 194,000 employees the difference between right and wrong in the aerospace industry.[38] Ethics training becomes even more credible when top managers teach the initial ethics classes to their subordinates, who in turn teach their subordinates.[39] Unfortunately, though, 25 percent of large companies don't require top managers to attend, much less teach, ethics training.[40]

The third objective of ethics training is to teach employees a practical model of ethical decision making. A basic model should help them think about the consequences their choices will have on others and consider how they will choose between different solutions. Exhibit 4.5 presents a basic model of ethical decision making.

4.4 Ethical Climate

In study after study, when researchers ask, "What is the most important influence on your ethical behavior at work?" the answer comes back, "My manager." The first step in establishing an ethical climate is for managers, especially top managers, to act ethically themselves. The National Business Ethics Survey found that unethical misconduct occurred in just 15 percent of the organizations where top managers talked about the importance of ethics, kept their promises to others, and modeled ethical behavior themselves. By contrast, unethical misconduct occurred in 56 percent of the organizations in which top management only talked about the importance of ethics, but did nothing else.[41]

A second step in establishing an ethical climate is for top management to be active in and committed to the company ethics program.[42] Business writer Dayton Fandray says, "You can have ethics offices and officers and training programs and reporting systems, but if the CEO

Exhibit 4.5

A Basic Model of Ethical Decision Making

1. **Identify the problem.** What makes it an ethical problem? Think in terms of rights, obligations, fairness, relationships, and integrity. How would you define the problem if you stood on the other side of the fence?

2. **Identify the constituents.** Who has been hurt? Who could be hurt? Who could be helped? Are they willing players, or are they victims? Can you negotiate with them?

3. **Diagnose the situation.** How did it happen in the first place? What could have prevented it? Is it going to get worse or better? Can the damage now be undone?

4. **Analyze your options.** Imagine the range of possibilities. Limit yourself to the two or three most manageable. What are the likely outcomes of each? What are the likely costs? Look to the company mission statement or code of ethics for guidance.

5. **Make your choice.** What is your intention in making this decision? How does it compare with the probable results? Can you discuss the problem with the affected parties before you act? Could you disclose without qualm your decision to your boss, the CEO, the board of directors, your family, or society as a whole?

6. **Act.** Do what you have to do. Don't be afraid to admit errors. Be as bold in confronting a problem as you were in causing it.

Source: L. A. Berger, "Train All Employees to Solve Ethical Dilemmas," *Best's Review—Life-Health Insurance Edition* 95 (1995): 70–80.

> Amazingly, though, **not all companies** fire ethics violators.

doesn't seem to care, it's all just a sham. It's not surprising to find that the companies that really do care about ethics make a point of including senior management in all of their ethics and compliance programs."[43]

A third step is to put in place a reporting system that encourages managers and employees to report potential ethics violations. **Whistleblowing,** that is, reporting others' ethics violations, is a difficult step for most people to take.[44] Potential whistleblowers often fear that they, and not the ethics violators, will be punished.[45] This is exactly what happened to Sandy Baratta, who used to be a vice president at Oracle, which makes database software used by most large companies. Baratta was fired, she alleges, for complaining about Oracle's treatment of women and its unethical business practices. Under California's whistleblower protection laws, a jury awarded her $2.6 million in damages.[46]

Today, many federal and state laws protect the rights of whistleblowers (see **http://www.whistleblowers.org** for more information). In particular, the Sarbanes-Oxley Act of 2002 (see **http://www.aicpa.org/info/sarbanes_oxley_summary.htm**) made it a serious crime to retaliate in any way against corporate whistleblowers in publicly owned companies. Managers who punish whistleblowers can be imprisoned for up to 10 years.

Some companies, including defense contractor Northrop Grumman, have made it easier for whistleblowers to report possible violations by establishing anonymous, toll-free corporate ethics hot lines. The Sarbanes-Oxley Act also requires all publicly held companies to establish anonymous hot lines to encourage reporting of unethical and illegal behaviors.[47]

The factor that does the most to discourage whistleblowers from reporting problems, however, is lack of company action on their complaints.[48] Thus, the final step in developing an ethical climate is for management to fairly and consistently punish those who violate the company's code of ethics. Amazingly, though, not all companies fire ethics violators. In fact, 8 percent of surveyed companies admit that they would promote top performers even if they violated ethical standards.[49]

Whistleblowing reporting others' ethics violations to management or legal authorities

Social responsibility a business's obligation to pursue policies, make decisions, and take actions that benefit society

What Is Social Responsibility?

Social responsibility is a business's obligation to pursue policies, make decisions, and take actions that benefit society.[50] Unfortunately, because there are strong disagreements over to whom and for what in society organizations are responsible, it can be difficult for managers to know what is or will be perceived as socially responsible corporate behavior. In a recent McKinsey & Co. study of 1,144 top global executives, 79 percent predicted that at least some responsibility for dealing with future social and political issues would fall on corporations, but only 3 percent said they do a good job of dealing with these issues.[51]

©Stockbyte/Getty Images

After reading the next four sections, you should be able to explain

5 to whom organizations are socially responsible.

6 for what organizations are socially responsible.

7 how organizations can choose to respond to societal demands for social responsibility.

8 whether social responsibility hurts or helps an organization's economic performance.

5 To Whom Are Organizations Socially Responsible?

There are two perspectives regarding to whom organizations are socially responsible: the shareholder model and the stakeholder model. According to the late Nobel Prize–winning economist Milton Friedman, the only social responsibility that organizations have is to satisfy their owners, that is, company shareholders. This view—called the **shareholder model**—holds that the only social responsibility that businesses have is to maximize profits. By maximizing profit, the firm maximizes shareholder wealth and satisfaction. More specifically, as profits rise, the company stock owned by shareholders generally increases in value.

Friedman argued that it is socially irresponsible for companies to divert time, money, and attention from maximizing profits to social causes and charitable organizations. The first problem, he believed, is that organizations cannot act effectively as moral agents for all

holders can then use their time and increased wealth to contribute to the social causes, charities, or institutions they want, rather than those that companies want.

The second major problem, Friedman said, is that the time, money, and attention diverted to social causes undermine market efficiency.[52] In competitive markets, companies compete for raw materials, talented workers, customers, and investment funds. A company that spends money on social causes will have less money to purchase quality materials or to hire talented workers who can produce a valuable product at a good price. If customers find the company's product less desirable, its sales

Among primary stakeholders, are some **more important** than others?

company shareholders. Although shareholders are likely to agree on investment issues concerning a company, it's highly unlikely that they have common views on what social causes a company should or should not support. Rather than act as moral agents, Friedman argued, companies should maximize profits for shareholders. Share-

Exhibit 4.6

Stakeholder Model of Corporate Social Responsibility

PRIMARY STAKEHOLDERS: ____

SECONDARY STAKEHOLDERS: – – – –

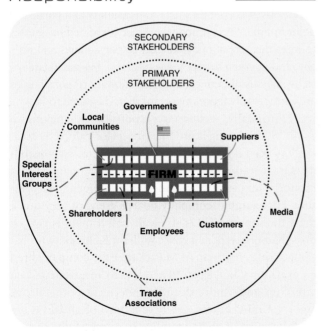

Source: Republished with permission of Academy of Management, P.O. Box 3020, Briar Cliff Manor, NY, 10510-8020. "The Stakeholder Theory of the Corporation: Concepts, Evidence and Implications" (Figure), T. Donaldson & L. E. Preston, *Academy of Management Review.* 1995, Vol. 20. Reproduced by permission of the publisher via Copyright Clearance Center, Inc.

and profits will fall. If profits fall, the company's stock price will decline, and the company will have difficulty attracting investment funds that could be used to fund long-term growth. In the end, Friedman argues, diverting the firm's money, time, and resources to social causes hurts customers, suppliers, employees, and shareholders. Russell Roberts, an economist at George Mason University, agrees, saying, "Doesn't it make more sense to have companies do what they do best, make good products at fair prices, and then let consumers use the savings for the charity of their choice?"[53]

By contrast, under the **stakeholder model**, management's most important responsibility is the firm's long-term survival (not just maximizing profits), which is achieved by satisfying the interests of multiple corporate stakeholders (not just shareholders).[54] **Stakeholders** are persons or groups with a legitimate interest in a company.[55] Since stakeholders are interested in and affected by the organization's actions, they have a "stake" in what those actions are. Consequently, stakeholder groups may try to influence the firm to act in their own interests. Exhibit 4.6 shows the various stakeholder groups that the organization must satisfy to ensure its long-term survival.

Shareholder model a view of social responsibility that holds that an organization's overriding goal should be profit maximization for the benefit of shareholders

Stakeholder model a theory of corporate responsibility that holds that management's most important responsibility, long-term survival, is achieved by satisfying the interests of multiple corporate stakeholders

Stakeholders persons or groups with a "stake" or legitimate interest in a company's actions

Being responsible to multiple stakeholders raises two basic questions. First, how does a company identify organizational stakeholders? Second, how does a company balance the needs of different stakeholders? Distinguishing between primary and secondary stakeholders can help answer these questions.[56]

Some stakeholders are more important to the firm's survival than others. **Primary stakeholders** are groups on which the organization depends for its long-term survival; they include shareholders, employees, customers, suppliers, governments, and local communities. When managers are struggling to balance the needs of different stakeholders, the stakeholder model suggests that the needs of primary stakeholders take precedence over the needs of secondary stakeholders. But among primary stakeholders, are some more important than others? In practice, yes, as CEOs typically give somewhat higher priority to shareholders, employees, and customers than to suppliers, governments, and local communities.[57] Addressing the concerns of primary stakeholders is important because if a stakeholder group becomes dissatisfied and terminates its relationship with the company, the company could be seriously harmed or go out of business.

Secondary stakeholders, such as the media and special interest groups, can influence or be influenced by the company. Unlike the primary stakeholders, however, they do not engage in regular transactions with the company and are not critical to its long-term survival. Consequently, meeting the needs of primary stakeholders is usually more important than meeting the needs of secondary stakeholders. Nevertheless, secondary stakeholders are still important because they can affect public perceptions and opinions about socially responsible behavior. For instance, after hundreds of protests by animal-rights activists, including groups such as the People for the Ethical Treatment of Animals (PETA), Smithfield Foods, the nation's largest pork producer, announced that it will phase out small "gestation crates" in which it confines pregnant female pigs at its company-owned farms. In this case, a secondary stakeholder, animal-rights activists, was able to mobilize public opinion and convince Smithfield Foods' primary stakeholders and large customers, such as McDonald's and Wal-Mart, to exert pressure on Smithfield to discontinue the practice.[58]

So, to whom are organizations socially responsible? Many commentators, especially economists and financial analysts, continue to argue that organizations are responsible only to shareholders. Increasingly, however, top managers have come to believe that they and their companies must be socially responsible to their stakeholders. Today, surveys show that as many as 80 percent of top-level managers believe that it is unethical to focus just on shareholders. Twenty-nine states have changed their laws to allow company boards of directors to consider the needs of employees, creditors, suppliers, customers, and local communities, as well as those of shareholders.[59] So, although there is not complete agreement, a majority of opinion makers would argue that companies must be socially responsible to their stakeholders.

6 For What Are Organizations Socially Responsible?

If organizations are to be socially responsible to stakeholders, what are they to be socially responsible for? Well, companies can best benefit their stakeholders by fulfilling their economic, legal, ethical, and discretionary responsibilities.[60] Economic and legal responsibilities play a larger part in a company's social responsibility than do ethical and discretionary responsibilities. However, the relative importance of these various responsibilities depends on society's expectations of corporate social responsibility at a particular point in time.[61] A century ago, society expected businesses to meet their economic and legal responsibilities and little else. Today, when society judges whether businesses are socially responsible, ethical and discretionary responsibilities are considerably more important than they used to be.

Historically, **economic responsibility,** making a profit by producing a product or service valued by society, has been a business's most basic social responsibility. Organizations that don't meet their financial and economic expectations come under tremendous pressure. For example, company boards are very, very quick these days to fire CEOs. Typically, all it takes is two or three bad quarters in a row. William Rollnick, who became acting chairman of Mattel after the company fired its previous CEO, says, "There's zero forgiveness. You screw up and you're dead."[62] Indeed, in both Europe and the United States, nearly one-third of all CEOs are fired because of their inability to successfully change their companies.[63] In fact, CEOs are three times more likely to be fired today than two decades ago.

Primary stakeholder any group on which an organization relies for its long-term survival

Secondary stakeholder any group that can influence or be influenced by a company and can affect public perceptions about its socially responsible behavior

Economic responsibility the expectation that a company will make a profit by producing a valued product or service

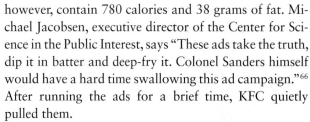

A survey by Booz Allen Hamilton revealed that CEOs are more likely to be fired for underperformance than for ethical violations—in other words, for not fulfilling the company's economic responsibilities. And the CEO attrition rate, which used to be much smaller than that of the general working population, has now pulled even with it. That is, the departure rate for U.S. CEOs is the same as general employee turnover, or about 12 percent. Ironically, one of the contributing factors in this shift is increased shareholder activism, which causes CEOs to focus on short-term results at the expense of long-term shareholder value.

Source: "Underperformance, Not Ethics, Gets CEOs Fired," *SmartPro.com*, 20 May 2005, http://accounting.smartpros.com/x48322.xml. Booz Allen Hamilton, http://www.boozallen.com/publications/article/658375?lpid=827466.

Legal responsibility is a company's social responsibility to obey society's laws and regulations as it tries to meet its economic responsibilities. For example, under the 1990 Clean Air Act, the smell of fresh baked bread is now illegal. Actually, it's not the smell that is illegal, but the ethanol that is emitted when bread is baked.[64] Although ethanol itself is nontoxic, it contributes to pollution by promoting the formation of the harmful atmospheric compound ozone. Consequently, to meet the law, large bakery plants spent millions to purchase catalytic oxidizers that remove ethanol emissions.[65]

Ethical responsibility is a company's social responsibility not to violate accepted principles of right and wrong when conducting its business. For example, most people believe that KFC was wrong to run ads implying that its fried chicken was good for you and could help you lose weight. In one ad, one friend said to another, "Is that you? Man you look fantastic! What the heck you been doin'?" With his mouth full, the friend says, "Eatin' chicken." A voice-over then says, "So if you're watching carbs and going high protein, go KFC!" Two of KFC's fried chicken breasts,

Deep-fried truth not so ethical.

©Image Source/Getty Images

however, contain 780 calories and 38 grams of fat. Michael Jacobsen, executive director of the Center for Science in the Public Interest, says "These ads take the truth, dip it in batter and deep-fry it. Colonel Sanders himself would have a hard time swallowing this ad campaign."[66] After running the ads for a brief time, KFC quietly pulled them.

Discretionary responsibilities pertain to the social roles that businesses play in society beyond their economic, legal, and ethical responsibilities. For example, dozens of companies support the fight against hunger at The Hunger Site, **http://www.thehungersite.com**. Each time someone clicks on the "donate free food" button (only one click per day per visitor), sponsors of The Hunger Site donate money to pay for food to be sent to Bosnia, Indonesia, Mozambique, or wherever people suffer from hunger. Thanks to the corporate sponsors and the clicks of 284 million visitors nearly 49 million pounds of food have been distributed thus far.[67] Discretionary responsibilities such as these are voluntary. Companies are not considered unethical if they don't perform them. Today, however, corporate stakeholders expect companies to do much more than in the past to meet their discretionary responsibilities.

7 Responses to Demands for Social Responsibility

Social responsiveness refers to a company's strategy to respond to stakeholders' economic, legal, ethical, or discretionary expectations concerning social responsibility. A social responsibility problem exists whenever company actions do not meet stakeholder expectations. One model of social responsiveness identifies four strategies for responding to social responsibility problems: reactive, defensive, accommodative, and proactive. These strategies differ in the extent to which the company is willing to act to meet or exceed society's expectations.

Legal responsibility a company's social responsibility to obey society's laws and regulations

Ethical responsibility a company's social resonsibility not to violate accepted principles of right and wrong when conducting its business

Discretionary responsibility the expectation that a company will voluntarily serve a social role beyond its economic, legal, and ethical responsibilities

Social responsiveness refers to a company's strategy to respond to stakeholders' economic, legal, ethical, or discretionary expectations concerning social responsibility

©Alan Ramey/PhotoEdit Inc.

A company using a **reactive strategy** will do less than society expects. It may deny responsibility for a problem or fight any suggestions that the company should solve a problem. By contrast, a company using a **defensive strategy** would admit responsibility for a problem but would do the least required to meet societal expectations. Second Chance Body Armor makes bulletproof vests for police officers. According to company founder Richard Davis, tests indicated that the protective material in its vests deteriorated quickly under high temperatures and humidity, conditions under which they're typically used. As a result, Davis concluded that even vests that were only two years old were potentially unsafe. Nevertheless, he couldn't convince the company's executive committee to recall the vests (an accommodative strategy). Davis says he told the committee that it had three choices: recall the vests and stop selling them, do nothing and wait "until a customer is injured or killed," or wait until the problem becomes public and "be forced to make excuses as to why we didn't recognize and correct the problem."[68] After two vests were pierced by bullets, killing one police officer and wounding another, Second Chance announced that it would fix or replace 130,000 potentially defective vests. Although the company finally admitted responsibility for the problem, management decided to do only the minimum of what society expects (fix a defective product). Second Chance, therefore, used a defensive strategy.

A company using an **accommodative strategy** will accept responsibility for a problem and take a progressive approach by doing all

that could be expected to solve the problem. For example, when an F4 tornado with winds of over 200 mph destroyed the Parsons Manufacturing plant in Roanoke, Illinois, the owner, Bob Parsons, continued paying workers their paychecks as they helped with cleanup and reconstruction, and with community service projects. A year later, the plant reopened. Parsons could have collected the insurance money and left, but he felt that workers were part of his extended family and the right thing was to rebuild.[69]

Finally, a company using a **proactive strategy** will anticipate responsibility for a problem before it occurs, do more than expected to address the problem, and lead the industry in its approach. Honda Motors announced that it will include side-curtain air bags (that drop from the roof and protect passengers' heads) and front-side air bags (that come out of the door to protect against side-impact collisions) as standard equipment on all of its cars. Although more expensive car brands, such as Lexus and Volvo, already included these safety features, Honda was the first to make them standard on all models. Charlie Baker, Honda's vice president for U.S. research and development, says, "We are convinced this is the right direction and will save lives."[70] Exhibit 4.7 summarizes the discussion of social responsiveness.

8 Social Responsibility and Economic Performance

One question that managers often ask is, "Does it pay to be socially responsible?" Though understandable, asking whether social responsibility pays is a bit like asking if giving to your favorite charity will help you get a better-

Reactive strategy a social responsiveness strategy in which a company does less than society expects

Defensive strategy a social responsiveness strategy in which a company admits responsibility for a problem but does the least required to meet societal expectations

Accommodative strategy a social responsiveness strategy in which a company accepts responsibility for a problem and does all that society expects to solve that problem

Proactive strategy a social responsiveness strategy in which a company anticipates responsibility for a problem before it occurs and does more than society expects to address the problem

Big Blue Turns Green

Rather than wait for legislation or other external pressure, IBM is taking a proactive approach to reducing energy consumption—for itself and its clients. IBM has launched a program called "Project Big Green" to help its customers slash the energy usage associated with their data centers and computer networks and cooling the facilities where those systems are stored. Big Blue will train 1,000 service representatives to help clients redesign their systems. By 2010, IBM plans to double the computing capacity of its own centers—without using any more energy—and has introduced new technology and software to help it achieve its aggressive goals.

Source: W. Bulkeley, "IBM to Launch Push for Green," *Wall Street Journal*, 10 May 2007, B4.

©Susan Van Etten

Exhibit 4.7

Social Responsiveness

Reactive	Defensive	Accommodative	Proactive
Fight all the way	Do only what is required	Be progressive	Lead the industry
Withdrawal	Public Relations Approach	Legal Approach	Bargaining	Problem Solving

DO   DO

Source: Republished with permission of Academy of Management, P.O. Box 3020, Briar Cliff Manor, NY, 10510-8020. "A Three-Dimensional Conceptual Model of Corporate Performance." (Figure 3.3) A. B. Carroll, *Academy of Management Review*, 1979, Vol. 4. Reproduced by permission of the publisher via Copyright Clearance Center, Inc.

paying job. The obvious answer is no. There is not an inherent relationship between social responsibility and economic performance.[71] Nevertheless, this doesn't stop supporters of corporate social responsibility from claiming a positive relationship. For example, one study shows that the Domini 400 Social Index, which is a stock fund consisting of 400 socially responsible companies, has outperformed the Standard & Poor's 500 (an index of 500 stocks representative of the entire economy) by nearly 5 percent. At the same time, though, critics have plenty of facts to support their claim that social responsibility hurts economic performance. For example, another study of 42 socially responsible mutual funds found that they underperformed the Standard & Poor's 500 by 8 percent.[72]

When it comes to social responsibility and economic performance, the first reality is that being socially responsible can sometimes cost a company significantly. Boston-based Timberland, which makes an assortment of work and outdoor clothing and shoes, gives each of its employees a paid (yes, paid) week off each year to help local charities. Each year, Timberland also gives four workers six months of paid leave so that they can work full-time for nonprofit organizations. Finally, Timberland closes the entire company for one day each year so that all of its 5,400 workers can spend the day working on charitable projects sponsored by the company. This commitment to giving back doesn't come cheap. Indeed, closing down for one day costs Timberland $2 million. Furthermore, assuming that the average employee makes $50,000 a year, the cost of giving each employee a paid week off to do charitable work is at least $5 million. That's $7 million a year that doesn't go to Timberland's bottom line.[73]

The second reality of social responsibility and economic performance is that sometimes it does pay to be socially responsible. The mission of Worldwise, which sells environmentally friendly consumer products, is "to make environmentally responsible products that work as well or better, look as good or finer, and cost the same or less as the competition." For example, its water bowls for pets are made out of 125 recycled bottle caps. Likewise, its ecoplanter, which looks like a heavy terra-cotta planter, is light, cheap, and made from 100 percent recycled plastic. In short, Worldwise doesn't think you should have to pay more for environmentally friendly products. In fact, its products are priced competitively enough to be sold in Wal-Mart, Target, and Home Depot. The company, which is only 13 years old, has been profitable each of the last eight years.[74]

The third reality of social responsibility and economic performance is that although socially responsible behavior may be "the right thing to do," it does not guarantee profitability. Socially responsible companies experience the same ups and downs in economic performance that traditional businesses do. Being socially responsible may be the "right thing to do," but it doesn't guarantee business success.

In the end, if company management chooses a proactive or accommodative strategy toward social responsibility (rather than a defensive or reactive strategy), it should do so because it wants to benefit society and its corporate stakeholders, not because it expects a better financial return.

Timberland closes the entire company for one day each year so that all of its 5,400 workers can spend the day working on charitable projects sponsored by the company.

PLANNING AND DECISION MAKING

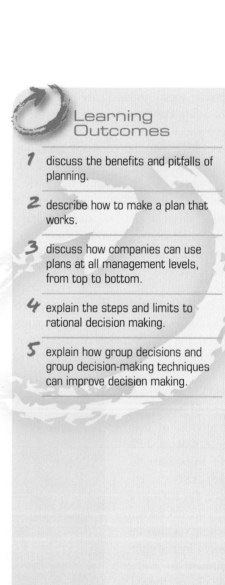
©Jupiter Images

Even inexperienced managers know that planning and decision making are central parts of their jobs. Figure out what the problem is. Generate potential solutions or plans. Pick the best one. Make it work. Experienced managers, however, know how hard it really is to make good plans and decisions. One seasoned manager says: "I think the biggest surprises are the problems. Maybe I had never seen it before. Maybe I was protected by my management when I was in sales. Maybe I had delusions of grandeur, I don't know. I just know how disillusioning and frustrating it is to be hit with problems and conflicts all day and not be able to solve them very cleanly."[1]

Learning Outcomes

1 discuss the benefits and pitfalls of planning.

2 describe how to make a plan that works.

3 discuss how companies can use plans at all management levels, from top to bottom.

4 explain the steps and limits to rational decision making.

5 explain how group decisions and group decision-making techniques can improve decision making.

Planning

Planning is choosing a goal and developing a method or strategy to achieve that goal. Toyota established a goal to increase its U.S. market share to 15 percent by 2010. Achieving that goal would move Toyota, which at that time was the fourth largest car maker in the United States, ahead of DaimlerChrysler, which has a 14.1 percent market share. How did Toyota plan to meet its 15 percent market share goal? Two words: geography and trucks. In terms of geography, Toyota already had an 18 percent market share in California but saw an opportunity in the Midwest where it had only 5 to 6 percent of the market. Manager Yuki Funo believed that the only sure way for Toyota to get

Planning choosing a goal and developing a strategy to achieve that goal a 15 percent market share nationally was with pickup trucks. In 2006, Toyota rolled out its first full-size pickup truck, the Toyota Tundra, and saw its national market share jump to 13.3 percent, well on the way to the 15 percent goal.[2]

After reading the next three sections, you should be able to

1   discuss the benefits and pitfalls of planning.

2   describe how to make a plan that works.

3   discuss how companies can use plans at all management levels, from top to bottom.

1 Benefits and Pitfalls of Planning

Are you one of those naturally organized people who always make a daily to-do list, and never miss a deadline? Or are you one of those flexible, creative, go-with-the-flow people who dislike planning because it restricts their freedom? Some people are natural planners. They love it and can see only its benefits. Others dislike planning and can see only its disadvantages. It turns out that both views have real value.

*Planning has advantages and disadvantages. Let's learn about **1.1 the benefits** and **1.2 the pitfalls of planning**.*

1.1 Benefits of Planning

Planning offers several important benefits: intensified effort, persistence, direction, and creation of task strategies.[3] First, managers and employees put forth greater effort when following a plan. Take two workers. Instruct one to "do your best" to increase production, and instruct the other to achieve a 2 percent increase in production each month. Research shows that the one with the specific plan will work harder.[4]

Second, planning leads to persistence, that is, working hard for long periods. In fact, planning encourages persistence even when there may be little chance of short-term success.[5] McDonald's founder Ray Kroc, a keen believer in the power of persistence, had this quotation from President Calvin Coolidge hung in all of his executives' offices: "Nothing in the world can take the place of persistence. Talent will not; nothing is more common than unsuccessful men with talent. Genius will not; unrewarded genius is almost a proverb. Education will not; the world is full of educated derelicts. Persistence and determination alone are omnipotent."[6]

The third benefit of planning is direction. Plans encourage managers and employees to direct their persistent efforts *toward* activities that help accomplish their goals and *away* from activities that don't.[7] The fourth benefit of planning is that it encourages the development of task strategies. In other words, planning not only encourages people to work hard for extended periods and to engage in behaviors directly related to goal accomplishment, it also encourages them to think of better ways to do their jobs. Finally, perhaps the most compelling benefit of planning is that it has been proved to work for both companies and individuals. On average, companies with plans have larger profits and grow much faster than companies that don't.[8] The same holds true for individual managers and employees: There is no better way to improve the performance of the people who work in a company than to have them set goals and develop strategies for achieving those goals.

> ## DESPITE THE SIGNIFICANT BENEFITS ASSOCIATED WITH PLANNING, PLANNING IS NOT A CURE-ALL.

Planning . . .

Working for you by:	Working against you by:
• intensifying effort	• impeding change
• increasing persistence	• creating a false sense of certainty
• providing direction	• allowing planners to plan things they don't understand how to accomplish
• creating task strategies	

1.2 Planning Pitfalls

Despite the significant benefits associated with planning, planning is not a cure-all. Plans won't fix all organizational problems. In fact, many management authors and consultants believe that planning can harm companies in several ways.[9]

The first pitfall of planning is that it can impede change and prevent or slow needed adaptation. Sometimes companies become so committed to achieving the goals set forth in their plans, or on following the strategies and tactics spelled out in them, that they fail to see that their plans aren't working or that their goals need to change. Ironically, Sony, one of the world's best known electronics innovators which famously introduced its breakthrough Trinitron (picture tube) televisions, was one of the last major TV manufacturers to develop a line of flat-screen TVs. Sony's TV division was so committed to the old—and now outdated—Trinitron picture tube technology that its engineers were reluctant to turn to Sony's audio, videogame, and computer monitor divisions for help and expertise in designing new flat-screen TVs.[10]

The second pitfall is that planning can create a false sense of certainty. Planners sometimes feel that they know exactly what the future holds for their competitors, their suppliers, and their companies. However, all plans are based on assumptions. "The price of gasoline will increase by 4 percent per year." "Exports will continue to rise." For plans to work, the assumptions on which they are based must hold true. If the assumptions turn out to be false, then the plans based on them are likely to fail.

The third potential pitfall of planning is the detachment of planners. In theory, strategic planners and top-level managers are supposed to focus on the big picture and not concern themselves with the details of implementation, that is, carrying out the plan. According to management professor Henry Mintzberg, detachment leads planners to plan for things they don't understand.[11] Plans are meant to be guidelines for action, not abstract theories. Consequently, planners need to be familiar with the daily details of their businesses if they are to produce plans that can work.

2 How to Make a Plan That Works

Planning is a double-edged sword. If done right, planning brings about tremendous increases in individual and organizational performance. If planning is done wrong, however, it can have just the opposite effect and harm individual and organizational performance.

In this section, you will learn how to make a plan that works. As depicted in Exhibit 5.1, planning consists of *2.1 setting goals, 2.2 developing commitment to the goals, 2.3 developing effective action plans, 2.4 tracking progress toward goal achievement,* and *2.5 maintaining flexibility in planning.*

2.1 Setting Goals

Since planning involves choosing a goal and developing a method or strategy to achieve that goal, the first step in planning is to set goals. To direct behavior and increase effort, goals need to be specific and challenging.[12] For example, deciding to "increase sales this year" won't direct and energize workers as much as deciding to "increase North American sales by 4 percent in the next six months." Specific, challenging goals provide a target for which to aim and a standard against which to measure success.

One way of writing effective goals for yourself, your job, or your company is to use the S.M.A.R.T. guidelines. **S.M.A.R.T. goals** are Specific, Measurable, Attainable, Realistic, and Timely.[13] Let's see how a heating, ventilation, and air-conditioning (HVAC) company might use S.M.A.R.T. goals in its business.

The HVAC business is cyclical. It's extremely busy at the beginning of summer, when homeowners find that their air-conditioning isn't working, and at the beginning of winter, when furnaces and heat pumps need repair. During these times, most HVAC companies have more business than they can handle, while at other times of year their business can

Exhibit 5.1
How to Make a Plan That Works

| 1 Set goals | 2 Develop commitment | 3 Develop effective action plans | 4 Track progress toward goal achievement | 5 Maintain flexibility |

✓ Who
✓ What
✓ When
  How

Revise existing plan
or
Begin planning process
anew

be very slow. So a *specific* goal would be to increase sales by 50 percent during the fall and spring, when business is slower. This goal could be *measured* by keeping track of the number of annual maintenance contracts sold to customers. This goal of increasing sales during the off-seasons is *attainable* because maintenance contracts typically include spring tune-ups (air-conditioning systems) and fall tune-ups (furnace or heating systems). Moreover, a 50 percent increase in sales during the slow seasons appears to be *realistic*. Because customers want their furnaces and air conditioners to work the first time it gets cold (or hot) each year, a well-designed pitch may make them very open to buying service contracts that ensure their equipment is in working order. Tune-up work can then be scheduled during the slow seasons, increasing sales at those times. Finally, this goal can be made *timely* by asking the staff to push sales of maintenance contracts before Labor Day, the traditional end of summer, when people start thinking about the cold days ahead, and in March, when winter-weary people start longing for hot days in air-conditioned comfort. The result should be more work during the slow fall and spring seasons.

2.2 Developing Commitment to Goals

Just because a company sets a goal doesn't mean that people will try to accomplish it. If workers don't care about a goal, that goal won't encourage them to work harder or smarter. Thus, the second step in planning is to develop commitment to goals.[14]

Goal commitment is the determination to achieve a goal. Commitment to achieve a goal is not automatic. Managers and workers must choose to commit themselves to a goal. Edwin Locke, professor emeritus of management at the University of Maryland and the foremost expert on how, why, and when goals work, tells a story about an overweight friend who finally lost 75 pounds. Locke says, "I asked him how he did it, knowing how hard it was for most people to lose so much weight." His friend responded, "Actually, it was quite simple. I simply decided that I *really wanted* to do it."[15] Put another way, goal commitment is really wanting to achieve a goal.

So how can managers bring about goal commitment? The most popular approach is to set goals participatively. Rather than assigning goals to workers ("Johnson, you've got till Tuesday of next week to redesign the flux capacitor so it gives us 10 percent more output"), managers and employees choose goals together. The goals are more likely to be realistic and attainable if employees participate in setting them. Another technique for gaining commitment to a goal is to make the goal public by having individuals or work units tell others about their goals. Another way to increase goal commitment is to obtain top management's support. Top management can show support for a plan or program by providing funds, speaking publicly about the plan, or participating in the plan itself.

2.3 Developing Effective Action Plans

The third step in planning is to develop effective action plans. An **action plan** lists the specific steps (how), people (who), resources (what), and time period (when) for accomplishing a goal. Unlike most CEOs, Randy Papadellis has a unique goal that requires an extraordinary action plan. As the CEO of Ocean Spray, Papadellis has to buy all of the cranberries that his farmers produce (Ocean Spray is a farmer cooperative) and must buy the crop at the highest possible price. Then, it's Papadellis's job to figure out how to sell the entire crop of high-cost berries. He says, "Imagine if Pepsi had to maximize the aluminum it used, and at the highest price it could afford!" Under Papadellis's direction, Ocean Spray began looking for alternative uses for cranberries beyond the traditional juice and canned products. The company invented driedfruit Craisins by reinfusing juice into husks that used to be thrown away. Craisins have grown into a $100 million product line. Ocean Spray also developed a set of light drinks that had just 40 calories, mock berries that could be infused with other flavors (blueberry, strawberry, etc.) and used in muffins and cereals, and was the first company to introduce juice boxes. Because of these effective actions, Ocean Spray has been able to increase the price it pays its farmers over 100 percent in the past three years.[16]

2.4 Tracking Progress

The fourth step in planning is to track progress toward goal achievement. There are two accepted methods of tracking progress. The first is to set proximal goals and distal goals. **Proximal goals** are short-term goals or subgoals, whereas **distal goals** are long-term or primary goals.[17] The idea behind setting proximal goals is that achieving them may be more motivating and rewarding than waiting to reach far-off distal goals.

The second method of tracking progress is to gather and provide performance feedback. Regular, frequent performance feedback allows workers and managers to track their progress toward goal achievement and make adjustments in effort, direction, and strategies.[18] For example, Exhibit 5.2 shows the result of providing feedback on safety behavior to the makeup and wrapping workers in a large bakery company. During the baseline period, workers in the wrapping department, who measure and mix ingredients, roll the bread dough, and put it into baking pans, performed their jobs safely about 70 percent of the time (see arrow 1 in Exhibit 5.2). The baseline safety record for workers in the makeup department, who bag and seal baked bread and assemble, pack, and tape cardboard cartons for shipping, was somewhat better at 78 percent (see arrow 2). After the company gave workers 30 minutes of safety training, set a goal of 90 percent safe behavior, and then provided daily feedback (such as a chart similar to Exhibit 5.2), performance improved dramatically. During the intervention period,

Action plan the specific steps, people, and resources needed to accomplish a goal

Proximal goals short-term goals or subgoals

Distal goals long-term or primary goals

Ocean Spray has been able to increase the price it pays its farmers over 100 percent in the past 3 years.

©Tetra Images/Jupiter Images

©Landov

Exhibit 5.2

Effects of Goal Setting, Training, and Feedback on Safe Behavior in a Bread Factory

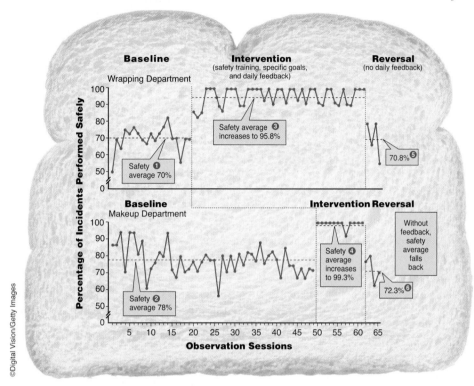

Baseline | **Intervention** (safety training, specific goals, and daily feedback) | **Reversal** (no daily feedback)

Wrapping Department

Safety ❶ average 70%

Safety average ❸ increases to 95.8%

70.8% ❺

Baseline Makeup Department | **Intervention** | **Reversal**

Safety ❷ average 78%

Safety ❹ average increases to 99.3%

Without feedback, safety average falls back

72.3% ❻

Percentage of Incidents Performed Safely

Observation Sessions

©Digital Vision/Getty Images

Source: © 1978 by the American Psychological Association. "A Behavioral Approach to Occupational Safety: Pinpointing and Reinforcing Safe Performance in a Food Manufacturing Plant." Komaki, J., Barwick K. D., & Scott, L. R., *Journal of Applied Psychology*, 1978, V63. Reprinted with permission.

the percentage of safely performed behaviors rose to an average of 95.8 percent for wrapping workers (see arrow 3) and 99.3 percent for workers in the makeup department (see arrow 4), and never fell below 83 percent. Thus, the combination of training, a challenging goal, and feedback led to a dramatic increase in performance.

The importance of feedback alone can be seen in the reversal stage, when the company quit posting daily feedback on safe behavior. Without daily feedback, the percentage of safely performed behavior returned to baseline levels, 70.8 percent for the wrapping department (see arrow 5) and 72.3 percent for the makeup department (see arrow 6). For planning to be effective, workers need both a specific, challenging goal and regular feedback to track their progress. Indeed, further research indicates that the effectiveness of goal setting can be doubled by the addition of feedback.[19]

2.5 Maintaining Flexibility

Because action plans are sometimes poorly conceived and goals sometimes turn out not to be achievable, the last step in developing an effective plan is to maintain flexibility. One method of maintaining flexibility while planning is to adopt an options-based approach.[20] The goal of **options-based planning** is to keep options open by making small, simultaneous investments in many alternative plans. Then, when one or a few of these plans emerge as likely winners, you invest even more in these plans while discontinuing or reducing investment in the others. In part, options-based planning is the opposite of traditional planning. Whereas the purpose of an action plan is to commit people and resources to a particular course of action, the purpose of options-based planning is to leave those commitments open by maintaining **slack resources**, that is, a cushion of resources, such as extra time, people, money, or production capacity, that can be used to address and adapt to unanticipated changes, problems, or opportunities.[21] Holding options open gives you choices, and choices, combined with slack resources, give you flexibility.

3 Planning from Top to Bottom

Planning works best when the goals and action plans at the bottom and middle of the organization support the goals and action plans at

Options-based planning maintaining planning flexibility by making small, simultaneous investments in many alternative plans

Slack resources a cushion of extra resources that can be used with options-based planning to adapt to unanticipated change, problems, or opportunities

Exhibit 5.3

Planning from Top to Bottom

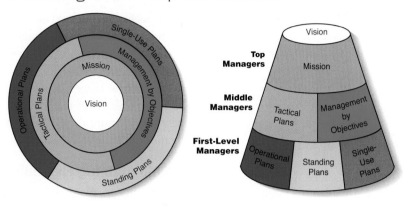

the top of the organization. In other words, planning works best when everybody pulls in the same direction. Exhibit 5.3 illustrates this planning continuity, beginning at the top with a clear definition of the company vision and ending at the bottom with the execution of operational plans.

*Let's see how **3.1 top managers create the organizational vision and mission, 3.2 middle managers develop tactical plans and use management by objectives to motivate employee efforts toward the overall vision and mission,** and **3.3 first-level managers use operational, single-use, and standing plans to implement the tactical plans.***

3.1 Starting at the Top

Top management is responsible for developing long-term **strategic plans** that make clear how the company will serve customers and position itself against competitors in the next two to five years. Strategic planning begins with the creation of an organizational vision and an organizational mission.

A **vision** is a statement of a company's purpose or reason for existing.[22] Vision statements should be brief—no more than two sentences. They should also be enduring, inspirational, clear, and consistent with widely shared company beliefs and values. An excellent example of a well-crafted vision statement is that of Avon, the cosmetics company: To be the company that best understands and satisfies the product, service, and self-fulfillment needs of women—globally. That state-

Strategic plans overall company plans that clarify how the company will serve customers and position itself against competitors over the next two to five years

Vision a statement of a company's purpose or reason for existing

Mission a statement of a company's overall goal that unifies company-wide efforts toward its vision, stretches and challenges the organization, and possesses a finish line and a time frame

ment guides everyone in the organization and provides a focal point for the delivery of beauty products and services to the customer, women around the world. The vision is the same whether Avon is selling lipstick to women in India, shampoo packets to women in the Amazon, or jewelry to women in the United States. Understanding the needs of women—globally—does not change. Furthermore, Avon's vision is clear, inspirational, and consistent with Avon's company values and the principles that guide the company. Other examples of organizational visions that have been particularly effective include Walt Disney Company's "to make people happy" and Schlage Lock Company's "to make the world more secure."[23]

The **mission,** which flows from the vision, is a more specific goal that unifies company-wide efforts, stretches and challenges the organization, and possesses a finish line and a time frame. For example, in 1961, President John F. Kennedy established an organizational mission for NASA with this simple statement: "Achieving the goal, before this decade is out, of landing a man on the moon and returning him safely to earth."[24] NASA achieved this goal on July 20, 1969, when astronaut Neil Armstrong walked on the moon. Once a mission has been accomplished, a new one should be chosen. Again, however, the new mission must grow out of the organization's vision, which does not change significantly over time. For example, NASA's new mission is to return to the moon "as early as 2015 and no later than 2020" and to use the moon "as a stepping stone for more ambitious missions" to Mars and beyond."[25]

©Reuters/China News Photo/Landov

Missions and Visions—from the Ridiculous to the Sublime

Jeffrey Abrahams's 2007 book assembles in one location the single most difficult pieces of corporate communication to unearth through regular research—visions. But even having such a rich repository of vision statements is still confusing. Alcoa's vision, "to be the best company in the world" is as vague in its brevity as Hershey's 65-word vision is in its detail. Progressive Insurance has a vision that seems perfectly fitting: "to reduce the human trauma and economic costs associated with automobile accidents." And same for Kellogg's, which even though it doesn't mention cereal—or even food—leaves no doubt about the company's direction: "We build *Gr-r-r-eat* brands and make the world a little happier by bringing our best to you."

Source: R. J. Tofel, "Telling a Big Story in a Few Words," *Wall Street Journal*, 2 May 2007, D14.

3.2 Bending in the Middle

Middle management is responsible for developing and carrying out tactical plans to accomplish the organization's mission. **Tactical plans** specify how a company will use resources, budgets, and people to accomplish specific goals within its mission. Whereas strategic plans and objectives are used to focus company efforts over the next two to five years, tactical plans and objectives are used to direct behavior, efforts, and attention over the next six months to two years. For example, Craig Knouf, CEO of Associated Business Systems, a 110-person business that sells office equipment in Portland, Oregon, reviews his company's 30-page business plan monthly to compare the company's actual performance with the goals set forth in the plan. He is especially focused at the six- and twelve-month markers. When Knouf noticed that over a six-month period the company had sold more high-volume scanners than before, he changed his business plan to put more emphasis on scanners and scanning software. As a result, sales of scanning products, which will double this year over last, now account for one-third of all sales. Working without his business plan, says Knouf, "would be like driving a car with no steering wheel."[26]

Management by objectives is a management technique often used to develop and carry out tactical plans. **Management by objectives,** or MBO, is a four-step process in which managers and their employees (1) discuss possible goals; (2) participatively select goals that are challenging, attainable, and consistent with the company's overall goals; (3) jointly develop tactical plans that lead to the accomplishment of tactical goals and objectives; and (4) meet regularly to review progress toward accomplishment of those goals.

3.3 Finishing at the Bottom

Lower-level managers are responsible for developing and carrying out **operational plans,** which are the day-to-day plans for producing or delivering the organization's products and services. Operational plans direct the behavior, efforts, and priorities of operative employees for periods ranging from 30 days to six months. There are three kinds of operational plans: single-use plans, standing plans, and budgets.

Single-use plans deal with unique, one-time-only events. For example, Philip Morris is relocating its headquarters and 682 employees from Park Avenue in New York City to Henrico County, Virginia. Although the move will cost $120 million, the company will save $60 million a year in operating costs. The move will happen once; it requires a single-use plan.

Unlike single-use plans that are created, carried out, and then never used again, **standing plans** save managers time because once the plans are created, they can be used repeatedly to handle frequently recurring events. If you encounter a problem that you've seen before, someone in your company has probably written a standing plan that explains how to address it. There are three kinds of standing plans: policies, procedures, and rules and regulations.

Policies indicate the general course of action that

Tactical plans plans created and implemented by middle managers that specify how the company will use resources, budgets, and people over the next six months to two years to accomplish specific goals within its mission

Management by objectives (MBO) a four-step process in which managers and employees discuss and select goals, develop tactical plans, and meet regularly to review progress toward goal accomplishment

Operational plans day-to-day plans, developed and implemented by lower-level managers, for producing or delivering the organization's products and services over a 30-day to six-month period

Single-use plans plans that cover unique, one-time-only events

Standing plans plans used repeatedly to handle frequently recurring events

Policy a standing plan that indicates the general course of action that should be taken in response to a particular event or situation company managers should take in response to a particular event or situation. A well-written policy will also specify why the policy exists and what outcome the policy is intended to produce. Because the average employee surfs the Internet 11.1 hours per week, many companies have policies of either monitoring or blocking access to non-work-related Web sites. After its monitoring policy failed, Chaparral Energy, an oil and gas company, switched to software that blocks access to religious, political, or sexually oriented Web sites. Employee Web surfing has now dropped from an hour to less than 15 minutes a day.[27]

Procedures are more specific than policies because they indicate the series of steps that should be taken in response to a particular event. A manufacturer's procedure for handling defective products might include the following steps. Step 1: Rejected material is locked in a secure area with "reject" documentation attached. Step 2: Material Review Board (MRB) identifies the defect and how far outside the standard the rejected products are. Step 3: MRB determines the disposition of the defective product as either scrap or as rework. Step 4: Scrap is either discarded or recycled, and rework is sent back through the production line to be fixed. Step 5: If delays in delivery will result, MRB member notifies customer.[28]

Rules and regulations are even more specific than procedures because they specify what must happen or not happen. They describe precisely how a particular action should be performed. For instance, many companies have rules and regulations forbidding managers from writing job reference letters for employees who have worked at their firms because a negative reference may prompt a former employee to sue for defamation of character.[29]

Budgets are the third kind of operational plan. **Budgeting** is quantitative planning because it forces managers to decide how to allocate available money to best accomplish company goals. According to Jan King, author of *Business Plans to Game Plans,* "Money sends a clear mes-

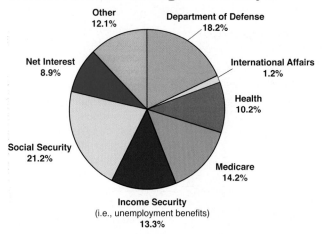

2007 U.S. Federal Government Budget Outlays

- Other 12.1%
- Department of Defense 18.2%
- International Affairs 1.2%
- Net Interest 8.9%
- Health 10.2%
- Social Security 21.2%
- Medicare 14.2%
- Income Security (i.e., unemployment benefits) 13.3%

Source: "B-80. Federal Receipts and Outlays, by Major Category, and Surplus or Deficit, Fiscal Years 1940–2007," Economic Report of the President: 2006 Report Spreadsheet Tables, [Online] Available at http://a257.g.akamaitech.net/7/257/24222/15feb20061000/www.gpoaccess.gov/eop/2006/B80.xls

sage about your priorities. Budgets act as a language for communicating your goals to others."

What Is Rational Decision Making?

Decision making is the process of choosing a solution from available alternatives.[30] **Rational decision making** is a systematic process in which managers define problems, evaluate alternatives, and choose optimal solutions that provide maximum benefits to their organizations.

After reading the next two sections, you should be able to

4 explain the steps and limits to rational decision making.

5 explain how group decisions and group decision-making techniques can improve decision making.

4 Steps and Limits to Rational Decision Making

There are six steps of the rational decision-making process. Let's learn more about each of these steps: **4.1**

Procedure a standing plan that indicates the specific steps that should be taken in response to a particular event

Rules and regulations standing plans that describe how a particular action should be performed, or what must happen or not happen in response to a particular event

Budgeting quantitative planning through which managers decide how to allocate available money to best accomplish company goals

Decision making the process of choosing a solution from available alternatives

Rational decision making a systematic process of defining problems, evaluating alternatives, and choosing optimal solutions

define the problem, 4.2 identify decision criteria, 4.3 weight the criteria, 4.4 generate alternative courses of action, 4.5 evaluate each alternative, and 4.6 compute the optimal decision. Then we'll consider 4.7 limits to rational decision making.

4.1 Define the Problem

The first step in decision making is identifying and defining the problem. A **problem** exists when there is a gap between a desired state (what is wanted) and an existing state (the situation you are actually facing). Because it can hold 550 to 850 passengers, Airbus's new A380 super-jumbo jetliner could generate tremendous revenues for airlines. But with wings larger than a small passenger jet and wheels so large that it takes a crane to move them, the A380 was several tons too heavy. Randy Baseler of Boeing, Airbus's competitor, says, "If the plane's heavier, it consumes more fuel. That drives up landing and navigation fees, and also maintenance costs, especially for wheels, tires, and brakes."[31] Fearing exorbitant costs, the airlines told Airbus they wouldn't buy the A380 unless it was substantially lighter.[32]

The existence of a gap between an existing state and a desired state is no guarantee that managers will make decisions to solve problems. Two things must occur for this to happen.[33] First, managers have to be aware of the gap. But that isn't enough. Managers also have to be motivated to reduce the gap. In other words, managers have to know there is a problem and *want* to solve it. Finally, it's not enough to be aware of a problem and be motivated to solve it. Managers must also have the knowledge, skills, abilities, and resources to fix the problem. So, how did Airbus reduce the weight of its A380 super-jumbo jet? Engineers achieved the biggest weight savings by substituting a light carbon-fiber composite material for heavier aluminum in the rear fuselage and the large structural ribs in the wings. Altogether, these changes and others reduced the A380's weight by four tons.[34]

4.2 Identify Decision Criteria

Decision criteria are the standards used to guide judgments and decisions. Typically, the more criteria a potential solution meets, the better that solution will be.

Imagine that your boss asks for a recommendation on outfitting the sales force, many of whom travel regularly, with new computers. What general factors would be important when purchasing these computers? Reliability, price, warranty, on-site service, and compatibility with existing software, printers, and computers would all be important, but you must also consider the technical details. With technology changing so quickly, you'll probably want to buy laptops with as much capability and flexibility as you can afford. What are your options? Well, laptops come in four distinct model types. There are budget models that are good for routine office work, but are usually saddled with a slower processor; workhorse models that are not lightweight, but have everything included; slim models for traveling but that usually require an exernal drive to read/write to a DVD/CD; and tablet models that include extra features like handwriting-recognition software.[35] But what will the sales force really need? Will they need to burn CDs and DVDs, or just read them? How much memory will the users need? How many files and programs will they need to store on their hard drives? Answering questions like these will help you identify the criteria that will guide the purchase of the new equipment.

4.3 Weight the Criteria

After identifying decision criteria, the next step is deciding which criteria are more or less important. Although there are numerous mathematical models for weighting decision criteria,

---

Steps of the Rational Decision-Making Process

1 Define the Problem
2 Identify Decision Criteria
3 Weight the Criteria
4 Generate Alternative Courses of Action
5 Evaluate Each Alternative
6 Compute the Optimal Decision

Problem a gap between a desired state and an existing state

Decision criteria the standards used to guide judgments and decisions all require the decision maker to provide an initial ranking of the criteria. Some use **absolute comparisons,** in which each criterion is compared to a standard or ranked on its own merits. For example, *Consumer Reports* uses this checklist when it rates and recommends new cars: predicted reliability, previous owners' satisfaction, predicted depreciation (the price you could expect if you sold the car), ability to avoid an accident, fuel economy, crash protection, acceleration, ride, and front seat comfort.[36]

Exhibit 5.4 shows the absolute weights that someone buying a car might use. Because these weights are absolute, each criterion is judged on its own importance, using a five-point scale, with "5" representing "critically important" and "1" representing "completely unimportant." In this instance, predicted reliability, fuel economy, and front seat comfort were rated most important, and acceleration and predicted depreciation were rated least important.

Another method uses **relative comparisons,** in which each criterion is compared directly to every other criterion.[37] For example, Exhibit 5.5 shows six criteria that someone might use when buying a house. Moving down the first column of Exhibit 5.5, we see that the time of the daily commute has been rated less important (-1) than school system quality; more important ($+1$) than having an inground pool, sun room, or a quiet street, and just as important as the house being brand new (0). Total weights, which are obtained by summing the scores in each column, indicate that the daily commute and school system quality are the most important factors to this home buyer, while an inground pool, sun room, and a quiet street are the least important. So with relative comparison, criteria are directly compared to each other.

Exhibit 5.4

Absolute Weighting of Decision Criteria for a Car Purchase

5 critically important
4 important
3 somewhat important
2 not very important
1 completely unimportant

1.	Predicted reliability	1	2	3	4	**5**
2.	Owner satisfaction	1	**2**	3	4	5
3.	Predicted depreciation	**1**	2	3	4	5
4.	Avoiding accidents	1	2	3	**4**	5
5.	Fuel economy	1	2	3	4	**5**
6.	Crash protection	1	2	3	**4**	5
7.	Acceleration	**1**	2	3	4	5
8.	Ride	1	2	**3**	4	5
9.	Front seat comfort	1	2	3	4	**5**

4.4 Generate Alternative Courses of Action

After identifying and weighting the criteria that will guide the decision-making process, the next step is to identify possible courses of action that could solve the problem. In general, at this step, the idea is to generate as many alternatives as possible. For instance, let's assume that you're trying to select a city in Europe to be the location of a major office. After meeting with your staff, you generate a list of possible alternatives: Amsterdam, the Netherlands; Barcelona or Madrid, Spain; Berlin or Frankfurt, Germany; Brussels, Belgium; Lon-

Exhibit 5.5

Relative Comparison of Home Characteristics

HOME CHARACTERISTICS	L	SSQ	IP	SR	QS	NBH
Daily commute (L)		+1	−1	−1	−1	0
School system quality (SSQ)	−1		−1	−1	−1	−1
Inground pool (IP)	+1	+1		0	0	+1
Sun room (SR)	+1	+1	0		0	0
Quiet street (QS)	+1	+1	0	0		0
Newly built house (NBH)	0	+1	−1	0	0	
Total weight	**+2**	**+5**	**−3**	**−2**	**−2**	**0**

Absolute comparisons a process in which each decision criterion is compared to a standard or ranked on its own merits

Relative comparisons a process in which each decision criterion is compared directly to every other criterion don, England; Milan, Italy; Paris, France; and Zurich, Switzerland.

4.5 Evaluate Each Alternative

The next step is to systematically evaluate each alternative against each criterion. Because of the amount of information that must be collected, this step can take much longer and be much more expensive than other steps in the decision-making process. For example, in selecting a European city for your office, you could contact economic development offices in each city, systematically interview businesspeople or executives who operate there, retrieve and use published government data on each location, or rely on published studies such as Cushman & Wakefield Healy & Baker's *European Cities Monitor*, which conducts an annual survey of more than 500 senior European executives who rate 30 European cities on 12 business-related criteria.[38]

No matter how you gather the information, once you have it, the key is to systematically use that information to evaluate each alternative against each criterion. For example, Exhibit 5.6 shows how each of the 10 cities on your staff's list fared on each of the 12 criteria (higher scores are better), from qualified staff to freedom from pollution. Although Paris has good access to markets and very good travel to and from the city, it has a poor business climate and relatively few different languages are spoken in its business community. On the other hand, Barcelona has the lowest costs for employing staff, but weak access to markets and poor ease of travel to and from the city.

©EMPICS/Landov

And the winner is . . . London. When all the weights are calculated and compared, London is the best city in Europe for business.

4.6 Compute the Optimal Decision

The final step in the decision-making process is to compute the optimal decision by determining each alternative's optimal value. This is done by multiplying the rating for each criterion (Step 5) by the weight for that criterion (Step 3), and then summing those scores for each alternative course of action that you generated (Step 4). For example, the 500 executives participating in Cushman & Wakefield Healy & Baker's survey of the best European cities for business rated the 12 decision criteria in terms of importance as follows: qualified staff (57 percent), access to major markets (60 percent), travel to and from the city (52 percent), good telecommunications (50 percent), positive business climate (32 percent), cost of staff (35 percent), cost and value of office space (31 percent), availability of office space (30 percent), travel within the city (22 percent), languages spoken in the business community (24 percent), quality of life (16 percent), and freedom from pollution (13 percent). Those weights are then multiplied by the ratings in each category. For example, Amsterdam's optimal value of 1.68 (that is, its weighted average) is determined by the following calculation:

$$(.57 \times .35) + (.60 \times .39) + (.52 \times .66) +$$
$$(.50 \times .32) + (.32 \times .34) + (.35 \times .16) +$$
$$(.31 \times .28) + (.30 \times .26) + (.22 \times .34) +$$
$$(.24 \times 1.00) + (.16 \times .30) +$$
$$(.13 \times .41) = 1.68$$

The weighted average (or optimal) scores in the next to last row of Exhibit 5.6 show that London clearly ranks as the best location for your company's new European office because of its large number of qualified staff; easy access to markets; outstanding ease of travel to, from, and within the city; excellent telecommunications; and top-notch business climate.

4.7 Limits to Rational Decision Making

In general, managers who diligently complete all six steps of the rational decision-making model will make better decisions than those who don't. So, when they can, managers should try to follow the steps in the rational decision-making model, especially for big decisions with long-range consequences.

To make perfect decisions, managers have to operate in perfect worlds with no real-world constraints. Of course, it never works like that in the real world. Managers face time and money constraints. They often don't have time to make extensive lists of decision criteria. And they often don't have the resources to test all possible solutions against all possible criteria.

In theory, fully rational decision makers **maximize** decisions by choosing the optimal solution. In practice, however, limited resources,

Maximizing choosing the best alternative

Exhibit 5.6

Criteria Ratings Used to Determine the Best Locations in Europe for a New Office

	WEIGHTS	Amsterdam	Barcelona	Berlin	Brussels	Frankfurt	London	Madrid	Milan	Paris	Zurich
QUALIFIED STAFF	57%	0.35	0.30	0.40	0.44	0.58	1.32	0.30	0.33	0.78	0.41
ACCESS TO MARKETS	60%	0.39	0.30	0.28	0.54	0.71	1.36	0.41	0.38	1.18	0.24
TRAVEL TO/ FROM CITY	52%	0.66	0.26	0.19	0.55	1.19	1.74	0.30	0.23	1.42	0.27
TELECOMMU- NICATIONS	50%	0.32	0.21	0.33	0.40	0.58	1.22	0.24	0.20	0.80	0.34
BUSINESS CLIMATE	32%	0.34	0.40	0.36	0.35	0.11	0.51	0.52	0.11	0.20	0.51
COST OF STAFF	35%	0.16	0.73	0.27	0.19	0.05	0.15	0.60	0.21	0.11	0.07
COST & VALUE OF OFFICE SPACE	31%	0.28	0.57	0.52	0.44	0.26	0.18	0.48	0.17	0.20	0.18
AVAILABLE OFFICE SPACE	30%	0.26	0.46	0.63	0.42	0.45	0.55	0.58	0.21	0.39	0.25
TRAVEL WITHIN CITY	22%	0.34	0.45	0.53	0.34	0.41	1.09	0.38	0.19	1.19	0.38
LANGUAGES SPOKEN	24%	1.00	0.22	0.34	1.13	0.53	1.41	0.21	0.17	0.50	0.66
QUALITY OF LIFE	16%	0.30	1.21	0.24	0.38	0.14	0.39	0.61	0.26	0.67	0.55
FREEDOM FROM POLLUTION	13%	0.41	0.44	0.17	0.18	0.12	0.06	0.16	0.03	0.10	0.94
WEIGHTED AVERAGE [OPTIMAL SCORE]		1.68	1.69	1.48	1.93	2.20	4.17	1.63	0.99	3.07	1.36
RANKING		6	5	8	4	3	1	7	11	2	10

Source: "European Cities Monitor," Cushman & Wakefield Healy & Baker, [Online] available at http://www.frankfurt.de/sixcms_upload/media, 26 April 2004.

Satisficing choosing a "good enough" alternative

along with attention, memory, and expertise problems, make it nearly impossible for managers to maximize decisions. Consequently, most managers don't maximize—they "satisfice." Whereas maximizing is choosing the best alternative, **satisficing** is choosing a "good enough" alternative. In reality, however, the manager's limited time, money, and expertise mean that only a few alternatives will be assessed against a few decision criteria. In practice, the manager will visit two or three computer or electronic stores, read a few recent computer reviews, and get bids from Dell, Lenovo, Gateway, and Hewlett-Packard. The decision will be complete when the manager finds a "good enough" laptop computer that meets a few decision criteria.

5 Using Groups to Improve Decision Making

According to a study reported in *Fortune* magazine, 91 percent of U.S. companies use teams and groups to solve specific problems (i.e., make decisions).[39] Why so many?

> (91 percent of U.S. companies use **teams** and **groups** to solve specific problems.)

Because when done properly, group decision making can lead to much better decisions than decisions typically made by individuals. In fact, numerous studies show that groups consistently outperform individuals on complex tasks.

Let's explore the *5.1 advantages and pitfalls of group decision making* and see how the following group decision-making methods—*5.2 structured conflict, 5.3 the nominal group technique, 5.4 the Delphi technique, and*

REASONS GROUPS ARE BETTER AT DEFINING PROBLEMS AND GENERATING POSSIBLE SOLUTIONS

1 Group members usually possess different knowledge, skills, abilities, and experiences, so groups are able to view problems from multiple perspectives. Being able to view problems from different perspectives, in turn, can help groups perform better on complex tasks and make better decisions than individuals.[40]

2 Groups can find and access much more information than can individuals alone.

3 The increased knowledge and information available to groups make it easier for them to generate more alternative solutions. Studies show that generating lots of alternative solutions is critical to improving the quality of decisions.

4 If groups are involved in the decision-making process, group members will be more committed to making chosen solutions work.

5.6 electronic brainstorming—can be used to improve decision making.

5.1 Advantages and Pitfalls of Group Decision Making

Groups can do a much better job than individuals in two important steps of the decision-making process: defining the problem and generating alternative solutions.

Still, group decision making is subject to some pitfalls that can quickly erase these gains. One possible pitfall is groupthink. **Groupthink** occurs in highly cohesive groups when group members feel intense pressure to agree with each other so that the group can approve a proposed solution.[41] Because groupthink leads to consideration of a limited number of solutions and restricts discussion of any considered solutions, it usually results in poor decisions. Groupthink is most likely to occur under the following conditions:

- The group is insulated from others with different perspectives.
- The group leader begins by expressing a strong preference for a particular decision.
- The group has no established procedure for systematically defining problems and exploring alternatives.
- Group members have similar backgrounds and experiences.[42]

Groupthink is considered one of the reasons that Merck's prescription drug Vioxx stayed on the market for over five years despite a large body of evidence indicating the drug had fatal side effects. Merck viewed Vioxx as a miracle pain reliever, and over 100 million prescriptions for the drug were written while it was on the market. The *New England Journal of Medicine*, however, had reported that Vioxx users were suffering from significant heart problems almost from the beginning, and the drug was withdrawn from the market. Court documents revealed that Merck's own internal studies showed a link between Vioxx and elevated incidence of heart attacks. However, managers chose to listen to positive feedback about how

> **Groupthink** a barrier to good decision making caused by pressure within the group for members to agree with each other

well the drug worked as a pain killer rather than act on the information about the drug's risky side effects.[43]

A second potential problem with group decision making is that it takes considerable time. Reconciling schedules so that group members can meet takes time. Furthermore, it's a rare group that consistently holds productive task-oriented meetings to effectively work through the decision process. Some of the most common complaints about meetings (and thus decision making) are that the meeting's purpose is unclear, participants are unprepared, critical people are absent or late, conversation doesn't stay focused on the problem, and no one follows up on the decisions that were made. As Google's vice president of search products and user experience, Marissa Mayer (pictured right), holds over 70 meetings a week and is the last executive to hear a pitch before it is made to the cofounders. To keep meetings on track, Mayer has set down six guidelines. Meetings must (1) have a firm agenda and (2) an assigned note-taker. Meetings must occur (3) during established office hours, and (4) preferably in short, 10-minute micromeetings. Those running the meeting should (5) discourage office politics and rely on data, and above all, they should (6) stick to the clock. Mayer's guidelines help meetings stay focused and productive.[44]

A third possible pitfall to group decision making is that sometimes one or two people, perhaps the boss or a strong-willed, vocal group member, dominate group discussion, restricting consideration of different problem definitions and alternative solutions. Another potential problem is that, unlike with their own decisions and actions, group members may not feel accountable for the decisions made and actions taken by the group.

Although these pitfalls can lead to poor decision making, this doesn't mean that managers should avoid using groups to make decisions. When done properly, group decision making can lead to much better decisions. The pitfalls of group decision making are not inevitable. Managers can overcome most of them by using the various techniques described next.

5.2 Structured Conflict

C-type conflict (cognitive conflict) disagreement that focuses on problem- and issue-related differences of opinion

A-type conflict (affective conflict) disagreement that focuses on individuals or personal issues

Most people view conflict negatively. Yet the right kind of conflict can lead to much better group decision making. **C-type conflict,** or "cognitive conflict," focuses on problem- and issue-related differences of opinion.[45] In c-type conflict, group members disagree because their different

©Landov

experiences and expertise lead them to view the problem and its potential solutions differently. C-type conflict is also characterized by a willingness to examine, compare, and reconcile those differences to produce the best possible solution. Alteon WebSystems, now a division of Nortel Networks, makes critical use of c-type conflict. Top manager Dominic Orr described Alteon's c-type conflict this way:

After an idea is presented, we open the floor to objective, and often withering, critiques. And if the idea collapses under scrutiny, we move on to another: no hard feelings. We're judging the idea, not the person. At the same time, we don't really try to regulate emotions. Passionate conflict means that we're getting somewhere, not that the discussion is out of control. But one person does act as referee—by asking basic questions like "Is this good for the customer?" or "Does it keep our time-to-market advantage intact?" By focusing relentlessly on the facts, we're able to see the strengths and weaknesses of an idea clearly and quickly.[46]

By contrast, **a-type conflict,** meaning "affective conflict," refers to the emotional reactions that can occur when disagreements become personal rather than professional. A-type conflict often results in hostility, anger, resentment, distrust, cynicism, and apathy. Unlike c-type conflict, a-type conflict undermines team effectiveness by preventing teams from engaging in the activities characteristic of c-type conflict that are critical to team effectiveness. Examples of a-type conflict statements are "your idea," "our idea," "my department," "you don't know what you are talking about," or "you don't understand our situation." Rather than focusing on issues and ideas, these statements focus on individuals.[47]

The **devil's advocacy** approach can be used to create c-type conflict by assigning an individual or a subgroup the role of critic. The following five steps establish a devil's advocacy program:

1. Generate a potential solution.
2. Assign a devil's advocate to criticize and question the solution.
3. Present the critique of the potential solution to key decision makers.
4. Gather additional relevant information.
5. Decide whether to use, change, or not use the originally proposed solution.[48]

When properly used, the devil's advocacy approach introduces c-type conflict into the decision-making process. Further, contrary to the common belief that conflict is bad, studies show that this leads to less a-type conflict, improved decision quality, and greater acceptance of decisions once they have been made.[49]

5.3 Nominal Group Technique

"Nominal" means "in name only." Accordingly, the **nominal group technique** received its name because it begins with "quiet time," in which group members independently write down as many problem definitions and alternative solutions as possible. In other words, the nominal group technique begins by having group members act as individuals. After the "quiet time," the group leader asks each group member to share one idea at a time with the group. As they are read aloud, ideas are posted on flipcharts or wallboards for all to see. This step continues until all ideas have been shared. In the next step, the group discusses the advantages and disadvantages of the ideas. The nominal group technique closes with a second "quiet time," in which group members independently rank the ideas presented. Group members then read their rankings aloud, and the idea with the highest average rank is selected.[50]

The nominal group technique improves group decision making by decreasing a-type conflict. In doing so, however, it also restricts c-type conflict. Consequently, the nominal group technique typically produces poorer decisions than does the devil's advocacy approach. Nonetheless, more than 80 studies have found that nominal groups produce better ideas than those produced by traditional groups.[51]

5.4 Delphi Technique

In the **Delphi technique,** the members of a panel of experts respond to questions and to each other until reaching agreement on an issue. The first step is to assemble a panel of experts. Unlike other approaches to group decision making, however, it isn't necessary to bring

Avoiding Blamestorming and Coblabberation

Without serious planning and adherence to brainstorming guidelines and procedures, brainstorming can quickly degenerate into blamestorming (where zero progress is made) or coblabberation (settling for an unimaginative solution just to get the session over with). Indeed, Professor Paul Paulus of the University of Texas at Arlington conducted a study comparing the number and quality of ideas of four people brainstorming versus four individuals working alone. Results: the brainstormers were only half as effective as the solo thinkers. Professor David Perkins of Harvard is not surprised. He prefers having people write down their ideas then bring them in. That way, you get diversity without all the politicking.

Source: J. Sandberg, "Brainstorming Works Best If People Scramble for Ideas on Their Own," *Wall Street Journal,* 13 June 2006, B1.

©Riser/Getty Images

Devil's advocacy a decision-making method in which an individual or a subgroup is assigned the role of a critic

Nominal group technique a decision-making method that begins and ends by having group members quietly write down and evaluate ideas to be shared with the group

Delphi technique a decision-making method in which members of a panel of experts respond to questions and to each other until reaching agreement on an issue the panel members together in one place. Because the Delphi technique does not require the experts to leave their offices or disrupt their schedules, they are more likely to participate.

The second step is to create a questionnaire consisting of a series of open-ended questions for the experts. In Step 3, the panel members' written responses are analyzed, summarized, and fed back to the panel for reactions until the members reach agreement. Asking the members why they agree or disagree is important because it helps uncover their unstated assumptions and beliefs. Again, this process of summarizing panel feedback and obtaining reactions to that feedback continues until the panel members reach agreement.

5.5 Electronic Brainstorming

Brainstorming, in which group members build on others' ideas, is a technique for generating a large number of alternative solutions. Brainstorming has four rules:

1. The more ideas, the better.
2. All ideas are acceptable, no matter how wild or crazy they might seem.
3. Other group members' ideas should be used to come up with even more ideas.
4. Criticism or evaluation of ideas is not allowed.

Though brainstorming is great fun and can help managers generate a large number of alternative solutions, it does have a number of disadvantages. Fortunately, **electronic brainstorming,** in which group members use computers to communicate and generate alternative solutions, overcomes the disadvantages associated with face-to-face brainstorming.[52]

The first disadvantage that electronic brainstorming overcomes is **production blocking,** which occurs when you have an idea but have to wait to share it because someone else is already presenting an idea to the group. During this short delay, you may forget your idea or decide that it really wasn't worth sharing. With electronic brainstorming, production blocking doesn't happen. All group members are seated at computers, so everyone can type in ideas whenever they occur. There's no "waiting your turn" to be heard by the group.

The second disadvantage that electronic brainstorming overcomes is **evaluation apprehension,** that is, being afraid of what others will think of your ideas. With electronic brainstorming, all ideas are anonymous. When you type in an idea and hit the "Enter" key to share it with the group, group members see only the idea. Furthermore, many brainstorming software programs also protect anonymity by displaying ideas in random order. So, if you laugh maniacally when you type "Cut top management's pay by 50 percent!" and then hit the "Enter" key, it won't show up immediately on everyone's screen. This makes it doubly difficult to determine who is responsible for which comments.

In the typical layout for electronic brainstorming, all participants sit in front of computers around a U-shaped table. This configuration allows them to see their computer screens, the other participants, a large main screen, and a meeting leader or facilitator. The first step in electronic brainstorming is to anonymously generate as many ideas as possible. Groups commonly generate 100 ideas in a half-hour period. Step 2 is to edit the generated ideas, categorize them, and eliminate redundancies. Step 3 is to rank the categorized ideas in terms of quality. Step 4, the last step, has three parts: generate a series of action steps, decide the best order for accomplishing these steps, and identify who is responsible for each step. All four steps are accomplished with computers and electronic brainstorming software.[53]

Studies show that electronic brainstorming is much more productive than face-to-face brainstorming. Four-person electronic brainstorming groups produce 25 to 50 percent more ideas than four-person regular brainstorming groups, and 12-person electronic brainstorming groups produce 200 percent more ideas than regular groups of the same size! In fact, because production blocking (i.e., waiting your turn) is not a problem for electronic brainstorming, the number and quality of ideas generally increase with group size.[54]

Even though it works much better than traditional brainstorming, electronic brainstorming has disadvantages, too. An obvious problem is the expense of computers, networks, software, and other equipment. As these costs continue to drop, however, electronic brainstorming will become cheaper.

Another problem is that the anonymity of ideas may bother people who are used to having their ideas accepted by virtue of their position (i.e., the boss). On

Brainstorming a decision-making method in which group members build on each others' ideas to generate as many alternative solutions as possible

Electronic brainstorming a decision-making method in which group members use computers to build on each others' ideas and generate many alternative solutions

Production blocking a disadvantage of face-to-face brainstorming in which a group member must wait to share an idea because another member is presenting an idea

Evaluation apprehension fear of what others will think of your ideas the other hand, one CEO said, "Because the process is anonymous, the sky's the limit in terms of what you can say, and as a result it is more thought-provoking. As a CEO, you'll probably discover things you might not want to hear but need to be aware of."[55]

A third disadvantage is that outgoing individuals who are more comfortable expressing themselves verbally may find it difficult to express themselves in writing. Finally, the most obvious problem is that participants have to be able to type. Those who can't type, or who type slowly, may be easily frustrated and find themselves at a disadvantage to experienced typists.

Whose Big Idea Was Brainstorming?

Advertising executive and co-founder of BBDO, Alex Osborn is considered the father of brainstorming. His book *Your Creative Power*, published in 1948, introduced to America the idea generation technique BBDO had been using in-house for years. Osborn advocated having employees storm corporate problems "in commando fashion." Eventually, Osborn's career as a writer overtook his advertising career, and after more than 40 years at the helm, he retired from BBDO.

Alex Faickney Osborn, http://www.wikipedia.org, May 2007.

©Image Source/Jupiter Images

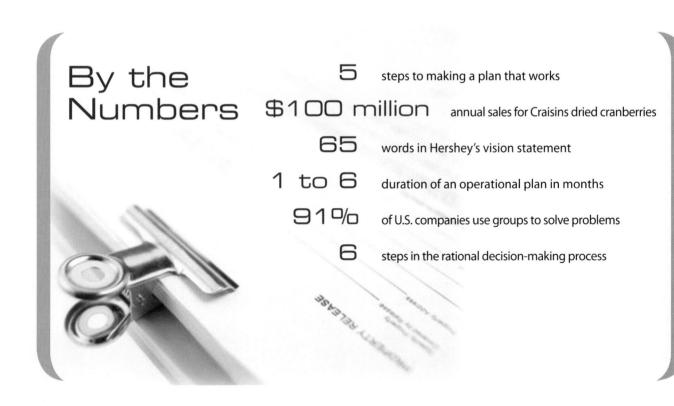

By the Numbers

5	steps to making a plan that works
$100 million	annual sales for Craisins dried cranberries
65	words in Hershey's vision statement
1 to 6	duration of an operational plan in months
91%	of U.S. companies use groups to solve problems
6	steps in the rational decision-making process

ORGANIZATIONAL STRATEGY

Basics of Organizational Strategy

L Less than a decade ago, Apple Computer was not in the music business. And then it released the iPod, which quickly set the standard for all other digital music devices. Designed around a 1.8-inch-diameter hard drive, the iPod boasted low battery consumption and enough storage to hold literally thousands of songs in an easy-to-use product smaller than a deck of cards. Because Apple used existing technology to make the iPod, Sony, Samsung, Dell, Creative, and Microsoft moved quickly to produce their own MP3 players.

As the market has matured, competitors have tried to steal—or at least minimize—Apple's competitive advantage by adding unique features to their MP3 players. Sony's new Walkman includes software that examines the user's taste in music and, at the push of a button labeled "Artist Link," the device will suggest new artists the user might like. SanDisk, best known as a maker of basic flash drive memory, has entered the MP3 market with its Sansae 280, which has twice the storage of an iPod Nano yet sells at roughly the same price. Microsoft's Zune player can store the same number of songs as a video iPod, but holds 100 hours of video compared with the iPod's 40. Plus the Zune allows users to wirelessly share music. Still, Apple still holds a commanding 75 percent of the market for digital music players; SanDisk, its nearest competitor, has less than 10 percent.[1]

Learning Outcomes

1 specify the components of sustainable competitive advantage and explain why it is important.

2 describe the steps involved in the strategy-making process.

3 explain the different kinds of corporate-level strategies.

4 describe the different kinds of industry-level strategies.

5 explain the components and kinds of firm-level strategies.

©Jupiter Images

How can a company like Apple, which dominates a particular industry, maintain its competitive advantage as strong, well-financed competitors enter the market? What steps can Apple and other companies take to better manage their strategy-making process? How does strategy relate to sustainable competitive advantage?

After reading the next two sections, you should be able to

1 specify the components of sustainable competitive advantage and explain why it is important.

2 describe the steps involved in the strategy-making process.

1 Sustainable Competitive Advantage

Resources are the assets, capabilities, processes, employee time, information, and knowledge that an organization controls. Firms use their resources to improve organizational effectiveness and efficiency. Resources are critical to organizational strategy because they can help companies create and sustain an advantage over competitors.[2]

> **Resources** the assets, capabilities, processes, information, and knowledge that an organization uses to improve its effectiveness and efficiency, create and sustain competitive advantage, and fulfill a need or solve a problem

Organizations can achieve a **competitive advantage** by using their resources to provide greater value for customers than competitors can. For example, the iPod's competitive advantage came from its simple, attractive design relative to its price. But Apple's most important advantage was being the first company to make it easy to use MP3 players to legally buy and download music from iTunes.com. (Prior to the iTunes store at iTunes.com, the only means of acquiring digital music was illegal file swapping.)

tions, and technology can make once-valuable resources much less valuable. Throughout the 1980s, Sony controlled the portable music market with its Sony Walkman, which has sold over 230 million units worldwide since its introduction in 1979. Sony leveraged the capabilities of its engineers and inventors (more resources) to make incremental changes to the Walkman that were unmatched by the competition—until the MP3 player came along. With the introduction of Apple's iPod to the market, So-

> To achieve a **sustainable** competitive **advantage**, the resources must be valuable, rare, imperfectly imitable, *and* nonsubstitutable.

Apple negotiated agreements with nearly all of the major record labels to sell their music, and iTunes.com quickly became the premier platform for music downloading. The easy-to-understand site came with free downloadable software customers could use to organize and manage their digital music libraries.[3]

The goal of most organizational strategies is to create and then sustain a competitive advantage. A competitive advantage becomes a **sustainable competitive advantage** when other companies cannot duplicate the value a firm is providing to customers. Sustainable competitive advantage is *not* the same as a long-lasting competitive advantage, though companies obviously want a competitive advantage to last a long time. Instead, a competitive advantage is *sustained* if competitors have tried unsuccessfully to duplicate the advantage and have, for the moment, stopped trying to

duplicate it. It's the corporate equivalent of your competitors saying, "We give up. You win. We can't do what you do, and we're not even going to try to do it any more." Four conditions must be met if a firm's resources are to be used to achieve a sustainable competitive advantage. The resources must be valuable, rare, imperfectly imitable, *and* nonsubstitutable.

Valuable resources allow companies to improve their efficiency and effectiveness. Unfortunately, changes in customer demand and preferences, competitors' ac-

ny's previous valuable technology lost nearly all its value. Sony finally changed the Walkman to a portable digital device and created its own online music store (Connect), which does not yet match iTunes' simplicity of song selection.[4]

For sustained competitive advantage, valuable resources must also be rare resources. Think about it: How can a company sustain a competitive advantage if all of its competitors have similar resources and capabilities? Consequently, **rare resources,** resources that are not controlled or possessed by many competing firms, are necessary to sustain a competitive advantage. When Apple introduced the iPod, no other portable music players on the market used existing hard drive technology in their design. The iPod gained an immediate advantage over competitors because it was able to satisfy the desire of consumers to carry large numbers of songs in a portable device, something the newer MP3 systems and older individual CD players could not do. The technology that powered the iPod, however, was readily available, so competitors were able to quickly imitate iPod's basic storage capacity. As competitors began introducing iPod look-alikes, Apple released a model with double the storage and replaced the original mechanical wheel with a solid-state touch wheel. Once again, Apple used its design talents (resources) to gain an advantage over the competition.

As this shows, valuable and rare resources can create temporary competitive advantage. For sustained competitive advantage, however, other firms must be unable to imitate or find substitutes for those valuable,

©Chapel House Photography

©Chapel House Photography

Competitive advantage providing greater value for customers than competitors can

Sustainable competitive advantage a competitive advantage that other companies have tried unsuccessfully to duplicate and have, for the moment, stopped trying to duplicate

Valuable resource a resource that allows companies to improve efficiency and effectiveness

Rare resources resources that are not controlled or possessed by many competing firms rare resources. **Imperfectly imitable resources** are those resources that are impossible or extremely costly or difficult to duplicate. For example, despite numerous attempts by competitors to imitate it, iTunes has retained its competitive lock on the music download business. Capitalized on Apple's reputation for developing customer-friendly software, and its library of music, movies, and podcasts, iTunes is still two to three times larger than those of other music download sites. Because the company has developed a closed system for its iTunes and iPod, iPod owners can only download music from Apple's iTunes store. But consumers don't seem to mind. Kelly Moore, a sales representative for a Texas software company, takes her pink iPod mini everywhere she goes and keeps it synchronized with her iBook laptop. She says, "Once I find something I like, I don't switch brands."[5] She's not alone: since iTunes was launched, customers have downloaded over a billion songs. No other competitor comes close to those numbers.

Valuable, rare, imperfectly imitable resources can produce sustainable competitive advantage only if they are also **nonsubstitutable resources,** meaning that no other resources can replace them and produce similar value or competitive advantage. To compete effectively against iTunes, competitors may need to change their business model by developing substitutes for iTunes that consumers will accept. For example, Napster founders Shawn Fanning and Wayne Rosso have created a subscription-based service called Mashboxx that charges $15 a month for unlimited downloads. Yahoo! music uses a similar model but charges as little as $6 per month for complete access to its entire library of 2 million songs.[6] In addition to straight subscription models, some companies are experimenting with price. Where iTunes charges 99 cents per song, period, Amazon's new online store will allow the record companies to charge different amounts for different songs based upon popularity. At Amie Street, a newly posted track can be downloaded for free, but as the number of downloads increases, so does the song's price, until it reaches the maximum of 98 cents.[7] In response to competitors' experimentation, Apple has stated that its one-flat-price model has been both effective and lucrative and has no plans to change. It will take years to find out whether competing music download sites will be an effective substitute to iTunes.[8]

In summary, Apple has reaped the rewards of a first mover advantage from its interdependent iPod and iTunes. The company's history of developing customer-friendly software,

the innovative capabilities of the iPod, the simple 99-cent-pay-as-you-go sales model of iTunes, and the unmatched list of music and movies available for download provide customers with a service that has been valuable, rare, relatively non-substitutable, and, in the past, imperfectly imitable. Past success is, however, no guarantee of future success: Apple needs to continually change and develop its offerings or risk being unseated by a more nimble competitor whose products are more relevant and have higher perceived value to consumers.

2 Strategy-Making Process

Companies use a *strategy-making process* to create strategies that produce sustainable competitive advantage.[9] Exhibit 6.1 displays the three steps of the strategy-making process: ***2.1 assess the need for strategic change, 2.2 conduct a situational analysis,*** and then ***2.3 choose strategic alternatives.*** Let's examine each of these steps in more detail.

2.1 Assessing the Need for Strategic Change

The external business environment is much more turbulent than it used to be. With customers' needs constantly growing and changing, and with competitors working harder, faster, and smarter to meet those needs, the first step in strategy making is determining the need for strategic change. In other words, the company should determine whether it needs to change its strategy to sustain a competitive advantage.[10]

Determining the need for strategic change might seem easy to do, but in reality, it's not. There's a great deal of uncertainty in strategic business environments. Furthermore, top-level managers are often slow to recognize the need for strategic change, especially at successful companies that have created and sustained competitive advantages. Because they are acutely aware of the strategies that made their companies successful, they continue to rely on those strategies, even as the competition changes. In other words, success often leads to **competitive inertia**—a reluctance to change strategies or competitive practices that have been successful in the past.

Imperfectly imitable resources resources that are impossible or extremely costly or difficult for other firms to duplicate

Nonsubstitutable resource a resource that produces value or competitive advantage and has no equivalent substitutes or replacements

Competitive inertia a reluctance to change strategies or competitive practices that have been successful in the past

Besides being aware of the dangers of competitive inertia, what can managers do to improve the speed and accuracy with which they determine the need for strategic change? One method is to actively look for signs of strategic dissonance. **Strategic dissonance** is a discrepancy between a company's intended strategy and the strategic actions managers take when actually implementing that strategy.[11]

For example, when Edgar Bronfman, Jr., bought the struggling Warner Music Group, his strategy was to cut costs and change a company culture where excessive spending—not uncommon in the entertainment industry—was the norm. Accordingly, he laid off 1,200 employees to save $250 million and cut remaining salaries by as much as 50 percent. A few weeks later, however, he contradicted his new cost-cutting strategy. First, he signed off on a $13,000 bill to charter a private jet to fly top company managers and the agents of the company's best-selling artists to the Grammy awards in Los Angeles. Then, despite his insistence that music industry professionals shouldn't be paid more than their counterparts in other industries, Bronfman quietly restored the salary cuts he had made after top executives complained.[12]

Finally, while strategic dissonance can indicate that managers are not doing what they should to carry out company strategy, it can also mean that the intended strategy is out of date and needs to be changed.

2.2 Situational Analysis

A situational analysis can also help managers determine the need for strategic change. A **situational analysis**, also called a **SWOT analysis** for *strengths, weaknesses, opportunities,* and *threats,* is an assessment of the strengths and weaknesses in an organization's internal environment and the opportunities and threats in its external environment.[13] Ideally, as shown in Step 2 of Exhibit 6.1, a SWOT analysis helps a company determine how to increase internal strengths and minimize internal weaknesses

Strategic dissonance a discrepancy between a company's intended strategy and the strategic actions managers take when implementing that strategy

Situational (SWOT) analysis an assessment of the strengths and weaknesses in an organization's internal environment and the opportunities and threats in its external environment

Distinctive competence what a company can make, do, or perform better than its competitors

Core capabilities the internal decision-making routines, problem-solving processes, and organizational cultures that determine how efficiently inputs can be turned into outputs

Exhibit 6.1

Three Steps of the Strategy-Making Process

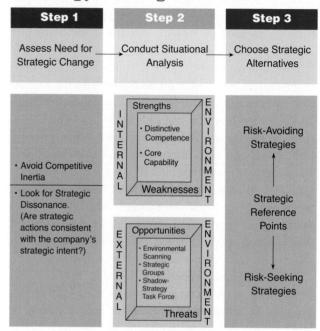

Step 1	Step 2	Step 3
Assess Need for Strategic Change	Conduct Situational Analysis	Choose Strategic Alternatives

• Avoid Competitive Inertia

• Look for Strategic Dissonance. (Are strategic actions consistent with the company's strategic intent?)

INTERNAL — Strengths — ENVIRONMENT
• Distinctive Competence
• Core Capability
Weaknesses

EXTERNAL — Opportunities — ENVIRONMENT
• Environmental Scanning
• Strategic Groups
• Shadow-Strategy Task Force
Threats

Risk-Avoiding Strategies
↑
Strategic Reference Points
↓
Risk-Seeking Strategies

while maximizing external opportunities and minimizing external threats.

An analysis of an organization's internal environment, that is, a company's strengths and weaknesses, often begins with an assessment of its distinctive competencies and core capabilities. A **distinctive competence** is something that a company can make, do, or perform better than its competitors. For example, *Consumer Reports* magazine consistently ranks Toyota cars number one in quality and reliability.[14] Similarly, for 13 of the last 15 years, *PC Magazine* readers have ranked Dell's desktop computers best in terms of service and reliability.[15]

Whereas distinctive competencies are tangible—for example, a product or service is faster, cheaper, or better—the core capabilities that produce distinctive competencies are not. **Core capabilities** are the less visible, internal decision-making routines, problem-solving processes, and organizational cultures that determine how efficiently inputs can be turned into outputs.[16] Distinctive competencies cannot be sustained for long without superior core capabilities. IKEA's core capability is the way it works with 1,800 suppliers in 55 countries that make products exclusively for IKEA. IKEA employees in 43 local trading offices work closely with these suppliers to improve quality, cut costs, and improve worker safety. When IKEA develops a new product, such as the $650 small kitchen, the trading offices, with the help

©Susan Van Etten

IKEA's core capabilities help it keep its stores stocked with the merchandise customers want to buy.

of their suppliers, compete to earn the right to produce that product. IKEA uses the same approach for product design. This ability to work with so many suppliers and designers, and to keep suppliers happy by guaranteeing them a high volume of work is the core capability that generates IKEA's distinctive competence, selling good-value, low-cost furniture, which it does better than anyone else in the world.[17]

After examining internal strengths and weaknesses, the second part of a situational analysis is to look outside the company and assess the opportunities and threats in the external environment. In Chapter 3, you learned that *environmental scanning* involves searching the environment for important events or issues that might affect the organization, such as pricing trends, or new products and technology. In a situational analysis, however, managers use environmental scanning to identify specific opportunities and threats that can either improve or harm the company's ability to sustain its competitive advantage. Identification of strategic

groups and formation of shadow-strategy task forces are two ways to do this.

Strategic groups are not actual groups; they are companies, usually competitors, that managers closely follow. More specifically, a **strategic group** is a group of other companies within an industry that top managers choose for comparing, evaluating, and benchmarking their company's strategic threats and opportunities.[18] (*Benchmarking* involves identifying outstanding practices, processes, and standards at other companies and adapting them to your own company.) Typically, managers include companies as part of their strategic group if they compete directly with those companies for customers or if those companies use strategies similar to theirs. It's likely that the managers at Home Depot, the largest U.S. home improvement and hardware retailer, assess

> **Strategic group** a group of companies within an industry that top managers choose to compare, evaluate, and benchmark strategic threats and opportunities

strategic threats and opportunities by comparing their company to a strategic group consisting of the other home improvement and hardware retailers.

	# of Stores	# of States	Other Countries	Size of Modern Store (Sq. Feet)
Home Depot	2,079	50	3	130,000
Lowe's	1,325	49	2	117,000
Ace Hardware	4,700	50	70	17,000
84 Lumber	500	40	0	33,000

In fact, when scanning the environment for strategic threats and opportunities, managers tend to categorize the different companies in their industries as core or secondary firms.[19] **Core firms** are the central companies in a strategic group. Home Depot operates 2,079 stores covering all 50 states, Puerto Rico, the U.S. Virgin Islands, Mexico, and all 10 provinces of Canada. The company has more than 350,000 employees and annual revenue of over $85 billion. By comparison, Lowe's has 1,325 stores in 49 states, stocks more than 40,000 products in each store, and has total annual sales of more than $43 billion.[20] Clearly, Lowe's is the closest competitor to Home Depot and would probably be classified as the core firm in Home Depot's strategic group. While Ace Hardware has more stores than Home Depot and appears to be bigger internationally, Ace's franchise structure and small, individualized stores keep it from being a core firm in Home Depot's strategic group.[21] Likewise, Home Depot's management probably doesn't concern itself much with Aubuchon Hardware, which has only 140 stores in New England and upstate New York.[22]

Secondary firms are firms that use strategies related to but somewhat different from those of core firms. 84 Lumber has over 500 stores in 40 states, but even though its stores are open to the public, the company focuses on supplying professional contractors, to which it sells 95 percent of its products. While Home Depot does sell to professional contractors, because most of its sales are to consumers, it would likely classify 84 Lumber as a secondary firm

Core firms the central companies in a strategic group

Secondary firms the firms in a strategic group that follow strategies related to but somewhat different from those of the core firms

Strategic reference points the strategic targets managers use to measure whether a firm has developed the core competencies it needs to achieve a sustainable competitive advantage

in its strategic group analysis.[23] Managers need to be aware of the potential threats and opportunities posed by secondary firms, but they usually spend more time assessing the threats and opportunities associated with core firms.

2.3 Choosing Strategic Alternatives

After determining the need for strategic change and conducting a situational analysis, the last step in the strategy-making process is to choose strategic alternatives that will help the company create or maintain a sustainable competitive advantage. According to strategic reference point theory, managers choose between two basic alternative strategies. They can choose a conservative, *risk-avoiding strategy* that aims to protect an existing competitive advantage. Or they can choose an aggressive, *risk-seeking strategy* that aims to extend or create a sustainable competitive advantage.

The choice to seek risk or avoid risk typically depends on whether top management views the company as falling above or below strategic reference points. **Strategic reference points** are the targets that managers use to measure whether their firm has developed the core competencies that it needs to achieve a sustainable competitive advantage. If a hotel chain decides to compete by providing superior quality and service, then top management will track the success of this strategy through customer surveys or published hotel ratings, such as those provided by the prestigious *Mobil Travel Guide*. By contrast, if a hotel chain decides to compete on price, it will regularly conduct market surveys to check the prices of other hotels. The competitors' prices are the hotel managers' strategic reference points against which to compare their own pricing strategy. If competitors can consistently underprice them, then the managers need to determine whether their staff and resources have the core competencies to compete on price.

As shown in Exhibit 6.2, when a company is performing above or better than its strategic reference points, top management will typically be satisfied with the company's strategy. Ironically, this satisfaction tends to make top management conservative and risk-averse. After all, since the company already has a sustainable competitive advantage, the worst thing that could happen would be to lose it. Consequently, new issues or changes in the company's external environments are viewed as threats. In contrast, when a company is performing below or worse than its strategic reference points, top management will typically be dissatisfied with the company's strategy. In this instance, managers

Exhibit 6.2

Strategic Reference Points

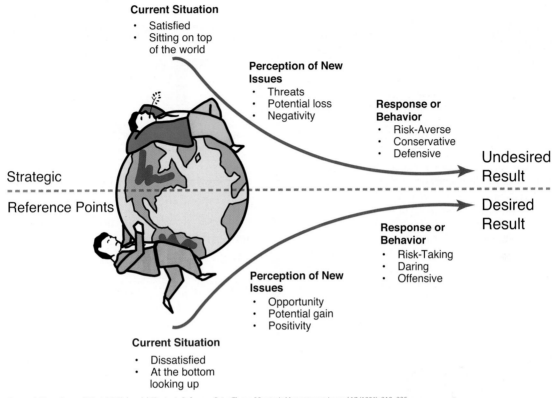

Current Situation
- Satisfied
- Sitting on top of the world

Perception of New Issues
- Threats
- Potential loss
- Negativity

Response or Behavior
- Risk-Averse
- Conservative
- Defensive

Undesired Result

Strategic

Reference Points

Desired Result

Response or Behavior
- Risk-Taking
- Daring
- Offensive

Perception of New Issues
- Opportunity
- Potential gain
- Positivity

Current Situation
- Dissatisfied
- At the bottom looking up

Source: A. Fiegenbaum, S. Hart, & D. Schendel, "Strategic Reference Point Theory," *Strategic Management Journal* 17 (1996): 219–235.

are much more likely to choose a daring, risk-taking strategy. After all, if the current strategy is producing substandard results, the company has nothing to lose by switching to risky new strategies in the hopes that it can create a sustainable competitive advantage. Consequently, managers of companies in this situation view new issues or changes in external environments as opportunities for potential gain.

Strategic reference point theory is not deterministic, however. Managers are not predestined to choose risk-averse or risk-seeking strategies for their companies. Indeed, one of the most important elements of the theory is that managers can influence the strategies chosen by their company by *actively changing and adjusting* the strategic reference points they use to judge strategic performance. To illustrate, if a company has become complacent after consistently surpassing its strategic reference points, then top management can change from a risk-averse to a risk-taking orientation by raising the standards of performance (i.e., strategic reference points). Indeed, this is what happened at Menards.

Menards is a hardware store chain with 170 locations throughout the Midwest. Instead of being satisfied with just protecting its existing stores (a risk-averse strategy), founder John Menard changed the strategic reference points the company had been using to assess strategic performance. To encourage a daring, offensive-minded strategy, he determined that Menards would have to beat Home Depot on four strategic reference points: price, products, sales per square foot, and "friendly accessibility." The strategy appears to be succeeding. In terms of price, market research indicates that a 100-item shopping cart of goods is consistently cheaper at Menards.[24] In terms of products, Menards sells 50,000 products per store, the same as Home Depot. In terms of sales per square foot, Menards ($407 per square foot) outsells Home Depot ($371 per square foot).[25] Finally, unlike Home Depot's warehouse-like stores, Menards' stores are built to resemble grocery stores. Shiny tiled floors, wide aisles, and easy-to-reach products all make Menards a "friendlier" place for shoppers.[26] And now with Lowe's, the second largest hardware store chain in the nation, also entering its markets,

Menards has added a fifth strategic reference point, store size. At 225,000 square feet, most new Menards stores are more than double the size of Home Depot's stores and 75,000 square feet larger than Lowe's.[27]

So even when (perhaps *especially* when) companies have achieved a sustainable competitive advantage, top managers must adjust or change strategic reference points to challenge themselves and their employees to develop new core competencies for the future. In the long run, effective organizations will frequently revise their strategic reference points to better focus managers' attention on the new challenges and opportunities that occur in their ever-changing business environments.

Corporate-level strategy the overall organizational strategy that addresses the question "What business or businesses are we in or should we be in?"

Diversification a strategy for reducing risk by owning a variety of items (stocks or, in the case of a corporation, types of businesses) so that the failure of one stock or one business does not doom the entire portfolio

Corporate-, Industry-, and Firm-Level Strategies

To formulate effective strategies, companies must be able to answer these three basic questions:

- What business are we in?
- How should we compete in this industry?
- Who are our competitors, and how should we respond to them?

These simple, but powerful questions are at the heart of corporate-, industry-, and firm-level strategies.

After reading the next three sections, you should be able to

3 explain the different kinds of corporate-level strategies.

4 describe the different kinds of industry-level strategies.

5 explain the components and kinds of firm-level strategies.

3 Corporate-Level Strategies

Corporate-level strategy is the overall organizational strategy that addresses the question "What business or businesses are we in or should we be in?"

There are two major approaches to corporate-level strategy that companies use to decide which businesses they should be in: **3.1 portfolio strategy**[28] *and* **3.2 grand strategies.**

3.1 Portfolio Strategy

One of the standard strategies for stock market investors is **diversification**: owning stocks in a variety of companies in different industries. The purpose of this strategy is to reduce risk in the overall stock portfolio (the entire collection of stocks). The basic idea is simple: if you invest in 10 companies in 10 different industries, you won't lose your entire investment if one company performs poorly. Furthermore, because they're in different industries, one company's losses are likely to be offset by another company's gains. Portfolio strategy is based on these same ideas. We'll start by taking a look at the theory and ideas behind portfolio strategy and then proceed with a critical review that suggests that some of the key ideas behind portfolio strategy are *not* supported.

Portfolio strategy is a corporate-level strategy that minimizes risk by diversifying investment among various businesses or product lines. Just as a diversification strategy guides an investor who invests in a variety of stocks, portfolio strategy guides the strategic decisions of corporations that compete in a variety of businesses. For example, portfolio strategy could be used to guide the strategy of a company like 3M, which makes 55,000 products for seven different business sectors: consumers and offices (Post-its, Scotch tape, etc.); display and graphics (for computers, cell phones, PDAs, TVs); electronics and communications (flexible circuits used in printers and electronic displays); health care (medical, surgical, dental, and personal care products); industrial (tapes, adhesives, supply chain software); safety, security, and protection services (glass safety, fire protection, respiratory products); and transportation (products and components for the manufacture, repair, and maintenance of autos, aircraft, boats, and other vehicles).[29] Furthermore, just as investors consider the mix of stocks in their stock portfolio when deciding which stocks to buy or sell, managers following portfolio strategy try to acquire companies that fit well with the rest of their corporate portfolio and to sell those that don't. Portfolio strategy provides the following guidelines to help companies make these difficult decisions.

First, according to portfolio strategy, the more businesses in which a corporation competes, the smaller its overall chances of failing. Think of a corporation as a stool and its businesses as the legs of the stool. The more legs or businesses added to the stool, the less likely it is to tip over. Using this analogy, portfolio strategy reduces 3M's risk of failing because the corporation's survival depends on essentially seven different business sectors. Because the emphasis is on adding "legs to the stool," managers who use portfolio strategy are often on the lookout for acquisitions, that is, other companies to buy.

Second, beyond adding new businesses to the corporate portfolio, portfolio strategy predicts that companies can reduce risk even more through unrelated diversification—creating or acquiring companies in completely unrelated businesses (more on the accuracy of this prediction later). According to portfolio strategy, when businesses are unrelated, losses in one business or industry should have minimal effect on the performance of other companies in the corporate portfolio. One of the best examples of unrelated diversification is Samsung of Korea. Samsung has businesses in electronics, machinery and heavy industries, chemicals, financial services, and other areas ranging from automobiles to hotels and entertainment.[30] Because most internally grown businesses tend to be related to existing products or services, portfolio strategy suggests that acquiring new businesses is the preferred method of unrelated diversification.

Third, investing the profits and cash flows from mature, slow-growth businesses into newer, faster-growing businesses can reduce long-term risk. The best-known portfolio strategy for guiding investment in a corporation's businesses is the Boston Consulting Group (BCG) matrix. The **BCG matrix** is a portfolio strategy that managers use to categorize their corporation's businesses by growth rate and relative market share, helping them decide how to invest corporate funds. The matrix, shown in Exhibit 6.3, separates businesses into four categories based on how fast the market is growing (high-growth or low-growth) and the size of the business's share of that market (small or large). **Stars** are companies that have a large share of a fast-growing market. To take advantage of a star's fast-growing market and its strength in that market (large share), the

Corporate-Level Strategies	
PORTFOLIO STRATEGY	**GRAND STRATEGIES**

• Acquisitions, unrelated diversification, related diversification, single businesses
• Boston Consulting Group matrix
  • Stars
  • Question marks
  • Cash cows
  • Dogs
	• Growth
	
	• Stability
	
	• Retrenchment/recovery

Portfolio strategy a corporate-level strategy that minimizes risk by diversifying investment among various businesses or product lines

Acquisition the purchase of a company by another company

Unrelated diversification creating or acquiring companies in completely unrelated businesses

BCG matrix a portfolio strategy, developed by the Boston Consulting Group, that categorizes a corporation's businesses by growth rate and relative market share, and helps managers decide how to invest corporate funds

Star a company with a large share of a fast-growing market corporation must invest substantially in it. The investment is usually worthwhile, however, because many stars produce sizable future profits. **Question marks** are companies that have a small share of a fast-growing market. If the corporation invests in these companies, they may eventually become stars, but their relative weakness in the market (small share) makes investing in question marks more risky than investing in stars. **Cash cows** are companies that have a large share of a slow-growing market. Companies in this situation are often highly profitable, hence the name "cash cow." Finally, **dogs** are companies that have a small share of a slow-growing market. As the name "dogs" suggests, having a small share of a slow-growth market is often not profitable.

Since the idea is to redirect investment from slow-growing to fast-growing companies, the BCG matrix starts by recommending that while the substantial cash flows from cash cows last, they should be reinvested in stars (see arrow 1 in Exhibit 6.3) to help them grow even faster and obtain even more market share. Using this strategy, current profits help produce future profits. Over time, as their market growth slows, some stars may turn into cash cows (see arrow 2). Cash flows should also be directed to some question marks (see arrow 3). Though riskier than stars, question marks have great potential because of their fast-growing market. Managers must decide which question marks are most likely to turn into stars, and therefore warrant further investment, and which ones are too risky and should be sold. Over time, it is hoped that some question marks will become stars as their small markets become large ones (see arrow 4). Finally, because dogs lose money, the corporation should "find them new owners" or "take them to the pound." In other words, dogs should either be sold to other companies or be closed down and liquidated for their assets (see arrow 5).

Although the BCG matrix and other forms of portfolio strategy are relatively popular among managers, portfolio strategy has some drawbacks. The most significant is that contrary to the predictions of portfolio strategy, the evidence does *not* support the usefulness of acquiring unrelated businesses.

Question mark a company with a small share of a fast-growing market

Cash cow a company with a large share of a slow-growing market

Dog a company with a small share of a slow-growing market

Exhibit 6.3

Boston Consulting Group Matrix

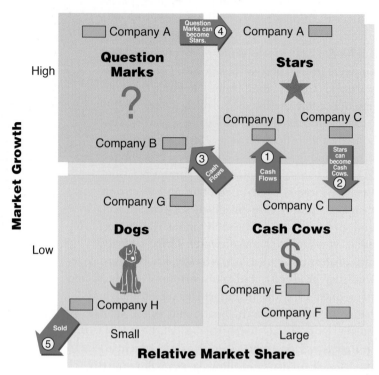

As shown in Exhibit 6.4, there is a U-shaped relationship between diversification and risk. The left side of the curve shows that single businesses with no diversification are extremely risky (if the single business fails, the entire business fails). So, in part, the portfolio strategy of diversifying is correct—competing in a variety of different businesses can lower risk. However, portfolio strategy is partly wrong, too—the right side of the curve shows that conglomerates composed of completely unrelated businesses are even riskier than single, undiversified businesses.

A second set of problems with portfolio strategy has to do with the dysfunctional consequences that occur when companies are categorized as stars, cash cows, question marks, or dogs. Contrary to expectations, the BCG matrix often yields incorrect judgments about a company's potential. This is because it relies on past performance (i.e., previous market share and previous market growth), which is a notoriously poor predictor of future company performance.

Furthermore, using the BCG matrix can also weaken the strongest performer in the corporate portfolio, the cash cow. As funds are redirected from cash cows to stars, corporate managers essentially take away the resources needed to take advantage of the cash cow's new business opportunities. As a result, the cash cow becomes less aggressive in seeking new business or in defending its present business. Finally, labeling a top performer as a cash cow can harm employee morale. Cash cow employees realize that they have inferior status and that instead of working for themselves, they are now working to fund the growth of stars and question marks.

So, what kind of portfolio strategy does the best job of helping managers decide which companies to buy or sell? The U-shaped curve in Exhibit 6.4 indicates that,

Exhibit 6.4

U-Shaped Relationship between Diversification and Risk

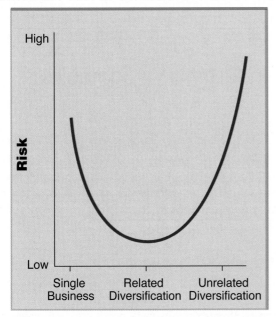

Source: Republished with permission of Academy of Management, P.O. Box 3020, Briar Cliff Manor, NY, 10510-8020. M. Lubatkin & P. J. Lane, "Psst . . . The Merger Mavens Still Have It Wrong!" *Academy of Management Executive* 10 (1996): 21–39. Reproduced with permission of the publisher via Copyright Clearance Center, Inc.

contrary to the predictions of portfolio strategy, the best approach is probably **related diversification,** in which the different business units share similar products, manufacturing, marketing, technology, or cultures. The key to related diversification is to acquire or create new companies with core capabilities that complement the core capabilities of businesses already in the corporate portfolio. We began this section with the example of 3M and its 55,000 products sold in over seven different business sectors. While seemingly different, most of 3M's product divisions are based in some fashion on its distinctive competencies in adhesives and tape (e.g., wet or dry sandpaper, Post-it notes, Scotchgard fabric protector, transdermal skin patches, reflective material used in traffic signs, etc.). Furthermore, all of 3M's divisions share its strong corporate culture that promotes and encourages risk taking and innovation. In sum, in contrast to a single, undiversified business or unrelated diversification, related diversification reduces risk because the different businesses can work as a team, relying on each other for needed experience, expertise, and support.

3.2 Grand Strategies

A **grand strategy** is a broad strategic plan used to help an organization achieve its strategic goals.[31] Grand strategies guide the strategic alternatives that managers of individual businesses or subunits may use in deciding what businesses they should be in. There are three kinds of grand strategies: growth, stability, and retrenchment/recovery.

The purpose of a **growth strategy** is to increase profits, revenues, market share, or the number of places (stores, offices, locations) in which the company does business. Companies can grow in several ways. They can grow externally by merging with or acquiring other companies in the same or different businesses.

Another way to grow is internally, directly expanding the company's existing business or creating and

> **Related diversification** creating or acquiring companies that share similar products, manufacturing, marketing, technology, or cultures
>
> **Grand strategy** a broad corporate-level strategic plan used to achieve strategic goals and guide the strategic alternatives that managers of individual businesses or subunits may use
>
> **Growth strategy** a strategy that focuses on increasing profits, revenues, market share, or the number of places in which the company does business

Method, the innovative branding concept in household cleaning, was launched by two roommates who saw tremendous growth opportunity in a stagnant product category. Because household cleaning products were all competing on price, and the products had all been formulated and promoted the same way since the 1950s, Method decided to apply design principles to environmentally-friendly cleaning formulas. The result? High-style design; fresh, organic scents (lavender, eucalyptus); 3,390 percent growth in 3 years; and a ranking of #7 on the *Inc.* 500 list.

Source: "Where the Action Is," *Inc.,* September 2006, 106.

© South-Western

growing new businesses. Walgreens one of the largest pharmacy chains in the United States, opened 425 new stores last year and will shoot for 500 this year. In fact, with 4,582 stores in 44 states, it hopes to have 7,000 stores by 2010.[32] Because Walgreens stores tend to draw customers from only a one- to two-mile radius, each additional store should add significant revenues and profits without cannibalizing existing stores' sales.[33]

The purpose of a **stability strategy** is to continue doing what the company has been doing, but just do it better. Consequently, companies following a stability strategy try to improve the way in which they sell the same products or services to the same customers. For example, Subaru has been making four-wheel-drive station wagons for 30 years. Over the last decade, it strengthened this focus by manufacturing only all-wheel-drive vehicles, like the Subaru Legacy and Outback (both come in four-door sedans or two-door coupes), which are popular in snowy and mountainous regions.[34] Companies often choose a stability strategy when their external environment doesn't change

Stability strategy a strategy that focuses on improving the way in which the company sells the same products or services to the same customers

Retrenchment strategy a strategy that focuses on turning around very poor company performance by shrinking the size or scope of the business

Recovery the strategic actions taken after retrenchment to return to a growth strategy

Industry-level strategy a corporate strategy that addresses the question "How should we compete in this industry?"

much or after they have struggled with periods of explosive growth.

The purpose of a **retrenchment strategy** is to turn around very poor company performance by shrinking the size or scope of the business or, if a company is in multiple businesses, by closing or shutting down different lines of the business. The first step of a typical retrenchment strategy might include making significant cost reductions; laying off employees; closing poorly performing stores, offices, or manufacturing plants; or closing or selling entire lines of products or services.[35]

After cutting costs and reducing a business's size or scope, the second step in a retrenchment strategy is recovery. **Recovery** consists of the strategic actions that a company takes to return to a growth strategy. This two-step process of cutting and recovery is analogous to pruning roses. Prior to each growing season, roses should be cut back to two-thirds their normal size. Pruning doesn't damage the roses; it makes them stronger and more likely to produce beautiful, fragrant flowers. The retrenchment-and-recovery process is similar. Cost reductions, layoffs, and plant closings are sometimes necessary to restore companies to "good health." But like pruning, those cuts are intended to allow companies to eventually return to growth strategies (i.e., recovery). So, when company performance drops significantly, a strategy of retrenchment and recovery may help the company return to a successful growth strategy.

4 Industry-Level Strategies

Industry-level strategy addresses the question "How should we compete in this industry?"

*Let's find out more about industry-level strategies by discussing **4.1 the five industry forces that determine overall levels of competition in an industry** and **4.2 the positioning strategies** and **4.3 adaptive strategies that companies can use to achieve sustained competitive advantage and above-average profits**.*

4.1 Five Industry Forces

According to Harvard professor Michael Porter, five industry forces—character of the rivalry, threat of new entrants, threat of substitute products or services, bargaining power of suppliers, and bargaining power of buyers—determine an industry's overall attractiveness and potential for long-term profitability. The stronger these forces, the less attractive the industry becomes to corporate investors because it is more difficult for companies to be profitable. Porter's industry forces are illustrated in Exhibit 6.5. Let's examine how these industry forces are bringing changes to several kinds of industries.

Character of the rivalry is a measure of the intensity of competitive behavior between companies in an industry. Is the competition among firms aggressive and cutthroat, or do competitors focus more on serving customers than on attacking each other? Both industry attractiveness and profitability decrease when rivalry is cutthroat.

The **threat of new entrants** is a measure of the degree to which barriers to entry make it easy or difficult for new companies to get started in an industry. If new companies can easily enter the industry, then competition will increase, and prices and profits will fall. However, if there are sufficient barriers to entry, such as large capital requirements to buy expensive equipment or plant facilities or the need for specialized knowledge,

then competition will be weaker, and prices and profits will generally be higher. For instance, high costs and intense competition make it very difficult to enter the video-game business. With today's average video game taking 12 to 36 months to create, $5 million to $10 million to develop, and teams of high-paid creative workers to develop realistic graphics, captivating story lines, and innovative game capabilities, the barriers to entry for this business are obviously extremely high.

The **threat of substitute products or services** is a measure of the ease with which customers can find substitutes for an industry's products or services. If customers can easily find substitute products or services, the competition will be greater, and profits will be lower. If there are few or no substitutes, competition will be weaker, and profits will be higher. Generic medicines are some of the best-known examples of substitute products. Under U.S. patent law, a company that develops a drug has exclusive rights to produce and market that drug for 20 years. During this time, if the drug sells well, prices and profits are generally high. After 20 years, however, the patent will expire, and any pharmaceutical company can manufacture and sell the same drug. When this happens, drug prices drop substantially, and the company that developed the drug typically sees its revenues drop sharply.

Bargaining power of suppliers is a measure of the influence that suppliers of parts, materials, and services to firms in an industry

Exhibit 6.5

Porter's Five Industry Forces

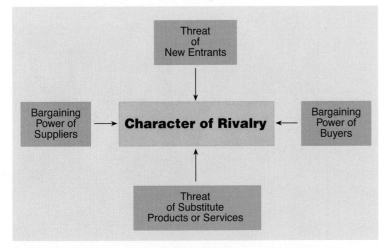

Source: Adapted with permission of The Free Press, a Division of Simon & Schuster, Inc. M. E. Porter, *Competitive Strategy: Techniques for Analyzing Industries and Competitors* (New York: Free Press, 1980). (c) 1980 by the Free Press.

Character of the rivalry a measure of the intensity of competitive behavior between companies in an industry

Threat of new entrants a measure of the degree to which barriers to entry make it easy or difficult for new companies to get started in an industry

Threat of substitute products or services a measure of the ease with which customers can find substitutes for an industry's products or services

Bargaining power of suppliers a measure of the influence that suppliers of parts, materials, and services to firms in an industry have on the prices of these inputs have on the prices of these inputs. When companies can buy parts, materials, and services from numerous suppliers, the companies will be able to bargain with the suppliers to keep prices low. Today, there are so many suppliers of inexpensive, standardized parts, computer chips, and video screens that dozens of new companies are beginning to manufacture flat-screen TVs. In other words, the weak bargaining power of suppliers has made it easier for new firms to enter the HDTV business. On the other hand, if there are few suppliers, or if a company is dependent on a supplier with specialized skills and knowledge, then the suppliers will have the bargaining power to dictate price levels.

Weak bargaining power of suppliers = more HDTV makers.

Bargaining power of buyers is a measure of the influence that customers have on the firm's prices. If a company sells a popular product or service to multiple buyers, then the company has more power to set prices. By contrast, if a company is dependent on just a few high-volume buyers, those buyers will typically have enough bargaining power to dictate prices. For example, with more than 6,200 stores and 176 million weekly shoppers, Wal-Mart is the largest single buyer in the history of retailing.[36] Wal-Mart buys 30 percent of all toothpaste, shampoo, and paper towels made by retail suppliers; 15 to 20 percent of all CDs, videos, and DVDs; 15 percent of all magazines; 14 percent of all groceries; and 20 percent of all toys. And, of course, Wal-Mart uses its purchasing power as a buyer to push down prices.[37]

4.2 Positioning Strategies

After analyzing industry forces, the next step in industry-level strategy is to protect your company from the negative effects of industry-wide competition and to create a sustainable competitive advantage. Ac-

cording to Michael Porter, there are three positioning strategies: cost leadership, differentiation, and focus.

Cost leadership means producing a product or service of acceptable quality at consistently lower production costs than competitors so that the firm can offer the product or service at the lowest price in the industry. Cost leadership protects companies from industry forces by deterring new entrants, who will have to match low costs and prices. Cost leadership also forces down the prices of substitute products and services, attracts bargain-seeking buyers, and increases bargaining power with suppliers, who have to keep their prices low if they want to do business with the cost leader.[38]

Differentiation means making your product or service sufficiently different from competitors' offerings such that customers are willing to pay a premium price for the extra value or performance that it provides. Differentiation protects companies from industry forces by reducing the threat of substitute products. It also protects companies by making it easier to retain customers and more difficult for new entrants trying to attract new customers. For example, why would anyone pay $2,300 for Whirlpool's Duet, a deluxe washer-dryer combination, when they could purchase a regular washer-dryer combination for $700 or less? The answer is that the Duet washer does huge loads, almost twice what normal washers hold, with just 16 gallons of water, compared to 40 gallons for conventional washers. So it's incredibly efficient in terms of water and

Bargaining power of buyers a measure of the influence that customers have on a firm's prices

Cost leadership the positioning strategy of producing a product or service of acceptable quality at consistently lower production costs than competitors can, so that the firm can offer the product or service at the lowest price in the industry

Differentiation the positioning strategy of providing a product or service that is sufficiently different from competitors' offerings that customers are willing to pay a premium price for it energy and saves consumers time because they can wash and dry twice as many clothes at the same time.[39]

With a **focus strategy,** a company uses either cost leadership or differentiation to produce a specialized product or service for a limited, specially targeted group of customers in a particular geographic region or market segment. Focus strategies typically work in market niches that competitors have overlooked or have difficulty serving. With 38 stores nationwide, the Container Store sells products to reorganize and rebuild your closets, sort out your kitchen drawers and cabinets, or add shelves, hooks, and storage anywhere in your home, office, or dorm room.[40] But, unlike Wal-Mart or Target, that's all it does.

4.3 Adaptive Strategies

Adaptive strategies are another set of industry-level strategies. Whereas the aim of positioning strategies is to minimize the effects of industry competition and build a sustainable competitive advantage, the purpose of adaptive strategies is to choose an industry-level strategy that is best suited to changes in the organization's external environment. There are four kinds of adaptive strategies: defenders, prospectors, analyzers, and reactors.[41]

Defenders seek moderate, steady growth by offering a limited range of products and services to a well-defined set of customers. In other words, defenders aggressively "defend" their current strategic position by doing the best job they can to hold on to customers in a particular market segment.

Prospectors seek fast growth by searching for new market opportunities,

Differentiation is what makes Whirlpool's $2,300 washer-dryer combination a hot product.

Gore-y Prospects

W.L. Gore, creator of GoreTex, encourages its employees to spend at least 10 percent of their work time on speculative ventures. The Elixir acoustic guitar string, a coated plastic string that is now the market leader, started out as one of those ventures. An employee working on bicycle cabling and gearing drafted another employee who had recently developed Glide dental floss. After two years of experimentation, their team launched Elixir. When music stores refused to carry it because it cost $15 per string, or 3 to 5 times more than traditional strings, Gore decided to give away 20,000 free samples valued at $15 each. Within a year, Elixir had a 35 percent market share.[42]

©Spencer Grant/PhotoEdit Inc.

encouraging risk taking, and being the first to bring innovative new products to market. Prospectors are analogous to gold miners who "prospect" for gold nuggets (i.e., new products) in hopes that the nuggets will lead them to a rich deposit of gold (i.e., fast growth).

Analyzers are a blend of the defender and prospector strategies. Analyzers seek moderate, steady growth *and* limited opportunities for fast growth. Analyzers are rarely first to market with new products or services. Instead, they try to simultaneously minimize risk and maximize profits by following or imitating the proven successes of prospectors. India-based Ranbaxy Pharmaceuticals follows an analyzer strategy by making low-priced generic

Focus strategy the positioning strategy of using cost leadership or differentiation to produce a specialized product or service for a limited, specially targeted group of customers in a particular geographic region or market segment

Defenders an adaptive strategy aimed at defending strategic positions by seeking moderate, steady growth and by offering a limited range of high-quality products and services to a well-defined set of customers

Prospectors an adaptive strategy that seeks fast growth by searching for new market opportunities, encouraging risk taking, and being the first to bring innovative new products to market

Analyzers an adaptive strategy that seeks to minimize risk and maximize profits by following or imitating the proven successes of prospectors copies of already popular patented drugs. And, with $80 billion of patented drugs losing their patent protection in the next four years, Ranbaxy, whose costs are just one-fifth those of U.S. pharmaceutical firms, plans to file applications with the U.S. Food and Drug Administration to make 20 more generic drugs.[43]

Finally, unlike defenders, prospectors, or analyzers, **reactors** do not follow a consistent strategy. Rather than anticipating and preparing for external opportunities and threats, reactors tend to "react" to changes in their external environment after they occur. Not surprisingly, reactors tend to be poorer performers than defenders, prospectors, or analyzers. A reactor approach is inherently unstable, and firms that fall into this mode of operation must change their approach or face almost certain failure.

©Creatas/Jupiter Images

5 Firm-Level Strategies

Microsoft brings out its Xbox 360 video-game console; Sony counters with its PlayStation 3. Sprint Nextel drops prices and increases monthly cell phone minutes; Verizon strikes back with better reception and even lower prices and more minutes. Attack and respond, respond and attack. **Firm-level strategy** addresses the question "How should we compete against a particular firm?"

Let's find out more about the firm-level strategies (i.e., direct competition between companies) by reading about **5.1 the basics of direct competition,** *and* **5.2 the strategic moves involved in direct competition between companies.**

5.1 Direct Competition

Although Porter's five industry forces indicate the overall level of competition in an industry, most companies do not compete directly with all the firms in their industry. For example,

McDonald's and Red Lobster are both in the restaurant business, but no one would characterize them as competitors. McDonald's offers low-cost, convenient fast food in a "seat yourself" restaurant, while Red Lobster offers mid-priced, sit-down seafood dinners complete with servers and a bar.

Instead of "competing" with the industry, most firms compete directly with just a few companies. **Direct competition** is the rivalry between two companies offering similar products and services that acknowledge each other as rivals and take offensive and defensive positions as they act and react to each other's strategic actions.[44] Two factors determine the extent to which firms will be in direct competition with each other: market commonality and resource similarity. **Market commonality** is the degree to which two companies have overlapping products, services, or customers in multiple markets. The more markets in which there is product, service, or customer overlap, the more intense the direct competition between the two companies. **Resource similarity** is the extent to which a competitor has similar amounts and kinds of resources, that is, similar assets, capabilities, processes, information, and knowledge used to create and sustain an advantage over competitors. From a competitive standpoint, resource similarity means that your direct competitors can probably match the strategic actions that your company takes.

Exhibit 6.6 shows how market commonality and resource similarity interact to determine when and where companies are in direct competition.[45] The overlapping

---

Reactors an adaptive strategy of not following a consistent strategy, but instead reacting to changes in the external environment after they occur

Firm-level strategy a corporate strategy that addresses the question "How should we compete against a particular firm?"

Direct competition the rivalry between two companies that offer similar products and services, acknowledge each other as rivals, and act and react to each other's strategic actions

Market commonality the degree to which two companies have overlapping products, services, or customers in multiple markets

Resource similarity the extent to which a competitor has similar amounts and kinds of resources area in each quadrant (between the triangle and the rectangle, or between the differently colored rectangles) depicts market commonality. The larger the overlap, the greater the market commonality. Shapes depict resource similarity, with rectangles representing one set of competitive resources and triangles representing another. Quadrant I shows two companies in direct competition because they have similar resources at their disposal and a high degree of market commonality. These companies try to sell similar products and services to similar customers. McDonald's and Burger King would clearly fit here as direct competitors.

In Quadrant II, the overlapping parts of the triangle and rectangle show two companies going after similar customers with some similar products or services, but doing so with different competitive resources. McDonald's and Wendy's restaurants would fit here. Wendy's is after the same lunchtime and dinner crowds that McDonald's is. Nevertheless, with its more expensive hamburgers, fries, shakes, and salads, Wendy's is less of a direct competitor to McDonald's than Burger King is. For example, Wendy's Garden Sensation salads (using fancy lettuce varieties, grape tomatoes, and mandarin oranges) bring in customers who would have eaten at more expensive casual dining restaurants like Applebee's.[46] A representative from Wendy's says, "We believe you win customers by consistently offering a better product at a strong, everyday value."[47]

In Quadrant III, the very small overlap shows two companies with different competitive resources and little market commonality. McDonald's and Luby's cafeterias fit here. Although both are in the fast-food busi-

Exhibit 6.6

A Framework of Direct Competition

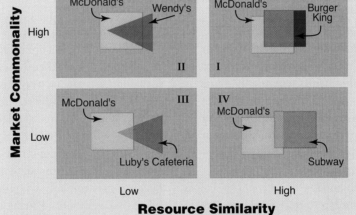

Source: Republished with permission of Academy of Management, P.O. Box 3020, Briar Cliff, NY, 10510-8020. M. Chen, "Competitor Analysis and Interfirm Rivalry: Toward a Theoretical Integration," *Academy of Management* Review 21. Reproduced by permission of the publisher via Copyright Clearance Center, Inc.

ness, there's almost no overlap in terms of products and customers. For example, Luby's sells baked chicken, turkey, roasts, meat loaf, and vegetables, none of which are available at McDonald's. Furthermore, Luby's customers aren't likely to eat at McDonald's. In fact, Luby's is not really competing with other fast-food restaurants, but with eating at home. Company surveys show that close to half of its customers would have eaten at home, not at another restaurant, if they hadn't come to Luby's.[48]

Finally, in Quadrant IV, the small overlap between the two rectangles shows that McDonald's and Subway compete with similar resources but with little market commonality. In terms of resources, McDonald's sales are much larger, but Subway, with its 27,270 stores worldwide, much faster growth, and plans to have 30,000 stores worldwide by 2010, will soon approach McDonald's 31,129 stores worldwide (just 13,000 in the United States).[49] Though Subway and McDonald's compete, they aren't direct competitors in terms of market commonality in the way that McDonald's and Burger King are, because Subway, unlike McDonald's, sells itself as a provider of healthy fast food. Thus, the overlap is much smaller in Quadrant IV than in Quadrant I.

5.2 Strategic Moves of Direct Competition

While corporate-level strategies help managers decide what business to be in and industry-level strategies help them determine how to compete within an industry, firm-level strategies help managers determine when, where, and what strategic actions should be taken against a direct competitor. Firms in direct competition can make two basic strategic moves: attacks and responses. These moves occur all the time in virtually every industry, but they are most noticeable in industries where multiple large competitors are pursuing customers in the same market space.

An **attack** is a competitive move designed to reduce a rival's market share or profits. For example, hoping to increase its market share at Burger King's expense, McDonald's began a brutal price war by putting eight items on a new $1 value menu, including two sandwiches, the Big N' Tasty quarter-pounder and the McChicken sandwich, that usually sold for $1.99.[50] Sales of those sandwiches doubled within weeks. By contrast, a **response** is a countermove, prompted by a rival's attack, that is designed to defend or improve a company's market share or profit. There are two kinds of responses.[51] The first is to match or mirror your competitor's move. This is what Burger King did to McDonald's by selling 11 menu items at 99 cents each, including its popular double cheeseburgers. The second kind of response, however, is to respond along a different dimension from your competitor's move or attack. For example, instead of cutting prices, Burger King could have introduced a new menu item to attract customers away from McDonald's.

Market commonality and resource similarity determine the likelihood of an attack or response, that is, whether a company is likely to attack a direct competitor or to strike back with a strong response when attacked. When market commonality is strong and companies have overlapping products, services, or customers in multiple markets, there is less motivation to attack and more motivation to respond to an attack. The reason for this is straightforward: when firms are direct competitors in a large number of markets, they have a great deal at stake. So when McDonald's launched an aggressive price war with its value menu, Burger King

had no choice but to respond by cutting its own prices.

Whereas market commonality affects the likelihood of an attack or a response to an attack, resource similarity largely affects response capability, that is, how quickly and forcefully a company can respond to an attack. When resource similarity is strong, the responding firm will generally be able to match the strategic moves of the attacking firm. Consequently, a firm is less likely to attack firms with similar levels of resources because it is unlikely to gain any sustained advantage when the responding firms strike back. On the other hand, if one firm is substantially stronger than another (i.e., low resource similarity), then a competitive attack is more likely to produce sustained competitive advantage. With over 30,000 stores to Burger King's 11,000 stores and much greater financial resources, McDonald's hoped its price war would inflict serious financial damage on Burger King while suffering minimal financial damage itself. This strategy worked to some extent. Although Burger King already sold 11 menu items for 99 cents, it wasn't willing or able to cut the price of its best-selling Whopper sandwiches to 99 cents (from $1.99). Basically admitting that it couldn't afford to match McDonald's price cuts on more expensive sandwiches, a Burger King spokesperson insisted, "McDonald's can't sell those sandwiches at $1 without losing money. It isn't sustainable." Thanks to its much

Red Ocean, Blue Ocean

Using the ocean as a metaphor, Professors Renée Mauborgne and W. Chan Kim describe highly competitive markets as shark-infested waters. The water is red with blood from continual attacks and responses, and any gains made by one company are incremental at best and bound to be ceded in the next shark fight.

The only hope for survival is to pursue innovations that take you out of the red ocean and into the deep blue ocean, where there are no competitors. If it sounds hard, it is; but it's not impossible. Cirque du Soleil created a whole new category of entertainment; Gmail lets you store unlimited email for free; and Nintendo's Wii has redefined videogaming with simple games that combine elements of virtual reality. Read more in *Blue Ocean Strategy* (Harvard University Press, 2005).

©Stone/Getty Images/ ©Reuters/Las Vegas Sun/Ethan Miller/Landov

Attack a competitive move designed to reduce a rival's market share or profits

Response a competitive countermove, prompted by a rival's attack, to defend or improve a company's market share or profit larger financial resources, McDonald's had the funds to outlast Burger King in the price war. As often happens, though, the price war ended up hurting both companies' profits.[52] McDonald's ended the price war when it became clear that lower prices didn't draw more customers to its restaurants.

In general, the more moves (i.e., attacks) a company initiates against direct competitors, and the greater a company's tendency to respond when attacked, the bet-ter its performance. More specifically, attackers and early responders (companies that are quick to launch a retaliatory attack) tend to gain market share and profits at the expense of late responders. This is not to suggest that a "full-attack" strategy always works best. In fact, attacks can provoke harsh retaliatory responses. Consequently, when deciding when, where, and what strategic actions to take against a direct competitor, managers should always consider the possibility of retaliation.

By the Numbers

1979	year Sony introduced the Walkman
2,711	number of Tim Horton's stores in Canada
50,000	number of products sold in each Menards store
3	number of grand strategies; number of positioning strategies
3,390%	growth at Method since in 2006
$2,300	price of Whirlpool Duet set
99¢	price of a Whopper during a price war

INNOVATION AND CHANGE

Organizational Innovation

W"When you're done, be sure to turn off the lights and lock the doors. We don't want anyone breaking into the tent." The tent? Because of their low cost and interesting architectural features, organizations are increasingly using tents as buildings. A 20,000 square foot church in Colorado Springs has heavy vinyl walls and ceilings instead of canvas, huge metal frames instead of tent poles, windows and doors that lock instead of zippered openings, central heating and air-conditioning instead of campfires, and wood floors and carpeting instead of hard, uneven ground, leading architect Todd Dalland, who has designed tents for 30 years, to ask, "At what point is it a tent? At what point is it a building?"[1]

Organizational innovation is the successful implementation of creative ideas in an organization.[2] **Creativity,** which is a form of organizational innovation, is the production of novel and useful ideas.[3] In the first part of this chapter, you will learn why innovation matters and how to manage innovation to create and sustain a competitive advantage. In the second part, you will learn about organizational change, which is a difference in the form, quality, or condition of an organization over time.[4] You will also learn about the risk of not changing and the ways in which companies can manage change. But first,

Organizational innovation the successful implementation of creative ideas in organizations

Creativity the production of novel and useful ideas

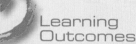

Learning Outcomes

1 explain why innovation matters to companies.

2 discuss the different methods that managers can use to effectively manage innovation in their organizations.

3 discuss why not changing can lead to organizational decline.

4 discuss the different methods that managers can use to better manage change as it occurs.

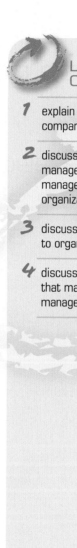

©Science Faction/Getty Images

let's get back to organizational innovation, like using tents for buildings.[5]

After reading the next two sections on organizational innovation, you should be able to

1 explain why innovation matters to companies.

2 discuss the different methods that managers can use to effectively manage innovation in their organizations.

1 Why Innovation Matters

We can only guess what changes technological innovations will bring in the next 20 years. Maybe we'll be listening to compact chips instead of compact discs. (Come to think of it, with iPods, we already do.) Maybe cars won't need tune-ups. And maybe TVs will be voice activated, so it won't matter if you lose the remote (just don't lose your voice). Who knows? The only thing we do know about the next 20 years is that innovation will continue to change our lives.

Let's begin our discussion of innovation by learning about: **1.1 technology cycles** and **1.2 innovation streams.**

1.1 Technology Cycles

In Chapter 3, you learned that *technology* is the knowledge, tools, and techniques used to transform inputs

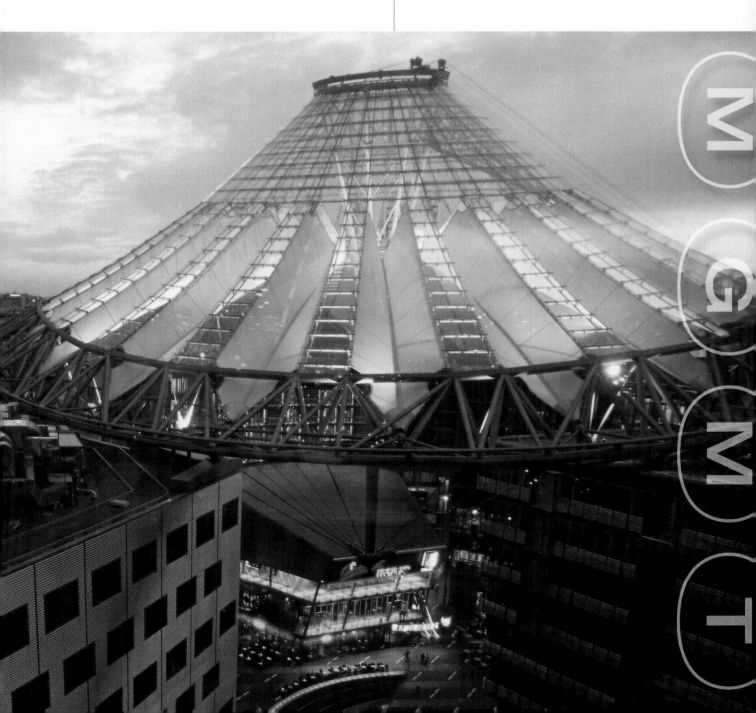

(raw materials, information, etc.) into outputs (products and services). A **technology cycle** begins with the "birth" of a new technology and ends when that technology reaches its limits and "dies" as it is replaced by a newer, substantially better technology.[6] For example, technology cycles occurred when air-conditioning supplanted fans, when Henry Ford's Model T replaced horse-drawn carriages, and when planes replaced trains as a means of cross-country travel.

From Gutenberg's invention of the printing press in the 1400s to the rapid advance of the Internet, studies of hundreds of technological innovations have shown that nearly all technology cycles follow the typical **S-curve pattern of innovation** shown in Exhibit 7.1.[7] Early in a technology cycle, there is still much to learn, so progress is slow, as depicted by point A on the S-curve. The flat slope indicates that increased effort (i.e., money, research and development) brings only small improvements in technological performance. Fortunately, as the new technology matures, researchers figure out how to get better performance from it. This is represented by point B of the S-curve in Exhibit 7.1. The steeper slope indicates that small amounts of effort will result in significant increases in performance. At point C, the flat slope again indicates that further efforts to develop this particular technology will result in only small increases in performance. More importantly, however, point C indicates that the performance limits of that particular technology are being reached. In other words, additional significant improvements in performance are highly unlikely.

Intel's technology cycles have followed this pattern. Intel spends billions to develop new computer chips and to build new production facilities to produce them. Intel has found that the technology cycle for its integrated circuits is about three years. In each three-year cycle, Intel spends billions to

Exhibit 7.1

S-Curves and Technological Innovation

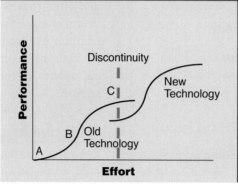

Source: R. N. Foster, *Innovation: The Attacker's Advantage* (New York: Summitt, 1986).

Technology cycle a cycle that begins with the "birth" of a new technology and ends when that technology reaches its limits and is replaced by a newer, substantially better technology

S-curve pattern of innovation a pattern of technological innovation characterized by slow initial progress, then rapid progress, and then slow progress again as a technology matures and reaches its limits

introduce a new chip, improves the chip by making it a little bit faster each year, and then replaces that chip at the end of the cycle with a brand new, different chip that is substantially faster than the old chip. At first, though (point A), the billions Intel spends typically produce only small improvements in performance. But after six months to a year with a new chip design, Intel's engineering and production people typically figure out how to make the new chips much faster than they were initially (point B). Yet, despite impressive gains in performance, Intel is unable to make a particular computer chip run any faster because it reaches its design limits.

After a technology has reached its limits at the top of the S-curve, significant improvements in performance usually come from radical new designs or new performance-enhancing materials (point C). In Exhibit 7.1, that new technology is represented by the second S-curve. The changeover or discontinuity between the old and new technologies is represented by the dotted line. At first, the old and new technologies will likely coexist. Eventually, however, the new technology will replace the old technology. When that happens, the old technology cycle will be complete, and a new one will have started. The changeover between Intel's newer and older computer chip designs typically takes about one year. Over time, improving existing technology (tweaking the performance of the current technology cycle), combined with replacing old technology with new technology cycles (i.e., new, faster computer chip

Joseph Balgazette designed the first interceptor sewers to carry London's sewage down the banks of the Thames to be dumped into the estuary.

©Getty Images Editorial

designs replacing older ones), has increased the speed of Intel's computer processors by a factor of 70 in just 19 years.

Though the evolution of Intel's Pentium chips has been used to illustrate S-curves and technology cycles, it's important to note that technology cycles and technological innovation don't necessarily mean "high technology." Remember, *technology* is simply the knowledge, tools, and techniques used to transform inputs into outputs. So a technology cycle occurs whenever there are major advances or changes in the *knowledge, tools,* and *techniques* of a field or discipline. For example, one of the most important technology cycles in the history of civilization occurred in 1859, when 1,300 miles of central sewer line were constructed throughout London to carry human waste to the sea more than 11 miles away. This sewer system replaced the practice of dumping raw sewage into streets where it drained into public wells that supplied drinking water. Preventing waste runoff from contaminating water supplies stopped the spread of cholera that had killed millions of people for centuries in cities throughout the world.[8] Indeed, the water you drink today is safe thanks to this "technology" breakthrough. So, when you think about technology cycles, don't automatically think "high technology." Instead, broaden your perspective by considering advances or changes in knowledge, tools, and techniques.

1.2 Innovation Streams

In Chapter 6, you learned that organizations can create *competitive advantage* for themselves if they have a *distinctive competence* that allows them to make, do, or perform something better than their competitors. Furthermore, a competitive advantage becomes sustainable if other companies cannot duplicate the benefits obtained from that distinctive competence. Technological innovation, however, not only can enable competitors to dupli-

cate the benefits obtained from a company's distinctive advantage but also can quickly turn a company's competitive advantage into a competitive disadvantage. For more than 110 years, Eastman Kodak was the dominant producer of photographic film worldwide. That is, until Kodak invented the digital camera (patent 4,131,919). But Kodak itself was unprepared for the rapid acceptance of its new technology, and its managers watched film quickly become obsolete for the majority of camera users. Technological innovation turned Kodak's competitive advantage into a competitive disadvantage.[9]

As the Kodak example shows, companies that want to sustain a competitive advantage must understand and protect themselves from the strategic threats of innovation. Over the long run, the best way for a company to do that is to create a stream of its own innovative ideas and products year after year. Consequently, we define **innovation streams** as patterns of innovation over time that can create sustainable competitive advantage.[10] Exhibit 7.2 shows a typical innovation consisting of a series of technology cycles. Recall that a technology cycle begins with a new technology and ends when that technology is replaced by a newer, substantially better technology. The innovation stream in Exhibit 7.2 shows three such technology cycles.

An innovation stream begins with a **technological discontinuity,** in which a scientific advance or a unique combination of existing technologies creates a significant breakthrough in performance or function. Technological discontinuities are followed by a **discontinuous change,** which is characterized by

Innovation streams patterns of innovation over time that can create sustainable competitive advantage

Technological discontinuity a scientific advance or a unique combination of existing technologies creates a significant breakthrough in performance or function

Discontinuous change the phase of a technology cycle characterized by technological substitution and design competition

Exhibit 7.2

Innovation Streams:
Technology Cycles over Time

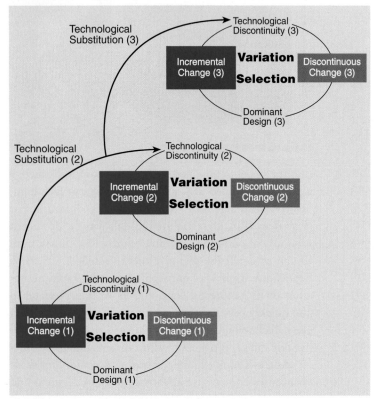

Source: Adapted from M. L. Tushman, P. C. Anderson, & C. O'Reilly, "Technology Cycles, Innovation Streams, and Ambidextrous Organizations," in *Managing Strategic Innovation and Change*, ed. M. L. Tushman & P. Anderson (1997), 3–23. © 1997 by Oxford University Press, Inc. Used by permission of Oxford University Press, Inc.

technological substitution and design competition. **Technological substitution** occurs when customers then purchase new technologies to replace older technologies.

Discontinuous change is also characterized by **design competition,** in which the old technology and several different new technologies compete to establish a new technological standard or dominant design. Because of large investments in old technology, and because the new and old technologies are often incompatible with each other, companies and consumers are reluctant to switch to a different technology during a design competition. Indeed, the telegraph was so widely used as a means of communication in the late 1800s that, at first, almost no one understood

Technological substitution the purchase of new technologies to replace older ones

Design competition competition between old and new technologies to establish a new technological standard or dominant design

Dominant design a new technological design or process that becomes the accepted market standard

why telephones would be a better way to communicate. In addition, during design competition, the older technology usually improves significantly in response to the competitive threat from the new technologies; this response also slows the changeover from older to newer technologies.

Discontinuous change is followed by the emergence of a **dominant design,** which becomes the new accepted market standard for technology.[11] Dominant designs emerge in several ways. One is critical mass, meaning that a particular technology can become the dominant design simply because most people use it. For example, even though Apple's AAC and Microsoft's WMA digital music file formats have better sound and smaller file sizes, the MP3 digital file format became dominant because millions of people across the world first used Napster to exchange MP3 digital music files.[12] As a result, today, nearly all new digital file formats are compatible with the MP3 format. If they weren't, digital music lovers wouldn't use them.

Likewise, a design can become dominant if it solves a practical problem. For example, the QWERTY keyboard (named for the top left line of letters) became the dominant design for typewriters because it slowed typists who, by typing too fast, caused mechanical typewriter keys to jam. Though computers can easily be switched to the DVORAK keyboard layout, which doubles typing speed and cuts typing errors by half, QWERTY lives on as the standard keyboard. Thus, the best technology doesn't always become the dominant design.

Dominant designs can also emerge through independent standards bodies. The International Telecommunications Union (**http://www.itu.ch**) is an independent organization that establishes standards for the communications industry. The ITU was founded in Paris in 1865 because European countries all had different telegraph systems that could not communicate with each other. After three months of negotiations, 20 countries signed the International Telegraph Conven-

tion, which standardized equipment and instructions, enabling telegraph messages to flow seamlessly from country to country. Today, as in 1865, various standards are proposed, discussed, negotiated, and changed until agreement is reached on a final set of standards that communication industries (i.e., Internet, telephony, satellites, radio, etc.) will follow worldwide.

No matter how it happens, the emergence of a dominant design is a key event in an innovation stream. First, the emergence of a dominant design indicates that there are winners and losers. Technological innovation is both competence enhancing and competence destroying. Companies that bet on the now-dominant design usually prosper. In contrast, when companies bet on the wrong design or the old technology, they may experience **technological lockout,** which occurs when a new dominant design (i.e., a significantly better technology) prevents a company from competitively selling its products or makes it difficult to do so.[13] In fact, more companies are likely to go out of business in a time of discontinuous change and changing standards than in an economic recession or slowdown. Second, the emergence of a dominant design signals a shift from design experimentation and competition to **incremental change,** a phase in which companies innovate by lowering the cost and improving the functioning and performance of the dominant design. For example, during a technology cycle, manufacturing efficiencies enable Intel to cut the cost of its chips by one-half to two-thirds, while doubling or tripling their speed. This focus on improving the dominant design continues until the next technological discontinuity occurs.

2 Managing Innovation

As the discussion of technology cycles and innovation streams showed, managers must be equally good at managing innovation in two very different circumstances. First, during discontinuous change, companies must find a way to anticipate and survive the technological changes that can suddenly transform industry leaders into losers and industry unknowns into powerhouses. Companies that can't manage innovation following technological discontinuities risk quick organizational decline and dissolution. Second, after a new dominant design emerges following discontinuous change, companies must manage the very different process of incre-

mental improvement and innovation. Companies that can't manage incremental innovation slowly deteriorate as they fall farther behind industry leaders.

Unfortunately, what works well when managing innovation during discontinuous change doesn't work well when managing innovation during periods of incremental change (and vice versa).

Consequently, to successfully manage innovation streams, companies need to be good at three things: *2.1 managing sources of innovation, 2.2 managing innovation during discontinuous change,* and *2.3 managing innovation during incremental change.*

2.1 Managing Sources of Innovation

Innovation comes from great ideas. So a starting point for managing innovation is to manage the sources of innovation, that is, where new ideas come from. One place that new ideas originate is with brilliant inventors. But only a few companies, however, have the likes of an Edison, Marconi, or Graham Bell working for them. Given that great thinkers and inventors are in short supply, what might companies do to ensure a steady flow of good ideas?

Well, when we say that innovation begins with great ideas, we're really saying that innovation begins with creativity. *Creativity* is the production of novel and useful ideas.[14] Although companies can't command employees to be creative ("You *will* be more creative!"), they can jump-start innovation by building **creative work environments,** in which workers perceive that creative thoughts and ideas are welcomed and valued. As Exhibit 7.3 shows, creative work environments have six components that encourage creativity: challenging work, organizational encouragement, supervisory encouragement, work group encouragement, freedom, and a lack of organizational impediments.[15]

Work is *challenging* when it requires effort, demands

Technological lockout when a new dominant design (i.e., a significantly better technology) prevents a company from competitively selling its products or makes it difficult to do so

Incremental change the phase of a technology cycle in which companies innovate by lowering costs and improving the functioning and performance of the dominant technological design

Creative work environments workplace cultures in which workers perceive that new ideas are welcomed, valued, and encouraged

Exhibit 7.3

Components of Creative Work Environments

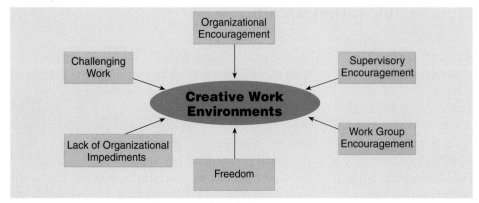

Sources: T. M. Amabile, R. Conti, H. Coon, J. Lazenby, & M. Herron, "Assessing the Work Environment for Creativity," *Academy of Management Journal* 39 (1996): 1154–1184.

attention and focus, and is perceived as important to others in the organization. According to researcher Mihaly Csikszentmihalyi (pronounced ME-high-ee CHICK-sent-me-high-ee), challenging work promotes creativity because it creates a rewarding psychological experience known as "flow." **Flow** is a psychological state of effortlessness, in which you become completely absorbed in what you're doing and time seems to fly.[16] A key part of creating flow experiences, and thus creative work environments, is to achieve a balance between skills and task challenge. When workers can do more than is required of them, they become bored, and when their skills aren't sufficient to accomplish a task, they become anxious. When skills and task challenge are balanced, however, flow and creativity can occur.

A creative work environment requires three kinds of encouragement: organizational, supervisory, and work group encouragement. *Organizational encouragement* of creativity occurs when management encourages risk taking and new ideas, supports and fairly evaluates new ideas, rewards and recognizes creativity, and encourages the sharing of new ideas throughout different parts of the company. *Supervisory encouragement* of creativity occurs when supervisors provide clear goals, encourage open interaction with subordinates, and actively support development teams' work and ideas. *Work group encouragement* occurs when group members have diverse experience, education, and backgrounds and the group fosters mutual openness to ideas, positive, constructive challenge to ideas, and shared commitment to ideas.

An example of organizational and supervisory

> **Flow** a psychological state of effortlessness, in which you become completely absorbed in what you're doing and time seems to pass quickly

encouragement can be found at Tractor Supply Company, which sells farm supplies, equipment, and tools. Tractor Supply encourages employees to take calculated risks, and it doesn't punish them if those risks don't work out. Chairman Joe Scarlett explains what happened after a company buyer took a gamble on a new line of "Iron Smith" power tools for its stores: "It was well put together as a program. But we imported the product and it was junk. We could have fired the buyer. But he did a wonderful job conceptually. We took our punch in the mouth and our financial losses. Today, that buyer is our VP of marketing. The only reason the line didn't work was because the outside people we relied on for a piece of the execution didn't work out. Most people who take risks are not doing crazy things. We just tell them to fix the problem. Nobody gets chewed out."[17]

Freedom means having autonomy over one's day-to-day work and a sense of ownership and control over one's ideas. Numerous studies have indicated that creative ideas thrive under conditions of freedom. At Royal Philips Electronics (Philips), all groups within the company have been given complete freedom to rethink every product with the goal of making it simpler for the end user to install and use.[18]

To foster creativity, companies may also have to *remove impediments* to creativity from their work environments. Internal conflict and power struggles, rigid management structures, and a conservative bias toward the status quo can all discourage creativity. They create the perception that others in the organization will decide which ideas are acceptable and deserve support.

Idea Champion Showcase

Every quarter, Adobe hosts the Idea Champion Showcase, an *American Idol*-style ideathon in which six presenters get 10 minutes each to pitch a new business idea, product concept, packaging, technology, whatever. Top executives are not invited to the showcase because their tendency to be cautious makes them want to "hurl rocks" at nascent ideas before they have a chance to develop. Rick Bess is an idea mentor at Adobe. He developed the showcase after an internal study showed too many roadblocks were being thrown in front of new ideas, keeping them from penetrating the organizational hierarchy.

Source: S. Kirsner, "Adobe Idol," *Fast Company*, May 2007, 95.

2.2 Experiential Approach: Managing Innovation during Discontinuous Change

A study of 72 product-development projects (i.e., innovation) in 36 computer companies across the United States, Europe, and Asia found that companies that succeeded in periods of discontinuous change (characterized by technological substitution and design competition, as described earlier) typically followed an experiential approach to innovation.[19] The **experiential approach to innovation** assumes that innovation is occurring within a highly uncertain environment and that the key to fast product innovation is to use intuition, flexible options, and hands-on experience to reduce uncertainty and accelerate learning and understanding. The experiential approach to innovation has five aspects: design iterations, testing, milestones, multifunctional teams, and powerful leaders.[20]

An "iteration" is a repetition. So a **design iteration** is a cycle of repetition in which a company tests a prototype of a new product or service, improves on the design, and then builds and tests the improved product or service prototype. A **product prototype** is a full-scale working model that is being tested for design, function, and reliability. **Testing** is a systematic comparison of different product designs or design iterations. Companies that want to create a new dominant design following a technological discontinuity quickly build, test, improve, and retest a series of different product prototypes. When Avery Dennison decided to build a new label printer for offices, it designed a prototype printer that prints and then partially peels each label. When Avery tested the prototype in offices, workers said that it was too heavy to move, its large electrical plug wouldn't fit a standard surge protector strip, and it was too loud. After numerous design iterations, Avery's Quick Peel Automatic Label Peeler is quiet, weighs just seven pounds, and can print 500 labels in just 30 minutes, as opposed to 54 minutes for earlier printers.[21]

By trying a number of very different designs, or by making successive improvements and changes in the same design, frequent design iterations reduce uncertainty and improve understanding. Simply put, the more prototypes you build, the more likely you are to learn what works and what doesn't. Also, when designers and engineers build a number of

© Photographer's Choice/Getty Images

prototypes, they are less likely to "fall in love" with a particular prototype. Instead, they'll be more concerned with improving the product or technology as much as they can. Testing speeds up and improves the innovation process, too. When two very different design prototypes are tested against each other, or the new design iteration is tested against the previous iteration, product design strengths and weaknesses quickly become apparent. Likewise, testing uncovers errors early in the design process when they are easiest to correct. Finally, testing accelerates learning and understanding by forcing engineers and product designers to examine hard data about product performance. When there's hard evidence that prototypes are testing well, the confidence of the design team grows. Also, personal conflict between design team members is less likely when testing focuses on hard measurements and facts rather than personal hunches and preferences.

Milestones are formal project review points used to assess progress and performance. For example, a company that has put itself on a 12-month schedule to complete a project might schedule milestones at the 3-month, 6-month, and 9-month points on the schedule. By making people regularly assess what they're doing, how well they're performing, and whether they need to take corrective action, milestones provide structure to the general chaos that follows technological discontinuities. Milestones also shorten the innovation process by creating a sense of urgency that keeps everyone on task.

Multifunctional teams are work teams composed of people from different departments. Multifunctional teams accelerate learning and understanding by mixing and integrating technical, marketing, and manufacturing activities. By involving all key departments in development from the start, multifunctional teams speed innovation through early identification of

Experiential approach to innovation an approach to innovation that assumes a highly uncertain environment and uses intuition, flexible options, and hands-on experience to reduce uncertainty and accelerate learning and understanding

Design iteration a cycle of repetition in which a company tests a prototype of a new product or service, improves on that design, and then builds and tests the improved prototype

Product prototype a full-scale, working model that is being tested for design, function, and reliability

Testing the systematic comparison of different product designs or design iterations

Milestones formal project review points used to assess progress and performance

Multifunctional teams work teams composed of people from different departments

new ideas or problems that would typically not have been generated or addressed until much later.

Powerful leaders provide the vision, discipline, and motivation to keep the innovation process focused, on time, and on target. Powerful leaders are able to get resources when they are needed, are typically more experienced, have high status in the company, and are held directly responsible for the product's success or failure. On average, powerful leaders can get innovation-related projects done nine months faster than leaders with little power or influence. One such powerful leader was Phil Martens, the former head of Ford's product development. With a year to go before introduction and Ford's hybrid Escape months behind schedule, he told the team, "We are going to deliver on time. . . . Anything you need you'll get."[22] Despite daily inquiries "from above," he promised no interruptions or interference from anyone—even top management. And, when the team members needed something, they got it without waiting.

2.3 Compression Approach: Managing Innovation during Incremental Change

Whereas the experiential approach is used to manage in-

Compression approach to innovation an approach to innovation that assumes that incremental innovation can be planned using a series of steps and that compressing those steps can speed innovation

Generational change change based on incremental improvements to a dominant technological design such that the improved technology is fully backward compatible with the older technology

novation in highly uncertain environments during periods of discontinuous change, the compression approach is used to manage innovation in more certain environments during periods of incremental change. Whereas the goals of the experiential approach are significant improvements in performance and the establishment of a *new* dominant design, the goals of the compression approach are lower costs and incremental improvements in the performance and function of the *existing* dominant design.

The general strategies in each approach are different, too. With the experiential approach, the general strategy is to build something new, different, and substantially better. Because there's so much uncertainty—no one knows which technology will become the market leader—companies adopt a winner-take-all approach by trying to create the market-leading, dominant design. With the compression approach, the general strategy is to compress the time and steps needed to bring about small, consistent improvements in performance and functionality. Because a dominant technology design already exists, the general strategy is to continue improving the existing technology as rapidly as possible.

In short, a **compression approach to innovation** assumes that innovation is a predictable process, that incremental innovation can be planned using a series of steps, and that compressing the time it takes to complete those steps can speed up innovation. The compression approach to innovation has five aspects: planning, supplier involvement, shortening the time of individual steps, overlapping steps, and multifunctional teams.[23]

In Chapter 5, *planning* was defined as choosing a goal and a method or strategy to achieve that goal. When *planning for incremental innovation,* the goal is to squeeze or compress development time as much as possible, and the general strategy is to create a series of planned steps to accomplish that goal. Planning for incremental innovation helps avoid unnecessary steps and enables developers to sequence steps in the right order to avoid wasted time and delays between steps. Planning also reduces misunderstandings and improves coordination.

Most planning for incremental innovation is based on the idea of generational change. **Generational change** occurs when incremental improvements are made to a dominant technological design such that the improved version of the technology is fully backward compatible with the older version.[24] Software is backward compatible if a new version of the software will work with files created by older versions. Likewise, one of the important features of gaming machines, like the Xbox 360 and the Nintendo Wii, is their ability to play games purchased for earlier machines. In fact, the latest Game Boy can play games originally purchased more than 20 years ago.[25]

Because the compression approach assumes that innovation can follow a series of preplanned steps, one of the ways to shorten development time is *supplier involvement*. Delegating some of the preplanned steps in the innovation process to outside suppliers reduces the amount of work that internal development teams must do. Plus, suppliers provide an alternative source of ideas and expertise that can lead to better designs. When Bombardier Aerospace designed its new Continental business jet, it relied heavily on 30 suppliers to design and test new parts and share in the $500 million development cost. In today's jets, it is essential that the various electronic components, most of which are computer controlled, do not interfere with each other. Bombardier relied on supplier Rockwell Collins, which built an electronics integration testing unit to ensure that the electronic controls for the throttles, wings and rudders, radar, and other components were compatible.[26] In general, the earlier suppliers are involved, the quicker they catch and prevent future problems, such as unrealistic designs or mismatched product specifications.

Another way to shorten development time is simply to *shorten the time of individual steps* in the innovation process. A common way to do that is through computer-aided design (CAD). CAD speeds up the design process by allowing designers and engineers to make and test design changes using computer models rather than physically testing expensive prototypes. CAD also speeds innovation by making it easy to see how design changes affect engineering, purchasing, and production.

In a sequential design process, each step must be completed before the next step begins. But sometimes multiple development steps can be performed at the same time. *Overlapping steps* shorten the development process by reducing delays or waiting time between steps. Warner Bros. is using overlapping steps to reduce the time it takes to make the entire series of seven *Harry Potter* films—one for each of the seven books in J.K. Rowling's series. Because the actors were aging and would soon resemble adults more than high school students, Warner Bros. used new directors and new production teams for each of the movies in the *Harry Potter* series so it could begin shooting the next film while the previous one was in post production and the one prior to that was in the theaters.[27]

Extreme Makeover

Standing in front of her mirror, Hana Zalal, the president of Cargo Cosmetics, was holding a tube of lipstick and wondering how to redesign it. Then came a packaging epiphany: make it completely biodegradable. An alumna of the University of Toronto's civil engineering program, she went to the university for help. Professor Mohini Sain took up the project and worked with Cargo and a local injection-molding company for two years to figure out how to form corn into a lipstick tube at a "fast and cheap commercial rate." They succeeded. Not only does the new PlantLove lipstick tube decompose in 47 days with composting, the box it comes in is embedded with wildflower seeds and can be planted instead of discarded. And as you would expect, the lipstick itself is environmentally friendly and uses no mineral or petroleum oils or derivatives.

Source: S. Bhattacharya, "Cosmetics Company Cargo Takes Green and Floral Path," *Toronto Star*, 16 January 2007; "Lipstick Maker Goes Green with Biodegradable Tube," *CBC Canada*, 20 April 2007, www.cbc.ca.

©Susan Van Etten

Organizational Change

The idea was simple. Build a series of electronics superstores and watch the customers and profits pour in. For a while, it seemed to work. Sales at Incredible Universe grew to $725 million in less than four years as the company grew to 17 stores, each of which stocked an average of 85,000 products in a 185,000-square-foot building. That's more than four times the size of rival Circuit City stores. Yet, because of the size, inventory, and extras, the breakeven point for each store was $70 million in sales per year, so despite rapid growth, the company was losing money at record rates. Managers were unable to change the store concept quickly enough to reverse the situation, so the parent company, Tandy Corporation, closed Incredible Universe just 4 years after its founding.[28]

After reading the next two sections on organizational change, you should be able to

3 discuss why not changing can lead to organizational decline.

4 discuss the different methods that managers can use to better manage change as it occurs.

3 Organizational Decline: The Risk of Not Changing

Businesses operate in a constantly changing environment. Recognizing and adapting to internal and external changes can mean the difference between continued success and going out of business. Companies that fail to change run the risk of organizational decline.[29]

Organizational decline occurs when companies don't anticipate, recognize, neutralize, or adapt to the internal or external pressures that threaten their survival.[30] In other words, decline occurs when organizations don't recognize the need for change. General Motors' loss of market share in the automobile industry (from 50 to 25 percent) is an example of organizational decline. There are five stages of organizational decline: blinded, inaction, faulty action, crisis, and dissolution.[31]

In the *blinded stage,* decline begins because key managers fail to recognize the internal or external changes that will harm their organizations. This "blindness" may be due to a simple lack of awareness about changes or an inability to understand their significance. It may also come from the overconfidence that can develop when a company has been successful.

In the *inaction stage,* as organizational performance problems become more visible, management may recognize the need to change but still take no action. The managers may be waiting to see if the problems will correct themselves. Or, they may find it difficult to change the practices and policies that previously led to success. Possibly, too, they wrongly assume that they can easily correct the problems, so they don't feel the situation is urgent.

In the *faulty action stage,* faced with rising costs and decreasing profits and market share, management will announce "belt-tightening" plans designed to cut costs, increase efficiency, and restore profits. In other words, rather than recognizing the need for fundamental changes, managers assume that if they just run

a "tighter ship," company performance will return to previous levels.

In the *crisis stage,* bankruptcy or dissolution (i.e., breaking up the company and selling its parts) is likely to occur unless the company completely reorganizes the way it does business. At this point, however, companies typically lack the resources to fully change how they run their businesses. Cutbacks and layoffs will have reduced the level of talent among employees. Furthermore, talented managers who were savvy enough to see the crisis coming will have found jobs with other companies (often with competitors).

In the *dissolution stage,* after failing to make the changes needed to sustain the organization, the company is dissolved through bankruptcy proceedings or by selling assets in order to pay suppliers, banks, and creditors. At this point, a new CEO may be brought in to oversee the closing of stores, offices, and manufacturing facilities, the final layoff of managers and employees, and the sale of assets.

Finally, note that because decline is reversible at each of the first four stages, not all companies in decline reach final dissolution. For example, GM is trying to aggressively cut costs, stabilize its shrinking market share, and use innovative production techniques in an effort to reverse a decline that has lasted nearly a decade and resulted in all-time low stock prices.

Organizational decline a large decrease in organizational performance that occurs when companies don't anticipate, recognize, neutralize, or adapt to the internal or external pressures that threaten their survival

Read All About It

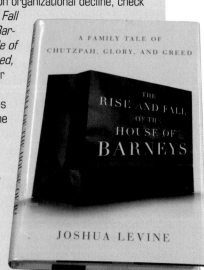

For a great story on organizational decline, check out *The Rise and Fall of the House of Barneys A Family Tale of Chutzpah, Glory, and Greed,* by Joshua Levine, a writer for *Forbes* magazine. In his book, Levine chronicles the trajectory of one of the most upscale retailers in the United States, from its humble origins as a tiny discount men's clothing store in New York to an international phenomenon to a bankrupt shell later to be revived and purchased by Jones New York. Not only a cautionary tale, but a great read.

mgmttale

©Susan Van Etten

4 Managing Change

According to social psychologist Kurt Lewin, change is a function of the forces that promote change and the opposing forces that slow or resist change.[32] **Change forces** lead to differences in the form, quality, or condition of an organization over time.

By contrast, **resistance forces** support the status quo, that is, the existing conditions in organizations. Change is difficult under any circumstances. Indeed, in a study of heart bypass patients, doctors told participants straight-forwardly to change their eating and health habits or they would die. Unbelievably, a full 90 percent of participants did *not* change their habits at all![33] This fierce resistance to change also applies to organizations.

Resistance to change, is caused by self-interest, misunderstanding and distrust, and a general intolerance for change.[34] People resist change out of *self-interest* because they fear that change will cost or deprive them of something they value. For example, resistance might stem from a fear that the changes will result in a loss of pay, power, responsibility or even perhaps one's job. People also resist change because of *misunderstanding and distrust;* they don't understand the change or the reasons for it, or they distrust the people, typically management, behind the change. Resistance isn't always visible at first, however. In fact, some of the strongest resisters may initially support the changes in public, nodding and smiling their agreement, but then ignore the changes in private and do their jobs as they always have. Management consultant Michael Hammer calls this deadly form of resistance the "Kiss of Yes."[35]

Resistance may also come from a generally low tolerance for change. Some people are simply less capable of handling change than others. People with a *low tolerance for change* feel threatened by the uncertainty associated with change and worry that they won't be able to learn the new skills and behaviors needed to successfully negotiate change in their companies.

Because resistance to change is inevitable, successful change efforts require careful management. In this section you will learn about *4.1 managing resistance to change, 4.2 what not to do when leading organizational change,* and *4.3 different change tools and techniques.*

4.1 Managing Resistance to Change

According to Kurt Lewin, managing organizational change is a basic process of unfreezing, change intervention, and refreezing. **Unfreezing** is getting the people affected by change to believe that change is needed.

©Stone/Getty Images

During the **change intervention** itself, workers and managers change their behavior and work practices. **Refreezing** is supporting and reinforcing the new changes so that they "stick."

Resistance to change is an example of frozen behavior. Given the choice between changing and not changing, most people would rather not change. Because resistance to change is natural and inevitable, managers need to unfreeze resistance to change to create successful change programs. The following methods can be used to manage resistance to change: education and communication, participation, negotiation, top management support, and coercion.[36]

When resistance to change is based on insufficient, incorrect, or misleading information, managers should *educate* employees about the need for change and *communicate* change-related information to them. Managers must also supply the information and funding or other support employees need to make changes. For example, resistance to change can be particularly

Change forces forces that produce differences in the form, quality, or condition of an organization over time

Resistance forces forces that support the existing state of conditions in organizations

Resistance to change opposition to change resulting from self-interest, misunderstanding and distrust, or a general intolerance for change

Unfreezing getting the people affected by change to believe that change is needed

Change intervention the process used to get workers and managers to change their behavior and work practices

Refreezing supporting and reinforcing new changes so that they "stick"

strong when one company buys another company. New York-Presbyterian Healthcare System, however, reduced resistance to change by designating mentors to coach individuals, groups, and departments in newly acquired companies about its procedures and practices. New York Presbyterian's Diane Iorfida said, "Keeping employees informed every step of the way is so important. It's also important to tell the truth, whatever you do. If you don't know, say you don't know."[37]

Another way to reduce resistance to change is to have those affected by the change *participate in planning and implementing the change process.* Employees who participate have a better understanding of the change and the need for it. Furthermore, employee concerns about change can be addressed as they occur if employees participate in the planning and implementation process. CEO A. G. Lafley turned around Procter

Coercion using formal power and authority to force others to change

& Gamble by refocusing the company on its billion-dollar brands (e.g., Tide, Pantene). Martin Nuechtern, then chief of global hair care, said, "A. G. made things very clear: Make sure you focus on Pantene."[38] While Lafley clearly shifted the focus to P&G's best brands, the strategies to reenergize those brands were generated through employee participation. At an informal luncheon with midlevel managers, Lafley said, "I don't have a speech planned. I thought we could talk. I'm searching for meaty issues. Give me some meaty issues."[39] Then, he listened to their ideas.

Employees are also less likely to resist change if they are allowed to discuss and agree on who will do what after change occurs. And, resistance to change decreases when change efforts receive *significant managerial support.* Managers must do more than talk about the importance of change, though. They must provide the training, resources, and autonomy needed to make change happen. For example, with a distinguished 70-year history of hand-drawing Hollywood's most successful animated films (*Snow White, Bambi, The Little Mermaid, Beauty and the Beast*), animators at Walt Disney Company naturally resisted the move to computer-generated (CG) animation. So Disney supported the difficult change by putting all of its animators through a six-month "CG Boot Camp," where they learned how to "draw" animated characters with computers.[40]

Finally, resistance to change can be managed through **coercion,** or the use of formal power and authority to force others to change. Because of the intense negative reactions it can create (e.g., fear, stress, resentment, sabotage of company products), coercion should be used only when a crisis exists or when all other attempts to reduce resistance to change have failed.

4.2 What *Not* to Do When Leading Change

So far, you've learned about the basic change process (unfreezing, change, refreezing) and managing resistance to change. However, Harvard Business School professor John Kotter argues that knowing what *not* to do is just as important as knowing what to do when it comes to achieving successful organizational change.[41]

Managers commonly make certain errors when they lead change. The first two errors occur during the unfreezing phase, when managers try to get the people affected by change to believe that change is really needed. The first and potentially most serious error is *not establishing a great enough sense of urgency.* Indeed, Kotter estimates that more than half of all change efforts fail because the people affected are not convinced that change is necessary. People will feel a greater sense of urgency if a leader in the company makes a public, candid assessment of the company's problems and weaknesses.

The second mistake that occurs in the unfreezing process is *not creating a powerful enough coalition.* Change often starts with one or two people, but to build enough momentum to change an entire department, division, or company, change has to be supported by a critical and growing group of people. Besides top management, Kotter recommends that key employees, managers, board members, customers, and even union leaders be members of a *core change coalition,* which guides and supports organizational change. Procter & Gamble's CEO A. G. Lafley says, "If you are going to make a significant change, you have to declare where are we going and why are we going there. Then you have to put together this guiding coalition. You have to put the true disciples together—the prophets who believe in it as passionately as you do. And they help you to carry the organization, because you can't carry a 100,000-person organization spread across 80 to 100 countries by yourself."[42]

The next four errors that managers make occur during the change phase, when a change intervention is used to try to get workers and managers to change their behavior and work practices. *Lacking a vision* for change is a significant error at this point. As you learned in Chapter 5, a *vision* is a statement of a company's purpose or reason for existing. A vision for change makes clear where a company or department is headed and why the change is occurring. Change efforts that lack vision tend to be confused, chaotic, and contradictory. By contrast, change efforts guided by visions are clear and easy to understand and can be effectively explained in five minutes or less.

Undercommunicating the vision by a factor of 10 is another mistake in the change phase. According to Kotter, companies mistakenly hold just one meeting to announce the vision. Or, if the new vision receives heavy emphasis in executive speeches or company newsletters, senior management then undercuts the vision by behaving in ways contrary to it. Successful communication of the vision requires that top managers link everything the company does to the new vision and that they "walk the talk" by behaving in ways consistent with the vision.

Furthermore, even companies that begin change with a clear vision sometimes make the mistake of *not removing obstacles to the new vision.* They leave formidable barriers to change in place by failing to redesign jobs, pay plans, and technology to support the new way of doing things. One way CEO Aylwin Lewis removed obstacles to Sears' new vision was by reorganizing how the work of store employees gets done so that they could spend less time with inventory in the back of the store and more time with customers in the front. Many employees at headquarters had never worked at a Sears store, so Lewis began requiring all 3,800 staff members at company headquarters to spend a day each year working in a store. Lewis himself spends every Thursday through Saturday visiting company stores. Without these store visits, management would be isolated from customers and less able to understand how customers perceive and use the store.[43]

Another error in the change phase is *not systematically planning for and creating short-term wins.* Most people don't have the discipline and patience to wait two years to see if the new change effort works. Change

CHANGE EFFORTS THAT LACK VISION TEND TO BE CONFUSED, CHAOTIC, AND CONTRADICTORY.

During his weekly store visits, Sears CEO Aylwin Lewis questions managers about their knowledge of the profit margins for various products. He asks them how they would run their stores better and pushes them to be financially literate. At today's Sears, one of the highest complements is to be called "commercial" meaning that the employee understands how to make money.[44]

is threatening and uncomfortable, so people need to see an immediate payoff if they are to continue to support it. Kotter recommends that managers create short-term wins by actively picking people and projects that are likely to work extremely well early in the change process. Even though Ford Motor Company was losing billions of dollars, CEO Alan Mulally announced that he would award blue-collar employees year-end bonuses ranging from $300 to $800. Admitting that the company did not meet profit or market share goals for the year, Mulally acknowledged that workers improved quality levels and reduced costs, and that those improvements were an important part of turning around the company. "These [financial] awards underscore the importance of working together as a unified team," Mulally said in an email, "That's the only way we'll make more progress down the road."[45]

The last two errors that managers make occur during the refreezing phase, when attempts are made to support and reinforce changes so that they "stick." *Declaring victory too soon* is a tempting mistake in the refreezing phase. Managers typically declare victory right after the first large-scale success in the change process. Declaring success too early has the same effect as draining the gasoline out of a car: It stops change efforts dead in their tracks. With success declared, supporters of the change process stop pushing to make change happen. After all, why push when success has been achieved? Rather than declaring victory, managers should use the momentum from short-term wins to push for even bigger or faster changes. This maintains urgency and prevents change supporters from slacking off before the changes are frozen into the company's culture.

The last mistake that managers make is *not anchoring changes in the corporation's culture*. An *organization's culture* is the set of key values, beliefs, and attitudes shared by organizational members that determines the "accepted way of doing things" in a company. As you learned in Chapter 3, changing cultures is extremely difficult and slow. According to Kotter, that two things help anchor changes in a corporation's culture. The first is directly showing people that the changes have actually improved performance. At Sears, this was easily demonstrated by the company's ability to drastically increase profits despite declining sales. The year after Lewis became CEO and Sears began seriously focusing on cost-cutting and profitability, the company tripled its annual profits.[46] The second is to make sure that the people who get promoted fit the new culture. If they don't, it's a clear sign that the changes were only temporary.

4.3 Change Tools and Techniques

Imagine that your boss came to you and said, "All right, genius, you wanted it. You're in charge of turning around the division." How would you start? Where would you begin? How would you encourage change-resistant managers to change? What would you do to include others in the change process? How would you get the change process off to a quick start? Finally, what long-term approach would you use to promote long-term effectiveness and performance? Results-driven change, the General Electric workout, and organizational development are different change tools and techniques that can be used to address these issues.

One of the reasons that organizational change efforts fail is that they are activity oriented, rather than results oriented meaning that they focus primarily on changing company procedures, management philosophy, or employee behavior. Typically, there is much buildup and preparation as consultants are brought in, presentations are made, books are read, and employees and managers are trained. There's a tremendous emphasis on "doing things the new way." But, with all the focus on activities, on "doing," almost no attention is paid to results, to seeing if all this activity has actually made a difference.

By contrast, **results-driven change** supplants the emphasis on activity with a laser-like focus on quickly measuring and improving results.[47] For example, top managers at Hyundai knew that if they were to compete successfully against the likes of Honda and Toyota, they would have to substantially improve the quality of their cars. So top managers guided the company's results-driven change process by increasing the number of quality teams from 100 to 865. Then, all employees were required to attend seminars on quality improvement and use the results of industry quality studies, like those published annually by J.D. Power and Associates, as their benchmark. Before the change, a new Hyundai averaged 23.4 initial quality problems; after the results-driven change efforts, that number dropped to 9.6.[48]

Another advantage of results-driven change is that managers introduce changes in procedures, philosophy, or behavior only if they are likely to improve measured performance. In other words, managers and workers actually test to see if changes make a difference. Consistent with this approach, Chairman Chung invested $30 million in a test center where cars were subjected to a sequence of extremely harsh conditions to allow engineers to pinpoint defects and fix problems.[49] A third advantage of results-driven change is that quick, visible improvements motivate employees to continue to make additional changes to improve measured performance. Exhibit 7.4 describes the basic steps of results-driven change.

> **Results-driven change** change created quickly by focusing on the measurement and improvement of results

Exhibit 7.4
Results-Driven Change Programs

1. Management should create measurable, short-term goals to improve performance.
2. Management should use action steps only if they are likely to improve measured performance.
3. Management should stress the importance of immediate improvements.
4. Consultants and staffers should help managers and employees achieve quick improvements in performance.
5. Managers and employees should test action steps to see if they actually yield improvements. Action steps that don't should be discarded.
6. It takes few resources to get results-driven change started.

Source: R. H. Schaffer & H. A. Thomson, J.D, "Successful Change Programs Begin with Results," *Harvard Business Review on Change* (Boston: Harvard Business School Press, 1998), 189–213.

The **General Electric workout** is a special kind of results-driven change. It is a three-day meeting that brings together managers and employees from different levels and parts of an organization to quickly generate and act on solutions to specific business problems.[50] On the first morning of a workout, the boss discusses the agenda and targets specific business problems that the group is to try to solve. Then, the boss leaves, and an outside facilitator breaks the group, typically 30 to 40 people, into five or six teams and helps them spend the next day and a half discussing and debating solutions. On day three, in what GE calls a "town meeting," the teams present specific solutions to their boss, who has been gone since day one. As each team's spokesperson makes specific suggestions, the boss has only three options: agree on the spot, say no, or ask for more information so that a decision can be made by a specific, agreed-on date.[51]

Organizational development is a philosophy and collection of planned change interventions designed to improve an organization's long-term health and performance. Organizational development takes a long-range approach to change; assumes that top management support is necessary for change to succeed; creates change by educating workers and managers to change ideas, beliefs, and behaviors so that problems can be solved in new ways; and emphasizes employee participation in diagnosing, solving, and evaluating problems.[52] As shown in Exhibit 7.5, organizational development interventions begin with the recognition of a problem. Then, the company designates a **change agent** to be formally in charge of guiding the change effort. This person can be someone from the company or a professional consultant. The change agent clarifies the problem, gathers information, works with decision makers to create and implement an action plan, helps to evaluate the plan's effectiveness, implements the plan throughout the company, and then leaves (if from outside the company) after making sure the change intervention will continue to work.

Organizational development interventions are aimed at changing large systems, small groups, or people.[53] More specifically, the purpose of *large system interventions* is to change the character and performance of an organization, business unit, or department. *Small group intervention* focuses on assessing how a group functions and helping it work more effectively to accomplish its goals. *Person-focused intervention* is intended to increase interpersonal effectiveness by helping people become aware of their attitudes and behaviors and acquire new skills and knowledge. Exhibit 7.6 describes the most frequently used organizational development interventions for large systems, small groups, and people.

General Electric workout a three-day meeting in which managers and employees from different levels and parts of an organization quickly generate and act on solutions to specific business problems

Organizational development a philosophy and collection of planned change interventions designed to improve an organization's long-term health and performance

Change agent the person formally in charge of guiding a change effort

Exhibit 7.5

General Steps for Organizational Development Interventions

1.	**Entry**	A problem is discovered and the need for change becomes apparent. A search begins for someone to deal with the problem and facilitate change.
2.	**Startup**	A change agent enters the picture and works to clarify the problem and gain commitment to a change effort.
3.	**Assessment & feedback**	The change agent gathers information about the problem and provides feedback about it to decision makers and those affected by it.
4.	**Action planning**	The change agent works with decision makers to develop an action plan.
5.	**Intervention**	The action plan, or organizational development intervention, is carried out.
6.	**Evaluation**	The change agent helps decision makers assess the effectiveness of the intervention.
7.	**Adoption**	Organizational members accept ownership and responsibility for the change, which is then carried out through the entire organization.
8.	**Separation**	The change agent leaves the organization after first ensuring that the change intervention will continue to work.

Source: W. J. Rothwell, R. Sullivan, & G. M. McLean, *Practicing Organizational Development: A Guide for Consultants* (San Diego: Pfeiffer & Co., 1995).

Exhibit 7.6

Different Kinds of Organizational Development Interventions

LARGE SYSTEM INTERVENTIONS	
Sociotechnical systems	An intervention designed to improve how well employees use and adjust to the work technology used in an organization.
Survey feedback	An intervention that uses surveys to collect information from the members, reports the results of that survey to the members, and then uses those results to develop action plans for improvement.
SMALL GROUP INTERVENTIONS	
Team building	An intervention designed to increase the cohesion and cooperation of work group members.
Unit goal setting	An intervention designed to help a work group establish short- and long-term goals.
PERSON-FOCUSED INTERVENTIONS	
Counseling/coaching	An intervention designed so that a formal helper or coach listens to managers or employees and advises them on how to deal with work or interpersonal problems.
Training	An intervention designed to provide individuals with the knowledge, skills, or attitudes they need to become more effective at their jobs.

Source: W. J. Rothwell, R. Sullivan, & G. M. McLean, *Practicing Organizational Development: A Guide for Consultants* (San Diego: Pfeiffer & Co., 1995).

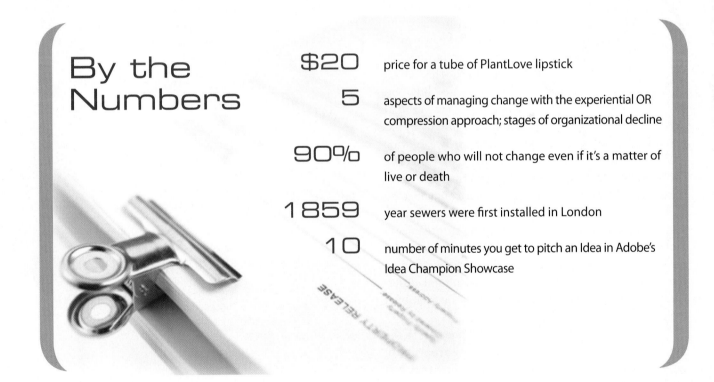

By the Numbers

$20 price for a tube of PlantLove lipstick

5 aspects of managing change with the experiential OR compression approach; stages of organizational decline

90% of people who will not change even if it's a matter of live or death

1859 year sewers were first installed in London

10 number of minutes you get to pitch an Idea in Adobe's Idea Champion Showcase

GLOBAL MANAGEMENT

What Is Global Business?

How can you be sure that the way you run your business in one country is the right way to run that business in another? This chapter discusses how organizations answer that question. We will start by examining global business in two ways: first, by exploring its impact on U.S. businesses, and then, by reviewing the basic rules and agreements that govern global trade. Next, we will examine how and when companies go global by examining the tradeoff between consistency and adaptation and by discussing how to organize a global company. Finally, we will look at how companies decide where to expand globally, including finding the best business climate, adapting to cultural differences, and better preparing employees for international assignments.

So, what is global business? **Global business** is the buying and selling of goods and services by people from different countries. The Timex watch on my wrist as I write this chapter was purchased at a Wal-Mart in Texas. But since it was made in the Philippines, I participated in global business when I wrote Wal-Mart a check. Wal-Mart, for its part, had already paid Timex, which had paid the company that employs the Filipino managers and workers who made my watch.

Global business the buying and selling of goods and services by people from different countries

Learning Outcomes

1 discuss the impact of global business and the trade rules and agreements that govern it.

2 explain why companies choose to standardize or adapt their business procedures.

3 explain the different ways that companies can organize to do business globally.

4 explain how to find a favorable business climate.

5 discuss the importance of identifying and adapting to cultural differences.

6 explain how to successfully prepare workers for international assignments.

©Susan Van Etten

Of course, there is more to global business than buying imported products at Wal-Mart. After reading the next section, you should be able to

1   discuss the impact of global business and the trade rules and agreements that govern it.

1 Global Business, Trade Rules, and Trade Agreements

If you want a simple demonstration of the impact of global business, look at the tag on your shirt, the inside of your shoes, and the inside of your cell phone (take your battery out). Chances are, all of these items were made in different places around the world. As I write this, my shirt, shoes, and cell phone were made in Thailand, China, and Korea. Where were yours made?

*Let's learn more about **1.1 the impact of global business, 1.2 how tariff and nontariff trade barriers have historically restricted global business, 1.3 how today global and regional trade agreements are reducing those trade barriers worldwide,** and **1.4 how consumers are responding to those changes in trade rules and agreements**.*

1.1 The Impact of Global Business

Multinational corporations are corporations that own businesses in two or more

> **Multinational corporation** a corporation that owns businesses in two or more countries

MGMT

Direct Foreign Investment in the United States

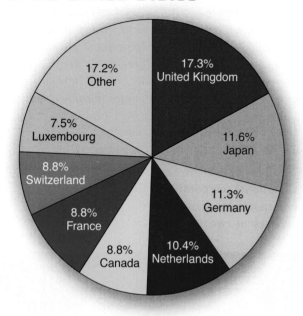

Source: J. Koncz & D. Yorgason, "Direct Investment Positions for 2005: Country and Industry Detail," [Online] available at http://www.bea.gov/bea/ARTICLES/2006/07July/0706_DIP_WEB.pdf, 7 February 2007.

U.S. Direct Foreign Investment Abroad

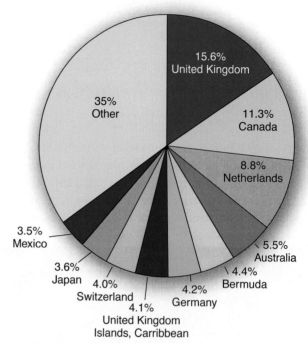

Source: J. Koncz & D. Yorgason, "Direct Investment Positions for 2005: Country and Industry Detail," [Online] available at http://www.bea.gov/bea/ARTICLES/2006/07July/0706_DIP_WEB.pdf, 7 February 2007.

countries. In 1970, more than half of the world's 7,000 multinational corporations were headquartered in just two countries: the United States and the United Kingdom. Today, there are 77,175 multinational corporations, nearly 11.25 times as many as in 1970, and only 2,418, or 3.1 percent, are based in the United States.[1] Today, 53,072 multinationals, or 68.8 percent, are based in other developed countries (e.g., Germany, Italy, Canada, and Japan), while 20,238, or 26.2 percent, are based in developing countries (e.g., Colombia, South Africa, and Tunisia). So, today, multinational companies can be found by the thousands all over the world!

Another way to appreciate the impact of global business is by considering direct foreign investment. **Direct foreign investment** occurs when a company builds a new business or buys an existing business in a foreign country. Brazilian steelmaker Gerdau S.A. made a direct foreign investment when it began purchasing U.S. steel companies such as International Steel Group.[2] Of course, companies from many other countries also own businesses in the United States. Companies from the United Kingdom, Japan, Germany, the Netherlands, Canada, France, Switzerland, and Luxembourg have the largest direct foreign investment in the United States. Overall,

Direct foreign investment a method of investment in which a company builds a new business or buys an existing business in a foreign country

foreign companies invest more than $1.6 trillion a year to do business in the United States.

At the same time, direct foreign investment in the United States is just half the picture. U.S. companies also have made large direct foreign investments in countries throughout the world. For example, Anheuser-Busch, the brewer of Budweiser Beer, paid $700 million to acquire Harbin Brewery Group, the fourth-largest beer company in China.[3] U.S. companies have made their largest direct foreign investments in the United Kingdom, Canada, the Netherlands, and Australia. Overall, U.S. companies invest more than $2 trillion a year to do business in other countries.

So, whether foreign companies invest in the United States or U.S. companies invest abroad, direct foreign investment is an increasingly important and common method of conducting global business.

1.2 Trade Barriers

Although today's consumers usually don't care where the products they buy come from (more on this in Section 1.4), national governments have traditionally preferred that consumers buy domestically made products in hopes that such purchases would increase the number of domestic businesses and workers. Indeed, governments have done much more than hope that you will buy from domestic companies. Historically, governments have actively used **trade barriers** to make it much more expensive or difficult (or sometimes impossible) for consumers to buy or consume imported goods. For example, the European Union places a 34 percent tax on frozen strawberries imported from China.[4] And the U.S. government imposes a tariff of 54 cents a gallon on imported ethanol, which is blended with gasoline for use in automobiles.[5] By establishing these restrictions and taxes, the European Union and the Chinese, and U.S. governments are engaging in **protectionism,** which is the use of trade barriers to protect local companies and their workers from foreign competition.

Governments have used two general kinds of trade barriers: tariff and nontariff barriers. A **tariff** is a direct tax on imported goods. Like the U.S. government's 54-cents-per-gallon tax on imported ethanol, tariffs increase the cost of imported goods relative to that of domestic goods. **Nontariff barriers** are nontax methods of increasing the cost or reducing the volume of imported goods. There are five types of nontariff barriers: quotas, voluntary export restraints, government import standards, government subsidies, and customs valuation/classification. Because there are so many different kinds of nontariff barriers, they can be an even more potent method of shielding domestic industries from foreign competition.

Quotas are specific limits on the number or volume of imported products. For example, because of strict import quotas, raw sugarcane imports into the United States are limited to approximately 1.2 million metric tons per year.[6] Since this is well below the demand for sugar in the United States, domestic U.S. sugar prices are twice as high as sugar prices in the rest of the world.[7] Like quotas, **voluntary export restraints** limit the amount of a product that can be imported annually. The difference is that the exporting country, rather than the importing country, imposes restraints. Usually, however, the "voluntary" offer to limit exports occurs because the importing country has implicitly threatened to impose quotas. According to the World Trade Organization (see the discussion in Section 1.3), however, voluntary export restraints are illegal and should not be used to restrict imports.[8]

In theory, **government import standards** are established to protect the health and safety of citizens. In reality, such standards are often used to restrict or ban imported goods. For example, Japan banned the importation of nearly all U.S. apples, which are one-third the cost of Japanese apples. Ostensibly, the ban was to prevent transmission of fire blight bacteria to Japanese apple orchards, but the Japanese government was actually using this government import standard to protect the economic health of its apple farmers. Only after the World Trade Organization ruled that there was no scientific basis for the ban did Japan allow U.S. apples to be imported without restrictions.[9]

Many nations also use **subsidies,** such as long-term, low-interest loans, cash grants, and tax deferments, to develop and protect companies in special industries. Not surprisingly, businesses complain about unfair trade practices when foreign companies receive government subsidies. For example, Boeing, the U.S. jet manufacturer, protested when Airbus received $4.5 billion in "launch aid" from nine European countries to build its new A380 superjumbo jet.[10]

To protect South African textile manufacturers from cheap and plentiful Chinese textile products, the South African government convinced China to "voluntarily" restrict the textiles it exports to South Africa each year.

Source: http://slate.msn.com/id/2116629/

©InsideOut/Jupiter Images

Trade barriers government-imposed regulations that increase the cost and restrict the number of imported goods

Protectionism a government's use of trade barriers to shield domestic companies and their workers from foreign competition

Tariff a direct tax on imported goods

Nontariff barriers nontax methods of increasing the cost or reducing the volume of imported goods

Quota a limit on the number or volume of imported products

Voluntary export restraints voluntarily imposed limits on the number or volume of products exported to a particular country

Government import standard a standard ostensibly established to protect the health and safety of citizens but, in reality, often used to restrict imports

Subsidies government loans, grants, and tax deferments given to domestic companies to protect them from foreign competition

The last type of nontariff barrier is **customs classification.** As products are imported into a country, they are examined by customs agents, who must decide into which of nearly 9,000 categories they should classify a product (see the Official Harmonized Tariff Schedule of the United States at **http://www. usitc.gov/tata/hts/index.htm** for more information). Classification is important because the category assigned by customs agents can greatly affect the size of the tariff and whether the item is subject to import quotas. For example, the U.S. Customs Service has several customs classifications for imported shoes. Tariffs on imported leather or "nonrubber" shoes are about 8.5 percent, whereas tariffs on imported rubber shoes, such as athletic footwear or waterproof shoes, range from 20 to 67 percent.[11] The difference is large enough that some importers try to make their rubber shoes look like leather in hopes of receiving the nonrubber customs classification and lower tariff.

1.3 Trade Agreements

Customs classification a classification assigned to imported products by government officials that affects the size of the tariff and imposition of import quotas

General Agreement on Tariffs and Trade (GATT) a worldwide trade agreement that reduced and eliminated tariffs, limited government subsidies, and established protections for intellectual property

World Trade Organization (WTO) as the successor to GATT, the only international organization dealing with the global rules of trade between nations. Its main function is to ensure that trade flows as smoothly, predictably, and freely as possible.

Regional trading zones areas in which tariff and nontariff barriers on trade between countries are reduced or eliminated

Thanks to the trade barriers described above, buying imported goods has often been much more expensive and difficult than buying domestic goods. During the 1990s, however, the regulations governing global trade were transformed. The most significant change was that 124 countries agreed to adopt the **General Agreement on Tariffs and Trade (GATT).** Although GATT itself was replaced by the **World Trade Organization (WTO)** in 1995, the changes that it made continue to encourage international trade.

Through tremendous decreases in tariff and nontariff barriers, GATT made it much easier and cheaper for consumers in all countries to buy foreign products. First, tariffs were cut

World Trade Organization

☑ **FACT FILE**

WORLD TRADE ORGANIZATION

Location: Geneva, Switzerland
Established: 1 January 1995
Created by: Uruguay Round negotiations (1986–1994)
Membership: 150 countries (on 11 January 2007)
Budget: 175 million Swiss francs for 2006
Secretariat staff: 635
Head: Pascal Lamy (Director-General)

Functions:
• Administering WTO trade agreements
• Forum for trade negotiations
• Handling trade disputes
• Monitoring national trade policies
• Technical assistance and training for developing countries
• Cooperation with other international organizations

Source: "WTO: About the Organization," World Trade Organization, [Online] available at http://www.wto.org/english/ thewto_e/whatis_e/whatis_e.htm, 7 February 2007.

40 percent on average worldwide by 2005. Second, tariffs were eliminated in 10 specific industries: beer, alcohol, construction equipment, farm machinery, furniture, medical equipment, paper, pharmaceuticals, steel, and toys. Third, stricter limits were put on government subsidies. Fourth, GATT established protections for intellectual property, such as trademarks, patents, and copyrights. Protection of intellectual property has become an increasingly important issue in global trade because of widespread product piracy. For example, 90 percent of the computer software and 95 percent of the video games in China are illegal pirated copies.[12] Finally, trade disputes between countries now are fully settled by arbitration panels from the WTO. In the past, countries could use their veto power to cancel a panel's decision, but now WTO rulings are complete and final.

The second major development that has reduced trade barriers has been the creation of **regional trading zones,** in which tariff and nontariff barriers are reduced or eliminated for countries within the trading zone. The largest and most important trading zones are in Europe (the Maastricht Treaty), North America (the North American Free Trade Agreement, or NAFTA), Central America (Central America Free Trade Agreement, or CAFTA-DR), South America (Mercosur, and the proposed South American Community of Nations, or SACN), and Asia (the Association of Southeast Asian Nations, or ASEAN, and Asia-Pacific Economic Cooperation, or APEC). The map in Exhibit 8.1 shows the extent to which free trade agreements govern global trade.

Exhibit 8.1

Global Map of Regional Trade Agreements

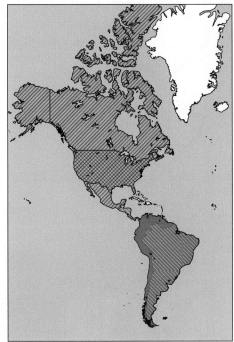

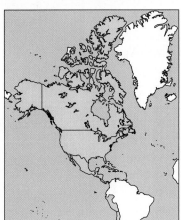

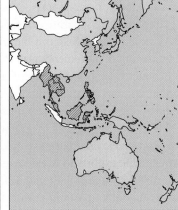

■ **Maastricht Treaty of Europe** Austria, Belgium, Bulgaria, Cyprus, the Czech Republic, Denmark, Estonia, Finland, France, Germany, Greece, Hungary, Ireland, Italy, Latvia, Lithuania, Luxembourg, Malta, the Netherlands, Poland, Portugal, Romania, Slovakia, Slovenia, Spain, Sweden, and the United Kingdom.

▨ **ASEAN** Brunei Darussalam, Cambodia, Indonesia, Lao PDR, Malaysia, Myanmar, the Philippines, Singapore, Thailand, and Vietnam.

□ **APEC** Australia, Canada, Chile, the People's Republic of China, Hong Kong (China), Japan, Mexico, New Zealand, Papua New Guinea, Peru, Russia, South Korea, Taiwan, the United States, and all members of ASEAN except Cambodia, Lao PDR, and Myanmar.

▨ **NAFTA (North American Free Trade Agreement)**
United States, Canada, and Mexico.

■ **SACN (South American Community of Nations)** (Proposed)
South America.

▨ **CAFTA-DR (Central America-Dominian Republic Free Trade Agreement)**
Costa Rica, the Dominican Republic, El Salvador, Guatemala, Honduras, Nicaragua, and the United States.

▨ **Mercosur**
Brazil, Argentina, Uruguay, and Paraguay.

In 1992, Belgium, Denmark, France, Germany, Greece, Ireland, Italy, Luxembourg, the Netherlands, Portugal, Spain, and the United Kingdom implemented the **Maastricht Treaty of Europe.** The purpose of this treaty was to transform their 12 different economies and 12 currencies into one common economic market, called the European Union (EU), with one common currency. Austria, Finland, and Sweden joined the EU in 1995, followed by Cyprus, the Czech Republic, Estonia, Hungary, Latvia, Lithuania, Malta, Poland, Slovakia, and Slovenia in 2004, and Bulgaria and Romania in 2007, bringing the total membership to 27 countries.[13] Croatia, Macedonia, and Turkey have applied and are still being considered for membership.[14] On 1 January 2002, a single common currency, the euro, went into circulation in 12 of the EU's members (Austria, Belgium, Finland, France, Germany, Greece, Ireland, Italy, Luxembourg, the Netherlands, Portugal, and Spain).

Prior to the treaty, trucks carrying products were stopped and inspected by customs agents at each border. Furthermore, since the required paperwork, tariffs, and government product specifications could be radically different in each country, companies often had to file 12 different sets of paperwork, pay 12 different tariffs, produce 12 different versions of their basic product to meet various government specifications, and exchange money in 12 different currencies. Likewise, open business travel from state to state, which we take for granted in

> **Maastricht Treaty of Europe** a regional trade agreement between most European countries

the United States, was complicated by inspections at each border crossing. If you lived in Germany, but worked in Luxembourg, your car was stopped and your passport was inspected twice every day, as you traveled to and from work. Also, every business transaction required a currency exchange, for example, from German deutsche marks to Italian lira, or from French francs to Dutch guilders. Imagine all of this happening to millions of trucks, cars, and businesspeople, and you can begin to appreciate the difficulty and cost of conducting business across Europe before the Maastricht Treaty.

NAFTA, the **North American Free Trade Agreement** between the United States, Canada, and Mexico, went into effect on 1 January 1994. More than any other regional trade agreement, NAFTA has liberalized trade between countries so that businesses can plan for one market, North America, rather than for three separate markets, the United States, Canada, and Mexico. One of NAFTA's most important achievements was to eliminate most product tariffs *and* prevent Canada, the United States, and Mexico from increasing existing tariffs or introducing new ones. Overall, both Mexican and Canadian exports to the United States have doubled since NAFTA went into effect. U.S. exports to Mexico and Canada have doubled, too, growing twice as fast as U.S. exports to any other part of the world.[15] In fact, Mexico and Canada now account for 36 percent of all U.S. exports.[16]

CAFTA-DR, the new **Central America Free Trade Agreement** between the United States, the Dominican Republic, and the Central American countries of Costa Rica, El Salvador, Guatemala, Honduras, and Nicaragua, went into effect in August 2005. With a combined

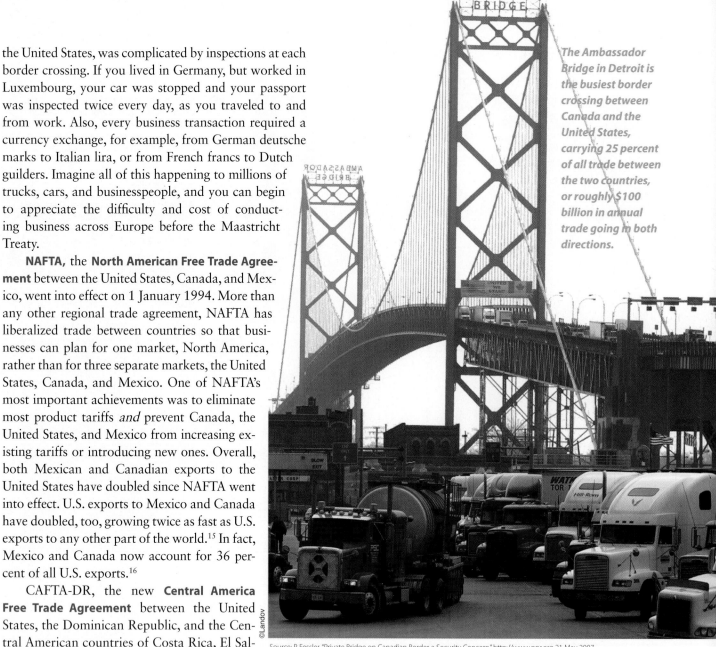

The Ambassador Bridge in Detroit is the busiest border crossing between Canada and the United States, carrying 25 percent of all trade between the two countries, or roughly $100 billion in annual trade going in both directions.

Source: P. Fessler, "Private Bridge on Canadian Border a Security Concern," http://www.npr.org 21 May 2007.

population of 347.6 million, the CAFTA-DR countries together are the 10th largest U.S. export market in the world, and the second-largest U.S. export market in Latin America, after Mexico. U.S. companies export more than $16 billion in goods each year to the CAFTA-DR countries. Furthermore, U.S. exports to CAFTA-DR countries, which are increasing at 16 percent per year, are by far the fastest growing export market for U.S. companies.[17]

One of the goals of the proposed SACN, the South American Community of Nations, is to establish a free trade zone throughout South America for the countries of Argentina, Bolivia, Brazil, Chile, Colombia, Ecuador, Guyana, Paraguay, Peru, Suriname, Uruguay, and Venezuela. If created, the SACN would likely supplant Mercosur, a free trade agreement between Brazil, Argentina, Uruguay, and Paraguay, which have been granted associate membership in SACN. If approved, SACN would become one of the largest trading zones in the world, encompassing 361 million people in 12 countries in South America with a combined gross domestic product of $1 trillion.[18]

North American Free Trade Agreement (NAFTA) a regional trade agreement between the United States, Canada, and Mexico

Central America Free Trade Agreement (CAFTA) a regional trade agreement between Costa Rica, the Dominican Republic, El Salvador, Guatemala, Honduras, Nicaragua, and the United States

ASEAN, the **Association of Southeast Asian Nations,** and APEC, the **Asia-Pacific Economic Cooperation,** are the two largest and most important regional trading groups in Asia. ASEAN is a trade agreement between Brunei Darussalam, Cambodia, Indonesia, Lao PDR, Malaysia, Myanmar, the Philippines, Singapore, Thailand, and Vietnam, which form a market of more than 558 million people. U.S. trade with ASEAN countries exceeds $153 billion a year.[19] In fact, the United States is ASEAN's largest trading partner, and ASEAN'S member nations constitute the fifth largest trading partner of the United States. ASEAN's members have agreed to create an ASEAN free trade area beginning in 2015 for the six original countries (Brunei Darussalam, Indonesia, Malaysia, the Philippines, Singapore, and Thailand) and in 2018 for the newer member countries (Cambodia, Lao PDR, Myanmar, and Vietnam).[20]

APEC is a broader agreement that includes Australia, Canada, Chile, the People's Republic of China, Hong Kong (China), Japan, Mexico, New Zealand, Papua New Guinea, Peru, Russia, South Korea, Taiwan, the United States, and all the members of ASEAN except Cambodia, Lao PDR, and Myanmar.[21] APEC's 21 member countries contain 2.6 billion people, account for 47 percent of all global trade, and have a combined gross domestic product of over $19 trillion.[22] APEC countries began reducing trade barriers in 2000, though all the reductions will not be completely phased in until 2020.

1.4 Consumers, Trade Barriers, and Trade Agreements

The average worker earns nearly $54,930 a year in Switzerland, $59,590 in Norway, $38,980 in Japan, and $43,749 in America.[23] Yet, after adjusting these incomes for how much they can buy, the Swiss income is equivalent to just $37,080, the Norwegian income to $40,420, and the Japanese income to $31,410![24] This is the same as saying that $1 of income can buy you only 68 cents' worth of goods in Switzerland and Norway, and 81 cents' worth in Japan. In other words, Americans can buy much more with their incomes than those in other countries can.

One reason that Americans get more for their money is that the U.S. marketplace has been one of the easiest for foreign companies to enter. Although some U.S. industries, such as textiles, have been heavily protected from foreign competition by trade bar-

riers, for the most part, American consumers (and businesses) have had plentiful choices among American-made and foreign-made products. More important, the high level of competition between foreign and domestic companies that creates these choices helps to keep prices low in the United States. Further-

What $1 gets you in the U.S.

What $1 gets you in Switzerland   *What $1 gets you in Japan*

more, it is precisely the lack of choice and the low level of competition that keep prices higher in countries that have not been as open to foreign companies and products. For example, Japanese trade barriers are estimated to cost Japanese consumers more than $100 billion a year.[25]

So why do trade barriers and free trade agreements matter to consumers? They're important because free trade agreements increase choices, competition, and purchasing power and thus decrease what people pay for food, clothing, necessities, and luxuries. Accordingly, today's consumers rarely care where their products and services come from. Peter Germano, a New York jeweler who sells diamonds, says people don't care where the diamonds are from; they "just want to know which is cheaper."

And why do trade barriers and free trade agreements matter to managers? The reason, as you're about to read, is that while free trade agreements create new business opportunities, they also intensify competition, and addressing that competition is a manager's job.

Association of Southeast Asian Nations (ASEAN) a regional trade agreement between Brunei Darussalam, Cambodia, Indonesia, Lao PDR, Malaysia, Myanmar, the Philippines, Singapore, Thailand, and Vietnam

Asia-Pacific Economic Cooperation (APEC) a regional trade agreement between Australia, Canada, Chile, the People's Republic of China, Hong Kong, Japan, Mexico, New Zealand, Papua New Guinea, Peru, Russia, South Korea, Taiwan, the United States, and all members of ASEAN, except Cambodia, Lao PDR, and Myanmar

Courtesy of Chapel House Photography

How to Go Global?

 Once a company has decided that it *will* go global, it must decide *how* to go global. For example, if you decide to sell in Singapore, should you try to find a local business partner who speaks the language, knows the laws, and understands the customs and norms of Singapore's culture, or should you simply export your products from your home country? What do you do if you are also entering eastern Europe, perhaps starting in Hungary? Should you use the same approach in Hungary that you used in Singapore?

Although there is no magical formula for answering these questions, after reading the next two sections, you should be able to

2 explain why companies choose to standardize or adapt their business procedures.

3 explain the different ways that companies can organize to do business globally.

2 Consistency or Adaptation?

In this section, we return to a key issue: How can you be sure that the way you run your business in one country is the right way to run that business in another? In other words, how can you strike the right balance between global consistency and local adaptation?

Global consistency
when a multinational company has offices, manufacturing plants, and distribution facilities in different countries and runs them all using the same rules, guidelines, policies, and procedures

Local adaptation
when a multinational company modifies its rules, guidelines, policies, and procedures to adapt to differences in foreign customers, governments, and regulatory agencies

Global consistency means that when a multinational company has offices, manufacturing plants, and distribution facilities in different countries, it will use the same rules, guidelines, policies, and procedures to run those offices, plants, and facilities. Managers at company headquarters value global consistency because it simplifies decisions. In contrast, a company with a **local adaptation** policy modifies its standard operating procedures to adapt to differences in foreign customers, governments, and regulatory agencies. Local adaptation is typically more important to local managers who are charged with making the international business successful in their countries.

If companies lean too much toward global consistency, they run the risk of using management procedures poorly suited to particular countries' markets, cultures, and employees (i.e., a lack of local adaptation). MTV made this mistake when going global. According to Divya Gupta, president of Media Edge, which helps companies buy advertising in India, "MTV, when it first entered the country, made the mistake of coming in as MTV. No changes." So MTV quickly learned from this

It Pays to Adapt

When Tommy Hilfiger opened its first store in London, it was a flop. The company barely changed its U.S. format, but Europeans weren't interested in designs popular in America. So, Hilfiger changed tactics. Hilfiger now has a design center in Amsterdam, staffed with 37 people who do nothing but design clothes and accessories for European consumers. Adapting to local tastes has paid off: European sales now account for 37 percent of Hilfiger's $1.78 billion in sales.

Source: T. Agins, "For U.S. Fashion Firms, A Global Makeover—Tommy Hilfiger Finds Assimilating in Europe Requires a New Look," *Wall Street Journal,* 2 February 2007.

©UPI/Ezio Petersen/Landov

Because Germans associate the word "idol" with Hitler, producers exporting the popular American Idol television show opted to change the name to Deutschland sucht den SuperStar (Germany Seeks the Superstar).

mistake and stopped showing Western videos in international locations and started featuring local music and shows like *Mochilão* in Brazil, a travel show hosted by a popular model who backpacks to famous sites.[26]

If companies focus too much on local adaptation, however, they run the risk of losing the cost efficiencies and productivity that result from using standardized rules and procedures throughout the world. A decade into its development, MTV International was profitable, but not by much. While it had access to huge markets—in fact, 80 percent of MTV viewers were outside the United States—access to those markets was slow to translate into large profits. Why? Because of the enormous cost of building new studios, acquiring new talent, and developing local content for so many different international markets.

3 Forms for Global Business

Historically, companies have generally followed the *phase model of globalization,* in which a company makes the transition from a domestic company to a global company in the following sequential phases: *3.1 exporting, 3.2 cooperative contracts, 3.3 strategic alliances, and 3.4 wholly owned affiliates.* At each step, the company grows much larger, uses those resources to enter more global markets, is less dependent on home country sales, and is more committed in its orientation to global business. Some companies, however, do not follow the phase model of globalization.[27] Some skip phases on their way to becoming more global and less domestic. Others don't follow the phase model at all. These are known as *3.5 global new ventures.* This section reviews these forms of global business.[28]

3.1 Exporting

When companies produce products in their home countries and sell those products to customers in foreign countries, they are **exporting.** For example, Fremantle-Media, the London-based company that orginally developed the *Pop Idol* TV show in Britain and then exported a nearly identical version to the United States as *American Idol,* now has exported similar versions of the show to 35 different countries.[29]

Exporting as a form of global business offers many advantages. It makes the company less dependent on sales in its home market and provides a greater degree of control over research, design, and production decisions. Though advantageous in a number of ways, exporting also has its disadvantages. The primary disadvantage is that many exported goods are subject to tariff and nontariff barriers that can substantially increase their final cost to consumers. A second disadvantage is that transportation costs can significantly increase the price of an exported product. Another disadvantage is that companies that export depend on foreign importers for product distribution. This means that if, for example,

> **Exporting** selling domestically produced products to customers in foreign countries

the foreign importer makes a mistake on the paperwork that accompanies a shipment of imported goods, those goods can be returned to the foreign manufacturer at the manufacturer's expense.

3.2 Cooperative Contracts

When an organization wants to expand its business globally without making a large financial commitment to do so, it may sign a **cooperative contract** with a foreign business owner, who pays the company a fee for the right to conduct that business in his or her country. There are two kinds of cooperative contracts: licensing and franchising.

Under a **licensing** agreement, a domestic company, the *licensor,* receives royalty payments for allowing another company, the *licensee,* to produce its product, sell its service, or use its brand name in a particular foreign market. For example, brands such as Peter Paul Mounds and Almond Joy, which consumers associate with American companies, are not really American products. A British company, Cadbury Schweppes, licenses those candy bars to Hershey for U.S. production.

One of the most important advantages of licensing is that it allows companies to earn additional profits without investing more money. As foreign sales increase, the royalties paid to the licensor by the foreign licensee increase. Moreover, the licensee, not the licensor, invests in production equipment and facilities to produce the licensed product. Licensing also helps companies avoid tariff and nontariff barriers. Since the licensee manufactures the product within the foreign country, tariff and nontariff barriers don't apply.

The biggest disadvantage associated with licensing is that the licensor gives up control over the quality of the product or service sold by the foreign licensee. Unless the licensing agreement contains specific restrictions, the licensee controls the entire business, from production to marketing to final sales. Many licensors include inspection clauses in their license contracts, but closely monitoring product or service quality from thousands of miles away can be difficult. An additional disadvantage is that licensees can eventually become competitors, especially when a licensing agreement includes access to important technology or proprietary business knowledge.

A **franchise** is a collection of networked firms in which the manufacturer or marketer of a product or service, the *franchisor,* licenses the entire business to another person or organization, the *franchisee.* For the price of an initial franchise fee plus royalties, franchisors provide franchisees with training, assistance with marketing and advertising, and an exclusive right to conduct business in a particular location. More than 400 U.S. companies franchise their businesses to foreign franchise partners. Overall, franchising is a fast way to enter foreign markets. Over the last 20 years, U.S. franchisors have more than doubled their global franchises for a total of more than 100,000 global franchise units.

Despite franchising's many advantages, franchisors face a loss of control when they sell businesses to franchisees who are thousands of miles away. And, while there are exceptions, franchising success may be somewhat culture-bound. In other words, because most global franchisors begin by franchising their businesses in similar countries or regions (Canada is by far the first choice for American companies taking their first step into global franchising), and because 65 percent of franchisors make absolutely no change in their business for overseas franchisees, that success may not generalize to cultures with different lifestyles, values, preferences, and technological infrastructures.

3.3 Strategic Alliances

Companies forming **strategic alliances** combine key resources, costs, risks, technology, and people. The most common strategic alliance is a **joint venture,** which oc-

---

Cooperative contract an agreement in which a foreign business owner pays a company a fee for the right to conduct that business in his or her country

Licensing an agreement in which a domestic company, the licensor, receives royalty payments for allowing another company, the licensee, to produce the licensor's product, sell its service, or use its brand name in a specified foreign market

Franchise a collection of networked firms in which the manufacturer or marketer of a product or service, the franchisor, licenses the entire business to another person or organization, the franchisee

Strategic alliance an agreement in which companies combine key resources, costs, risk, technology, and people

Joint venture a strategic alliance in which two existing companies collaborate to form a third, independent company

©Susan Van Etten

curs when two existing companies collaborate to form a third company. The two founding companies remain intact and unchanged, except that together they now own the newly created joint venture. One of the oldest and most successful global joint ventures is Fuji-Xerox, which is a joint venture between Fuji Film of Japan and U.S.-based Xerox Corporation, which makes copiers and automated office systems. More than 45 years after its creation, Fuji-Xerox employs nearly 37,000 employees and has close to $9.1 billion in revenues.[30]

One of the advantages of global joint ventures is that, like licensing and franchising, they help companies avoid tariff and nontariff barriers to entry. Another advantage is that companies participating in a joint venture bear only part of the costs and the risks of that business. Many companies find this attractive because of the expense of entering foreign markets or developing new products. Global joint ventures can be especially advantageous to smaller local partners that link up with larger, more experienced foreign firms that can bring advanced management, resources, and business skills to the joint venture. For instance, Venyon is a global joint venture between Finland-based cell phone giant Nokia and Germany-based Giesecke & Devrient (G&D), which specializes in secure smart cards, telecommunications, electronic payments and identification, and

joint ventures should carefully develop detailed contracts that specify the obligations of each party. This is important, because the rate of failure for global joint ventures is estimated to be as high as 50 percent.[32]

3.4 Wholly Owned Affiliates (Build or Buy)

Approximately one-third of multinational companies enter foreign markets through wholly owned affiliates. Unlike licensing arrangements, franchises, or joint ventures, **wholly owned affiliates** are 100 percent owned by the parent company. For example, Honda Motors of America in Marysville, Ohio, is 100 percent owned by Honda Motors of Japan.

The primary advantage of wholly owned businesses is that the parent company receives all of the profits and has complete control over the foreign facilities. The biggest disadvantage is the expense of building new operations or buying existing businesses. While the payoff can be enormous if wholly owned affiliates succeed, the losses can be immense if they fail because the parent company assumes all of the risk.

3.5 Global New Ventures

Companies used to evolve slowly from small operations selling in their home markets to large businesses selling to

> ## GLOBAL JOINT VENTURES ARE NOT WITHOUT PROBLEMS THOUGH.

IT security. Through their combined efforts in Venyon, Nokia and G&D will enable consumers to securely use their cellphones, blackberries, or personal digital assistants to buy airline, rail, or taxi service, or to make credit card purchases from retailers, banks, and providers of digital services and media.[31]

Global joint ventures are not without problems, though. Because companies share costs and risks with their joint venture partners, they must also share profits. Managing global joint ventures can also be difficult because they represent a merging of four cultures: the country and the organizational cultures of the first partner, and the country and organizational cultures of the second partner. Oftentimes, to be "fair" to all involved, each partner in the global joint venture will have equal ownership and power. But this can result in power struggles and a lack of leadership. Because of these problems, companies forming global

foreign markets. Furthermore, as companies went global, they usually followed the phase model of globalization. Recently, however, three trends have combined to allow companies to skip the phase model when going global. First, quick, reliable air travel can transport people to nearly any point in the world within one day. Second, low-cost communication technologies, such as international email, teleconferencing, phone conferencing, and the Internet, make it easier to communicate with global customers, suppliers, managers, and employees. Third, there is now a critical mass of businesspeople with extensive personal experience in all aspects of global business.[33] This combination of developments has made it possible to start companies that are global from inception.

Wholly owned affiliates foreign offices, facilities, and manufacturing plants that are 100 percent owned by the parent company

With sales, employees, and financing in different countries, **global new ventures** are companies that are founded with an active global strategy.[34]

Although there are several different kinds of global new ventures, all share two common factors. First, the company founders successfully develop and communicate the company's global vision from inception. Second, rather than going global one country at a time, new global ventures bring a product or service to market in several foreign markets at the same time. While headquartered in Lexington, Massachusetts, VistaPrint receives 15,000 orders a day from customers in 120 different countries who design their business cards, brochures, and invitations online using 17 different Vista-Print Web sites, each representing a different language or location. Printing happens at two automated production facilities, one in The Netherlands and the other in Canada. Once printed, the products are cut and sized by robots, and then packaged and delivered just three days after ordering. Regarding VistaPrint's commitment to worldwide customers, founder Robert Keane says, "It's often hard for startups to find their way out of their home nation. But you have to—it's not that type of world anymore."[35]

Where to Go Global?

Deciding where to go global is just as important as deciding how your company will go global.

After reading the next three sections, you should be able to

4 explain how to find a favorable business climate.

5 discuss the importance of identifying and adapting to cultural differences.

6 explain how to successfully prepare workers for international assignments.

Global new ventures new companies that are founded with an active global strategy and have sales, employees, and financing in different countries

Purchasing power a comparison of the relative cost of a standard set of goods and services in different countries

4 Finding the Best Business Climate

When deciding where to go global, companies try to find countries or regions with promising business climates.

An attractive global business climate **4.1 positions the company for easy access to growing markets, 4.2 is an effective but cost-efficient place to build an office or manufacturing facility,** *and* **4.3 minimizes the political risk to the company.**

4.1 Growing Markets

The most important factor in an attractive business climate is access to a growing market. Two factors help companies determine the growth potential of foreign markets: purchasing power and foreign competitors. **Purchasing power** is measured by comparing the relative cost of a standard set of goods and services in different countries. In Tokyo, a Coke costs $1.33.[36] Because a Coke costs only about $1.00 in the United States, the

The Big Mac Index

Every year since 1986, *The Economist* has published the Big Mac Index. The index compares the price for a Big Mac in dozens of countries around the world and uses its results to determine a country's purchasing power and value its exchange rate against the dollar (undervalued, overvalued, or right on the mark). Why the Big Mac? Well, like a Coke, the Big Mac is one of the few truly global consumer products. A McDonald's Big Mac sandwich costs an average of $3.22 in the United States, $3.90 in the United Kingdom, and $5.05 in Switzerland. Although not all products are more expensive in other countries (in some, they are cheaper; for example, a Big Mac costs $1.41 in China and $2.66 in Mexico), international studies find that American consumers get much more for their money than most other consumers in the world.

Source: "The Big Mac Index," *Economist*, http://www.economist.com/markets/indicators/displaystory.cfm?story_id=8649005, 10 February 2007.

Exhibit 8.2

How Consumption of Coca-Cola Varies with Purchasing Power around the World

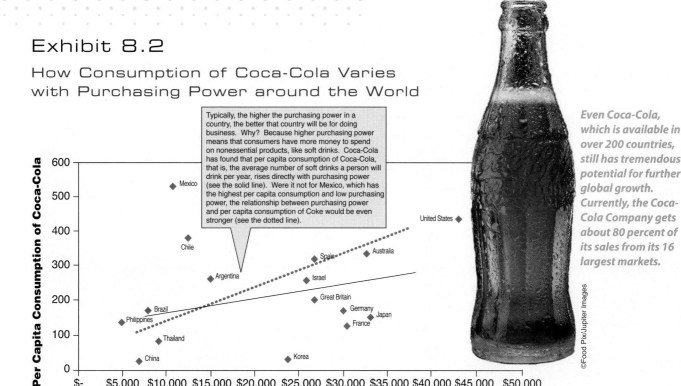

Typically, the higher the purchasing power in a country, the better that country will be for doing business. Why? Because higher purchasing power means that consumers have more money to spend on nonessential products, like soft drinks. Coca-Cola has found that per capita consumption of Coca-Cola, that is, the average number of soft drinks a person will drink per year, rises directly with purchasing power (see the solid line). Were it not for Mexico, which has the highest per capita consumption and low purchasing power, the relationship between purchasing power and per capita consumption of Coke would be even stronger (see the dotted line).

Even Coca-Cola, which is available in over 200 countries, still has tremendous potential for further global growth. Currently, the Coca-Cola Company gets about 80 percent of its sales from its 16 largest markets.

©Food Pix/Jupiter Images

Sources: "Rank Order—GDP—Per Capita," *The World Factbook*, [Online] available at http://www.cia.gov/cia/publications/ factbook/rankorder/2004rank.html, 12 February 2007; "2005 Annual Per Capita Consumption of All Company Beverage Products," *The Coca-Cola Company 2005 Annual Review*, [Online] available at http://www.thecoca-colacompany.com/investors/annualandotherreports/2005/companyToday_chart.html, 12 February 2007.

average American would have more purchasing power than the average Japanese. Purchasing power is strong in countries like Mexico, India, and China, which have low average levels of income. This is because basic living expenses, such as food, shelter, and transportation, are very inexpensive in those countries, so consumers still have money to spend after paying for necessities. Because basic living expenses are so low in China, Mexico, and India, purchasing power is strong, and millions of Chinese, Mexican, and Indian consumers increasingly have extra money to spend on what they want, in addition to what they need.[37]

Consequently, countries with high and growing levels of purchasing power are good choices for companies looking for attractive global markets. As Exhibit 8.2 shows, Coke has found that the per capita consumption of Coca-Cola, or the number of Cokes a person drinks per year, rises directly with purchasing power. The more purchasing power people have, the more likely they are to purchase soft drinks.[38]

The second part of assessing the growth potential of global markets involves analyzing the degree of global competition, which is determined by the number and quality of companies that already compete in a foreign market. Intel has been in China for 20 years not only because of the size of the potential market, but

also because there was almost no competition. But now that China is the third-largest computer chip market in the world, Intel faces competition from AMD, Intel's primary U.S. competitor, which entered China four years ago, and Shanghai Semiconductor Manufacturing International, a five-year-old Chinese company that manufactures low-end chips.[39]

4.2 Choosing an Office/ Manufacturing Location

Companies do not have to establish an office or manufacturing location in each country they enter. They can license, franchise, or export to foreign markets, or they can serve a larger region from one country. Thus, the criteria for choosing an office/manufacturing location are different from the criteria for entering a foreign market.

Rather than focusing on costs alone, companies should consider both qualitative and quantitative factors. Two key qualitative factors are work force quality and company strategy. Work force quality is important because it is often difficult to find workers with the specific skills, abilities, and experience that a company needs to run its business. Work force quality is one reason that many companies doing business in Europe locate their customer call centers in the Netherlands.

Exhibit 8.3

World's Best Cities for Business

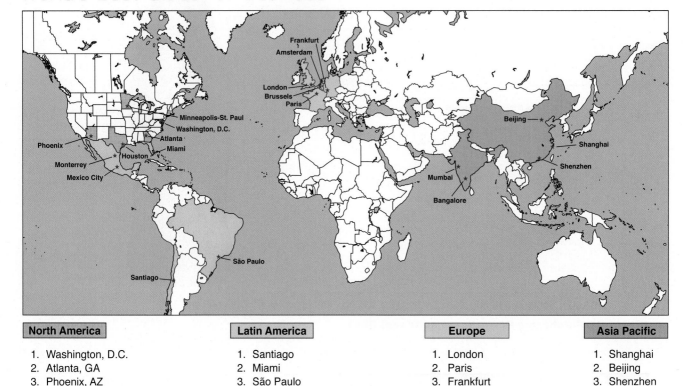

North America	Latin America	Europe	Asia Pacific
1. Washington, D.C.	1. Santiago	1. London	1. Shanghai
2. Atlanta, GA	2. Miami	2. Paris	2. Beijing
3. Phoenix, AZ	3. São Paulo	3. Frankfurt	3. Shenzhen
4. Houston, TX	4. Monterrey (Mexico)	4. Amsterdam	4. Bangalore
5. Minneapolis-St. Paul, MN	5. Mexico City	5. Brussels	5. Mumbai

Sources: "European Cities Monitor 2006," *Cushman & Wakefield*, http://www.cushmanwakefield.com/cwglobal/jsp/publication.jsp?Country=EMEA&Language=EN, 13 February 2007. K. Badenhausen, "Best Places for Business and Careers," http://www.forbes.com/lists/2005/05/05/05bestplaces.html, 17 February 2007. "Shanghai, Beijing, Shenzhen Top 3 in Best City Survey," *Fortune China*, http://www.fortunechina.com/pdf/Best%20Cities%20Press%20Release%20(English)%202004.12.01.pdf, 13 February 2007. R. Sridharan, "Best Cities, Really?" *Business Today*, 13 August 2006, 62. "Miami Is the Best City for Doing Business in Latin America, According to AmericaEconomia Magazine," *PR Newswire*, 24 April 2003;

Workers in the Netherlands are the most linguistically gifted in Europe, with 73 percent speaking two languages, 44 percent speaking three languages, and 12 percent speaking more than three.[40]

A company's strategy is also important when choosing a location. For example, a company pursuing a low-cost strategy may need plentiful raw materials, low-cost transportation, and low-cost labor. A company pursuing a differentiation strategy (typically a higher-priced, better product or service) may need access to high-quality materials and a highly skilled and educated work force.

Quantitative factors, such as the kind of facility being built, tariff and non-tariff barriers, exchange rates, and transportation and labor costs, should also be considered when choosing an office/manufactur-

ing location. Exhibit 8.3 shows the world's top cities for global business. This information is a good starting point if your company is trying to decide where to put an international office or manufacturing plant.

4.3 Minimizing Political Risk

When managers think about political risk in global business, they envision burning factories and riots in the streets. Although political events such as these receive dramatic and extended coverage from the media, the political risks that most companies face usually are not covered as breaking stories on Fox News and CNN. Nonetheless, the negative consequences of ordinary political risk can be just as devastating to companies that fail to identify and minimize that risk.[41]

When conducting global business, companies should attempt to identify two types of political risk: political uncertainty and policy uncertainty.[42] **Political uncertainty** is associated with the risk of major changes in political regimes that can result from war, revolution, death of

Political uncertainty
the risk of major changes in political regimes that can result from war, revolution, death of political leaders, social unrest, or other influential events

political leaders, social unrest, or other influential events. **Policy uncertainty** refers to the risk associated with changes in laws and government policies that directly affect the way foreign companies conduct business.

Policy uncertainty is the most common form of political risk in global business and perhaps the most frustrating, especially when changes in laws and government policies directly undercut sizable investments made by foreign companies. Royal Dutch Shell joined with Rus-

©Landov

sia-based Gazprom, a state-owned company controlled by the Kremlin, to develop Sakhalin II, one of the world's largest liquefied natural gas fields. Shell and its partners took the lead role with 55 percent ownership, and fronted a correspondingly larger amount of the estimated $20 billion in development costs. However, after years of development and billions in investment, the Russian government banned foreign companies from owning more than 49 percent of any energy development project. In the end, to avoid losing its investment, Royal Dutch Shell relinquished majority ownership to Gazprom in return for a $7.45 billion payment, well short of the $12 billion Shell had already invested.[43]

Several strategies can be used to minimize or adapt to the political risk inherent in global business. An *avoidance strategy* is used when the political risks associated with a foreign country or region are viewed as too great. If

firms are already invested in high-risk areas, they may divest or sell their businesses. If they have not yet invested, they will likely postpone their investment until the risk shrinks. Exhibit 8.4 shows the long-term political risk for various countries in the Middle East (higher scores indicate less political risk). The following factors, which were used to compile these ratings, indicate greater political risk: government instability, poor socioeconomic conditions, internal or external conflict, military involvement in politics, religious and ethnic tensions, high foreign debt as a percentage of gross domestic product, exchange rate instability, and high inflation.[44] An avoidance strategy would likely be used for the riskiest countries shown in Exhibit 8.4, such as Iran and Lebanon, but would probably not be needed for the least risky countries, such as Israel, Jordan, or Oman. Risk conditions and factors change, so be sure to make risk decisions with the latest available information from resources such as the PRS Group, **http://www.prsgroup.com**, which supplies information about political risk to 80 percent of the *Fortune* 500 companies.

Control is an active strategy to prevent or reduce political risks. Firms using a control strategy lobby foreign governments or international trade agencies to change laws, regulations, or trade barriers that hurt their business in that country.

Another method for dealing with political risk is *cooperation,* which involves using joint ventures and collaborative contracts, such as franchising and licensing. Although cooperation does not eliminate the political risk of doing business in a country, it can limit the risk associated with foreign ownership of a business. For example, a German company forming a joint venture with a Chinese company to do business in China may structure the joint venture contract so that the Chinese company owns 51 percent or more of the joint venture. Doing so qualifies the joint venture as a Chinese company and exempts it from Chinese laws that

Policy uncertainty the risk associated with changes in laws and government policies that directly affect the way foreign companies conduct business

Exhibit 8.4
Overview of Political Risk in the Middle East

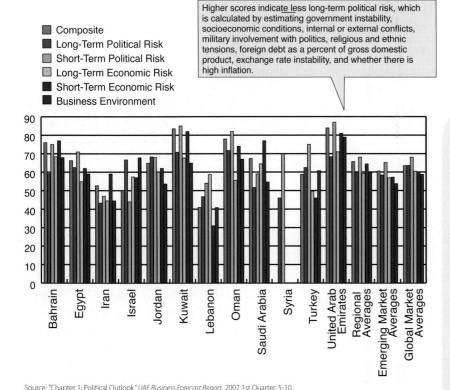

Legend:
- Composite
- Long-Term Political Risk
- Short-Term Political Risk
- Long-Term Economic Risk
- Short-Term Economic Risk
- Business Environment

Higher scores indicate less long-term political risk, which is calculated by estimating government instability, socioeconomic conditions, internal or external conflicts, military involvement with politics, religious and ethnic tensions, foreign debt as a percent of gross domestic product, exchange rate instability, and whether there is high inflation.

Countries: Bahrain, Egypt, Iran, Israel, Jordan, Kuwait, Lebanon, Oman, Saudi Arabia, Syria, Turkey, United Arab Emirates, Regional Averages, Emerging Market Averages, Global Market Averages

Source: "Chapter 1: Political Outlook," *UAE Business Forecast Report*, 2007 1st Quarter, 5-10.

Where in the World...?

In 2007, *Inc.* magazine published an interactive map with information on doing business around the world. The map shows annual GDP growth, identifies places with little regulation, and provides useful factoids. Most importantly, though, the map highlights the worst countries in which to do business: Afghanistan, Burkina Faso, Chad, Congo, Djibouti, East Timor, Egypt, Eritrea, and Venezuela. Three countries were singled out as the worst of the worst, where businesspeople "must proceed very carefully": Belarus, Guinea-Bissau, and Zimbabwe. See if the map is still online at **http://www.inc.com/ keyword/globalmap**.

Source: M. Chafkin and N. Tiku, "The 21st Century Treasure Map," *Inc.*, April 2007, unpaginated pullout.

---

apply to foreign-owned businesses. However, as we saw with Shell and Gazprom, the state-controlled Russian oil company, cooperation cannot always protect against *policy risk* if a foreign government changes its laws and policies to directly affect the way foreign companies conduct business.

5 Becoming Aware of Cultural Differences

National culture is the set of shared values and beliefs that affects the perceptions, decisions, and behavior of the people from a particular country. The first step in dealing with culture is to recognize that there are meaningful differences. Professor Geert Hofstede spent 20 years studying cultural differences in 53 different countries. His research shows that there are five consistent cultural dimensions across countries: power distance, individual-

National culture the set of shared values and beliefs that affects the perceptions, decisions, and behavior of the people from a particular country

ism, masculinity, uncertainty avoidance, and short-term versus long-term orientation.[45]

Power distance is the extent to which people in a country accept that power is distributed unequally in society and organizations. In countries where power distance is weak, such as Denmark and Sweden, employees don't like their organization or their boss to have power over them or tell them what to do. They want to have a say in decisions that affect them. As Exhibit 8.5 shows, Russia and China, with scores of 95 and 80, respectively, are much stronger in power distance than Germany (35), the Netherlands (38), and the United States (40).

Individualism is the degree to which societies believe that individuals should be self-sufficient. In individualistic societies, employees put loyalty to themselves first and loyalty to their company and work group second. In Exhibit 8.5, the United States (91), the Netherlands (80), France (71), and Germany (67) are the strongest in individualism, while Indonesia (14), West Africa (20), and China (20) are the weakest.

Masculinity and *femininity* capture the difference between highly assertive and highly nurturing cultures.

Exhibit 8.5

Hofstede's Five Cultural Dimensions

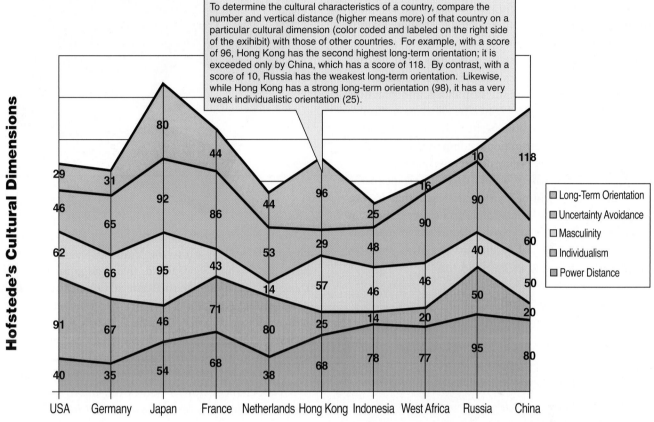

To determine the cultural characteristics of a country, compare the number and vertical distance (higher means more) of that country on a particular cultural dimension (color coded and labeled on the right side of the exihibit) with those of other countries. For example, with a score of 96, Hong Kong has the second highest long-term orientation; it is exceeded only by China, which has a score of 118. By contrast, with a score of 10, Russia has the weakest long-term orientation. Likewise, while Hong Kong has a strong long-term orientation (98), it has a very weak individualistic orientation (25).

Hofstede's Cultural Dimensions (y-axis label)

Legend:
- Long-Term Orientation
- Uncertainty Avoidance
- Masculinity
- Individualism
- Power Distance

Countries (x-axis): USA, Germany, Japan, France, Netherlands, Hong Kong, Indonesia, West Africa, Russia, China

Source: G. H. Hofstede, "Cultural Constraints in Management Theories," *Academy of Management Executive* 7, no. 1 (1993): 81–94.

Masculine cultures emphasize assertiveness, competition, material success, and achievement, whereas feminine cultures emphasize the importance of relationships, modesty, caring for the weak, and quality of life. In Exhibit 8.5, Japan (95), Germany (66), and the United States (62) have the most masculine orientations, while the Netherlands (14) has the most feminine orientation.

The cultural difference of *uncertainty avoidance* is the degree to which people in a country are uncomfortable with unstructured, ambiguous, unpredictable situations. In countries with strong uncertainty avoidance, like Greece and Portugal, people tend to be aggressive and emotional and seek security (rather than uncertainty). In Exhibit 8.5, Japan (92), France (86), West Africa (90), and Russia (90) are strongest in uncertainty avoidance, while Hong Kong (29) is the weakest.

Short-term/long-term orientation addresses whether cultures are oriented to the present and seek immediate gratification, or to the future and defer gratification. Not surprisingly, countries with short-term orientations are consumer driven, whereas countries with long-term

orientations are savings driven. In Exhibit 8.5, China (118) and Hong Kong (96) have very strong long-term orientations, while Russia (10), West Africa (16), Indonesia (25), the United States (29), and Germany (31) have very strong short-term orientations. To generate a graphical comparison of two different countries' cultures, go to **http://www.geert-hofstede.com/hofstede_dimensions.php**. Select a "home culture." Then select a "host culture." A graph comparing the countries on each of Hofstede's five cultural differences will automatically be generated.

Cultural differences affect perceptions, understanding, and behavior. Recognizing cultural differences is critical to succeeding in global business. Nevertheless, as Hofstede pointed out, descriptions of cultural differences are based on averages—the average level of uncertainty avoidance in Portugal, the average level of power distance in Argentina, and so forth. Accordingly, says Hofstede, "If you are going to spend time with a Japanese colleague, you shouldn't assume that overall cultural statements about Japanese society automatically apply to this person."[46] Similarly, cultural beliefs may differ significantly from one part of a country to another.[47]

After becoming aware of cultural differences, the second step is deciding how to adapt your company to those differences. Unfortunately, studies investigating the effects of cultural differences on management practice point more to difficulties than to easy solutions. One problem is that different cultures will probably perceive management policies and practices differently. For example, blue-collar workers in France and Argentina, all of whom performed the same factory jobs for the same multinational company, perceived its company-wide safety policy differently.[48] French workers perceived that safety wasn't very important to the company, but Argentine workers thought that it was. The fact that something as simple as a safety policy can be perceived differently across cultures shows just how difficult it can be to standardize management practices across different countries and cultures.

©Susan Van Etten

20 percent of American expatriates sent abroad by their companies will return to the United States before they have successfully completed their assignments.[49] Of those who do complete their international assignments, about one-third are judged by their companies to be no better than marginally effective.[50]

Since the average cost of sending an employee on a three-year international assignment is $1 million, failure in those assignments can be extraordinarily expensive.[51]

The chances for a successful international assignment can be increased through **6.1 language and cross-cultural training** and **6.2 consideration of spouse, family, and dual-career issues.**

6.1 Language and Cross-Cultural Training

Predeparture language and cross-cultural training can reduce the uncertainty that expatriates feel, the misunderstandings that take place between expatriates and natives, and the inappropriate behaviors that expatriates unknowingly commit when they travel to a foreign country. Indeed, simple things like using a phone, locating a public toilet, asking for directions, finding out how much things cost, exchanging greetings, or understanding what people want can become tremendously complex when expatriates don't know a foreign language or a country's customs and cultures.

Expatriates who receive predeparture language and cross-cultural training make faster adjustments to foreign cultures and perform better on their international assignments.[52] Unfortunately, only a third of the managers who go on international assignments are offered any kind of predeparture training, and only half of those actually participate in the training![53] This is somewhat surprising given the failure rates for expatriates and the high cost of those failures. Furthermore,

6 Preparing for an International Assignment

An **expatriate** is someone who lives and works outside his or her native country. The difficulty of adjusting to language, cultural, and social differences is the primary reason for expatriate failure in overseas assignments. For example, although there have recently been disagreements among researchers about these numbers, 5 to

Expatriate someone who lives and works outside his or her native country

> Only **a third** of the **managers** who go on international assignments are offered any kind of **predeparture training.**

with the exception of some language courses, predeparture training is not particularly expensive or difficult to provide. Three methods can be used to prepare workers for international assignments: documentary training, cultural simulations, and field experiences.

Documentary training focuses on identifying specific critical differences between cultures. For example, when 60 workers at Axcelis Technologies in Beverly, Massachusetts, were preparing to do business in India, they learned that while Americans make eye contact and shake hands firmly when greeting others, Indians, as a sign of respect, do just the opposite, avoiding eye contact and shaking hands limply.[54]

After learning specific critical differences through documentary training, trainees can then participate in *cultural simulations,* in which they practice adapting to cultural differences. After the workers at Axcelis Technologies learned about key differences between their culture and India, they practiced adapting to those differences by role playing. Some Axcelis workers would take the roles of Indian workers, while other Axcelis workers would play themselves and try to behave in a way consistent with Indian culture. As they role-played, Indian music played loudly in the background, and they were coached on what to do or not do. Axcelis human resources director Randy Longo says, "At first, I was skeptical and wondered what I'd get out of the class. But it was enlightening for me. Not everyone operates like we do in America."

Finally, *field simulation* training, a technique made popular by the U.S. Peace Corps, places trainees in an ethnic neighborhood for three to four hours to talk to residents about cultural differences. For example, a U.S. electronics manufacturer prepared workers for assignments in South Korea by having trainees explore a nearby South Korean neighborhood and talk to shopkeepers and people on the street about South Korean politics, family orientation, and day-to-day living practices.

6.2 Spouse, Family, and Dual-Career Issues

Not all international assignments are difficult for expatriates and their families, but the evidence clearly shows that how well an expatriate's spouse and family ad-

just to the foreign culture is the most important factor in determining the success or failure of an international assignment.[55] Barry Kozloff of Selection Research International says, "The cost of sending a family on a foreign assignment is around $1 million and their failure to adjust is an enormous loss."[56] Unfortunately, despite its importance, there has been little systematic research on what does and does not help expatriates' families successfully adapt. A number of companies, however, have found that adaptability screening and intercultural training for families can lead to more successful overseas adjustment.

Adaptability screening is used to assess how well managers and their families are likely to adjust to foreign cultures. For example, Prudential Relocation Management's international division has developed an "Overseas Assignment Inventory" to assess a spouse's and family's open-mindedness, respect for others' beliefs, sense of humor, and marital communication. Likewise, Pennsylvania-based AMP, a worldwide producer of electrical connectors, conducts extensive psychological screening on expatriates and their spouses when making international assignments.

Only 40 percent of expatriates' families receive language and cross-cultural training, yet such training is just as important for the families of expatriates as for the expatriates themselves.[57] In fact, it may be more important because, unlike expatriates, whose professional jobs often shield them from the full force of a country's culture, spouses and children are fully immersed in foreign neighborhoods and schools. Households must be run, shopping must be done, and bills must be paid. Unfortunately, expatriate spouse Laurel Larsen, despite two hours of Chinese lessons a week, hasn't learned enough of the language to communicate with the family's baby-sitter. She has to phone her husband, who became fluent in Chinese in his teens, to translate. Likewise, expatriates' children must deal with different cultural beliefs and practices, too. While the Larsens' three daughters love the private, international school that they attend, they still have had difficulty adapting to, from their perspective, the incredible differences in inner China.[58]

DESIGNING ADAPTIVE ORGANIZATIONS

Structure and Process

Organizational structure is the vertical and horizontal configuration of departments, authority, and jobs within a company. For example, Exhibit 9.1 shows Microsoft's organizational chart. From this chart, you can see the vertical dimensions of the company—who reports to whom, the number of management levels, who has authority over what, and so forth. Founder Bill Gates is the chairman and chief software architect. In this role, Gates focuses on Microsoft's product and technology strategies. CEO Steve Ballmer reports directly to him.[1] Three division presidents, each responsible for one of Microsoft's core businesses, report directly to Ballmer. In turn, each division has several group vice presidents who oversee a number of operations.[2] The organizational chart also displays Microsoft's horizontal dimensions—who does what jobs, the number of different departments, and so forth.

An **organizational process** is the collection of activities that transform inputs into outputs that customers value.[3] For example, Microsoft uses basic internal and external processes to write computer software, shown in Exhibit 9.2. The process starts when Microsoft gets feedback from customers through Internet newsgroups, email, phone calls, or letters. This information helps Microsoft understand customers' needs and problems and identify important software issues and needed changes and functions. Mi-

Learning Outcomes

1 describe the departmentalization approach to organizational structure.

2 explain organizational authority.

3 discuss the different methods for job design.

4 explain the methods that companies are using to redesign internal organizational processes (i.e., intraorganizational processes).

5 describe the methods that companies are using to redesign external organizational processes (i.e., interorganizational processes).

Organizational structure the vertical and horizontal configuration of departments, authority, and jobs within a company

Organizational process the collection of activities that transform inputs into outputs that customers value

©Austin Grote

crosoft then rewrites the software, testing it internally at the company and then externally through its beta-testing process where customers who volunteer or are selected by Microsoft give the company extensive feedback, which is then used to make improvements. After "final" corrections are made to the software, the company distributes and sells it to customers, who start the process again by giving Microsoft more feedback.

This process view of Microsoft, which focuses on how things get done, is very different from the hierarchical view of Microsoft (go back to Microsoft's organizational chart in Exhibit 9.1), which focuses on accountability, responsibility, and positions within the chain of command. Yet, both are important, and you'll learn about them in this chapter.

Designing Organizational Structures

With offices and operations in 58 countries, products in over 200, and more than 150,000 employees worldwide, Sara Lee Corporation owns some of the best-known brands (Sara Lee, Hillshire Farms, Ball Park, and Jimmy Dean) in the world. To improve company performance, Sara Lee changed its organizational structure to focus on

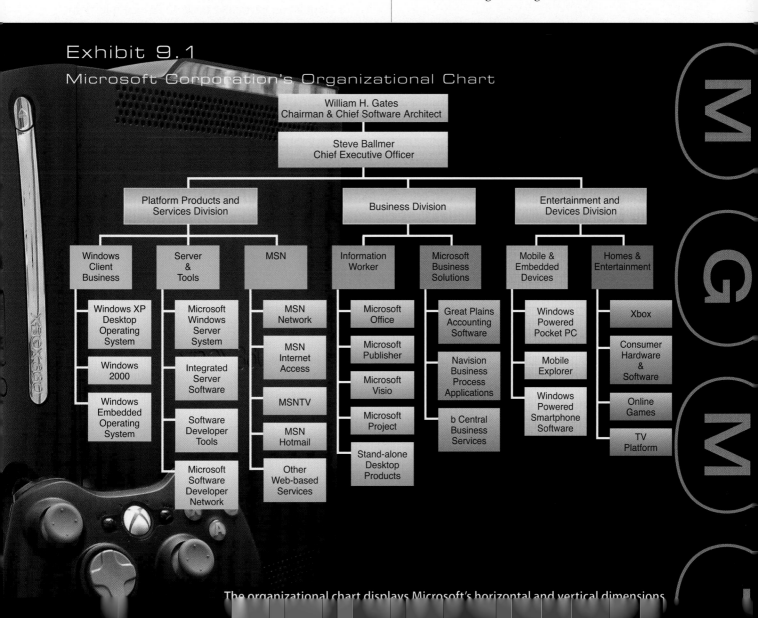

Exhibit 9.1
Microsoft Corporation's Organizational Chart

The organizational chart displays Microsoft's horizontal and vertical dimensions

Exhibit 9.2
Process View of Microsoft's Organization

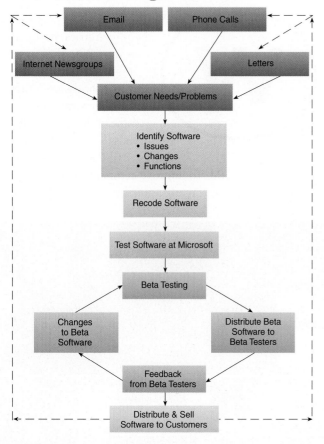

three key customer/geographic markets: North American retail (bakery, packaged meats, and Senseo coffee), North American food service (bakery goods, coffee, and meats sold to restaurants), and Sara Lee International (bakery and beverage businesses outside North America and global household products). Companies or divisions that didn't fit the new structure, like the European meats division and the branded apparel businesses (including Champion and Playtex) were sold. As a result, Sara Lee is now focused on its core businesses—food, beverage, and household and body care.[4]

Why would a large company like Sara Lee completely restructure its organizational design? What does it expect to gain from this change?

After reading the next three sections, you'll have a

Departmentalization subdividing work and workers into separate organizational units responsible for completing particular tasks

Functional departmentalization organizing work and workers into separate units responsible for particular business functions or areas of expertise

better understanding of the importance of organizational structure because you should be able to

1 describe the departmentalization approach to organizational structure.

2 explain organizational authority.

3 discuss the different methods for job design.

1 Departmentalization

Traditionally, organizational structures have been based on some form of departmentalization. **Departmentalization** is a method of subdividing work and workers into separate organizational units that take responsibility for completing particular tasks.[5] For example, Sony has separate departments or divisions for electronics, music, movies, computer games and game consoles, and theaters.[6]

Traditionally, organizational structures have been created by departmentalizing work according to five methods: 1.1 functional, 1.2 product, 1.3 customer, 1.4 geographic, and 1.5 matrix.

1.1 Functional Departmentalization

The most common organizational structure is functional departmentalization. Companies tend to use this structure when they are small or just starting out. **Functional departmentalization** organizes work and workers into separate units responsible for particular business functions or areas of expertise. A common functional structure might have individuals organized into accounting, sales, marketing, production, and human resources departments.

Not all functionally departmentalized companies have the same functions, however. The insurance company and the advertising agency shown in Exhibit 9.3 both have sales, accounting, human resources, and information systems departments, as indicated by the orange boxes. The purple and green boxes indicate the functions that are different. As would be expected, the insurance company has separate departments for life, auto, home, and health insurance. The advertising agency has departments for artwork, creative work, print advertising, and radio advertising. So the kind of functional departments in a functional structure depends, in part, on the business or industry a company is in.

Functional departmentalization has some advantages. First, it allows work to be done by highly qualified specialists. While the accountants in the accounting department take responsibility for producing accurate revenue and ex-

Exhibit 9.3

Functional Departmentalization

Insurance Company

Sales	Information Systems
Accounting	Human Resources
Life Insurance	Auto Insurance
Home Insurance	Health Insurance

Advertising Agency

Sales	Information Systems
Accounting	Human Resources
Art Department	Print Advertising
Creative Department	Radio Advertising

Exhibit 9.4

Product Departmentalization: United Technologies

United Technologies

- Carrier (heating, ventilating, & air-conditioning)
- Chubb (security, monitoring, & fire protection)
- Hamilton Sundstrand (aircraft systems)
- Otis (elevators & escalators)
  - Customer Service
  - Engineering
  - Human Resources
  - Information Technology
  - Legal
  - Maintenance & Field Operations
  - Manufacturing
  - Marketing & Sales
  - Sourcing & Logistics
- Pratt & Whitney (jet aircraft engines)
  - Administrative Services
  - Communication & Public Relations
  - Customer Service & Support
  - E-Business
  - Engineering
  - Enterprise Resource Planning
  - Environmental Health & Safety
  - Facilities & Services
  - Human Resources
  - Legal
  - Manufacturing
  - Procurement
  - Quality
- Sikorsky (helicopters)
- UTC Power (commercial heating, cooling, & power systems)

Source: *United Technologies Corporation 2004 Annual Report,* United Technologies, [Online] available at http://www.utc.com/annual_reports/2004/2004_ar.pdf,1 May 2005.

pense figures, the engineers in research and development can focus their efforts on designing a product that is reliable and simple to manufacture. Second, it lowers costs by reducing duplication. When the engineers in research and development come up with that fantastic new product, they don't have to worry about creating an aggressive advertising campaign to sell it. That task belongs to the advertising experts and sales representatives in marketing. Third, with everyone in the same department having similar work experience or training, communication and coordination are less problematic for departmental managers.

At the same time, functional departmentalization has a number of disadvantages. To start, cross-department coordination can be difficult. Managers and employees are often more interested in doing what's right for their function than in doing what's right for the entire organization. As companies grow, functional departmentalization may also lead to slower decision making and produce managers and workers with narrow experience and expertise.

1.2 Product Departmentalization

Product departmentalization organizes work and workers into separate units responsible for produc-

ing particular products or services. Exhibit 9.4 shows the product departmentalization structure used by United Technologies, which is organized along seven different product lines: Carrier, Chubb, Hamilton Sundstrand, Otis, Pratt & Whitney, Sikorsky, and UTC Power.[7]

One of the advantages of product departmentalization is that, like functional departmentalization, it allows managers and workers to specialize in one area of expertise. Unlike the narrow expertise and experiences in functional departmentalization, however, managers and workers develop a broader set of experiences and expertise related to an entire product line. Likewise, product departmentalization makes it easier for top managers to assess work-unit performance. For example, because of the clear separation of their seven

Product departmentalization organizing work and workers into separate units responsible for producing particular products or services different product divisions, United Technologies' top managers can easily compare the performance of its Otis elevators product division and its Pratt & Whitney aircraft engines division. The divisions had similar revenues—almost $8.99 billion for Otis and $8.3 billion for Pratt & Whitney—but Otis had a profit of $1.54 billion (a 17 percent profit margin) compared to just $1.1 billion (a 13 percent profit margin) for Pratt & Whitney.[8] Finally, decision making should be faster because managers and workers are responsible for the entire product line rather than for separate functional departments, and thus there are fewer conflicts (compared to functional departmentalization).

The primary disadvantage of product departmentalization is duplication. For example, you can see in Exhibit 9.4 that the Otis elevators and Pratt & Whitney divisions both have customer service, engineering, human resources, legal, manufacturing, and procurement (similar to sourcing and logistics) departments. Duplication like this often results in higher costs.

A second disadvantage is the challenge of coordinating across the different product departments. United Technologies would probably have difficulty standardizing its policies and procedures in product departments as different as the Carrier (heating, ventilating, and air-conditioning) and Sikorsky (military and commercial helicopters) divisions.

1.3 Customer Departmentalization

Customer departmentalization organizes work and workers into separate units responsible for particular kinds of customers. For example, as Exhibit 9.5 shows, the telecommunications company Sprint Nextel is organized into departments that cater to businesses, consum-

Exhibit 9.5

Customer Departmentalization: Sprint Corporation

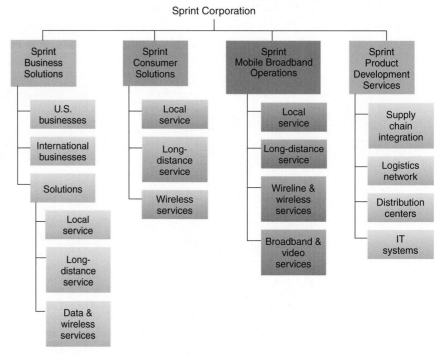

Source: "Overview," Sprint, [Online] available at http://www.sprint.com/sprint/fastfacts/overview/index.html, 1 May 2005.

ers, 4G mobile broadband operations, and product development.[9]

The primary advantage of customer departmentalization is that it focuses the organization on customer needs rather than on products or business functions. Furthermore, creating separate departments to serve specific kinds of customers allows companies to specialize and adapt their products and services to customer needs and problems.

The primary disadvantage of customer departmentalization is that, like product departmentalization, it leads to duplication of resources. Furthermore, as with product departmentalization, it can be difficult to achieve coordination across different customer departments. Finally, the emphasis on meeting customers' needs may lead workers to make decisions that please customers but hurt the business.

1.4 Geographic Departmentalization

Geographic departmentalization organizes work and workers into separate units responsible for doing business in particular geographic areas. For example, Exhibit 9.6 shows the geographic departmentalization used by Coca-Cola Enterprises (CCE), the largest bottler and distributor of Coca-Cola products in the world. As shown in

Exhibit 9.6

Geographic Departmentalization: Coca-Cola Enterprises

Territories of Operation

	POPULATION	PER CAPITA CONSUMPTION(1)	EMPLOYEES	FACILITIES(2)
North American Group	263 M	300	63,000	399
European Group	146 M	174	11,000	32
Total Company	409 M	255	74,000	431

(1) Number of 8-ounce servings consumed per person per year.

(2) Facilities include 18 production, 335 sales/distribution, and 46 combination sales and production plants in North America, and 3 production, 17 sales/distribution, and 12 combination plants in Europe.

Source: "Territories of Operation, 2004 Annual Report," Coca-Cola Enterprises, [Online] available at http://ir.cokecce.com/downloads/ar2004.pdf, 1 May 2005.

Exhibit 9.6, CCE has two regional groups: North America and Europe. As the table in the exhibit shows, each of these regions would be a sizable company by itself.

The primary advantage of geographic departmentalization is that it helps companies respond to the demands of different markets. This can be especially important when the company sells in different countries. For example, CCE's geographic divisions sell products suited to taste preferences in different countries. CCE bottles and distributes the following products in Europe but not in the United States: Aquarius, Bonaqua, Burn, Coca-Cola Light (which is somewhat different from Diet Coke), Cresta flavors, Five Alive, Kia-Ora, Kinley, Lilt, Malvern, and Oasis.[10] Another advantage is that geographic departmentalization can reduce costs by locating unique organizational resources closer to customers. For instance, it is much cheaper for CCE to build bottling plants in Belgium than to bottle Coke in England and then transport it across the English Channel to Belgium.

The primary disadvantage of geographic departmentalization is that it can lead to duplication of resources. For example, while it may be necessary to adapt products and marketing to different geographic locations, it's doubtful that CCE needs significantly different inventory tracking systems from location to location. Also, even more than with the other forms of departmentalization, it can be difficult to coordinate departments that are literally thousands of miles from each other and whose managers have very limited contact with each other.

1.5 Matrix Departmentalization

Matrix departmentalization is a hybrid structure in which two or more forms of departmentalization are used together. The most common matrix combines the product and functional forms of departmentalization, but other forms may also be used. Exhibit 9.7 shows the matrix structure used by Procter & Gamble, which has 98,000 employees working in 80 different countries. Across the top of Exhibit 9.7, you can see that the company uses a product unit structure with managers responsible for the global efforts of their branded products. The left side of the figure, however, shows that the company is also using a geographic structure. Geographic managers are responsible for taking P&G's globally positioned products and adapting them to fit the cultures of the countries where they are sold—more than 140 countries in all. P&G's roster of brands includes Pampers (diapers), Tide (laundry detergent), Always (feminine protection), Pantene (shampoo), Bounty (dryer sheets), Folgers (coffee), Pringles (snack food), Charmin (toilet paper), Downy (fabric softener), Iams (dog and cat food), Crest (toothpaste), Actonel (prescription drug), and Olay (body care).[11] The company also has two groups that cut across the entire matrix, taking care of customer service and administration.

The boxes in the figure represent the matrix structure, created by the combination of

> **Matrix departmentalization** a hybrid organizational structure in which two or more forms of departmentalization, most often product and functional, are used together

the geographic and product structures. For example, in the health care business in Central-Eastern Europe, Middle East, and Africa, country managers in Hungary, United Arab Emirates, or Kenya are responsible for developing P&G's business in products such as Metamucil, Pepto-Bismol, Prilosec OTC, and Vicks.

Several things distinguish matrix departmentalization from the other traditional forms of departmentalization.[12] First, most employees report to two bosses, one from each core part of the matrix. For example, in Exhibit 9.7, the manager responsible for Charmin in France would report both to the president for Global Baby Care/ Family Care and to the president for Western Europe. Second, by virtue of their hybrid design, matrix structures lead to much more cross-functional interaction than other forms of departmentalization. In fact, while matrix workers are typically members of only one functional department (based on their work experience and expertise), they are also commonly members of several ongoing project, product, or customer groups. Third, because of the high level of cross-functional interaction, matrix departmentalization requires significant coordination between managers in the different parts of the matrix. In particular, managers have the complex job of tracking and managing the multiple demands (project, product, customer, or functional) on employees' time.

The primary advantage of matrix departmentalization is that it allows companies to efficiently manage large, complex tasks like researching, developing, and marketing pharmaceuticals or carrying out complex global businesses. Efficiency comes from avoiding duplication. For example, rather than having an entire marketing function for each project, the company simply assigns and reassigns workers from the marketing department as they are needed at various stages of product completion. More specifically, an employee from a department may simultaneously be part of five different ongoing projects, but may be actively completing work on only a few projects at a time.

Exhibit 9.7

Matrix Departmentalization: Procter & Gamble

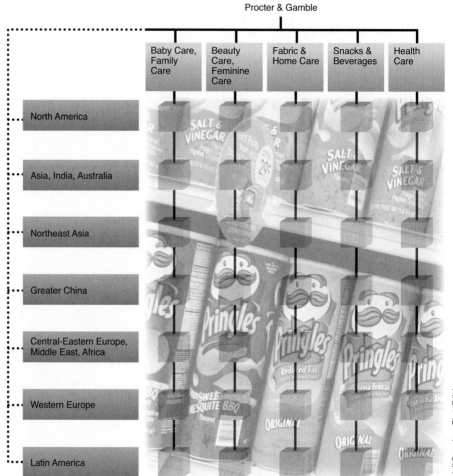

Sources: http://www.pg.com/jobs/corporate_structure/four_pillars.jhtml; http://www.pg.com/news/management/bios_photos.jhtml.

Another advantage is the pool of resources available to carry out large, complex tasks. Because of the ability to quickly pull in expert help from all the functional areas of the company, matrix project managers have a much more diverse set of expertise and experience at their disposal than do managers in the other forms of departmentalization.

The primary disadvantage of matrix departmentalization is the high level of coordination required to manage the complexity involved with running large, ongoing projects at various levels of completion. Matrix structures are notorious for confusion and conflict between project bosses in different parts of the matrix. At P&G, such confusion or conflict might occur between managers in the Global Fabric and Home Care Division and the president of operations in greater China. Disagreements or misunderstandings about schedules, budgets, available resources, and the availability of employees with particular functional expertise are common. Another disadvantage is that matrix structures require much more management skill than the other forms of departmentalization.

Because of these problems, many matrix structures evolve from a **simple matrix,** in which managers in different parts of the matrix negotiate conflicts and resources directly, to a **complex matrix,** in which specialized matrix managers and departments are added to the organizational structure. In a complex matrix, managers from different parts of the matrix might report to the same matrix manager, who helps them sort out conflicts and problems.

2 Organizational Authority

The second part of traditional organizational structures is authority. **Authority** is the right to give commands, take action, and make decisions to achieve organizational objectives.[13]

Traditionally, organizational authority has been characterized by the following dimensions: 2.1 chain of command, 2.2 line versus staff authority, 2.3 delegation of authority, and 2.4 degree of centralization.

2.1 Chain of Command

Turn back a few pages to Microsoft's organizational chart in Exhibit 9.1. If you place your finger on any position in the chart, say, Central Business Services (under Microsoft Business Solutions), you can trace a line upward to the company's CEO, Steve Ballmer. This line, which vertically connects every job in the company to higher levels of management, represents the chain of command. The **chain of command** is the vertical line of authority that clarifies who reports to whom throughout the organization. People higher in the chain of command have the right, *if they so choose,* to give commands, take action, and make decisions concerning activities occurring anywhere below them in the chain. In the following discussion about delegation and decentralization, you will learn that managers don't always choose to exercise their authority directly.[14]

One of the key assumptions underlying the chain of command is **unity of command,** which means that workers should report to just one boss.[15] In practical terms, this means that only one person can be in charge at a time. Matrix organizations, in which employees have two bosses, automatically violate this principle. This is one of the primary reasons that matrix organizations are difficult to manage. The purpose of unity of command is to prevent the confusion that might arise when an employee receives conflicting commands from two different bosses.

2.2 Line versus Staff Authority

A second dimension of authority is the distinction between line and staff authority. **Line authority** is the right to command immediate subordinates in the chain of command. For example, in the Microsoft organizational chart in Exhibit 9.1, CEO Steve Ballmer has line authority over the manager of the Business Division. Ballmer can issue orders to that division president and expect them to be carried out. In turn, the Business Division president can issue orders to the manager of the Information Worker group and expect them to be carried out.

Staff authority is the right to advise, but not command, others who are not subordinates in the chain of command. For example, at Microsoft, a manager in human resources might advise the vice president of MSN on a hiring decision but cannot order him or her to hire a certain applicant.

The terms *line* and *staff* are also used to describe different functions within the organization. A **line function** is an activity that contributes directly to creating or selling the company's products. So, for example, activities that take place within the manufacturing and marketing departments would be

---

Simple matrix a form of matrix departmentalization in which managers in different parts of the matrix negotiate conflicts and resources

Complex matrix a form of matrix departmentalization in which managers in different parts of the matrix report to matrix managers, who help them sort out conflicts and problems

Authority the right to give commands, take action, and make decisions to achieve organizational objectives

Chain of command the vertical line of authority that clarifies who reports to whom throughout the organization

Unity of command a management principle that workers should report to just one boss

Line authority the right to command immediate subordinates in the chain of command

Staff authority the right to advise, but not command, others who are not subordinates in the chain of command

Line function an activity that contributes directly to creating or selling the company's products

In practical terms, only **one person** can be in **charge at a time**.

considered line functions. A **staff function,** such as accounting, human resources, or legal services, does not contribute directly to creating or selling the company's products, but instead supports line activities. For example, marketing managers might consult with the legal staff to make sure the wording of a particular advertisement is legal.

2.3 Delegation of Authority

Managers can exercise their authority directly by completing the tasks themselves, or they can choose to pass on some of their authority to subordinates. **Delegation of authority** is the assignment of direct authority and responsibility to a subordinate to complete tasks for which the manager is normally responsible.

When a manager delegates work, three transfers occur, as illustrated in Exhibit 9.8. First, the manager transfers full responsibility for the assignment to the subordinate. Many managers find giving up full responsibility somewhat difficult. For example, Phil Knight, the charismatic founder of Nike, has made three unsuccessful attempts at turning over the reins of his multibillion-dollar corporation.[16] According to former CEO William Perez, Knight's name belongs near the top of the list of CEOs who can't delegate. Perez says, "From virtually the day I arrived, Phil was as engaged in the company as he ever was. He was talking to my direct reports. It was confusing for the people and frustrating for me."[17]

Another problem is that managers often fear that the task won't be done as well as if they did it themselves. However, one CEO says, "If you can delegate a task to somebody who can do it 75 percent to 80 percent as well as you can today, you delegate it

Exhibit 9.8

Delegation: Responsibility, Authority, and Accountability

Manager   Subordinate

Responsibility →

Authority →

← Accountability

Source: C. D. Pringle, D. F. Jennings, & J. G. Longenecker, *Managing Organizations: Functions and Behaviors* © 1990. Adapted by permission of Pearson Education, Inc., Upper Saddle River, NJ.

immediately." Why? The reason is that many tasks don't need to be done perfectly; they just need to be done. And delegating tasks that someone else can do frees managers to assume other important responsibilities.

Sometimes managers delegate only to later interfere with how the employee is performing the task. "Why are you doing it that way? That's not the way I do it." In contrast, delegating full responsibility means that the employee—not the manager—is now completely responsible for task completion.

The second transfer that occurs with delegation is that the manager gives the subordinate full authority over the budget, resources, and personnel needed to do the job. To do the job effectively, subordinates must have the same tools and information that managers had when they were responsible for the same task. In other words, for delegation to work,

Staff function an activity that does not contribute directly to creating or selling the company's products, but instead supports line activities

Delegation of authority the assignment of direct authority and responsibility to a subordinate to complete tasks for which the manager is normally responsible

How to Be a More Effective Delegator

1. Trust your staff to do a good job. Recognize that others have the talent and ability to complete projects.
2. Avoid seeking perfection. Establish a standard of quality and provide a time frame for reaching it.
3. Give effective job instructions. Make sure employees have enough information to complete the job successfully.
4. Know your true interests. Delegation is difficult for some people who actually prefer doing the work themselves rather than managing it.
5. Follow up on progress. Build in checkpoints to help identify potential problems.
6. Praise the efforts of your staff.
7. Don't wait until the last minute to delegate. Avoid crisis management by routinely delegating work.
8. Ask questions, expect answers, and assist employees to help them complete the work assignments as expected.
9. Provide the resources you would expect if you were doing an assignment yourself.
10. Delegate to the lowest possible level to make the best possible use of organizational resources, energy, and knowledge.

Source: S. B. Wilson, "Are You an Effective Delegator?" *Female Executive*, 1 November 1994, 19.

delegated authority must be commensurate with delegated responsibility.

The third transfer that occurs with delegation is the transfer of accountability. The subordinate now has the authority and responsibility to do the job and in return is accountable for getting the job done. In other words, delegate their managerial authority and responsibility to subordinates in exchange for results.

2.4 Degree of Centralization

If you've ever called a company's toll-free number with a complaint or a special request and been told by the customer service representative, "I'll have to ask my manager," or "I'm not authorized to do that," you know that centralization of authority exists in that company. **Centralization of authority** is the location of most authority at the upper levels of the organization. In a centralized organization, managers make most decisions, even the relatively small ones. That's why the customer

service representative you called couldn't make a decision without first asking the manager.

If you are lucky, however, you may have talked to a customer service representative at another company who said, "I can take care of that for you right now." In other words, the person was able to handle your problem without any input from or consultation with company management. **Decentralization** is the location of a significant amount of authority in the lower levels of the organization. An organization is decentralized if it has a high degree of delegation at all levels. In a decentralized organization, workers closest to problems are authorized to make the decisions necessary to solve the problems on their own.

Decentralization has a number of advantages. It develops employee capabilities throughout the company and leads to faster decision making and more satisfied customers and employees. Furthermore, a study of 1,000 large companies found that companies with a high degree of decentralization outperformed those with a low degree of decentralization in terms of return on assets (6.9 percent versus 4.7 percent), return on investment (14.6 percent versus 9.0 percent), return on equity (22.8 percent versus 16.6 percent), and return on sales (10.3 percent versus 6.3 percent). Surprisingly, the same study found that few large companies actually are decentralized. Specifically, only 31 percent of employees in these 1,000 companies were responsible for recommending improvements to management. Overall, just 10 percent of employees received the training and information needed to support a truly decentralized approach to management.[18]

> ## Stay centralized where standardization is important and decentralize where standardization is unimportant.

With results like these, the key question is no longer *whether* companies should decentralize, but *where* they should decentralize. One rule of thumb is to stay centralized where standardization is important and to decentralize where standardization is unimportant. **Standardization** is solving problems by consistently applying the same rules, procedures, and processes. Each year, General Motors purchases roughly $85 billion worth

Centralization of authority the location of most authority at the upper levels of the organization

Decentralization the location of a significant amount of authority in the lower levels of the organization

Standardization solving problems by consistently applying the same rules, procedures, and processes of automotive parts, many of which are only slightly different from each other. For instance, GM makes 26 different types of seat frames, 20 different fuel pumps, and a dozen V6 engines. GM, however, has started standardizing the parts it uses across its product lines and today uses only six types of fuel pump, and management wants to cut that number to five.[19]

3 Job Design

1. "Welcome to McDonald's. May I have your order please?"
2. Listen to the order. Repeat it for accuracy. State the total cost. "Please drive to the second window."
3. Take the money. Make change.
4. Give customers drinks, straws, and napkins.
5. Give customers food.
6. "Thank you for coming to McDonald's."

Could you stand to do the same simple tasks an average of 50 times per hour, 400 times per day, 2,000 times per week, 8,000 times per month? Few can. Fast-food workers rarely stay on the job more than six months. Indeed, McDonald's and other fast-food restaurants have well over 100 percent employee turnover each year.[20]

In this next section, you will learn about **job design**—the number, kind, and variety of tasks that individual workers perform in doing their jobs.

You will learn **3.1 why companies continue to use specialized jobs like the McDonald's drive-through job** *and* **3.2 how job rotation, job enlargement, job enrichment,** *and* **3.3 the job characteristics model are being used to overcome the problems associated with job specialization.**

3.1 Job Specialization

Job specialization occurs when a job is composed of a small part of a larger task or process. Specialized jobs are characterized by simple, easy-to-learn steps, low variety, and high repetition, like the McDonald's drive-through

window job just described. One of the clear disadvantages of specialized jobs is that, being so easy to learn, they quickly become boring. This, in turn, can lead to low job satisfaction and high absenteeism and employee turnover, all of which are very costly to organizations.

Why, then, do companies continue to create and use specialized jobs? The primary reason is that specialized jobs are very economical. Once a job has been specialized, it takes little time to learn and master. Consequently, when experienced workers quit or are absent, the company can replace them with new employees and lose little productivity. For example, next time you're at McDonald's, notice the pictures of the food on the cash registers. These pictures make it easy for McDonald's trainees to quickly learn to take orders. Likewise, to simplify and speed operations, the drink dispensers behind the counter are set to automatically fill drink cups. Put a medium cup below the dispenser. Punch the medium drink button. The soft drink machine then fills the cup to within a half-inch of the top while that same worker goes to get your fries. At McDonald's, every task has been simplified in this way. Because the work is designed to be simple, wages can remain low since it isn't necessary to pay high salaries to attract highly experienced, educated, or trained workers.

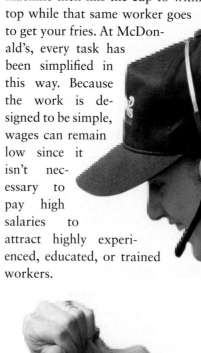

Job design the number, kind, and variety of tasks that individual workers perform in doing their jobs

Job specialization a job composed of a small part of a larger task or process

3.2 Job Rotation, Enlargement, and Enrichment

Because of the efficiency of specialized jobs, companies are often reluctant to eliminate them. Consequently, job redesign efforts have focused on modifying jobs to keep the benefits of specialized jobs, while reducing their obvious costs and disadvantages. Three methods—job rotation, job enlargement, and job enrichment—have been used to try to improve specialized jobs.[21]

Job rotation attempts to overcome the disadvantages of job specialization by periodically moving workers from one specialized job to another to give them more variety and the opportunity to use different skills. For example, an office receptionist who does nothing but answer phones could be systematically rotated to a different job, such as typing, filing, or data entry, every day or two. Likewise, a "mirror attacher" in an automobile plant might attach mirrors in the first half of the day's work shift and then install bumpers during the second half. Because employees simply switch from one specialized job to another, job rotation allows companies to retain the economic benefits of specialized work. At the same time, the greater variety of tasks makes the work less boring and more satisfying for workers.

Another way to counter the disadvantages of specialization is to enlarge the job. **Job enlargement** increases the number of different tasks that a worker performs within one particular job. So, instead of being assigned just one task, workers with enlarged jobs are given several tasks to perform. For example, an enlarged "mirror attacher" job might include attaching the mirror, checking to see that the mirror's power adjustment controls work, and then cleaning the mirror's surface. Though job enlargement increases variety, many workers report feeling more stress when their jobs are enlarged. Consequently, many workers view enlarged jobs as simply "more work," especially if they are not given additional time to complete the additional tasks. In comparison, **job enrichment** attempts to overcome the deficiencies in specialized work by increasing the number of tasks and by giving workers the authority and control to make meaningful decisions about their work.[22]

3.3 Job Characteristics Model

In contrast to job rotation, job enlargement, and job enrichment, which focus on providing variety in job tasks, the **job characteristics model (JCM)** is an approach to job redesign that seeks to formulate jobs in ways that motivate workers and lead to positive work outcomes.[23] As shown in Exhibit 9.9, the primary goal of the model is to create jobs that result in positive personal and work outcomes such as internal work motivation, satisfaction with one's job, and work effectiveness. Of these, the central concern of the JCM is internal motivation. **Internal motivation** is motivation that comes from the job itself rather than from outside

Exhibit 9.9

Job Characteristics Model

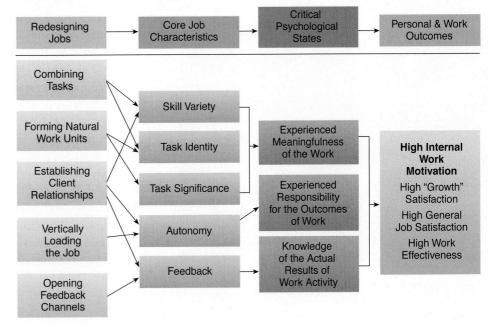

Source: J. R. Hackman and G. R. Oldham, *Work Redesign* (Reading, MA: Addison-Wesley, 1980). Reprinted by permission of Addison-Wesley Longman.

Job rotation periodically moving workers from one specialized job to another to give them more variety and the opportunity to use different skills

Job enlargement increasing the number of different tasks that a worker performs within one particular job

Job enrichment increasing the number of tasks in a particular job and giving workers the authority and control to make meaningful decisions about their work

Job characteristics model (JCM) an approach to job redesign that seeks to formulate jobs in ways that motivate workers and lead to positive work outcomes

Internal motivation motivation that comes from the job itself rather than from outside rewards

©Taxi/Getty Images

edge of results; that is, they must know how well they are performing their jobs. All three critical psychological states must occur for work to be internally motivating.

For example, grocery store cashiers usually have knowledge of results. When you're slow, your checkout line grows long. If you make a mistake, customers point it out: "No, I think that's on sale for $2.99, not $3.99." Likewise, cashiers experience responsibility for work outcomes. At the end of the day, the register is totaled and the money is counted. Ideally, the money matches the total sales in the register. If the money in the till is less than what's recorded in the register, most stores make the cashier pay the difference. Consequently, most cashiers are very careful to avoid being caught short at the end of the day. Nonetheless, despite knowing the results and experiencing responsibility for work outcomes, most grocery store cashiers (at least where I shop) aren't internally motivated because they don't experience the work as mean-

WHY ISN'T THE DRIVE-THROUGH JOB PARTICULARLY SATISFYING OR MOTIVATING?

Skill variety the number of different activities performed in a job

Task identity the degree to which a job, from beginning to end, requires the completion of a whole and identifiable piece of work

Task significance the degree to which a job is perceived to have a substantial impact on others inside or outside the organization

Autonomy the degree to which a job gives workers the discretion, freedom, and independence to decide how and when to accomplish the job

Feedback the amount of information the job provides to workers about their work performance

rewards, such as a raise or praise from the boss. If workers feel that performing the job well is itself rewarding, then the job has internal motivation. Statements such as "I get a nice sense of accomplishment" or "I feel good about myself and what I'm producing" are examples of internal motivation.

Moving to the left in Exhibit 9.9, you can see that the JCM specifies three critical psychological states that must occur for work to be internally motivating. First, workers must *experience the work as meaningful;* that is, they must view their job as being important. Second, they must *experience responsibility for work outcomes*—they must feel personally responsible for the work being done well. Third, workers must have *knowl-*

ingful. With scanners, it takes little skill to learn or do the job. Anyone can do it. In addition, cashiers have few decisions to make, and the job is highly repetitive.

Of course, this raises the question: What kinds of jobs produce the three critical psychological states? Moving another step to the left in Exhibit 9.9, you can see that these psychological states arise from jobs that are strong on five core job characteristics: skill variety, task identity, task significance, autonomy, and feedback. **Skill variety** is the number of different activities performed in a job. **Task identity** is the degree to which a job, from beginning to end, requires completion of a whole and identifiable piece of work. **Task significance** is the degree to which a job is perceived to have a substantial impact on others inside or outside the organization. **Autonomy** is the degree to which a job gives workers the discretion, freedom, and independence to decide how and when to accomplish the work. Finally, **feedback** is the amount of information the job provides to workers about their work performance.

To illustrate how the core job characteristics work together, let's use them to more thoroughly assess why the McDonald's drive-through window job is not particularly satisfying or motivating. To start, skill variety is low. Except for the size of an order or special requests ("no onions"), the process is the same for each customer. At best, task identity is moderate. Although you take the order, handle the money, and deliver the food, others are responsible for a larger part of the process—preparing the food. Task identity will be even lower if the McDonald's has two drive-through windows because each drive-through window worker will have an even more specialized task. The first is limited to taking the order and making change, while the second just delivers the food. Task significance, the impact you have on others, is probably low. Autonomy is also very low: McDonald's has strict rules about dress, cleanliness, and procedures. But the job does provide immediate feedback, such as positive and negative customer comments, car horns honking, the amount of time it takes to process orders, and the number of cars in the drive-through. With the exception of feedback, the low levels of the core job characteristics show why the drive-through window job is not internally motivating for many workers.

What can managers do when jobs aren't internally motivating? The far left column of Exhibit 9.9 lists five job redesign techniques that managers can use to strengthen a job's core characteristics. *Combining tasks* increases skill variety and task identity by joining separate, specialized tasks into larger work modules. For example, some trucking firms are now requiring truck drivers to load their rigs as well as drive them. The hope is that involving drivers in loading will ensure that trucks are properly loaded, thus reducing damage claims.

Work can be formed into *natural work units* by arranging tasks according to logical or meaningful groups. Although many trucking companies randomly assign drivers to trucks, some have begun assigning drivers to particular geographic locations (e.g., the Northeast or Southwest) or to truckloads that require special driving skill when being transported (e.g., oversized loads, chemicals, etc.). Forming natural work units increases task identity and task significance.

Establishing client relationships increases skill variety, autonomy, and feedback by giving employees direct contact with clients and customers. In some companies, truck drivers are expected to establish business relationships with their regular customers. When something goes wrong with a shipment, customers are told to call drivers directly.

Vertical loading means pushing some managerial authority down to workers. For truck drivers, this means that they have the same authority as managers to resolve customer problems. In some companies, if a late shipment causes problems for a customer, the driver has the authority to fully refund the cost of that shipment (without first obtaining management's approval).

The last job redesign technique offered by the model, *opening feedback channels,* means finding additional ways to give employees direct, frequent feedback about their job performance.

Designing Organizational Processes

More than 40 years ago, Tom Burns and G. M. Stalker described how two kinds of organizational designs, mechanistic and organic, are appropriate for different kinds of organizational environments.[24] **Mechanistic organizations** are characterized by specialized jobs and responsibilities; precisely defined, unchanging roles; and a rigid chain of command based on centralized authority and vertical communication. This type of organization works best in stable, unchanging business environments. By contrast, **organic organizations** are characterized by broadly defined jobs and responsibility; loosely defined, frequently changing roles; and decentralized authority and horizontal communication based on task knowledge. This type of organization works best in dynamic, changing business environments.

The organizational design techniques described in the first half of this chapter—departmentalization, authority, and job design—are better suited for mechanistic organizations and the stable business environments that were more prevalent before 1980. In contrast, the organizational design techniques discussed next, in the second part of the chapter, are more appropriate for organic organizations and the increasingly dynamic environments in which today's businesses compete.

The key difference between these approaches is that whereas mechanistic organizational designs focus on organizational structure, organic organizational designs are concerned with organizational process, the collection

Mechanistic organization an organization characterized by specialized jobs and responsibilities; precisely defined, unchanging roles; and a rigid chain of command based on centralized authority and vertical communication

Organic organization an organization characterized by broadly defined jobs and responsibility; loosely defined, frequently changing roles; and decentralized authority and horizontal communication based on task knowledge *of activities that transform inputs into outputs valued by customers.*

After reading the next two sections, you should be able to

4 explain the methods that companies are using to redesign internal organizational processes (i.e., intraorganizational processes).

5 describe the methods that companies are using to redesign external organizational processes (i.e., interorganizational processes).

4 Intraorganizational Processes

An **intraorganizational process** is the collection of activities that take place within an organization to transform inputs into outputs that customers value.

Let's take a look at how companies are using *4.1 reengineering* and *4.2 empowerment to redesign intraorganizational processes like these.*

4.1 Reengineering

In their best-selling book *Reengineering the Corporation*, Michael Hammer and James Champy define **reengineering** as "the *fundamental* rethinking and *radical* redesign of business *processes* to achieve *dramatic* improvements in critical, contemporary measures of performance, such as cost, quality, service and speed."[25] Hammer and Champy further explained the four key words shown in italics in this definition. The first key word is *fundamental*. When reengineering organizational designs, managers must ask themselves, "Why do we do what we do?" and "Why do we do it the way we do?" The usual answer is, "Because that's the way we've always done it." The second key word is *radical*. Reengineering is about significant change, about starting over by throwing out the old ways of getting work done. The third key word is *processes*. Hammer and Champy noted that "most business people are not process oriented; they are focused on tasks, on jobs, on people, on structures, but not on processes." The fourth key word is *dramatic*. Reengineering is about achieving "quantum" improvements in company performance.

In Plain English

The definition of intraorganizational process tells you exactly what it is, but here's a quick example to help you get to "Oh, that's it."

The steps involved in an automobile insurance claim are a good example of an intraorganizational process:
1. Document the loss (i.e., the accident).
2. Assign an appraiser to determine the dollar amount of damage.
3. Make an appointment to inspect the vehicle.
4. Inspect the vehicle.
5. Write an appraisal and get the repair shop to agree to the damage estimate.
6. Pay for the repair work.
7. Return the repaired car to the customer.

Intraorganizational process the collection of activities that take place within an organization to transform inputs into outputs that customers value

Reengineering fundamental rethinking and radical redesign of business processes to achieve dramatic improvements in critical measures of performance, such as cost, quality, service, and speed

An example from IBM Credit's operation illustrates how work can be reengineered.[26] IBM Credit lends businesses money to buy IBM computers. Previously, the loan process began when an IBM salesperson called the home office to obtain credit approval for a customer's purchase. The first department involved in the process took the credit information over the phone from the salesperson and recorded it on the credit form. The credit form was sent to the credit checking department, then to the pricing department (where the interest rate was determined), and on through a total of five departments. In all, it took the five departments six days to approve or deny the customer's loan. Of course, this delay cost IBM business. Some customers got their loans elsewhere. Others, frustrated by the wait, simply canceled their orders.

Finally, two IBM managers decided to walk a loan straight through each of the departments involved in the process. At each step, they asked the workers to stop what they were doing and immediately process their loan application. They were shocked by what they found. From start to finish, the entire process took just 90 minutes! The six-day turnaround time was almost entirely due to delays in handing off the work from one department to another. The solution: IBM redesigned the process so that one person, not five people in five separate departments, now handles the entire loan approval process without any handoffs. Approval time dropped from six days to four hours and allowed IBM Credit to increase the number of loans it handled by a factor of 100!

Reengineering changes an organization's orientation from vertical to horizontal. Instead of "taking orders" from upper management, lower- and middle-level managers and workers "take orders" from a customer who is at the beginning and end of each process. Instead of running independent functional departments, managers and workers in different departments take ownership of cross-functional processes. Instead of simplifying work so that it becomes increasingly specialized, reengineering complicates work by giving workers increased autonomy and responsibility for complete processes.

In essence, reengineering changes work by changing **task interdependence,** the extent to which collective action is required to complete an entire piece of work. There are three kinds of task

interdependence.[27] In **pooled interdependence,** each job or department independently contributes to the whole. In **sequential interdependence,** work must be performed in succession, as one group's or job's outputs become the inputs for the next group or job. Finally, in **reciprocal interdependence,** different jobs or groups work together in a back-and-forth manner to complete the process. By reducing the handoffs between different jobs or groups, reengineering decreases sequential interdependence. Likewise, reengineering decreases pooled interdependence by redesigning work so that formerly independent jobs or departments now work together to complete processes. Finally, reengineering increases reciprocal interdependence by making groups or individuals responsible for larger, more complete processes in which several steps may be accomplished at the same time.

As an organizational design tool, reengineering promises big rewards, but it has also come under severe criticism. The most serious complaint is that because it allows a few workers to do the work formerly done by many, reengineering is simply a corporate code word for cost cutting and worker layoffs.[28] Likewise, for that reason, detractors claim that reengineering hurts morale and performance. Today, even reengineering gurus Hammer and Champy admit that roughly 70 percent of all reengineering projects fail because of the effects on people in the workplace. Says Hammer, "I wasn't smart enough about that [the people issues]. I was reflecting my engineering background and was insufficiently appreciative of the human dimension. I've [now] learned that's critical."[29]

4.2 Empowerment

Another way of redesigning intraorganizational processes is

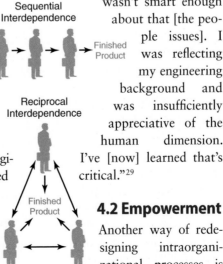

Reengineering and Task Interdependence

Pooled Interdependence

Finished Product

Sequential Interdependence

Finished Product

Reciprocal Interdependence

Finished Product

Task interdependence
the extent to which collective action is required to complete an entire piece of work

Pooled interdependence work completed by having each job or department independently contribute to the whole

Sequential interdependence work completed in succession, with one group's or job's outputs becoming the inputs for the next group or job

Reciprocal interdependence work completed by different jobs or groups working together in a back-and-forth manner through empowerment. **Empowering workers** means permanently passing decision-making authority and responsibility from managers to workers. For workers to be fully empowered, companies must give them the information and resources they need to make and carry out good decisions, and then reward them for taking individual initiative.[30] Unfortunately, this doesn't happen often enough. As Michael Schrage, author and MIT researcher, wrote:

> A warehouse employee can see on the intranet that a shipment is late but has no authority to accelerate its delivery. A project manager knows—and can mathematically demonstrate—that a seemingly minor spec change will bust both her budget and her schedule. The spec must be changed anyway. An airline reservations agent tells the Executive Platinum Premier frequent flier that first class appears wide open for an upgrade. However, the airline's yield management software won't permit any upgrades until just four hours before the flight, frequent fliers (and reservations) be damned. In all these cases, the employee has access to valuable information. Each one possesses the "knowledge" to do the job better. But the knowledge and information are irrelevant and useless. Knowledge isn't power; the ability to act on knowledge is power.[31]

When workers are given the proper information and resources and are allowed to make good decisions, they experience strong feelings of empowerment. **Empowerment** is a feeling of intrinsic motivation, in which workers perceive their work to have meaning and perceive themselves to be competent, having an impact, and capable of self-determination.[32] Work has meaning when it is consistent with personal standards and beliefs. Workers feel com-

Selling Shoes No Mean Feat

What sets Zappos.com apart from other online shoe sellers isn't its mind-numbing inventory or $184 million in annual sales. It's that Zappos employees are completely empowered to solve customer problems. If customers can't find the shoes they want, Zappos agents are encouraged to recommend another store. The company has a wiki to which employees can post complaints and propose solutions. And the company's training manual is a 156-page handbook on Zappos culture—written entirely by the employees themselves. According to chairman and founder Nick Swinmurn, empowerment isn't just about solving customer problems, however. It's about giving employees the power to make the company better. One of the entries in the handbook, written by an associate, reads, "I'm helping write the book. We all are."

Sources: J. Vilaga, "Employee Innovator Runner-up: Zappos", *Fast Company*, October 2005, 58; C. Thomson, "The See-Through CEO," *Wired*, March 2007, http://www.wired.com/wired/archive/15.04/wired40_ceo.html.

Empowering workers permanently passing decision-making authority and responsibility from managers to workers by giving them the information and resources they need to make and carry out good decisions

Empowerment feelings of intrinsic motivation, in which workers perceive their work to have impact and meaning and perceive themselves to be competent and capable of self-determination

Interorganizational process a collection of activities that take place among companies to transform inputs into outputs that customers value

Modular organization an organization that outsources noncore business activities to outside companies, suppliers, specialists, or consultants

---

petent when they believe they can perform an activity with skill. The belief that they are having an impact comes from a feeling that they can affect work outcomes. A feeling of self-determination arises from workers' belief that they have the autonomy to choose how best to do their work.

Empowerment can lead to changes in organizational processes because meaning, competence, impact, and self-determination produce empowered employees who take active, rather than passive, roles in their work.

5 Interorganizational Processes

An **interorganizational process** is a collection of activities that occur *among companies* to transform inputs into outputs that customers value. In other words, many companies work together to create a product or service that keeps customers happy. For example, when you purchase a Liz Claiborne outfit, you're not just buying from Liz Claiborne; you're also buying from a network of 250 suppliers in 35 countries and a sourcing team in Hong Kong that produces the right fabrics and the entire line of clothing. Those companies then manufacture the first product prototypes and send them back to the New York designers for final inspection and possibly last-minute changes.[33]

*In this section, you'll explore interorganizational processes by learning about **5.1 modular organizations** and **5.2 virtual organizations.**[34]*

5.1 Modular Organizations

Except for the core business activities that they can perform better, faster, and cheaper than others, **modular or-**

ganizations outsource all remaining business activities to outside companies, suppliers, specialists, or consultants. The term *modular* is used because the business activities purchased from outside companies can be added and dropped as needed, much like adding pieces to a three-dimensional puzzle. Exhibit 9.10 depicts a modular organization in which the company has chosen to keep training, human resources, sales, product design, manufacturing, customer service, research and development, and information technology as core business activities, but it has outsourced the noncore activities of product distribution, Web page design, advertising, payroll, accounting, and packaging.

Modular organizations have several advantages. First, because modular organizations pay for outsourced labor, expertise, or manufacturing capabilities only when needed, they can cost significantly less to run than traditional organizations. For example, when Apple came up with its iPod digital music player, it outsourced the audio chip design and manufacture to SigmaTel in Austin, Texas, and final assembly to Asutek Computers in Taiwan. Doing so not only reduced costs and sped up production (beating Sony's Network Walkman to market), but also allowed Apple to do what it does best—design innovative products with easy-to-use software.[35] To obtain these advantages, however, modular organizations need reliable partners—vendors and suppliers that they can work closely with and can trust.

Exhibit 9.10
Modular Organization

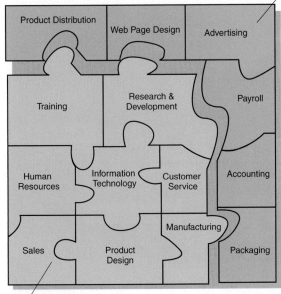

Outsourced Noncore Business Activities

Core Business Activities

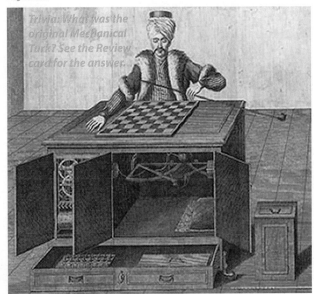

Trivia: What was the original Mechanical Turk? See the Review card for the answer.

mgmt trend

Modular organizations have disadvantages, too. The primary disadvantage is the loss of control that occurs when key business activities are outsourced to other companies. Also, companies may reduce their competitive advantage in two ways if they mistakenly outsource a core business activity. First, as a result of competitive and technological change, the noncore business activities a company has outsourced may suddenly become the basis for competitive advantage. Second, related to that point, suppliers to whom work is outsourced can sometimes become competitors.

5.2 Virtual Organizations

In contrast to modular organizations in which the interorganizational process revolves around a central company, a **virtual organization** is part of a network in which many companies share skills, costs, capabilities, markets, and customers with each other. Exhibit 9.11 shows a virtual organization in which, for "today," the parts of a virtual company consist of product design, purchasing, manufacturing, advertising, and information technology. Unlike modular organizations, in which the outside organizations are tightly linked to one central company, virtual organizations work with some companies in the network alliance, but not with all. So, whereas a puzzle with various pieces is a fitting metaphor for a modular organization, a potluck dinner is an appropriate metaphor for a virtual organization. All participants bring their finest food dish, but eat only what they want.

Another difference is that the working relationships between modular organizations and outside companies tend to be more stable and longer lasting than the shorter, often temporary relationships found among the virtual companies in a network alliance. The composition of a virtual organization is always changing. The combination of network partners that a virtual corporation has at any one time depends on the expertise needed to solve a particular problem or provide a specific product or service. This is why the businessperson in the network organization shown in the photo is saying, "Today, I'll have . . . ." Tomorrow, the business could want something completely different. In this sense, the term *virtual organization* means the organization that exists "at the moment." For example, 19 small companies in Pennsylvania have formed a network of virtual organizations that they call the Agile Web.[36] Together, the companies have ex-

pertise in product development and design, machining, metal fabrication, diecasting, plastic-injection molding, finishing and coating, and the design and manufacture of electronic components. Tony Nickel, who coordinates business opportunities for the 19 Agile Web members, says, "We do have multiple machine shops and multiple sheet-metal shops. If only one is needed, I make the decision based on the nature of the [customer's] request and the areas of specialization of the member firms." He adds, "We've already had one occasion where, while negotiating with a customer, we discovered that we really didn't have the right Web member for a particular part—so we changed members."[37]

Virtual organizations have a number of advantages. They let companies share costs. And, because members can quickly combine their efforts to meet customers' needs, they are fast and flexible.

As with modular organizations, a disadvantage of virtual organizations is that once work has been outsourced, it can be difficult to control the quality of work done by network partners. The greatest disadvantage, however, is that tremendous managerial skills are required to make a network of independent organizations work well together, especially since their relationships tend to be short and based on a single task or project.

Virtual organization
an organization that is part of a network in which many companies share skills, costs, capabilities, markets, and customers to collectively solve customer problems or provide specific products or services

Exhibit 9.11

Virtual Organizations

Today, I'll have...

Purchasing

Product Design

Information Technology

Manufacturing

Advertising

©Riser/Getty Images

Virtual organizations are using two methods to solve this problem. The first is to use a *broker,* like Tony Nickel. In traditional, hierarchical organizations, managers plan, organize, and control. But with the horizontal, interorganizational processes that characterize virtual organizations, the job of a broker is to create and assemble the knowledge, skills, and resources from different companies for outside parties, such as customers.[38] The second way to make networks of virtual organizations more manageable is to use a *virtual organization agreement* that, somewhat like a contract, specifies the schedules, responsibilities, costs, payouts, and liabilities for participating organizations.[39] The Agile Web has operationalized its virtual organization agreement on a day-to-day basis through Web-based software that is used by all 19 companies to schedule work, share design specifications, and provide anything else they need to complete their work for particular customers.[40]

By the Numbers

2 fewest number of bosses each employee has in a matrix system

98,000 number of employees at P&G

100+% annual employee turnover at fast-food restaurants

5 traditional departmental structures; redesign techniques for strengthening a job's core characteristics

3 types of task interdependence

MANAGING TEAMS

Why Work Teams?

A growing number of organizations are significantly improving their effectiveness by establishing work teams. In fact, 91 percent of U.S. companies use teams and groups of one kind or another to solve specific problems.[1] Nonetheless, with the exception of early adopters such as Procter & Gamble and Cummins Engine, which began using teams in 1962 and 1973, respectively, many companies did not establish work teams until the mid to late 1980s. Boeing, Caterpillar, Champion International, Ford Motor Company, and General Electric, for example, set up their first teams in the 1980s.[2] So, most companies have been using teams for only 20 to 25 years, if that long. In other words, teams are a relatively new phenomenon in companies, and there's still much for organizations to learn about managing them.

Work teams consist of a small number of people with complementary skills who hold themselves mutually accountable for pursuing a common purpose, achieving performance goals, and improving interdependent work processes.[3] Though work teams are not the answer for every situation or organization, if the right teams are used properly and in the right settings, teams can dramatically improve company performance over more traditional management approaches and instill a sense of vitality in the workplace that is otherwise difficult to achieve.

Learning Outcomes

1 explain the good and bad of using teams.

2 recognize and understand the different kinds of teams.

3 understand the general characteristics of work teams.

4 explain how to enhance work team effectiveness.

Work team a small number of people with complementary skills who hold themselves mutually accountable for pursuing a common purpose, achieving performance goals, and improving interdependent work processes

©Creatas/Jupiter Images

After reading the next two sections, you should be able to

1 explain the good and bad of using teams.

2 recognize and understand the different kinds of teams.

1 The Good and Bad of Using Teams

*Let's begin our discussion of teams by learning about **1.1 the advantages of teams, 1.2 the disadvantages of teams,** and **1.3 when to use and not use teams.***

1.1 The Advantages of Teams

Companies are making greater use of teams because teams have been shown to improve customer satisfaction, product and service quality, employee job satisfaction, and decision making.[4]

Teams help businesses increase *customer satisfaction* in several ways. One way is to create work teams that are trained to meet the needs of specific customers. Hewitt Associates, a consulting firm, manages benefits administration for hundreds of multinational client firms. To ensure customer satisfaction, Hewitt reengineered its customer service center and created specific teams to handle benefits-related questions posed by employees

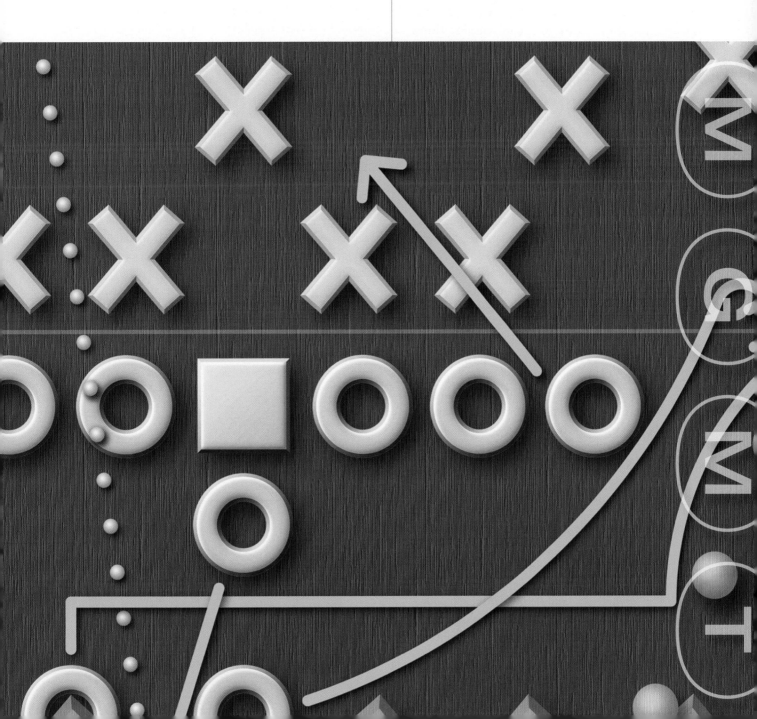

of specific client organizations.[5] Businesses also create problem-solving teams and employee involvement teams to study ways to improve overall customer satisfaction and make recommendations for improvements. Teams like these typically meet on a weekly or monthly basis.

Teams also help firms improve *product and service quality* in several ways.[6] In contrast to traditional organizational structures where management is responsible for organizational outcomes and performance, teams take direct responsibility for the quality of the products and service they produce. At Whole Foods, a supermarket chain that sells groceries and health foods, the 10 teams that manage each store are responsible for store quality and performance; they are also directly accountable because the size of their team bonus depends on the store's performance. Productive teams get an extra $1.50 to $2.00 per hour in every other paycheck.[7]

Another reason for using teams is that teamwork often leads to increased *job satisfaction*.[8] One reason that teamwork can be more satisfying than traditional work is that it gives workers a chance to improve their skills. This is often accomplished through **cross-training,** in which team members are taught how to do all or most of the jobs performed by the other team members. The advantage for the organization is that cross-training allows a team to function normally when one member is absent, quits, or is transferred. The advantage for workers is that cross-training broadens their skills and increases their capabilities while also making their work more varied and interesting. A second reason that teamwork is satisfying is that work teams often receive proprietary business information that is available only to managers at most companies. For example, at Whole Foods, the supermarket chain that sells groceries and health foods, team members are given full access to their store's financial information and everyone's salaries, including

Cross-training training team members to do all or most of the jobs performed by the other team members

those of the store manager and the CEO.[9] Team members also gain job satisfaction from unique leadership responsibilities that typically are not available in traditional organizations. For example, rotating leadership among team members can lead to more participation and cooperation in team decision making and improved team performance.[10]

Finally, teams share many of the advantages of group decision making discussed in Chapter 5. For instance, because team members possess different knowledge, skills, abilities, and experiences, a team is able to view problems from multiple perspectives. This diversity of viewpoints increases the odds that team decisions will solve the underlying causes of problems and not just address the symptoms. The increased knowledge and information available to teams also make it easier for them to generate more alternative solutions, which is a critical part of improving the quality of decisions. Because team members are involved in decision-making processes, they are also likely to be more committed to making those decisions work. In short, teams can do a much better job than individuals in two important steps of the decision-making process: defining the problem and generating alternative solutions.

1.2 The Disadvantages of Teams

Although teams can significantly improve customer satisfaction, product and service quality, speed and efficiency in product development, employee job satisfaction, and decision making, using teams does not guarantee these positive outcomes. In fact, if you've ever participated in team projects in your classes, you're probably

> Although teams can **significantly improve** customer satisfaction, using teams does **not guarantee** positive outcomes.

already aware of some of the problems inherent in work teams. Despite all of their promise, teams and teamwork are also prone to these significant disadvantages: initially high turnover, social loafing, and the problems associated with group decision making.

The first disadvantage of work teams is *initially high turnover*. Teams aren't for everyone, and some workers balk at the responsibility, effort, and learning required in team settings.

Social loafing is another disadvantage of work teams. **Social loafing** occurs when workers withhold their efforts and fail to perform their share of the work.[11] A 19th-century French engineer named Maximilian Ringlemann first documented social loafing when he found that one person pulling on a rope alone exerted an average of 63 kilograms of force on the rope. In groups of three, the average force dropped to 53 kilograms per person. In groups of eight, the average dropped to just 31 kilograms per person. Ringlemann concluded that the larger the team, the smaller the individual effort. In fact, social loafing is more likely to occur in larger groups, where identifying and monitoring the efforts of individual team members can be difficult.[12] In other words, social loafers count on being able to blend into the background, where their lack of effort isn't easily spotted. From team-based class projects, most students already know about social loafers or "slackers," who contribute poor, little, or no work whatsoever. Not surprisingly, a study of 250 stu-

dent teams found that the most talented students are typically the least satisfied with teamwork because of having to carry "slackers" and do a disproportionate share of their team's work. Perceptions of fairness are negatively related to the extent of social loafing within teams.[13]

FACTORS THAT ENCOURAGE PEOPLE TO WITHHOLD EFFORT IN TEAMS

1. **The presence of someone with expertise.** Team members will withhold effort when another team member is highly qualified to make a decision or comment on an issue.

2. **The presentation of a compelling argument.** Team members will withhold effort if the arguments for a course of action are very persuasive or similar to their own thinking.

3. **Lacking confidence in one's ability to contribute.** Team members will withhold effort if they are unsure about their ability to contribute to discussions, activities, or decisions. This is especially so for high-profile decisions.

4. **An unimportant or meaningless decision.** Team members will withhold effort by mentally withdrawing or adopting a "who cares" attitude if decisions don't affect them or their units, or if they don't see a connection between their efforts and their team's successes or failures.

5. **A dysfunctional decision-making climate.** Team members will withhold effort if other team members are frustrated or indifferent or if a team is floundering or disorganized.

Source: P. W. Mulvey, J. F. Veiga, & P. M. Elsass, "When Teammates Raise a White Flag," *Academy of Management Executive* 10, no. 1 (1996): 40–49.

Finally, teams share many of the *disadvantages of group decision making* discussed in Chapter 5, such as groupthink. In *groupthink*, members of highly cohesive groups feel intense pressure not to disagree with each other so that the group can approve a proposed solution. Because groupthink restricts discussion and leads to consideration of a limited number of alternative solutions, it usually results in poor decisions. Also, team decision making takes considerable time, and team meetings can often be unproductive and inefficient. Another possible pitfall is *minority domination*, where just one or two people dominate team discussions, thus restricting consideration of

Social loafing behavior in which team members withhold their efforts and fail to perform their share of the work

Exhibit 10.1

When to Use or Not Use Teams

USE TEAMS WHEN . . .	DON'T USE TEAMS WHEN . . .
✓ there is a clear, engaging reason or purpose.	✗ there isn't a clear, engaging reason or purpose.
✓ the job can't be done unless people work together.	✗ the job can be done by people working independently.
✓ rewards can be provided for teamwork and team performance.	✗ rewards are provided for individual effort and performance.
✓ ample resources are available.	✗ the necessary resources are not available.

Source: R. Wageman, "Critical Success Factors for Creating Superb Self-Managing Teams," *Organizational Dynamics* 26, no. 1 (1997): 49–61.

different problem definitions and alternative solutions. Finally, team members may not feel accountable for the decisions and actions taken by the "team."

1.3 When to Use Teams

As the two previous subsections made clear, teams have significant advantages *and* disadvantages. Therefore, the question is not *whether* to use teams, but *when* and *where* to use teams for maximum benefit and minimum cost. As Doug Johnson, associate director at the Center for the Study of Work Teams, puts it, "Teams are a means to an end, not an end in themselves."[14] Exhibit 10.1 provides some additional guidelines on when to use or not use teams.[15]

First, teams should be used when there is a clear, engaging reason or purpose for using them. Too many companies use teams because they're popular or because the companies assume that teams can fix all problems. Teams are much more likely to succeed if they know why they exist and what they are supposed to accomplish, and more likely to fail if they don't.

Second, teams should be used when the job can't be done unless people work together. This typically means that teams are needed when tasks are complex, require multiple perspectives, or require repeated interaction with others to complete. If tasks are simple and don't require multiple perspectives or repeated interaction with others, however, teams should not be used.[16] For instance, production levels dropped by 23 percent when Levi Strauss introduced teams in its factories. Levi Strauss's mistake was assuming that teams were appropriate for garment work, where workers perform single, specialized tasks, like sewing

zippers or belt loops. Because this kind of work does not require interaction with others, Levi Strauss unwittingly pitted the faster workers against the slower workers on each team. Arguments, infighting, insults, and threats were common between faster workers and the slower workers who held back team performance. One seamstress even had to physically restrain an angry coworker who was about to throw a chair at a faster worker who constantly nagged her about her slow pace.[17]

Third, teams should be used when rewards can be provided for teamwork and team performance. Team rewards that depend on team performance, rather than individual performance, are the key to rewarding team behaviors and efforts. You'll read more about team rewards later in the chapter, but for now it's enough to know that if the level of rewards (individual versus team) is not matched to the level of performance (individual versus team), groups won't work.

2 Kinds of Teams

Let's continue our discussion of teams by learning about the different kinds of teams that companies use to make themselves more competitive. We look first at *2.1 how*

If the work doesn't require interaction with others, don't use a team, or your employees are liable to come unzipped.

teams differ in terms of autonomy, which is the key dimension that makes one team different from another, and then at **2.2 some special kinds of teams.**

2.1 Autonomy, the Key Dimension

Teams can be classified in a number of ways, such as permanent or temporary, or functional or cross-functional. However, studies indicate that the key dimension that makes teams different from each another the amount of autonomy possessed by a team.[18] *Autonomy* is the degree to which workers have the discretion, freedom, and independence to decide how and when to accomplish their jobs.

Exhibit 10.2 shows how five kinds of teams differ in terms of autonomy. Moving left to right across the autonomy continuum at the top of the exhibit, tradi-

tional work groups and employee involvement groups have the least autonomy, semi-autonomous work groups have more autonomy, and, finally, self-managing teams and self-designing teams have the most autonomy. Moving from bottom to top along the left side of the exhibit, note that the number of responsibilities given to each kind of team increases directly with its autonomy. Let's review each of these kinds of teams and their autonomy and responsibilities in more detail.

The smallest amount of autonomy is found in **traditional work groups,** where two or more people work together to achieve a shared goal. In these groups, workers are responsible for doing

> **Traditional work group** a group composed of two or more people who work together to achieve a shared goal

Exhibit 10.2

Team Autonomy Continuum

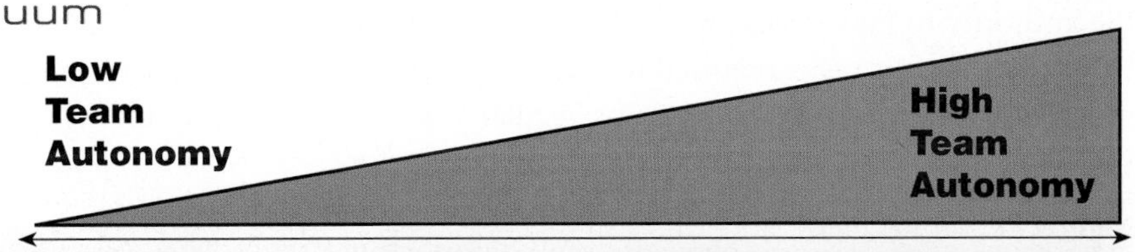

Low Team Autonomy → **High Team Autonomy**

RESPONSIBILITIES	TRADITIONAL WORK GROUPS	EMPLOYEE INVOLVEMENT GROUPS	SEMI-AUTONOMOUS WORK GROUPS	SELF-MANAGING TEAMS	SELF-DESIGNING TEAMS
Control Design of					
Team					✓
Tasks					✓
Membership					✓
Production/Service Tasks					
Make Decisions				✓	✓
Solve Problems				✓	✓
Major Production/Service Tasks					
Make Decisions			✓	✓	✓
Solve Problems			✓	✓	✓
Information			✓	✓	✓
Give Advice/Make Suggestions		✓	✓	✓	✓
Execute Task	✓	✓	✓	✓	✓

Sources: R. D. Banker, J. M. Field, R. G. Schroeder, & K. K. Sinha, "Impact of Work Teams on Manufacturing Performance: A Longitudinal Field Study," *Academy of Management Journal* 39 (1996): 867-890; J. R. Hackman, "The Psychology of Self-Management in Organizations," in *Psychology and Work: Productivity, Change, and Employment,* ed. M. S. Pallak & R. Perlof (Washington, DC: American Psychological Association), 85–136.

the work or "executing the task," but they do not have direct responsibility or control over their work. Workers report to managers, who are responsible for their performance and have the authority to hire and fire them, make job assignments, and control resources.

Employee involvement teams, which have somewhat more autonomy, meet on company time on a weekly or monthly basis to provide advice or make suggestions to management concerning specific issues, such as plant safety, customer relations, or product quality.[19] Though they offer advice and suggestions, they do not have the authority to make decisions. Membership on these teams is often voluntary, but members may be selected because of their expertise. The idea behind employee involvement teams is that the people closest to the problem or situation are best able to recommend solutions.

Semi-autonomous work groups not only provide advice and suggestions to management, but also have the authority to make decisions and solve problems related to the major tasks required to produce a product or service. Semi-autonomous groups regularly receive information about budgets, work quality and performance, and competitors' products. Furthermore, members of semi-autonomous work groups are typically cross-trained in a number of different skills and tasks. In short, semi-autonomous work groups give employees the authority to make decisions that are typically made by supervisors and managers.

That authority is not complete, however. Managers still play a role, though much reduced compared to traditional work groups, in supporting the work of semi-autonomous work groups. In semi-autonomous work groups, managers ask good questions, provide resources, and facilitate performance of group goals.

Self-managing teams differ from semi-autonomous work groups in that team members manage and control *all* of the major tasks

directly related to production of a product or service without first getting approval from management. This includes managing and controlling the acquisition of materials, making a product or providing a service, and ensuring timely delivery. At a Crown Cork aluminum can factory in Texas, "The teams make and implement decisions regarding production, product quality, training, attendance, safety, maintenance, and certain types of discipline. The teams can stop production lines without management approval, stop delivery of cans that do not meet quality standards, decide which workers should receive training, decide whether to grant leave requests, and investigate and correct safety problems."[20] Seventy-two percent for *Fortune* 1,000 companies have at least one self-managing team, up from 28 percent in 1987.[21]

Self-designing teams have all the characteristics of self-managing teams, but they can also control and change the design of the teams themselves, the tasks they do and how and when they do them, and the membership of the teams.

Two engineers assembled a team of 20 for the "thin calm" project at Motorola. Money and resources were no object, but secrecy and speed were. The team had complete control over all aspects of the project, and it delivered the Motorola RAZR. Since RAZR's launch in late 2004, it has sold almost as many units as Apple's iPod.[22]

©Courtesy, Motorola

2.2 Special Kinds of Teams

Companies are also increasingly using several other kinds of teams that can't easily be categorized in terms of autonomy: cross-functional teams, virtual teams, and project teams. Depending on how these teams are designed, they can be either low- or high-autonomy teams.

Cross-functional teams are intentionally composed of employees from different functional areas of the organization.[23] Because their members have different functional backgrounds, education, and experience, cross-functional teams usually attack problems from multiple perspectives and generate more ideas and alternative solutions, all of which are especially important when trying to innovate

---

Employee involvement team team that provides advice or makes suggestions to management concerning specific issues

Semi-autonomous work group a group that has the authority to make decisions and solve problems related to the major tasks of producing a product or service

Self-managing team a team that manages and controls all of the major tasks of producing a product or service

Self-designing team a team that has the characteristics of self-managing teams but also controls team design, work tasks, and team membership

Cross-functional team a team composed of employees from different functional areas of the organization or do creative problem solving.[24] Cross-functional teams can be used almost anywhere in an organization and are often used in conjunction with matrix and product organizational structures (see Chapter 9). They can also be used either with part-time or temporary team assignments or with full-time, long-term teams.

Cessna, which manufactures airplanes, created cross-functional teams for purchasing parts. With workers from purchasing, manufacturing engineering, quality engineering, product design engineering, reliability engineering, product support, and finance, each team addressed make-versus-buy decisions (make it themselves or buy from others), sourcing (who to buy from), internal plant and quality improvements, and the external training of suppliers to reduce costs and increase quality.[25]

Virtual teams are groups of geographically and/ or organizationally dispersed coworkers who use a combination of telecommunications and information technologies to accomplish an organizational task.[26] Members of virtual teams rarely meet face-to-face; instead, they use email, videoconferencing, and group communication software. For example, pLotDev Multimedia Developers is a Web site development company of 12 people that does work for Sean Jean, P. Diddy's clothing label, among others. Yet the people in the company have never met. As Max Oshman, who started the company, describes it, "Some of them live in the U.K., two in Croatia, two in Sweden and the rest are scattered around in southern California, New York, Texas, and Amsterdam."[27] Virtual teams can be employee involvement teams, self-managing teams, or nearly any kind of team discussed in this chapter. Virtual teams are often (but not necessarily) temporary teams that are set up to accomplish a specific task.[28]

The principal advantage of virtual teams is their flexibility. Employees can work with each other regardless of physical location, time zone, or organizational affiliation.[29] Because the team members don't meet in a physical location, virtual teams also find it much easier to include other key stakeholders, such as suppliers and customers. Plus, virtual teams have certain efficiency advantages over traditional team structures. Because the teammates do not meet face-to-face, a virtual team typically requires a smaller time commitment than a traditional team does.[30] A drawback of virtual teams is that the team members must learn to express themselves in new contexts.[31] The give-and-take that naturally occurs in face-to-face meetings is more difficult to achieve through video conferencing or other methods of

virtual teaming. Indeed, several studies have shown that physical proximity enhances information processing in teams.[32] Therefore, some companies bring virtual team members together in offices or special trips on a regular basis to try to minimize these problems.

Tips for Managing Successful Virtual Teams

- Select people who are self-starters and strong communicators.
- Keep the team focused by establishing clear, specific goals and by explaining the consequences and importance of meeting these goals.
- Provide frequent feedback so that team members can measure their progress.
- Keep team interactions upbeat and action-oriented by expressing appreciation for good work and completed tasks.
- "Personalize" the virtual team by periodically bringing team members together and by encouraging team members to share information with each other about their personal lives. This is especially important when the virtual team first forms.
- Improve communication through increased telephone calls, emails, and Internet messaging and videoconference sessions.
- Periodically ask team members how well the team is working and what can be done to improve performance.
- Empower virtual teams so they have the discretion, freedom, and independence to decide how and when to accomplish their jobs.

Sources: W. F. Cascio, "Managing a Virtual Workplace," *Academy of Management Executive* 14 (2000): 81–90; B. Kirkman, B. Rosen, P. Tesluk, & C. Gibson, "The Impact of Team Empowerment on Virtual Team Performance: The Moderating Role of Face-to-Face Interaction," *Academy of Management Journal* 47 (2004): 175–192; S. Furst, M. Reeves, B. Rosen, & R. Blackburn, "Managing the Life Cycle of Virtual Teams," *Academy of Management Executive* (May 2004): 6–20; C. Solomon, "Managing Virtual Teams," *Workforce* 80 (June 2001), 60.

Project teams are created to complete specific, one-time projects or tasks within a limited time.[33] Project teams are often used to develop new products, significantly improve existing products, roll out new information systems, or build new factories or offices. The project team is typically led

Virtual team a team composed of geographically and/or organizationally dispersed coworkers who use telecommunication and information technologies to accomplish an organizational task

Project team a team created to complete specific, one-time projects or tasks within a limited time by a project manager, who has the overall responsibility for planning, staffing, and managing the team, which usually includes employees from different functional areas. Effective project teams demand both individual and collective responsibility.[34] One advantage of project teams is that drawing employees from different functional areas can reduce or eliminate communication barriers. In turn, as long as team members feel free to express their ideas, thoughts, and concerns, free-flowing communication encourages cooperation among separate departments and typically speeds up the design process.[35] Another advantage of project teams is their flexibility. When projects are finished, project team members either move on to the next project or return to their functional units. For example, publication of this book required designers, editors, page compositors, and Web designers, among others. When the task was finished, these people applied their skills to other textbook projects. Because of this flexibility, project teams are often used with the matrix organizational designs discussed in Chapter 9.

Managing Work Teams

 "Why did I ever let you talk me into teams? They're nothing but trouble."[36] Lots of managers have this reaction after making the move to teams. Many don't realize that this reaction is normal, both for them and for workers. In fact, such a reaction is characteristic of the *storming* stage of team development (discussed in Section 3.5). Managers who are familiar with these stages and with the other important characteristics of teams will be better prepared to manage the predictable changes that occur when companies make the switch to team-based structures.

Norms informally agreed-on standards that regulate team behavior

Cohesiveness the extent to which team members are attracted to a team and motivated to remain in it

After reading the next two sections, you should be able to

3 understand the general characteristics of work teams.

4 explain how to enhance work team effectiveness.

3 Work Team Characteristics

Understanding the characteristics of work teams is essential for making teams an effective part of an organization. Therefore, in this section you'll learn about *3.1 team norms, 3.2 team cohesiveness, 3.3 team size, 3.4 team conflict,* and *3.5 the stages of team development.*

3.1 Team Norms

Over time, teams develop **norms,** informally agreed-on standards that regulate team behavior.[37] Norms are valuable because they let team members know what is expected of them. At Nucor Steel, work groups expect their members to get to work on time. To reinforce this norm, anyone who is late to work will not receive the team bonus for that day (assuming the team is productive). A worker who is more than 30 minutes late will not receive the team bonus for the entire week. At Nucor losing a bonus matters because work group bonuses can easily double the size of a worker's take-home pay.[38]

Studies indicate that norms are one of the most powerful influences on work behavior. Team norms are often associated with positive outcomes, such as stronger organizational commitment, more trust in management, and stronger job and organizational satisfaction.[39] In general, effective work teams develop norms about the quality and timeliness of job performance, absenteeism, safety, and honest expression of ideas and opinions. The power of norms also comes from the fact that they regulate the everyday behaviors that allow teams to function effectively.

Norms can also influence team behavior in negative ways. For example, most people would agree that damaging organizational property; saying or doing something to hurt someone at work; intentionally doing one's work badly, incorrectly, or slowly; griping about coworkers; deliberately bending or breaking rules; or doing something to harm the company or boss are negative behaviors. Nonetheless, a study of workers from 34 teams in 20 different organizations found that teams with negative norms strongly influenced their team members to engage in these negative behaviors. In fact, the longer individuals were members of a team with negative norms and the more frequently they interacted with their teammates, the more likely they were to perform negative behaviors. Since team norms typically develop early in the life of a team, these results indicate how important it is for teams to establish positive norms from the outset.[40]

3.2 Team Cohesiveness

Cohesiveness is another important characteristic of work teams. **Cohesiveness** is the extent to which team members are attracted to a team and motivated to remain in it.[41] The level of cohesiveness in a group is important for several reasons. To start, cohesive groups have a better chance of retaining their members. As a result, cohesive groups typically experience lower turnover.[42] In addition, team cohesiveness promotes cooperative behavior, generosity, and a willingness on the part of team members to assist each other.[43] When team cohesiveness is high, team members are more motivated to contribute to the team because they want to gain the approval of other team members. For these reasons and others, studies have clearly established that cohesive teams consistently perform better.[44] Furthermore, cohesive teams quickly achieve high levels of performance. By contrast, teams low in cohesion take much longer to reach the same levels of performance.[45]

What can be done to promote team cohesiveness? First, make sure that all team members are present at team meetings and activities. Team cohesiveness suffers when members are allowed to withdraw from the team and miss team meetings and events.[46] Second, create additional opportunities for teammates to work together by rearranging work schedules and creating common workspaces. When task interdependence is high and team members have lots of chances to work together, team cohesiveness tends to increase.[47] Third, engaging in nonwork activities as a team can help build cohesion. At a company where teams put in extraordinarily long hours coding computer software, the software teams maintained cohesion by doing "fun stuff" together. Team leader Tammy Urban says, "We went on team outings at least once a week. We'd play darts, shoot pool. Teams work best when you get to know each other outside of work—what people's interests are, who they are. Personal connections go a long way when you're developing complex applications in our kind of time frames."[48] Finally, companies build team cohesiveness by making

employees feel that they are part of a "special" organization. For example, all the new hires at Disney World in Orlando are required to take a course entitled "Traditions One," where they learn the traditions and history of the Walt Disney Company (including the names of the seven dwarfs!). The purpose of Traditions One is to instill a sense of team pride in working for Disney.

3.3 Team Size

There appears to be a curvilinear relationship between team size and performance. Very small or very large teams may not perform as well as moderately sized teams. For most teams, the right size is somewhere between six and nine members.[49] This size is conducive to high team cohesion, which has a positive effect on team performance, as discussed above. A team of this size is small enough for the team members to get to know each other and for each member to have an opportunity to contribute in a meaningful way to the success of the team. At the same time, the team is also large enough to take advantage of team members' diverse skills, knowledge, and perspectives. It is also easier to instill a sense of responsibility and mutual accountability in teams of this size.[50]

By contrast, when teams get too large, team members find it difficult to get to know one another, and the team may splinter into smaller subgroups. When this occurs, subgroups sometimes argue and disagree, weakening overall team cohesion. As teams grow, there is also a greater chance of *minority domination,* where just a few team members dominate team discussions. Even if minority domination doesn't occur, larger groups may not have time for all team members to share their input. And when team members feel that their contributions are unimportant or not needed, the result is

Teams work best when you get to know each other outside of work.

©Jupiter Images

High-Performance Team: Priceless

Most people are familiar with MasterCard's memorable "Priceless" ad campaigns. Each ad in the series features a list of ordinary transactions and the dollar amounts associated with those purchases. The final item in the series, however, is always pitched as "priceless." Those ads were created by a highly cohesive, yet very small, team. Joyce Thomas, one of the three-member team that conceived of and created those ads, says, "We were very comfortable working together, so we debated everything freely."

Source: E. Levenson, "The Power of an Idea," *Fortune*, 12 June 2006, 131.

less involvement, effort, and accountability to the team.[51] Large teams also face logistical problems, such as finding an appropriate time or place to meet. Finally, the incidence of social loafing, discussed earlier in the chapter, is much higher in large teams.

Just as team performance can suffer when a team is too large, it can also be negatively affected when a team is too small. Teams with just a few people may lack the diversity of skills and knowledge found in larger teams. Also, teams that are too small are unlikely to gain the advantages of team decision making (i.e., multiple perspectives, generating more ideas and alternative solutions, and stronger commitment) found in larger teams.

What signs indicate that a team's size needs to be changed? If decisions are taking too long, if the team has difficulty making decisions or taking action, if a few members dominate the team, or if the commitment or efforts of team members are weak, chances are the team is too big. In contrast, if a team is having difficulty coming up with ideas or generating solutions, or if the team does not have the expertise to address a specific problem, chances are the team is too small.

3.4 Team Conflict

Conflict and disagreement are inevitable in most teams. But this shouldn't surprise anyone. From time to time,

people who work together are going to disagree about what and how things get done. What causes conflict in teams? Although almost anything can lead to conflict—casual remarks that unintentionally offend a team member or fighting over scarce resources—the primary cause of team conflict is disagreement over team goals and priorities.[52] Other common causes of team conflict include disagreements over task-related issues, interpersonal incompatibilities, and simple fatigue.

Though most people view conflict negatively, the key to dealing with team conflict is not avoiding it, but rather making sure that the team experiences the right kind of conflict. In Chapter 5, you learned about *c-type conflict,* or *cognitive conflict,* which focuses on problem-related differences of opinion, and *a-type conflict,* or *affective conflict,* which refers to the emotional reactions that can occur when disagreements become personal rather than professional.[53] Cognitive conflict is strongly associated with improvements in team performance, whereas affective conflict is strongly associated with decreases in team performance.[54] Why does this happen? With cognitive conflict, team members disagree because their different experiences and expertise lead them to different views of the problem and solutions. Indeed, managers who participated on teams that emphasized cognitive conflict described their teammates as "smart," "team players," and "best in the business." They described their teams as "open," "fun," and "productive." One manager summed up the positive attitude that team members had about cognitive conflict by saying, "We scream a lot, then laugh, and then resolve the issue."[55] Thus, cognitive conflict is also characterized by a willingness to examine, compare, and reconcile differences to produce the best possible solution.

©InspireStock/Jupiter Images

By contrast, affective conflict often results in hostility, anger, resentment, distrust, cynicism, and apathy. Managers who participated on teams that emphasized affective conflict described their teammates as "manipulative," "secretive," "burned out," and "political."[56] Not surprisingly, affective conflict can make people uncomfortable and cause them to withdraw and decrease their commitment to a team.[57] Affective conflict also lowers the satisfaction of team members, may lead to personal hostility between coworkers, and can decrease team cohesiveness.[58] So, unlike cognitive conflict, affective conflict undermines team performance by preventing teams from engaging in the kinds of activities that are critical to team effectiveness.

So, what can managers do to manage team conflict? First, managers need to realize that emphasizing cognitive conflict alone won't be enough. Studies show that cognitive and affective conflicts often occur together in the same teams! Therefore, sincere attempts to reach agreement on a difficult issue can quickly deteriorate from cognitive to affective conflict if the discussion turns personal and tempers and emotions flare. So, while cognitive conflict is clearly the better approach to take, efforts to engage in cognitive conflict should be approached with caution.

Can teams disagree and still get along? Fortunately, they can. In an attempt to study this issue, researchers examined team conflict in 12 high-tech companies. In four of the companies, work teams used cognitive conflict to address work problems but did so in a way that minimized the occurrence of affective conflict.

There are several ways teams can have a "good fight."[59] First, work with more, rather than less, information. If data are plentiful, objective, and up-to-date, teams will focus on issues, not personalities. Second, develop mul-

tiple alternatives to enrich debate. Focusing on multiple solutions diffuses conflict by getting the team to keep searching for a better solution. Positions and opinions are naturally more flexible with five alternatives than with just two. Third, establish common goals. Remember, most team conflict arises from disagreements over team goals and priorities. Therefore, common goals encourage collaboration and minimize conflict over a team's purpose. Fourth, inject humor into the workplace. Humor relieves tension, builds cohesion, and just makes being in teams fun. Fifth, maintain a balance of power by involving as many people as possible in the decision process. And sixth, resolve issues without forcing a consensus. Consensus means that everyone must agree before decisions are finalized. Effectively, requiring consensus gives everyone on the team veto power. Nothing gets done until everyone agrees, which, of course, is nearly impossible. As a result, insisting on consensus usually promotes affective rather than cognitive conflict. If team members can't agree after constructively discussing their options, it's better to have the team leader make the final choice. Most team members can accept the team leader's choice if they've been thoroughly involved in the decision process.

Exhibit 10.3

Stages of Team Development

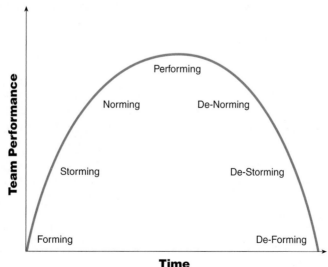

Sources: J. F. McGrew, J. G. Bilotta, & J. M. Deeney, "Software Team Formation and Decay: Extending the Standard Model for Small Groups," *Small Group Research* 30, no. 2 (1999): 209–234; B. W. Tuckman, "Development Sequence in Small Groups," *Psychological Bulletin* 63, no. 6 (1965): 384–399.

3.5 Stages of Team Development

As teams develop and grow, they pass through four stages of development. As shown in Exhibit 10.3, those stages are forming, storming, norming, and performing.[60] Although not every team passes through each of these stages, teams that do tend to be better performers.[61] This holds true even for teams composed of seasoned executives. After a period of time, however, if a team is not managed well, its performance may start to deteriorate as the team begins a process of decline and progresses through the stages of de-norming, de-storming, and de-forming.[62]

Forming is the initial stage of team development. This is the getting-acquainted stage, when team members first meet each other, form initial impressions, and try to get a sense of what it will be like to be part of the team. Some of the first team norms will be established during this stage, as team members begin to find out what behaviors will and won't be accepted by the team. During this stage, team leaders should allow time for team members to get to know each other, set early ground rules, and begin to set up a preliminary team structure.

Conflicts and disagreements often characterize the second stage of team development, **storming.** As team members begin working together, different personalities and work styles may clash. Team members become more assertive at this stage and more willing to state opinions. This is also the stage when team members jockey for position and try to establish a favorable role for themselves on the team. In addition, team members are likely to disagree about what the group should do and how it should do it. Team performance is still relatively low, given that team cohesion is weak and team members are still reluctant to support each other. Since teams that get stuck in the storming stage are almost always ineffective, it is important for team leaders to focus the team on team goals and on improving team performance. Team members need to be particularly patient and tolerant with each other in this stage.

During **norming,** the third stage of team development, team members begin to settle into their roles as team members. Positive team norms will have developed by this stage, and teammates should know what to expect from each other. Petty differences should have been resolved, friendships will have developed, and group cohesion will be relatively strong. At this point, team members will have accepted team goals, be operating as a unit, and, as indicated by the increase in performance, be working together effectively. This stage can be very short and is often characterized by someone on the team saying, "I think things are finally coming together." Note, however, that teams may also cycle back and forth between storming and norming several times before finally settling into norming.

In the last stage of team development, **performing,** performance improves because the team has finally matured into an effective, fully functioning team. At this point, members should be fully committed to the team and think of themselves as "members of a team" and not just "employees." Team members often become intensely loyal to one another at this stage and feel mutual accountability for team successes and failures. Trivial disagreements, which can take time and energy away from the work of the team, should be rare. At this stage, teams get a lot of work done, and it is fun to be a team member.

The team should not become complacent, however, because without effective management, its performance may begin to decline as the team passes through the stages of de-norming, de-storming, and de-forming.[63] Indeed, John Puckett, manufacturing vice president for circuit board manufacturer XEL Communications, says, "The books all say you start in this state of chaos and march through these various stages, and you end up in this state of ultimate self-direction, where everything is going just great. They never tell you it can go back in the other direction, sometimes just as quickly."[64]

4 Enhancing Work Team Effectiveness

Making teams work is a challenging and difficult process. Nonetheless, companies can increase the likelihood that

Forming the first stage of team development, in which team members meet each other, form initial impressions, and begin to establish team norms

Storming the second stage of development, characterized by conflict and disagreement, in which team members disagree over what the team should do and how it should do it

Norming the third stage of team development, in which team members begin to settle into their roles, group cohesion grows, and positive team norms develop

Performing the fourth and final stage of team development, in which performance improves because the team has matured into an effective, fully functioning team teams will succeed by carefully managing *4.1 the setting of team goals and priorities* and *4.2 how work team members are selected, 4.3 trained,* and *4.4 compensated.*[65]

4.1 Setting Team Goals and Priorities

In Chapter 5, you learned that having specific, measurable, attainable, realistic, and timely (i.e., S.M.A.R.T.) goals is one of the most effective means for improving individual job performance. Fortunately, team goals also improve team performance. In fact, team goals lead to much higher team performance 93 percent of the time.[66] For example, Nucor Steel sets specific, challenging *hourly* goals for each of its production teams, which consist of first-line supervisors and production and maintenance workers. The average in the steel industry is 10 tons of steel per hour. Nucor production teams have a goal of 8 tons per hour, but get a 5 percent bonus for *every* ton over 8 tons that they produce each hour. With no limit on the bonuses they can receive, Nucor's production teams produce an average of 35 to 40 tons of steel per hour![67]

Why is setting specific, challenging team goals so critical to team success? One reason is that increasing a team's performance is inherently more complex than just increasing one individual's job performance. For instance, consider that any team is likely to involve at least four different kinds of goals: each member's goal for the team, each member's goal for himself or herself on the team, the team's goal for each member, and the team's goal for itself.[68] In other words, without a specific, challenging goal for the team itself (the last of the four goals listed), team members may head off in all directions at once pursuing these other goals. Consequently, setting a specific, challenging goal *for the team* clarifies team priorities by providing a clear focus and purpose.

Specific, challenging team goals also affect how hard team members work. In particular, challenging team goals greatly reduce the incidence of social loafing. When faced with difficult goals, team members necessarily expect everyone to contribute. Consequently, they are much more likely to notice and complain if a teammate isn't doing his or her share. In fact, when teammates know each other well, when team goals are specific, when team communication is good, and when teams are rewarded for team performance (discussed below), there is only a 1 in 16 chance that teammates will be social loafers.[69]

What can companies and teams do to ensure that team goals lead to superior team performance? One increasingly popular approach is to give teams stretch goals. *Stretch goals* are extremely ambitious goals that workers don't know how to reach.[70] The purpose of stretch goals is to achieve extraordinary improvements in performance by forcing managers and workers to

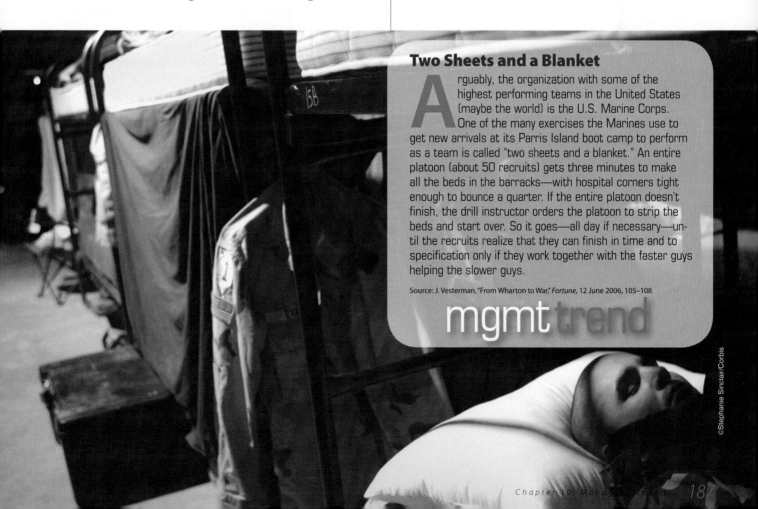

Two Sheets and a Blanket

Arguably, the organization with some of the highest performing teams in the United States (maybe the world) is the U.S. Marine Corps. One of the many exercises the Marines use to get new arrivals at its Parris Island boot camp to perform as a team is called "two sheets and a blanket." An entire platoon (about 50 recruits) gets three minutes to make all the beds in the barracks—with hospital corners tight enough to bounce a quarter. If the entire platoon doesn't finish, the drill instructor orders the platoon to strip the beds and start over. So it goes—all day if necessary—until the recruits realize that they can finish in time and to specification only if they work together with the faster guys helping the slower guys.

Source: J. Vesterman, "From Wharton to War," *Fortune,* 12 June 2006, 105–108.

mgmt trend

©Stephanie Sinclair/Corbis

throw away old, comfortable solutions and adopt radical, never-used-before solutions.[71]

Four things must occur for stretch goals to effectively motivate teams.[72] First, teams must have a high degree of autonomy or control over how they achieve their goals. Second, teams must be empowered with control over resources, such as budgets, workspaces, computers, or whatever else they need to do their jobs. Steve Kerr, Goldman Sachs' chief learning officer, says, "We have a moral obligation to try to give people the tools to meet tough goals. I think it's totally wrong if you don't give employees the tools to succeed, then punish them when they fail."[73]

Third, teams need structural accommodation. **Structural accommodation** means giving teams the ability to change organizational structures, policies, and practices if doing so helps them meet their stretch goals. Finally, teams need bureaucratic immunity. **Bureaucratic immunity** means that teams no longer have to go through the frustratingly slow process of multilevel reviews and sign-offs to get management approval before making changes. Once granted bureaucratic immunity, teams are immune from the influence of various organizational groups and are accountable only to top management. Therefore, teams can act quickly and even experiment with little fear of failure.

4.2 Selecting People for Teamwork

University of Southern California professor Edward Lawler says, "People are very naive about how easy it is to create a team. Teams are the Ferraris of work design. They're high performance but high maintenance and expensive."[74] It's almost impossible to have an effective work team without carefully selecting people who are suited for teamwork or for working on a particular team. A focus on teamwork (individualism-collectivism), team level, and team diversity can help companies choose the right team members.[75]

Are you more comfortable working alone or with others? If you strongly prefer to work alone, you may not be well suited for teamwork.

Indeed, studies shaow that job satisfaction is higher in teams when team members prefer working with others.[76] An indirect way to measure someone's *preference for teamwork* is to assess the person's degree of individualism or collectivism. **Individualism-collectivism** is the degree to which a person believes that people should be self-sufficient and that loyalty to one's self is more important than loyalty to one's team or company.[77] *Individualists,* who put their own welfare and interests first, generally prefer independent tasks in which they work alone. In contrast, *collectivists,* who put group or team interests ahead of self-interests, generally prefer interdependent tasks in which they work with others. Collectivists would also rather cooperate than compete and are fearful of disappointing team members or of being ostracized from teams. Given these differences, it makes sense to select team members who are collectivists rather than individualists. Indeed, many companies use individualism-collectivism as an initial screening device for team members. If team diversity is desired, however, individualists may also be appropriate, as discussed below. To determine your preference for teamwork, take the Team Player Inventory shown in Exhibit 10.4.

Team level is the average level of ability, experience, personality, or any other factor on a team. For example, a high level of team experience means that a team has particularly experienced team members. This does not mean that every member of the team has considerable experience, but that enough team members do to significantly raise the average level of experience on the team. Team level is used to guide selection of teammates when teams need a particular set of skills or capabilities to do their jobs well. For example, at GE's Aerospace Engines manufacturing plant in Durham, North Carolina, everyone hired had to have an FAA-certified mechanic's license.[78]

Whereas team level represents the average level or capability on a team, **team diversity** represents the variances or differences in ability, experience, personality, or any other factor on a team.[79] From a practical perspective, why is team diversity important? Professor John Hollenbeck explains, "Imagine if you put all the extroverts together. Everyone is talking, but nobody is listening. [By contrast,] with a team of [nothing but] introverts, you can hear the clock ticking on the wall."[80] Strong teams not only have talented members (i.e., team level), but those talented members are also different in terms of ability, experience, or personality. For example, teams with strong team diversity on job experience have a mix of team members, ranging from seasoned veterans to people with three or four years of

Structural accommodation the ability to change organizational structures, policies, and practices in order to meet stretch goals

Bureaucratic immunity the ability to make changes without first getting approval from managers or other parts of an organization

Individualism-collectivism the degree to which a person believes that people should be self-sufficient and that loyalty to one's self is more important than loyalty to team or company

Team level the average level of ability, experience, personality, or any other factor on a team

Team diversity the variances or differences in ability, experience, personality, or any other factor on a team

Exhibit 10.4

The Team Player Inventory

	STRONGLY DISAGREE				STRONGLY AGREE
1. I enjoy working on team/group projects.	1	2	3	4	5
2. Team/group project work easily allows others to not "pull their weight."	1	2	3	4	5
3. Work that is done as a team/group is better than the work done individually.	1	2	3	4	5
4. I do my best work alone rather than in a team/group.	1	2	3	4	5
5. Team/group work is overrated in terms of the actual results produced.	1	2	3	4	5
6. Working in a team/group gets me to think more creatively.	1	2	3	4	5
7. Teams/groups are used too often, when individual work would be more effective.	1	2	3	4	5
8. My own work is enhanced when I am in a team/group situation.	1	2	3	4	5
9. My experiences working in team/group situations have been primarily negative.	1	2	3	4	5
10. More soultions/ideas are generated when working in a team/group situation than when working alone.	1	2	3	4	5

Reverse score items 2, 4, 5, 7, and 9. Then add the scores for items 1 to 10. Higher scores indicate a preference for teamwork, whereas lower total scores indicate a preference for individual work.

experience to rookies with little or no experience. Team diversity is used to guide the selection of team members when teams must complete a wide range of different tasks or when tasks are particularly complex.

Once the right team has been put together in terms of individualism-collectivism, team level, and team diversity, it's important to keep the team together as long as practically possible. Interesting research by the National Transportation Safety Board shows that 73 percent of the serious mistakes made by jet cockpit crews are made the very first day that a crew flies together as a team and that 44 percent of serious mistakes occur on their very first flight together (pilot teams fly two to three flights per day). Moreover, research has shown that fatigued pilot crews who have worked together before make significantly fewer errors than rested crews who have never worked together.[81] Their experience working together helps them overcome their fatigue and outperform new teams that have not worked together before. So, once you've created effective teams, keep them together as long as possible.

4.3 Team Training

After selecting the right people for teamwork, you need to train them. And, to be successful, teams need significant training, particularly in interpersonal skills, decision making and problem solving, conflict resolution, and technical training. Team leaders need training, too.

Organizations that create work teams *often underestimate the amount of training* required to make teams effective. This mistake occurs frequently in successful organizations, where managers assume that if employees can work effectively on their own, they can work effectively in teams. In reality, companies that successfully use teams provide thousands of hours of training to make behavior is creating a problem within a team, the team is expected to work it out without involving the team leader. Two team members will meet with the 'problem' team member and work toward a resolution. If this is unsuccessful, the whole team meets and confronts the issue. If necessary, the team leader can be brought in to make a decision, but . . . it is a rare occurrence for a team to reach that stage."[83] Firms must also provide team members with the *technical training* they need to do their jobs, particularly if they are being cross-trained to perform all of the different jobs on the team. Cross-training is less appropriate for teams of highly skilled workers. For instance, it is unlikely that a group of engineers, computer programmers, and systems analysts would be cross-trained for each other's jobs.

Finally, companies need to provide *training for team leaders,* who often feel unprepared for their new duties. New team leaders face myriad problems, ranging from confusion about their new roles as team leaders (compared to their old jobs as managers or employees) to not knowing where to go for help when their teams have problems. The solution is extensive training for team leaders.

4.4 Team Compensation and Recognition

Compensating teams correctly is very difficult. For instance, one survey found that only 37 percent of companies were satisfied with their team compensation plans and even fewer, just 10 percent, reported being "very positive."[84] One of the problems, according to Monty Mohrman of the Center for Effective Organizations, is that "there is a very strong set of beliefs in most organizations that people should be paid for how well they do. So when people first get put into team-based organizations, they really balk at being paid for how well the team does. It sounds illogical to them. It sounds like their individuality and their sense of self-worth are being threatened."[85] Consequently, companies need to carefully choose a team compensation plan and then fully explain how teams will be rewarded. One basic requirement for team compensation to work is that the level of rewards (individual versus team) must match the level of performance (individual versus team).

Employees can be compensated for team participation and accomplishments in three ways: skill-based pay, gainsharing, and nonfinancial rewards. **Skill-based pay** programs pay employees for learning additional skills or knowledge.[86] These programs encourage employees to acquire the additional skills they will need to perform multiple jobs within a team and to share knowledge with others within their work groups.[87]

sure that teams work. Stacy Myers, a consultant who helps companies implement teams, says, "When we help companies move to teams, we also require that employees take basic quality and business knowledge classes as well. Teams must know how their work affects the company, and how their success will be measured."[82]

Most commonly, members of work teams receive training in interpersonal skills. **Interpersonal skills,** such as listening, communicating, questioning, and providing feedback, enable people to have effective working relationships with others. Because of teams' autonomy and responsibility, many companies also give team members training in *decision-making and problem-solving skills* to help them do a better job of cutting costs and improving quality and customer service. Many organizations also teach teams *conflict resolution skills.* "Teams at Delta Faucet have specific protocols for addressing conflict. For example, if an employee's

Interpersonal skills skills, such as listening, communicating, questioning, and providing feedback, that enable people to have effective working relationships with others

Skill-based pay compensation system that pays employees for learning additional skills or knowledge

> The more each **team member** knows and can do,
> the better the **whole team** performs.

In **gainsharing** programs, companies share the financial value of performance gains, such as productivity increases, cost savings, or quality improvements, with their workers.[88] *Nonfinancial rewards* are another way to reward teams for their performance. These rewards, which can range from vacation trips to T-shirts, plaques, and coffee mugs, are especially effective when coupled with management recognition, such as awards, certificates, and praise.[89] Nonfinancial awards tend to be most effective when teams or team-based interventions, such as total quality management (see Chapter 18), are first introduced.[90]

Which team compensation plan should your company use? In general, skill-based pay is most effective for self-managing and self-directing teams performing complex tasks. In these situations, the more each team member knows and can do, the better the whole team performs. By contrast, gainsharing works best in relatively stable environments where employees can focus on improving the productivity, cost savings, or quality

> **Gainsharing** a compensation system in which companies share the financial value of performance gains, such as productivity, cost savings, or quality, with their workers

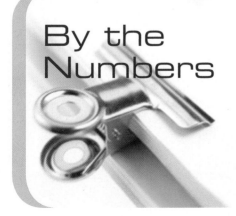

By the Numbers

4	stages of team development
6–9	ideal number of members on a team
$2.00	hourly bonus for Whole Foods' most productive teams
37%	of companies surveyed satisfied with their team compensation plans.

MANAGING HUMAN RESOURCE SYSTEMS

Human resource management (HRM), or the process of finding, developing, and keeping the right people to form a qualified work force, is one of the most difficult and important of all management tasks. This chapter is organized around the three parts of the human resource management process shown in Exhibit 11.1: attracting, developing, and keeping a qualified work force.

Exhibit 11.1

The Human Resource Management Process

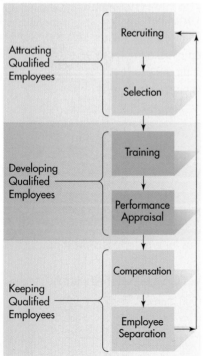

Attracting Qualified Employees
- Recruiting
- Selection

Developing Qualified Employees
- Training
- Performance Appraisal

Keeping Qualified Employees
- Compensation
- Employee Separation

Learning Outcomes

1 explain how different employment laws affect human resource practice.

2 explain how companies use recruiting to find qualified job applicants.

3 describe the selection techniques and procedures that companies use when deciding which applicants should receive job offers.

4 describe how to determine training needs and select the appropriate training methods.

5 discuss how to use performance appraisal to give meaningful performance feedback.

6 describe basic compensation strategies and discuss the four kinds of employee separations.

The chapter begins by reviewing the federal laws that govern human resource management decisions. Next, we explore how companies use recruiting and selection techniques to attract and hire qualified employees to fulfill those needs. The next part of the chapter discusses how training and performance appraisal can develop the knowledge, skills, and abilities of the work force. The chapter concludes with a review of compensation and employee separation, that is, how companies can keep their best workers through effective compensation practices and how they can manage the separation process when employees leave the organization.

Before exploring how human resource systems work, you need to better understand the complex legal environment in which they exist.

 After reading the next section, you should be able to

1 explain how different employment laws affect human resource practice.

1 Employment Legislation

Since their inception, Hooters restaurants have hired only female servers. Moreover, consistent with the company's marketing theme, the servers wear short nylon shorts and cutoff T-shirts that

Human resource management (HRM) the process of finding, developing, and keeping the right people to form a qualified work force

MGMT

show their midriffs. The Equal Employment Opportunity Commission (EEOC) began an investigation of Hooters when a Chicago man filed a sex-based discrimination charge. The man alleged that he had applied for a server's job at a Hooters restaurant and was rejected because of his sex. The dispute between Hooters and the EEOC quickly gained national attention. One sarcastic letter to the EEOC printed in *Fortune* magazine read as follows:

Dear EEOC:

Hi! I just wanted to thank you for investigating those Hooters restaurants, where the waitresses wear those shorty shorts and midriffy T-shirts. I think it's a great idea that you have decided to make Hooters hire men as—how do you say it?—waitpersons. Gee, I never knew so many men wanted to be waitpersons at Hooters. No reason to let them sue on their own either. You're right, the government needs to take the lead on this one.[1]

This letter characterized public sentiment at the time. Given its backlog of 100,000 job discrimination cases, many wondered if the EEOC didn't have better things to do with its scarce resources.

Three years after the initial complaint, the EEOC ruled that Hooters had violated antidiscrimination laws and offered to settle the case if the company would agree to pay $22 million to the EEOC for distribution to male victims of the "Hooters Girl" hiring policy, establish a scholarship fund to enhance opportunities or education for men, and provide sensitivity training to teach Hooters' employees how to be more sensitive to men's needs. Hooters responded with a $1 million publicity campaign, criticizing the EEOC's investigation. Billboards featuring "Vince," a man dressed in a Hooters Girl uniform and blond wig, sprang up all over the country. Hooters customers were given postcards to send complaints to the EEOC. Of course, Hooters

Bona fide occupational qualification (BFOQ) an exception in employment law that permits sex, age, religion, and the like to be used when making employment decisions, but only if they are "reasonably necessary to the normal operation of that particular business." BFOQs are strictly monitored by the Equal Employment Opportunity Commission.

paid the postage. As a result of the publicity campaign, restaurant sales increased by 10 percent. Soon thereafter, the EEOC announced that it would not pursue discriminatory hiring charges against Hooters.[2] Nonetheless, the company ended up paying $3.75 million to settle a class-action suit brought by seven men who claimed that their inability to get a job at Hooters violated federal law.[3] Under the settlement, Hooters maintained its women-only policy for server jobs, but had to create additional support jobs, such as hosts and bartenders, that would also be open to men.

As the Hooters example illustrates, the human resource planning process occurs in a very complicated legal environment. Let's explore employment legislation by reviewing *1.1 the major federal employment laws that affect human resource practice, 1.2 how the concept of adverse impact is related to employment discrimination,* and *1.3 the laws regarding sexual harassment in the workplace.*

1.1 Federal Employment Laws

Exhibit 11.2 lists the major federal employment laws and their Web sites, where you can find more detailed information. Except for the Family and Medical Leave Act and the Uniformed Services Employment and Reemployment Rights Act, which are administrated by the Department of Labor (**http://www.dol.gov**), all of these laws are administered by the EEOC (**http://www.eeoc. gov**). The general effect of this body of law, which is still evolving through court decisions, is that employers may not discriminate in employment decisions on the basis of sex, age, religion, color, national origin, race, or disability. The intent is to make these factors irrelevant in employment decisions. Stated another way, employment decisions should be based on factors that are "job related," "reasonably necessary," or a "business necessity" for successful job performance. The only time that sex, age, religion, and the like can be used to make employment decisions is when they are considered a bona fide occupational qualification.[4] Title VII of the 1964 Civil Rights Act says that it is not unlawful to hire and employ someone on the basis of gender, religion, or national origin when there is a **bona fide occupational qualification (BFOQ)** that is "reasonably necessary to the normal operation of that particular business." For example, a Baptist church hiring a new minister can reasonably specify that being a Baptist rather than a Catholic or Presbyterian is a BFOQ for the position.

However, it's unlikely that the church could specify race or national origin as a BFOQ. In general, the courts and the EEOC take a hard look when a business claims that sex, age, religion, color, national origin, race, or disability is a BFOQ.

It is important to understand, however that these laws apply to the entire HRM process and not just to selection decisions (i.e., hiring and promotion). Thus, these laws also cover all training and development activities, performance appraisals, terminations, and compensation decisions. Employers who use sex, age, race, or religion to make employment-related decisions when those factors are unrelated to an applicant's or employee's ability to perform a job may face charges of discrimination from employee lawsuits or the EEOC. For example, Morgan Stanley, an investment bank, agreed to pay $54 million in damages after the EEOC filed a sex discrimination suit on behalf of 300 of the firm's female employees. The women were paid less and promoted less often than comparable male employees with whom they worked.[5]

In addition to the laws presented in Exhibit 11.2, there are two other important sets of federal laws: labor laws and laws and regulations governing safety standards. Labor laws regulate the interaction between management and labor unions that represent groups of employees. These laws guarantee employees the right to form and join unions of their own choosing. The Occupational Safety and Health Act (OSHA) requires that employers provide employees with a workplace that is "free from recognized hazards that are causing or are likely to cause death or serious physical harm." This law is administered by the Occupational Safety and Health Administration (which, like the act, is referred to as OSHA). OSHA sets safety and health standards for employers and conducts inspections to determine whether those standards are being met. Employers who do not meet OSHA standards may be fined.[6]

1.2 Adverse Impact and Employment Discrimination

The EEOC has investigatory, enforcement, and informational responsibilities. Therefore, it investigates charges of discrimination, enforces the employment discrimination laws in federal court, and publishes guidelines that organizations can use to ensure they are in compliance with the law. One of the most important guidelines jointly issued by the EEOC, the Department of Labor, the U.S.

Exhibit 11.2

Summary of Major Federal Employment Laws

Law	URL	Description
■ Equal Pay Act of 1963	http://www.eeoc.gov/policy/epa.html	Prohibits unequal pay for males and females doing substantially similar work.
■ Civil Rights Act of 1964	http://www.eeoc.gov/policy/vii.html	Prohibits discrimination on the basis of race, color, religion, gender, or national origin.
■ Age Discrimination in Employment Act of 1967	http://www.eeoc.gov/policy/adea.html	Prohibits discrimination in employment decisions against persons age 40 and over.
■ Pregnancy Discrimination Act of 1978	http://www.eeoc.gov/facts/fs-preg.html	Prohibits discrimination in employment against pregnant women.
■ Americans with Disabilities Act of 1990	http://www.eeoc.gov/policy/ada.html	Prohibits discrimination on the basis of physical or mental disabilities.
■ Civil Rights Act of 1991	http://www.eeoc.gov/policy/cra91.html	Strengthened the provisions of the Civil Rights Act of 1964 by providing for jury trials and punitive damages.
■ Family and Medical Leave Act of 1993	http://www.dol.gov/esa/whd/fmla/index.html	Permits workers to take up to 12 weeks of unpaid leave for pregnancy and/or birth of a new child, adoption or foster care of a new child, illness of an immediate family member, or personal medical leave.
■ Uniformed Services Employment and Reemployment Rights Act of 1994	http://www.osc.gov/userra.htm	Prohibits discrimination against those serving in the Armed Forces Reserve, the National Guard, or other uniformed services; guarantees that civilian employers will hold and then restore civilian jobs and benefits for those who have completed uniformed service.

Justice Department, and the federal Office of Personnel Management is the *Uniform Guidelines on Employee Selection Procedures.* These guidelines define two important criteria, disparate treatment and adverse impact, that are used in determining whether companies have engaged in discriminatory hiring and promotion practices.

Disparate treatment, which is *intentional* discrimination, occurs when people, despite being qualified, are *intentionally* not given the same hiring, promotion, or membership opportunities as other employees, because of their race, color, age, sex, ethnic group, national origin, or religious beliefs.[7] Legally, a key element of discrimination lawsuits is establishing motive, meaning that the employer intended to discriminate. If no motive can be established, then a claim of disparate treatment may actually be a case of adverse impact. **Adverse impact,** which is *unintentional* discrimination, occurs when members of a particular race, sex, or ethnic group are *unintentionally* harmed or disadvantaged because they are hired, promoted, or trained (or any other employment decision) at substantially lower rates than others. The courts and federal agencies use the **four-fifths (or 80 percent) rule** to determine if adverse impact has occurred. Adverse impact occurs if the decision rate for a protected group of people is less than four-fifths (or 80 percent) of the decision rate for a nonprotected group (usually white males). So, if 100 white applicants and 100 black applicants apply for entry-level jobs, and 60 white applicants are hired (60/100 = 60%), but only 20 black applicants are hired (20/100 = 20%), adverse impact has occurred (0.20/0.60 = 0.33). The criterion for the four-fifths rule in this situation is 0.48 ($0.60 \times 0.80 = 0.48$). Since 0.33 is less than 0.48, the four-fifths rule has been violated.

Violation of the four-fifths rule is not an automatic indication of discrimination, however. If an employer can demonstrate that a selection procedure or test is valid, meaning that the test accurately predicts job performance or that the test is job related because it assesses applicants on specific tasks actually used in the job, then the organization may continue to use the test. If validity cannot be established, however, then a violation of the four-fifths rule may likely result in a lawsuit brought by employees, job applicants, or the EEOC itself.

1.3 Sexual Harassment

According to the EEOC, **sexual harassment** is a form of discrimination in which unwelcome sexual advances, requests for sexual favors, or other verbal or physical conduct of a sexual nature occurs. From a legal perspective, there are two kinds of sexual harassment, quid pro quo and hostile work environment.[8]

Quid pro quo sexual harassment occurs when employment outcomes, such as hiring, promotion, or simply keeping one's job, depend on whether an individual submits to being sexually harassed. For example, in a quid pro quo sexual harassment lawsuit against Costco, a female employee alleged that her boss groped her and bumped into her from behind to simulate sex. "He would tell her: 'You work with me and I'll work with you,' motioning to his private area."[9] The supervisor also allegedly told her that he would fire her if she reported his activities to upper management. In quid pro quo cases, requests for sexual acts are linked to economic outcomes (that is, keeping a job). A **hostile work environment** occurs when unwelcome and demeaning sexually related behavior creates an intimidating, hostile, and offensive work environment. There may be no economic injury, that is, requests for sexual acts aren't tied to economic outcomes. However, they can lead to psychological injury from a stressful work environment.

What should companies do to make sure that sexual harassment laws are followed and not violated?[10] First, respond immediately when sexual harassment is reported. A quick response encourages victims of sexual harassment to report problems to management rather than to lawyers or the EEOC. Furthermore, a quick and fair investigation may serve as a deterrent to future harassment. Next, take the time to write a clear, understandable sexual harassment

Disparate treatment intentional discrimination that occurs when people are purposely not given the same hiring, promotion, or membership opportunities because of their race, color, sex, age, ethnic group, national origin, or religious beliefs

Adverse impact unintentional discrimination that occurs when members of a particular race, sex, or ethnic group are unintentionally harmed or disadvantaged because they are hired, promoted, or trained (or any other employment decision) at substantially lower rates than others

Four-fifths (or 80 percent) rule a rule of thumb used by the courts and the EEOC to determine whether there is evidence of adverse impact. A violation of this rule occurs when the selection rate for a protected group is less than 80 percent or four-fifths of the selection rate for a nonprotected group.

Sexual harassment a form of discrimination in which unwelcome sexual advances, requests for sexual favors, or other verbal or physical conduct of a sexual nature occurs while performing one's job

Quid pro quo sexual harassment a form of sexual harassment in which employment outcomes, such as hiring, promotion, or simply keeping one's job, depend on whether an individual submits to sexual harassment

Hostile work environment a form of sexual harassment in which unwelcome and demeaning sexually related behavior creates an intimidating and offensive work environment policy that is strongly worded, gives specific examples of what constitutes sexual harassment, spells outs sanctions and punishments, and is widely publicized within the company. This lets potential harassers and victims know what will not be tolerated and how the firm will deal with harassment should it occur.

Next, establish clear reporting procedures that indicate how, where, and to whom incidents of sexual harassment can be reported. The best procedures ensure that a complaint will receive a quick response, that impartial parties will handle the complaint, and that the privacy of the accused and accuser will be protected. At DuPont, Avon, and Texas Industries, employees can call a confidential hotline 24 hours a day, 365 days a year.[11]

Finally, managers should also be aware that most states and many cities or local governments have their own employment-related laws and enforcement agencies. So compliance with federal law is often not enough. In fact, organizations can be in full compliance with federal law and at the same time be in violation of state or local sexual harassment laws.

Finding Qualified Workers

As Gail Hyland-Savage, the CEO of real estate and marketing firm Michaelson, Connor & Boul, says "Staffing is absolutely critical to the success of every company. To be competitive in today's economy, companies need the best people to create ideas and execute them for the organization. Without a competent and talented workforce, organizations will stagnate and eventually perish. The right employees are the most important resources of companies today."[12]

After reading the next two sections, you should be able to

2 explain how companies use recruiting to find qualified job applicants.

3 describe the selection techniques and procedures that companies use when deciding which applicants should receive job offers.

2 Recruiting

Recruiting is the process of developing a pool of qualified job applicants. Let's examine *2.1 what job analysis is and how it is used in recruiting* and *2.2 how companies use internal recruiting* and *2.3 external recruiting to find qualified job applicants*.

2.1 Job Analysis and Recruiting

Job analysis is a "purposeful, systematic process for collecting information on the important work-related aspects of a job."[13] Typically, a job analysis collects four kinds of information:

- work activities, such as what workers do and how, when, and why they do it
- the tools and equipment used to do the job
- the context in which the job is performed, such as the actual working conditions or schedule
- the personnel requirements for performing the job, meaning the knowledge, skills, and abilities needed to do a job well[14]

Job analysis information can be collected by having job incumbents and/or supervisors complete questionnaires about their jobs, by direct observation, by interviews, or by filming employees as they perform their jobs.

Job descriptions and job specifications are two of the most important results of a job analysis. A **job description** is a written description of the basic tasks, duties, and responsibilities required of an employee holding a particular job. **Job specifications,** which are often included as a separate section of a job description, are a summary of the qualifications needed to successfully perform the job. Exhibit 11.3 shows a job description and the job specifications for a helicopter pilot for the city of Little Rock, Arkansas.

Because a job analysis specifies what a job entails, as well as the knowledge, skills, and abilities that are needed to do the job well, companies must complete a

Recruiting the process of developing a pool of qualified job applicants

Job analysis a purposeful, systematic process for collecting information on the important work-related aspects of a job

Job description a written description of the basic tasks, duties, and responsibilities required of an employee holding a particular job

Job specifications a written summary of the qualifications needed to successfully perform a particular job

Exhibit 11.3

Job Description and Job Specifications for a
Helicopter Pilot for the City of Little Rock, Arkansas

DESCRIPTION FOR HELICOPTER PILOT

To provide assistance for air searches, river rescues, high-rise building rescues, and other assignments, by providing air survey and aviation response. Pilots a rotary-wing aircraft, serving as pilot or co-pilot, to assist in air searches, river rescues, high-rise building rescues, and other assignments. Ensures that aircraft is properly outfitted for each assignment (equipment, rigging tools, supplies, etc.). Performs preflight inspection of aircraft; checks rotors, fuel, lubricants, controls, etc. Prepares written reports on assignments; maintains flight logs. Obtains weather reports; determines to proceed with assignments given forecasted weather conditions. Operates a radio to maintain contact with and to report information to airport personnel and police department personnel.

JOB SPECIFICATIONS FOR HELICOPTER PILOT

Must possess a valid Commercial Pilot's License for rotary-wing aircraft before employment and maintain licensure for the duration of employment in this position. Must have considerable knowledge of Federal Aviation Administration (FAA) laws and regulations, rotary-wing aircraft operating procedures, air traffic safety, flying procedures and navigational techniques, and FAA and police radio operation and procedures. Must have some knowledge of preventive maintenance methods, repair practices, safety requirements and inspection procedures. Must have skill in the operation of a rotary-wing aircraft, radio equipment, the ability to conduct safety inspections of aircraft, to maintain aircraft maintenance logs and prepare reports, to detect and identify aircraft malfunction symptoms, to detect and recognize ground conditions and characteristics (i.e., utility line breaks, river currents, etc.), to read maps and air navigation charts, and to communicate effectively, both orally and in writing. Must have completed high school; at least one-thousand hours of flight time experience in piloting rotary-wing aircraft; OR any equivalent combination of experience and training which provides the required knowledge, skills, and abilities.

Source: "Job Description: Helicopter Pilot," City of Little Rock, Arkansas, [Online] available at http://www.accesslittlerock.org/HumanResources/h000274.htm, 31 May 2003.

job analysis *before* beginning to recruit job applicants. Job analysis, job descriptions, and job specifications are the foundation on which all critical human resource activities are built. They are used during recruiting and selection to match applicant qualifications with the requirements of the job. They are used throughout the staffing process to ensure that selection devices and the decisions based on these devices are job related. For example, the questions asked in an interview should be based on the most important work activities identified by a job analysis. Likewise, during performance appraisals, employees should be evaluated in areas that a job analysis has identified as the most important in a job.

Job analyses, job descriptions, and job specifications also help companies meet the legal requirement that their human resource decisions be job related. To be judged *job related*, recruitment, selection, training, performance appraisals, and employee separations must be valid and be directly related to the important aspects of the job, as identified by a careful job analysis. In fact, in *Griggs v. Duke Power Co.* and *Albemarle Paper Co. v. Moody*, the U.S. Supreme Court stated that companies should use job analyses to help establish the job relatedness of their human resource procedures.[15] The EEOC's *Uniform Guidelines on Employee Selection Procedures* also recommend that companies base their human resource procedures on job analysis.

FIND A STAR
IN THE CROWD

Sponsored by
monster
today's the day™
Special Discounts for Inc.com Users!

Inc. Hiring Center
http://hiring.inc.com

©Created by Haewon Kye & Edward Sussman, ©Inc.com

2.2 Internal Recruiting

Internal recruiting is the process of developing a pool of qualified job applicants from people who already work in the company. Internal recruiting, sometimes called "promotion from within," improves employee commitment, morale, and motivation. Recruiting current employees also reduces recruitment startup time and costs, and because employees are already familiar with the company's culture and procedures, they are more likely to succeed in new jobs. Job posting and career paths are two methods of internal recruiting.

Job posting is a procedure for advertising job openings within the company to existing employees. A job description and requirements are typically posted on a bulletin board, in a company newsletter, or in an internal computerized job bank that is accessible only to employees.

A *career path* is a planned sequence of jobs through which employees may advance within an organization. For example, a person who starts as a sales representative may move up to sales manager and then to district or regional sales manager. Career paths help employees focus on long-term goals and development while also helping companies increase employee retention.

2.3 External Recruiting

External recuiting is the process of developing a pool of qualified job applicants from outside the company. External recruitment methods include advertising (newspapers, magazines, direct mail, radio, or television), employee referrals (asking current employees to recommend possible job applicants), walk-ins (people who apply on their own), outside organizations (universities, technical/trade schools, professional societies), employment services (state or private employment agencies, temporary help agencies, and professional search firms), special events (career conferences or job fairs), and Internet job sites. Which external recruiting method should you use? Studies show that employee referrals, walk-ins, newspaper advertisements, and state employment agencies tend to be used most frequently for office/clerical and production/service employees. By contrast, newspaper advertisements and college/university recruiting are used most frequently for professional/technical employees. When recruiting managers, organizations tend to rely most heavily on newspaper advertisements, employee referrals, and search firms.[16]

In the last few years, the biggest change in external recruiting has been the increased use of the Internet. Some companies now recruit applicants through Internet job sites such as Monster.com, HotJobs.com, Hire.com, and CareerBuilder.com. Companies can post job openings for 30 days on one of these sites for about half of the cost of running an advertisement just once in a Sunday newspaper. Plus, Internet job listings generate nine times as many résumés as one ad in the Sunday newspaper.[17] And because these sites attract so many applicants and offer so many services, companies save by finding qualified applicants without having to use more expensive recruitment and search firms, which typically charge one-third or more of a new hire's salary.[18]

3 Selection

Once the recruitment process has produced a pool of qualified applicants, the selection process is used to determine which applicants have the best chance of performing well on the job. More specifically, **selection** is the process

Internal recruiting
the process of developing a pool of qualified job applicants from people who already work in the company

External recruiting
the process of developing a pool of qualified job applicants from outside the company

Selection the process of gathering information about job applicants to decide who should be offered a job

Recruiting Challenges

According to a survey by Deloitte & Touche, executives at fast-growing technology companies say their greatest operational challenge is finding, hiring, and retaining workers. About 41 percent of respondents listed the shortage of qualified workers as their biggest obstacle, more significant than the combined concerns of developing a strong sales strategy, managing cash flow, and building internal systems. And 66 percent of the CEOs surveyed said that high-quality employees are the biggest contributors to growth, more so than even strategy and leadership.

Source: J. Badal, "Surveying the Field—Tapping Tech Talent," *Wall Street Journal*, 26 June 2006, B5.

mgmt trend

©Ingram Publishing/Jupiter Images

---

of gathering information about job applicants to decide who should be offered a job. To make sure that selection decisions are accurate and legally defensible, the EEOC's *Uniform Guidelines on Employee Selection Procedures* recommend that all selection procedures be validated. **Validation** is the process of determining how well a selection test or procedure predicts future job performance. The better or more accurate the prediction of future job performance, the more valid a test is said to be.

Let's examine common selection procedures, such as 3.1 application forms and résumés, 3.2 references and background checks, 3.3 selection tests, and 3.4 interviews.

Validation the process of determining how well a selection test or procedure predicts future job performance. The better or more accurate the prediction of future job performance, the more valid a test is said to be.

Employment references sources such as previous employers or coworkers who can provide job-related information about job candidates

Background checks procedures used to verify the truthfulness and accuracy of information that applicants provide about themselves and to uncover negative, job-related background information not provided by applicants

3.1 Application Forms and Résumés

The first selection devices that most job applicants en-counter when they seek a job are application forms and résumés. Both contain similar information about an applicant, such as name, address, job and educational history, and so forth. Though an organization's application form often asks for information already provided by the applicant's résumé, most organizations prefer to collect this information in their own format for entry into a human resource information system.

Employment laws apply to application forms, just as they do to all selection devices. Application forms may ask applicants for only valid, job-related information. Nonetheless, application forms commonly ask applicants for non-job-related information, such as marital status, maiden name, age, or date of high school graduation. Indeed, one study found that 73 percent of organizations had application forms that violated at least one federal or state law.[19] There's quite a bit of information that companies may not request in application forms, during job interviews, or in any other part of the selection process. Courts will assume that you consider all of the information you request of applicants, even if you don't. Be sure to ask only those questions that directly relate to the candidate's ability and motivation to perform the job.

Résumés also pose problems for companies, but in a different way. Studies show that as many as one-third of job applicants intentionally falsify some information on their résumés and that 80 percent of the information on résumés may be misleading. Therefore, managers should verify the information collected via résumés and application forms by comparing it with additional information collected during interviews and other stages of the selection process, such as references and background checks, which are discussed next.

3.2 References and Background Checks

Nearly all companies ask an applicant to provide **employment references**, such as previous employers or coworkers, that they can contact to learn more about the candidate. **Background checks** are used to verify the truthfulness and accuracy of information that applicants provide about themselves and to uncover negative, job-related background information not provided by applicants. Background checks are conducted by contacting "educational institutions, prior employers, court records, police and governmental agencies, and other informational sources, either by telephone, mail, remote computer access, or through in-person investigations."[20]

Unfortunately, previous employers are increasingly reluctant to provide references or background check information for fear of being sued by previous employees

Don't Ask! (Topics to Avoid in an Interview)

1. *Children.* Don't ask applicants if they have children, plan to have them, or have or need child care. Questions about children can unintentionally single out women.

2. *Age.* Because of the Age Discrimination in Employment Act, employers cannot ask job applicants their age during the hiring process. Since most people graduate high school at the age of 18, even asking for high school graduation dates could violate the law.

3. *Disabilities.* Don't ask if applicants have physical or mental disabilities. According to the Americans with Disabilities Act, disabilities (and reasonable accommodations for them) cannot be discussed until a job offer has been made.

4. *Physical characteristics.* Don't ask for information about height, weight, or other physical characteristics. Questions about weight could be construed as leading to discrimination toward overweight people, who studies show are less likely to be hired in general.

5. *Name.* Yes, you can ask an applicant's name, but you cannot ask a female applicant for her maiden name because it indicates marital status. Asking for a maiden name could also lead to charges that the organization was trying to establish a candidate's ethnic background.

6. *Citizenship.* Asking applicants about citizenship could lead to claims of discrimination on the basis of national origin. However, according to the Immigration Reform and Control Act, companies may ask applicants if they have a legal right to work in the United States.

7. *Lawsuits.* Applicants may not be asked if they have ever filed a lawsuit against an employer. Federal and state laws prevent this to protect whistleblowers from retaliation by future employers.

8. *Arrest records.* Applicants cannot be asked about their arrest records. Arrests don't have legal standing. However, applicants can be asked whether they have been convicted of a crime.

9. *Smoking.* Applicants cannot be asked if they smoke. Smokers might be able to claim that they weren't hired because of fears of higher absenteeism and medical costs. However, they can be asked if they are aware of company policies that restrict smoking at work.

10. *AIDS/HIV.* Applicants can't be asked about AIDS, HIV, or any other medical condition. Questions of this nature would violate the Americans with Disabilities Act, as well as federal and state civil rights laws.

Source: J. S. Pouliot, "Topics to Avoid with Applicants," *Nation's Business* 80, no. 7 (1992): 57.

---

for defamation. If former employers provide potential employers with unsubstantiated information that damages applicants' chances of being hired, applicants can (and do) sue for defamation. As a result, 54 percent of employers will not provide information about previous employees.[21] Many provide only dates of employment, positions held, and date of separation.

valuable goods, or access to the elderly, children with disabilities, or people's homes.[23] According to the Society for Human Resource Management, 96 percent of companies conduct background checks and 80 percent of companies go further and conduct criminal record checks.[24]

Next, ask applicants to sign a waiver that permits you to check references, run a background check, or

> 54 percent of employers will not provide information about previous employees.

When previous employers decline to provide meaningful references or background information, they put other employers at risk of *negligent hiring* lawsuits, in which an employer is held liable for the actions of an employee who would not have been hired if the employer had conducted a thorough reference search and background check.[22]

With previous employers generally unwilling to give full, candid references and with negligent hiring lawsuits awaiting companies that don't get such references and background information, what can companies do? Conduct criminal record checks, especially if the job for which the person is applying involves money, drugs, control over

contact anyone else with knowledge of their work performance or history. Likewise, ask applicants if there is anything they would like the company to know or if they expect you to hear anything "unusual" when contacting references.[25] This in itself is often enough to get applicants to share information that they typically withhold. When you've finished checking, keep the findings confidential to minimize the chances of a defamation charge.

Finally, consider hiring private investigators to conduct background checks. They can often uncover surprising information not revealed by traditional background checks.[26]

3.3 Selection Tests

Selection tests give organizational decision makers a chance to know who will likely do well in a job and who won't. The basic idea behind selection testing is to have applicants take a test that measures something directly or indirectly related to doing well on the job. The selection tests discussed here are specific ability tests, cognitive ability tests, biographical data, personality tests, work sample tests, and assessment centers.

Specific ability tests measure the extent to which an applicant possesses the particular kind of ability needed to do a job well. Specific ability tests are also called **aptitude tests** because they measure aptitude for doing a particular task well. For example, if you took the SAT to get into college, then you've taken the aptly named Scholastic Aptitude Test, which is one of the best predictors of how well students will do in college (i.e., scholastic performance). Specific ability tests also exist for mechanical, clerical, sales, and physical work. For example, clerical workers have to be good at accurately reading and scanning numbers as they type or enter data. Exhibit 11.4 shows items similar to those found on the Minnesota Clerical Test, in which applicants have only a short time to determine if the two columns of numbers and letters are identical. Applicants who are good at this are likely to do well as clerical or data-entry workers.

Cognitive ability tests measure the extent to which applicants have abilities in perceptual speed, verbal comprehension, numerical aptitude, general reasoning, and spatial aptitude. In other words, these tests indicate how quickly and how well people understand words, numbers, logic, and spatial dimensions. Whereas specific ability tests predict job performance in only particular types of jobs, cognitive ability tests accurately predict job performance in almost all kinds of jobs.[27] Why is this so? The reason is that people with strong cognitive or mental abilities are usually good at learning new things, processing complex information, solving problems, and making decisions, and these abilities are important in almost all jobs.[28] In fact, cognitive ability tests are almost always the best predictors of job performance. Consequently, if you were allowed to use just one selection test, a cognitive ability test would be the one to use.[29] (In practice, though, companies use a battery of different tests because doing so leads to much more accurate selection decisions.)

Biographical data, or **biodata,** are extensive surveys that ask applicants questions about their personal backgrounds and life experiences. The basic idea behind biodata is that past behavior (personal background and life experience) is the best predictor of future behavior. Most biodata questionnaires have over 100 items that gather information about habits and attitudes, health, interpersonal relations, money, what it was like growing up in your family (parents, siblings, childhood years, teen years), personal habits, current home (spouse, children), hobbies, education and training, values, preferences, and work.[30] In general, biodata are very good predictors of future job performance, especially in entry-level jobs.

You may have noticed that some of the information requested in biodata surveys is related to those topics employers should avoid in applications, interviews, or other parts of the selection process. This information can be requested in biodata questionnaires provided that the company can demonstrate that the information is job related (i.e., valid) and does not result in adverse impact against protected groups of job applicants. Biodata surveys should be validated and tested

Specific ability tests (aptitude tests) tests that measure the extent to which an applicant possesses the particular kind of ability needed to do a job well

Cognitive ability tests tests that measure the extent to which applicants have abilities in perceptual speed, verbal comprehension, numerical aptitude, general reasoning, and spatial aptitude

Biographical data (biodata) extensive surveys that ask applicants questions about their personal backgrounds and life experiences

Exhibit 11.4

Clerical Test Items Similar to Those Found on the Minnesota Clerical Test

NUMBERS/LETTERS		SAME	
1. 3468251	3467251	Yes O	No O
2. 4681371	4681371	Yes O	No O
3. 7218510	7218520	Yes O	No O
4. ZXYAZAB	ZXYAZAB	Yes O	No O
5. ALZYXMN	ALZYXNM	Yes O	No O
6. PRQZYMN	PRQZYMN	Yes O	No O

Source: N. W. Schmitt & R. J. Klimoski, *Research Methods in Human Resource Management* (Mason, OH: South-Western, 1991). Used with permission.

for adverse impact before they are used to make selection decisions.[31]

Work sample tests, also called *performance tests,* require applicants to perform tasks that are actually done on the job. So, unlike specific ability, cognitive ability, biographical data, and personality tests, which are indirect predictors of job performance, work sample tests directly measure job applicants' capability to do the job. For example, a computer-based work sample test has applicants assume the role of a real estate agent who must decide how to interact with "virtual clients" in a gamelike scenario. And, as in real life, the clients can be frustrating, confusing, demanding, or indecisive. In one situation, the wife loves the "house" but the husband hates it. The applicants, just like actual real estate agents, must demonstrate what they would do in these realistic situations.[32] This work sample simulation gives real estate companies direct evidence of whether applicants can do the job if they are hired. Work sample tests are generally very good at predicting future job performance; however, they can be expensive to administer and can be used for only one kind of job. For example, an auto dealership could not use a work sample test for mechanics as a selection test for sales representatives.

Assessment centers use a series of job-specific simulations that are graded by multiple trained observers to determine applicants' ability to perform managerial work. Unlike the previously described selection tests that are commonly used for specific jobs or entry-level jobs, assessment centers are most often used to select applicants who have high potential to be good managers. Assessment centers often last two to five days and require participants to complete a number of tests and exercises that simulate managerial work.

Some of the more common assessment center exercises are in-basket exercises, role-plays, small-group presentations, and leaderless group discussions. An *in-basket exercise* is a paper-and-pencil test in which an applicant is given a manager's "in-basket" containing memos, phone messages, organizational policies, and other communications normally received by and available to managers. Applicants have a limited time to read through the in-basket, prioritize the items, and decide how to deal with each item. Experienced managers then score the applicants' decisions and recommendations. Exhibit 11.5 shows an item that could be used in an assessment center for evaluating applicants for a job as a store manager.

In a *leaderless group discussion,* another common assessment center exercise, a group of six applicants is

Exhibit 11.5

In-Basket Item for an Assessment Center for Store Managers

```
February 28
Sam & Dave's Discount Warehouse
Orange, California


Dear Store Manager,


Last week, my children and I were shopping in your store.
After doing our grocery shopping, we stopped in the
electronics department and asked the clerk, whose name
is Donald Block, to help us find a copy of the latest
version of the Madden NFL video game. Mr. Block was rude,
unhelpful, and told us to find it for ourselves as he
was busy.


I've been a loyal customer for over six years and expect
you to immediately do something about Mr. Block's
behavior. If you don't, I'll start doing my shopping
somewhere else.


Sincerely,
Margaret Quinlan
```

Source: Adapted from N. W. Schmitt & R. J. Klimoski, *Research Methods in Human Resource Management* (Mason, OH: South-Western 1991).

given approximately two hours to solve a problem, but no one is put in charge (hence the name "leaderless" group discussion). Trained observers watch and score each participant on the extent to which he or she facilitates discussion, listens, leads, persuades, and works well with others.

Are tests perfect predictors of job performance? No, they aren't. Some people who do well on selection tests will do poorly in their jobs. Likewise, some people who do poorly on selection tests (and therefore weren't hired) would have been very good performers. Nonetheless, valid tests will minimize these selection errors (hiring people who should not have been hired, and not hiring people who should have been hired) while maximizing correct selection decisions (hiring people who should have been hired, and not hiring people who should not have been hired).

In short, tests increase the chances that you'll hire the right person for the job, that is, someone who turns out to be a good performer. So, although tests aren't perfect, almost nothing predicts future job performance as well as the selection tests discussed here.

Work sample tests
tests that require applicants to perform tasks that are actually done on the job

Assessment centers
a series of managerial simulations, graded by trained observers, that are used to determine applicants' capability for managerial work

3.4 Interviews

In **interviews,** company representatives ask job applicants job-related questions to determine whether they are qualified for the job. Interviews are probably the most frequently used and relied on selection device. There are several basic kinds of interviews: unstructured, structured, and semistructured.

In **unstructured interviews,** interviewers are free to ask applicants anything they want, and studies show that they do. Because interviewers often disagree about which questions should be asked during interviews, different interviewers tend to ask applicants very different questions.[33] Furthermore, individual interviewers even seem to have a tough time asking the same questions from one interview to the next. This high level of inconsistency lowers the validity of unstructured interviews as a selection device because comparing applicant responses can be difficult. As a result, unstructured interviews are about half as accurate as structured interviews at predicting which job applicants should be hired.

By contrast, with **structured interviews,** standardized interview questions are prepared ahead of time so that all applicants are asked the same job-related questions.[34] The primary advantage of structured interviews is that comparing applicants is much easier because they are all asked the same questions. Structuring interviews also ensures that interviewers ask only for important, job-related information. Not only are the accuracy, usefulness, and validity of the interview improved, but the chances that interviewers will ask questions about topics that violate employment laws (the "Don't Ask!" box on page 205 has a list of these topics) are reduced.

Semistructured interviews are in between structured and unstructured interviews. A major part of the semistructured interview (perhaps as much as 80 percent) is based on structured questions, but some time is set aside for unstructured interviewing to allow the interviewer to probe into ambiguous or missing information uncovered during the structured portion of the interview.

How well do interviews predict future job performance? Contrary to what you've probably heard, recent evidence indicates that

Interviews a selection tool in which company representatives ask job applicants job-related questions to determine whether they are qualified for the job

Unstructured interviews interviews in which interviewers are free to ask the applicants anything they want

Structured interviews interviews in which all applicants are asked the same set of standardized questions, usually including situational, behavioral, background, and job-knowledge questions

---

Kinds of Questions Typically Asked in Structured Interviews:

- *situational questions,* which ask applicants how they would respond in a hypothetical situation (e.g., "What would you do if . . . ?"). These questions are more appropriate for hiring new graduates, as they are unlikely to have encountered real-work situations because of their limited work experience.
- *behavioral questions,* which ask applicants what they did in previous jobs that were similar to the job for which they are applying (e.g., "In your previous jobs, tell me about . . . "). These questions are more appropriate for hiring experienced individuals.
- *background questions,* which ask applicants about their work experience, education, and other qualifications (e.g., "Tell me about the training you received at . . . ").
- *job-knowledge questions,* which ask applicants to demonstrate their job knowledge (e.g., for nurses, "Give me an example of a time when one of your patients had a severe reaction to a medication. How did you handle it?")[35]

---

even unstructured interviews do a fairly good job.[36] When conducted properly, however, structured interviews can lead to much more accurate hiring decisions than unstructured interviews. In some cases, the validity of structured interviews can rival that of cognitive ability tests. But even more important, because interviews are especially good at assessing applicants' interpersonal skills, they work particularly well with cognitive ability tests. The combination (i.e., smart people who work well in conjunction with others) leads to even better selection decisions than using either alone.[37] Exhibit 11.6 provides a set of guidelines for conducting effective structured employment interviews.

Developing Qualified Workers

According to the American Society for Training and Development, a typical investment in employee training increases productivity by an average of 17 percent, reduces employee turnover, and makes companies more profitable.[38] Giving employees the knowledge and skills they need to improve their per-

Exhibit 11.6
Guidelines for Conducting Effective Structured Interviews

Interview Stage	What to Do

Planning the Interview

- Identify and define the knowledge, skills, abilities, and other (KSAO) characteristics needed for successful job performance.
- For each essential KSAO, develop key behavioral questions that will elicit examples of past accomplishments, activities, and performance.
- For each KSAO, develop a list of things to look for in the applicant's responses to key questions.

Conducting the Interview

- Create a relaxed, nonstressful interview atmosphere.
- Review the applicant's application form, résumé, and other information.
- Allocate enough time to complete the interview without interruption.
- Put the applicant at ease; don't jump right into heavy questioning.
- Tell the applicant what to expect. Explain the interview process.
- Obtain job-related information from the applicant by asking those questions prepared for each KSAO.
- Describe the job and the organization to the applicant. Applicants need adequate information to make a selection decision about the organization.

After the Interview

- Immediately after the interview, review your notes and make sure they are complete.
- Evaluate the applicant on each essential KSAO.
- Determine each applicant's probability of success and make a hiring decision.

Source: B. M. Farrell, "The Art and Science of Employment Interviews," *Personnel Journal* 65 (1986): 91–94.

---

formance is just the first step in developing employees, however. The second step, and not enough companies do this, is giving employees formal feedback about their actual job performance.

After reading the next two sections, you should be able to

4 describe how to determine training needs and select the appropriate training methods.

5 discuss how to use performance appraisal to give meaningful performance feedback.

4 Training

Training means providing opportunities for employees to develop the job-specific skills, experience, and knowledge they need to do their jobs or improve their performance. American companies spend more than $60 billion a year on training. To make sure those training dollars are well spent, companies need to **4.1 determine specific training needs, 4.2 select appropriate training methods,** and **4.3 evaluate training.**

> **Training** developing the skills, experience, and knowledge employees need to perform their jobs or improve their performance

4.1 Determining Training Needs

Needs assessment is the process of identifying and prioritizing the learning needs of employees. Needs assessments can be conducted by identifying performance deficiencies, listening to customer complaints, surveying employees and managers, or formally testing employees' skills and knowledge.

Note that training should never be conducted without first performing a needs assessment. Sometimes, training isn't needed at all or isn't needed for all employees. Unfortunately, however, many organizations simply require all employees to attend training, whether they need to or not. As a result, employees who are not interested or don't need the training may react negatively during or after training. Likewise, employees who should be sent for training but aren't may also react negatively. Consequently, a needs assessment is an important tool for deciding who should or should not attend training. In fact, employment law restricts employers from discriminating on the basis of age, sex, race, color, religion, national origin, or disability when selecting training participants. Just like hiring decisions, the selection of training participants should be based on job-related information.

4.2 Training Methods

Assume that you're a training director for a bank and that you're in charge of making sure that all bank employees know what to do in case of a robbery. Exhibit 11.7 lists a number of training methods you could use: films and videos, lectures, planned readings, case studies, coaching and mentoring, group discussions, on-the-job training, role-playing, simulations and games, vestibule training, and computer-based learning. Which method would be best?

To choose the best method, you should consider a number of factors, such as the number of people to be trained, the cost of training, and the objectives of the training. For instance, if the training objective is to impart information or knowledge to trainees, then you should use films and videos, lectures, and planned readings. In our robbery training example, trainees would hear, see, or read about what to do in case of a robbery.

If developing analytical and problem-solving skills is the objective, then use case studies, coaching and mentoring, and group discussions. In our example, trainees would read about a real robbery, talk to people who had been through robberies, and discuss what to do.

Needs assessment the process of identifying and prioritizing the learning needs of employees

Training bank tellers to handle a robbery attempt could take several different forms depending on which part of the robbery the training were meant to address.

If practicing, learning, or changing job behaviors is the objective, then use on-the-job training, role-playing, simulations and games, and vestibule training. In our example, trainees would learn about robbery situations on the job, pretend that they were in a robbery situation, or participate in a highly realistic mock robbery.

If training is supposed to meet more than one of these objectives, then your best choice may be to combine one of the previous methods with computer-based training.

These days, many companies are adopting Internet training, or "e-learning." E-learning can offer several advantages. Because employees don't need to leave their jobs, travel costs are greatly reduced. Also, because employees can take training modules when it is convenient (in other words, they don't have to fall behind at their jobs to attend week-long training courses), workplace productivity should increase and employee stress should decrease. Finally, if the company's technology infrastructure can support it, e-learning can be much faster than traditional training methods.

There are, however, several disadvantages to e-learning. First, despite its increasing popularity, it's not always the appropriate training method. E-learning can be a good way to impart information, but it isn't always as effective for changing job behaviors or de-

Exhibit 11.7
Training Objectives and Methods

TRAINING OBJECTIVE	TRAINING METHODS
Impart Information and Knowledge	• *Films and videos*. Films and videos share information, illustrate problems and solutions, and effectively hold trainees' attention.
	• *Lectures*. Trainees listen to instructors' oral presentations.
	• *Planned readings*. Trainees read about concepts or ideas before attending training.
Develop Analytical and Problem-Solving Skills	• *Case studies*. Cases are analyzed and discussed in small groups. The cases present a specific problem or decision, and trainees develop methods for solving the problem or making the decision.
	• *Coaching and mentoring*. Coaching and mentoring of trainees by managers involves informal advice, suggestions, and guidance. This method is helpful for reinforcing other kinds of training and for trainees who benefit from support and personal encouragement.
	• *Group discussions*. Small groups of trainees actively discuss specific topics. The instructor may perform the role of discussion leader.
Practice, Learn, or Change Job Behaviors	• *On-the-job training (OJT)*. New employees are assigned to experienced employees. The trainee learns by watching the experienced employee perform the job and eventually by working alongside the experienced employee. Gradually, the trainee is left on his or her own to perform the job.
	• *Role-playing*. Trainees assume job-related roles and practice new behaviors by acting out what they would do in job-related situations.
	• *Simulations and games*. Experiential exercises place trainees in realistic job-related situations and give them the opportunity to experience a job-related condition in a relatively low-cost setting. The trainee benefits from "hands-on experience" before actually performing the job, where mistakes may be more costly.
	• *Vestibule training*. Procedures and equipment similar to those used in the actual job are set up in a special area called a "vestibule." The trainee is then taught how to perform the job at his or her own pace without disrupting the actual flow of work, making costly mistakes, or exposing the trainee and others to dangerous conditions.
Impart Information and Knowledge; Develop Analytical and Problem-Solving Skills; and Practice, Learn, or Change Job Behaviors	• *Computer-based learning*. Interactive videos, software, CD-ROMs, personal computers, teleconferencing, and the Internet may be combined to present multimedia-based training.

Source: A. Fowler, "How to Decide on Training Methods," *People Management* 25, no. 1 (1995): 36.

veloping problem-solving and analytical skills. Second, e-learning requires a significant investment in computers and high-speed Internet and network connections for all employees. Finally, though e-learning can be faster, many employees find it so boring and unengaging that they may choose to do their jobs rather than complete e-learning courses when sitting alone at their desks. E-learning may become more interesting, how-

ever, as more companies incorporate gamelike features in training, such as avatars and competition, into their e-learning courses.

4.3 Evaluating Training

After selecting a training method and conducting the training, the last step is to evaluate the training. Training can be evaluated in four ways: on *reactions*, how satisfied

ow Chemical now has the ability to provide electronic learning or training to all 40,000 employees in 70 countries using its Learn@dow.now Web-based training system.[39] Likewise, Cisco Systems offers 4,500 e-learning courses to its managers and employees.[40] And British Telecom used an avatar-based course to train 4,500 salespeople in just over a month. Traditional classroom training would have cost twice as much and taken twice as long to deliver.[41] These companies all determined that the advantages of e-learning far outnumbered the disadvantages.

mgmt trend

trainees were with the program; on *learning,* how much employees improved their knowledge or skills; on *behavior,* how much employees actually changed their on-the-job behavior because of training; or on *results,* how much training improved job performance, such as increased sales or quality, or decreased costs.[42] In general, if done well, training provides meaningful benefits for most companies. For example, a study by the American Society for Training and Development shows that a training budget as small as $680 per employee can increase a company's total return on investment by 6 percent.[43]

5 Performance Appraisal

Performance appraisal is the process of assessing how well employees are doing their jobs. Most employees and managers intensely dislike the performance appraisal process. One manager says "I hate annual performance reviews. I hated them when I used to get them, and I hate them now that I give them. If I had to choose between performance reviews and paper cuts, I'd take paper cuts every time. I'd even take razor

Performance appraisal
the process of assessing how well employees are doing their jobs

Objective performance measures measures of job performance that are easily and directly counted or quantified

burns and the sound of fingernails on a blackboard."[44] Unfortunately, attitudes like this are all too common. In fact, 70 percent of employees are dissatisfied with the performance appraisal process in their companies. Likewise, according to the Society for Human Resource Management, 90 percent of human resource managers are dissatisfied with the performance appraisal systems used by their companies.[45]

*Let's explore how companies can avoid some of these problems with performance appraisals by **5.1 accurately measuring job performance** and **5.2 effectively sharing performance feedback with employees**.*

5.1 Accurately Measuring Job Performance

Workers often have strong doubts about the accuracy of their performance appraisals—and they may be right. For example, it's widely known that assessors are prone to errors when rating worker performance. One of the reasons that managers make these errors is that they often don't spend enough time gathering or reviewing performance data. What can be done to minimize rating errors and improve the accuracy with which job performance is measured? In general, two approaches have been used: improving performance appraisal measures themselves and training performance raters to be more accurate.

One of the ways companies try to improve performance appraisal measures is to use as many objective performance measures as possible. **Objective performance measures** are measures of performance that are easily and directly counted or quantified. Common objective performance measures include output, scrap,

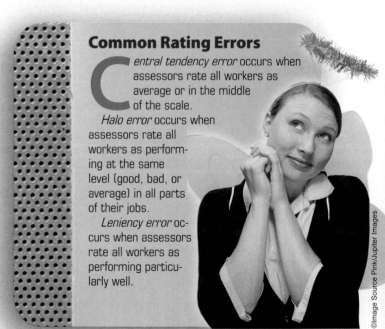

Common Rating Errors

Central tendency error occurs when assessors rate all workers as average or in the middle of the scale.

Halo error occurs when assessors rate all workers as performing at the same level (good, bad, or average) in all parts of their jobs.

Leniency error occurs when assessors rate all workers as performing particularly well.

waste, sales, customer complaints, and rejection rates.

But when objective performance measures aren't available, and frequently they aren't, subjective performance measures have to be used instead. Subjective performance measures require that someone judge or assess a worker's performance. The most common kind of subjective performance measure is the Graphic Rating Scale (GRS) shown in Exhibit 11.8. Graphic rating scales are most widely used because they are easy to construct, but they are very susceptible to rating errors.

A popular alternative to graphic rating scales is the **Behavior Observation Scale (BOS).** BOS requires raters to rate the frequency with which workers perform specific behaviors representative of the job dimensions that are critical to successful job performance. Exhibit 11.8 shows a BOS for two important job dimensions for a retail salesperson: customer service and money handling. Notice that each dimension lists several specific behaviors characteristic of a worker who excels in that dimension of job performance. (Normally, the scale would list 7 to 12 items per dimension, not 3 as in the exhibit.) Notice also that the behaviors are good behaviors, meaning they indicate good performance, and the rater is asked to judge how frequently an employee engaged in those good behaviors. The logic behind the BOS is that better performers engage in good behaviors more often.

Not only do BOSs work well for rating critical dimensions of performance, but studies also show that managers strongly prefer BOSs for giving performance feedback; accurately differentiating between poor, average, and good workers; identifying training needs; and accurately measuring performance. And in response to the statement, "If I were defending a company, this rating format would be an asset to my case," attorneys strongly preferred BOSs over other kinds of subjective performance appraisal scales.[46]

The second approach to improving the measurement of workers' job performance is **rater training**. The most effective is frame-of-reference training in which a group of trainees learns how to do performance appraisals by watching a videotape of an employee at work. Next, they evaluate the performance of the person in the videotape. A trainer (i.e., subject matter expert) then shares his or her evaluations, and trainees' evaluations are compared with

the expert's. The expert then explains rationales behind his or her evaluations. This process is repeated until the difference in evaluations given by trainees and evaluations by the expert are minimized. The underlying logic behind the frame-of-reference training is that by adopting the frame of reference used by an expert, trainees will be able to accurately observe, judge, and use the scale to evaluate performance of others.[47]

Exhibit 11.8

Subjective Performance Appraisal Scales

Graphic Rating Scale

	Very poor	Poor	Average	Good	Very good
Example 1: Quality of work performed is	1	2	3	4	5

	Very poor (20% errors)	Poor (15% errors)	Average (10% errors)	Good (5% errors)	Very good (less than 5% errors)
Example 2: Quality of work performed is	1	2	3	4	5

Behavioral Observation Scale

Dimension: Customer Service

	Almost Never				Almost Always
1. Greets customers with a smile and a "hello."	1	2	3	4	5
2. Calls other stores to help customers find merchandise that is not in stock.	1	2	3	4	5
3. Promptly handles customer concerns and complaints.	1	2	3	4	5

Dimension: Money Handling

	Almost Never				Almost Always
1. Accurately makes change from customer transactions.	1	2	3	4	5
2. Accounts balance at the end of the day, no shortages or surpluses.	1	2	3	4	5
3. Accurately records transactions in computer system.	1	2	3	4	5

Behavioral observation scales (BOSs) rating scales that indicate the frequency with which workers perform specific behaviors that are representative of the job dimensions critical to successful job performance

Rater training training performance appraisal raters in how to avoid rating errors and increase rating accuracy

5.2 Sharing Performance Feedback

After gathering accurate performance data, the next step is to share performance feedback with employees. Unfortunately, even when performance appraisal ratings are accurate, the appraisal process often breaks down at the feedback stage. Employees become defensive and dislike hearing any negative assessments of their work, no matter how small. Managers become defensive, too, and dislike giving appraisal feedback as much as employees dislike receiving it.

What can be done to overcome the inherent difficulties in performance appraisal feedback sessions? Since performance appraisal ratings have traditionally been the judgments of just one person, the boss, one possibility is to use **360-degree feedback.** In this approach, feedback comes from four sources: the boss, subordinates, peers and coworkers, and the employees themselves. The data, which are obtained anonymously (except for the boss's), are compiled into a feedback report comparing the employee's self-ratings with those of the boss, subordinates, and peers and coworkers. Usually, a consultant or human resource specialist discusses the results with the employee. The advantage of 360-degree programs is that negative feedback ("You don't listen.") is often more credible when it comes from several people.

Herbert Meyer, who has been studying performance appraisal feedback for more than 30 years, recommends a list of topics for discussion in performance appraisal feedback sessions (see Exhibit 11.9).[48] First, managers should separate developmental feedback, which is designed to improve future performance, from administrative feedback, which is used as a reward for past performance, such as for raises. When managers give developmental feedback, they're acting as coaches, but when they give administrative feedback, they're acting as judges. These roles, coaches and judges, are clearly incompatible. As coaches, managers are encouraging, pointing out opportunities for growth and improvement, and employees are typically open and receptive to feedback. But as judges, managers are evaluative, and employees are typically defensive and closed to feedback.

Second, Meyer suggests that performance appraisal feedback sessions be based on self-appraisals, in which employees carefully assess their own strengths, weaknesses, successes, and failures in writing. Because

360-degree feedback
a performance appraisal process in which feedback is obtained from the boss, subordinates, peers and coworkers, and the employees themselves

Exhibit 11.9

What to Discuss in a Performance Appraisal Feedback Session

- ✔ Overall progress—an analysis of accomplishments and shortcomings.
- ✔ Problems encountered in meeting job requirements.
- ✔ Opportunities to improve performance.
- ✔ Long-range plans and opportunities— for the job and for the individual's career.
- ✔ General discussion of possible plans and goals for the coming year.

Source: H. H. Meyer, "A Solution to the Performance Appraisal Feedback Enigma," *Academy of Management Executive* 5, no. 1 (1991): 68–76.

employees play an active role in the review of their performance, managers can be coaches rather than judges. Also, because the focus is on future goals and development, both employees and managers are likely to be more satisfied with the process and more committed to future plans and changes. And, because the focus is on development and not administrative assessment, studies show that self-appraisals lead to more candid self-assessments than traditional supervisory reviews.[49] See Exhibit 11.9 for a list of topics that Meyer recommends for discussion in performance appraisal feedback sessions.

Finally, what people do with the performance feedback they receive really matters. A study of 1,361 senior managers found that managers who reviewed their 360-degree feedback with an executive coach (hired by the company) were more likely to set specific goals for improvement, ask their bosses for ways to improve, and subsequently improve their performance.[50]

Also, a five-year study of 252 managers found that their performance improved dramatically if they met with their subordinates to discuss their 360-degree feedback ("You don't listen") and how they were going to address it ("I'll restate what others have said before stating my opinion"). Performance was dramatically lower for managers who never discussed their 360-degree feedback with subordinates and for managers who did not routinely do so (some managers did not review their 360-degree feedback with subordinates each year of the study). Why is discussing 360-degree feedback with subordinates so effective? These discussions help managers better understand their weaknesses, force them to develop a plan to improve, and demonstrate to the subordinates the managers' public commitment to improving.[51] In short, it helps to have people discuss their performance feedback with others, but it particularly helps to have them discuss their feedback with the people who provided it.

Keeping Qualified Workers

China has a population of 1.3 billion people, but in the Pearl River delta there aren't enough workers to meet the skyrocketing demand for manufacturing workers. Consequently, companies such as Chigo Air-Conditioning are having to work hard to keep their employees. In the last five years, Chigo has raised salaries, started giving bonuses to workers who stay longer than three years, and built brand new housing with TV sets and swimming pools to entice workers to stay.[52] All this may not be enough, however, as Chinese economists estimate that companies will have to pay wages 40 to 50 percent higher to keep the workers they have and to fill the two million job openings in this part of China.

> After reading the next section, you should be able to
>
> 6 describe basic compensation strategies and discuss the four kinds of employee separations.

6 Compensation and Employee Separation

Compensation includes both the financial and the non-financial rewards that organizations give employees in exchange for their work. **Employee separation** is a broad term covering the loss of an employee for any reason. *Involuntary separation* occurs when employers decide to terminate or lay off employees. *Voluntary separation* occurs when employees decide to quit or retire. Because employee separations affect recruiting, selection, training, and compensation, organizations should forecast the number of employees they expect to lose through terminations, layoffs, turnover, or retirements when doing human resource planning.

*Let's learn more about compensation and employee separation by examining the **6.1 compensation decisions that managers must make,** as well as **6.2 terminations, 6.3 downsizing, 6.4 retirements,** and **6.5 turnover.***

6.1 Compensation Decisions

There are three basic kinds of compensation decisions: pay level, pay variability, and pay structure.[53]

Pay-level decisions are decisions about whether to pay workers at a level that is below, above, or at current market wages. Companies use job evaluation to set their pay structures. **Job evaluation** determines the worth of each job by determining the market value of the knowledge, skills, and requirements needed to perform it. After conducting a job evaluation, most companies try to pay the "going rate," meaning the current market wage. There are always companies, however, whose financial situation causes them to pay considerably less than current market wages. The child-care industry, for example, has chronic difficulties filling jobs because it pays well below market wages. Also, because wages are so low (an average of $7.86 an hour, or $16,350 a year), the applicants it attracts are increasingly less qualified.[54] Donna Krause, who runs Creative Learning and Child Care in Dundalk, Maryland, lost five child-care teachers one August when all were hired away by higher-paying public school systems. All of the teachers who left had college degrees, but none of their replacements did.[55]

Some companies choose to pay above-average wages to attract and keep employees. *Above-market wages* can attract a larger, more qualified

Compensation the financial and nonfinancial rewards that organizations give employees in exchange for their work

Employee separation the voluntary or involuntary loss of an employee

Job evaluation a process that determines the worth of each job in a company by evaluating the market value of the knowledge, skills, and requirements needed to perform it pool of job applicants, increase the rate of job acceptance, decrease the time it takes to fill positions, and increase the time that employees stay.[56]

Pay-variability decisions concern the extent to which employees' pay varies with individual and organizational performance. Linking pay to performance is intended to increase employee motivation, effort, and job performance. Piecework, sales commissions, profit sharing, employee stock ownership plans, and stock options are common pay-variability options. For instance, under **piecework** pay plans, employees are paid a set rate for each item produced up to some standard (e.g., 35 cents per item produced for output up to 100 units per day). Once productivity exceeds the standard, employees are paid a set amount for each unit of output over the standard (e.g., 45 cents for each unit above 100 units). Under a sales **commission** plan, salespeople are paid a percentage of the purchase price of items they sell. The more they sell, the more they earn.

Because pay plans such as piecework and commissions are based on individual performance, they can reduce the incentive that people have to work together. Therefore, companies also use group incentives (discussed in Chapter 10) and organizational incentives, such as profit sharing, employee stock ownership plans, and stock options, to encourage teamwork and cooperation.

With **profit sharing** employees receive a portion of the organization's profits over and above their regular compensation. The more profitable the company, the more profit is shared. Renault SAS, the French automaker, has a profit sharing agreement that distributes 6 percent of its net income to employees, with a minimum payout of $2,134 Euros per employee.[57]

Employee stock ownership plans (ESOPs) compensate employees by awarding them shares of the company stock in addition to their regular compensation. By contrast, **stock options** give employees the right to purchase shares of stock

Piecework a compensation system in which employees are paid a set rate for each item they produce

Commission a compensation system in which employees earn a percentage of each sale they make

Profit sharing a compensation system in which a company pays a percentage of its profits to employees in addition to their regular compensation

Employee stock ownership plan (ESOP) a compensation system that awards employees shares of company stock in addition to their regular compensation

Stock options a compensation system that gives employees the right to purchase shares of stock at a set price, even if the value of the stock increases above that price

How Do Options Work?

Options work like this. Let's say that you are awarded the right (or option) to buy 100 shares of stock from the company for $5 a share. If the company's stock price rises to $15 a share, you can exercise your options and make $1,000. When you exercise your options, you pay the company $500 (100 shares at $5 a share), but because the stock is selling for $15 in the stock market, you can sell your 100 shares for $1,500 and make $1,000. Of course, as the company's profits and share values increase, stock options become even more valuable to employees. Stock options have no value, however, if the company's stock falls below the option "grant price," the price at which the options have been issued to you. For instance, the options you have on 100 shares of stock with a grant price of $5 aren't going to do you a lot of good if the company's stock is worth $2.50. Why exercise your stock options and pay $5 a share for stock that sells for $2.50 a share in the stock market? (Stock options are said to be "underwater" when the grant price is lower than the market price.)

©Getty Images News

at a set price. Proponents of stock options argue that this gives employees and managers a strong incentive to work hard to make the company successful. If they do, the company's profits and stock price increase, and their stock options increase in value. If they don't, profits stagnate or turn into losses, and their stock options decrease in value or become worthless.

Pay-structure decisions are concerned with internal pay distributions, meaning the extent to which people in the company receive very different levels of pay.[58] With *hierarchical pay structures,* there are big differences from one pay level to another. The highest pay levels are for people near the top of the pay distribution. The basic idea behind hierarchical pay structures is that large differences in pay between jobs or organizational levels should motivate people to work harder to obtain those higher-paying jobs. Many publicly owned companies have hierarchical pay structures by virtue of the huge amounts they pay their top managers and CEOs. For example, the average CEO now makes 289 times as much as the average worker, down from 475 times the pay of average workers just five years ago. But with CEO pay packages averaging $9.6 million per year and average workers earning just $33,176, the difference is still incredible.[59]

By contrast, *compressed pay structures* typically have fewer pay levels and smaller differences in pay between levels. Pay is less dispersed and more similar across jobs in the company. The basic idea behind compressed pay structures is that similar pay levels should lead to higher levels of cooperation, feelings of fairness and a common purpose, and better group and team performance.

So should companies choose hierarchical or compressed pay structures? The evidence isn't straightforward, but studies seem to indicate that there are significant problems with the hierarchical approach. The most damaging finding is that there appears to be little link between organizational performance and the pay of top managers.[60] Furthermore, studies of professional athletes indicate that hierarchical pay structures (e.g., paying superstars 40 to 50 times more than the lowest-paid athlete on the team) hurt the performance of teams and individual players.[61] Likewise, managers are twice as likely to quit their jobs when their companies have very strong hierarchical pay structures (i.e., when they're paid dramatically less than the people above them).[62] For now, it seems that hierarchical pay structures work best for independent work, where it's easy to determine the contributions of individual performers and little coordination with others is needed to get the job done. In other words, hierarchical pay structures work best when clear links can be drawn between individual performance and individual rewards. By contrast, compressed pay structures, in which everyone receives similar pay, seem to work best for interdependent work, which requires employees to work together. Some companies are pursuing a middle ground: combining hierarchical and compressed pay structures by giving ordinary workers the chance to earn more through ESOPs, stock options, and profit sharing.

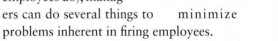

6.2 Terminating Employees

Hopefully, the words "You're fired!" have never been directed at you. Lots of people hear them, however, as more than 400,000 people a year get fired from their jobs. Getting fired is a terrible thing, but many managers make it even worse by bungling the firing process, needlessly provoking the person who was fired and unintentionally inviting lawsuits. Though firing is never pleasant (and managers hate firings nearly as much as employees do), managers can do several things to minimize the problems inherent in firing employees.

First, in most situations, firing should not be the first option. Instead, employees should be given a chance to change their behavior. When problems arise, employees should have ample warning and must be specifically informed as to the nature and seriousness of the trouble they're in. After being notified, they should be given sufficient time to change. If the problems continue, the employees should again be counseled about their job performance, what could be done to improve it, and the possible consequences if things don't change (e.g., written reprimand, suspension without pay, or firing). Sometimes this is enough to solve the problem. If the problem isn't corrected after several rounds of warnings and discussions, however, the employee may be terminated.[63]

Second, employees should be fired only for a good reason. Employers used to hire and fire employees under the legal principle of "employment at will," which allowed them to fire employees for a good reason, a bad reason, or no reason at all. (Employees could also quit for a good reason, a bad reason, or no reason whenever they desired.) As employees began contesting their firings in court, however, the principle of wrongful discharge emerged. **Wrongful discharge** is a legal doctrine that requires employers to have a job-related reason to terminate employees. In other words, like other major human resource decisions, termination decisions should be made on the basis of job-related factors, such as violating company rules or consistently poor performance.

6.3 Downsizing

Downsizing is the planned elimination of jobs in a company. Whether it's because of cost cutting, declining market share, previous overaggressive hiring and growth, or outsourcing, companies typically eliminate 1 million to 1.9 million jobs a year.[64] Two-thirds of companies that downsize will downsize a second time within a year.

Does downsizing work? In theory, downsizing is supposed to lead to higher productivity and profits, better stock performance, and increased organizational flexibility. However, numerous studies demonstrate that it doesn't. For instance, a 15-year study of downsizing found that downsizing 10 percent of a company's work force produced only a 1.5 percent decrease in costs; that firms that downsized increased their stock price by only 4.7 percent over three years, compared with 34.3 percent for firms that didn't; and that profitability and productivity were generally not improved by downsizing.[65] These results make it clear that the best strategy is to conduct effective human resource planning and avoid downsizing altogether. Indeed, downsizing should always be a last resort.

If companies do find themselves in financial or strategic situations where downsizing is required for survival, however, they should train managers in how to break the news to downsized employees, have senior managers explain in detail why downsizing is necessary, and time the announcement so that employees hear it from the company and not from other sources, such as TV or newspaper reports.[66] Fi-

Guidelines for Conducting Layoffs

1. Provide clear reasons and explanations for the layoffs.
2. To avoid laying off employees with critical or irreplaceable skills, knowledge, and expertise, get input from human resources, the legal department, and several levels of management.
3. Train managers in how to tell employees that they are being laid off (i.e., stay calm; make the meeting short; explain why, but don't be personal; and provide information about immediate concerns, such as benefits, job search, and collecting personal goods).
4. Give employees the bad news early in the day, and try to avoid laying off employees before holidays.
5. Provide outplacement services and counseling to help laid-off employees find new jobs.
6. Communicate with survivors to explain how the company and their jobs will change.

Source: M. Boyle, "The Not-So-Fine Art of the Layoff," *Fortune*, 19 March 2001, 209.

nally, companies should do everything they can to help downsized employees find other jobs. One of the best ways to do this is to use **outplacement services** that provide employment-counseling services for employees faced with downsizing. Outplacement services often include advice and training in preparing résumés, getting ready for job interviews, and even identifying job opportunities in other companies.

6.4 Retirement

Early retirement incentive programs (ERIPs) offer financial benefits to employees to encourage them to retire early. Companies use ERIPs to reduce the number of employees in the organization, to lower costs by eliminating positions after employees retire, to lower costs by replacing high-paid retirees with lower-paid, less-experienced employees, or to create openings and job opportunities for people inside the company.

Although ERIPs can save companies money, they can pose a big problem for managers if they fail to accurately predict which employees—the good performers or the poor performers—and how many will retire early. Consultant Ron Nicol says, "The thing that doesn't work is just asking for volunteers. You get the wrong volunteers. Some of your best people will feel they can get a job anywhere. Or you have people who are close to retirement and are a real asset to the company."[67] When Ameritech Corporation (now part of AT&T) offered an ERIP, it carefully identified the number of employees near retirement age and estimated that 5,000 to 6,000 of its 48,000 employees would take advantage of the program.

Wrongful discharge a legal doctrine that requires employers to have a job-related reason to terminate employees

Downsizing the planned elimination of jobs in a company

Outplacement services employment-counseling services offered to employees who are losing their jobs because of downsizing

Early retirement incentive programs (ERIPs) programs that offer financial benefits to employees to encourage them to retire early

Instead, nearly 22,000 employees accepted the ERIP offer and applied for early retirement![68]

Because of the problems associated with ERIPs, many companies are now offering **phased retirement,** in which employees transition to retirement by working reduced hours over a period of time before completely retiring. The advantage for employees is that they have more free time, but continue to earn salaries and benefits without changing companies or careers. The advantage for companies is that it allows them to reduce salaries and hiring and training costs and retain experienced, valuable workers.[69]

6.5 Employee Turnover

Employee turnover is the loss of employees who voluntarily choose to leave the company. In general, most companies try to keep the rate of employee turnover low to reduce recruiting, hiring, training, and replacement costs. Not all kinds of employee turnover are bad for organizations, however. In fact, some turnover can actually be good. For instance, **functional turnover** is the loss of poor-performing employees who choose to leave the organization.[70] Functional turnover gives the organization a chance to replace poor performers with better workers. In fact, one study found that simply replacing poor-performing leavers with average workers would increase the revenues produced by retail salespeople in an upscale department store by $112,000 per person per year.[71] By contrast, **dysfunctional turnover,** the loss of high performers who choose to leave, is a costly loss to the organization.

Employee turnover should be carefully analyzed to determine whether good or poor performers are choosing to leave the organization. If the company is losing too many high performers, managers should determine the reasons and find ways to reduce the loss of valuable employees. The company may have to raise salary levels, offer enhanced benefits, or improve working conditions to retain skilled workers. One of the best ways to influence functional and dysfunctional turnover is to link pay directly to performance. A study of four sales forces found that when pay was strongly linked to performance via sales commissions and bonuses, poor performers were much more likely to leave (i.e., functional turnover). By contrast, poor performers were much more likely to stay when paid large, guaranteed monthly salaries and small sales commissions and bonuses.[72]

Phased retirement employees transition to retirement by working reduced hours over a period of time before completely retiring

Employee turnover loss of employees who voluntarily choose to leave the company

Functional turnover loss of poor-performing employees who voluntarily choose to leave a company

Dysfunctional turnover loss of high-performing employees who voluntarily choose to leave a company

By the Numbers

$3.75 million amount Hooters paid to settle class-action lawsuit brought by 7 men

80% of companies conduct criminal record checks

$680 smallest training budget per employee that can increase company's ROI by 6%

$7.86 average hourly wage for a U.S. child-care worker

2 million number of job openings in Pearl River delta region of China

MANAGING INDIVIDUALS AND A DIVERSE WORK FORCE

Workplace diversity as we know it today is changing. Exhibit 12.1 (on page 222) shows predictions from the U.S. Bureau of the Census of how the U.S. population will change over the next 65 years. The percentage of white, non-Hispanic Americans in the general population is expected to decline from 69.3 percent in 2005 to 46.8 percent by the year 2070. By contrast, the percentage of African Americans will increase (from 12.3 percent to 13.2 percent), as will the percentage of Asian Americans (from 4.3 percent to 10.6 percent). Meanwhile the proportion of Native Americans will hold steady (at 0.8 percent). The fastest-growing group by far, though, is Hispanics, who are expected to increase from 13.3 percent of the total population in 2005 to 28.6 percent by 2070.

Other significant changes have already occurred. For example, today women hold half the jobs in the United States, up from 38.2 percent in 1970.[1] Furthermore, white males, who composed 63.9 percent of the work force in 1950, hold just 38.2 percent of today's jobs.[2]

These rather dramatic changes have taken place in a relatively short time. And, as these trends clearly show, the work force of the near future will be increasingly Hispanic, Asian American, African American, and female. It will also be older, as the average baby boomer approaches the age of 60 around 2010. Since many boomers are likely to postpone retirement and work well into their 70s to offset predicted reductions in Social Security and Medicare benefits, the work force may become even older than expected.[3]

Learning Outcomes

1 describe diversity and explain why it matters.

2 understand the special challenges that the dimensions of surface-level diversity pose for managers.

3 explain how the dimensions of deep-level diversity affect individual behavior and interactions in the workplace.

4 explain the basic principles and practices that can be used to manage diversity.

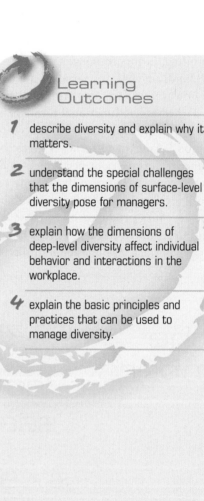

©Radius Images/Jupiter Images

Diversity and Why It Matters

Diversity means variety. Therefore, **diversity** exists in organizations when there is a variety of demographic, cultural, and personal differences among the people who work there and the customers who do business there. For example, step into Longo Toyota in El Monte, California, one of Toyota's top-selling dealerships, and you'll find diversity in the form of salespeople who speak Spanish, Korean, Arabic, Vietnamese, Hebrew, and Mandarin Chinese. In fact, the 60 salespeople at Longo Toyota speak 30 different languages. Surprisingly, this level of diversity was achieved without a formal diversity plan in place.[4]

After reading the next section, you should be able to

1 describe diversity and explain why it matters.

Diversity a variety of demographic, cultural, and personal differences among an organization's employees and customers

Exhibit 12.1

Predicted U.S. Population, Distributed by Race, 2005-2070

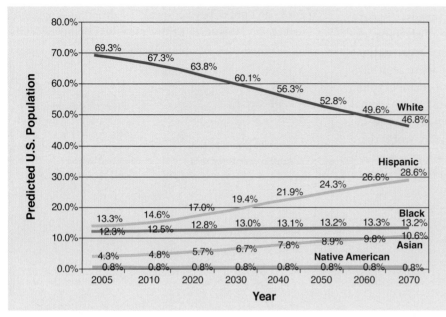

Sources: "Projections of the Resident Population by Race, Hispanic Origin, and Nativity: Middle Series, 2001–2005, 2006–2010, 2011–2015, 2016–2020, 2025–2045, 2050–2070," U.S. Census Bureau, [Online] available at http://www.census.gov/population/projections/nation/summary/np-t5-b.txt, ttp://www.census.gov/population/projections/nation/summary/np-t5-c.txt, http://www.census.gov/population/projections/nation/summary/np-t5-e.txt, http://www.census.gov/population/projections/nation/summary/np-t5-f.txt, http://www.census.gov/population/projections/nation/summary/np-t5-g.txt.

1 Diversity: Differences That Matter

You'll begin your exploration of diversity by learning **1.1 that diversity is not affirmative action** and **1.2 how to build a business case for diversity.**

1.1 Diversity Is Not Affirmative Action

A common misconception is that workplace diversity and affirmative action are the same, yet these concepts differ in several critical ways. To start, **affirmative action** refers to purposeful steps taken by an organization to create employment opportunities for minorities and women.[5] By contrast, diversity exists in organizations when there is a variety of demographic, cultural, and personal differences among the people who work there and the customers who do business there. So one key difference is that affirmative action is more narrowly focused on demographics such as sex and race, while diversity has a broader focus that includes demographic, cultural, and personal

Affirmative action
purposeful steps taken by an organization to create employment opportunities for minorities and women

differences. Furthermore, diversity can exist even if organizations don't take purposeful steps to create it. For example, as mentioned earlier, Longo Toyota achieved a high level of diversity without having a formal affirmative action program. Likewise, a local restaurant located near a university in a major city is likely to have a more diverse group of employees than one located in a small town. So, organizations can achieve diversity without affirmative action. Likewise, organizations that take affirmative action to create employment opportunities for women and minorities may not yet have diverse work forces.

Another important difference is that affirmative action is required by law for private employers with 15 or more employees, while diversity is not. Affirmative action originated with the 1964 Civil Rights Act, which bans discrimination in voting, public places, federal government programs, federally supported public education, and employment. Title VII of the Civil Rights Act (**http://www.eeoc.gov/policy/vii.html**) requires that workers have equal employment opportunities when being hired or promoted. More specifically, Title VII prohibits companies

©Rachel Epstein/PhotoEdit Inc.

> A common misconception is that workplace **diversity** and **affirmative** action are the same.

from discriminating on the basis of race, color, religion, sex or national origin. Furthermore, Title VII created the Equal Employment Opportunity Commission, or EEOC (**http://www.eeoc.gov**), to administer these laws. By contrast, there is no federal law or agency to oversee diversity. Organizations that pursue diversity goals and programs do so voluntarily.

Affirmative action programs and diversity programs also have different purposes. The purpose of affirmative action programs is to compensate for past discrimination, which was widespread when legislation was introduced in the 1960s; to prevent ongoing discrimination; and to provide equal opportunities to all, regardless of race, color, religion, sex, or national origin. Organizations that fail to uphold these laws may be required to

- hire, promote, or give back pay to those not hired or promoted
- reinstate those who were wrongly terminated
- pay attorneys' fees and court costs for those who bring charges against them
- take other actions that make individuals whole by returning them to the condition or place they would have been had it not been for discrimination[6]

Consequently, affirmative action is basically a punitive approach.[7] By contrast, the general purpose of diversity programs is to create a positive work environ-

ment where no one is advantaged or disadvantaged, where "we" is everyone, where everyone can do his or her best work, where differences are respected and not ignored, and where everyone feels comfortable.[8] So, unlike affirmative action, which punishes companies for not achieving specific sex and race ratios in their work forces, diversity programs seek to benefit both organizations and their employees by encouraging organizations to value all kinds of differences.

Despite affirmative action's overall success in making workplaces much fairer than they used to be,[9] many people argue that some affirmative action programs unconstitutionally offer preferential treatment to females and minorities at the expense of other employees—a view accepted by some courts.[10] In California and Michigan, voters approved propositions that ban race- and sex-based affirmative action in college admissions, government hiring, and government contracting programs. Christopher Katzenbach, an attorney in a San Francisco law firm, said, "I think people want to be evaluated on their merits, not their race or gender, and that is the driving force behind a lot of this [reverse discrimination] litigation."[11]

Furthermore, research shows that people who have gotten a job or promotion as a result of affirmative action are frequently viewed as unqualified, even when clear evidence of their qualifications exists.[12] So, while affirmative action programs have created opportunities for minorities and women, those same minorities and women are frequently presumed to be unqualified when others believe they obtained their jobs as a result of affirmative action.

In summary, affirmative action and diversity are not the same thing. Not only are they fundamentally different, but they also differ in purpose, practice, and the reactions they produce.

1.2 Diversity Makes Good Business Sense

Those who support the idea of diversity in organizations often ignore its business aspects altogether, claiming instead that diversity is simply the "right thing to do." Yet diversity actually makes good business sense in several ways: cost savings, attracting and retaining talent, and driving business growth.[13]

Diversity helps companies with *cost savings* by reducing turnover, decreasing absenteeism, and enabling them to avoid expensive lawsuits.[14] Because of lost productivity and the cost of recruiting and selecting new workers, companies lose substantial amounts of money when employees quit their jobs. In fact, turnover costs typically amount to more than 90 percent of employees' salaries. Since turnover rates for African Americans average 40 percent higher than for whites, and since women quit their jobs at twice the rate men do, companies that manage diverse work forces well can cut costs by reducing the turnover rates of these employees.[15]

Diversity programs also save companies money by helping them avoid discrimination lawsuits, which have increased by a factor of 20 since 1970 and quadrupled just since 1995. In one survey conducted by the Society for Human Resource Management, 78 percent of respondents reported that diversity efforts helped them avoid lawsuits and litigation costs.[16] Indeed, because companies lose two-thirds of all discrimination cases that go to trial, the best strategy from a business perspective is not to be sued for discrimination at all. When companies lose, the average individual settlement amounts to more than $600,000.[17] And settlement costs can be substantially higher in class-action lawsuits, in which individuals join together to sue a company as a group. In fact, the average class-action lawsuit costs companies $58.9 million for racial discrimination and $24.9 million for gender discrimination.[18]

Diversity also makes business sense by helping companies *attract and retain talented workers.*[19] Indeed, diversity-friendly companies tend to attract better and more diverse job applicants. Very simply, diversity begets more diversity. Companies that make *Fortune* magazine's list of the 50 best companies for minorities already attract a diverse and talented pool of job applicants. But, after being recognized by *Fortune* for their efforts, they experience even bigger increases in both the quality and the diversity of people who apply for jobs. Indeed, research shows that companies with acclaimed diversity programs not only attract more talented workers, but also have higher stock market performance.[20]

The third way that diversity makes business sense is by *driving business growth.* Diversity helps companies grow by improving their understanding of the marketplace. When companies have diverse work forces, they are better able to understand the needs of their increasingly diverse customer bases.

A recent survey conducted by the Society for Human Resource Management found that tapping into "di-verse customers and markets" was the number one reason managers gave for implementing diversity programs.[21]

Diversity also helps companies grow through higher-quality problem solving. Though diverse groups initially have more difficulty working together than homogeneous groups, after several months diverse groups do a better job of identifying problems and generating alternative solutions, the two most important steps in problem solving.[22] In short, "diversity is no longer about counting heads; it's about making heads counts," says Amy George, vice president of diversity and inclusion at PepsiCo.[23]

Diversity and Individual Differences

A survey that asked managers, "What is meant by diversity to decision-makers in your organization?" found that they most frequently mentioned race, culture, sex, national origin, age, religion, and regional origin.[24] When managers describe workers this way, they are focusing on surface-level diversity. **Surface-level diversity** consists of differences that are immediately observable, typically unchangeable, and easy to measure.[25] In other words,

Surface-level diversity differences such as age, sex, race/ethnicity, and physical disabilities that are observable, typically unchangeable, and easy to measure

MGMT INPUT

The Latino employee network at Frito-Lay proved invaluable during the development of Doritos Guacamole Flavored Tortilla Chips. Members of the network, called Adelante, provided feedback on the taste and packaging to ensure that the product would be regarded as authentic in the Latino community. The Adelante members' insights helped make the guacamole-flavored Doritos one of the most successful new-product launches in the company's history, generating more than $100 million in sales in its first year alone.

Source: R. Rodriguez, "Diversity Finds Its Place: More Organizations Are Dedicating Senior-Level Executives to Drive Diversity Initiatives for Bottom-Line Effect," *HR Magazine,* August 2006.

©Susan Van Etten

independent observers can usually agree on dimensions of surface-level diversity, such as another person's age, sex, race/ethnicity, or physical capabilities.

And while most people start by using easily observable characteristics, such as surface-level diversity, to categorize or stereotype other people, those initial, surface-level categorizations typically give way to deeper impressions formed from knowledge of others' behavior and psychological characteristics, such as personality and attitudes.[26] When you think of others this way, you are focusing on deep-level diversity. **Deep-level diversity** consists of differences that are communicated through verbal and nonverbal behaviors and are learned only through extended interaction with others.[27] Examples of deep-level diversity include personality differences, attitudes, beliefs, and values. In other words, as people in diverse workplaces get to know each other, the initial focus on surface-level differences such as age, race/ethnicity, sex, and physical capabilities is replaced by deeper, more accurate knowledge of coworkers.

If managed properly, the shift from surface- to deep-level diversity can accomplish two things.[28] First, coming to know and understand each other better can result in reduced prejudice and conflict. Second, it can lead to stronger social integration. **Social integration** is the degree to which group members are psychologically attracted to working with each other to accomplish a common objective, or, as one manager put it, "working together to get the job done."

After reading the next two sections, you should be able to

2 understand the special challenges that the dimensions of surface-level diversity pose for managers.

3 explain how the dimensions of deep-level diversity affect individual behavior and interactions in the workplace.

2 Surface-Level Diversity

Because age, sex, race/ethnicity, and disabilities are usually immediately observable, many managers and workers use these dimensions of surface-level diversity to form initial impressions and categorizations of coworkers, bosses, customers, or job applicants. Whether

intentionally or not, sometimes those initial categorizations and impressions lead to decisions or behaviors that discriminate. Consequently, these dimensions of surface-level diversity pose special challenges for managers who are trying to create positive work environments where everyone feels comfortable and no one is advantaged or disadvantaged.

Let's learn more about those challenges and the ways that **2.1 age, 2.2 sex, 2.3 race/ethnicity, and 2.4 mental or physical disabilities can affect decisions and behaviors in organizations.**

2.1 Age

Age discrimination is treating people differently (e.g., in hiring and firing, promotion, and compensation decisions) because of their age. According to the Society for Human Resource Management, 53 percent of 428 surveyed managers believed that older workers "didn't keep up with technology," and 28 percent said that older workers were "less flexible."[29] For example, when 57-year-old Sam Horgan, a former chief financial officer, was interviewing for a job, he was asked by a 30-something job interviewer, "Would you have trouble working with young bright people?"[30]

So, what's reality and what's myth? Do older employees actually cost more? In some ways, they do. The older people are and the longer they stay with a company, the more the company pays for salaries, pension plans, and vacation time. But older workers cost companies less, too, because they show better judgment, care more about the quality of their work, and are less likely to quit, show up late, or be absent, the cost of which can be substantial.[31] A survey by Chicago outplacement firm Challenger, Gray & Christmas found that only 3 percent of employees age 50 and over

Deep-level diversity
differences such as personality and attitudes that are communicated through verbal and nonverbal behaviors and are learned only through extended interaction with others

Social integration
the degree to which group members are psychologically attracted to working with each other to accomplish a common objective

Age discrimination
treating people differently (e.g., in hiring and firing, promotion, and compensation decisions) because of their age

Surface-Level Diversity

Age

Personality   Attitudes

Physical
Capabilities   **Deep-Level Diversity**   Gender

Values/Beliefs

Race/
Ethnicity

©Goodshoot/Jupiter Images

> Interviewers rate **younger job candidates** as more qualified (even when they aren't).

changed jobs in any given year, compared to 10 percent of the entire work force and 12 percent of workers ages 25 to 34. The study also found that while older workers make up about 14 percent of the work force, they suffer only 10 percent of all workplace injuries and use fewer health-care benefits than younger workers with school-age children.[32] As for the widespread belief that job performance declines with age, the scientific evidence clearly refutes this stereotype. Performance does not decline with age, regardless of the type of job.[33]

What can companies do to reduce age discrimination?[34] To start, managers need to recognize that age discrimination is much more pervasive than they probably think. Whereas "old" used to mean mid-50s, in today's workplace, "old" is closer to 40. When 773 CEOs were asked, "At what age does a worker's productivity peak?" the average age they gave was 43. Thus, age discrimination may be affecting more workers because perceptions about age have changed. In addition, with the aging of the baby boomers, age discrimination is more likely to occur simply because there are millions more older workers than there used to be. And, because studies show that interviewers rate younger job candidates as more qualified (even when they aren't), companies need to train managers and recruiters to make hiring and promotion decisions on the basis of qualifications, not age. Companies also need to monitor the extent to which older workers receive training. The Bureau of Labor Statistics found that the number of training courses and number of hours spent in training drops dramatically after employees reach the age of 44.[35] Finally, companies need to ensure that younger and older workers interact with each other. One study found that younger workers generally hold positive views of older workers and that the more time they spent working with older coworkers, the more positive their attitudes became.[36]

2.2 Sex

Sex discrimination occurs when people are treated differently because of their sex. Sex discrimination and racial/ethnic discrimination (discussed in the next section) are often associated with the so-called **glass ceiling,** the in-

visible barrier that prevents women and minorities from advancing to the top jobs in organizations.

To what extent do women face sex discrimination in the workplace? In some ways, there is much less sex discrimination than there used to be. For example, whereas women held only 17 percent of managerial jobs in 1972, today they now outnumber men with 50.6 percent of managerial jobs, a percentage that is nearly equal to their representation in the work force.[37] Likewise, women own 47 percent of all U.S. businesses.[38] Whereas women owned 700,000 businesses in 1977 and 4.1 million businesses in 1987, today they own 9 million![39] Finally, though women still earn less than men on average, the differential is narrowing. Women earned 79.5 percent of what men did in 2003, up from 63 percent in 1979.

Women's Earnings as a Percentage of Men's

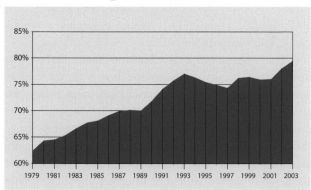

Sources: "Highlights of Women's Earnings in 2001, 2002, 2003," U.S. Department of Labor, Bureau of Labor Statistics, [Online] available at http://www.bls.gov/cps/cpswom2001.pdf and http://www.bls.gov/opub/ted/2004/oct/wk4/art01.htm, 25 May 2005.

Although progress is being made, sex discrimination continues to operate via the glass ceiling at higher levels in organizations. For instance, a woman had the highest salary (i.e., was the top earner) in only 5.2 percent of *Fortune* 500 companies, and only 15.7 percent of corporate officers (i.e., top management) were women. Indeed, only 9 of the 500 largest companies in the United States have women CEOs.[40] Similarly, just 13.6 percent of the members of corporate boards of directors are women.[41]

Is sex discrimination the sole reason for the slow rate at which women have been promoted to middle and upper levels of management and corporate boards? Some studies indicate that it's not.[42] In some instances, the slow

Women at *Fortune* 500 and 1000 Companies

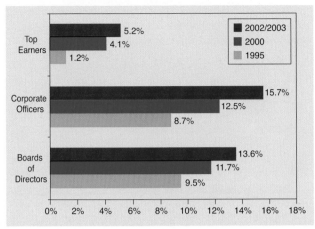

	2002/2003	2000	1995
Top Earners	5.2%	4.1%	1.2%
Corporate Officers	15.7%	12.5%	8.7%
Boards of Directors	13.6%	11.7%	9.5%

Sources: "Census of Women Corporate Officers and Top Earners" Catalyst, [Online] available at http://www.catalystwomen.org/knowledge/titles/title.php? page=cen WOTE02, 26 May 2005; "2003 Catalyst Census of Women Board Directors of the Fortune 1000," Catalyst, [Online] available at http://www.catalystwomen.org/knowledge/titles/title.php?page=cen_WBD03, 26 May 2005.

progress appears to be due to career and job choices. Whereas men's career and job choices are often driven by the search for higher pay and advancement, women are more likely to choose jobs or careers that also give them a greater sense of accomplishment, more control over their work schedules, and easier movement in and out of the workplace.[43] Furthermore, women are historically much more likely than men to prioritize family over work at some time in their careers. For example, 96 percent of 600 female Harvard MBAs held jobs while they were in their 20s. That dropped to 71 percent in their late 30s when they had children, but then increased to 82.5 percent in their late 40s as their children became older.[44]

Beyond these reasons, however, it's likely that sex discrimination does play a role in women's slow prog-

ress into the higher levels of management. And even if you don't think so, many of the women you work with probably do. Indeed, one study found that more than 90 percent of executive women believed that the glass ceiling had hurt their careers.[45] In another study, 80 percent of women said they left their last organization because the glass ceiling had limited their chances for advancement.[46] A third study indicated that the glass ceiling is prompting more and more women to leave companies to start their own businesses.[47]

So, what can companies do to make sure that women have the same opportunities for development and advancement as men? One strategy is mentoring, or pairing promising female executives with senior executives from whom they can seek advice and support. A vice president at a utility company says "I think it's the single most critical piece to women advancing career-wise. In my experience you need somebody to help guide you and . . . go to bat for you."[48] In fact, 91 percent of female executives have a mentor at some point and feel their mentor was critical to their advancement.

Another strategy is to make sure that male-dominated social activities don't unintentionally exclude women.

The Golf Divide

For decades, golf has been known as the great executive pastime—the white, male executive pastime. Today, however, many executive positions are held by women, who are less likely to be avid golfers, and techies and Silicon Valley executives, who prefer mountain biking, so corporate outings are becoming as diverse as their employees (soccer, cycling, etc.). Still, golf reigns as the activity of choice in many industries and is considered an ideal place to build and sustain business relationships. To get all types of businesspeople prepared to play, the PGA of America has a program called "Golf: For Business and for Life" that sponsors courses at colleges and universities, and the nonprofit Executive Women's Golf Association teaches the game to businesswomen, a growing number of whom are middle managers with executive aspirations.

Source: J.P. Newport & R. Adams, "Business Gold Changes Course," *Wall Street Journal*, 26-27 May 2007, P1.

Nearly half (47 percent) of women in the work force believe that "exclusion from informal networks" makes it more difficult to advance their careers. By contrast, just 18 percent of CEOs thought this was a problem.[49] One final strategy is to designate a "go-to person," other than their supervisors, that women can talk to if they believe that they are being held back or discriminated against because of their sex. Make sure this person has the knowledge and authority to conduct a fair, confidential internal investigation.[50]

2.3 Race/Ethnicity

Racial and ethnic discrimination occurs when people are treated differently because of their race or ethnicity. To what extent is racial and ethnic discrimination a factor in the workplace? Every year, the EEOC receives between 26,000 and 30,000 charges of race discrimination, which is more than any other type of charge of discrimination (**http://www.eeoc.gov/stats/race.html**). However, thanks to the 1964 Civil Rights Act and Title VII, there is much less racial and ethnic discrimination than there used to be. For example, 18 *Fortune* 500 firms had an African American or Hispanic CEO in 2005, whereas none did in 1988.[51] Nonetheless, strong racial and ethnic disparities still exist. For instance, whereas about 12 percent of Americans are black, only 5.9 percent of managers and 3.2 percent of top managers are black. Similarly, about 13 percent of Americans are Hispanic, but only 6.3 percent are managers and 3.7 percent are CEOs. By contrast, Asians, who constitute about 4 percent of the population, are better represented, holding 4 percent of management jobs and 3.4 percent of CEO jobs.[52]

What accounts for the disparities between the percentages of minority groups in the general population and their smaller representation in management positions? Some studies have found that the disparities are due to preexisting differences in training, education, and skills; when African Americans, Hispanics, Asian Americans, and whites have similar skills, training, and education, they are much more likely to have similar jobs and salaries.[53]

Other studies, however, provide increasingly strong direct evidence of racial or ethnic discrimination in the workplace. For example, one study directly tested hiring discrimination by sending pairs of black and white males and pairs of Hispanic and non-Hispanic males to apply for the same jobs. Each pair had résumés with identical qualifications, and all were trained to present

Racial and ethnic discrimination treating people differently because of their race or ethnicity

themselves in similar ways to minimize differences during interviews. The researchers found that the white males got three times as many job offers as the black males, and that the non-Hispanic males got three times as many offers as the Hispanic males.[54]

Another study, which used similar methods to test hiring procedures at 149 different companies, found that whites received 10 percent more interviews than blacks. Half of the whites interviewed received job offers, but only 11 percent of the blacks. And when job offers were made, blacks were much more likely to be offered lower-level positions, while whites were more likely to be offered jobs at higher levels than the jobs they had applied for.[55]

Critics of these studies point out that it's nearly impossible to train different applicants to give identical responses in job interviews and that differences in interviewing skills may have somehow accounted for the results. However, British researchers found similar kinds of discrimination just by sending letters of inquiry to prospective employers. As in the other studies, the letters were identical except for the applicant's race. Employers frequently responded to letters from Afro-Caribbean, Indian, or Pakistani "applicants" by indicating that the positions had been filled. By contrast, they often responded to white, Anglo-Saxon "applicants" by inviting them to face-to-face interviews. Similar results were found with Vietnamese and Greek "applicants" in

©Susan Van Etten

2.4 Mental or Physical Disabilities

According to the Americans with Disabilities Act (**http://www.usdoj.gov/crt/ada/adahom1.htm**), a **disability** is a mental or physical impairment that substantially limits one or more major life activities.[59] One in every five Americans, or more than 54 million people, has a disability.[60] **Disability discrimination** occurs when people are treated differently because of their disabilities.

To what extent is disability discrimination a factor in the workplace? According to the U.S. Census Bureau, 80 percent of able men have jobs, compared to only 60 percent of those with disabilities. For women, the statistics show a similar pattern with 67 percent of able women being employed versus only 51 percent of disabled women. More specifically, only 47 percent of those who have a sensory disability, 32 percent of those who have a physical disability, and 28 percent of those who have a mental disability have jobs.[61] Furthermore, people with disabilities are disproportionately employed in low-status or part-time jobs, have little chance for advancement, and, on average, are twice as likely to live in poverty as able people.[62] Numerous studies also indicate that managers and the general public believe that discrimination against people with disabilities is common and widespread.[63]

What accounts for the disparities between the employment and income levels of able people and people with disabilities? Contrary to popular opinion, it has nothing to do with the ability of people with disabilities to do their jobs well. Studies show that as long as companies make reasonable accommodations for disabilities (e.g., changing procedures or equipment), people with disabilities perform their jobs just as well as able people. Furthermore, they have better safety records and are not any more likely to be absent or quit their jobs.[64]

What can companies do to make sure that people with disabilities have the same opportunities as everyone else? Beyond educational efforts to address incorrect stereotypes and expectations, a good place to start is to commit to reasonable workplace accommodations such as changing work schedules, reassigning jobs, acquiring or modifying equipment, or providing assistance when needed. Accommodations for disabilities needn't be expensive. According to the Job Accommodation Network, 71 percent of accommodations cost employers $500 or less, and 20 percent of accommodations don't cost anything at all.[65]

Disability a mental or physical impairment that substantially limits one or more major life activities

Disability discrimination treating people differently because of their disabilities

Australia.[56] In short, the evidence strongly indicates that there is strong and persistent racial and ethnic discrimination in the hiring processes of many organizations.

What can companies do to make sure that people of all racial and ethnic backgrounds have the same opportunities?[57] Start by looking at the numbers. Compare the hiring rates of whites to the hiring rates for racial and ethnic applicants. Do the same thing for promotions within the company. See if nonwhite workers quit the company at higher rates than white workers. Also, survey employees to compare white and nonwhite employees' satisfaction with jobs, bosses, and the company, as well as their perceptions concerning equal treatment. Next, if the numbers indicate racial or ethnic disparities, consider employing a private firm to test your hiring system by having applicants of different races with identical qualifications apply for jobs in your company.[58] Although disparities aren't proof of discrimination, it's much better to investigate hiring and promotion disparities yourself than to have the EEOC or a plaintiff's lawyer do it for you.

Another step companies can take is to eliminate unclear selection and promotion criteria. Vague criteria allow decision makers to focus on non-job-related characteristics that may unintentionally lead to employment discrimination. Instead, selection and promotion criteria should spell out the specific knowledge, skills, abilities, education, and experience needed to perform a job well.

Work Force Health on the Decline

According to the Council for Disability Awareness, the general health of the American work force is declining because of age and questionable lifestyle choices (poor diet, lack of exercise, etc.). Rising obesity rates are causing back pain, hip and knee injury (often leading to joint replacement), and diabetes. Claims for depression and other nervous disorders, chronic bronchitis, and asthma are also increasing. Many companies are finding ways to accommodate workers. American Express has made its cafeteria wheelchair accessible and rearranged work schedules to coincide with the paratransit system. Sylvania has created flexible shifts for disabled employees, and General Motors enlists the help of an ergonomic specialist to help assign disabled workers to jobs that won't aggravate their ailments.

Source: M. P. McQueen, "Workplace Disabilities Are on the Rise," *Wall Street Journal,* 1 May 2007, D1.

Finally, companies should actively recruit qualified workers with disabilities. Numerous organizations, such as Mainstream, Kidder Resources, theAmerican Council of the Blind (**http://www.acb.org**), the National Federation of the Blind (**http://www.nfb.org**), the National Association of the Deaf (**http://www.nad.org**), the Epilepsy Foundation of America (**http://www.epilepsyfoundation. org**), and the National Amputation Foundation (**http:// www.nationalamputation.org**), actively work with employers to find jobs for qualified people with disabilities. Companies can also place advertisements in publications, such as *Careers and the Disabled*, that specifically target workers with disabilities.[66]

3 Deep-Level Diversity

As you learned in Section 2, people often use the dimensions of surface-level diversity to form initial impressions about others. Over time, however, as people have a chance to get to know each other, initial impressions based on age, sex, race/ethnicity, and mental or physical disabilities give way to deeper impressions based on behavior and psychological characteristics. When we think of others this way, we are focusing on deep-level diversity. *Deep-level diversity* represents differences that can be learned only through extended interaction with others. Examples of deep-level diversity include differences in personality, attitudes, beliefs, and values. In short, recognizing deep-level diversity requires getting to know and understand one another better. And that matters, because it can result in less prejudice, discrimination, and conflict in the workplace. These changes can then lead to better *social integration*, the degree to which organizational or group members are psychologically attracted to working with each other to accomplish a common objective.

Stop for a second and think about your boss (or the boss you had in your last job). What words would you use to describe him or her? Is your boss introverted or extraverted? Emotionally stable or unstable? Agreeable or disagreeable? Organized or disorganized? Open or closed to new experiences? When you describe your boss or others in this way, what you're really doing is describing dispositions and personality.

A **disposition** is the tendency to respond to situations and events in a predetermined manner. **Personality** is the relatively stable set of behaviors, attitudes, and emotions displayed over time that makes people different from each other.[67] For example, which of your aunts or uncles is a little offbeat, a little out of the ordinary? What was that aunt or uncle like when you were small? What is she or he like now? Chances are she or he is pretty much the same wacky person. In other words, the person's core personality hasn't changed. For years, personality researchers studied thousands of different ways to describe people's personalities. In the last decade, however, personality research conducted in different cultures, different settings, and different languages has shown that five basic dimensions of personality account for most of the differences in peoples' behaviors, attitudes, and emotions. The *Big Five Personality Dimensions* are extraversion, emotional stability, agreeableness, conscientiousness, and openness to experience.[68]

Disposition the tendency to respond to situations and events in a predetermined manner

Personality the relatively stable set of behaviors, attitudes, and emotions displayed over time that makes people different from each other

Extraversion is the degree to which someone is active, assertive, gregarious, sociable, talkative, and energized by others. In contrast to extraverts, introverts are less active, prefer to be alone, and are shy, quiet, and reserved. For the best results in the workplace, introverts and extraverts should be correctly matched to their jobs.

> (Under only moderately **stressful situations,** emotionally unstable people find it difficult to handle the most **basic demands** of their jobs.)

Emotional stability is the degree to which someone is not angry, depressed, anxious, emotional, insecure, or excitable. People who are emotionally stable respond well to stress. In other words, they can maintain a calm, problem-solving attitude in even the toughest situations (e.g., conflict, hostility, dangerous conditions, or extreme time pressures). By contrast, under only moderately stressful situations, emotionally unstable people find it difficult to handle the most basic demands of their jobs and become distraught, tearful, self-doubting, and anxious. Emotional stability is particularly important for high-stress jobs, such as police work, fire fighting, emergency medical treatment, piloting planes, or commanding rockets.

Agreeableness is the degree to which someone is cooperative, polite, flexible, forgiving, good-natured, tolerant, and trusting. Basically, agreeable people are easy to work with and be around, whereas disagreeable people are distrusting and difficult to work with and be around.

Conscientiousness is the degree to which someone is organized, hardworking, responsible, persevering, thorough, and achievement oriented. One management consultant wrote about his experiences with a conscientious employee: "He arrived at our first meeting with a typed copy of his daily schedule, a sheet bearing his home and office phone numbers, addresses, and his email address. At his request, we established a timetable for meetings for the next four months. He showed up on time every time, day planner in hand, and carefully listed tasks and due dates. He questioned me exhaustively if he didn't understand an assignment and returned on schedule with the completed work or with a clear explanation as to why it wasn't done."[69]

Openness to experience is the degree to which someone is curious, broad-minded, and open to new ideas, things, and experiences; is spontaneous; and has a high tolerance for ambiguity. People in marketing, advertising, research, or other creative jobs need to be curious, open to new ideas, and spontaneous. By contrast, openness to experience is not particularly important to accountants, who need to consistently apply stringent rules and formulas to make sense out of complex financial information.

Which of the Big Five Personality Dimensions has the largest impact on behavior in organizations? The

Indeed, 92 studies across five occupational groups (professionals, police, managers, sales, and skilled/semiskilled jobs) with a combined total of 12,893 study participants indicated that, on average, conscientious people are inherently more motivated and are better at their jobs.[70]

©AbleStock/Jupiter Images

Extraversion the degree to which someone is active, assertive, gregarious, sociable, talkative, and energized by others

Emotional stability the degree to which someone is not angry, depressed, anxious, emotional, insecure, and excitable

Agreeableness the degree to which someone is cooperative, polite, flexible, forgiving, good-natured, tolerant, and trusting

Conscientiousness the degree to which someone is organized, hardworking, responsible, persevering, thorough, and achievement oriented

Openness to experience the degree to which someone is curious, broad-minded, and open to new ideas, things, and experiences; is spontaneous; and has a high tolerance for ambiguity cumulative results indicate that conscientiousness is related to job performance across five different occupational groups (professionals, police, managers, sales, and skilled or semiskilled jobs).[71] In short, people "who are dependable, persistent, goal directed, and organized tend to be higher performers on virtually any job; viewed negatively, those who are careless, irresponsible, low-achievement striving, and impulsive tend to be lower performers on virtually any job."[72] The results also indicate that extraversion is related to performance in jobs, such as sales and management, that involve significant interaction with others. In people-intensive jobs like these, it helps to be sociable, assertive, and talkative and to have energy and be able to energize others. Finally, people who are extraverted and open to experience seem to do much better in training. Being curious and open to new experiences, as well as sociable, assertive, talkative, and full of energy, helps people perform better in learning situations.[73]

How Can Diversity Be Managed?

How much should companies change their standard business practices to accommodate the diversity of their workers? What do you do when a talented top executive has a drinking problem that only seems to affect his behavior at company business parties (for entertaining clients), where he has made inappropriate advances toward female employees? What do you do when, despite aggressive company policies against racial discrimination, employees continue to tell racial jokes and publicly post cartoons displaying racial humor? And, since many people confuse diversity with affirmative action, what do you do to make sure that your company's diversity practices and policies are viewed as benefiting all workers and not just some workers?

No doubt about it, questions like these make managing diversity one of the toughest challenges that managers face.[74] Nonetheless, there are steps companies can take to begin to address these issues.

After reading the next section, you should be able to

4 explain the basic principles and practices that can be used to manage diversity.

White Males Lead Diversity?

At PricewaterhouseCoopers (PwC), the chief diversity officer, Chris Simmons, who is black, asked Keith Ruth to help lead the company's diversity effort. Ruth was surprised to be asked—because he is white. An emerging trend in managing diversity is to put white males in charge. The rationale is that unless white males are heavily involved and even champion diversity efforts, those efforts will not ever become part of the mainstream. PwC, Coca-Cola, and Georgia Power all have white men running diversity programs. For PwC's Simmons, it's an important step away from thinking that only women and minorities should be leading the diversity movement.

Source: E. White, "Diversity Programs Look to Involve White Males as Leaders," *Wall Street Journal*, 7 May 2007, B4.

©BananaStock/Jupiter Images

4 Managing Diversity

As discussed earlier, diversity programs try to create a positive work environment where no one is advantaged or disadvantaged, where "we" is everyone, where everyone can do his or her best work, where differences are respected and not ignored, and where everyone feels comfortable. *Let's begin to address those goals by learning about* **4.1 different diversity paradigms, 4.2 diversity principles,** *and* **4.3 diversity training and practices.**

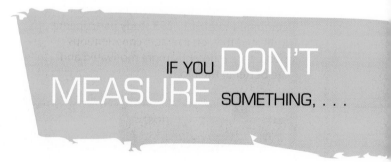

IF YOU DON'T MEASURE SOMETHING, . . .

4.1 Diversity Paradigms

There are several different methods or paradigms for managing diversity: the discrimination and fairness paradigm, the access and legitimacy paradigm, and the learning and effectiveness paradigm.[75] The *discrimination and fairness paradigm,* which is the most common method of approaching diversity, focuses on equal opportunity, fair treatment, recruitment of minorities, and strict compliance with the equal employment opportunity laws. Under this approach, success is usually measured by how well companies achieve recruitment, promotion, and retention goals for women, people of different racial/ethnic backgrounds, or other under-represented groups. According to a recent workplace diversity practices survey conducted by the Society for Human Resource Management, 77 percent of companies with more than 500 employees systematically collect measurements on diversity-related practices.[76] For example, one manager says "If you don't measure something, it doesn't count. You measure your market share. You measure your profitability. The same should be true for diversity. There has to be some way of measuring whether you did, in fact, cast your net widely, and whether the company is better off today in terms of the experience of people of color than it was a few years ago. I measure my market share and my profitability. Why not this?"[77] The primary benefit of the discrimination and fairness paradigm is that it generally brings about fairer treatment of employees and increases demographic diversity. The primary limitation is that the focus of diversity remains on the surface-level diversity dimensions of sex, race, and ethnicity.

The *access and legitimacy paradigm* focuses on the acceptance and celebration of differences to ensure that the diversity within the company matches the diversity found among primary stakeholders, such as customers, suppliers, and local communities. This is similar to the *business growth* advantage of diversity discussed earlier in the chapter. The basic idea behind this approach is "We are living in an increasingly multicultural country, and new ethnic groups are quickly gaining consumer

IT DOESN'T COUNT.

> **Creating a Learning and Effectiveness Diversity Paradigm in an Organization**
>
> 1. The leadership must understand that a diverse work force will embody different perspectives and approaches to work, and must truly value variety of opinion and insight.
> 2. The leadership must recognize both the learning opportunities and the challenges that the expression of different perspectives presents for an organization.
> 3. The organizational culture must create an expectation of high standards of performance for everyone.
> 4. The organizational culture must stimulate personal development.
> 5. The organizational culture must encourage openness and a high tolerance for debate and support constructive conflict on work-related matters.
> 6. The culture must make workers feel valued.
> 7. The organization must have a well-articulated and widely understood mission. This keeps discussions about work differences from degenerating into debates about the validity of people's perspectives.
> 8. The organization must have a relatively egalitarian, nonbureaucratic structure.
>
> Source: D. A. Thomas & R. J. Ely, "Making Differences Matter: A New Paradigm for Managing Diversity," *Harvard Business Review* 74 (September–October 1996): 79–90.

power. Our company needs a demographically more diverse work force to help us gain access to these differentiated segments."[78] Consistent with this goal, Ed Adams, vice president of human resources for Enterprise Rent-a-Car, says "We want people who speak the same language, literally and figuratively, as our customers. We don't set quotas. We say [to our managers], 'Reflect your local market.'"[79] The primary benefit of this approach is that it establishes a clear business reason for diversity. Like the discrimination and fairness paradigm, however, it focuses only on the surface-level diversity dimensions of sex, race, and ethnicity. Furthermore, employees who are assigned responsibility for customers and stakeholders on the basis of their sex, race, or ethnicity may eventually feel frustrated and exploited.

While the discrimination and fairness paradigm focuses on assimilation (having a demographically representative work force), and the access and legitimacy paradigm focuses on differentiation (having demographic differences inside the company match those of key customers and stakeholders), the *learning and effectiveness paradigm* focuses on integrating deep-level diversity differences, such as personality, attitudes, beliefs, and values, into the actual work of the organization. Aetna's 28,000 employees are diverse not only in terms of sex, ethnicity and race, but also by age group, sexual orientation, work styles and levels, perspective, education, skills, and other characteristics. Raymond Arroyo, head of diversity at Aetna, says, "Diversity at Aetna means treating individuals individually, leveraging everyone's best, and maximizing the powerful potential of our workforce." He adds, "Part of a top diversity executive's role in any organization is to integrate diversity into every aspect of a business, including the workforce, customers, suppliers, products, services and even into the community a business serves."[80]

The learning and effectiveness paradigm is consistent with achieving organizational plurality. **Organizational plurality** is a work environment where (1) all members are empowered to contribute in a way that maximizes the benefits to the organization, customers, and themselves, and (2) the individuality of each member is respected by not segmenting or polarizing people on the basis of their membership in a particular group.[81]

The learning and effectiveness diversity paradigm offers four benefits.[82] First, it values common ground. Dave Thomas of the Harvard Business School explains: "Like the fairness paradigm, it promotes equal opportunity for all individuals. And like the access paradigm, it acknowledges cultural differences among people and recognizes the value in those differences. Yet this new model for managing diversity lets the organization internalize differences among employees so that it learns and grows because of them. Indeed, with the model fully in place, members of the organization can say, 'We are all on the same team, with our differences—not despite them.'"[83]

Second, this paradigm makes a distinction between individual and group differences. When diversity focuses only on differences between groups, such as females versus males, large differences within groups are ignored.[84] For example, think of the women you know at work. Now, think for a second about what they have in common. After that, think about how they're different. If your situation is typical, the list of differences should be just as long as the list of commonalties, if not longer. In short, managers can achieve a greater understanding of diversity and their employees by treating them as individuals and by realizing that not all African Americans, Hispanics, women, or white males want the same things at work.[85]

Organizational plurality a work environment where (1) all members are empowered to contribute in a way that maximizes the benefits to the organization, customers, and themselves, and (2) the individuality of each member is respected by not segmenting or polarizing people on the basis of their membership in a particular group

Diversity Principles

1. Carefully and faithfully follow and enforce federal and state laws regarding equal employment opportunity.
2. Treat group differences as important, but not special.
3. Find the common ground.
4. Tailor opportunities to individuals, not groups.
5. Reexamine, but maintain, high standards.
6. Solicit negative as well as positive feedback.
7. Set high but realistic goals.

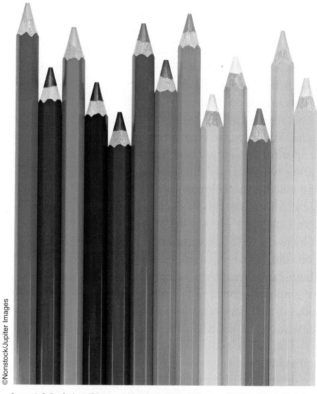

©Nonstock/Jupiter Images

Source: L. S. Gottfredson, "Dilemmas in Developing Diversity Programs," in *Diversity in the Workplace*, ed. S. E. Jackson & Associates (New York: Guildford Press, 1992).

Third, because the focus is on individual differences, the learning and effectiveness paradigm is less likely to encounter the conflict, backlash, and divisiveness sometimes associated with diversity programs that focus only on group differences. Ray Haines, a consultant who has helped companies deal with the aftermath of diversity programs that became divisive, says, "There's a large amount of backlash related to diversity training. It stirs up a lot of hostility, anguish, and resentment but doesn't give people tools to deal with [the backlash]. You have people come in and talk about their specific ax to grind."[86] Certainly, not all diversity programs are divisive or lead to conflict. But, by focusing on individual rather than group differences, the learning and effectiveness paradigm helps to minimize these potential problems.

Finally, unlike the other diversity paradigms that simply focus on the value of being different (primarily in terms of surface-level diversity), the learning and effectiveness paradigm focuses on bringing different talents and perspectives *together* (i.e., deep-level diversity) to make the best organizational decisions and to produce innovative, competitive products and services.

4.2 Diversity Principles

While diversity paradigms represent general approaches or strategies for managing diversity, several diversity principles will help managers do a better job of *managing company diversity programs,* no matter which diversity paradigm they choose.[87]

Begin by *carefully and faithfully following and enforcing federal and state laws regarding equal opportunity employment.* Diversity programs can't and won't succeed if the company is being sued for discriminatory actions and behavior. Faithfully following the law will also reduce the time and expense associated with EEOC investigations or lawsuits. Start by learning more at the EEOC Web site (**http://www.eeoc.gov**). Following the law also means strictly and fairly enforcing company policies.

Treat group differences as important, but not special. Surface-level diversity dimensions such as age, sex, and race/ethnicity should be respected, but should not be treated as more important than other kinds of differences (i.e., deep-level diversity). Remember, the shift from surface- to deep-level diversity helps people know and understand each other better, reduces prejudice and conflict, and leads to stronger social integration with people wanting to work together and get the job done. Also, *find the common ground.* While respecting differences is important, it's just as important, especially with diverse work forces, to actively find ways for employees to see and share commonalities.

Tailor opportunities to individuals, not groups. Special programs for training, development, mentoring, or promotions should be based on individual strengths and weaknesses, not on group status. Instead of making mentoring available for just one group of workers, create mentoring opportunities for everyone who wants to be mentored. For example, at Pacific Enterprises, all programs, including Career Conversations forums, in which upper-level managers are publicly interviewed about themselves and how they got their jobs, are open to all employees.[88]

Solicit negative as well as positive feedback. Diversity is one of the most difficult management issues. No company or manager gets it right from the start. Consequently, companies should aggressively seek positive and negative feedback about their diversity programs. One way to do that is to use a series of measurements to see if progress is being made. L'Oréal, the cosmetics firm, has goals and measurements to track its progress in diversity with respect to recruitment, retention, and advancement, as well as the extent to which the company buys goods and services from minority- and women-owned suppliers.[89]

Set high but realistic goals. Just because diversity is difficult doesn't mean that organizations shouldn't try to accomplish as much as possible. The general purpose of diversity programs is to try to create a positive work environment where no one is advantaged or disadvantaged, where "we" is everyone, where everyone can do his or her best work, where differences are respected and not ignored, and where everyone feels comfortable. Even if progress is slow, companies should not shrink from these goals.

©Susan Van Etten

4.3 Diversity Training and Practices

Organizations use diversity training and several common diversity practices to manage diversity. There are two basic types of diversity training programs. **Awareness training** is designed to raise employees' awareness of diversity issues, such as the dimensions discussed in this chapter, and to get employees to challenge underlying assumptions or stereotypes they may have about others. As a starting point in awareness training, some companies have begun using the Implicit Association Test (IAT), which measures the extent to which people associate positive or negative thoughts (i.e., underlying assumptions or stereotypes) with blacks or whites, men or women, homosexuals or heterosexuals, young or old, or other groups. For example, test takers are shown black or white faces that they must instantly pair with various words. Response times (shorter responses generally indicate stronger associations) and the pattern of associations indicates the extent to which people are biased. Most people are, and strongly so. For example, 88 percent of whites have a more positive mental association toward whites than toward blacks, but, surprisingly, so do blacks, 48 percent of whom show the same bias. Taking the IAT is a good way to increase awareness of diversity issues. To take the IAT and to learn more about the decade of research behind it, go to **http://implicit.harvard.edu**.[90] By contrast, **skills-based diversity training** teaches employees the practical skills they need for managing a diverse work force, such as flexibility and adaptability, negotiation, problem solving, and conflict resolution.[91]

Companies also use diversity audits, diversity pairing, and minority experiences for top executives to better manage diversity. **Diversity audits** are formal assessments that measure employee and management attitudes, investigate the extent to which people are advantaged or disadvantaged with respect to hiring and promotions, and review companies' diversity-related policies and procedures. For example, the results of a formal diversity audit prompted BRW, an architecture and engineering firm, to increase job advertising in minority publications, set up a diversity committee to make recommendations to upper management, provide diversity training for all employees, and rewrite the company handbook to make a stronger statement about the company's commitment to a diverse work force.[92]

Earlier in the chapter you learned that *mentoring,* pairing a junior employee with a senior employee, is a common strategy for creating learning and promotional opportunities for women. Diversity pairing is a special kind of mentoring. In **diversity pairing,** people of different cultural backgrounds, sexes, or races/ethnicities are paired for mentoring. The hope is that stereotypical beliefs and attitudes will change as people get to know each other as individuals.[93] Pat Carmichael, an African American female vice president at JPMorgan Chase, who was mentored early in her career by a white male, mentors men and women of all backgrounds. Regarding a current mentee, John Imperiale, a white assistant branch manager, she says, "My hope is that the exposure John has to me will give him insights when he's managing a diverse group of employees."[94]

Finally, because top managers are still overwhelmingly white and male, a number of companies believe that it is worthwhile to *have top executives experience what it is like to be in the minority.* This can be done by having top managers go to places or events where nearly everyone else is of a different sex or racial/ethnic background. At Hoechst Celanese (which has now split into two companies), top managers would join two organizations in which they were a minority. For instance, the CEO, a white male, joined the board of Hampton University, a historically African American college, and Jobs for Progress, a Hispanic organization that helps people prepare for jobs. Commenting on his experiences, he said, "The only way to break out of comfort zones is to be exposed to other people. When we are, it becomes clear that all people are similar." A Hoechst vice president who joined three organizations in which he was in the minority said, "Joining these organizations has been more helpful to me than two weeks of diversity training."[95]

Awareness training training that is designed to raise employees' awareness of diversity issues and to challenge the underlying assumptions or stereotypes they may have about others

Skills-based diversity training training that teaches employees the practical skills they need for managing a diverse work force, such as flexibility and adaptability, negotiation, problem solving, and conflict resolution

Diversity audits formal assessments that measure employee and management attitudes, investigate the extent to which people are advantaged or disadvantaged with respect to hiring and promotions, and review companies' diversity-related policies and procedures

Diversity pairing a mentoring program in which people of different cultural backgrounds, sexes, or races/ethnicities are paired together to get to know each other and change stereotypical beliefs and attitudes

By the Numbers

7 diversity principles

5 personality dimensions

60 age of average baby boomer in 2010

$58.9 million average costs to company for a class-action racial discrimination lawsuit

Good business is built on diversity.

Each day Cargill does business around the world in food, nutrition, agriculture, and supply chain management. Our work in diverse communities has made us very aware of the importance of diversity in our supply chain. We've learned that no one has a monopoly on good ideas and that they can come from anyone, anywhere. We're committed to supplier diversity because we know it's good business. It adds value to what we do for our customers, as well as promoting prosperity in communities where we live and work. For more information, visit www.cargill.com/about

More and more companies are embracing diversity because it makes good business sense. As this ad for Cargill puts it, "no one has a monopoly on good ideas."

Cargill™
Nourishing Ideas. Nourishing People.™

MOTIVATION

What Is Motivation?

What makes people happiest and most productive at work? Is it money, benefits, opportunities for growth, interesting work, or something else altogether? And if people desire different things, how can a company keep everyone motivated? It takes insight and hard work to motivate workers to join the company, perform well, and then stay with the company. Indeed, when asked to name their biggest management challenge, nearly one-third of executives polled by Creative Group, a specialized staffing service in Menlo Park, California, cited "motivating employees."[1]

So what is motivation? **Motivation** is the set of forces that initiates, directs, and makes people persist in their efforts to accomplish a goal.[2] In terms of this definition, *initiation of effort* is concerned with the choices that people make about how much effort to put forth in their jobs. ("Do I really knock myself out for these performance appraisals or just do a decent job?") *Direction of effort* is concerned with the choices that people make in deciding where to put forth effort in their jobs. ("I should be spending time with my high-dollar accounts instead of learning this new computer system!") *Persistence of effort* is concerned with the choices that people make about how long they will put forth effort in their jobs before reducing or eliminating those efforts. ("I'm only halfway through the project, and I'm exhausted. Do I plow

Motivation the set of forces that initiates, directs, and makes people persist in their efforts to accomplish a goal

Learning Outcomes

1 explain the basics of motivation.

2 use equity theory to explain how employees' perceptions of fairness affect motivation.

3 use expectancy theory to describe how workers' expectations about rewards, effort, and the link between rewards and performance influence motivation.

4 explain how reinforcement theory works and how it can be used to motivate.

5 describe the components of goal-setting theory and how managers can use them to motivate workers.

6 discuss how the entire motivation model can be used to motivate workers.

through to the end, or just call it quits?") Initiation, direction, and persistence are at the heart of motivation.

Initiation + Direction + Persistence ⟶ Motivation

After reading the next section, you should be able to

1 explain the basics of motivation.

1 Basics of Motivation

Take your right hand and point the palm toward your face. Keep your thumb and pinky finger straight and bend the three middle fingers so the tips are touching your palm. Now rotate your wrist back and forth. If you were in the Regent Square Tavern in Pittsburgh, Pennsylvania, that hand signal would tell waitress Marjorie Landale that you wanted a Yuengling beer. Marjorie, who isn't deaf, would not have understood that sign a few years ago. But with a state school for the deaf nearby, the tavern always has its share of deaf customers, so she decided on her own to take classes to learn how to sign. At first, deaf customers would signal for a pen and paper to write out their orders. But after Marjorie signaled that she was learning to sign, "their eyes [would] light up, and they [would] finger-spell their order." Word quickly spread as the students started bringing in their friends, classmates, teachers, and hearing friends as well. Says Marjorie, "The deaf customers are patient with my amateur signing. They appreciate the effort."[3]

What would motivate an employee like Marjorie to voluntarily learn a new language like American Sign Language? (Sign language is every bit as much of a language as French or Spanish.) She wasn't paid to take classes in her free time. She chose to do it on her own. And while she undoubtedly makes more tip money with a full bar than with an empty one, it's highly unlikely that she began her classes with the objective of making more money. Just what is it that motivates employees like Marjorie Landale?

*Let's learn more about motivation by building a basic model of motivation out of **1.1 effort and performance, 1.2 need satisfaction,** and **1.3 extrinsic and intrinsic rewards** and then discussing **1.4 how to motivate people with this basic model of motivation**.*

1.1 Effort and Performance

When most people think of work motivation, they think that working hard (effort) should lead to a good job (performance). Exhibit 13.1 shows a basic model of work motivation and performance, displaying this process.

The first thing to notice about Exhibit 13.1 is that this is a basic model of work motivation *and* performance. In practice, it's almost impossible to talk about one without mentioning the other. Not surprisingly, managers often assume motivation to be the only determinant of performance saying things such as "Your performance was really terrible last quarter. What's the matter? Aren't you as motivated as you used to be?" In fact, motivation is just one of three primary determinants of job performance. In industrial psychology, job performance is frequently represented by this equation:

$$\text{Job Performance} = \text{Motivation} \times \text{Ability} \times \text{Situational Constraints}$$

In this formula, *job performance* is how well someone performs the requirements of the job. *Motivation,* as defined above, is effort, the degree to which someone works hard to do the job well. *Ability* is the degree to which workers possess the knowledge, skills, and talent needed to do a job well. And *situational constraints* are factors beyond the control of individual employees, such as tools, policies, and resources that have an effect on job performance.

Since job performance is a multiplicative function of motivation times ability times situational constraints, job performance will suffer if any one of

Needs the physical or psychological requirements that must be met to ensure survival and well-being

Exhibit 13.1

A Basic Model of Work Motivation and Performance

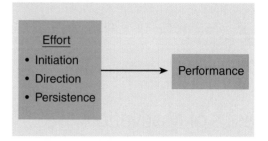

these components is weak. Does this mean that motivation doesn't matter? No, not at all. It just means that all the motivation in the world won't translate into high performance when you have little ability and high situational constraints.

1.2 Need Satisfaction

In Exhibit 13.1, we started with a very basic model of motivation in which effort leads to job performance. However, managers want to know, "What leads to effort?" Determining employee needs is the first step to answering that question.

Needs are the physical or psychological requirements that must be met to ensure survival and well-being.[4] As shown on the left side of Exhibit 13.2, a person's unmet need creates an uncomfortable, internal state of tension that must be resolved. For example, if you normally skip breakfast, but then have to work through lunch, chances are you'll be so hungry by late afternoon that the only thing you'll be motivated to do is find something to eat. So, according to needs theories, people are motivated by unmet needs. But once a need is met, it no longer motivates. When this occurs, people become satisfied, as shown on the right side of Exhibit 13.2.

Note: Throughout the chapter, as we build on this basic model, the parts of the model that we've already discussed will appear shaded in color. For example, since we've already discussed the effort ⟶ performance part of the model, those components are shown with a colored background. When we add new parts to the model, they will have a white background. For instance, since we're adding need satisfaction to the model at this step, the need-satisfaction components of unsatisfied need, tension, energized to take action, and satisfaction are shown with a white background. This shading convention should make it easier to understand the work motivation model as we add to it in each section of the chapter.

Exhibit 13.2

Adding Need Satisfaction to the Model

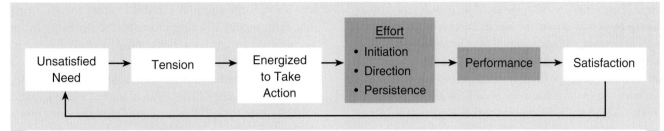

| Unsatisfied Need | → | Tension | → | Energized to Take Action | → | **Effect**
• Initiation
• Direction
• Persistence | → | Performance | → | Satisfaction |

As shown on the left side of this exhibit, a person's unsatisfied need creates an uncomfortable, internal state of tension that must be resolved. So, according to needs theories, people are motivated by unmet needs. But once a need is met, it no longer motivates. When this occurs, people become satisfied, as shown on the right side of the exhibit.

Since people are motivated by unmet needs, managers must learn what those unmet needs are and address them. This is not always a straightforward task, however, because different needs theories suggest different needs categories. Consider three well-known needs theories. Maslow's Hierarchy of Needs suggests that people are motivated by *physiological* (food and water), *safety* (physical and economic), *belongingness* (friendship, love, needs), *relatedness* (belongingness), and *growth* (esteem and self-actualization).[6] McClelland's Learned Needs Theory suggests that people are motivated by the need for *affiliation* (to be liked and accepted), the need for *achievement* (to accomplish challenging goals), or the need for *power* (to influence others).[7]

Things become even more complicated when we consider the different predictions made by these theo-

> Since people are motivated by **unmet needs**, managers must learn what those unmet needs are and **address them**.

social interaction), *esteem* (achievement and recognition), and *self-actualization* (realizing your full potential) needs.[5] Alderfer's ERG Theory collapses Maslow's five needs into three: *existence* (safety and physiological

ries. According to Maslow, needs are arranged in a hierarchy from low (physiological) to high (self-actualization). Within this hierarchy, people are motivated by their lowest unsatisfied need. As each need is met, they

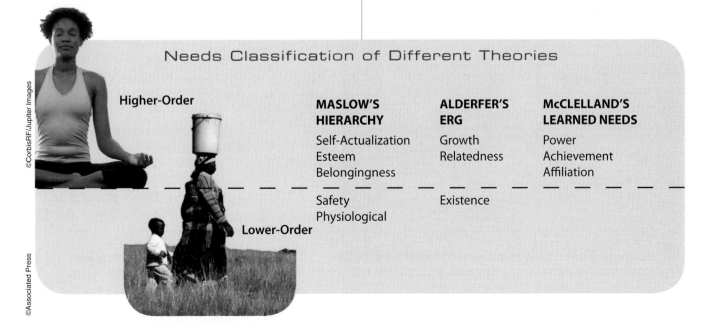

Needs Classification of Different Theories

Higher-Order

	MASLOW'S HIERARCHY	ALDERFER'S ERG	McCLELLAND'S LEARNED NEEDS
	Self-Actualization	Growth	Power
	Esteem	Relatedness	Achievement
	Belongingness		Affiliation
	Safety	Existence	
	Physiological		

Lower-Order

©CorbisRF/Jupiter Images

©Associated Press

work their way up the hierarchy from physiological to self-actualization needs. By contrast, Alderfer says that people can be motivated by more than one need at a time. Furthermore, he suggests that people are just as likely to move down the needs hierarchy as up, particularly when they are unable to achieve satisfaction at the next higher need level. McClelland argues that the degree to which particular needs motivate varies tremendously from person to person, with some people being motivated primarily by achievement and others by power or affiliation. Moreover, McClelland says that needs are learned, not innate. For instance, studies show that children whose parents own a small business or hold a managerial position are much more likely to have a high need for achievement.[8]

So, with three different sets of needs and three very different ideas about how needs motivate, how do we provide a practical answer to managers who just want to know "What leads to effort?" Fortunately, the research evidence simplifies things a bit. To start, studies indicate that there are two basic kinds of needs categories.[9] As you would expect, *lower-order needs* are concerned with safety and with physiological and existence requirements, whereas *higher-order needs* are concerned with relationships (belongingness, relatedness, and affiliation); challenges and accomplishments (esteem, self-actualization, growth, and achievement); and influence (power). Studies generally show that higher-

Extrinsic reward a reward that is tangible, visible to others, and given to employees contingent on the performance of specific tasks or behaviors

order needs will not motivate people as long as lower-order needs remain unsatisfied.[10]

For example, imagine that you graduated from college six months ago and are still looking for your first job. With money running short (you're probably living on your credit cards) and the possibility of having to move back in with your parents looming (if this doesn't motivate you, what will?), your basic needs for food, shelter, and security drive your thoughts, behavior, and choices at this point. But once you land that job, find a great place (of your own!) to live, and put some money in the bank, these basic needs should decrease in importance as you begin to think about making new friends and taking on challenging work assignments. In fact, once lower-order needs are satisfied, it's difficult for managers to predict which higher-order needs will motivate behavior.[11] Some people will be motivated by affiliation, while others will be motivated by growth or esteem. Also, the relative importance of the various needs may change over time, but not necessarily in any predictable pattern. So, what leads to effort? In part, needs do. After we discuss rewards in subsection 1.3, in subsection 1.4 we discuss how managers can use what we know from need-satisfaction theories to motivate workers.

1.3 Extrinsic and Intrinsic Rewards

No discussion of motivation would be complete without considering rewards. Let's add two kinds of rewards, extrinsic and intrinsic, to the model, as shown in Exhibit 13.3.[12]

Extrinsic rewards are tangible and visible to others and are given to employees contingent on the perfor-

Exhibit 13.3

Adding Rewards to the Model

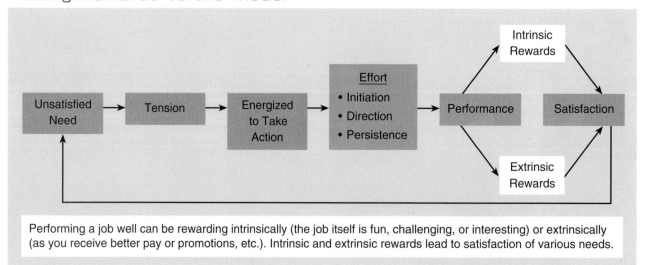

Performing a job well can be rewarding intrinsically (the job itself is fun, challenging, or interesting) or extrinsically (as you receive better pay or promotions, etc.). Intrinsic and extrinsic rewards lead to satisfaction of various needs.

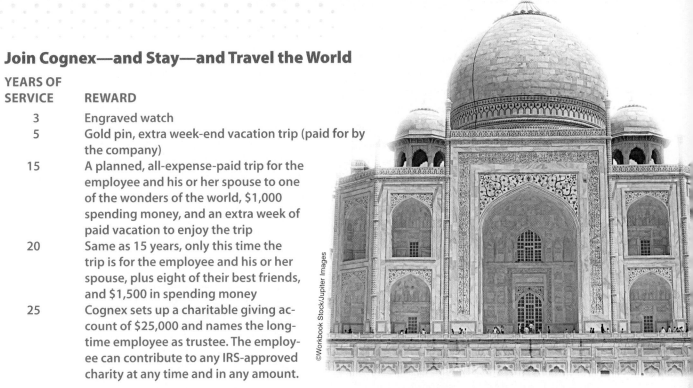

Join Cognex—and Stay—and Travel the World

YEARS OF SERVICE	REWARD
3	Engraved watch
5	Gold pin, extra week-end vacation trip (paid for by the company)
15	A planned, all-expense-paid trip for the employee and his or her spouse to one of the wonders of the world, $1,000 spending money, and an extra week of paid vacation to enjoy the trip
20	Same as 15 years, only this time the trip is for the employee and his or her spouse, plus eight of their best friends, and $1,500 in spending money
25	Cognex sets up a charitable giving account of $25,000 and names the long-time employee as trustee. The employee can contribute to any IRS-approved charity at any time and in any amount.

©Workbook Stock/Jupiter Images

Source: J. S. Lublin, "Creative Compensation: A CEO Talks about His Company's Innovative Pay Ideas. Free Ice Cream, Anyone?" *Wall Street Journal*, 10 April 2006, R6.

mance of specific tasks or behaviors.[13] External agents (managers, for example) determine and control the distribution, frequency, and amount of extrinsic rewards, such as pay, company stock, benefits, and promotions. For example, Wal-Mart paid $529.8 million in bonuses to 813,759 hourly U.S. employees at Wal-Mart and Sam's Club stores. Lois Honeycutt, a 46-year-old customer service manager at Wal-Mart in Altamonte Springs, Florida, says the bonus program will help increase employee performance and boost employee spirits and morale.[14]

Why do companies need extrinsic rewards? To get people to do things they wouldn't otherwise do. Companies use extrinsic rewards to motivate people to perform four basic behaviors: join the organization, regularly attend their jobs, perform their jobs well, and stay with the organization.[15] Think about it. Would you show up to work every day to do the best possible job that you could just out of the goodness of your heart? Very few people would. This is why Cognex, maker of industrial vision systems (robots that "see"), rewards its employees for perseverance, or staying with the company—for a long time. To Dr. Robert Shillman, perseverance means not only longevity, but the willingess and ability to keep working on difficult issues for an extended period. The longer an employee perseveres, the greater the rewards.[16]

By contrast, **intrinsic rewards** are the natural rewards associated with performing a task or activity for its own sake. For example, aside from the external

rewards management offers for doing something well, employees often find the activities or tasks they perform interesting and enjoyable. Examples of intrinsic rewards include a sense of accomplishment or achievement, a feeling of responsibility, the chance to learn something new or interact with others, or simply the fun that comes from performing an interesting, challenging, and engaging task.

Which types of rewards are most important to workers in general? A number of surveys suggest that both extrinsic and intrinsic rewards are important. One survey found that the most important rewards were good benefits and health insurance, job security, a week or more of vacation (all extrinsic rewards), interesting work, the opportunity to learn new skills, and independent work situations (all intrinsic rewards). And employee preferences for intrinsic and extrinsic rewards appear to be relatively stable. Studies conducted over the last three decades have consistently found that employees are twice as likely to indicate that "important and meaningful work" matters more to them than what they are paid.[17]

1.4 Motivating with the Basics

So, given the basic model of work motivation in Exhibit 13.3, what practical steps can managers take to motivate employees to increase their effort?

Intrinsic reward a natural reward associated with performing a task or activity for its own sake

Well, *start by asking people what their needs are.* If managers don't know what workers' needs are, they won't be able to provide them the opportunities and rewards that can satisfy those needs. Linda Connor, vice president of corporate culture at Technology Professionals Corp. (TPC) in Grand Rapids, Michigan, keeps careful notes about TPC employees' needs. She says, "I sit down at employees' 30-day reviews and ask specific questions about hobbies and interests for each member of their families."[18]

Next, *satisfy lower-order needs first.* Since higher-order needs will not motivate people as long as lower-order needs remain unsatisfied, companies should satisfy lower-order needs first. In practice, this means providing the equipment, training, and knowledge to create a safe workplace free of physical risks, paying employees well enough to provide financial security, and offering a benefits package that will protect employees and their families through good medical coverage and health and disability insurance. Indeed, a survey based on a representative sample of Americans found that when people choose jobs or organizations, three of the four most important factors—starting pay/salary (62 percent), employee benefits (57 percent), and job security (47 percent)—are lower-order needs.[19]

Third, managers should *expect people's needs to change.* As some needs are satisfied or situations change, what motivated people before may not motivate them now. Likewise, what motivates people to accept a job (pay and benefits), may not necessarily motivate them once they have the job (the job itself, opportunities for advancement). Managers should also expect needs to change as people mature.[20] For older employees benefits are as important as pay, which is always ranked as more important by younger employees. Also, older employees rank job security as more important than personal and family time, which is more important to younger employees.[21]

Finally, *as needs change and lower-order needs are satisfied, create opportunities for employees to satisfy higher-order needs.* Recall that intrinsic rewards, such as accomplishment, achievement, learning something new, and interacting with others, are the natural rewards associated with performing a task or activity for its own sake. And, with the exception of influence (power), intrinsic rewards correspond very closely to higher-order needs that are con-

Equity theory a theory that states that people will be motivated when they perceive that they are being treated fairly

cerned with relationships (belongingness, relatedness, and affiliation) and challenges and accomplishments (esteem, self-actualization, growth, and achievement). Therefore, one way for managers to meet employees' higher-order needs is to create opportunities for employees to experience intrinsic rewards by providing challenging work, encouraging employees to take greater responsibility for their work, and giving employees the freedom to pursue tasks and projects they find naturally interesting.

How Perceptions and Expectations Affect Motivation

As previously discussed, people are motivated to achieve intrinsic and extrinsic rewards. When employees believe that rewards are not fairly awarded, or if they don't believe they can achieve the performance goals the company has set for them, they won't be very motivated.

After reading the next two sections, you should be able to

2 use equity theory to explain how employees' perceptions of fairness affect motivation.

3 use expectancy theory to describe how workers' expectations about rewards, effort, and the link between rewards and performance influence motivation.

2 Equity Theory

Fairness, or what people perceive to be fair, is a critical issue in organizations. **Equity theory** says that people

On average, CEOs of the 500 largest U.S. companies make $10.9 million a year.

Source: S. DeCarlo, "Special Report: CEO Compensation," *Forbes Magazine,* 26 March 2007.

©Susan Van Etten

will be motivated at work when they *perceive* that they are being treated fairly. In particular, equity theory stresses the importance of perceptions. So, regardless of the actual level of rewards people receive, they must also perceive that, relative to others, they are being treated fairly. For example, you learned in Chapter 11 that the average CEO now makes 289 times more than the average worker.[22] Many people believe that CEO pay is obscenely high and unfair. Others believe that CEO pay is fair because if it were easier to find good CEOs, then CEOs would be paid much less.

As explained below, equity theory doesn't focus on objective equity (i.e., that CEOs make 289 times more than blue-collar workers). Instead, equity theory says that equity, like beauty, is in the eye of the beholder.

Let's learn more about equity theory by examining **2.1 the components of equity theory, 2.2 how people react to perceived inequities,** *and* **2.3 how to motivate people using equity theory.**

2.1 Components of Equity Theory

The basic components of equity theory are inputs, outcomes, and referents. **Inputs** are the contributions employees make to the organization. Inputs include education and training, intelligence, experience, effort, number of hours worked, and ability. **Outcomes** are what employees receive in exchange for their contributions to the organization. Outcomes include pay, fringe benefits, status symbols, and job titles and assignments. And, since perceptions of equity depend on comparisons, **referents** are others with whom people compare themselves to determine if they have been treated fairly. The referent can be a single person (comparing yourself with a coworker), or a generalized other (comparing yourself with "students in general," for example), or could be with yourself over time ("I was better off last year than I am this year"). Usually, people choose to compare themselves to referents who hold the same or similar jobs or who are otherwise similar in gender, race, age, tenure, or other characteristics.[23]

According to the equity theory process, employees compare their outcomes, the rewards they receive from the organization, to their inputs, their contributions to the organization. This comparison of outcomes to inputs is called the **outcome/input (O/I) ratio.**

$$\frac{\text{OUTCOMES}_{\text{SELF}}}{\text{INPUTS}_{\text{SELF}}} = \frac{\text{OUTCOMES}_{\text{REFERENT}}}{\text{INPUTS}_{\text{REFERENT}}}$$

After an internal comparison in which they compare their outcomes to their inputs, employees then make an external comparison in which they compare their O/I ratio with the O/I ratio of a referent.[24] When people perceive that their O/I ratio is equal to the referent's O/I ratio, they conclude that they are being treated fairly. But, when people perceive that their O/I ratio is different from their referent's O/I ratio, they conclude that they have been treated inequitably or unfairly.

Inequity can take two forms, underreward and overreward. **Underreward** occurs when your O/I ratio is worse than your referent's O/I ratio. In other words, you are getting fewer outcomes relative to your inputs than the referent you compare yourself to is getting. When people perceive that they have been underrewarded, they tend to experience anger or frustration.

By contrast, **overreward** occurs when your O/I ratio is better than your referent's O/I ratio. In this case, you are getting more outcomes relative to your inputs than your referent is. In theory, when people perceive that they have been overrewarded, they experience guilt. But, not surprisingly, people have a very high tolerance for overreward. It takes a tremendous amount of overpayment before people decide that their pay or benefits are more than they deserve.

2.2 How People React to Perceived Inequity

So what happens when people perceive that they have been treated inequitably at work? Exhibit 13.4 shows that perceived inequity affects satisfaction. In the case of underreward, this usually translates into frustration or anger; with overreward, the reaction is guilt. These reactions lead to tension and a strong need to take action to restore equity in some way. At first, a slight inequity may not be strong enough to motivate an employee to take immediate action. If the inequity continues or there are multiple inequities, however, tension may build over time until a point of intolerance is reached, and the person is energized to take action.[25]

Inputs in equity theory, the contributions employees make to the organization

Outcomes in equity theory, the rewards employees receive for their contributions to the organization

Referents in equity theory, others with whom people compare themselves to determine if they have been treated fairly

Outcome/input (O/I) ratio in equity theory, an employee's perception of how the rewards received from an organization compare with the employee's contributions to that organization

Underreward a form of inequity in which you are getting fewer outcomes relative to inputs than your referent is getting

Overreward a form of inequity in which you are getting more outcomes relative to inputs than your referent

Exhibit 13.4

Adding Equity Theory to the Model

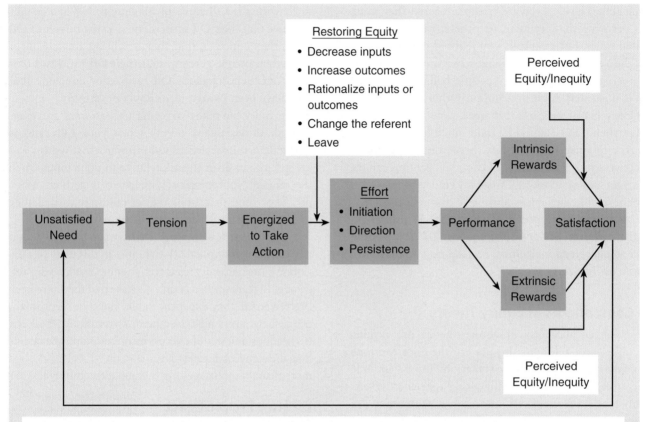

Restoring Equity
- Decrease inputs
- Increase outcomes
- Rationalize inputs or outcomes
- Change the referent
- Leave

When people perceive that they have been treated inequitably at work because of the intrinsic or extrinsic rewards they receive relative to their efforts, they are dissatisfied (or frustrated or angry), their needs aren't met, and those reactions lead to tension and a strong need to take action to restore equity in some way (as explained in the "Restoring Equity" box).

When people perceive that they have been treated unfairly, they may try to restore equity by reducing inputs, increasing outcomes, rationalizing inputs or outcomes, changing the referent, or simply leaving. We will discuss these possible responses in terms of the inequity associated with underreward, which is much more common than the inequity associated with overreward.

People who perceive that they have been underrewarded may try to restore equity by *decreasing or withholding their inputs (i.e., effort)*. For example, when Iberia, the Spanish airline, was near bankruptcy seven years ago, it pressured its pilots to take substantial pay cuts. When Iberia's finances improved, the pilots requested that the pay cuts, which had cost them $140 million, be reversed. They also asked for annual pay increases substantially higher than the rate of inflation. When Iberia management refused, the pilots staged a work slowdown at the peak of the busy summer tourism season. Over the course of 10 separate days throughout the summer, 30 to 40 percent of Iberia's pilots called in sick, disrupting the airline's flight schedule, customers, and profits.[26]

Increasing outcomes is another way people try to restore equity. This might include asking for a raise or pointing out the inequity to the boss and hoping that he or she takes care of it. Sometimes, however, employees may go to external organizations, such as labor unions, federal agencies, or the courts for help in increasing outcomes to restore equity.

Another method of restoring equity is to *rationalize or distort inputs or outcomes*. Instead of decreasing inputs or increasing outcomes, employees restore equity by making mental or emotional "adjustments" in their O/I ratios or the O/I ratios of their referents. For example, suppose that a company downsizes 10 percent of its work force. It's likely that the survivors, the people who still have jobs, will be angry or frustrated with company management because of the layoffs. If alternative jobs are difficult to find, however, these survivors may rationalize or distort their O/I ratios and conclude, "Well, things could be worse. At least I still have my job." Rationalizing or distorting outcomes may be used when other ways to restore equity aren't available.

Changing the referent is another way of restoring equity. In this case, people compare themselves to someone other than the referent they had been using for previous O/I ratio comparisons. Since people usually choose to compare themselves to others who hold the same or similar jobs or who are otherwise similar (i.e., friends, family members, neighbors who work at other companies), they may change referents to restore equity when their personal situations change, such as a decrease in job status or pay.[27]

Finally, when none of these methods—reducing inputs, increasing outcomes, rationalizing inputs or outcomes, or changing referents—are possible or restore equity, *employees may leave* by quitting their jobs, transferring, or increasing absenteeism.[28] For example, attorneys and accountants at the Securities and Exchange Commission (SEC) quit their jobs at twice the rate of employees in other federal agencies. Why? One reason is that the SEC's attorneys and accountants are paid 40 percent less than their counterparts at other government agencies. Furthermore, they can get jobs in the private sector that pay $180,000 to $250,000 per year.[29]

2.3 Motivating with Equity Theory

What practical steps can managers take to use equity theory to motivate employees? They can *start by looking for and correcting major inequities*. Among other things, equity theory makes us aware that an employee's sense of fairness is based on subjective perceptions. What one

©Radius Images/Jupiter Images

employee considers grossly unfair may not affect another employee's perceptions of equity at all. Although these different perceptions make it difficult for managers to create conditions that satisfy all employees, it's critical that they do their best to take care of major inequities that can energize employees to take disruptive, costly, or harmful actions, such as decreasing inputs or leaving. So, whenever possible, managers should look for and correct major inequities.

Second, managers can *reduce employees' inputs.* Increasing outcomes is often the first and only strategy that companies use to restore equity, yet reducing employee inputs is just as viable a strategy. In fact, with dual-career couples working 50-hour weeks, more and more employees are looking for ways to reduce stress and restore a balance between work and family. Consequently, it may make sense to ask employees to do less, not more; to have them identify and eliminate the 20 percent of their jobs that doesn't increase productivity or add value for customers; and to eliminate company-imposed requirements that really aren't critical to the performance of managers, employees, or the company (e.g., unnecessary meetings and reports).

Finally, managers should *make sure decision-making processes are fair*. Equity theory focuses on **distributive justice**, the degree to which outcomes and rewards are fairly distributed or allocated. However, **procedural justice**, the fairness of the procedures used to make reward allocation decisions, is just as important.[30] Procedural justice matters because even when employees are unhappy with their outcomes (i.e., low pay), they're much less likely to be unhappy with company management if they believe that the procedures used to allocate outcomes were fair. For example, employees who are laid off tend to be hostile toward their employer when they perceive

Distributive justice the perceived degree to which outcomes and rewards are fairly distributed or allocated

Procedural justice the perceived fairness of the process used to make reward allocation decisions that the procedures leading to the layoffs were unfair. By contrast, employees who perceive layoff procedures to be fair tend to continue to support and trust their employers.[31] Also, if employees perceive that their outcomes are unfair (i.e., distributive injustice), but that the decisions and procedures leading to those outcomes were fair (i.e., procedural justice), they are much more likely to seek constructive ways of re- storing equity, such as discussing these matters with their manager. In contrast, if employees perceive both distributive and procedural injustice, they may resort to more destructive tactics, such as withholding effort, absenteeism, tardiness, or even sabotage and theft.[32]

3 Expectancy Theory

One of the hardest things about motivating people is that rewards that are attractive to some employees are unattractive to others. **Expectancy theory** says that people will be motivated to the extent to which they believe that their efforts will lead to good performance, that good performance will be rewarded, and that they will be offered attractive rewards.[33]

Let's learn more about expectancy theory by examining **3.1 the components of expectancy theory** *and* **3.2 how to use expectancy theory as a motivational tool.**

3.1 Components of Expectancy Theory

Expectancy theory
a theory that states that people will be motivated to the extent to which they believe that their efforts will lead to good performance, that good performance will be rewarded, and that they will be offered attractive rewards

Valence the attractiveness or desirability of a reward or outcome

Expectancy the perceived relationship between effort and preformance

Instrumentality the perceived relationship between performance and rewards

Expectancy theory holds that people make conscious choices about their motivation. The three factors that affect those choices are valence, expectancy, and instrumentality.

Valence is simply the attractiveness or desirability of various rewards or outcomes. Expectancy theory recognizes that the same reward or outcome, say, a promotion, will be highly attractive to some people, will be highly disliked by others, and will not make much difference one way or the other to still others. Accordingly, when people are

deciding how much effort to put forth, expectancy theory says that they will consider the valence of all possible rewards and outcomes that they can receive from their jobs. The greater the sum of those valences, each of which can be positive, negative, or neutral, the more effort people will choose to put forth on the job.

Expectancy is the perceived relationship between effort and performance. When expectancies are strong, employees believe that their hard work and efforts will result in good performance, so they work harder. By contrast, when expectancies are weak, employees figure that no matter what they do or how hard they work, they won't be able to perform their jobs successfully, so they don't work as hard.

Instrumentality is the perceived relationship between performance and rewards. When instrumentality is strong, employees believe that improved performance will lead to better and more rewards, so they choose to work harder. When instrumentality is weak, employees don't believe that better performance will result in more or better rewards, so they choose not to work as hard.

Expectancy theory holds that for people to be highly motivated, all three variables—valence, expectancy, and instrumentality—must be high. Thus, expectancy theory can be represented by the following simple equation:

$$\text{Motivation} = \text{Valence} \times \text{Expectancy} \times \text{Instrumentality}$$

If any one of these variables (valence, expectancy, or instrumentality) declines, overall motivation will decline, too.

Exhibit 13.5 incorporates the expectancy theory variables into our motivation model. Valence and instrumentality combine to affect employees' willingness to put forth effort (i.e., the degree to which they are energized to take action), while expectancy transforms intended effort ("I'm really going to work hard in this job") into actual effort. If you're offered rewards that you desire and you believe that you will in fact receive these rewards for good performance, you're highly likely to be energized to take action. However, you're not likely to actually exert effort unless you also believe that you can do the job (i.e., that your efforts will lead to successful performance).

3.2 Motivating with Expectancy Theory

What practical steps can managers take to use expectancy theory to motivate employees? First, they can *systematically gather information to find out what employees want*

Exhibit 13.5

Adding Expectancy Theory to the Model

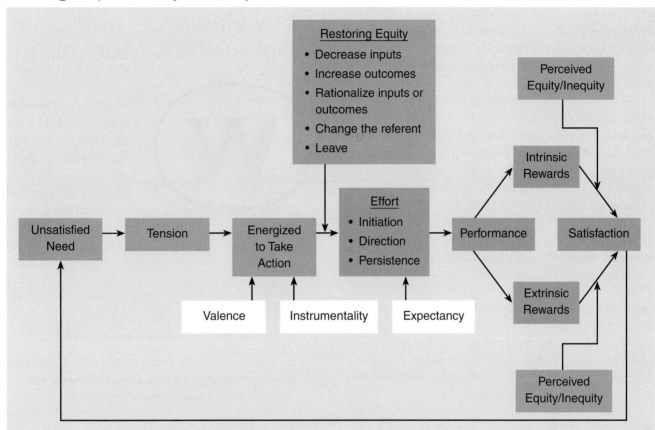

Restoring Equity
- Decrease inputs
- Increase outcomes
- Rationalize inputs or outcomes
- Change the referent
- Leave

Perceived Equity/Inequity

Unsatisfied Need → Tension → Energized to Take Action → **Effort** • Initiation • Direction • Persistence → Performance → Satisfaction

Intrinsic Rewards

Extrinsic Rewards

Perceived Equity/Inequity

Valence   Instrumentality   Expectancy

If rewards are attractive (valence) and linked to performance (instrumentality), then people are energized to take action. In other words, good performance gets them rewards that they want. Intended effort (i.e., energized to take action) turns into actual effort when people believe that their hard work and efforts will result in good performance. After all, why work hard if that hard work is wasted?

from their jobs. In addition to individual managers directly asking employees what they want from their jobs (see Subsection 1.4 "Motivating with the Basics"), companies need to survey their employees regularly to determine their wants, needs, and dissatisfactions. Since people consider the valence of all the possible rewards and outcomes

$50 Windfall?

Employees at Kimley-Horn, a big civil-engineering firm in North Carolina, can at any time, for any reason, award a bonus of $50 to another employee. Bonuses don't have to be approved by anyone, and there are no strings attached. An employee who wants to award a bonus to a coworker downloads a form, fills it out, and often delivers it to the awardee in person. The awardee then redeems the form at the payroll department for a $50 check. Kimley-Horn employees give out over 6,100 bonuses per year for a total corporate expense nearing $340,000.

Source: A. C. Pasquariello, "Grant Makers," *Fast Company*, April 2007, 32.

that they can receive from their jobs, regular identification of wants, needs, and dissatisfactions gives companies the chance to turn negatively valent rewards and outcomes into positively valent rewards and outcomes, thus raising overall motivation and effort. Therefore, employers should routinely survey employees to identify not only the range of rewards that are valued by most employees but also to understand preferences of specific employees.

Second, managers can *take specific steps to link rewards to individual performance in a way that is clear and understandable to employees.* Unfortunately, most employees are extremely dissatisfied with the link between pay and performance in their organizations. In one study, based on a representative sample, 80 percent of the employees surveyed wanted to be paid according to a different kind of pay system! Moreover, only 32 percent of employees were satisfied with how their annual pay raises were determined, and only 22 percent were happy with the way the starting salaries for their jobs were determined.[34] One way to make sure that employees see the connection between pay and performance (see Chapter 11 for a discussion of compensation strategies) is for managers to publicize the way in which pay decisions are made. This is especially important given that only 41 percent of employees know how their pay increases are determined.[35]

Finally, managers should *empower employees to make decisions if management really wants them to believe that their hard work and effort will lead to good performance.* If valent rewards are linked to good performance, people should be energized to take action. However, this works only if they also believe that their efforts will lead to good performance. One of the ways that managers destroy the expectancy that hard work and effort will lead to good performance is by restricting what employees can do or by ignoring employees' ideas. In Chapter 9, you learned that *empowerment* is a feeling of intrinsic motivation, in which workers perceive their work to have meaning and perceive themselves to be competent, to have an impact, and to be capable of self-determination.[36] So, if managers want workers to have strong expectancies, they should empower them to make decisions. Doing so will motivate employees to take active rather than passive roles in their work.

How Rewards and Goals Affect Motivation

When used properly, rewards motivate and energize employees. But when used incorrectly, they can demotivate, baffle, and even anger them. Goals are also supposed to motivate employees. But leaders who focus blindly on meeting goals at all costs often find that they destroy motivation.

After reading the next three sections, you should be able to

4 explain how reinforcement theory works and how it can be used to motivate.

5 describe the components of goal-setting theory and how managers can use them to motivate workers.

6 discuss how the entire motivation model can be used to motivate workers.

4 Reinforcement Theory

Reinforcement theory says that behavior is a function of its consequences, that behaviors followed by positive consequences (i.e., reinforced) will occur more frequently, and that behaviors followed by negative consequences, or not followed by positive consequences, will occur less frequently.[37] More specifically, **reinforcement** is the process of changing behavior by changing the consequences that follow behavior.[38]

Reinforcement theory a theory that states that behavior is a function of its consequences, that behaviors followed by positive consequences will occur more frequently, and that behaviors followed by negative consequences, or not followed by positive consequences, will occur less frequently

Reinforcement the process of changing behavior by changing the consequences that follow behavior

©Image Source Pink/Jupiter Images

Reinforcement has two parts: reinforcement contingencies and schedules of reinforcement. **Reinforcement contingencies** are the cause-and-effect relationships between the performance of specific behaviors and specific consequences. For example, if you get docked an hour's pay for being late to work, then a reinforcement contingency exists between a behavior, being late to work, and a consequence, losing an hour's pay. A **schedule of reinforcement** is the set of rules regarding reinforcement contingencies, such as which behaviors will be reinforced, which consequences will follow those behaviors, and the schedule by which those consequences will be delivered.[39]

Exhibit 13.6 incorporates reinforcement contingencies and reinforcement schedules into our motivation model. First, notice that extrinsic rewards and the schedules of reinforcement used to deliver them are the primary method for creating reinforcement contingencies in organizations. In turn, those reinforcement contingencies directly affect valences (the attractiveness of rewards), instrumentality (the perceived link between rewards and performance), and effort (how hard employees will work).

*Let's learn more about reinforcement theory by examining **4.1 the components of reinforcement theory, 4.2 the different schedules for***

Reinforcement contingencies cause-and-effect relationships between the performance of specific behaviors and specific consequences

Schedule of reinforcement rules that specify which behaviors will be reinforced, which consequences will follow those behaviors, and the schedule by which those consequences will be delivered

Exhibit 13.6

Adding Reinforcement Theory to the Model

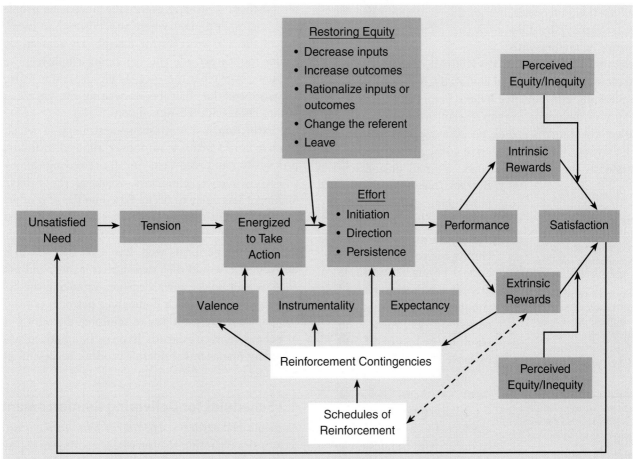

Extrinsic rewards and the schedules of reinforcement used to deliver them are the primary method for creating reinforcement contingencies in organizations. In turn, those reinforcement contingencies directly affect valences (the attractiveness of rewards), instrumentality (the perceived link between rewards and performance), and effort (how hard employees will work).

delivering reinforcement, and 4.3 how to motivate with reinforcement theory.

4.1 Components of Reinforcement Theory

As just described, *reinforcement contingencies* are the cause-and-effect relationships between the performance of specific behaviors and specific consequences. There are four kinds of reinforcement contingencies: positive reinforcement, negative reinforcement, punishment, and extinction.

Positive reinforcement strengthens behavior (i.e., increases its frequency) by following behaviors with desirable consequences. By contrast, **negative reinforcement** strengthens behavior by withholding an unpleasant consequence when employees perform a specific behavior. Negative reinforcement is also called avoid*ance learning* because workers perform a behavior to *avoid* a negative consequence. For example, at the Florist Network, a small business in Buffalo, New York, company management instituted a policy of requiring good attendance for employees to receive their annual bonuses. Employee attendance has improved significantly now that excessive absenteeism can result in the loss of $1,500 or more.[40]

By contrast, **punishment** weakens behavior (i.e., decreases its frequency) by following behaviors with undesirable consequences. For example, the standard disciplinary or punishment process in most companies is an oral warning ("Don't ever do that again"), followed by a written warning ("This letter is to discuss the serious problem you're having with . . . "), followed by three days off without pay ("While you're at home not being paid, we want you to think hard about . . . "), followed by being fired ("That was your last chance"). Though punishment can weaken behavior, managers have to be careful to avoid the backlash that sometimes occurs when employees are punished at work. For example, Frito-Lay began getting complaints from customers that they were finding potato chips with obscene messages written on them. Frito-Lay eventually traced the problem to a potato chip plant where supervisors had fired 58 out of the 210 workers for disciplinary reasons over a nine-month period. The remaining employees were so angry over what they saw as unfair treatment from management that they began writing the phrases on potato chips with felt-tipped pens.[41]

Extinction is a reinforcement strategy in which a positive consequence is no longer allowed to follow a previously reinforced behavior. By removing the positive consequence, extinction weakens the behavior, making it less likely to occur. Based on the idea of positive reinforcement, most companies give company leaders and managers substantial financial rewards when the company performs well. Based on the idea of extinction, you would then expect that leaders and managers would not be rewarded (i.e., removing the positive consequence) when companies perform poorly. If companies really want pay to reinforce the right kinds of behaviors, then rewards have to be removed when company management doesn't produce successful performance.

4.2 Schedules for Delivering Reinforcement

As mentioned earlier, a *schedule of reinforcement* is the set of rules regarding reinforcement contingencies, such as which behaviors will be reinforced, which consequences will follow those behaviors, and the schedule by which those consequences will be delivered. There are two categories of reinforcement schedules: continuous and intermittent.

Positive reinforcement reinforcement that strengthens behavior by following behaviors with desirable consequences

Negative reinforcement reinforcement that strengthens behavior by withholding an unpleasant consequence when employees perform a specific behavior

Punishment reinforcement that weakens behavior by following behaviors with undesirable consequences

Extinction reinforcement in which a positive consequence is no longer allowed to follow a previously reinforced behavior, thus weakening the behavior

©Food Pix/Jupiter Images

Exhibit 13.7

Intermittent Reinforcement Schedules

INTERMITTENT REINFORCEMENT SCHEDULES		
	FIXED	**VARIABLE**
INTERVAL (TIME)	Consequences follow behavior after a fixed time has elapsed.	Consequences follow behavior after different times, some shorter and some longer, that vary around a specific average time.
RATIO (BEHAVIOR)	Consequences follow a specific number of behaviors.	Consequences follow a different number of behaviors, sometimes more and sometimes less, that vary around a specified average number of behaviors.

With **continuous reinforcement schedules,** a consequence follows every instance of a behavior. For example, employees working on a piece-rate pay system earn money (consequence) for every part they manufacture (behavior). The more they produce, the more they earn. By contrast, with **intermittent reinforcement schedules,** consequences are delivered after a specified or average time has elapsed or after a specified or average number of behaviors has occurred. As Exhibit 13.7 shows, there are four types of intermittent reinforcement schedules. Two of these are based on time and are called *interval reinforcement schedules,* while the other two, known as *ratio schedules,* are based on behaviors.

With **fixed interval reinforcement schedules,** consequences follow a behavior only after a fixed time has elapsed. For example, most people receive their paychecks on a fixed interval schedule (e.g., once or twice per month). As long as they work (behavior) during a specified pay period (interval), they get a paycheck (consequence). With **variable interval reinforcement schedules,** consequences follow a behavior after different times, some shorter and some longer, that vary around a specified average time. On a 90-day variable interval reinforcement schedule, you might receive a bonus after 80 days or perhaps after 100 days, but the average interval between performing your job well (behavior) and receiving your bonus (consequence) would be 90 days.

With **fixed ratio reinforcement schedules,** consequences are delivered following a specific number of behaviors. For example, a car salesperson might receive a $1,000 bonus after every 10 sales. Therefore, a salesperson with only 9 sales would not receive the bonus until he or she finally sold a 10th car.

With **variable ratio reinforcement schedules,** consequences are delivered following a different number of behaviors, sometimes more and sometimes less, that vary around a specified average number of behaviors. With a 10-car variable ratio reinforcement schedule, a salesperson might receive the bonus after 7 car sales, or after 12, 11, or 9 sales, but the average number of cars sold before receiving the bonus would be 10 cars.

Which reinforcement schedules work best? In the past, the standard advice was to use continuous reinforcement when employees were learning new behaviors because reinforcement after each success leads to faster learning. Likewise, the standard advice was to use intermittent reinforcement schedules to maintain behavior after it is learned because intermittent rewards are supposed to make behavior much less subject to extinction.[42] Research shows, however, that except for interval-based systems, which usually produce weak results, the effectiveness of continuous reinforcement, fixed ratio, and variable ratio schedules differs very little.[43] In organizational settings, all three produce consistently large increases over noncontingent reward schedules. So managers should choose whichever of these three is easiest to use in their companies.

4.3 Motivating with Reinforcement Theory

What practical steps can managers take to use reinforcement theory to motivate employees? University of Nebraska business professor Fred Luthans, who

Continuous reinforcement schedule a schedule that requires a consequence to be administered following every instance of a behavior

Intermittent reinforcement schedule a schedule in which consequences are delivered after a specified or average time has elapsed or after a specified or average number of behaviors has occurred

Fixed interval reinforcement schedule an intermittent schedule in which consequences follow a behavior only after a fixed time has elapsed

Variable interval reinforcement schedule an intermittent schedule in which the time between a behavior and the following consequences varies around a specified average

Fixed ratio reinforcement schedule an intermittent schedule in which consequences are delivered following a specific number of behaviors

Variable ratio reinforcement schedule an intermittent schedule in which consequences are delivered following a different number of behaviors, sometimes more and sometimes less, that vary around a specified average number of behaviors has been studying the effects of reinforcement theory in organizations for more than a quarter of a century, says that there are five steps to motivating workers with reinforcement theory: *identify, measure, analyze, intervene,* and *evaluate* critical performance-related behaviors.[44]

Identify means identifying critical, observable, performance-related behaviors. These are the behaviors that are most important to successful job performance. In addition, they must also be easily observed so that they can be accurately measured. *Measure* means measuring the baseline frequencies of these behaviors. In other words, find out how often workers perform them. *Analyze* means analyzing the causes and consequences of these behaviors. Analyzing the causes helps managers create the conditions that produce these critical behaviors, and analyzing the consequences helps them determine if these behaviors produce the results that they want. *Intervene* means changing the organization by using positive and negative reinforcement to increase the frequency of these critical behaviors. *Evaluate* means evaluating the extent to which the intervention actually changed workers' behavior. This is done by comparing behavior after the intervention to the original baseline of behavior before the intervention.

In addition to these five steps, managers should remember three other key things when motivating with reinforcement theory. *Don't reinforce the wrong behaviors.* Although reinforcement theory sounds simple, it's actually very difficult to put into practice. One of the most common mistakes is accidentally reinforcing the wrong behaviors. In fact, sometimes managers reinforce behaviors that they don't want!

Managers should also *correctly administer punishment at the appropriate time.* Many managers believe that punishment can change workers' behavior and help them improve their job performance. Furthermore, managers believe that fairly punishing workers also lets other workers know what is or isn't acceptable.[45] A danger of using punishment is that it can produce a backlash against managers and companies, but if administered properly, punishment can weaken the frequency of undesirable behaviors without creating a backlash.[46] To be effective, the punishment must be strong enough to stop the undesired behavior and must be administered objectively (same rules applied to everyone), impersonally (without emotion or anger), consistently and

contingently (each time improper behavior occurs), and quickly (as soon as possible following the undesirable behavior). In addition, managers should clearly explain what the appropriate behavior is and why the employee is being punished. Employees typically respond well when punishment is administered this way.[47]

Finally, managers should *choose the simplest and most effective schedule of reinforcement.* When choosing a schedule of reinforcement, managers need to balance effectiveness against simplicity. In fact, the more complex the schedule of reinforcement, the more likely it is to be misunderstood and resisted by managers and employees. Since continuous reinforcement, fixed ratio, and variable ratio schedules are about equally effective, continuous reinforcement schedules may be the best choice in many instances by virtue of their simplicity.

Praise as a Motivator

Today's companies are using compliments, prizes, and public displays of appreciation as motivation and retention tools. The Container Store has something called "Celebration Voice Mailboxes" especially for messages of praise. By company estimates, every 20 seconds, one of the Container Store's 4,000 employees receives praise. The Scooter Store, which sells power wheelchairs, has a "celebrations assistant" whose job it is to throw confetti at employees (she throws over 25 pounds per week) and pass out celebratory helium balloons (she hands out 100 to 500 per week).

Source: J. Zaslow, "The Most-Praised Generation Goes to Work," *Wall Street Journal,* 20 April 2007.

©Nonstock/Jupiter Images

Choose the **simplest** and **most effective** schedule of reinforcement.

5 Goal-Setting Theory

The basic model of motivation with which we began this chapter showed that individuals feel tension after becoming aware of an unfulfilled need. Once they experience tension, they search for and select courses of action that they believe will eliminate this tension. In other words, they direct their behavior toward something. This something is a goal. A **goal** is a target, objective, or result that someone tries to accomplish.

Goal-setting theory says that people will be motivated to the extent to which they accept specific, challenging goals and receive feedback that indicates their progress toward goal achievement.

Let's learn more about goal setting by examining **5.1 the components of goal-setting theory** *and* **5.2 how to motivate with goal-setting theory.**

5.1 Components of Goal-Setting Theory

The basic components of goal-setting theory are goal specificity, goal difficulty, goal acceptance, and performance feedback.[48] **Goal specificity** is the extent to which goals are detailed, exact, and unambiguous. Specific goals, such as "I'm going to have a 3.0 average this semester," are more motivating than general goals, such as "I'm going to get better grades this semester."

Goal difficulty is the extent to which a goal is hard or challenging to accomplish. Difficult goals, such as "I'm going to have a 3.5 average and make the Dean's List this semester," are more motivating than easy goals, such as "I'm going to have a 2.0 average this semester."

Goal acceptance, which is similar to the idea of goal commitment discussed in Chapter 5, is the extent to which people consciously understand and agree to goals. Accepted goals, such as "I really want to get a 3.5 average this semester to show my parents how much I've improved," are more motivating than unaccepted goals, such as "My parents really want me to get a 3.5 average this semester, but there's so much more I'd rather do on campus than study!"

Performance feedback is information about the quality or quantity of past performance and indicates whether progress is being made toward the accomplishment of a goal. Performance feedback, such as "My prof said I need a 92 on the final to get an 'A' in that class," is more motivating than no feedback, "I have no idea what my grade is in that class." In short, goal-setting theory says that people will be motivated to the extent to which they accept specific, challenging goals and receive feedback that indicates their progress toward goal achievement.

How does goal setting work? To start, challenging goals focus employees' attention (i.e., direction of effort) on the critical aspects of their jobs and away from unimportant areas. Goals also energize behavior. When faced with unaccomplished goals, employees typically develop plans and strategies to reach those goals. Goals also create tension between the goal, which is the desired future state of affairs, and where the employee or company is now, meaning the current state of affairs. This tension can be satisfied only by achieving or abandoning the goal. Finally, goals influence persistence. Since goals only "go away" when they are accomplished, employees are more likely to persist in their efforts in the presence of goals. Exhibit 13.8 incorporates goals into the motivation model by showing how goals directly affect tension, effort, and the extent to which employees are energized to take action.

5.2 Motivating with Goal-Setting Theory

What practical steps can managers take to use goal-setting theory to motivate employees? One of the simplest, most effective ways to motivate workers is to *assign them specific, challenging goals.*

Second, managers should *make sure workers truly accept organizational goals.* Specific, challenging goals won't motivate workers unless they really accept, understand, and agree to the organization's goals. For this to occur, people must see the goals as fair and reasonable. Plus, they must trust management and believe that managers are using goals to clarify what is expected from them rather than to exploit or threaten them ("If you don't achieve these goals . . . "). Participative goal setting, in which managers and employees generate goals together, can help increase trust and understanding and thus acceptance of goals. Furthermore, providing workers with training can help increase goal acceptance, particularly when workers don't believe they are capable of reaching the organization's goals.[49]

Goal a target, objective, or result that someone tries to accomplish

Goal-setting theory a theory that states that people will be motivated to the extent to which they accept specific, challenging goals and receive feedback that indicates their progress toward goal achievement

Goal specificity the extent to which goals are detailed, exact, and unambiguous

Goal difficulty the extent to which a goal is hard or challenging to accomplish

Goal acceptance the extent to which people consciously understand and agree to goals

Performance feedback information about the quality or quantity of past performance that indicates whether progress is being made toward the accomplishment of a goal

Exhibit 13.8
Adding Goal-Setting Theory to the Model

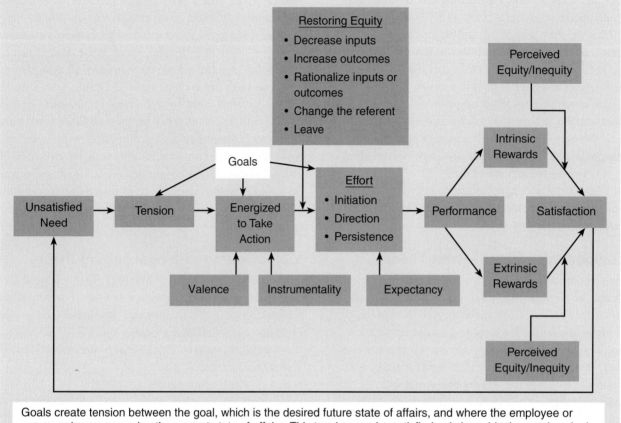

Goals create tension between the goal, which is the desired future state of affairs, and where the employee or company is now, meaning the current state of affairs. This tension can be satisfied only by achieving or abandoning the goal. Goals also energize behavior. When faced with unaccomplished goals, employees typically develop plans and strategies to reach those goals. Finally, goals influence persistence.

Finally, managers should *provide frequent, specific, performance-related feedback.* Once employees have accepted specific, challenging goals, they should receive frequent performance-related feedback so that they can track their progress toward goal completion. Feedback leads to stronger motivation and effort in three ways.[50] Receiving specific feedback that indicates how well they're performing can encourage employees who don't have specific, challenging goals to set goals to improve their performance. Once people meet goals, performance feedback often encourages them to set higher, more difficult goals. And, feedback lets people know whether they need to increase their efforts or change strategies in order to accomplish their goals. So, to motivate employees with goal-setting theory, make sure they receive frequent performance-related feedback so that they can track their progress toward goal completion.

6 Motivating with the Integrated Model

We began this chapter by defining motivation as the set of forces that initiates, directs, and makes people persist in their efforts to accomplish a goal. We also asked the basic question that managers ask when they try to figure out how to motivate their workers: "What leads to effort?" Though the answer to that question is likely to be somewhat different for each employee, the diagram on your Review Card for this chapter helps you begin to answer it by consolidating the practical advice from the theories reviewed in this chapter in one convenient location. So, if you're having difficulty figuring out why people aren't motivated where you work, check your review card for a useful, theory-based starting point.

Speak Up!

MGMT was built on a simple principle: to create a new teaching and learning solution that reflects the way today's faculty teach and the way you learn.

Through conversations, focus groups, surveys, and interviews, we collected data that drove the creation of the current version of *MGMT* that you are using today. But it doesn't stop there – in order to make *MGMT* an even better learning experience, we'd like you to SPEAK UP and tell us how worked for you. What did you like about it? What would you change? Are there additional ideas you have that would help us build a better product for next semester's principles of management students?

At **www.mgmt4me.com** you'll find all of the resources you need to succeed in principles of management – **video podcasts, audio downloads, flash cards, cell phone quizzes** and more!

Speak Up! Go to **www.mgmt4me.com/survey.**

[Faculty, check out **www.mgmt4me.com** for great ideas on how to incorporate student feedback as an example of management research in your classroom!]

THOMSON
SOUTH-WESTERN

LEADERSHIP

What Is Leadership?

Do I have what it takes to lead? What are the most important things leaders do? How can I transform a poorly performing department, division, or company? Do I need to adjust my leadership depending on the situation and the employee? Why doesn't my leadership inspire people? If you've ever been "in charge," or even just thought about it, chances are you've considered similar questions. Well, you're not alone—millions of leaders in organizations across the world struggle with fundamental leadership issues on a daily basis.

Southwest Airlines flies two to three times as many passengers per employee as other airlines at a cost 25 to 40 percent that of its competitors.[1] Why is Southwest able to achieve such incredible results? It takes care of its employees. For instance, with most ticket sales moving to its Web site, Southwest closed reservation centers in Dallas, Little Rock, and Salt Lake City. But instead of laying off employees, it paid for them to commute or relocate to places it had jobs. Regarding layoffs, Colleen Barrett, Southwest's president, says, "We don't do those kind of things. That's what our competitors do. At Southwest, our employees come first."[2] The result, says Southwest spokesperson Paula Berg, is, "We work hard. I'll stay here until 10 P.M., if necessary. But we do it because the company takes care of us, so we want to take care of the company."[3] As Colleen Barrett and the rest of the managers at Southwest Airlines have discovered, **leadership** is the process of influencing others to achieve group or organizational goals.

Leadership the process of influencing others to achieve group or organizational goals

Learning Outcomes

1 explain what leadership is.

2 describe who leaders are and what effective leaders do.

3 explain Fiedler's contingency theory.

4 describe how path-goal theory works.

5 explain the normative decision theory.

6 explain how visionary leadership (i.e., charismatic and transformational leadership) helps leaders achieve strategic leadership.

©Stone+/Getty Images

After reading the next two sections, you should be able to

1   explain what leadership is.

2   describe who leaders are and what effective leaders do.

1 Leaders versus Managers

According to University of Southern California business professor Warren Bennis, the primary difference between leaders and managers is that leaders are concerned with doing the right thing, while managers are concerned with doing things right.[4] In other words, leaders begin with the question, "What should we be doing?" while managers start with "How can we do what we're already doing better?" Leaders focus on vision, mission, goals, and objectives, while managers focus on productivity and efficiency. Managers see themselves as preservers of the status quo, while leaders see themselves as promoters of change and challengers of the status quo in that they encourage creativity and risk taking. Four years ago, McDonald's was losing money and closing down stores. Today, with faster, friendlier service, healthier, better-tasting food, and a focus on quality rather than growth, McDonald's stock is up 45 percent. Furthermore, 50 million customers walk into its restaurants each day, 3.5 million more per day than four years ago. Despite these successes, CEO Jim Skinner is not happy with the status quo. Says Skinner, "I worry about complacency. We're not satisfied. We have a lot [more] work to do."[5]

Another difference is that managers have a relatively short-term perspective, while leaders take a long-term view. Managers are also more concerned with *means,* how to get things done, while leaders are more concerned with *ends,* what gets done. Managers are concerned with control and limiting the choices of others, while leaders are more concerned with expanding people's choices and options.[6] Finally, managers solve problems so that others can do their work, while leaders inspire and motivate others to find their own solutions.

Though leaders are different from managers, organizations need them both. Managers are critical to getting out the day-to-day work, and leaders are critical to inspiring employees and setting the organization's long-term direction. The key issue for any organization is the extent to which it is properly led and properly managed. As Warren Bennis said in summing up the difference between leaders and managers, "American organizations (and probably those in much of the rest of the industrialized world) are underled and overmanaged. They do not pay enough attention to doing the right thing, while they pay too much attention to doing things right."[7]

2 Who Leaders Are and What Leaders Do

Indra Nooyi, PepsiCo's new CEO, talks straight, has a sharp sense of humor, and sings in the hallways wherever she is. Nooyi is an extrovert. By contrast, J.C. Penney's CEO, Mike Ullman, who is soft-spoken and easy to approach, is an introvert.[8] Which one is likely to be successful as a CEO? According to a survey of 1,542 senior managers, it's the extrovert. Forty-seven percent of those 1,542 senior managers felt that extroverts make better CEOs, while 65 percent said that being an introvert hurts a CEO's chances of success.[9] So clearly senior managers believe that extroverted CEOs are better leaders. But are they? Not necessarily. In fact, a relatively high percentage of CEOs, 40 percent, are introverts. Sara Lee CEO Brenda Barnes says, "I've always been shy. . . . People wouldn't call me that [an introvert], but I am."[10] Indeed, Barnes turns down all speaking requests and rarely gives interviews.

So, what makes a good leader? Does leadership success depend on who leaders are, such as introverts or extroverts, or on what leaders do and how they behave? Let's learn more about who leaders are by investigating 2.1 leadership traits and 2.2 leadership behaviors.

2.1 Leadership Traits

Trait theory is one way to describe who leaders are. **Trait theory** says that effective leaders possess a similar set of traits or characteristics. **Traits** are relatively stable characteristics, such as abilities, psychological motives, or consistent patterns of behavior. For example, according to trait theory, leaders are taller and more confident and have greater physical stamina (i.e., higher energy levels) than nonleaders. Indeed, while just 14.5 percent of men are six feet tall, 58 *percent* of *Fortune* 500 CEOs are six foot or taller.[11] Trait theory is also known as the "great person" theory because early versions of the theory stated that leaders are born, not made. In other words,

Trait theory a leadership theory that holds that effective leaders possess a similar set of traits or characteristics

Traits relatively stable characteristics, such as abilities, psychological motives, or consistent patterns of behavior you either have the "right stuff" to be a leader, or you don't. And if you don't, there is no way to get "it."

For some time, it was thought that trait theory was wrong and that there are no consistent trait differences between leaders and nonleaders, or between effective and ineffective leaders. However, more recent evidence shows that "successful leaders are not like other people," that successful leaders are indeed different from the rest of us.[12] More specifically, leaders are different from nonleaders in the following traits: drive, the desire to lead, honesty/integrity, self-confidence, emotional stability, cognitive ability, and knowledge of the business.[13]

Drive refers to high levels of effort and is characterized by achievement, motivation, initiative, energy, and tenacity. In terms of achievement and ambition, leaders always try to make improvements or achieve success in what they're doing. Because of their initiative, they have strong desires to promote change or solve problems. Leaders typically have more energy, and they have to, given the long hours they put in and followers' expectations that they be positive and "up." Leaders are also more tenacious than nonleaders and are better at overcoming obstacles and problems that would deter most of us.

Successful leaders also have a stronger *desire to lead.* They want to be in charge and think about ways to influence or convince others about what should or shouldn't be done. *Honesty/integrity* is also important to leaders. *Honesty,* being truthful with others, is a cornerstone of leadership. Without honesty, leaders won't be trusted. When leaders have it, subordinates are willing to overlook other flaws. *Integrity* is the extent to which leaders do what they said they would do. Leaders may be honest and have good intentions, but if they don't consistently deliver on what they promise, they won't be trusted.

Because we think we know what a leader should look like, we become blind to other considerations.[14]

She has:
- Honesty & integrity
- Self-confidence
- Emotional stability
- Cognitive ability
- Knowledge of the business
- Drive
- Desire to lead

Leaders are shaped by the decisions they make.

Self-confidence, believing in one's abilities, also distinguishes leaders from nonleaders. Self-confident leaders are more decisive and assertive and are more likely to gain others' confidence. Moreover, self-confident leaders will admit mistakes because they view them as learning opportunities rather than as refutation of their leadership capabilities. This also means that leaders have *emotional stability.* Even when things go wrong, they remain even-tempered and consistent in their outlook and in the way they treat others. Leaders who can't control their emotions, who anger quickly or attack and blame others for mistakes, are unlikely to be trusted.

Leaders are also smart. Leaders typically have strong *cognitive abilities.* This doesn't mean that leaders are geniuses, far from it. But it does mean that leaders have the capacity to analyze large amounts of seemingly unrelated, complex information and see patterns, opportunities, or threats where others might not see them. Finally, leaders also "know their stuff," which means they have superior technical knowledge about the businesses they run. Leaders who have a good *knowledge of the business* understand the key technological decisions and concerns facing their companies. More often than not, studies indicate that effective leaders have long, extensive experience in their industries.

2.2 Leadership Behaviors

Thus far, you've read about who leaders *are.* Traits alone are not enough to make a successful leader, however, though they are a precondition for success. After all, it's hard to imagine a truly successful leader who lacks all of these qualities. Leaders who have these traits (or many of them) must then take actions that encourage people to achieve group or organizational goals.[15] Accordingly, we now examine what leaders *do,* meaning the behaviors they perform or the actions they take to

It's pretty common to complain about bad bosses, but if you take a minute to think about what it is you don't like about their behavior, you can improve your own leadership style. For example, the president of the University of Illinois used to work as a consultant for a Silicon Valley entrepreneur, who had a consideration deficit (a diplomatic way of saying he had a tendency to humiliate people in front of co-workers). At one meeting, the entrepreneur attacked one of his manager's proposals, saying, "That's the g****** stupidest thing I've ever heard in my life. I'm disappointed in you." The woman was shaken for hours and never did really recover. What did the university president take away from that experience? A greater awareness of people's vulnerabilities.

Source: Joann S. Lublin, "Recall the Mistakes of Your Past Bosses, So You Can Do Better," *Wall Street Journal*, 2 January 2007, B1.

influence others to achieve group or organizational goals. When she interviewed the CEO of Procter & Gamble on the subject of leadership, Associated Press reporter Elise Amendola asked, "Are leaders born or made?" Debunking the "great person" theory, A.G. Lafley answered, "Clearly made. You choose to lead. You choose to want to make a difference, to make the world better in some meaningful way. Until that choice is made, you don't have a leader. You have a lump of clay."[16]

Researchers at the University of Michigan, Ohio State University, and the University of Texas examined the specific behaviors that leaders use to improve subordinate satisfaction and performance. Hundreds of studies were conducted and hundreds of leader behaviors were examined. At all three universities, two basic leader behaviors emerged as central to successful leadership: initiating structure (called *job-centered leadership* at the University of Michigan and *concern for production* at the University of Texas) and considerate

There isn't one "best" leadership style.

Initiating structure the degree to which a leader structures the roles of followers by setting goals, giving directions, setting deadlines, and assigning tasks

Consideration the extent to which a leader is friendly, approachable, and supportive and shows concern for employees

leader behavior (called *employee-centered leadership* at the University of Michigan and *concern for people* at the University of Texas).[17] These two leader behaviors form the basis for many of the leadership theories discussed in this chapter.

Initiating structure is the degree to which a leader structures the roles of followers by setting goals, giving directions, setting deadlines, and assigning tasks. A leader's ability to initiate structure primarily affects subordinates' job performance. When Jamie Dimon became CEO of JPMorgan Chase, the financial services company had four different computer systems from previously acquired companies. Branch bankers couldn't access checking histories or determine whether customers qualified for credit cards or mortgages. Dimon initiated structure by telling his executives to put one system in place, and, "If you don't do it in six weeks, I'll make all the choices myself."[18] The deadline was met.

Consideration is the extent to which a leader is friendly, approachable, and supportive and shows concern for employees. Consideration primarily affects subordinates' job satisfaction. Specific leader consideration behaviors include listening to employees' problems and concerns, consulting with employees before making decisions, and treating employees as equals. Twenty-five years ago Wal-Mart's CEO, Lee Scott, received a lesson in the importance of consideration from founder Sam Walton. Scott, who was then in charge of a transportation unit, was known for his tough management style and for sending "blistering memos." When "Mr. Sam" called him into his office, Scott found nine of his truck drivers there waiting for him. The drivers, who were taking advantage of Wal-Mart's open-door policy, had complained to Walton about the way Scott treated them and asked that he be fired. According to Scott, "They just wanted to do their work and be appreciated for it. So Mr. Walton asked me, with them there, if I could do it differently."[19] After agreeing that he could, Scott said that Walton "had me stand at the door as they were leaving and thank each one for having the courage to use the open door, which is one of the very basic principles of Wal-Mart."[20] That office is now Scott's, and Wal-Mart has the same open door through which any Wal-Mart employee can walk to talk with the CEO.

Although researchers at all three universities generally agreed that initiating structure and consideration were basic leader behaviors, their interpretation of the

©Photodisc/Getty Images

Exhibit 14.1

Blake/Mouton Leadership Grid

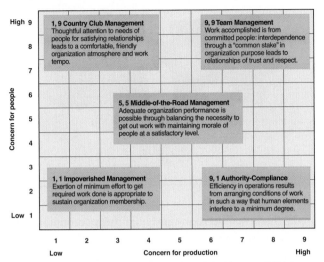

Source: R. R. Blake & A. A. McCanse, "The Leadership Grid®," *Leadership Dilemmas—Grid Solutions* (Houston: Gulf Publishing Company), 21. Copyright © 1991, by Scientific Methods, Inc. Reproduced by permission of the owners.

interaction and effectiveness of these behaviors differed. The University of Michigan studies indicated that initiating structure and consideration were mutually exclusive behaviors on opposite ends of the same continuum. In other words, leaders who wanted to be more considerate would have to do less initiating of structure (and vice versa). The University of Michigan studies also indicated that only considerate leader behaviors (i.e., employee-centered behaviors) were associated with successful leadership. By contrast, researchers at Ohio State University and the University of Texas found that initiating structure and consideration were independent behaviors, meaning that leaders can be considerate and initiate structure at the same time. Additional evidence confirms this finding.[21] The same researchers also concluded that the most effective leaders excelled at both initiating structure and considerate leader behaviors.

This "high-high" approach can be seen in the upper right corner of the Blake/Mouton leadership grid, shown in Exhibit 14.1. Blake and Mouton used two leadership behaviors, concern for people (i.e., consideration) and concern for production (i.e., initiating structure), to categorize five different leadership styles. Both behaviors are rated on a 9-point scale, with 1 representing "low" and 9 representing "high." Blake and Mouton suggest that a "high-high" or 9,9 leadership style is the best. They call this style *team management* because leaders who use it display a high concern for people (9) and a high concern for production (9).

By contrast, leaders use a 9,1 *authority-compliance* leadership style when they have a high concern for pro-

duction and a low concern for people. A 1,9 *country club* style occurs when leaders care about having a friendly enjoyable work environment but don't really pay much attention to production or performance. The worst leadership style, according to the grid, is the 1,1 *impoverished* leader, who shows little concern for people or production and does the bare minimum needed to keep his or her job. Finally, the 5,5 *middle-of-the-road* style occurs when leaders show a moderate amount of concern for both people and production.

Is the team management style, with a high concern for production and a high concern for people, the "best" leadership style? Logically, it would seem so. Why wouldn't you want to show high concern for both people and production? Nonetheless, nearly 50 years of research indicates that there isn't one "best" leadership style. The "best" leadership style depends on the situation. In other words, no one leadership behavior by itself and no one combination of leadership behaviors works well across all situations and employees.

Situational Approaches to Leadership

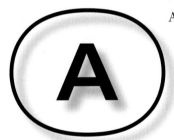

After leader traits and behaviors, the situational approach to leadership is the third major method used in the study of leadership. We review three major situational approaches to leadership—Fiedler's contingency theory, path-goal theory, and Vroom and Yetton's normative decision model. All assume that the effectiveness of any **leadership style,** the way a leader generally behaves toward followers, depends on the situation.[22]

According to situational leadership theories, there is no one "best" leadership style. But, one of these situational theories differs from the other three in one significant way. Fiedler's contingency theory assumes that leadership styles are consistent and difficult to change. Therefore, leaders must be placed in or "matched" to a situation that fits their leadership style. In contrast, the other situational theories assume that leaders are capable of adapting and adjusting their leadership styles to fit the demands of different situations.

> **Leadership style** the way a leader generally behaves toward followers

After reading the next three sections, you should be able to

3 explain Fiedler's contingency theory.

4 describe how path-goal theory works.

5 explain the normative decision theory.

3 Putting Leaders in the Right Situation: Fiedler's Contingency Theory

Fiedler's Contingency Theory

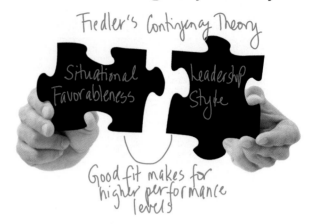

Fiedler's **contingency theory** states that in order to maximize work group performance, leaders must be matched to the right leadership situation.[23] More specifically, the first basic assumption of Fiedler's theory is that leaders are effective when the work groups they lead perform well. So, instead of judging leaders' effectiveness by what the leaders do (i.e., initiating structure and consideration) or who they are (i.e., trait theory), Fiedler assesses leaders by the conduct and performance of the people they supervise. Second, Fiedler assumes that leaders are generally unable to change their leadership styles and that they will be more effective when their styles are matched to the proper situation. Third, Fiedler assumes that the favorableness of a situation for a leader depends on the degree to which the situation permits the leader to influence the behavior of group members. Thus, Fiedler's third assumption is consistent with our definition of leadership, which is the process of influencing others to achieve group or organizational goals.

*Let's learn more about Fiedler's contingency theory by examining **3.1 the least preferred coworker** and **leadership styles, 3.2 situational favorableness**, and **3.3 how to match leadership styles to situations.***

3.1 Leadership Style: Least Preferred Coworker

When Fiedler refers to *leadership style,* he means the way that leaders generally behave toward their followers. Do the leaders yell and scream and blame others when things go wrong? Or do they correct mistakes by listening and then quietly but directly, making their point? Do they let others

Contingency theory a leadership theory that states that in order to maximize work group performance, leaders must be matched to the situation that best fits their leadership style

make their own decisions and hold them accountable for the results? Or do they micromanage, insisting that all decisions be approved first by them? Fiedler also assumes that leadership styles are tied to leaders' underlying needs and personalities. And since personality and needs are relatively stable, he assumes that leaders are generally incapable of changing their leadership styles. In other words, the way that leaders treat people now is probably the way they've always treated others.

Fiedler uses a questionnaire called the Least Preferred Coworker (LPC) scale to measure leadership style. When completing the LPC scale, people are instructed to consider all of the people with whom they have ever worked and then to choose the one person with whom they have worked *least* well. Fiedler explains, "This does not have to be the person you liked least well, but should be the one person with whom you have the most trouble getting the job done."[24]

Would you describe your LPC as pleasant, friendly, supportive, interesting, cheerful, and sincere? Or would you describe the person as unpleasant, unfriendly, hostile, boring, gloomy, and insincere? People

How would you rank your least-preferred coworker? He or she is:

Pleasant									Unpleasant
Pleasant	⑧	⑦	⑥	⑤	④	③	②	①	**Unpleasant**
Friendly	⑧	⑦	⑥	⑤	④	③	②	①	**Unfriendly**
Supportive	⑧	⑦	⑥	⑤	④	③	②	①	**Hostile**
Boring	①	②	③	④	⑤	⑥	⑦	⑧	**Interesting**
Gloomy	①	②	③	④	⑤	⑥	⑦	⑧	**Cheerful**
Insincere	①	②	③	④	⑤	⑥	⑦	⑧	**Sincere**

Source: F. E. Fiedler & M. M. Chemers, *Improving Leadership Effectiveness: The Leader Match Concept,* 2nd ed. (New York: John Wiley & Sons, 1984). Available at http://depts.washington.edu/psych/faculty/*cv/fiedler_cv.pdf, 23 March 2002. Reprinted by permission of the authors.

Exhibit 14.2
Situational Favorableness

Leader-Member Relations	Good	Good	Good	Good	Poor	Poor	Poor	Poor
Task Structure	High	High	Low	Low	High	High	Low	Low
Position Power	Strong	Weak	Strong	Weak	Strong	Weak	Strong	Weak
Situation	I	II	III	IV	V	VI	VII	VIII
		Favorable			Moderately Favorable		Unfavorable	

who describe their LPC in a positive way (scoring 64 and above on the full inventory of 18 oppositional pairs) have *relationship-oriented* leadership styles. After all, if they can still be positive about their least preferred coworker, they must be people oriented. By contrast, people who describe their LPC in a negative way (scoring 57 or below) have *task-oriented* leadership styles. Given a choice, they'll focus first on getting the job done and second on making sure everyone gets along. Finally, those with moderate scores (from 58 to 63) have a more flexible leadership style and can be somewhat relationship oriented or somewhat task oriented.

3.2 Situational Favorableness

Fiedler assumes that leaders will be more effective when their leadership styles are matched to the proper situation. More specifically, Fiedler defines **situational favorableness** as the degree to which a particular situation either permits or denies a leader the chance to influence the behavior of group members.[25] In highly favorable situations, leaders find that their actions influence followers, but in highly unfavorable situations, leaders have little or no success influencing the people they are trying to lead.

Three situational factors determine the favorability of a situation: leader-member relations, task structure, and position power. The most important situational factor is **leader-member relations,** which refers to how well followers respect, trust, and like their leaders. When leader-member relations are good, followers trust the leader and there is a friendly work atmosphere. **Task structure** is the degree to which the requirements of a subordinate's tasks are clearly specified. With highly structured tasks, employees have clear job responsibilities, goals, and procedures. **Position power** is the degree to which leaders are able to hire, fire, reward, and punish workers. The more influence leaders have over hiring, firing, rewards, and punishments, the greater their power.

Exhibit 14.2 shows how leader-member relations, task structure, and position power can be combined into eight situations that differ in their favorability to leaders. In general, Situation I, on the left side of Exhibit 14.2, is the most favorable leader situation. Followers like and trust their leaders and know what to do because their tasks are highly structured. Also, the leaders have the formal power to influence workers through hiring, firing, rewarding, and punishing them. Therefore, in Situation I, it's relatively easy for a leader to influence followers. By contrast, Situation VIII, on the right side of Exhibit 14.2, is the least favorable situation for leaders. Followers don't like or trust their leaders. Plus, followers are not sure what they're supposed to be doing because their tasks or jobs are highly unstructured. Finally, leaders find it difficult to influence followers without the ability to hire, fire, reward, or punish the people who work for them. In short, it's very difficult to influence followers given the conditions found in Situation VIII.

3.3 Matching Leadership Styles to Situations

After studying thousands of leaders and followers in hundreds of different situations, Fiedler found that the performance of relationship- and task-oriented leaders followed the pattern displayed in Exhibit 14.3.

Relationship-oriented leaders, with high LPC scores, were better leaders (i.e., their groups performed more effectively) under moderately favorable situations. In moderately favorable situations,

Situational favorableness the degree to which a particular situation either permits or denies a leader the chance to influence the behavior of group members

Leader-member relations the degree to which followers respect, trust, and like their leaders

Task structure the degree to which the requirements of a subordinate's tasks are clearly specified

Position power the degree to which leaders are able to hire, fire, reward, and punish workers

Exhibit 14.3

Matching Leadership Styles to Situations

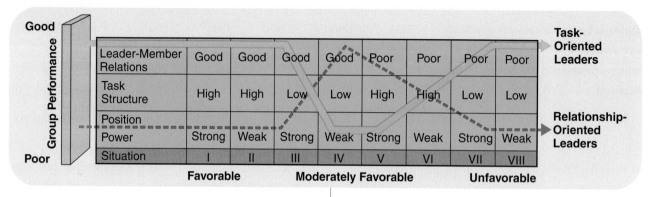

Leader-Member Relations	Good	Good	Good	Good	Poor	Poor	Poor	Poor	**Task-Oriented Leaders**
Task Structure	High	High	Low	Low	High	High	Low	Low	
Position Power	Strong	Weak	Strong	Weak	Strong	Weak	Strong	Weak	**Relationship-Oriented Leaders**
Situation	I	II	III	IV	V	VI	VII	VIII	

Group Performance: Good / Poor

Favorable — Moderately Favorable — Unfavorable

the leader may be liked somewhat, tasks may be somewhat structured, and the leader may have some position power. In this situation, a relationship-oriented leader improves leader-member relations, which is the most important of the three situational factors. In turn, morale and performance improve. By contrast, as Exhibit 14.3 shows, task-oriented leaders, with low LPC scores, are better leaders in highly favorable and unfavorable situations. Task-oriented leaders do well in favorable situations where leaders are liked, tasks are structured, and the leader has the power to hire, fire, reward, and punish. In these favorable situations, task-oriented leaders effectively step on the gas of a well-tuned car. Their focus on performance sets the goal for the group, which then charges forward to meet it. But task-oriented leaders also do well in unfavorable situations where leaders are disliked, tasks are unstructured, and the leader doesn't have the power to hire, fire, reward, and punish. In these unfavorable situations, the task-oriented leader sets goals, which focus attention on performance, and clarifies what needs to be done, thus overcoming low task structure. This is enough to jump-start performance, even if workers don't like or trust the leader. Finally, though not shown in Exhibit 14.3, people with moderate LPC scores, who can be somewhat relationship oriented or somewhat task oriented, tend to do fairly well in all situations because they can adapt their behavior. Typically, though, they don't perform quite as well as relationship-oriented or task-oriented leaders whose leadership styles are well matched to the situation.

Recall, however, that Fiedler assumes that leaders are incapable of changing their leadership styles. Accordingly, the key to applying Fiedler's contingency theory in the workplace is to accurately measure and match leaders to situations or to teach leaders how to change situational favorableness by changing leader-member relations, task structure, or position power. Though matching or placing leaders in appropriate situations works particularly well, practicing managers have had little luck with "reengineering situations" to fit their leadership styles. The primary problem, as you've no doubt realized, is the complexity of the theory. In a study designed to teach leaders how to reengineer their situations to fit their leadership styles, Fiedler found that most of the leaders simply did not understand what they were supposed to do to change their leadership situations. Furthermore, if they didn't like their LPC profile (perhaps they felt they were more relationship oriented than their scores indicated), they arbitrarily changed it to better suit their view of themselves. Of course, the theory won't work as well if leaders are attempting to change situational factors to fit their perceived leadership style and not their real leadership style.[26]

4 Adapting Leader Behavior: Path-Goal Theory

Just as its name suggests, **path-goal theory** states that leaders can increase subordinate satisfaction and performance by clarifying and clearing the paths to goals and by increasing the number and kinds of rewards available for goal attainment. Said another way, leaders need to clarify how followers can achieve organizational goals, take care of problems that prevent followers from achieving goals, and then find more and varied rewards to motivate followers to achieve those goals.[27]

Path-goal theory a leadership theory that states that leaders can increase subordinate satisfaction and performance by clarifying and clearing the paths to goals and by increasing the number and kinds of rewards available for goal attainment

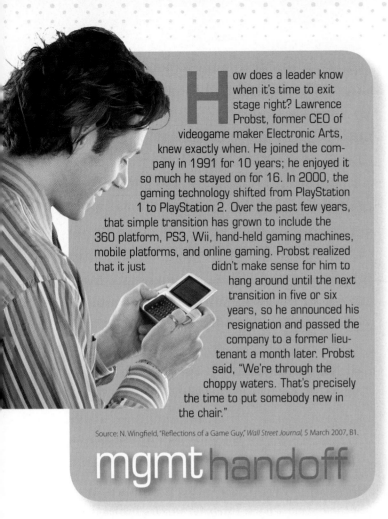

How does a leader know when it's time to exit stage right? Lawrence Probst, former CEO of videogame maker Electronic Arts, knew exactly when. He joined the company in 1991 for 10 years; he enjoyed it so much he stayed on for 16. In 2000, the gaming technology shifted from PlayStation 1 to PlayStation 2. Over the past few years, that simple transition has grown to include the 360 platform, PS3, Wii, hand-held gaming machines, mobile platforms, and online gaming. Probst realized that it just didn't make sense for him to hang around until the next transition in five or six years, so he announced his resignation and passed the company to a former lieutenant a month later. Probst said, "We're through the choppy waters. That's precisely the time to put somebody new in the chair."

Source: N. Wingfield, "Reflections of a Game Guy," *Wall Street Journal*, 5 March 2007, B1.

mgmt handoff

cess, showing that leaders change and adapt their leadership styles contingent on their subordinates or the environment in which those subordinates work.

*Let's learn more about path-goal theory by examining **4.1 the four kinds of leadership styles that leaders use, 4.2 the subordinate and environmental contingency factors that determine when different leader styles are effective,** and **4.3 the outcomes of path-goal theory in improving employee satisfaction and performance.***

4.1 Leadership Styles

As illustrated in Exhibit 14.4, the four leadership styles in path-goal theory are directive, supportive, participative, and achievement oriented.[28] **Directive leadership** involves letting employees know precisely what is expected of them, giving them specific guidelines for the performance of their tasks, scheduling work, setting standards of performance, and making sure that people follow standard rules and regulations.

Supportive leadership involves being approachable and friendly to employees, showing concern for them and their welfare, treating them as equals, and creating a friendly climate. Supportive leadership is very similar to considerate leader behavior. Supportive leadership often results in employee satisfaction with the job and with leaders. This leadership style may also result in improved performance when it increases employee confidence, lowers employee job stress, or improves relations and trust between employees and leaders.[29]

Participative leadership involves consulting employees for their suggestions and input before making decisions. Participation in decision making should help followers understand which goals are most important and clarify the paths to accomplishing

For path clarification, path clearing, and rewards to increase followers' motivation and effort, however, leaders must meet two conditions. First, leader behavior must be a source of immediate or future satisfaction for followers. Therefore, the things you do as a leader must please your followers today or lead to activities or rewards that will satisfy them in the future.

Second, while providing the coaching, guidance, support, and rewards necessary for effective work performance, leader behaviors must complement and not duplicate the characteristics of followers' work environments. Thus, leader behaviors must offer something unique and valuable to followers beyond what they're already experiencing as they do their jobs or what they can already do for themselves.

In contrast to Fiedler's contingency theory, path-goal theory assumes that leaders can change and adapt their leadership styles. Exhibit 14.4 illustrates this pro-

---

Directive leadership a leadership style in which the leader lets employees know precisely what is expected of them, gives them specific guidelines for performing tasks, schedules work, sets standards of performance, and makes sure that people follow standard rules and regulations

Supportive leadership a leadership style in which the leader is friendly and approachable, shows concern for employees and their welfare and treats them as equals, and creates a friendly climate

Participative leadership a leadership style in which the leader consults employees for their suggestions and input before making decisions

---

(The things you do as a **leader must please** your **followers today** or **satisfy them** in the future.)

6 CEOs a day leave their position!

©Polka Dot Images

them. Furthermore, when people participate in decisions, they become more committed to making them work.

Achievement-oriented leadership means setting challenging goals, having high expectations of employees, and displaying confidence that employees will assume responsibility and put forth extraordinary effort. Simon Cooper, president and COO of the Ritz-Carlton luxury hotel chain, uses the phrase "He who says it, does" to describe achievement-oriented leadership, Cooper explains, "I use this phrase whenever someone convinces me that they can achieve something I consider to be unachievable. In the past I've been known to add focus to a goal by making a bet to see if they can make it—sometimes with amusing consequences. I remember being at a mountain resort in Canada and proposing an incredible goal for the season. The team convinced me that they could achieve it, and I offered to jump into the lake if they did. It's a long story, but they made it. There's a great scene of a hole being cut in the ice and an ambulance on standby while I gave a whole new meaning to the term 'dunking'. The cognac [afterwards] was very welcome."[30]

4.2 Subordinate and Environmental Contingencies

Achievement-oriented leadership a leadership style in which the leader sets challenging goals, has high expectations of employees, and displays confidence that employees will assume responsibility and put forth extraordinary effort

As shown in Exhibit 14.4, path-goal theory specifies that leader behaviors should be fitted to subordinate characteristics. The theory identifies three kinds of subordinate contingencies: perceived ability, experience, and locus of control. *Perceived ability* is

simply how much ability subordinates believe they have for doing their jobs well. Subordinates who perceive that they have a great deal of ability will be dissatisfied with directive leader behaviors. Experienced employees are likely to react in a similar way. Since they already know how to do their jobs (or perceive that they do), they don't need or want close supervision. By contrast, subordinates with little experience or little perceived ability will welcome directive leadership.

Locus of control is a personality measure that indicates the extent to which people believe that they have control over what happens to them in life. *Internals* believe that what happens to them, good or bad, is largely a result of their choices and actions. *Externals*, on the other hand, believe that what happens to them is caused by external forces beyond their control. Accordingly, externals are much more comfortable with a directive leadership style, while internals greatly prefer a participative leadership style because they like to have a say in what goes on at work.

Path-goal theory specifies that leader behaviors should complement rather than duplicate the character-

Exhibit 14.4

Path-Goal Theory

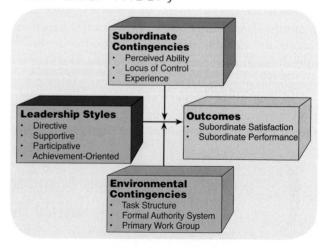

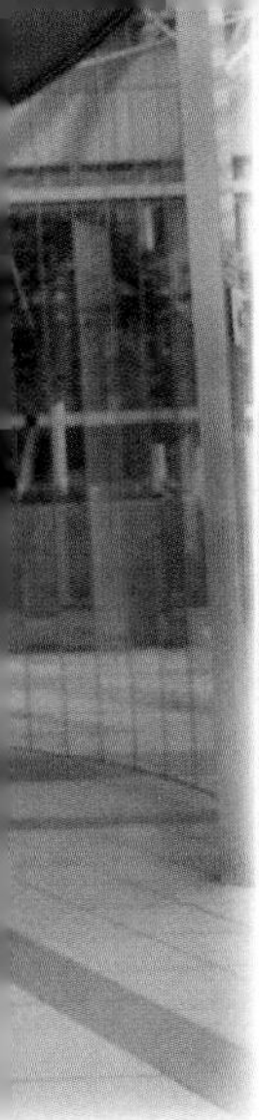

Turnover Stats

In 2005, 1,322 CEOs changed at U.S. companies, for an average of five exits per business day. The first half of 2006 proved just as robust, with 728 CEOs leaving (or losing) their positions—an average of six per day. By early 2007, though, CEO departures had mercifully slowed by nearly 20 percent.

Sources: T. Demos, "Leading Indicators," *Fortune*, August 7, 2006, 15; L. Perelman, "Executive-Level Turnover Down in January," *eWeek*, February 6, 2007, http://www.eweek.com/article2/0,1895,2091007,00.asp.

istics of followers' work environments. There are three kinds of environmental contingencies: task structure, the formal authority system, and the primary work group. As in Fiedler's contingency theory, *task structure* is the degree to which the requirements of a subordinate's tasks are clearly specified. When task structure is low and tasks are unclear, directive leadership should be used because it complements the work environment. When task structure is high and tasks are clear, however, directive leadership is not needed because it duplicates what task structure provides. Alternatively, when tasks are stressful, frustrating, or dissatisfying, leaders should respond with supportive leadership.

The *formal authority system* is an organization's set of procedures, rules, and policies. When the formal authority system is unclear, directive leadership complements the situation by reducing uncertainty and increasing clarity. But when the formal authority system is clear, directive leadership is redundant and should not be used.

Primary work group refers to the amount of work-oriented participation or emotional support that is provided by an employee's immediate work group. Participative leadership should be used when tasks are complex and there is little existing work-oriented participation in the primary work group. When tasks are stressful, frustrating, or repetitive, supportive leadership is called for.

Finally, since keeping track of all of these subordinate and environmental contingencies can get a bit confusing, Exhibit 14.5 provides a summary of when directive, supportive, participative, and achievement-oriented leadership styles should be used.

4.3 Outcomes

Does following path-goal theory improve subordinate satisfaction and performance? Preliminary evidence suggests that it does.[31] In particular, people who work for supportive leaders are much more satisfied with their jobs and their bosses. Likewise, people who work for directive leaders are more satisfied with their jobs and bosses (but not quite as much as when their bosses are supportive) and perform their jobs better, too. Does adapting one's leadership style to subordinate and environmental characteristics improve subordinate satisfaction and performance? At this point, because of the difficulty of completely testing this complex theory, it's too early to tell.[32] However, since the data clearly show that it makes sense for leaders to be both supportive *and* directive, it also makes sense that leaders could improve subordinate satisfaction and performance by adding participative and achievement-oriented leadership styles to their capabilities as leaders.

Exhibit 14.5

Path-Goal Theory: When to Use Directive, Supportive, Participative, or Achievement-Oriented Leadership

DIRECTIVE LEADERSHIP	SUPPORTIVE LEADERSHIP	PARTICIPATIVE LEADERSHIP	ACHIEVEMENT-ORIENTED LEADERSHIP
Unstructured tasks	Structured, simple, repetitive tasks; Stressful, frustrating tasks	Complex tasks	Unchallenging tasks
Workers with external locus of control	Workers lack confidence	Workers with internal locus of control	
Unclear formal authority system	Clear formal authority system	Workers not satisfied with rewards	
Inexperienced workers		Experienced workers	
Workers with low perceived ability		Workers with high perceived ability	

Exhibit 14.6

Normative Theory, Decision Styles and Levels of Employee Participation

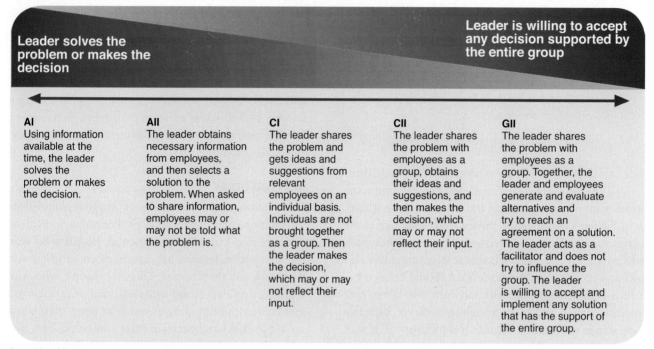

AI	**AII**	**CI**	**CII**	**GII**
Using information available at the time, the leader solves the problem or makes the decision.	The leader obtains necessary information from employees, and then selects a solution to the problem. When asked to share information, employees may or may not be told what the problem is.	The leader shares the problem and gets ideas and suggestions from relevant employees on an individual basis. Individuals are not brought together as a group. Then the leader makes the decision, which may or may not reflect their input.	The leader shares the problem with employees as a group, obtains their ideas and suggestions, and then makes the decision, which may or may not reflect their input.	The leader shares the problem with employees as a group. Together, the leader and employees generate and evaluate alternatives and try to reach an agreement on a solution. The leader acts as a facilitator and does not try to influence the group. The leader is willing to accept and implement any solution that has the support of the entire group.

Source: Adapted from V. H. Vroom & P. W. Yetton, *Leadership and Decision Making* (Pittsburgh: University of Pittsburgh Press, 1973), 13.

5 Adapting Leader Behavior: Normative Decision Theory

Many people believe that making tough decisions is at the heart of leadership. Yet experienced leaders will tell you that deciding how to make decisions is just as important. The **normative decision theory** (also known as the *Vroom-Yetton-Jago model*) helps leaders decide how much employee participation (from none to letting employees make the entire decision) should be used when making decisions.[33]

Let's learn more about normative decision theory by investigating 5.1 decision styles and 5.2 decision quality and acceptance.

5.1 Decision Styles

Unlike nearly all of the other leadership theories discussed in this chapter, which have specified leadership styles, that is, the way a leader generally behaves toward followers, the normative decision theory specifies five different decision styles, or ways of making decisions. (See Chapter 5 for a more complete review of de-

Normative decision theory a theory that suggests how leaders can determine an appropriate amount of employee participation when making decisions

cision making in organizations.) As shown in Exhibit 14.6, those styles vary from *autocratic* decisions (AI or AII) on the left, in which leaders make the decisions by themselves, to *consultative decisions* (CI or CII), in which leaders share problems with subordinates but still make the decisions themselves, to *group decisions* (GII) on the right, in which leaders share the problems with subordinates and then have the group make the decisions. GE Aircraft Engines in Durham, North Carolina, uses this approach when making decisions. According to *Fast Company* magazine, "At GE/Durham, every decision is either an 'A' decision, a 'B' decision, or a 'C' decision. An 'A' decision is one that the plant manager makes herself, without consulting anyone."[34] Plant manager Paula Sims says, "I don't make very many of those, and when I do make one, everyone at the plant knows it. I make maybe 10 or 12 a year."[35] "B" decisions are also made by the plant manager, but with input from the people affected. "C" decisions, the most common type, are made by consensus, by the people directly involved, with plenty of discussion. With "C" decisions, the view of the plant manager doesn't necessarily carry more weight than the views of those affected."[36]

5.2 Decision Quality and Acceptance

According to the normative decision theory, using the right degree of employee participation improves the

Exhibit 14.7

Normative Theory Decision Rules

DECISION RULES TO INCREASE DECISION QUALITY

Quality Rule. If the quality of the decision is important, then don't use an autocratic decision style.

Leader Information Rule. If the quality of the decision is important, and if the leader doesn't have enough information to make the decision on his or her own, then don't use an autocratic decision style.

Subordinate Information Rule. If the quality of the decision is important, and if the subordinates don't have enough information to make the decision themselves, then don't use a group decision style.

Goal Congruence Rule. If the quality of the decision is important, and subordinates' goals are different from the organization's goals, then don't use a group decision style.

Problem Structure Rule. If the quality of the decision is important, the leader doesn't have enough information to make the decision on his or her own, and the problem is unstructured, then don't use an autocratic decision style.

DECISION RULES TO INCREASE DECISION ACCEPTANCE

Commitment Probability Rule. If having subordinates accept and commit to the decision is important, then don't use an autocratic decision style.

Subordinate Conflict Rule. If having subordinates accept the decision is important and critical to successful implementation and subordinates are likely to disagree or end up in conflict over the decision, then don't use an autocratic or consultative decision style.

Commitment Requirement Rule. If having subordinates accept the decision is absolutely required for successful implementation and subordinates share the organization's goals, then don't use an autocratic or consultative style.

Sources: Adapted from V. H. Vroom, "Leadership," in *Handbook of Industrial and Organizational Psychology*, ed. M. D. Dunnette (Chicago: Rand McNally, 1976); V. H. Vroom & A. G. Jago, *The New Leadership: Managing Participation in Organizations* (Englewood Cliffs, NJ: Prentice Hall, 1988).

quality of decisions and the extent to which employees accept and are committed to decisions. Exhibit 14.7 lists the decision rules that normative decision theory uses to increase decision quality and employee acceptance and commitment. The quality, leader information, subordinate information, goal congruence, and problem structure rules are used to increase decision quality. For example, the leader information rule states that if a leader doesn't have enough information to make a decision on his or her own, then the leader should not use an autocratic decision style.

The commitment probability, subordinate conflict, and commitment requirement rules shown in Exhibit 14.7 are used to increase employee acceptance and commitment to decisions. For example, the commitment requirement rule says that if decision acceptance and commitment are important, and the subordinates share the organization's goals, then you shouldn't use an autocratic or consultative style. In other words, if followers want to do what's best for the company and you need their acceptance and commitment to make a decision work, then use a group decision style and let them make the decision.

As you can see, these decision rules help leaders improve decision quality and follower acceptance and commitment by eliminating decision styles that don't fit the decision or situation they're facing. Normative decision theory then operationalizes these decision rules in the form of yes/no questions, which are shown in the decision tree displayed in Exhibit 14.8. You start at the left side of the model and answer the first question, "How important is the technical quality of this decision?" by choosing "high" or "low." Then you continue by answering each question as you proceed along the decision tree until you get to a recommended decision style.

Let's use the model to make the decision of whether to change from a formal business attire policy to a casual wear policy. The problem sounds simple, but it is actually more complex than you might think. Follow the yellow line in Exhibit 14.8 as we work through the decision in the discussion below.

Problem: Change to Casual Wear?

1. *Quality requirement: How important is the technical quality of this decision?* High. This question has to do with whether there are quality differences in the alternatives and whether those quality differences matter. Although most people would assume that quality isn't an issue here, it really is, given the overall positive changes that generally accompany changes to casual wear.

2. *Commitment requirement: How important is subordinate commitment to the decision?* High.

Exhibit 14.8

Normative Decision Theory Tree for
Determining the Level of Participation in Decision Making

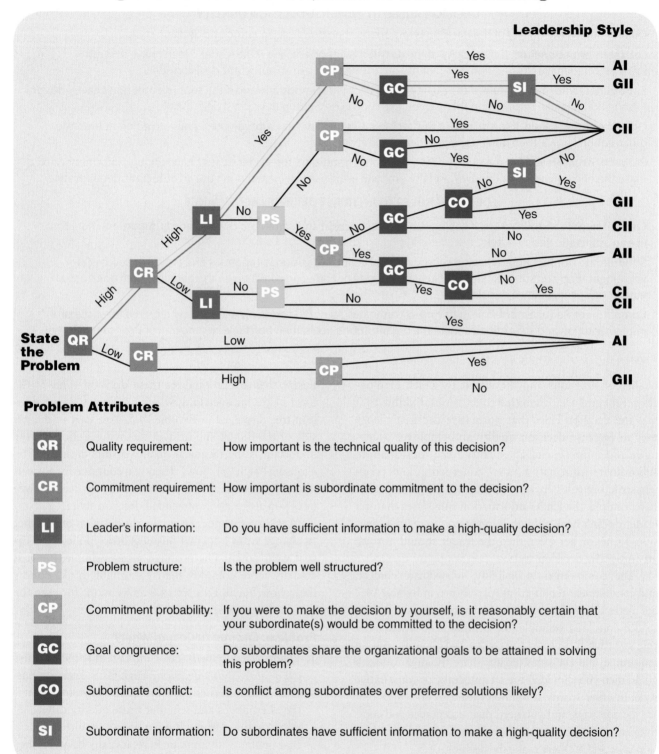

Leadership Style

Problem Attributes

QR	Quality requirement:	How important is the technical quality of this decision?
CR	Commitment requirement:	How important is subordinate commitment to the decision?
LI	Leader's information:	Do you have sufficient information to make a high-quality decision?
PS	Problem structure:	Is the problem well structured?
CP	Commitment probability:	If you were to make the decision by yourself, is it reasonably certain that your subordinate(s) would be committed to the decision?
GC	Goal congruence:	Do subordinates share the organizational goals to be attained in solving this problem?
CO	Subordinate conflict:	Is conflict among subordinates over preferred solutions likely?
SI	Subordinate information:	Do subordinates have sufficient information to make a high-quality decision?

Source: V. H. Vroom & P. W. Yetton, *Leadership and Decision Making* (Pittsburgh, University of Pittsburgh Press, 1973). Adapted and reprinted by permission of University of Pittsburgh Press.

©Digital Vision/Getty Images

tions (remember, different managers won't necessarily answer these questions the same way), the normative decision theory recommends that leaders consult with their subordinates before deciding whether to change to a casual wear policy.

How well does the normative decision theory work? A prominent leadership scholar has described it as the best supported of all leadership theories.[37] In general, the more managers violate the decision rules in Exhibit 14.7, the less effective their decisions are, especially with respect to subordinate acceptance and commitment.[38]

Strategic Leadership

Strategic leadership is the ability to anticipate, envision, maintain flexibility, think strategically, and work with others to initiate changes that will create a positive future for an organization.[39] Thus, strategic leadership captures how leaders inspire their companies to change and their followers to give extraordinary effort to accomplish organizational goals.

After reading the next section, you should be able to

6 explain how visionary leadership (i.e., charismatic and transformational leadership) helps leaders achieve strategic leadership.

Changes in culture, like dress codes, require subordinate commitment or they fail.

3. *Leader's information: Do you have sufficient information to make a high-quality decision?* Yes. Let's assume that you've done your homework. Much has been written about casual wear, from how to make the change to the effects it has in companies (almost all positive).

4. *Commitment probability: If you were to make the decision by yourself, is it reasonably certain that your subordinate(s) would be committed to the decision?* No. Studies of casual wear find that employees' reactions are almost uniformly positive. Nonetheless, employees are likely to be angry if you change something as personal as clothing policies without consulting them.

5. *Goal congruence: Do subordinates share the organizational goals to be attained in solving this problem?* Yes. The goals that usually accompany a change to casual dress policies are a more informal culture, better communication, and less money spent on business attire.

6. *Subordinate information: Do subordinates have sufficient information to make a high-quality decision?* No. Most employees know little about casual wear policies or even what constitutes casual wear in most companies. Consequently, most companies have to educate employees about casual wear practices and policies before making a decision.

7. *CII is the answer:* With a CII, or consultative decision process, the leader shares the problem with employees as a group, obtains their ideas and suggestions, and then makes the decision, which may or may not reflect their input. So, given the answers to these ques-

6 Visionary Leadership

In Chapter 5, we defined vision as a statement of a company's purpose or reason for existing. Similarly, **visionary leadership** creates a positive image of the future that motivates organizational members and provides direction for future planning and goal setting.[40]

*Two kinds of visionary leadership are **6.1 charismatic leadership** and **6.2 transformational leadership**.*

Strategic leadership
the ability to anticipate, envision, maintain flexibility, think strategically, and work with others to initiate changes that will create a positive future for an organization

Visionary leadership
leadership that creates a positive image of the future that motivates organizational members and provides direction for future planning and goal setting

6.1 Charismatic Leadership

Charisma is a Greek word meaning "divine gift." The ancient Greeks saw people with charisma as inspired by the gods and capable of incredible accomplishments. German sociologist Max Weber viewed charisma as a special bond between leaders and followers.[41] Weber wrote that the special qualities of charismatic leaders enable them to strongly influence followers. For example, Richard Scrushy, a founder and the former CEO of HealthSouth, a worldwide provider of health care (outpatient surgery, diagnostic imaging, and rehabilitation), was undoubtedly a charismatic leader. Says one employee, "When he was talking, you could be hypnotized by him."[42] Weber also noted that charismatic leaders tend to emerge in times of crisis and that the radical solutions they propose enhance the admiration that followers feel for them. Indeed, charismatic leaders tend to have incredible influence over their followers, who may be inspired by their leaders and become fanatically devoted to them. From this perspective, charismatic leaders are often seen as larger-than-life or uniquely special.

Charismatic leaders have strong, confident, dynamic personalities that attract followers and enable the leaders to create strong bonds with their followers. Followers trust charismatic leaders, are loyal to them, and are inspired to work toward the accomplishment of the leader's vision. Followers who become devoted to charismatic leaders may go to extraordinary lengths to please them. Therefore, we can define **charismatic leadership** as the behavioral tendencies and personal characteristics of leaders that create an exceptionally strong relationship between them and their followers. Charismatic leaders also

- articulate a clear vision for the future that is based on strongly held values or morals
- model those values by acting in a way consistent with the vision
- communicate high performance expectations to followers
- display confidence in followers' abilities to achieve the vision[43]

Does charismatic leadership work? Studies indicate that it often does. In general, the followers of charismatic leaders are more committed and satisfied, are better performers, are more likely to trust their leaders, and simply work harder.[44] Nonetheless, charismatic leadership also has risks that are at least as large as its benefits. The problems are likely to occur with ego-driven charismatic leaders who take advantage of fanatical followers.

In general, there are two kinds of charismatic leaders, ethical charismatics and unethical charismatics.[45] **Ethical charismatics** provide developmental opportunities for followers, are open to positive and negative feedback, recognize others' contributions, share information, and have moral standards that emphasize the larger interests of the group, organization, or society.

By contrast, **unethical charismatics** control and manipulate followers, do what is best for themselves instead of their organizations, want to hear only positive feedback, share only information that is beneficial to themselves, and have moral standards that put their interests before everyone else's. Because followers can become just as committed to unethical charismatics as to ethical char-

Charismatic leadership the behavioral tendencies and personal characteristics of leaders that create an exceptionally strong relationship between them and their followers

Ethical charismatics charismatic leaders who provide developmental opportunities for followers, are open to positive and negative feedback, recognize others' contributions, share information, and have moral standards that emphasize the larger interests of the group, organization, or society

Unethical charismatics charismatic leaders who control and manipulate followers, do what is best for themselves instead of their organizations, want to hear only positive feedback, share only information that is beneficial to themselves, and have moral standards that put their interests before everyone else's

Why do we fall for charismatics? According to **Fast Company**, *"We're worshipful of top executives who seem charismatic, visionary, and tough. So long as they're lifting profits and stock prices, we're willing to overlook that they can also be callous, cunning, manipulative, deceitful, verbally and psychologically abusive, remorseless, exploitative, self-delusional, irresponsible, and megalomaniacal."[46]*

©Luke Bosworth/iStockphoto

acteristics, unethical charismatics pose a tremendous risk for companies.

Exhibit 14.9 shows the stark differences between ethical and unethical charismatics on several leader behaviors: exercising power, creating the vision, communicating with followers, accepting feedback, stimulating followers intellectually, developing followers, and living by moral standards. For example, when creating a vision, ethical charismatics include followers' concerns and wishes by having them participate in the development of the company vision. By contrast, unethical charismatics develop a vision by themselves solely to meet their personal agendas. One unethical charismatic said, "The key thing is that it is my idea; and I am going to win with it at all costs."[47]

> ### Reduce the Risks Associated with Unethical Charismatics?[48]
>
> 1. Have a clearly written code of conduct that is fairly and consistently enforced for all managers.
> 2. Recruit, select, and promote managers with high ethical standards.
> 3. Train leaders to value, seek, and use diverse points of view.
> 4. Train leaders and subordinates regarding ethical leader behaviors so that abuses can be recognized and corrected.
> 5. Reward people who exhibit ethical behaviors, especially ethical leader behaviors.[49]

6.2 Transformational Leadership

While charismatic leadership involves articulating a clear vision, modeling values consistent with that vision, communicating high performance expectations, and establishing very strong relationships with their followers, **transformational leadership** goes further by generating awareness and acceptance of a group's purpose and mission and by getting employees to see beyond their own needs and self-interest for the good of the group.[50] Like charismatic leaders, transformational leaders are visionary, but they transform their organizations by getting their followers to accomplish more than they intended and even more than they thought possible.

Transformational leaders make their followers feel that they are a vital part of the organization and help them see how their jobs fit with the organization's vision. By linking individual and organizational interests, transformational leaders encourage followers to make sacrifices for the organization because they know that they will prosper when the organization prospers.

Transformational leadership has four components: charismatic leadership or idealized influence, inspirational motivation, intellectual stimulation, and individualized consideration.[51]

Charismatic leadership or idealized influence means that transformational leaders act as role models for their followers. Because transformational leaders put others' needs ahead of their own and share risks with their followers, they are admired, respected, and trusted, and followers want to emulate them. Thus, in contrast to purely charismatic leaders (especially unethical charismatics), transformational leaders can be counted on to do the right thing and maintain high standards for ethical and personal conduct.

Inspirational motivation means that transformational leaders motivate and inspire followers by providing meaning and challenge to their work. By clearly communicating expectations and demonstrating commitment to goals, transformational leaders help followers envision future states, such as the organizational vision or mission. In turn, this leads to greater enthusiasm and optimism about the future. *Intellectual stimulation* means that transformational leaders encourage followers to be creative and innovative, to question assumptions, and to look at problems and situations in new ways, even if their ideas are different from the leader's.

Individualized consideration means that transformational leaders pay special attention to followers' individual needs by creating learning opportunities, accepting and tolerating individual differences, encouraging two-way communication, and being good listeners. Roy Pelaez, who supervises 426 Aramark employees who clean airplanes, believes in attending to employees' needs. He says, "Managers are not supposed to get involved with the personal problems of their employees, but I take the opposite view."[52] With morale low and turnover high, he hired a tutor to improve his employees' English skills. To keep absences low, he found government programs that provided certified babysitters for his low-paid employees. And he set up three computers so that employees could teach each other to use word processors and spreadsheets. Says Pelaez, "All of these things are important, because we want employees who really feel connected to the company." Clearly, they do. Turnover, once almost 100 percent per year, dropped to 12 percent after Pelaez began paying attention to his employees' needs.

Transformational leadership leadership that generates awareness and acceptance of a group's purpose and mission and gets employees to see beyond their own needs and self-interests for the good of the group

Exhibit 14.9

Ethical and Unethical Charismatics

CHARISMATIC LEADER BEHAVIORS	ETHICAL CHARISMATICS	UNETHICAL CHARISMATICS
Exercising power	Power is used to serve others.	Power is used to dominate or manipulate others for personal gain.
Creating the vision	Followers help develop the vision.	Vision comes solely from leader and serves his or her personal agenda.
Communicating with followers	Two-way communication: Seek out viewpoints on critical issues.	One-way communication: Not open to input and suggestions from others.
Accepting feedback	Open to feedback. Willing to learn from criticism.	Inflated ego thrives on attention and admiration of sycophants. Avoid or punish candid feedback.
Stimulating followers	Want followers to think and question status quo as well as leader's views.	Don't want followers to think. Want uncritical, intellectually unquestioning acceptance of leader's ideas.
Developing followers	Focus on developing people with whom they interact. Express confidence in them and share recognition with others.	Insensitive and unresponsive to followers' needs and aspirations.
Living by moral standards	Follow self-guided principles that may go against popular opinion. Have three virtues: courage, a sense of fairness or justice, and integrity.	Follow standards only if they satisfy immediate self-interests. Manipulate impressions so that others think they are "doing the right thing." Use communication skills to manipulate others to support their personal agenda.

Source: J. M. Howell & B. J. Avolio, "The Ethics of Charismatic Leadership: Submission or Liberation?" *Academy of Management Executive* 6, no. 2 (1992): 43–54.

Finally, a distinction needs to be drawn between transformational leadership and transactional leadership. While transformational leaders use visionary and inspirational appeals to influence followers, **transactional leadership** is based on an exchange process, in which followers are rewarded for good performance and punished for poor performance. When leaders administer rewards fairly and offer followers the rewards that they want, followers will often reciprocate with effort. A problem, however, is that transactional leaders often rely too heavily on discipline or threats to bring performance up to standards. Though this may work in the short run, it's much less effective in the long run. Also, as discussed in Chapters 11 and 13, many leaders and organizations have difficulty successfully linking pay practices to individual performance. As a result, studies consistently show that transformational leadership is much more effective on average than transactional leadership. In the United States, Canada, Japan, and India and at all organizational levels, from first-level supervisors to upper-level executives, followers view transformational leaders as much better leaders and are much more satisfied when working for them. Furthermore, companies with transformational leaders have significantly better financial performance.[53]

Transactional leadership leadership based on an exchange process, in which followers are rewarded for good performance and punished for poor performance

MANAGING COMMUNICATION

What Is Communication?

 It's estimated that managers spend over 80 percent of their day communicating with others.[1] Indeed, much of the basic management process—planning, organizing, leading, and controlling—cannot be performed without effective communication. If this weren't reason enough to study communication, consider that effective oral communication, such as listening, following instructions, conversing, and giving feedback, is the most important skill for college graduates who are entering the work force.[2] Furthermore, across all industries, poor communication skills rank as the single most important reason that people do not advance in their careers.[3]

Communication is the process of transmitting information from one person or place to another. While some bosses sugarcoat bad news, smart managers understand that in the end effective, straightforward communication between managers and employees is essential for success.

 After reading the next two sections, you should be able to

1 explain the role that perception plays in communication and communication problems.

2 describe the communication process and the various kinds of communication in organizations.

Communication the process of transmitting information from one person or place to another

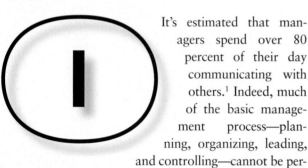

Learning Outcomes

1 explain the role that perception plays in communication and communication problems.

2 describe the communication process and the various kinds of communication in organizations.

3 explain how managers can manage effective one-on-one communication.

4 describe how managers can manage effective organization-wide communication.

©Blend Images/Jupiter Images

1 Perception and Communication Problems

One study found that when *employees* were asked whether their supervisor gave recognition for good work, only 13 percent said their supervisor gave a pat on the back, and a mere 14 percent said their supervisor gave sincere and thorough praise. But when the *supervisors* of these employees were asked if they gave recognition for good work, 82 percent said they gave pats on the back, while 80 percent said that they gave sincere and thorough praise.[4] How could managers and employees have had such different perceptions of something as simple as praise?

*Let's learn more about perception and communication problems by examining **1.1 the basic perception process, 1.2 perception problems, 1.3 how we perceive others,** and **1.4 how we perceive ourselves.** We'll also consider how all of these factors make it difficult for managers to achieve effective communication.*

1.1 Basic Perception Process

As shown in Exhibit 15.1, **perception** is the process by which individuals attend to, organize, interpret, and retain information from their

> **Perception** the process by which individuals attend to, organize, interpret, and retain information from their environments

Exhibit 15.1

Basic Perception Process

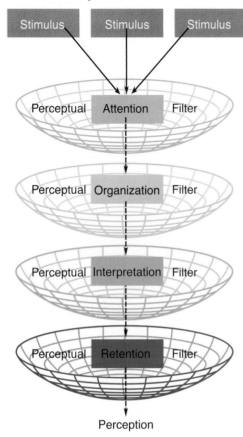

Stimulus   Stimulus   Stimulus

Perceptual   **Attention**   Filter

Perceptual   Organization   Filter

Perceptual   Interpretation   Filter

Perceptual   **Retention**   Filter

Perception

environments. And since communication is the process of transmitting information from one person or place to another, perception is obviously a key part of communication. Yet, perception can also be a key obstacle to communication.

As people perform their jobs, they are exposed to a wide variety of informational stimuli, such as emails, direct conversations with the boss or coworkers, rumors heard over lunch, stories about the company in the press, or a video broadcast of a speech from the CEO to all employees. Just being exposed to an informational stimulus, however, is no guarantee that an individual will pay attention or attend to that stimulus. People experience stimuli through their own **perceptual filters**—the personality-, psychology-, or experience-based differences that influence them to ignore or pay attention to particular stimuli. Because of filtering, people exposed to the same information will often disagree about what they saw or heard. As shown in Exhibit 15.1, perceptual filters affect each part of the *perception process:* attention, organization, interpretation, and retention.

Attention is the process of noticing or becoming aware of particular stimuli. Because of perceptual filters, we attend to some stimuli and not others. *Organization* is the process of incorporating new information (from the stimuli that you notice) into your existing knowledge. Because of perceptual filters, we are more likely to incorporate new knowledge that is consistent with what we already know or believe. *Interpretation* is the process of attaching meaning to new knowledge. Because of perceptual filters, our preferences and beliefs strongly influence the meaning we attach to new information (e.g., "This must mean that top management supports our project."). Finally, *retention* is the process of remembering interpreted information. In other words, retention is what we recall and commit to memory after we have perceived something. Of course, perceptual filters also affect retention, that is, what we're likely to remember in the end.

For instance, imagine that you miss the first 10 minutes of a TV show and turn on your TV to see two people talking to each other in a living room. As they

This play probably elicited both cheers and boos. The same perceptual filters that affect whether we think our team was "robbed" also affect management communication.

Perceptual filters the personality-, psychology-, or experience-based differences that influence people to ignore or pay attention to particular stimuli

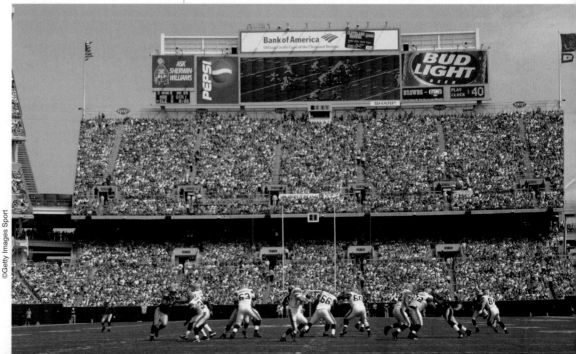

©Getty Images Sport

talk, they walk around the room, picking up and putting down various items; some items, such as a ring, watch, and credit card, appear to be valuable, and others appear to be drug related, such as a water pipe for smoking marijuana. In fact, this situation was depicted on videotape in a well-known study that manipulated people's perceptual filters.[5] Before watching the video, one-third of the study participants were told that the people were there to rob the apartment. Another third of the participants were told that police were on their way to conduct a drug raid and that the people in the apartment were getting rid of incriminating evidence. The remaining third of the participants were told that the people were simply waiting for a friend.

After watching the video, participants were asked to list all of the objects from the video that they could remember. Not surprisingly, the different perceptual filters (theft, drug raid, and waiting for a friend) affected what the participants attended to, how they organized the information, how they interpreted it, and ultimately which objects they remembered. Participants who thought a theft was in progress were more likely to remember the valuable objects in the video. Those who thought a drug raid was imminent were more likely to remember the drug-related objects. There was no discernible pattern to the items remembered by those who thought that the people in the video were simply waiting for a friend.

In short, because of perception and perceptual filters, people are likely to pay attention to different things, organize and interpret what they pay attention to differently, and, finally, remember things differently. Consequently, even when people are exposed to the same communications (e.g., organizational memos, discussions with managers or customers), they can end up with very different perceptions and understandings. This is why communication can be so difficult and frustrating for managers. Let's review some of the communication problems created by perception and perceptual filters.

1.2 Perception Problems

Perception creates communication problems for organizations because people exposed to the same communication and information can end up with completely different ideas and understandings. Two of the most common perception problems in organizations are selective perception and closure.

At work, we are constantly bombarded with sensory stimuli—phones ringing, people talking in the background, computers dinging as new email arrives, people calling our names, and so forth. As limited processors of information, we cannot possibly notice, receive, and interpret all of this information. As a result, we attend to and accept some stimuli but screen out and reject others. This isn't a random process, however. **Selective perception** is the tendency to notice and accept objects and information consistent with our values, beliefs, and expectations, while ignoring or screening out inconsistent information. For example, when Jack Smith, the former CEO of General Motors, was a junior-level executive, he traveled to Japan to learn why Toyota's cars were so reliable and why Toyota was so productive. When he learned that Toyota could build a car with half as many people as GM, he wrote a report and shared his findings with GM's all-powerful executive committee. But no one on the committee believed what he told them. The executives just couldn't accept that a Japanese company was so much more effective than GM. Says Smith, "Never in my life have I been so quickly and unceremoniously blown out of the water."[6]

Once we have initial information about a person, event, or process, **closure** is the tendency to fill in the gaps where information is missing, that is, to assume that what we don't know is consistent with what we already know. If employees are told that budgets must be cut by 10 percent, they may automatically assume that 10 percent of employees will lose their jobs, too, even if that isn't the case. Not surprisingly, when closure occurs, people sometimes "fill in the gaps" with inaccurate information, and this can create problems for organizations.

1.3 Perceptions of Others

Attribution theory says that we all have a basic need to understand and explain the causes of other people's behavior.[7] In other words, we need to know why people do what they do. According to attribution theory, we use two general reasons or attributions to explain people's behavior: an *internal attribution,* in which behavior is thought to be voluntary or under the control of the individual, and an *external attribution,* in which behavior is thought to be involuntary and outside of the control of the individual.

For example, have you ever seen someone changing a flat tire on the side of the

road and thought to yourself, "What rotten luck—somebody's having a bad day"? If you did, you perceived the person through an external attribution known as the defensive bias. The **defensive bias** is the tendency for people to perceive themselves as personally and situationally similar to someone who is having difficulty or trouble.[8] And, when we identify with the person in a situation, we tend to use external attributions (i.e., the situation) to explain the person's behavior. For instance, since flat tires are common, it's easy to perceive ourselves in that same situation and put the blame on external causes, such as running over a nail.

Now, let's assume a different situation, this time in the workplace:

A utility company worker puts a ladder on a utility pole and then climbs up to do his work. As he's doing his work, he falls from the ladder and seriously injures himself.[9]

Answer this question: Who or what caused the accident? If you thought, "It's not the worker's fault. Anybody could fall from a tall ladder," then you're still operating from a defensive bias in which you see yourself as personally and situationally similar to someone who is having difficulty or trouble. In other words, you made an external attribution by attributing the accident to an external cause, meaning the situation.

In reality, however, most accident investigations initially blame the worker (i.e., an internal attribution) and not the situation (i.e., an external attribution). Typically, 60 to 80 percent of workplace accidents each year are blamed on "operator error," that is, the employees themselves. More complete investigations, however, usually show that workers are responsible for only 30 to 40 percent of all workplace accidents.[10] Why are accident investigators so quick to blame workers? The

©Image 100/Jupiter Images

reason is that they are committing the **fundamental attribution error,** which is the tendency to ignore external causes of behavior and to attribute other people's actions to internal causes.[11] In other words, when investigators examine the possible causes of an accident, they're much more likely to assume that the accident is a function of the person and not the situation.

Which attribution, the defensive bias or the fundamental attribution error, are workers likely to make when something goes wrong? In general, as shown in Exhibit 15.2, employees and coworkers are more likely to perceive events and explain behavior from a defensive bias. Because they do the work themselves and see themselves as similar to others who make mistakes, have accidents, or are otherwise held responsible for things that go wrong at work, employees and coworkers are likely to attribute problems to external causes, such as failed machinery, poor support, or inadequate training. By contrast, because they are typically observers (who don't do

Defensive bias the tendency for people to perceive themselves as personally and situationally similar to someone who is having difficulty or trouble

Fundamental attribution error the tendency to ignore external causes of behavior and to attribute other people's actions to internal causes

Exhibit 15.2

Defensive Bias and Fundamental Attribution Error

The Coworker
How can they expect us to make sales if they don't have hot-selling inventory in stock? We can't sell what's not there.

The Employee
That's the third sale I've lost this week because company management doesn't keep enough inventory in stock. I can't sell it if we don't have it.

The Boss
That new employee isn't very good. I may have to get rid of him if his sales don't improve.

Defensive Bias—
the tendency for people to perceive themselves as personally and situationally similar to someone who is having difficulty or trouble

Defensive Bias—
the tendency for people to perceive themselves as personally and situationally similar to someone who is having difficulty or trouble

Fundamental Attribution Error—
the tendency to ignore external causes of behavior and to attribute other people's actions to internal causes

the work themselves) and see themselves as situationally and personally different from workers, managers (i.e., the boss) tend to commit the fundamental attribution error and blame mistakes, accidents, and other things that go wrong on workers (i.e., an internal attribution).

Consequently, in most workplaces, when things go wrong, workers and managers can be expected to take opposite views. Therefore, together, the defensive bias, which is typically used by workers, and the fundamental attribution error, which is typically made by managers, present a significant challenge to effective communication and understanding in organizations.

1.4 Self-Perception

The **self-serving bias** is the tendency to overestimate our value by attributing successes to ourselves (internal causes) and attributing failures to others or the environment (external causes).[12] The self-serving bias can make it especially difficult for managers to talk to employees about performance problems. In general, people have a need to maintain a positive self-image. This need is so strong that when people seek feedback at work, they typically want verification of their worth (rather than information about performance deficiencies) or assurance that mistakes or problems weren't their fault.[13] And, when managerial communication threatens people's positive self-image, they can become defensive and emotional. They quit listening, and communication becomes ineffective. In the second half of the chapter, which focuses on improving communication, we'll explain ways in which managers can minimize this self-serving bias and improve effective one-on-one communication with employees.

2 Kinds of Communication

There are many kinds of communication—formal, informal, coaching/counseling, and nonverbal—but they all follow the same fundamental process.

Let's learn more about the different kinds of communication by examining **2.1 the communication process, 2.2 formal communication channels, 2.3 informal communication channels, 2.4 coaching and counseling, or one-on-one communication,** *and* **2.5 nonverbal communication.**

2.1 The Communication Process

Earlier in the chapter, we defined *communication* as the process of transmitting information from one person or

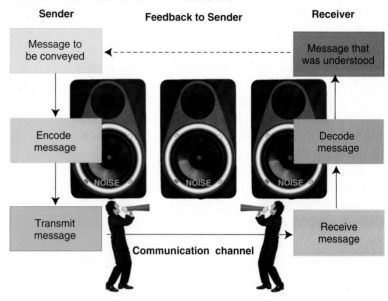

Exhibit 15.3
The Interpersonal Communication Process

Sender   **Feedback to Sender**   **Receiver**

Message to be conveyed → Message that was understood

Encode message → Decode message

Transmit message → Receive message

Communication channel

NOISE

place to another. Exhibit 15.3 displays a model of the communication process and its major components: the sender (message to be conveyed, encoding the message, transmitting the message); the receiver (receiving message, decoding the message, and the message that was understood); and noise, which interferes with the communication process.

The communication process begins when a *sender* thinks of a message he or she wants to convey to another person. The next step is to encode the message. **Encoding** means putting a message into a written, verbal, or symbolic form that can be recognized and understood by the receiver. The sender then *transmits the message* via *communication channels*. With some communication channels such as the telephone and face-to-face communication, the sender receives immediate feedback, whereas with others such as email (text messages and file attachments), fax, beepers, voice mail, memos, and letters, the sender must wait for the receiver to respond.

Unfortunately, because of technical difficulties (e.g., fax down, dead battery on the mobile phone, inability to read email attachments) or people-based transmission problems (e.g., forgetting to pass on the message),

Self-serving bias the tendency to overestimate our value by attributing successes to ourselves (internal causes) and attributing failures to others or the environment (external causes)

Encoding putting a message into a written, verbal, or symbolic form that can be recognized and understood by the receiver messages aren't always transmitted. If the message is transmitted and received, however, the next step is for the receiver to decode it. **Decoding** is the process by which the receiver translates the written, verbal, or symbolic form of the message into an understood message. However, the message, as understood by the receiver, isn't always the same message that was intended by the sender. Because of different experiences or perceptual filters, receivers may attach a completely different meaning to a message than was intended.

The last step of the communication process occurs when the receiver gives the sender feedback. **Feedback to sender** is a return message to the sender that indicates the receiver's understanding of the message (of what the receiver was supposed to know, to do, or to not do). Feedback makes senders aware of possible miscommunications and enables them to continue communicating until the receiver understands the intended message.

Unfortunately, feedback doesn't always occur in the communication process. Complacency and overconfidence about the ease and simplicity of communication can lead senders and receivers to simply assume that they share a common understanding of the message and to not use feedback to improve the effectiveness of their communication. This is a serious mistake, especially since messages and feedback are always transmitted with and against a background of noise. **Noise** is anything that interferes with the transmission of the intended message. Noise can occur in any of the following situations:

- The sender isn't sure what message to communicate.
- The message is not clearly encoded.
- The wrong communication channel is chosen.
- The message is not received or decoded properly.
- The receiver doesn't have the experience or time to understand the message.

Any idea what "rightsizing," "delayering," "unsiloing," and "knowledge acquisition" mean? Rightsizing means laying off workers. Delayering means firing man-

Decoding the process by which the receiver translates the written, verbal, or symbolic form of a message into an understood message

Feedback to sender in the communication process, a return message to the sender that indicates the receiver's understanding of the message

Noise anything that interferes with the transmission of the intended message

Jargon vocabulary particular to a profession or group

Formal communication channel the system of official channels that carry organizationally approved messages and information

Downward communication communication that flows from higher to lower levels in an organization

Bucket Full of Jargon

There's a hot old word in meeting rooms across the country: bucket. Trumping basket and the decades-old favorite silo, the centuries-old bucket has taken on new layers of metaphoric meaning. Anything that is a large category can become a bucket. The CEO of Dow has publicly talked about energy in terms of a supply bucket and a conservation bucket; analysts at Citigroup think of cash flows in terms of how many buckets they use; large blocks of stocks can even be bucket-y for a securities trader at UBS. Even in human resources, managers have been heard to talk about a young worker's potential as "How should we bucket this person?" Other popular jargon in 2007: business model (How are we going to make money at this?) and value drivers (reasons why a customer would buy your product).

Source: C. Rhoades, "Business Types Get a New Kick Out of the Bucket," *Wall Street Journal*, 27 March 2007, A1.

agers, or getting rid of layers of management. Unsiloing means getting workers in different parts of the company (i.e., different vertical silos) to work with others outside their own areas. Knowledge acquisition means teaching workers new knowledge or skills. **Jargon,** which is vocabulary particular to a profession or group, is another form of noise that interferes with communication in the workplace. Unfortunately, the business world is rife with jargon. Carol Hymowitz of the *Wall Street Journal* points out that, "A new crop of buzzwords usually sprouts every three to five years, or about the same length of time many top executives have to prove themselves. Some can be useful in swiftly communicating, and spreading, new business concepts. Others are less useful, even devious."[14]

2.2 Formal Communication Channels

An organization's **formal communication channel** is the system of official channels that carry organizationally approved messages and information. Organizational objectives, rules, policies, procedures, instructions, commands, and requests for information are all transmitted via the formal communication system or "channel." There are three formal communication channels: downward communication, upward communication, and horizontal communication.[15]

Downward communication flows from higher to lower levels in an organization. Downward communi-

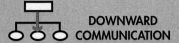
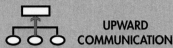

Common Problems with Downward, Upward, and Horizontal Communication

DOWNWARD COMMUNICATION

- Overusing downward communication by sending too many messages

- Issuing contradictory messages

- Hurriedly communicating vague, unclear messages

- Issuing messages that indicate management's low regard for lower-level workers

UPWARD COMMUNICATION

- The risk involved with telling upper management about problems (i.e., fear of retribution)

- Managers reacting angrily and defensively when workers report problems

- Not enough opportunities or channels for lower-level workers to contact upper levels of management

HORIZONTAL COMMUNICATION

- Management discouraging or punishing horizontal communication, viewing it as small talk

- Not giving managers and workers the time or opportunity for horizontal communication

- Not enough opportunities or channels for lower-level workers to engage in horizontal communication

Source: G. L. Kreps, *Organizational Communication: Theory and Practice* (New York: Longman, 1990).

cation is used to issue orders down the organizational hierarchy, to give organizational members job-related information, to give managers and workers performance reviews from upper managers, and to clarify organizational objectives and goals.[16]

Upward communication flows from lower levels to higher levels in an organization. Upward communication is used to give higher-level managers feedback about operations, issues, and problems; to help higher-level managers assess organizational performance and effectiveness; to encourage lower-level managers and employees to participate in organizational decision making; and to give those at lower levels the chance to share their concerns with higher-level authorities. At Cisco Systems, the manufacturer of the switches, routers, and computer equipment that form the backbone of the Internet and company computer networks, CEO John Chambers uses monthly birthday breakfasts to create upward communication. Says Chambers, "As for how I hear from employees, I host a monthly birthday breakfast. Anybody who has a birthday in that month gets to come and quiz me for an hour and 15 minutes. No directors or VPs in the room. It's how I keep my finger on the pulse of what's working and what's not. It's brutal, but it's my most enjoyable session."[17]

Horizontal communication flows among managers and workers who are at the same organizational level, such as when a day shift nurse comes in at 7:30 A.M. for a half-hour discussion with the midnight nurse supervisor who leaves at 8:00 A.M. Horizontal communication

helps facilitate coordination and cooperation between different parts of a company and allows coworkers to share relevant information. It also helps people at the same level resolve conflicts and solve problems without involving high levels of management. Studies show that communication breakdowns, which occur most often during horizontal communication, such as when patients are handed over from one nurse or doctor to another, are the largest source of medical errors in hospitals.[18]

In general, what can managers do to improve formal communication? First, decrease reliance on downward communication. Second, increase chances for upward communication by increasing personal contact with lower-level managers and workers. Third, encourage much better use of horizontal communication.

2.3 Informal Communication Channels

An organization's **informal communication channel,** sometimes called the **grapevine,** is the transmission of messages from employee to employee outside of formal communication channels. The grapevine arises out of curiosity, that is, the need to

Upward communication communication that flows from lower to higher levels in an organization

Horizontal communication communication that flows among managers and workers who are at the same organizational level

Informal communication channel ("grapevine") the transmission of messages from employee to employee outside of formal communication channels know what is going on in an organization and how it might affect you or others. To satisfy this curiosity, employees need a consistent supply of relevant, accurate, in-depth information about "who is doing what and what changes are occurring within the organization."[19] Employee Paul Haze agrees, saying, "If employees don't have a definite explanation from management, they tend to interpret for themselves."[20]

Grapevines arise out of informal communication networks, such as the gossip or cluster chains shown in Exhibit 15.4. In a *gossip chain,* one "highly connected" individual shares information with many other managers and workers. By contrast, in a *cluster chain,* numerous people simply tell a few of their friends. The result in both cases is that information flows freely and quickly through the organization. Some believe that grapevines are a waste of employees' time, that they promote gossip and rumors that fuel political speculation, and that they are sources of highly unreliable, inaccurate information. Yet studies clearly show that grapevines are highly accurate sources of information for a number of reasons.[21] First, because grapevines typically carry "juicy" information that is interesting and timely, information spreads rapidly. At Meghan De Goyler Hauser's former company, the word on the grapevine was that her boss drank on the job, the company accountant was stealing the company blind, and one of her coworkers was a nude model. She says, "The rumors all turned out to be true."[22] Second, since information is typically spread by face-to-face conversation, receivers can send feedback to make sure they understand the message that is being communicated. This reduces misunderstandings and increases accuracy. Third, since most of the information

Because grapevines typically carry "juicy" information that is interesting and timely, information spreads rapidly.

©Nonstock/Jupiter Images

in a company moves along the grapevine, as opposed to formal communication channels, people can usually verify the accuracy of information by "checking it out" with others.

What can managers do to "manage" organizational grapevines? The very worst thing managers can do is withhold information or try to punish those who share information with others. The grapevine abhors a vacuum, and in the absence of information from company management, rumors and anxiety will flourish. Why

Exhibit 15.4

Grapevine Communication Networks

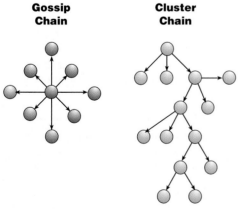

Gossip Chain

Cluster Chain

Source: K. Davis & J. W. Newstrom, *Human Behavior at Work: Organizational Behavior,* 8th ed. (New York: McGraw-Hill, 1989).

How to Deal with Internet Gripe Sites

1. Correct misinformation. Put an end to false rumors and set the record straight. Don't be defensive.
2. Don't take angry comments personally.
3. Give your name and contact number to show employees that you're concerned and that they can contact you directly.
4. Hold a town meeting to discuss the issues raised on the gripe site.
5. Set up anonymous internal discussion forums on the company server. Then encourage employees to gripe anonymously on the company intranet, rather than on the Web.[23]

does this occur? According to workplace psychologist Nicholas DiFonzo, "The main focus of rumor is to figure out the truth. It's the group trying to make sense of something that's important to them."[24] A better strategy is to embrace the grapevine and keep employees informed about possible changes and strategies. Failure to do so will just make things worse. And, in addition to using the grapevine to communicate with others, managers should not overlook the grapevine as a tremendous source of valuable information and feedback. In fact, information flowing through organizational grapevines is estimated to be 75 to 95 percent accurate.[25]

2.4 Coaching and Counseling: One-on-One Communication

When the Wyatt Company surveyed 531 U.S. companies undergoing major changes and restructuring, it asked their CEOs, "If you could go back and change one thing, what would it be?" The answer? "The way we communicated with our employees." The CEOs said that instead of flashy videos, printed materials, or formal meetings, they would make greater use of one-on-one communication, especially with employees' immediate supervisors instead of with higher-level executives that employees didn't know.[26]

Coaching and counseling are two kinds of one-on-one communication. **Coaching** is communicating with

PROBLEM OR NEED	SERVICE PROVIDED
Stress, depression, relationships, substance abuse	Counseling
Pregnancy, adoption, day care, nutrition, fertility	Child care
Health and nutrition, care options, Alzheimer's disease	Senior care
Wills, leases, estate plans, adoptions	Legal services
Referrals and discounts on chiropractic care, acupuncture, massage therapy, vitamins	Health/lifestyle assistance
Pet-sitting resources, obedience training, veterinarians	Pet care
Retirement planning, debt consolidation, budgeting	Financial services

Source: "You Can Do It. We Can Help," CIGNA Behavioral Health, [Online] available at http://www.hr.tcu.edu/eappages/core/html/default.html, 30 March 2002.

someone for the direct purpose of improving the person's on-the-job performance or behavior.[27] Managers tend to make several mistakes when coaching employees, however. First, they wait for a problem before coaching. Jim Concelman, who is manager for leadership development at Development Dimensions International, says, "Of course, a boss has to coach an employee if a mistake has been made, but they shouldn't be waiting for the error. While it is a lot easier to see a mistake and correct it, people learn more through success than through failure, so bosses should ensure that employees are experiencing as many successes as possible. Successful employees lead to a more successful organization."[28] Second, when mistakes *are* made, managers wait much too long before talking to the employee about the problem. Management professor Ray Hilgert says, "A manager must respond as soon as possible after an incident of poor performance. Don't bury your head.... When employees are told nothing, they assume everything is okay."[29]

By contrast, **counseling** is communicating with someone about non-job-related issues that may be affecting or interfering with the person's performance. However, counseling does not mean that managers should try to be clinicians, even though an estimated 20 percent of employees are dealing with personal problems at any

Coaching communicating with someone for the direct purpose of improving the person's on-the-job performance or behavior

Counseling communicating with someone about non-job-related issues that may be affecting or interfering with the person's performance

Hey Coach!

Management coaching has grown into an estimated $1 billion business and is no longer just for the likes of General Electric's Jeffrey Immelt and eBay's Meg Whitman, both of whom have sought tips on being better leaders. Many companies use coaching as a means to help overachievers (i.e., task-oriented managers) develop their people skills. Yahoo, Inc. and Genentech enlist coaching services to groom internal candidates for future executive positions within the company.

Source: Phred Dyorak, "Construction Firm Rebuilds Managers to Make Them Softer," *Wall Street Journal*, 16 May 2006, A1.

RIGHT TRENDS

one time. Dana Kiel, who works for CIGNA Behavioral Health, says, "We call it the quicksand. If you're a good supervisor, you do care about your employees, but it's not your job to be a therapist."[30] Instead, managers should discuss specific performance problems, listen if the employee chooses to share personal issues, and then recommend that the employee call the company's *Employee Assistance Program (EAP)*. EAPs are typically free when provided as part of a company's benefit package. In emergencies or times of crisis, EAPs can offer immediate counseling and support; they can also provide referrals to organizations and professionals that can help employees and their family members address personal issues.

2.5 Nonverbal Communication

Nonverbal communication is any communication that doesn't involve words. Nonverbal communication and messages almost always accompany verbal communication and may support and reinforce the verbal message or contradict it. The importance of nonverbal communication is well established. Researchers have estimated that as much as 93 percent of any message is transmitted nonverbally, with 55 percent coming from body language and facial expressions and 38 percent coming from the tone and pitch of the voice.[31] Since many nonverbal cues are unintentional, receivers often consider nonverbal communication to be a more accurate representation of what senders are thinking and feeling than the words they use.

Kinesics and paralanguage are two kinds of nonverbal communication.[32] **Kinesics** (from the Greek word *kinesis,* meaning "movement") are movements of the body and face.[33] These movements include arm and hand gestures, facial expressions, eye contact, folding arms, crossing legs, and leaning toward or away from another person.

It turns out that kinesics play an incredibly important role in communication. Studies of married couples' kinesic interactions can predict whether they will stay married with 93 percent accuracy.[34] The key is the ratio of positive to negative kinesic interactions that husbands and wives make as they communicate. Negative kinesic expressions such as eye rolling suggest contempt, whereas positive kinetic expressions such as maintaining eye contact and nodding suggest listening and caring. When the ratio of positive to negative interactions drops below 5 to 1, the chances for divorce quickly increase. Kinesics operate

Nonverbal communication any communication that doesn't involve words

Kinesics movements of the body and face

Paralanguage the pitch, rate, tone, volume, and speaking pattern (i.e., use of silences, pauses, or hesitations) of one's voice

similarly in the workplace, providing clues about people's true feelings, over and beyond what they say (or don't say). For instance, Louis Giuliano, former CEO of ITT, which makes heavy use of teams, says, "When you get a team together and say to them we're going to change a process, you always have people who say, 'No, we're not.'" They usually don't say it out loud, but "the body language is there," making it clear that their real answer is "no."[35]

Paralanguage includes the pitch, rate, tone, volume, and speaking pattern (i.e., use of silences, pauses, or hesitations) of one's voice. For example, when people are unsure what to say, they tend to decrease their communication effectiveness by speaking softly. When people are nervous, they tend to talk faster and louder. These characteristics have a tremendous influence on whether listeners are receptive to what speakers are saying.

In short, because nonverbal communication is so informative, especially when it contradicts verbal communication, managers need to learn how to monitor and control their nonverbal behavior.

How to Improve Communication

When it comes to improving communication, managers face two primary tasks, managing one-on-one communication and managing organization-wide communication.

After reading the next two sections, you should be able to

3 explain how managers can manage effective one-on-one communication.

4 describe how managers can manage effective organization-wide communication.

3 Managing One-on-One Communication

In Chapter 1, you learned that, on average, first-line managers spend 57 percent of their time with people, middle managers spend 63 percent of their time directly with people, and top managers spend as much as 78 percent of their time dealing with people.[36] These numbers make it clear that managers spend a great deal of time in one-on-one communication with others.

*Learn more about managing one-on-one communication by reading how to **3.1 choose the right communication medium, 3.2 be a good listener,** and **3.3 give effective feedback.***

3.1 Choosing the Right Communication Medium

Sometimes messages are poorly communicated simply because they are delivered using the wrong **communication medium,** which is the method used to deliver a message. For example, the wrong communication medium is being used when an employee returns from lunch, picks up the note left on her office chair, and learns she has been fired.

There are two general kinds of communication media: oral and written communication. *Oral communication* includes face-to-face and group meetings through telephone calls, videoconferencing, or any other means of sending and receiving spoken messages. Studies show that managers generally prefer oral communication over written because it provides the opportunity to ask questions about parts of the message that they don't understand. Oral communication is also a rich communication medium because it allows managers to receive and assess the nonverbal communication that accompanies spoken messages (i.e., body language, facial expressions, and the voice characteristics associated with paralanguage). Furthermore, you don't need a personal computer and an Internet connection to conduct oral communication. Oral communication should not be used for all communication, however. In general, when the message is simple, such as a quick request or a presentation of straightforward information, a memo or email is often the better communication medium.

©Brand X Pictures/Jupiter Images

Written communication includes letters, email, and memos. Although most managers still like and use oral communication, email in particular is changing how they communicate with workers, customers, and each other. Email is the fastest-growing form of communication in organizations primarily because of its convenience and speed. For instance, because people read six times faster than they can listen, they usually can read 30 email messages in 10 to 15 minutes.[37] By contrast, dealing with voice messages can take a considerable amount of time.

Written communication, such as email, is well suited for delivering straightforward messages and information. Furthermore, with email accessible at the office, at home, and on the road (by laptop computer, cell phone, or Web-based email), managers can use email to stay in touch from anywhere at almost any time. And, since email and other written communications don't have to be sent and received simultaneously, messages can be sent and stored for reading at any time. Consequently, managers can send and receive many more messages using email than using oral communication, which requires people to get together in person or by phone or videoconference.

Although written communication is well suited for delivering straightforward messages and information, it is not well suited to complex, ambiguous, or emotionally laden messages, which are better delivered through oral communication.

3.2 Listening

Are you a good listener? You probably think so. But, in fact, most people, including managers, are terrible listeners, retaining only about 25 percent of what they hear.[38] You qualify as a poor listener if you frequently interrupt others, jump to conclusions about what people will say before they've said it, hurry the speaker to finish his or her point, are a passive listener (not actively working at your listening), or simply don't pay attention to what people are saying.[39] On this last point, attentiveness, college students were periodically asked to record their thoughts during a psychology course. On average, 20 percent of the students were paying attention (only 12 percent were actively working at being good listeners), 20 percent were thinking about sex, 20

> **Communication medium** the method used to deliver an oral or written message

I'M LISTENING

Radio callers were encouraged to share their troubles when psychiatrist Dr. Frasier Crane (Kelsey Grammar) greeted them with a calm, "I'm listening."

percent were thinking about things they had done before class, and the remaining 40 percent were thinking about other things unrelated to the class (e.g., worries, religion, lunch, daydreaming).[40]

How important is it to be a good listener? In general, about 45 percent of the total time you spend communicating with others is spent listening. Furthermore, listening is important for managerial and business success, even for those at the top of an organization. As Feargal Quinn, CEO of Irish grocery chain Superquinn's, points out, "Listening is not an activity you can delegate—no matter who you are."[41] In fact, managers with better listening skills are rated as better managers by their employees and are much more likely to be promoted.[42]

So, what can you do to improve your listening ability? First, understand the difference between hearing and listening. According to *Webster's New World Dictionary,* **hearing** is the "act or process of perceiving sounds," whereas **listening** is "making a conscious effort to hear." In other words, we react to sounds, such as bottles breaking or music being played too loud, because hearing is an involuntary physiological process. By contrast, listening is a voluntary behavior. So, if you want to be a good listener, you have to choose to be a good listener. Typically, that means choosing to be an active, empathetic listener.[43]

Active listening means assuming half the responsibility for successful com-

munication by actively giving the speaker nonjudgmental feedback that shows you've accurately heard what he or she said. Active listeners make it clear from their behavior that they are listening carefully to what the speaker has to say. Active listeners put the speaker at ease, maintain eye contact, and show the speaker that they are attentively listening by nodding and making short statements.

Several specific strategies can help you be a better active listener. First, *clarify responses* by asking the speaker to explain confusing or ambiguous statements. Second, when there are natural breaks in the speaker's delivery, use this time to paraphrase or summarize what has been said. *Paraphrasing* is restating what has been said in your own words. *Summarizing* is reviewing the speaker's main points or emotions. Paraphrasing and summarizing give the speaker the chance to correct the message if the active listener has attached the wrong meaning to it. Paraphrasing and summarizing also show the speaker that the active listener is interested in the speaker's message. Exhibit 15.5 lists specific statements that listeners can use to clarify responses, paraphrase, or summarize what has been said.

Active listeners also avoid evaluating the message or being critical until the message is complete. They recognize that their only responsibility during the transmission of a message is to receive it accurately and derive the intended meaning from it. Evaluation and criticism can take place after the message is accurately received. Finally, active listeners also recognize that a large portion of any message is transmitted nonverbally and thus pay very careful attention to the nonverbal cues transmitted by the speaker.

Hearing the act or process of perceiving sounds

Listening making a conscious effort to hear

Active listening assuming half the responsibility for successful communication by actively giving the speaker nonjudgmental feedback that shows you've accurately heard what he or she said

Tread Lightly

Section 3.2 gives you important tools to help you become a better listener. Applying them insincerely—or indiscriminately—may cause you to seem patronizing and derail your attempt to build better working relationships. Not everyone appreciates having what they said repeated back to them—even if you've repeated it in your own words. The key is to *respond,* rather than *repeat* or *react,* in a manner appropriate for the situation and the person with whom you're speaking.

Source: J. Sandberg, "Not Communicating with Your Boss? Count Your Blessings," *Wall Street Journal,* 22 May 2007, B1.

Exhibit 15.5

Clarifying, Paraphrasing, and
Summarizing Responses for Active Listeners

CLARIFYING RESPONSES	PARAPHRASING RESPONSES	SUMMARIZING RESPONSES
Could you explain that again?	What you're really saying is	Let me summarize . . . .
I don't understand what you mean.	If I understand you correctly	Okay, your main concerns are . . . .
I'm not sure how	In other words	To recap what you've said . . . .
I'm confused. Would you run through that again?	So your perspective is that	Thus far, you've discussed . . . .
	Tell me if I'm wrong, but what you're saying is	

Source: E. Atwater, *I Hear You*, revised ed. (New York: Walker, 1992).

Empathetic listening means understanding the speaker's perspective and personal frame of reference and giving feedback that conveys that understanding to the speaker. Empathetic listening goes beyond active listening because it depends on our ability to set aside our own attitudes or relationships to be able to see and understand things through someone else's eyes. Empathetic listening is just as important as active listening, especially for managers, because it helps build rapport and trust with others.

The key to being a more empathetic listener is to show your desire to understand and to reflect people's feelings. You can *show your desire to understand* by listening, that is, asking people to talk about what's most important to them and then giving them sufficient time to talk before responding or interrupting.

Reflecting feelings is also an important part of empathetic listening because it demonstrates that you understand the speaker's emotions. Unlike active listening, in which you restate or summarize the informational content of what has been said, the focus is on the affective part of the message. As an empathetic listener, you can use the following statements to *reflect the speaker's emotions:*

- So, right now it sounds like you're feeling . . . .
- You seem as if you're . . . .
- Do you feel a bit . . . ?
- I could be wrong, but I'm sensing that you're feeling . . . .

In the end, says management consultant Terry Pearce, empathetic listening can be boiled down to these three steps. First, wait 10 seconds before you answer or respond. It will seem an eternity, but waiting prevents you from interrupting others and rushing your response. Second, to be sure you understand what the speaker wants, ask questions to clarify the speaker's intent.

Third, only then should you respond first with feelings and then facts (notice that facts *follow* feelings).[44]

3.3 Giving Feedback

In Chapter 11, you learned that performance appraisal feedback (i.e., judging) should be separated from developmental feedback (i.e., coaching).[45] At this point, we now focus on the steps needed to communicate feedback one-on-one to employees.

To start, managers need to recognize that feedback can be constructive or destructive. **Destructive feedback** is disapproving without any intention of being helpful and almost always causes a negative or defensive reaction in the recipient. In fact, one study found that 98 percent of employees responded to destructive feedback from their bosses with either verbal aggression (two-thirds) or physical aggression (one-third).[46]

By contrast, **constructive feedback** is intended to be helpful, corrective, and/or encouraging. It is aimed at correcting performance deficiencies and motivating employees. When providing constructive feedback, Jenet Noriega Schwind, vice president and chief people officer of Zantaz, an e-business archiving company, tells employees, "What I'm going to tell you may be upsetting to you—but it's important to your success." She says, "When you are telling people things they don't

Empathetic listening understanding the speaker's perspective and personal frame of reference and giving feedback that conveys that understanding to the speaker

Destructive feedback feedback that disapproves without any intention of being helpful and almost always causes a negative or defensive reaction in the recipient

Constructive feedback feedback intended to be helpful, corrective, and/or encouraging

Giving **feedback does not** give managers the right to personally attack workers.

98 percent of employees responded to destructive feedback from their bosses with either verbal aggression or physical aggression.

©Asia Images/Jupiter Images

For instance, instead of telling an employee that he or she is "always late for work," it's much more constructive to say, "In the last three weeks, you have been 30 minutes late on four occasions and more than an hour late on two others." Furthermore, specific feedback isn't very helpful unless employees have control over the problems that the feedback addresses. Indeed, giving negative feedback about behaviors beyond someone's control is likely to be seen as unfair. Similarly, giving positive feedback about behaviors beyond someone's control may be viewed as insincere.

Last, *problem-oriented feedback* focuses on the problems or incidents associated with the poor performance rather than on the worker or the worker's personality. Giving feedback does not give managers the right to personally attack workers. Though managers may be frustrated by a worker's poor performance, the point of problem-oriented feedback is to draw attention to the problem in a nonjudgmental way so that the employee has enough information to correct it.

4 Managing Organization-Wide Communication

Although managing one-on-one communication is important, managers must also know how to communicate effectively with a larger number of people throughout an organization.

*Learn more about organization-wide communication by reading the following sections about **4.1 improving transmission by getting the message out** and **4.2 improving reception by finding ways to hear what others feel and think.***

4.1 Improving Transmission: Getting the Message Out

Several methods of electronic communication—email, online discussion forums, televised/videotaped speeches and conferences, and broadcast voice mail—now make it easier for managers to communicate with people throughout the organization and "get the message out."

Although we normally think of *email,* the transmission of messages via computers, as a means of one-on-one communication, it also plays an important role in organization-wide communication. With the click of a

necessarily want to hear, you have to deliver your message in a way that gets their attention and acceptance."[47]

For feedback to be constructive rather than destructive, it must be immediate, focused on specific behaviors, and problem oriented. *Immediate feedback* is much more effective than delayed feedback because manager and worker can recall the mistake or incident more accurately and discuss it in detail. For example, if a worker is rude to a customer and the customer immediately reports the incident to management, and the manager, in turn, immediately discusses the incident with the employee, there should be little disagreement over what was said or done. By contrast, if the manager waits several weeks to discuss the incident, it's unlikely that either the manager or the worker will be able to accurately remember the specifics of what occurred. When that happens, it's usually too late to have a meaningful conversation.

Specific feedback focuses on particular acts or incidents that are clearly under the control of the employee.

button, managers can send email to everyone in the company via email distribution lists. Many CEOs now use this capability regularly to keep employees up to date on changes and developments. On his first day as CEO of Diebold, which makes ATM machines, Thomas Swidarski emailed Diebold's 14,500 employees a message about improving customer loyalty, increasing the speed with which products were manufactured and delivered, and "providing quality products and outstanding service." Swidarski concluded his email by writing that leading Diebold, "does not rest with one person—it rests with each and every one of us."[48] Many CEOs and top executives also make their email addresses public and encourage employees to contact them directly.

Discussion forums are another means of electronically promoting organization-wide communication. **Online discussion forums** are the in-house equivalent of Internet newsgroups; by using Web- or software-based discussion tools that

are available across the company, employees can easily ask questions and share knowledge with each other. The point is to share expertise and not duplicate solutions already "discovered" by others in the company. Furthermore, because online discussion forums remain online, they provide a historical database for people who are dealing with particular problems for the first time.

Exhibit 15.6 lists the steps companies need to take to establish successful online discussion forums. First, pinpoint your company's top intellectual assets through a knowledge audit; then spread that knowledge throughout the organization. Second, create an online directory detailing the expertise of individual

Exhibit 15.6

Establishing Online Discussion Forums

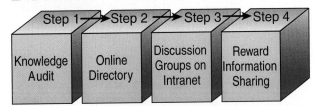

Step 1	Step 2	Step 3	Step 4
Knowledge Audit	Online Directory	Discussion Groups on Intranet	Reward Information Sharing

Source: Based on G. McWilliams & M. Stepanek, "Knowledge Management: Taming the Info Monster," *Business Week*, 22 June 1998, 170.

> **Online discussion forums** the in-house equivalent of Internet newsgroups. By using Web- or software-based discussion tools that are available across the company, employees can easily ask questions and share knowledge with each other.

Televised interview with Michael Dell to get the word out.

©Associated Press

workers and make it available to all employees. Third, set up discussion groups on the intranet so that managers and workers can collaborate on problem solving. Finally, reward information sharing by making the online sharing of knowledge a key part of performance ratings.

Televised/videotaped speeches and meetings are a third electronic method of organization-wide communication. **Televised/videotaped speeches and meetings** are simply speeches and meetings originally made to a smaller audience that are either simultaneously broadcast to other locations in the company or videotaped for subsequent distribution and viewing. Cisco's CEO, John Chambers, tapes ten to fifteen videos a quarter to communicate with his employees and customers.[49]

Voice messaging, or voice mail, is a telephone answering system that records audio messages. In one survey, 89 percent of respondents said that voice messaging is critical to business communication, 78 percent said that it improves productivity, and 58 percent said they would rather leave a message on a voice messaging system than with a receptionist.[50] Nonetheless, most people are unfamiliar with the ability to *broadcast voice mail* by sending a recorded message to everyone in the company. Broadcast voice mail gives top managers a quick, convenient way to address their work forces via oral communication. Harry Kraemer, CEO of pharmaceutical giant Baxter International, describes Baxter's broadcast voice mail system: "We have more than 30,000 Baxter team members hooked onto the same voice-mail system. That includes everybody but

the folks on the factory line. This is hooked up in over 50 countries."[51]

4.2 Improving Reception: Hearing What Others Feel and Think

When people think of "organization-wide" communication, they think of the CEO and top managers getting their message out to people in the company. But organization-wide communication also means finding ways to hear what people throughout the organization are feeling and thinking. This is important because most employees and managers are reluctant to share their thoughts and feelings with top managers. Surveys indicate that only 29 percent of first-level managers feel that their companies encourage employees to express their opinions openly. Another study of 22 companies found that 70 percent of the people surveyed were afraid to speak up about problems they knew existed at work.

Withholding information about organizational problems or issues is called **organizational silence.** Organizational silence occurs when employees believe that telling management about problems won't make a difference or that they'll be punished or hurt in some way for sharing such information.[52] Company hotlines, survey feedback, frequent informal meetings, surprise visits, and blogs are ways of overcoming organizational silence.

Company hotlines are phone numbers that anyone in the company can call anonymously to leave information for upper management. For example, Deloitte Touche Tohmatsu has a toll-free hotline for employees to call to report any kind of problem or issue within the company. Hotlines are particularly important because 44 percent of employees will not report misconduct. Why not? The reason is twofold: They don't believe anything will be done, and they "fear that the report will not be kept confidential."[53]

Survey feedback is information that is collected by survey from organization members and then compiled, disseminated, and used to develop action plans for improvement. Many organizations make use of survey feedback by surveying their managers and em-

Televised/video-taped speeches and meetings speeches and meetings originally made to a smaller audience that are either simultaneously broadcast to other locations in the company or videotaped for subsequent distribution and viewing

Organizational silence when employees withhold information about organizational problems or issues

Company hotlines phone numbers that anyone in the company can call anonymously to leave information for upper management

Survey feedback information that is collected by surveys from organizational members and then compiled, disseminated, and used to develop action plans for improvement

©Martin Parr/Magnum

ployees several times a year. FedEx, for example, runs its own Survey Feedback Action program. The online survey, which is completely anonymous, includes sections for employees to evaluate their managers and the overall environment at FedEx, including benefits, incentives, and working conditions. The results are compiled and then fed back to each FedEx work group to decide where changes and improvements need to be made and to develop specific action plans to address those problems. The final step is to look for improvements in subsequent employee surveys to see if those plans worked.[54]

Frequent, *informal meetings* between top managers and lower-level employees are one of the best ways for top managers to hear what others feel and think. Many people assume that top managers are at the center of everything that goes on in organizations, but top managers commonly feel isolated from most of their lower-level managers and employees. Consequently, more and more top managers are scheduling frequent, informal meetings with people throughout their companies.

Have you ever been around when a supervisor learns that upper management is going to be paying a visit? First there's panic, as everyone is told to drop what he or she is doing to polish, shine, and spruce up the workplace so that it looks perfect for the visit. Then, of course, top managers don't get a realistic look at what's going on in the company. Consequently, one of the ways to get an accurate picture is to pay *surprise visits* to various parts of the organization. These visits should not just be surprise inspections, but should also be used as an opportunity to encourage meaningful upward communication from those who normally don't get a chance to communicate with upper management. Such surprise visits are now part of the culture at the Royal Mail, the United Kingdom's postal service. Chairman Allan Leighton frequently shows up unannounced at Royal Mail delivery offices. Leighton says the initial reaction is always the same, "Oh s***, it's the chairman." However, Leighton isn't there to catch his employees doing something wrong. He's there to find out, right or wrong, what's really going on. Says Leighton, "Those visits at half past five in the morning [with employees] are the most important part" of turning around the Royal Mail, which was once losing 1.5 million pounds a day.[55] Today, thanks in part to his communication with employees, the Royal Mail delivers 95 percent of first class mail in one day, better than any other postal service in the world, and now earns, not loses, a profit of 1.5 million pounds per day.

Blogs are another way to hear what people are thinking and saying, both inside and outside the organization. A **blog** is a personal Web site that provides personal opinions or recommendations, news summaries, and reader comments. At Google, which owns the blog-hosting service Blogger, hundreds of employees are writing *internal blogs*. One employee even wrote a blog for posting all the notes from the brainstorming sessions used to redesign the search page used by millions each day.[56] *External blogs,* written by people outside the company, can be a good way to find out what others are saying or thinking about your organization or its products or actions. Tim Holmes, Ford's executive director of public affairs, believes that companies have to pay attention to what is being said about them online. Says Holmes, "Like most big companies, we monitor the press, but the problem with that is it's always retrospective, everything's a few weeks old. The real value of searching the net, including blogs, is that you get a live picture of what people are thinking about certain issues. It means that you can predict if there is going to be an issue that's going to grow and become something you need to respond to before it gets to the mainstream press."[57] Some companies have created the new position of chief blogging officer to manage internal company blogs and to monitor what is said about the company and its products on external blogs.[58]

Blog a personal Web site that provides personal opinions or recommendations, news summaries, and reader comments

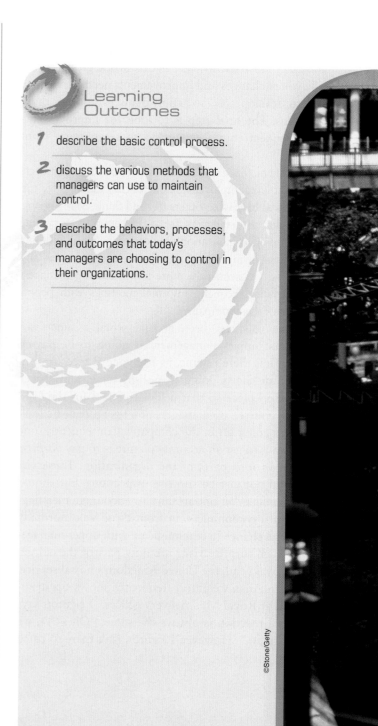

CONTROL

For all companies, past success is no guarantee of future success. Even successful companies fall short, face challenges, and have to make changes. **Control** is a regulatory process of establishing standards to achieve organizational goals, comparing actual performance against the standards, and taking corrective action when necessary to restore performance to those standards. Control is achieved when behavior and work procedures conform to standards and company goals are accomplished.[1] Control is not just an after-the-fact process, however. Preventive measures are also a form of control.

Learning Outcomes

1 describe the basic control process.

2 discuss the various methods that managers can use to maintain control.

3 describe the behaviors, processes, and outcomes that today's managers are choosing to control in their organizations.

Basics of Control

(W) With many empty stores and a dated look, the Coventry Mall in Pottstown, Pennsylvania, just 22 miles from the gigantic King of Prussia Mall, *was* dying, but mall manager Rene Daniel has it on the mend. With the mall down to just six food vendors (e.g., Hot Dogs & More and Egg Roll Hut), he convinced McDonald's, Subway, and Saladworks to open restaurants. When the lease expired on the "Everything 99 Cent" store, he convinced Gap to lease the adjacent space, knock out the wall, and replace the aging blue Formica with blond wood and modern glass. Changes like this have increased mall sales by a third, and they are now above the national average. Nevertheless, de-

Control a regulatory process of establishing standards to achieve organizational goals, comparing actual performance against the standards, and taking corrective action when necessary

©Stone/Getty

spite the changes, Vickey Sihler, who started shopping at the Coventry Mall again because of Gap and the new Children's Place store, still sees room for improvement. "This place really needs to be fixed up," she says.[2] So, by working the control process (standards, comparison to standards, and corrective action), Rene Daniel is slowly but surely fixing Coventry Mall.

After reading the next section, you should be able to

1   describe the basic control process.

1 The Control Process

The basic control process **1.1 begins with the establishment of clear standards of performance,** *1.2 involves* **a comparison of performance to those standards,** *1.3* **takes corrective action, if needed, to repair performance deficiencies,** *1.4 is a dynamic, cybernetic process,* **and** *1.5 consists of three basic methods: feedback control, concurrent control, and feedforward control.* *However, as much as managers would like,* **1.6 control isn't always worthwhile or possible.**

1.1 Standards

The control process begins when managers set goals, such as satisfying 90 percent of customers or increasing sales by 5 percent. Companies then specify the performance standards that must be met to accomplish those goals. **Standards** are a basis of comparison for measuring the extent to which organizational performance is satisfactory or unsatisfactory. For example, many pizzerias use 30–40 minutes as the standard for delivery times. Since anything longer is viewed as unsatisfactory, they'll typically reduce the price if they can't deliver a hot pizza to you within that time period.

So how do managers set standards? How do they decide which levels of performance are satisfactory and which are unsatisfactory? The first criterion for a good standard is that it must enable goal achievement. If you're meeting the standard, but still not achieving company goals, then the standard may have to be changed. For example, with the amount of unreimbursed medical care totaling $22.3 billion nationwide, hospitals are changing payment standards by asking that insurance copayments be paid *before* the patient leaves the hospital rather than *after.* Anyone who can't afford the entire copayment at once is asked to at least make a down payment (those who do are much more likely to pay their entire bill).[3]

Companies also determine standards by listening to customers' comments, complaints, and suggestions, or by observing competitors' products and services. After hearing from consumers that they were interested in machines that would automate routine household tasks, iRobot, a manufacturer of industrial and government (military) robots, created the Scooba, a robot that washes floors. Founder Colin Angle says, "People just hated to mop, so we saw a real opportunity."[4] The Scooba vacuums up dirt and debris, sprays a bleach cleaning solution, and then squeegees and sucks up the dirty water from the floor. At about $250, the Scooba can mop a typical kitchen in 45 minutes.

Standards can also be determined by benchmarking other companies. **Benchmarking** is the process of determining how well other companies (though not just competitors) perform business functions or tasks. In other words, benchmarking is the process of determining other companies' standards. When setting standards by benchmarking, the first step is to determine what to benchmark. Companies can benchmark anything, from cycle time (how fast) to quality (how well) to price (how much). The next step is to identify the companies against which to benchmark your standards. The last step is to collect data to determine other companies' performance standards.

©Associated Press

1.2 Comparison to Standards

The next step in the control process is to compare actual performance to performance standards. Although this sounds straightforward, the quality of the comparison largely depends on the measurement and information systems a company uses to keep track of performance. The better the system, the easier it is for companies to track their progress and identify problems that need to be fixed. One way for retailers to verify that performance standards are being met is to use "secret shoppers," who visit stores pretending to be customers, but are really there to determine whether employees provide helpful customer service. Secret shopper Cliff Fill recalls the fast-food restaurant where the workers discussed their dating plans as he stood in front of them ready to order. After ignoring him for 90 seconds (secret shoppers often carry timers with them), they turned to him and said, "We'll be done with our conversation in a minute and be with you."[5]

1.3 Corrective Action

The next step in the control process is to identify performance deviations, analyze those deviations, and then develop and implement programs to correct them.

Beta versions of software programs are a classic tool that developers use to monitor deviations from the

Standards a basis of comparison for measuring the extent to which various kinds of organizational performance are satisfactory or unsatisfactory

Benchmarking the process of identifying outstanding practices, processes, and standards in other companies and adapting them to your company standard and take corrective action—before the product is released on the market. Microsoft has an internal program called Software Quality Metrics (SQM) that company software developers use when creating new software releases. SQM helps the developers determine how each change in the software code will affect the functionality of the program and uses a system of comparison charts to show how the changes will affect users of new software.[6]

1.4 Dynamic, Cybernetic Process

As shown in Exhibit 16.1, control is a continuous, dynamic, cybernetic process. Control begins by setting standards, measuring performance, and then comparing performance to the standards. If the performance deviates from the standards, then managers and employees analyze the deviations and develop and implement corrective programs that (hopefully) achieve the desired performance by meeting the standards. Managers must repeat the entire process again and again in an endless feedback loop (a continuous process). Thus, control is not a onetime achievement or result. It continues over time (i.e., it is dynamic) and requires daily, weekly, and monthly attention from managers to maintain performance levels at the standard (i.e., it is cybernetic). **Cybernetic** derives from the Greek word *kubernetes*, meaning "steersman," that is, one who steers or keeps on course.[7] Therefore, the control process shown in Exhibit 16.1 is cybernetic because of the feedback loop in

Exhibit 16.1
Cybernetic Control Process

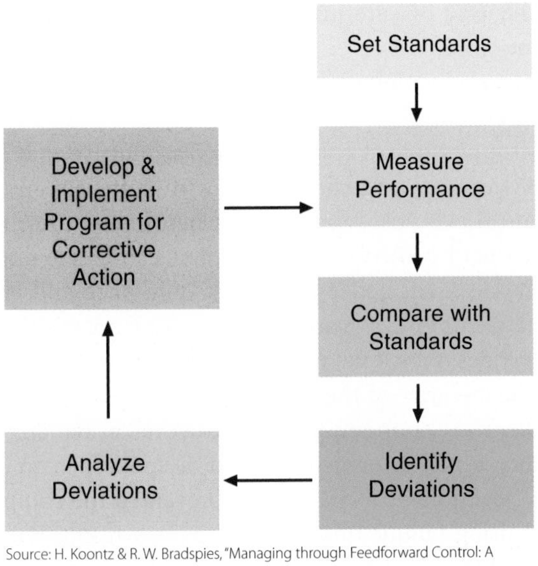

Source: H. Koontz & R. W. Bradspies, "Managing through Feedforward Control: A Future-Directed View," *Business Horizons*, June 1972, 25–36. Reprinted with permission from *Business Horizons*, © 1972 by the Trustees at Indiana University, Kelley School of Business.

which actual performance is compared to standards so that deviations from those standards can be minimized or corrected.

1.5 Feedback, Concurrent, and Feedforward Control

The three basic control method are feedback control, concurrent control, and feedforward control. **Feedback control** is a mechanism for gathering information about performance deficiencies *after* they occur. This information is then used to correct or prevent performance deficiencies. Study after study has clearly shown that feedback improves both individual and organizational performance. In most instances, any feedback is better than no feedback. But, if there is a downside to feedback, it is that it is always after the fact, in other words, after performance deficiencies occur.

Concurrent control addresses the problems inherent in feedback control by gathering information about performance deficiencies *as* they occur. Thus, it is an improvement over feedback because it attempts to eliminate or shorten the delay between performance and feedback about the performance. Apple and Nike teamed up to create a real-time exercise feedback system called Nike + iPod. After a runner installs the system in her shoes, it transmits concurrent information to her iPod. The system measures time, distance, calories burned, and pace. Runners can actually track their efforts every moment of their run and make changes on the fly.[8]

Feedforward control is a mechanism for gathering information about performance deficiencies *before* they occur. In contrast to feedback and concurrent

©Associated Press

Cybernetic the process of steering or keeping on course

Feedback control a mechanism for gathering information about performance deficiencies after they occur

Concurrent control a mechanism for gathering information about performance deficiencies as they occur, thereby eliminating or shortening the delay between performance and feedback

Feedforward control a mechanism for monitoring performance inputs rather than outputs to prevent or minimize performance deficiencies before they occur control, which provide feedback on the basis of outcomes and results, feedforward control provides information about performance deficiencies by monitoring inputs, not outputs. Thus, feedforward control seeks to prevent or minimize performance deficiencies *before* they happen. Microsoft uses feedforward controls to try to prevent software problems before they occur. For example, when developing the latest version of its Windows Server software (for network and Internet computer servers), Microsoft taught 8,500 experienced programmers new methods for writing more reliable software code *before* asking them to develop new features for Windows Server software. Microsoft has also developed new software testing tools that let the programmers thoroughly test the code they've written (i.e., input) before passing the code on to others to be used in beta testing and then in final products.[9]

1.6 Control Isn't Always Worthwhile or Possible

Control is achieved when behavior and work procedures conform to standards and goals are accomplished. By contrast, **control loss** occurs when behavior and work procedures do not conform to standards.[10] Maintaining control is important because control loss prevents goal achievement. When control loss occurs, managers need to find out what, if anything, they could have done to prevent it. Usually, as discussed above, that means identifying deviations from standard performance, analyzing the causes of those deviations, and taking corrective action. Implementing controls, however, isn't always worthwhile or possible. Let's look at regulation costs and cybernetic feasibility to see why.

To determine whether control is worthwhile, managers need to carefully assess **regulation costs,** that is, whether the costs and both the intended and unintended consequences of control exceed its benefits. For example, one of the reasons that the number of U.S. pharmaceutical companies producing major vaccines has dropped significantly is that the *cost of controlling* legal risk (through liability insurance and in-house legal staffs) is just too high. In the 1960s, 37 U.S. companies produced 380 licensed vaccines. In 1984, 15 U.S. companies produced 88 licensed vaccines. In theory, the cost of lawsuits was supposed to encourage pharmaceutical companies to develop safer vaccines. Today, because of exorbitant legal costs and liability insurance, just five U.S. companies produce vaccines.[11] The unintended consequence is that parents and doctors face severe shortages in 8 of the 11 recommended vaccines that prevent children from contracting diseases like diphtheria, tetanus, whooping cough, measles, mumps, rubella, and chickenpox.[12]

Another factor to consider is **cybernetic feasibility,** the extent to which it is possible to implement each step in the control process: clear standards of performance, comparison of performance to standards, and corrective action. If one or more steps cannot be implemented, then maintaining effective control may be difficult or impossible. For example, many retail companies provide significant employee discounts, which can be used by entering special codes at the company's online store. However, those codes have leaked out via email to nonemployees and are also published at various Web sites.[13]

Is it possible to control these discounts so that only employees can use them? Yes, with sufficient money, technical expertise, and the proper software tools (i.e., the costs of control), online retailers can create unique online discount codes that work only once and email them to employees. A spokesperson for Gap, which uses such codes, says, "We want to make sure we're protecting the integrity of the [sales] event. We really consider it a benefit to our employees." However, at Banana Republic, which is owned by Gap, a spokesperson said that "technological challenges" prevented the company from using unique one-time codes. As a result, Banana Republic's 25 percent employee discount was being widely used by people who aren't employees.

Control loss the situation in which behavior and work procedures do not conform to standards

Regulation costs the costs associated with implementing or maintaining control

Cybernetic feasibility the extent to which it is possible to implement each step in the control process

How and What to Control

At about 10 percent of Sam's Club and Wal-Mart stores, the doors are locked on midnight-shift employees to keep out robbers and, some say, also to prevent employee theft. According to Mona Williams, Wal-Mart's vice president for communications, "Wal-Mart secures these stores just as any other business does that has employees working overnight. Doors are locked to protect associates and the store from intruders."[14] But many employees dislike the policy. When Michael Rodriguez injured his ankle at 3 A.M., he had to wait an hour for a store manager to show up to unlock the doors. Says Rodriguez, "Being locked in in an emergency like that, that's not right."[15] Wal-Mart's Mona Williams responds, "Fire doors are always accessible [and unlocked from the inside] for safety, and there will always be at least one manager in the store with a set of keys to unlock the doors."[16]

If you managed a Wal-Mart store, would you lock in your midnight employees? Would doing so jeopardize or improve their safety? Or is this policy a reasonable response to employee theft, which can often exceed a store's profits? If you were a Wal-Mart or Sam's Club store manager, what would you do?

 After reading the next two sections, you should be able to

2 discuss the various methods that managers can use to maintain control.

3 describe the behaviors, processes, and outcomes that today's managers are choosing to control in their organizations.

2 Control Methods

*Managers can use five different methods to achieve control in their organizations: **2.1 bureaucratic**, **2.2 objective**, **2.3 normative**, **2.4 concertive**, and **2.5 self-control**.*

2.1 Bureaucratic Control

When most people think of managerial control, what they have in mind is bureaucratic control. **Bureaucratic control** is top-down control, in which managers try to influence employee behavior by rewarding or punishing employees for compliance or noncompliance with organizational policies, rules, and procedures. Most employees, however, would argue that bureaucratic managers emphasize punishment for noncompliance much more than rewards for compliance. For instance, when visiting the company's regional offices and managers, the president of a training company, who was known for his temper and for micromanaging others, would get some toilet paper from the restrooms and aggressively ask, "What's this?" When the managers answered, "Toilet paper," the president would scream that it was two-ply toilet paper that the company couldn't afford. When told of a cracked toilet seat in one of the women's restrooms, he said, "If you don't like sitting on that seat, you can stand up like I do!"[17]

Ironically, bureaucratic management and control were created to prevent just this type of managerial behavior. By encouraging managers to apply well-thought-out rules, policies, and procedures in an impartial, consistent manner to everyone in the organization, bureaucratic control is supposed to make companies more efficient, effective, and fair. Perversely, it frequently has just the opposite effect. Managers who use bureaucratic control often emphasize following the rules above all else.

Another characteristic of bureaucratically controlled companies is that due to their rule- and policy-driven decision making, they are highly resistant to change and slow to respond to customers and competitors. Recall from Chapter 2 that even Max Weber, the German philosopher who is largely credited with popularizing bureaucratic ideals in the late 19th century, referred to bureaucracy as the "iron cage." He said, "Once fully established, bureaucracy is among those social structures which are the hardest to destroy."[18]

2.2 Objective Control

In many companies, bureaucratic control has evolved into **objective control**, which is the use of observable measures of employee behavior or output to assess performance and influence behavior. Whereas bureaucratic control focuses on whether policies and rules are followed, objective control focuses on the observation or measurement of

Bureaucratic control the use of hierarchical authority to influence employee behavior by rewarding or punishing employees for compliance or noncompliance with organizational policies, rules, and procedures

Objective control the use of observable measures of worker behavior or outputs to assess performance and influence behavior worker behavior or output. There are two kinds of objective control: behavior control and output control.

Behavior control is regulating behaviors and actions that workers perform on the job. The basic assumption of behavior control is that if you do the right things (i.e., the right behaviors) every day, then those things should lead to goal achievement. Behavior control is still management-based, however, which means that managers are responsible for monitoring and rewarding or punishing workers for exhibiting desired or undesired behaviors. Companies that use global positioning satellite (GPS) technology to track where workers are and what they're doing are using behavior control. For example, after getting complaints that his police officers weren't always on the job, Sergeant John Kuczynsky quietly put GPS tracking devices in his Clinton Township, New Jersey, officers' cars. Contrary to the officers' reports indicating that they were patrolling streets or using radar to catch speeding drivers, the GPS tracking software soon showed that five officers were sitting for long periods in parking lots or taking long breaks for meals. All five are now barred from law enforcement jobs.[19]

Instead of measuring what managers and workers do, **output control** measures the results of their efforts. Whereas behavior control regulates, guides, and measures how workers behave on the job, output control gives managers and workers the freedom to behave as they see fit as long as they accomplish prespecified, measurable results. Output control is often coupled with rewards and incentives.

Three things must occur for output control and rewards to lead to improved business results. First, output control measures must be reliable, fair, and accurate. Second, employees and managers must believe that they can produce the desired results. If they don't, then the output controls won't affect their

behavior. Third, the rewards or incentives tied to outcome control measures must truly be dependent on achieving established standards of performance. For example, Smithfield Foods CEO Joseph Luter doesn't earn a bonus unless pretax profits exceed $100 million. Ray Goldberg, chairman of the company's compensation committee, says that, "We were trying to make sure [Luter's] rewards are based on the ups and downs of the company."[20] So, with pretax profits of $227.1 million, Luter's bonus, based on 2 percent of earnings between $100 million and $300 million, and 3 percent of profits over $300 million, would total just over $2.5 million. For output control to work with rewards, the rewards must truly be at risk if performance doesn't measure up.

2.3 Normative Control

Rather than monitoring rules, behavior, or output, another way to control what goes on in organizations is to use normative control to shape the beliefs and values of the people who work there. With **normative controls,** a company's widely shared values and beliefs guide workers' behavior and decisions. For example, at Nordstrom, a Seattle-based department store chain, one value permeates the entire work force from top to bottom: extraordinary customer service. On the first day of work at Nordstrom, trainees begin their transformation to the "Nordstrom way" by reading the employee handbook. Sounds boring, doesn't it? But Nordstrom's handbook is printed on one side of a 3-by-5-inch note card. In its entirety, it reads:

Welcome to Nordstrom's. We're glad to have you with our company. Our Number One goal is to provide outstanding customer service. Set both your personal and professional goals high. We have great confidence in your ability to achieve them. Nordstrom Rules: Rule #1: Use your good judgment in all situations. There will be no additional rules. Please feel free to ask your

Behavior control the regulation of the behaviors and actions that workers perform on the job

Output control the regulation of workers' results or outputs through rewards and incentives

Normative control the regulation of workers' behavior and decisions through widely shared organizational values and beliefs

©Getty Images

department manager, store manager, or division general manager any question at any time.[21]

That's it. No lengthy rules. No specifics about what behavior is or is not appropriate. Use your judgment.[22]

Normative controls are created in two ways. First, companies that use normative controls are very careful about whom they hire. While many companies screen potential applicants on the basis of their abilities, normatively controlled companies are just as likely to screen potential applicants based on their attitudes and values. For example, before building stores in a new city, Nordstrom sends its human resource team into town to interview prospective applicants. In a few cities, the company canceled its expansion plans when it could not find enough qualified applicants who embodied the service attitudes and values for which Nordstrom is known.[23]

shaped and negotiated by work groups.[26] Whereas normative controls are driven by strong organizational cultures, concertive controls usually arise when companies give autonomous work groups complete autonomy and responsibility for task completion. The most autonomous groups operate without managers and are completely responsible for controlling work group processes, outputs, and behavior. Such groups do their own hiring, firing, worker discipline, work schedules, materials ordering, budget making and meeting, and decision making.

Concertive control is not established overnight. Highly autonomous work groups evolve through two phases as they develop concertive control. In phase one, group members learn to work with each other, supervise each other's work, and develop the values and beliefs that will guide and control their behavior. And because

 Concertive control is not established overnight.

Second, with normative controls, managers and employees learn what they should and should not do by observing experienced employees and by listening to the stories they tell about the company. At Nordstrom, many of these stories, which employees call "heroics," have been inspired by the company motto, "Respond to Unreasonable Customer Requests!"[24] "Nordies," as Nordstrom employees call themselves, like to tell the story about a customer who just had to have a pair of burgundy Donna Karan slacks that had gone on sale, but she could not find her size. The sales associate who was helping her contacted five nearby Nordstrom stores, but none had the customer's size. So rather than leave the customer dissatisfied with her shopping experience, the sales associate went to her manager for petty cash and then went across the street and paid full price for the slacks at a competitor's store. She then resold them to the customer at Nordstrom's lower sale price.[25] Obviously, Nordstrom would quickly go out of business if this were the norm. Nevertheless, this story makes clear the attitude that drives employee performance at Nordstrom in ways that rules, behavioral guidelines, or output controls could not.

2.4 Concertive Control

Whereas normative controls are based on beliefs that are strongly held and widely shared throughout a company, **concertive controls** are based on beliefs that are

they develop these values and beliefs themselves, work group members feel strongly about following them.

In the steel industry, Nucor was long considered an upstart compared to the "biggies," U.S. Steel and Bethlehem Steel. Today, however, not only has Nucor managed to outlast many other mills, the company has bought out 13 other mills in the past five years. But Nucor has a unique culture that gives real power to employees on the line and fosters teamwork throughout the organization. This type of teamwork can be a difficult thing for a newly acquired group of employees to get used to. For example, at Nucor's first big acquisition in Auburn, New York, David Hutchins is a frontline supervisor or "lead man" in the rolling mill, where steel from the furnace is spread thin enough to be cut into sheets. When the plant was under the previous ownership, if the guys doing the cutting got backed up, the guys doing the rolling—including Hutchins—would just take a break. He says, "We'd sit back, have a cup of coffee, and complain: 'Those guys stink.'" It took six months to convince the employees at the Auburn plant that the Nucor teamwork way was better than the old way. Now, Hutchins says, "At Nucor, we're not 'you guys' and 'us guys.' It's all of us guys. Wherever the bottleneck is, we go there, and everyone works on it."[27]

Concertive control
the regulation of workers' behavior and decisions through work group values and beliefs

The second phase in the development of concertive control is the emergence and formalization of objective rules to guide and control behavior. The beliefs and values developed in phase one usually develop into more objective rules as new members join teams. The clearer those rules, the easier it becomes for new members to figure out how and how not to behave.

Ironically, concertive control may lead to even more stress for workers to conform to expectations than bureaucratic control. Under bureaucratic control, most workers only have to worry about pleasing the boss. But with concertive control, their behavior has to satisfy the rest of their team members. For example, one team member says, "I don't have to sit there and look for the boss to be around; and if the boss is not around, I can sit there and talk to my neighbor or do what I want. Now the whole team is around me and the whole team is observing what I'm doing."[28] Plus, with concertive control, team members have a second, much more stressful role to perform—that of making sure that their team members adhere to team values and rules.

2.5 Self-Control

Self-control, also known as **self-management,** is a control system in which managers and workers control their own behavior.[29] Self-control does not result in anarchy in which everyone gets to do whatever he or she wants. In self-control or self-management, leaders and managers provide workers with clear boundaries within which they may guide and control their own goals and behaviors.[30] Leaders and managers also contribute to self-control by teaching others the skills they need to maximize and monitor their own work effectiveness. In turn, individuals who manage and lead themselves establish self-control by setting their own goals, monitoring their own progress, rewarding or punishing themselves for achieving or for not achieving their self-set goals, and constructing positive thought patterns that remind them of the importance of their goals and their ability to accomplish them.[31]

For example, let's assume you need to do a better job of praising and recognizing the good work that your staff does for you. You can use goal setting, self-observation, and self-reward to self-manage this behavior. For self-observation, write "praise/recognition" on a 3-by-5-inch card. Put the card in your pocket. Put a check on the card each time you praise or recognize someone (wait until the person has left before you do this). Keep track for a week. This serves as your baseline or starting point. Simply keeping track will probably increase how often you do this. After a week, assess your baseline or starting point, and then set a specific goal. For instance, if your baseline was twice a day, you might set a specific goal to praise or recognize others' work five times a day. Continue monitoring your performance with your cards. Once you've achieved your goal every day for a week, give yourself a reward (perhaps a CD, a movie, lunch with a friend at a new restaurant) for achieving your goal.[32]

As you can see, the components of self-management, self-set goals, self-observation, and self-reward have their roots in the motivation theories you read about in Chapter 13. The key difference, though, is that the goals, feedback, and rewards originate from employees themselves and not from their managers or organizations.

3 What to Control?

In the first section of this chapter, we discussed the basics of the control process and that control isn't always worthwhile or possible. In the second section, we looked at the various ways in which control can be obtained. In this third and final section, we address an equally important issue, "What should managers control?" The way managers answer this question has critical implications for most businesses.

If you control for just one thing, such as costs, then other dimensions, like marketing, customer service, and quality, are likely to suffer. If you try to control for too many things, then managers and employees become confused about what's really important. In the end, successful companies find a balance that comes from doing three or four things right, like managing costs, providing value, and keeping customers and employees satisfied.

After reading this section, you should be able to explain **3.1 the balanced scorecard approach to control and how companies can achieve balanced control of company performance by choosing to control 3.2 budgets, cash flows, and economic value added, 3.3 customer defections, 3.4 quality,** *and* **3.5 waste and pollution**.

3.1 The Balanced Scorecard

Most companies measure performance using standard financial and accounting measures such as return on capital, return on assets, return on investments, cash flow,

Self-control (self-management) a control system in which managers and workers control their own behavior by setting their own goals, monitoring their own progress, and rewarding themselves for goal achievement

If you control for just one thing, such as costs,
then **other dimensions,** *like marketing, customer service,*
and quality are likely to **suffer.**

net income, and net margins. The **balanced scorecard** encourages managers to look beyond traditional financial measures to four different perspectives on company performance. How do customers see us (the customer perspective)? At what must we excel (the internal perspective)? Can we continue to improve and create value (the innovation and learning perspective)? How do we look to shareholders (the financial perspective)?[33]

The balanced scorecard has several advantages over traditional control processes that rely solely on financial measures. First, it forces managers at each level of the company to set specific goals and measure performance in each of the four areas. For example, Exhibit 16.2 shows that Southwest Airlines uses nine different measures in its balanced scorecard. Of those, only three, market value, seat revenue, and plane lease costs (at various compounded annual growth rates, or CAGR), are standard financial measures of performance. In addition, Southwest measures its Federal Aviation Administration (FAA) on-time arrival rating and the cost of its airfares compared to competitors' (customer perspec-

tive); how much time each plane spends on the ground after landing and the percentage of planes that depart on time (internal business perspective); and the percentage of its ground crew workers, such as mechanics and luggage handlers, who own company stock and have received job training (learning perspective).

The second major advantage of the balanced scorecard approach to control is that it minimizes the chances of **suboptimization,** which occurs when performance improves in one area, but at the expense of decreased performance in others. Jon Meliones, chief medical director at Duke Children's Hospital, says, ". . . we could increase productivity . . . by assigning more patients to a nurse, but doing so would raise the likelihood of errors—an unacceptable trade-off."[34]

Let's examine some of the ways in which companies are controlling the four basic parts of the balanced scorecard: the financial perspective (budgets, cash flows, and economic value added), the customer perspective (customer defections), the internal perspective (total quality management), and the innovation and learning perspective (waste and pollution).

Exhibit 16.2

Southwest Airlines' Balanced Scorecard

	OBJECTIVES	MEASURES	TARGETS	INITIATIVES
FINANCIAL	Profitability	Market Value	30% CAGR	
	Increased Revenue	Seat Revenue	20% CAGR	
	Lower Costs	Plane Lease Cost	5% CAGR	
CUSTOMER	On-Time Flights	FAA On-Time Arrival Rating	#1	Quality Management, Customer Loyalty Program
	Lowest Prices	Customer Ranking (Market Survey)	#1	
INTERNAL	Fast Ground Turnaround	Time on Ground	30 Minutes	Cycle Time Optimization Program
		On-Time Departure	90%	
LEARNING	Ground Crew Alignment with Company Goals	% Ground Crew Shareholders	Year 1: 70% Year 3: 90% Year 5: 100%	Employee Stock Option Plan Ground Crew Training
		% Ground Crew Trained		

©Image 100/Jupiter Images

Sources: G. Anthes, "ROI Guide: Balanced Scorecard," *Computer World* [Online] available at http://www.computerworld.com/managementtopics/roi/story/0,10801,78512,00.html, 5 May 2003.

Balanced scorecard
measurement of organizational performance in four equally important areas: finances, customers, internal operations, and innovation and learning

Suboptimization
performance improvement in one part of an organization but at the expense of decreased performance in another part

3.2 The Financial Perspective: Controlling Budgets, Cash Flows, and Economic Value Added

The traditional approach to controlling financial performance focuses on accounting tools, such as cash flow analysis, balance sheets, income statements, financial ratios, and budgets. **Cash flow analysis** predicts how changes in a business will affect its ability to take in more cash than it pays out. **Balance sheets** provide a snapshot of a company's financial position at a particular time (but not the future). **Income statements,** also called profit and loss statements, show what has happened to an organization's income, expenses, and net profit (income less expenses) over a period of time. **Financial ratios** are typically used to track a business's liquidity (cash), efficiency, and profitability over time compared to other businesses in its industry. Finally, **budgets** are used to project costs and revenues, prioritize and control spending, and ensure that expenses don't exceed available funds and revenues. The Financial Review Card bound in the the back of this book contains tables that (a) show the basic steps or parts for cash flow analyses, balance sheets, and income statements; (b) list a few of the most common financial ratios and explain how they are calculated, what they mean, and when to use them; and (c) review the different kinds of budgets managers can use to track and control company finances.

By themselves, none of these tools—cash flow anal-

Cash flow analysis a type of analysis that predicts how changes in a business will affect its ability to take in more cash than it pays out

Balance sheets accounting statements that provide a snapshot of a company's financial position at a particular time

Income statements accounting statements, also called "profit and loss statements," that show what has happened to an organization's income, expenses, and net profit over a period of time

Financial ratios calculations typically used to track a business's liquidity (cash), efficiency, and profitability over time compared to other businesses in its industry

Budgets quantitative plans through which managers decide how to allocate available money to best accomplish company goals

Economic value added (EVA) the amount by which company profits (revenues, minus expenses, minus taxes) exceed the cost of capital in a given year

yses, balance sheets, income statements, financial ratios, or budgets—tell the whole financial story of a business. They must be used together when assessing a company's financial performance. Since these tools are reviewed in detail in your accounting and finance classes, only a brief overview is provided here. Still, these are necessary tools for controlling organizational finances and expenses, and they should be part of your business toolbox.

Though no one would dispute the importance of cash flow analyses, balance sheets, income statements, financial ratios, or budgets, accounting research also indicates that the complexity and sheer amount of information contained in these accounting tools can shut down the brain and glaze over the eyes of even the most experienced manager.[35] Sometimes, there's simply too much information to make sense of. The balanced scorecard simplifies things by focusing on one simple question when it comes to finances: How do we look to shareholders? One way to answer that question is through something called economic value added.

Conceptually, **economic value added (EVA)** is not the same thing as profits. It is the amount by which profits exceed the cost of capital in a given year. It is based on the simple idea that capital is necessary to run a business and that capital comes at a cost. Although most people think of capital as cash, capital, once invested (i.e., spent), is more likely to be found in a business in the form of computers, manufacturing plants, employees, raw materials, and so forth. And just like the interest that a homeowner pays on a mortgage or that a college student pays on a student loan, there is a cost to that capital.

The most common costs of capital are the interest paid on long-term bank loans used to buy all those resources, the interest paid to bondholders (who lend organizations their money), and the dividends (cash payments) and growth in stock value that accrue to shareholders. EVA is positive when company profits (revenues minus expenses minus taxes) exceed the cost of capital in a given year. In other words, if a business is to truly grow, its revenues must be large enough to cover both short-term costs (annual expenses and taxes) and long-term costs (the cost of borrowing capital from bondholders and shareholders). If you're a bit confused, the late Roberto Goizueta, the former CEO of Coca-Cola, explained it this way: "You borrow money at a certain rate and invest it at a higher rate and pocket the difference. It is simple. It is the essence of banking."[36]

Exhibit 16.3 shows how to calculate EVA. First, starting with a company's income statement, you calculate the net operating profit after taxes (NOPAT) by subtracting taxes owed from income from operations. (Remember, a quick review of an income statement is on the Financial Review Card bound at the back of your book). The NOPAT shown in Exhibit 16.3 is $3,500,000. Second, identify how much capital the company has invested (i.e., spent). Total liabilities (what the company owes) less accounts payable and less accrued expenses, neither of which you pay interest on, provides a rough approximation of this amount. In Exhibit 16.3, total capital invested is $16,800,000. Third, calculate the cost (i.e., rate) paid for capital by determining the interest paid to bondholders (who lend organizations their money), which is usually somewhere between 5 and 8 percent, and the return that stockholders want in terms of dividends and stock price appreciation, which is historically about 13 percent. Take a weighted average of the two to determine the overall cost of capital. In Exhibit 16.3, the cost of capital is 10 percent. Fourth, multiply the total capital ($16,800,000) from Step 2 by the cost of capital (10 percent) from Step 3. In Exhibit 16.3, this amount is $1,680,000. Fifth, subtract the total dollar cost of capital in Step 4 from the NOPAT in Step 1. In Exhibit 16.3, this value is $1,820,000, which means that our example company has created economic value or wealth this year. If our EVA number had been negative, meaning that the company didn't make enough profit to cover the cost of capital from bondholders and shareholders, then the company would have destroyed economic value or wealth by taking in more money than it returned.[37]

Exhibit 16.3

Calculating Economic Value Added (EVA)

1. Calculate net operating profit after taxes (NOPAT).	$3,500,000
2. Identify how much capital the company has invested (i.e., spent).	$16,800,000
3. Determine the cost (i.e., rate) paid for capital (usually between 5 percent and 13 percent).	10%
4. Multiply capital used (Step 2) times cost of capital (Step 3).	(10% × $16,800,000) = $1,680,000
5. Subtract the total dollar cost of capital from net profit after taxes.	$3,500,000 NOPAT −$1,680,000 Total cost of capital $1,820,000 Economic value added

But why is EVA so important? First and most importantly, because it includes the cost of capital, it shows whether a business, division, department, profit center, or product is really paying for itself. The key is to make sure that managers and employees can see how their choices and behavior affect the company's EVA.

Second, because EVA can easily be determined for subsets of a company, such as divisions, regional offices, manufacturing plants, and sometimes even departments, it makes managers and workers at all levels pay much closer attention to their segment of the business. When company offices were being refurbished at Genesco, a shoe company, a worker who had EVA training handed CEO Ben Harris $4,000 in cash. The worker explained that he now understood the effect his job had on the company's ability to survive and prosper. And since the company was struggling, he had sold the old doors that had been removed during remodeling so that the company could have the cash.[38] In other words, EVA motivates managers and workers to think like small-business owners who

Top Ten U.S. Companies by Market Value Added and Economic Value Added

MVA RANKING	COMPANY	MARKET VALUE ADDED ($ MILLIONS)	ECONOMIC VALUE ADDED/(LOST) ($ MILLIONS)
1	General Electric	$299,810	$5,288
2	ExxonMobil	197,782	14,456
3	Microsoft	178,032	6,426
4	Wal-Mart	161,693	4,972
5	Johnson & Johnson	138,199	5,655
6	United Health Group	112,755	1,897
7	Procter & Gamble	105,858	3,951
8	CitiGroup	99,485	4,536
9	Intel	97,468	1,720
10	Dell	88,086	1,891

Source: R. Grizzetti, "U.S. Performance 1000," Stern Stewart & Co, [Online] available by request, http://www.sternstewart.com, 20 June 2005.

must scramble to contain costs and generate enough business to meet their bills each month. And, unlike many kinds of financial controls, EVA doesn't specify what should or should not be done to improve performance. Thus, it encourages managers and workers to be creative in looking for ways to improve EVA performance.

Remember that EVA is the amount by which profits exceed the cost of capital in a given year. So the more that EVA exceeds the total dollar cost of capital, the better a company has used investors' money that year. Market value added (MVA) is simply the cumulative

EVA created by a company over time. Thus, MVA indicates how much value or wealth a company has created or destroyed in total during its existence.

3.3 The Customer Perspective: Controlling Customer Defections

The second aspect of organizational performance that the balanced scorecard helps managers monitor is customers. It does so by forcing managers to address the question, "How do customers see us?" Unfortunately, most companies try to answer this question through customer satisfaction surveys, but these are often misleadingly positive. Most customers are reluctant to talk about their problems because they don't know who to complain to or think that complaining will not do any good. Indeed, a study by the federal Office of Consumer Affairs found that 96 percent of unhappy customers never complain to anyone in the company.[39]

One reason that customer satisfaction surveys can be misleading is that sometimes even very satisfied customers will leave to do business with competitors. Rather than poring over customer satisfaction surveys from current customers, studies indicate that companies may do a better job of answering the question "How do customers see us?" by closely monitoring **customer defections,** that is, by identifying which customers are

> Obtaining a new customer costs five times as much as keeping a current one.

Customer defections
a performance assessment in which companies identify which customers are leaving and measure the rate at which they are leaving

leaving the company and measuring the rate at which they are leaving. Unlike the results of customer satisfaction surveys, customer defections and retention do have a great effect on profits.

For example, very few managers realize that obtaining a new customer costs five times as much as keeping a current one. In fact, the cost of replacing old customers with new ones is so great that most companies could double their profits by increasing the rate of customer retention by just 5 to 10 percent per year.[40] And, if a company can keep a customer for life, the benefits are even larger. According to Stew Leonard, owner of the Connecticut-based Stew Leonard's grocery store chain, "The lifetime value of a customer in a supermarket is about $246,000. Every time a customer comes through our front door I see, stamped on their forehead in big red numbers, '$246,000.' I'm never going to make that person unhappy with me. Or lose her to the competition."[41]

Beyond the clear benefits to the bottom line, the second reason to study customer defections is that customers who have left are much more likely than current customers to tell you what you were doing wrong. Finally, companies that understand why customers leave can not only take steps to fix ongoing problems, but can also identify which customers are likely to leave and make changes to prevent them from leaving.

3.4 The Internal Perspective: Controlling Quality

The third part of the balanced scorecard, the internal perspective, consists of the processes, decisions, and actions that managers and workers make within the organization. In contrast to the financial perspective of EVA and the outward-looking customer perspective, the internal perspective asks the question "At what must we excel?" Consequently, the internal perspective of the balanced scorecard usually leads managers to a focus on quality.

Quality is typically defined and measured in three ways: excellence, value, and conformance to expectations.[42] When the company defines its quality goal as *excellence,* then managers must try to produce a product or service of unsurpassed performance and features. For example, by almost any standard, Singapore Airlines is the best airline in the world. It has been named "best" 18 years in a row by readers of *Conde Nast Traveler* magazine.[43] It has also received various "best airline" awards from the *Asian Wall Street Journal, Business Traveler International, Germany Business Traveler, Travel and Leisure,* and *Fortune.*[44] Whereas many airlines try to cram passengers into every available inch on a plane, Singapore Airlines delivers creature comforts to encourage repeat business and customers willing to pay premium prices. On its newer planes, the first-class cabin is divided into eight private mini-rooms, each with an unusually wide leather seat that folds down flat for sleeping, a 23-inch LCD TV that doubles as a computer monitor, and an adjustable table. These

MGMT TRENDS

An Old Standby Is a Hot Trend

Vertical integration is making a comeback. In an effort to better control resources—namely, raw materials—some companies are buying suppliers who furnish critical components for important product lines. In 2006, Armor Holdings bought the North Carolina textile manufacturer that supplied the super-strong fibers used in its armored cars. Toyota took control of a key battery supplier for hybrid gasoline-electric engines, and Bridgestone Tire bought a rubber plantation in Indonesia. Watch the business press for articles on companies expanding vertically rather than horizontally.

Source: Timothy Aeppel, "A Hot Commodities Market Spurs Buying Spree by Manufacturers," *Wall Street Journal,* 14 August 2006, A1, A7.

amenities and services are common for private jets but truly unique in the commercial airline industry.[45] Singapore Airlines was the first airline, in the 1970s, to introduce a choice of meals, complimentary drinks, and earphones in coach class. It was the first to introduce worldwide video, news, telephone, and fax services, and the first to feature personal video monitors for movies, news, documentaries, and games. Singapore Airlines has had AC power for laptop computers for some time, and recently it became the first airline to introduce on-board, *high-speed* Internet access.[46]

©AFP/Getty

Value is the customer perception that the product quality is excellent for the price offered. At a higher price, for example, customers may perceive the product to be less of a value. When a company emphasizes value as its quality goal, managers must simultaneously control excellence, price, durability, or other features of a product or service that customers strongly associate with value. Aldi, a grocery store company with 7,500 stores worldwide, operates on the single principle of bringing maximum value to customers. Aldi stocks only 3 percent of the products that a typical grocery store carries, and most of its products are store brands. Customers bring their own bags and pick products off pallets rather than store shelves. Yet, Aldi's store brands have consistently beaten the name

Value customer perception that the product quality is excellent for the price offered

brand rivals in taste and quality, and in Germany, Aldi was voted the most trusted name in the grocery business.[47]

When a company defines its quality goal as conformance to specifications, employees must base decisions and actions on whether services and products measure up to standard specifications. In contrast to excellence and value-based definitions of quality that can be somewhat ambiguous, measuring whether products and services are "in spec" is relatively easy. Furthermore, while conformance to specifications (i.e., precise tolerances for a part's weight or thickness) is usually associated with manufacturing, it can be used equally well to control quality in nonmanufacturing jobs. Exhibit 16.4 shows a checklist that a cook or restaurant owner would use to ensure quality when buying fresh fish.

The way in which a company defines quality affects the methods and measures that workers use to control quality. Accordingly, Exhibit 16.5 shows the advantages and disadvantages associated with the excellence, value, and conformance to specification definitions of quality.

3.5 The Innovation and Learning Perspective: Controlling Waste and Pollution

The last part of the balance scorecard, the innovation and learning perspective, addresses the question "Can we continue to improve and create value?" Thus, the innovation and learning perspective involves continuous improvement in ongoing products and services (discussed in Chapter 18), as well as relearning and redesigning the processes by which products and services are created (discussed in Chapter 7). Since these are discussed in more detail elsewhere in the text, this section reviews an increasingly important topic, waste and pollution minimization.

Exhibit 16.6 shows the four levels of waste minimization, from waste disposal, which produces the smallest minimization of waste, to waste prevention and reduction, which produces the greatest minimization.[48] The goals of the top level, *waste prevention and reduction,* are to prevent waste and pollution before they occur, or to reduce them when they do occur. There are three strategies for waste prevention and reduction.

1. *Good housekeeping*—performing regularly scheduled preventive maintenance for offices, plants, and equipment. Quickly fixing leaky valves and making sure machines are running properly so that they don't use more fuel than necessary are examples of good housekeeping.

Exhibit 16.4

Conformance to Specifications Checklist for Buying Fresh Fish

QUALITY CHECKLIST FOR BUYING FRESH FISH		
FRESH WHOLE FISH	**ACCEPTABLE**	**NOT ACCEPTABLE**
Gills	✓ bright red, free of slime, clear mucus	✗ brown to grayish, thick, yellow mucus
Eyes	✓ clear, bright, bulging, black pupils	✗ dull, sunken, cloudy, gray pupils
Smell	✓ inoffensive, slight ocean smell	✗ ammonia, putrid smell
Skin	✓ opalescent sheen, scales adhere tightly to skin	✗ dull or faded color, scales missing or easily removed
Flesh	✓ firm and elastic to touch, tight to the bone	✗ soft and flabby, separating from the bone
Belly cavity	✓ no viscera or blood visible, lining intact, no bone protruding	✗ incomplete evisceration, cuts or protruding bones, off-odor

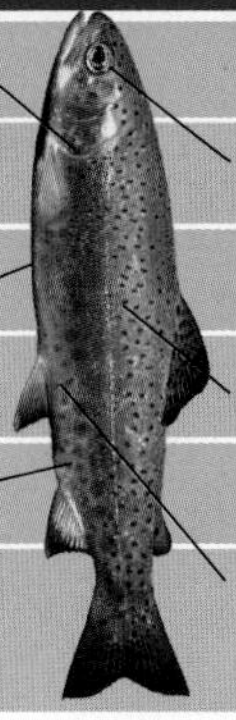

©Oxford Scientific/Jupiter Images

Sources: "A Closer Look: Buy It Fresh, Keep It Fresh," *Consumer Reports Online*, [Online] available at http://www.seagrant.sunysb.edu/SeafoodTechnology/SeafoodMedia/CR02-2001/CR-SeafoodII020101.htm, 20 June 2005; "How to Purchase: Buying Fish," AboutSeaFood Web site, [Online] available at http://www.aboutseafood.com/faqs/purchase1.html, 20 June 2005.

Exhibit 16.5

Advantages and Disadvantages of Different Measures of Quality

QUALITY MEASURE	ADVANTAGES	DISADVANTAGES
Excellence	Promotes clear organizational vision.	Provides little practical guidance for managers.
	Being/providing the "best" motivates and inspires managers and employees.	Excellence is ambiguous. What is it? Who defines it?
Value	Appeals to customers, who "know excellence when they see it."	Difficult to measure and control.
	Customers recognize differences in value.	Can be difficult to determine what factors influence whether a product/service is seen as having value.
	Easier to measure and compare whether products/services differ in value.	Controlling the balance between excellence and cost (i.e., affordable excellence) can be difficult.
Conformance to Specifications	If specifications can be written, conformance to specifications is usually measurable.	Many products/services cannot be easily evaluated in terms of conformance to specifications.
	Should lead to increased efficiency.	Promotes standardization, so may hurt performance when adapting to changes is more important.
	Promotes consistency in quality.	May be less appropriate for services, which are dependent on a high degree of human contact.

Source: Republished with permission of Academy of Management, PO Box 3020, Briar Cliff Manor, NY, 10510-8020. C. A. Reeves & D. A. Bednar, "Defining Quality: Alternatives and Implications," *Academy of Management Review* 19 (1994): 419–445. Reproduced by permission of the publisher via Copyright Clearance Center, Inc.

Exhibit 16.6

Four Levels of Waste Minimization

Waste Prevention & Reduction

Recycle & Reuse

Waste Treatment

Waste Disposal

Source: D. R. May & B. L. Flannery, "Cutting Waste with Employee Involvement Teams," *Business Horizons*, September–October 1995, 28–38. Reprinted with permission from *Business Horizons*, © 1995 by the Trustees at Indiana University, Kelley School of Business.

plant food in new bottles, Terracycle packages its product in used beverage containers and ships the bottles in recycled boxes to the retailers. The company's entire process operation is 100 percent geared toward reducing or eliminating waste.[50]

At the second level of waste minimization, *recycle and reuse*, wastes are reduced by reusing materials as long as possible or by collecting materials for on- or off-site recycling. A growing trend in recycling is *design for disassembly*, where products are designed from the start for easy disassembly, recycling, and reuse once they are no longer usable. For example, the European Union (EU) is moving toward prohibiting companies from selling products unless most of the product and its packaging can be recycled.[51] Since companies, not consumers, will be held responsible for recycling the products they manufacture, they must design their products from the start with recycling in mind.[52] At reclamation centers throughout Europe, companies will have to be able to recover and recycle 80 percent of the parts that go into their original products.[53] Already, under the EU's end-of-life vehicle program, all cars built in Europe since June 2002 are subject to the 80 percent requirement, which rose to 85 percent in 2006 and will be 95 percent by 2015 for autos. Moreover, effective in 2007, the EU requires auto manufacturers to pay to recycle all the cars they made between 1989 and 2002.[54] Today, roughly 160 million cars in Europe are covered by these strict end-of-life regulations.[55]

At the third level of waste minimization, *waste treatment*, companies use biological, chemical, or other processes to turn potentially harmful waste into harmless compounds or useful by-products. For example, during "pickling," a process in the manufacture of steel sheets, the steel is bathed in an acid solution to clean impurities and oxides (which would rust) from its surface. Fortunately, Magnetics International has found a safe, profitable way to treat the pickle juice, which it sprays into a 100-foot-high chamber at 1,200 degrees Fahrenheit to form

2. *Material/product substitution*—replacing toxic or hazardous materials with less harmful materials. As part of its Pollution Prevention Pays program over the last 30 years, 3M eliminated 2.2 billion pounds of pollutants and saved $1 billion by using benign substitutes for toxic solvents in its manufacturing processes.[49]

3. *Process modification*—changing steps or procedures to eliminate or reduce waste. Terracycle is a manufacturer of plant food made from the castings (that is, the droppings) of red worms that have feasted on various types of organic waste. But rather than package the

pure iron oxide that can be transformed into a useful magnetic powderwhich is reused in electric motors, stereo speakers, and refrigerator gaskets.[56]

The fourth and lowest level of waste minimization is *waste disposal.* Wastes that cannot be prevented, reduced, recycled, reused, or treated should be safely disposed of in processing plants or in environmentally secure landfills that prevent leakage and contamination of soil and underground water supplies. For example, with the average computer lasting just three years, approximately 60 million computers come out of service each year.[57] But with lead-containing cathode ray tubes in the monitors, toxic metals in the circuit boards, paint-coated plastic, and metal coatings that can contaminate ground water, old computers can't just be thrown away.[58] Hewlett-Packard has started a unique computer disposal program that allows companies or individual computer users to recycle PCs and electronic equipment. The service is available at **http://www.hp.com/hpinfo/globalcitizenship/environment /recycle/index.html.** With three clicks and a credit card number (prices range from $13 to $34 per item), the old PC equipment will be picked up and properly disposed of.[59] HP makes no profit from this service.

©AP World Wide Photos

By the Numbers

5	ways to achieve control
4	areas to the balanced scorecard
$250	price of a Scooba
$246,000	lifetime value of a supermarket customer
18	years in a row Singapore Airlines has been ranked the best airline in the world

MANAGING INFORMATION

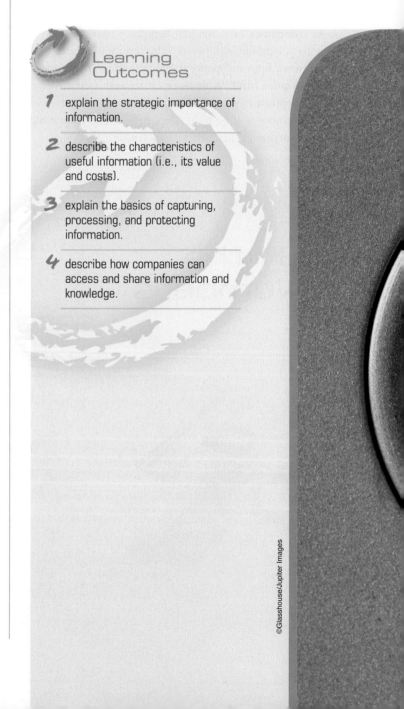

A generation ago, computer hardware and software had little to do with managing business information. Rather than storing information on hard drives, managers stored it in filing cabinets. Instead of uploading daily sales and inventory levels by satellite to corporate headquarters, they mailed hard-copy summaries to headquarters at the end of each month. Instead of word processing, reports were typed on an electric typewriter. Instead of spreadsheets, calculations were made on adding machines. Managers communicated by sticky notes, not email. Phone messages were written down by assistants and coworkers, not left on voice mail. Workers did not use desktop or laptop computers as a daily tool to get work done; they scheduled limited access time to run batch jobs on the mainframe computer (and prayed that the batch job computer code they wrote would work).

Today, a generation later, computer hardware and software are an integral part of managing business information. In large part, this is due to something called **Moore's law.** Gordon Moore is one of the founders of Intel Corporation, which makes 75 percent of the integrated processors used in personal computers. In 1965, Moore predicted that about every two years, computer-processing power would double and its cost would drop by 50 percent.[1] As Exhibit 17.1 shows, Moore was right. Every few years, computer power, as measured by the number of transistors per computer chip, *has* more than doubled. Consequently, the computer sitting in your lap on your desk is not only smaller, but also much cheaper and more powerful than the large mainframe computers used by *Fortune* 500 companies 15 years ago. In fact, if car manufacturers had achieved the same power increases and cost decreases attained by computer manufacturers, a fully outfitted Lexus or Mercedes sedan would cost less than $1,000!

Learning Outcomes

1 explain the strategic importance of information.

2 describe the characteristics of useful information (i.e., its value and costs).

3 explain the basics of capturing, processing, and protecting information.

4 describe how companies can access and share information and knowledge.

Moore's law the prediction that every 18 months, the cost of computing will drop by 50 percent as computer-processing power doubles

Why Information Matters

Raw data are facts and figures. For example, 11, $452, 4, and 26,100 are some data that I used the day I wrote this section of the chapter. However, facts and figures aren't particularly useful unless they have meaning. For example, you probably can't guess what these four pieces of raw data represent, can you? And if you can't, these data are useless. That's why researchers make the distinction between raw data and information. Whereas raw data consist of facts and figures, **information** is useful data that can influence someone's choices and behavior. So what did those four pieces of data mean to me? Well, 11 stands for Channel 11, the local CBS affiliate on which I watched part of the men's PGA golf tournament; $452 is how much it would cost me to rent a minivan for a week if I go skiing over spring break; 4 is for the 4-gigabyte storage card that I want to add to my digital camera (prices

Raw data facts and figures

Information useful data that can influence people's choices and behavior

MGMT

POWER

Exhibit 17.1

Moore's Law

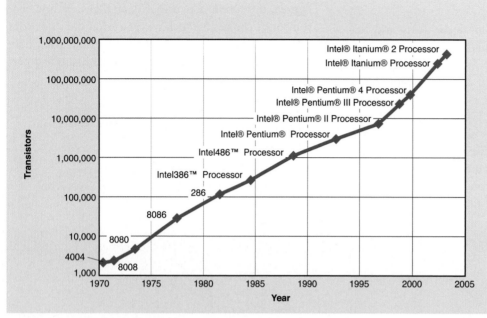

Source: "Moore's Law: Overviews," © Intel Corporation, [Online] available at http://www.intel.com/research/silicon/mooreslaw.htm, 27 June 2005. Reprinted with permission of Intel Corporation.

are low, so I'll probably buy it); and 26,100 means that it's time to get the oil changed in my car.

After reading the next two sections, you should be able to

1 explain the strategic importance of information.

2 describe the characteristics of useful information (i.e., its value and costs).

1 Strategic Importance of Information

In today's hypercompetitive business environments, information, whether it's about furniture delivery, product inventory, pricing, or costs, is as important as capital (i.e., money) for business success. It takes money to get businesses started, but businesses can't survive and grow without the right information. Information has strategic importance for organizations because it can be used to **1.1 obtain first-mover advantage** and

First-mover advantage the strategic advantage that companies earn by being the first to use new information technology to substantially lower costs or to make a product or service different from that of competitors

1.2 sustain a competitive advantage once it has been created.

1.1 First-Mover Advantage

First-mover advantage is the strategic advantage that companies earn by being the first in an industry to use new information technology to substantially lower costs or to differentiate a product or service from that of competitors. By investing $90 billion over the last decade to replace copper coaxial lines with digital lines that feed high-speed cable modems and digital TV cable channels, cable companies convinced two out of every three high-speed Internet subscribers to choose "cable" over DSL service provided by phone companies.[2] While the phone companies are beginning to catch up—they now sign up more new high-speed Internet subscribers than cable providers—does that mean that cable companies' first-mover advantage is slipping away? Well, not yet, as 57 percent of high-speed Internet subscribers still choose cable.[3] And with a grow-

©Sport/Jupiter Images

ing subscriber base for residential phone service, the cable companies are now going after the phone companies' business customers, offering them high-speed Internet and business phone service.[4]

In all, first-mover advantages, like those established by high-speed Internet cable companies, can be sizable. On average, first movers earn a 30 percent market share, compared to 19 percent for the companies that follow.[5] Likewise, over 70 percent of market leaders started as first movers.[6]

1.2 Sustaining a Competitive Advantage

As described above, companies that use information technology to establish first-mover advantage usually have higher market shares and profits. According to the resource-based view of information technology shown in Exhibit 17.2, companies need to address three critical issues in order to sustain a competitive advantage through information technology. First, does the information technology create value for the firm by lowering costs or providing a better product or service? If an information technology doesn't add value, then investing in it would put the firm at a competitive disadvantage to companies that choose information technologies that do add value.

Second, is the information technology the same or different across competing firms? If all the firms have access to the same information technology and use it in the same way, then no firm has an advantage over another (i.e., competitive parity).

Third, is it difficult for another company to create or buy the information technology used by the firm? If so, then the firm has established a sustainable competitive advantage over competitors through information technology. If not, then the competitive advantage is just temporary, and competitors should eventually be able to duplicate the advantages the leading firm has gained from information technology. For more about sustainable competitive advantage and its sources, see Chapter 6 on organizational strategy.

In short, the key to sustaining a competitive advantage is not faster computers, more memory, and larger hard drives. The key is using information technology to continuously improve and support the core functions of a business. Thanks to innovative use of information technology and the largest private satellite network and database system in the world, Wal-Mart's costs are 10 percent lower than its competitors'.[7] Wal-Mart was one of the first retailers to use computers and bar codes to track sales and inventory data and then share those data with suppliers. Today, Wal-Mart's $4 billion supplier network, Retail Link, allows vendors like Ted Haedicke of Coca-Cola to "look at how

Exhibit 17.2

Using Information Technology to Sustain a Competitive Advantage

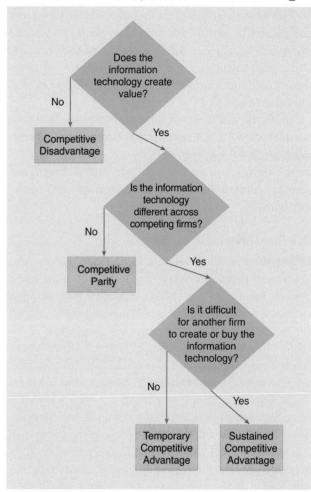

Source: Adapted from F. J. Mata, W. L. Fuerst, & J. B. Barney, "Information Technology and Sustained Competitive Advantage: A Resource-Based Analysis," *MIS Quarterly* 19, no. 4 (December 1995): " 487–505. Reprinted by special permission by the Society for Information Management and the Management Information Systems Research Center at the University of Minnesota.

much [and what kind of] Coke [has] sold . . . and at what prices at any store in the Wal-Mart system." He went on to say, "You can't do that with any other retailer today."[8]

Companies like Wal-Mart that achieve first-mover advantage with information technology and then sustain it with continued investment create a moving target that competitors have difficulty hitting.

2 Characteristics and Costs of Useful Information

Portsmouth, a scenic city of 190,000 on the southern coast of England, attracts 6.5 million visitors a year, primarily because of its historic role as the home of the British Royal Navy. To handle the crush of visitors, Portsmouth relies on 320 buses, all equipped with computers and QDMA (quad-division multiple access) radio communication, which works reliably at speeds up to 250 miles per hour. Because the buses are networked, passengers waiting at bus stops can access a weatherproof computer terminal to find out when the next bus will arrive and what route that bus is taking. They can also check their email, use trip planning software to determine which bus routes to take, or swipe a credit card to purchase tickets.[9]

As Portsmouth's bus system demonstrates, information is useful when it is **2.1 accurate, 2.2 complete, 2.3 relevant,** and **2.4 timely.** However, there can be significant **2.5 acquisition, 2.6 processing, 2.7 storage, 2.8 retrieval,** and **2.9 communication costs associated with useful information.**

2.1 Accurate Information

Information is useful when it is accurate. Before relying on information to make decisions, you must know that the information is correct. But what if it isn't? For example, the restaurant business is notoriously difficult for two reasons. First, it's extremely competitive. Customers in any location typically have hundreds of restaurants from which to choose when dining out. Second, 60 percent of restaurants go out of business within three years. Why? Restaurant owners and managers typically have little accurate information about their businesses. Sure, they know whether they're losing money or not, but they don't know why. Most restaurants don't have accurate information regarding how much alcohol they sell, for example, wine versus beer versus hard liquor, nor do they have information regarding which food dishes, lobster versus swordfish, sell more or are more expensive to prepare. With Avero's Slingshot software, however, restaurants can track this information and more. John Stinson, the head chef at Antonio's in Las Vegas, says, "My bosses keep asking, 'How many did you sell? How many did you sell?' I constantly need to provide the numbers." So Stinson uses Slingshot to examine the data and plan his menus accordingly. For instance, he found out that sea bass sold 196 times in one month, whereas ahi tuna sold 89 times. Since they both cost the same and sell for $29, Stinson reduced costs and eliminated unsold food by cutting his ahi tuna orders from suppliers in half.[10]

2.2 Complete Information

Information is useful when it is complete. Incomplete or missing information makes it difficult to recognize problems and identify potential solutions. For example, dispatchers at Con-way, a freight transportation company, are responsible for choosing truck routes that maximize trailer loads, minimize expenses (time, miles, and fuel), and get drivers home as soon as possible. On a typical day, Con-way's dispatchers must consider the number of trucks (2,100) and available drivers (varies), locations (200 across 25 states), shipments (typically 50,000), and the tonnage and trailer capacity for that day. Though Con-way's dispatchers do extremely well, they typically have only 85 percent of the information they need. Because they lack information about last-minute changes in orders, weather, accidents, driver no-shows, and breakdowns, they end up assigning longer, less efficient truck routes with less than full trucks that ultimately increase costs by $5 million per year.[11]

2.3 Relevant Information

You can have accurate, complete information, but if it doesn't pertain to the problems you're facing, then it's irrelevant and not very useful. Con-way dispatchers not only lacked complete information, they also lacked relevant information about their problems. To address these issues, the company spent $3 million over five years to build a computerized truck route optimization system. This system tracks all customer shipment requests (which can be made as late as 5:15 P.M. each day for the next day's delivery) and communicates by satellite with each truck to monitor truck availability, loads, miles, fuel, weather, and accidents. Then, armed with all of this relevant information, it cranks out optimal truck routes in just seven minutes. On an average day, this system allows Con-way to use 111 fewer trucks and 68 fewer drivers, drive 26,000 fewer miles, and increase the load in each truck by 370 revenue-generating pounds.[12]

2.4 Timely Information

Finally, information is useful when it is timely. To be timely, the information must be available when needed to define a problem or to begin to identify possible solutions. If you've ever thought, "I wish I had known that earlier," then you understand the importance of timely information and the opportunity cost of not having it.

Before relying on information to make decisions, you must know that the information is correct.

2.5 Acquisition Costs

Acquisition cost is the cost of obtaining data that you don't have. For example, among other things, Acxiom, a billion-dollar company, gathers and processes data for direct-mail marketing companies. If you've received an unsolicited, "preapproved" credit card application recently (and who hasn't?), chances are Acxiom helped the credit card company gather information about you. Where does Acxiom get that information? Companies that sell consumer credit reports at a wholesale cost of $1 each. Acxiom also obtains information from retailers. Each time you use your credit card, retailers' checkout scanners gather information about your spending habits and product preferences. Many retailers sell this information to companies like Acxiom that use it for market research. So why pay for this information? The reason is that acquiring it can help credit card companies do a better job of identifying who will mail back a signed credit card application and who will rip the credit card application in half and toss it in the trash.[13]

2.6 Processing Costs

Companies often have massive amounts of data, but not in the form or combination they need. Consequently, **processing cost** is the cost of turning raw data into usable information. For example, Hewlett-Packard, which sells everything from handheld personal digital assistants to personal computers to large computer servers to high definition TVs, has 150,000 employees worldwide. HP also has 85 different data centers in 29 countries, many of which can't "talk" to each other or share data. Why is this so? HP's chief information officer, Randy Mott, explains, "Think about all of the steps involved from actually taking the order to having that order arrive on time, at all of the right locations, with all of the right components included and then promptly follow[ing]-up with accurate line-item billing, taxes, shipping costs, etc." Consequently, because of high processing costs, it's difficult for HP executives located throughout the world to obtain accurate, up-to-date information. It's Mott's job over the next three years to reduce HP's processing costs (i.e., turning raw data into usable information) by consolidating those 85 data centers into just six data warehouses in the United States.[14]

2.7 Storage Costs

Storage cost is the cost of physically or electronically archiving information for later use and retrieval. For instance, Google and Yahoo! and Microsoft Live have incurred large storage costs to make it easy and fast for you to retrieve archived information. How costly can the storage for a simple web search be? Well, consider that each time you conduct a web search at Yahoo, 7,000 computers are activated to return the results of your search to you in less than 18/100 of a second.[15]

> Companies often have **massive amounts** of data,
> but not in the form or combination they **need**.

Acquisition cost the cost of obtaining data that you don't have

Processing cost the cost of turning raw data into usable information

Storage cost the cost of physically or electronically archiving information for later use and retrieval

And with the need for data storage doubling every 14 months, Yahoo!, Google, Microsoft, and other *Fortune* 500 companies are building server farms, large collections of networked computer servers in 750,000 square foot buildings (seven times the size of a Costco), to keep up with demand.

©Jupiter Images

2.8 Retrieval Costs

Retrieval cost is the cost of accessing already-stored and processed information. One of the most common misunderstandings about information is that it is easy and cheap to retrieve once the company has it. Not so. First, you have to find the information. Then, you've got to convince whoever has it to share it with you. Then the information has to be processed into a form that is useful for you. By the time you get the information you need, it may not be timely anymore.

2.9 Communication Costs

Communication cost is the cost of transmitting information from one place to another. For example, the most important information that an electric utility company collects each month is the information from the electric meter attached to the side of your house. Traditionally, electric companies employed meter readers to walk from house to house to gather information that would then be entered into company computers. Now, however, meter readers are losing their jobs to water, gas, and electric meters built with radio frequency (RF) transmitters (see Section 3.1 for more on this technology). The transmitters turn on when a meter reader drives by the house in a utility company van that has a laptop computer specially equipped to receive the RF signals. Such a van, traveling at legal speeds, can read 12,000 to 13,000 meters in an eight-hour day. By contrast, a meter reader on foot would record data from 500 meters per day.[16]

Retrieval cost the cost of accessing already-stored and processed information

Communication cost the cost of transmitting information from one place to another

Getting and Sharing Information

In 1907, Metropolitan Life Insurance built a huge office building in New York City for its brand new, state-of-the-art information technology system. What was this great breakthrough in information management? Card files. That's right, the same card file systems that every library in America used before computers. Metropolitan Life's information "technology" consisted of 20,000 separate file drawers that sat in hundreds of file cabinets more than 15 feet tall. This filing system held 20 million insurance applications, 700,000 accounting books, and 500,000 death certificates. Metropolitan Life employed 61 workers who did nothing but sort, file, and climb ladders to pull files as needed.[17]

Today, if storms, fire, or accidents damage policyholders' property, insurance companies write checks on the spot to cover the losses. When policyholders buy a car, they call their insurance agent from the dealership to activate their insurance before driving off in their new car. And now, insurance companies are marketing their products and services to customers directly from the Internet.

©Stock Connection/Jupiter Images

From card files to Internet files in just under a century, the rate of change in information technology is spectacular. After reading the next two sections, you should be able to

3 explain the basics of capturing, processing, and protecting information.

4 describe how companies can access and share information and knowledge.

3 Capturing, Processing, and Protecting Information

*In this section, you will learn about the information technologies that companies use to **3.1 capture, 3.2 process,** and **3.3 protect information.***

3.1 Capturing Information

There are two basic methods of capturing information: manual and electronic. Manual capture of information is a slow, costly, labor-intensive process, which entails recording and entering data by hand into a data storage device. Consequently, companies are relying more on electronic capture, in which data are electronically recorded and entered into electronic storage devices. Bar codes, radio frequency identification tags, and document scanners are methods of electronically capturing data.

Bar codes represent numerical data by varying the thickness and pattern of vertical bars. The primary advantage that bar codes offer is that the data they represent can be read and recorded in an instant with a handheld or pen-type scanner. Bar codes cut checkout times in half, reduce data entry errors by 75 percent, and save stores money because stockers don't have to go through the labor-intensive process of putting a price tag on each item in the store.[18]

Radio frequency identification (RFID) tags contain minuscule microchips and antennas that transmit information via radio waves.[19] Unlike bar codes, which require direct line-of-sight scanning, RFID tags are read by turning on an RFID reader that, like a radio, tunes into a specific frequency to determine the number *and* location of products, parts, or anything else to which the RFID tags are attached. Turn on an RFID reader, and every RFID tag within the reader's range (from several hundred to several thousand feet) is accounted for. Each year, airlines mishandle or lose four million of the 700 million luggage bags checked by U.S. airline passengers. Las Vegas's McCarran International Airport is reducing those costs by attaching luggage tags with embedded RFID chips. RFID readers accurately read 99 percent of RFID-tagged bags, compared with 80 to 90 percent of bar-coded tags read by optical scanners. That means that of the 70,000 outbound bags that are handled each day at McCarran, only 700 (1%) have to be sorted by hand now that RFID chips are used, compared to 7,000 (10%) to 14,000 (20%) of bags that must be hand sorted when using bar-coded tags.[20]

Because they are inexpensive and easy to use, **electronic scanners,** which convert printed text and pictures into digital images, have become an increasingly popular method of electronically capturing data. The first requirement for a good scanner is a *document feeder* that automatically feeds document pages into the scanner or turns the pages (often with a puff of air) when scanning books or bound documents.[21] Text that has been digitized cannot be searched or edited like the regular text in your word processing software, however, so the second requirement for a good scanner is **optical character recognition** software to scan and convert original or digitized documents into ASCII (American Standard Code for Information Interchange) text or Adobe PDF documents. ASCII text can be searched, read, and edited with standard word processing, email, desktop publishing, database management, and spreadsheet software, and PDF documents can be searched and edited with Adobe's Acrobat software.

Bar code a visual pattern that represents numerical data by varying the thickness and pattern of vertical bars

Radio frequency identification (RFID) tags tags containing minuscule microchips that transmit information via radio waves and can be used to track the number and location of the objects into which the tags have been inserted

Electronic scanners an electronic device that converts printed text and pictures into digital images

Optical character recognition the ability of software to convert digitized documents into ASCII (American Standard Code for Information Interchange) text that can be searched, read, and edited by word processing and other kinds of software

3.2 Processing Information

Processing information means transforming raw data into meaningful information that can be applied to business decision making. Evaluating sales data to determine the best- and worst-selling products, examining repair records to determine product reliability, and monitoring the cost of long-distance phone calls are all examples of processing raw data into meaningful information. And with automated, electronic capture of data, increased processing power, and cheaper and more plentiful ways to store data, managers no longer worry about getting data. Instead, they scratch their heads about how to use the overwhelming amount of data that pours into their businesses every day. Furthermore, most managers know little about statistics and have neither the time nor the inclination to learn how to use them to analyze data.

One promising tool to help managers dig out from under the avalanche of data is data mining. **Data mining** is the process of discovering patterns and relationships in large amounts of data.[22] Data mining works by using complex algorithms such as neural networks, rule induction, and decision trees. If you don't know what those are, that's okay. With data mining, you don't have to. Most managers only need to know that data mining looks for patterns that are already in the data but are too complex for them to spot on their own.

Data mining typically splits a data set in half, finds patterns in one half, and then tests the validity of those patterns by trying to find them again in the second half of the data set. The data typically come from a **data warehouse** that stores huge amounts of data that have been prepared for data mining analysis by being cleaned of errors and redundancy. The data in a data warehouse can then be analyzed using two kinds of data mining. **Supervised data mining** usually begins with the user telling the data mining software to look and test for specific patterns and relationships in a data set. Typically, this is done through a series of "what if?" questions or statements. For instance, a grocery store manager might instruct the data mining software to determine if coupons placed in the Sunday paper increase or decrease sales. By contrast, with **unsupervised data mining,** the user simply tells the data mining software to uncover whatever patterns and relationships it can find in a data set. For example, State Farm Insurance used to have three pricing categories for car insurance, depending on your driving record: preferred for the best drivers, standard for typical drivers, and nonstandard for the worst drivers. Now, however, it has moved to "tiered pricing" based on the 300 different kinds of driving records that its data mining software was able to discover. This allows State Farm to be much more precise in matching 300 different price levels to 300 different kinds of driving records.[23]

Unsupervised data mining is particularly good at identifying association or affinity patterns, sequence patterns, and predictive patterns. It can also identify what data mining "techies" call data clusters.[24] **Association or affinity patterns** occur when two or more database elements tend to occur together in a significant way. Surprisingly, Osco Drugs, based in Chicago, found that beer and diapers tended to be bought together between 5 and 7 p.m. The question, of course, was "why?" The answer, on further review, was fairly straightforward: fathers, who were told by their wives to buy some diapers on their way home, decided to pick up a six-pack for themselves, too.[25]

Sequence patterns occur when two or more database elements occur together in a significant pattern, but with one of the elements preceding the other. StratBridge provides data mining capability to professional sports teams, like basketball's Boston Celtics, to analyze their ticket sales in real time. One of its products is a "live" color-coded graphic of the Celtics stadium seating chart. Prior to a game, colors will change every few seconds to show whether a seat has been sold, at what price, and whether the seat was bought as part of a group purchase or an individual purchase. One season, after the Celtics had been eliminated from playoff eligibility, StratBridge's data mining software connected demographic data, sales data, seat location, and the timing of the seats to indicate that families typically bought tickets behind the basket just a few hours before tipoff. When the Celtics noticed that sales were lagging

---

Processing information transforming raw data into meaningful information

Data mining the process of discovering patterns and relationships in large amounts of data

Data warehouse stores huge amounts of data that have been prepared for data mining analysis by being cleaned of errors and redundancy

Supervised data mining the process when the user tells the data mining software to look and test for specific patterns and relationships in a data set

Unsupervised data mining the process when the user simply tells the data mining software to uncover whatever patterns and relationships it can find in a data set

Association or affinity patterns when two or more database elements tend to occur together in a significant way

Sequence patterns when two or more database elements occur together in a significant pattern, but one of the elements precedes the other for those seats, they bundled those seats together in a family four-pack, dropped the prices, added food coupons, and then emailed a list of local families who had previously purchased tickets to the game. As a result, all of those unsold seats sold. Says Shawn Sullivan, a vice-president for the team, "If we'd done our usual newspaper ad [for those seats], there'd have been no return at all."[26]

Predictive patterns are just the opposite of association or affinity patterns. Whereas association or affinity patterns look for database elements that seem to go together, **predictive patterns** help identify database elements that are different. On the day after Thanksgiving, typically the busiest shopping day of the year, Wal-Mart's data mining indicated that sales were unexpectedly slow for a boxed computer and printer combination that was offered at an extremely good price. Sales were slow everywhere, except one Wal-Mart store where sales greatly exceeded expectations. After noting the difference, headquarters called the store manager who said that the products were displayed in an open box that made it clear to customers that the low price was for the computer *and* the printer. Sales took off at all stores after headquarters relayed this simple message, "Open the box."[27]

Data clusters are the last kind of pattern found by data mining. **Data clusters** occur when three or more database elements occur together (i.e., cluster) in a significant way. For example, after analyzing several years' worth of repair and warranty claims, Ford Motor Company might find that, compared with cars built in its Chicago plant, the cars it builds in Atlanta (first element) are more likely to have problems with overtightened fan belts (second element) that break (third element) and result in overheated engines (fourth element), ruined radiators (fifth element), and payments for tow trucks (sixth element), which are paid for by Ford's three-year, 36,000 mile warranty.

Traditionally, data mining has been very expensive and very complex. Today, however, data mining services and analysis are much more affordable and within reach of most companies' budgets. And, if it follows the path of most technologies, it will become even easier and cheaper to use in the future.

3.3 Protecting Information

Protecting information is the process of ensuring that data are reliably and consistently retrievable in a usable format for authorized users, but no one else. For instance, when customers purchase prescription medicine

at Drugstore.com, an online drugstore and health-aid retailer, they want to be confident that their medical and credit card information is available only to them, the pharmacists at Drugstore.com, and their doctors. In fact, Drugstore.com has an extensive privacy policy (click "Privacy Policy" at **http://www.drugstore.com**) to make sure this is the case.

Companies like Drugstore.com find it necessary to protect information because of the numerous security threats to data and data security listed in Exhibit 17.3. People inside and outside companies can steal or destroy company data in various ways including denial-of-service Web server attacks that can bring down some of the busiest and best-run sites on the Internet; viruses and spyware/adware that spread quickly and can result in data loss and business disruption; keystroke monitoring in which every mouse click and keystroke you make is monitored, stored, and sent to unauthorized users; password cracking software that steals supposedly secure passwords; and phishing, where fake but real-looking emails and Web sites trick users into sharing personal information (user names, passwords, account numbers) that leads to unauthorized account access. Indeed, on average, 19 percent of computers are infected with viruses, 80 percent have spyware, and only one-third are running behind a protected firewall (discussed shortly). Studies show that the threats listed in Exhibit 17.3 are so widespread that automatic attacks will begin on an unprotected computer just 15 seconds after it connects to the Internet.[28]

As shown in the right-hand column of Exhibit 17.3, numerous steps can be taken to secure data and data networks. Some of the most important are authentication and authorization, firewalls, antivirus software for PCs and email servers, data encryption, and virtual private networks.[29] We will review those steps and then finish this section with a brief review of the dangers of wireless networks, which are exploding in popularity.

Two critical steps are required to make sure that

Predictive patterns patterns that help identify database elements that are different

Data clusters when three or more database elements occur together (i.e., cluster) in a significant way

Protecting information the process of ensuring that data are reliably and consistently retrievable in a usable format for authorized users, but no one else

Exhibit 17.3

Security Threats to Data and Data Networks

Security Problem	Source	Affects	Severity	The Threat	The Solution
Denial of service Web server attacks and corporate network attacks	Internet hackers	All servers	High	Loss of data, disruption of service, and theft of service.	Implement firewall, password control, server-side review, threat monitoring, and bug fixes, and turn PCs off when not in use.
Password cracking software and unauthorized access to PCs	Local area network, Internet	All users, especially digital subscriber line and cable Internet users	High	Hackers take over PCs. Privacy can be invaded. Corporate users' systems are exposed to other machines on the network.	Close ports and firewalls, disable file and print sharing, and use strong passwords.
Viruses, worms, Trojan horses, and rootkits	Email, downloaded and distributed software	All users	Moderate to high	Monitor activities and cause data loss and file deletion: compromise security by sometimes concealing their presence.	Use antivirus software and firewalls, and control Internet access.
Spyware, adware, malicious scripts and applets	Rogue Web pages	All users	Moderate to high	Invade privacy, intercept passwords, and damage files or file system.	Disable browser script support and use security, blocking, and spyware/adware software.
Email snooping	Hackers on your network and the Internet	All users	Moderate to high	People read your email from intermediate servers or packets, or they physically access your machine.	Encrypt message, ensure strong password protection, and limit physical access to machines.
Keystroke monitoring	Trojan horses, people with direct access to PCs	All users	High	Records everything typed at the keyboard and intercepts keystrokes before password masking or encryption occurs.	Use antivirus software to catch Trojan horses, control Internet access to transmission, and implement system monitoring and physical access control.
Phishing	Hackers on your network and the Internet	All users, including customers	High	Fake, but real-looking, emails and Web sites that trick users into sharing personal information on what they wrongly thought was the company's Web site. This leads to unauthorized account access.	Educate and warn users and customers about the dangers. Encourage both not to click on potentially fake URLs, which might take them to phishing Web sites. Instead, have them type your company's URL into the Web browser.
Spam	Email	All users and corporations	Mild to high	Clogs and overloads email servers and inboxes with junk mail. HTML-based spam may be used for profiling and identifying users.	Filter known spam sources and senders on email servers, and have users create further lists of approved and unapproved senders on their personal computers.
Cookies	Web sites you visit	Individual users	Mild to moderate	Trace Web usage and permit the creation of personalized Web pages that track behavior and interest profiles.	Use cookie managers to control and edit cookies, and use ad blockers.

Sources: K. Bannan, "Look Out: Watching You, Watching Me," *PC Magazine*, July 2002, 99; A. Dragoon, "Fighting Phish, Fakes, and Frauds," *CIO*, 1 September 2004, 33; B. Glass, "Are You Being Watched?" *PC Magazine*, 23 April 2002, 54; K. Karagiannis, "DDoS: Are You Next?" *PC Magazine*, January 2003, 79; B. Machrone, "Protect & Defend," *PC Magazine*, 27 June 2000, 168–181.

You Are How You Type

A new form of biometrics involves identifying people by the way they type. After entering your ID and a code, BioPassword's artificial-intelligence software monitors your speed, how long you take before selecting the keys, and the rhythm you use to pound out your text. The more you use the software, the better it can identify you as the typist, making it nearly impossible for someone to hack into your computer. BioPassword is as accurate as finger and iris scans.

Source: J. Manez, "We Got the Beat," *Fast Company*, September 2006.

©Thinkstock/Jupiter Images

data can be accessed by authorized users and no one else. One is **authentication,** that is, making sure users are who they claim to be.[30] The other is **authorization,** that is, granting authenticated users approved access to data, software, and systems.[31] For example, when an ATM prompts you to enter your personal identification number (PIN), the bank is authenticating that you are you. Once you've been authenticated, you are authorized to access your funds and no one else's. Of course, as anyone who has lost a PIN or password or had one stolen knows, user authentication systems are not foolproof. In particular, users create security risks by not changing their default account passwords (such as birth dates) or by using weak passwords such as names ("Larry") or complete words ("football") that are quickly guessed by password cracker software.[32]

This is why many companies are now turning to **two-factor authentication,** which is based on what users know, such as a password, and what they have, such as a secure ID card. For example, to log onto their computer accounts, employees at Bloomberg, a global provider of business news, data, and analysis, must enter a password, such as a four-digit personal identification number, plus a secure number that changes every 60 seconds and is displayed on the tiny screen of the secure electronic ID (about the

size of a pack of gum) they carry. For these same reasons, some companies are turning to biometrics for authentication. With **biometrics** such as fingerprint recognition or iris scanning, users are identified by unique, measurable body features.[33] Of course, since some fingerprint scanners can be fooled by fingerprint molds, some companies take security measures even further by requiring users to simultaneously scan their fingerprint *and* insert a secure, smart card containing a digital file of their fingerprint. This is another form of two-factor authentication.

Unfortunately, stolen or cracked passwords are not the only way for hackers and electronic thieves to gain access to an organization's computer resources. Unless special safeguards are put in place, every time corporate users are online there's literally nothing between their personal computers and the Internet (home users with high-speed DSL or cable Internet access face the same risks). Hackers can access files, run programs, and control key parts of computers if precautions aren't taken. To reduce these risks, companies use **firewalls,** hardware or software devices that sit between the computers in an internal organizational network and outside networks, such as the Internet. Firewalls filter and check incoming and outgoing data. They prevent company insiders from accessing unauthorized sites or from sending confidential company information to people outside the company. Firewalls also prevent outsiders from identifying and gaining access to company computers and data. Indeed, if a firewall is working properly, the computers behind the company firewall literally cannot be seen or accessed by outsiders.

A **virus** is a program or piece of code that, without your knowledge, attaches itself to other programs on your computer and can trigger anything from a harmless flashing message to the reformatting of your hard

Authentication making sure potential users are who they claim to be

Authorization granting authenticated users approved access to data, software, and systems

Two-factor authentication authentication based on what users know, such as a password, and what they have in their possession, such as a secure ID card or key

Biometrics identifying users by unique, measurable body features, such as fingerprint recognition or iris scanning

Firewall a protective hardware or software device that sits between the computers in an internal organizational network and outside networks, such as the Internet

Virus a program or piece of code that, against your wishes, attaches itself to other programs on your computer and can trigger anything from a harmless flashing message to the reformatting of your hard drive to a systemwide network shutdown

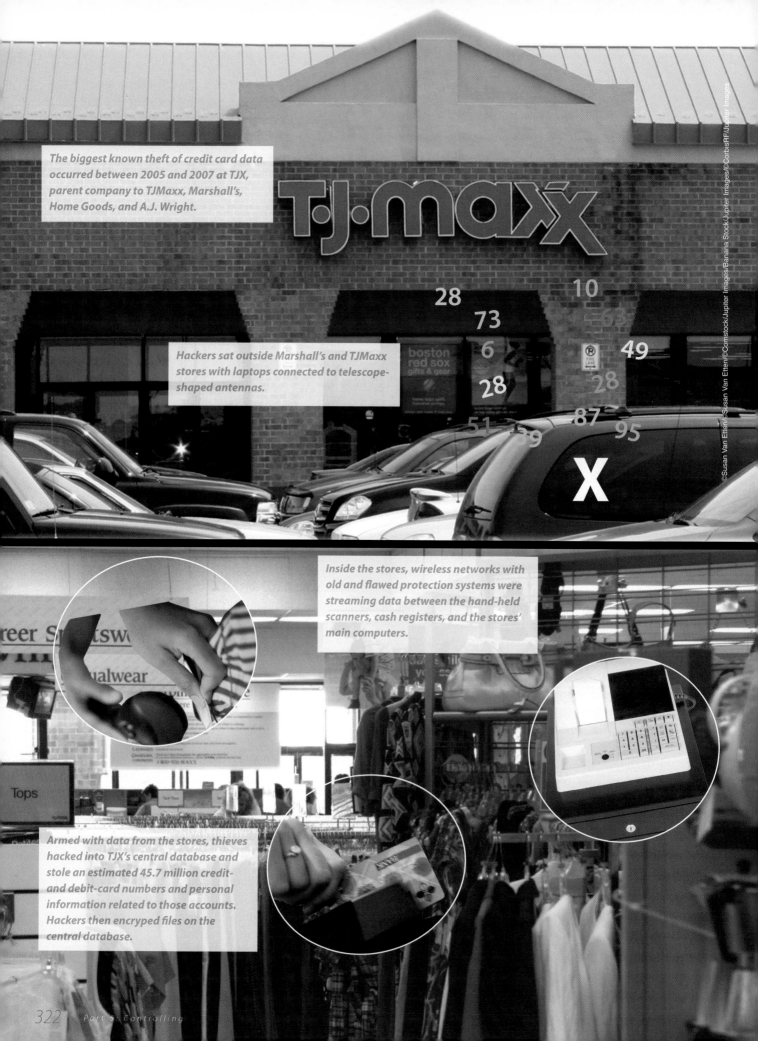

The biggest known theft of credit card data occurred between 2005 and 2007 at TJX, parent company to TJMaxx, Marshall's, Home Goods, and A.J. Wright.

Hackers sat outside Marshall's and TJMaxx stores with laptops connected to telescope-shaped antennas.

Inside the stores, wireless networks with old and flawed protection systems were streaming data between the hand-held scanners, cash registers, and the stores' main computers.

Armed with data from the stores, thieves hacked into TJX's central database and stole an estimated 45.7 million credit- and debit-card numbers and personal information related to those accounts. Hackers then encryped files on the central database.

drive to a systemwide network shutdown. You used to have to do or run something to get a virus, such as double-clicking an infected email attachment. Today's viruses are much more threatening. In fact, with some viruses, just being connected to a network can infect your computer. *Antivirus software for personal computers* scans email, downloaded files, and computer hard drives, disk drives, and memory to detect and stop computer viruses from doing damage. However, this software is effective only to the extent that users of individual computers have and use up-to-date versions. With new viruses appearing all the time, users should update their antivirus software weekly or, even better, configure their virus software to automatically check for, download, and install updates. By contrast, *corporate antivirus software* automatically scans email attachments, such as Microsoft Word documents, graphics, or text files, as they come across the company email server. It also monitors and scans all file downloads across company databases and network servers. So, while antivirus software for personal computers prevents individual computers from being infected, corporate antivirus software for email servers, databases, and network servers adds another layer of protection by preventing infected files from multiplying and being sent to others.

Another way of protecting information is to encrypt sensitive data. **Data encryption** transforms data into complex, scrambled digital codes that can be unencrypted only by authorized users who possess unique decryption keys. One method of data encryption is to use products by PGP (Pretty Good Privacy) (**http://www.pgp.com**) to encrypt the files stored on personal computers or network servers and databases. This is especially important with laptop computers, which are easily stolen. After a Boeing employee's laptop PC was stolen from his hotel room, the company implemented a training program that requires managers and employees to have data encryption software installed on their laptops and become certified in using it. Those not following the encryption procedures can be reprimanded and even fired.[34]

And, with people increasingly gaining unauthorized access to email messages—email snooping—it's also important to encrypt sensitive email messages and file attachments. You can use a system called "public key encryption" to do so. First, give copies of your "public key" to anyone who sends you files or email. Have the sender use the public key, which is actually a piece of software, to encrypt files before sending them to you. The only way to decrypt the files is with a companion "private key" that

you keep to yourself. If you want to learn more or want to begin encrypting your own files, download a free copy of Pretty Good Privacy from **http://web.mit.edu/pgp/**.

Although firewalls can protect personal computers and network servers connected to the corporate network, people away from their offices (e.g., salespeople, business travelers, telecommuters who work at home) who interact with their company networks via the Internet face a security risk. Because Internet data are not encrypted, packet sniffer software (see Exhibit 17.3) easily allows hackers to read everything sent or received, except files that have been encrypted before sending. Previously, the only practical solution was to have employees dial in to secure company phone lines for direct access to the company network. Of course, with international and long-distance phone calls, the costs quickly added up. Now, **virtual private networks (VPNs)** have solved this problem by using software to encrypt all Internet data at both ends of the transmission process. Instead of making long-distance calls, employees connect to the Internet. But, unlike typical Internet connections in which Internet data packets are unencrypted, the VPN encrypts the data sent by employees outside the company computer network, decrypts the data when they arrive within the company network, and does the same when data are sent back to the computer outside the network.

Alternatively, many companies are now adopting Web-based **secure sockets layer (SSL) encryption** to provide secure off-site access to data and programs. If you've ever entered your credit card in a Web browser to make an online purchase, you've used SSL technology to encrypt and protect that information. SSL encryption is being used if a gold lock (Internet Explorer) or a gold key (Netscape) appears along the bottom of your Web browser. SSL encryption works the same way in the workplace. Managers and employees who aren't at the office simply connect to the Internet, open a Web browser, and then enter a user name and password to gain access to SSL encrypted data and programs.

Data encryption the transformation of data into complex, scrambled digital codes that can be unencrypted only by authorized users who possess unique decryption keys

Virtual private network (VPN) software that securely encrypts data sent by employees outside the company network, decrypts the data when they arrive within the company computer network, and does the same when data are sent back to employees outside the network

Secure sockets layer (SSL) encryption Internet browser–based encryption that provides secure off-site Web access to some data and programs

Finally, many companies now have wireless networks, which make it possible for anybody with a laptop and a wireless card to access the company network from anywhere in the office. Though wireless networks come equipped with security and encryption capabilities that, in theory, permit only authorized users to access the wireless network, those capabilities are easily bypassed with the right tools. Furthermore, for ease of installation, many wireless networks are shipped with their security and encryption capabilities turned off.[35] Plus, although it's better to have it turned on than off, be wary of the WEP (Wired Equivalent Privacy) security protocol, which is easily compromised. See the Wi-Fi Alliance Web site at **http://www.wi-fi.org** for the latest information on wireless security and encryption protocols that provide much stronger protection for your company's wireless network.

4 Accessing and Sharing Information and Knowledge

Today, information technologies are letting companies communicate data, share data, and provide data access to workers, managers, suppliers, and customers in ways that were unthinkable just a few years ago. *After reading this section, you should be able to explain how companies use information technology to improve 4.1 internal access and sharing of information, 4.2 external access and sharing of information, and 4.3 the sharing of knowledge and expertise.*

4.1 Internal Access and Sharing

Executives, managers, and workers inside the company use three kinds of information technology to access and share information: executive information systems, intranets, and portals. An **executive information system (EIS)** uses internal and external sources of data to provide managers and executives the information they need to monitor

and analyze organizational performance.[36] The goal of an EIS is to provide accurate, complete, relevant, and timely information to managers.

Managers at Lands' End, the Web/mail-order company, use their EIS, which they call their "dashboard," to see how well the company is running. With just a few mouse clicks and basic commands such as *find, compare,* and *show,* the EIS displays costs, sales revenues, and other kinds of data in color-coded charts and graphs. Managers can drill down to view and compare data by region, state, time period, and product. Frank Giannantonio, Lands' End's CIO, says, "Our dashboards include an early alert system that utilizes key performance metrics to target items selling faster than expected and gives our managers the ability to adjust product levels far earlier than they were able to do in the past."[37]

Intranets are private company networks that allow employees to easily access, share, and publish information using Internet software. Intranet Web sites are just like external Web sites, but the firewall separating the internal company network from the Internet permits only authorized internal access.[38] Companies typically use intranets to share information (e.g., about benefits) and to replace paper forms with online forms. At IBM, however, the company intranet is used for electronic meetings, instant messaging, online libraries of policies and procedures, distance learning and training, online reimbursement of travel expenses, and travel schedules and reservations.[39]

Finally, corporate portals are a hybrid of executive information systems and intranets. While an EIS provides

Executive information system (EIS) a data processing system that uses internal and external data sources to provide the information needed to monitor and analyze organizational performance

Intranets private company networks that allow employees to easily access, share, and publish information using Internet software

Intranets Are Evolving to Include:

- collaboration tools, like wikis, where team members can post all relevant information for a project they're working on together
- customizable email accounts
- presence awareness (whether someone you are looking for on the network is in the office, in a meeting, working from home, etc.)
- instant messaging
- simultaneous access to files for virtual team members

managers and executives with the information they need to monitor and analyze organizational performance, and intranets help companies distribute and publish information and forms within the company, **corporate portals** allow company managers and employees to access customized information *and* complete specialized transactions using a Web browser. Hillman Group is the company that sells the nuts, bolts, fasteners, keys, and key cutting machines that you find in Home Depot, Lowes, Ace, and nearly every other hardware store. Hillman's 1,800 employees produce products for 25,000 customers. Hillman's portal contains a real-time revenue report for every product with updated sales and production numbers on a continuous basis. Today, Hillman's portal contains 75 specialized reports that are accessed by 800 managers and employees.[40]

4.2 External Access and Sharing

Historically, companies have been unable or reluctant to let outside groups have access to corporate information. Now, however, a number of information technologies—electronic data interchange, extranets, Web services, and the Internet—are making it easier to share company data with external groups like suppliers and customers. They're also reducing costs, increasing productivity by eliminating manual information processing (70 percent of the data output from one company, like a purchase order, ends up as data input at another company, such as a sales invoice or shipping order), reducing data entry errors, improving customer service, and speeding communications.

With **electronic data interchange,** or **EDI,** two companies convert purchase and ordering information to a standardized format to enable direct electronic transmission of that information from one company's computer system to the other company's system. For example, when a Wal-Mart checkout clerk drags an Apple iPod across the checkout scanner, Wal-Mart's computerized inventory system automatically reorders another iPod through the direct EDI connection that its computer has with Apple's manufacturing and shipping computer. No one at Wal-Mart or Apple fills out paperwork. No one makes phone calls. There are no delays to wait to find out whether Apple has the iPod in stock. The transaction takes place instantly and automatically because the data from both companies were translated into a standardized, shareable, compatible format.

In EDI, the different purchasing and ordering applications in each company interact automatically without any human input. No one has to lift a finger to click a mouse, enter data, or hit the "return" key. An **extranet,** by contrast, allows companies to exchange information and conduct transactions by purposely providing outsiders with direct, Web browser–based access to authorized parts of a company's intranet or information system. Typically, user names and passwords are required to access an extranet.[41] For example, to make sure that its distribution trucks don't waste money by running half empty (or make late deliveries to customers because it waited to ship until the trucks were full), General Mills uses an extranet to

Corporate portal a hybrid of executive information systems and intranets that allows managers and employees to use a Web browser to gain access to customized company information and to complete specialized transactions

Electronic data interchange (EDI) when two companies convert their purchase and ordering information to a standardized format to enable the direct electronic transmission of that information from one company's computer system to the other company's computer system

Extranets networks that allow companies to exchange information and conduct transactions with outsiders by providing them direct, Web-based access to authorized parts of a company's intranet or information system provide Web-based access to its trucking database to 20 other companies that ship their products over similar distribution routes. When other companies are ready to ship products, they log on to General Mills' trucking database, check the availability, and then enter the shipping load, place, and pickup time. Thus, by sharing shipping capacity on its trucks, General Mills can run its trucks fully loaded all the time. In several test areas, General Mills saved 7 percent on shipping costs, or nearly $2 million in the first year. Expanding the program company-wide is producing even larger cost savings.[42]

Finally, similar to the way in which extranets are used to handle transactions with suppliers and distributors, companies are reducing paperwork and manual

comfortable using the check-in kiosk for flights. Using a self-service kiosk for car rental is a natural progression."[43] Alamo has found that kiosks reduce check-in times by 50 percent.

In the long run, the goal is to link customer Internet sites with company intranets (or EDI) and extranets so that everyone—all the employees and managers within a company, and the suppliers and distributors outside the company—who is involved in providing a service or making a product for a customer is automatically notified when a purchase is made. Companies that use EDI, extranets, and the Internet to share data with customers and suppliers achieve increases in productivity 2.7 times larger than those that don't.[44]

4.3 Sharing Knowledge and Expertise

At the beginning of the chapter, we distinguished between raw data, which consist of facts and figures, and information, which consists of useful data that influence someone's choices and behavior. One more important distinction needs to be made, namely, that data and information are

> Knowledge does not reside in information.
> Knowledge resides in **people**.

information processing by using the Internet to electronically automate transactions with customers. For example, most airlines have automated the ticketing process by eliminating paper tickets altogether. Simply buy an e-ticket via the Internet, and then check yourself in online by printing your boarding pass from your personal computer or from a kiosk at the airport. Together, Internet purchases, ticketless travel, and automated check-ins have fully automated the purchase of airline tickets. Self-service kiosk uses are expanding, too. For example, Alamo Rent-a-Car has introduced kiosks that print rental agreements, permit upgrades to nicer cars, and allow customers to add additional drivers or buy rental insurance. Jerry Dow, Alamo's chief marketing officer, says, "Customers are already

not the same as knowledge. **Knowledge** is the understanding that one gains from information. Importantly, knowledge does not reside in information. Knowledge resides in people. That's why companies hire consultants and why family doctors refer patients to specialists. Unfortunately, it can be quite expensive to employ consultants, specialists, and experts. So companies have begun using two information technologies, decision support systems and expert systems, to capture and share the knowledge of consultants, specialists, and experts with other managers and workers.

Knowledge the understanding that one gains from information

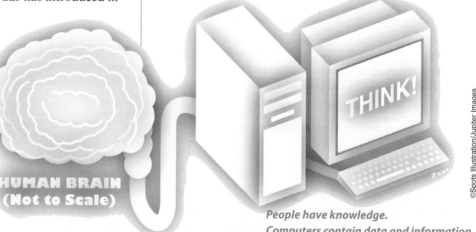

HUMAN BRAIN (Not to Scale)

THINK!

People have knowledge.
Computers contain data and information.

Whereas an executive information system speeds up and simplifies the acquisition of information, a **decision support system (DSS)** helps managers understand problems and potential solutions by acquiring and analyzing information with sophisticated models and tools.[45] Furthermore, whereas EIS programs are broad in scope and permit managers to retrieve all kinds of information about a company, DSS programs are usually narrow in scope and targeted toward helping managers solve specific kinds of problems. DSS programs have been developed to help managers pick the shortest and most efficient routes for delivery trucks, select the best combination of stocks for investors, and schedule the flow of inventory through complex manufacturing facilities.

©Topham/The Image Works

It's important to understand that DSS programs don't replace managerial decision making; they improve it by furthering managers' and workers' understanding of the problems they face and the solutions that might work. Though used by just 2 percent of physicians, medical DSS programs hold the promise of helping doctors make more accurate patient diagnoses. A British study of 88 cases misdiagnosed or initially misdiagnosed (to be correctly diagnosed much later) found that a medical DSS made the right diagnosis 69 percent of the time.[46] With a medical DSS, doctors enter patient data, such as age, gender, weight, and medical symptoms. The medical DSS then produces a list of diseases and conditions, ranked by probability, low or high, or by medical specialty, such as cardiology or oncology. For instance, when emergency room physician Dr. Harold Cross treated a 10-year-old boy who had been ill with nausea and dizziness for two weeks, he wasn't sure what was wrong, given that the boy had a healthy appetite, no abdominal pain, and just one brief headache. However, when the medical DSS that Dr. Cross used suggested a possible problem in the back of the boy's brain, he ordered an MRI scan that revealed a tumor, which was successfully removed two days later. Says Dr. Cross, "My personal knowledge of the literature and physical findings would not have prompted me to suspect a brain tumor."[47]

Expert systems are created by capturing the specialized knowledge and decision rules used by experts and experienced decision makers. They permit nonexpert em-

ployees to draw on this expert knowledge base to make decisions. Most expert systems work by using a collection of "if–then" rules to sort through information and recommend a course of action. For example, let's say that you're using your American Express card to help your spouse celebrate a promotion. After dinner and a movie, the two of you stroll by a travel office with a Las Vegas poster in its window. Thirty minutes later, caught up in the moment, you find yourselves at the airport ticket counter trying to purchase last-minute tickets to Vegas. But there's just one problem. American Express didn't approve your purchase. In fact, the ticket counter agent is now on the phone with an American Express customer service agent.

So what put a temporary halt to your weekend escape to Vegas? An expert system that American Express calls "Authorizer's Assistant."[48] The first "if–then" rule that prevented your purchase was the rule "*if* a purchase is much larger than the cardholder's regular spending habits, *then* deny approval of the purchase." This if–then rule, just one of 3,000, is built into American Express's transaction-processing system that handles thousands of purchase requests per second. Now that the American Express customer service agent is on the line, he or she is prompted by the Authorizer's Assistant to ask the ticket counter agent to examine your identification. You hand over your driver's license and another credit card to prove you're you. Then the ticket agent asks for your address, phone number, Social Security number, and your mother's maiden name and relays the information to American Express. Finally, your ticket purchase is approved. Why? Because you met the last series of "if–then" rules. *If* the purchaser can provide proof of identity and *if* the purchaser can provide personal information that isn't common knowledge, *then* approve the purchase.

Decision support system (DSS) an information system that helps managers understand specific kinds of problems and potential solutions and analyze the impact of different decision options using "what if" scenarios

Expert system an information system that contains the specialized knowledge and decision rules used by experts and experienced decision makers so that nonexperts can draw on this knowledge base to make decisions

MANAGING SERVICE AND MANUFACTURING OPERATIONS

Managing for Productivity and Quality

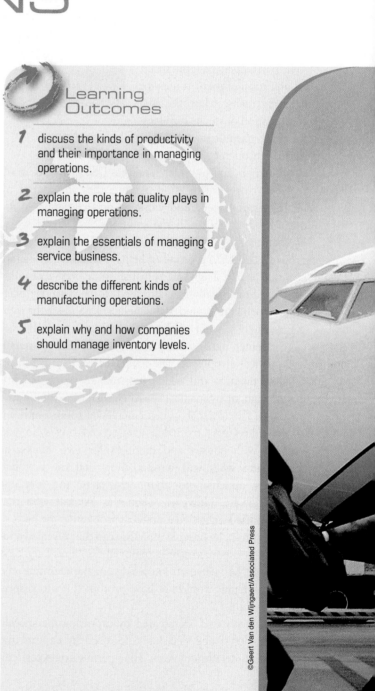

Furniture manufacturers, hospitals, restaurants, automakers, airlines, and many other kinds of businesses struggle to find ways to efficiently produce quality products and services and then deliver them in a timely manner. Modeled after U.S.-based Southwest Airlines, Ryanair achieves dramatically lower prices through aggressive price cutting, much higher productivity, and quality customer service. Want a frequent-flier plan? You won't find one at Ryanair. It's too expensive. Want a meal on your flight? Pack a lunch. Ryanair doesn't even serve peanuts because it takes too much time (i.e., expense) to get them out of the seat cushions. Passengers enter and exit the planes using old-fashioned, rolling stairs because they're quicker and cheaper than extendable boarding gates. As a result of such cost-cutting moves, Ryanair does more with less and thus has higher productivity. For example, most airlines break even on their flights when they're 75 percent full, but even with its incredibly low prices, Ryanair's productivity allows it to break even when its planes are only half full. And with this low breakeven point, Ryanair attracts plenty of customers who enable it to fill most of its seats (84 percent) and earn 20 percent net profit margins. Finally, because of its extremely low prices (and its competitors' extremely high prices), Ryanair has increased passenger traffic and profits for 17 straight years.[1]

Learning Outcomes

1 discuss the kinds of productivity and their importance in managing operations.

2 explain the role that quality plays in managing operations.

3 explain the essentials of managing a service business.

4 describe the different kinds of manufacturing operations.

5 explain why and how companies should manage inventory levels.

©Geert Van den Wijngaert/Associated Press

After reading the next two sections, you should be able to

1   discuss the kinds of productivity and their importance in managing operations.

2   explain the role that quality plays in managing operations.

1 Productivity

At their core, organizations are production systems. Companies combine inputs, such as labor, raw materials, capital, and knowledge, to produce outputs in the form of finished products or services. **Productivity** is a measure of performance that indicates how many inputs it takes to produce or create an output.

$$\text{Productivity} = \frac{\text{Outputs}}{\text{Inputs}}$$

The fewer inputs it takes to create an output (or the greater the output from one input), the higher the productivity. For example, a car's gas mileage is a common measure of productivity. A car that gets 35 miles (output) per gallon (input) is more productive and fuel efficient than a car that gets 18 miles per gallon.

Productivity a measure of performance that indicates how many inputs it takes to produce or create an output

*Let's examine **1.1 why productivity matters** and **1.2 the different kinds of productivity**.*

1.1 Why Productivity Matters

Why does productivity matter? For companies, higher productivity, that is, doing more with less, results in lower costs. In turn, doing more with less can lead to lower prices, faster service, higher market share, and higher profits. For example, at fast-food restaurants, every second saved in the drive-through lane increases sales by 1 percent. Furthermore, increasing the efficiency of drive-through service by 10 percent adds nearly 10 percent to a fast-food restaurant's sales. And with 65 percent of all fast-food restaurant sales coming from the drive-through window, it's no wonder that Wendy's (average drive-through time of 135.1 seconds), McDonald's (average time of 163.9 seconds), and Burger King (average time of 166 seconds) continue to look for ways to shorten the time it takes to process a drive-through order.[2] Productivity matters so much at the drive-through that McDonald's is experimenting with outsourcing. At roughly 50 McDonald's franchises around the country, drive-through orders are taken by someone at a California call center. An operator can take orders from customers at restaurants in Honolulu one minute, and from Gulfport, Mississippi the next. During the 10 seconds it takes for a car to pull away from the microphone at the drive-through, a call center operator can take the order of a different customer who has pulled up to the microphone at another

less, they can raise employee wages without increasing prices or sacrificing normal profits. For instance, when I wrote this chapter, recent government economic data indicated that companies were paying workers 3.5 percent more than in the previous year. But, since workers were producing 5.1 percent more than they had the year before, real labor costs had actually decreased by 1.6 percent.[4] For example, the average American family earned approximately $56,914 in 2005. If productivity grows 1 percent a year, that family's income will increase to $71,351 in 2030. But if productivity grows 2 percent a year, their annual income in 2030 will be $90,384, more than $18,000 higher, and that's without working longer hours.[5] Thanks to long-term increases in business productivity, the average American family today earns 33 percent more than the average family in 1980 and 223 percent more than the average family in 1953—and that's after accounting for inflation.[6]

Rising income stemming from increased productivity creates numerous other benefits as well. For example, with productivity increases exceeding 3.8 percent per year from 1999 to 2005, the U.S. economy created three million new jobs.[7] In 2005 alone, the economy added two million jobs.[8] And when more people have jobs that pay more, they give more to charity. For example, in 2005 Americans donated over $260 billion to charities, 6.1 percent more than they gave in 2004.[9]

Another benefit of productivity is that it makes products more affordable or better. For example, while infla-

> **Productivity matters** because it results in a **higher standard** of living.

restaurant, even if it's thousands of miles away. According to Jon Anton, co-founder of Bronco Communications, which operates the call center for McDonald's, the goal is "saving seconds to make millions," because more efficient service can lead to more sales and lower labor costs.[3]

For countries, productivity matters because it results in a higher standard of living. One way productivity leads to a higher standard of living is through increased wages. When companies can do more with

tion has pushed the average cost of a car to about $29,400 (after incentives and discounts), increases in productivity have actually made cars cheaper.[10] In 1960, the average family needed 26 weeks of income to pay for the average car. Today, the average family needs only 23.6 weeks of income—and today's car is loaded with accessories that weren't even available in 1960, including air bags, power steering and brakes, power windows, cruise control, stereo/CD/DVD players, seat warmers, air-conditioning, and satellite navigation.[11] So, in terms of real purchasing power, productivity gains have actually made today's $29,400 car cheaper than that $2,000 car in 1960.[12]

1.2 Kinds of Productivity

Two common measures of productivity are partial productivity and multifactor productivity. **Partial productivity** indicates how much of a particular kind of input it takes to produce an output.

$$\text{Partial Productivity} = \frac{\text{Outputs}}{\text{Single Kind of Input}}$$

Labor is one kind of input that is frequently used when determining partial productivity. *Labor productivity* typically indicates the cost or number of hours of labor it takes to produce an output. In other words, the lower the cost of the labor to produce a unit of output, or the less time it takes to produce a unit of output, the higher the labor productivity. For example, the automobile industry often measures labor productivity by determining the average number of hours of labor needed to completely assemble a car. The three most productive auto manufacturers can assemble a car with 32 or fewer hours of labor. Toyota assembles a car in only 27.9 hours of labor, Nissan does it in 29.4 hours, and Honda in 32 hours. These manufacturers have higher labor productivity than General Motors, which needs 34.3 hours of labor to assemble a car, DaimlerChrysler, which needs 35.8 hours, and Ford, which needs 36.9 hours.[13] These lower labor costs give Nissan, Honda, and Toyota an average cost advantage of $350 to $500 per car.[14]

Partial productivity assesses how efficiently companies use only one input, such as labor, when creating outputs. Multifactor productivity is an overall measure of productivity that assesses how efficiently companies use all the inputs it takes to make outputs. More specifically, **multifactor productivity** indicates how much labor, capital, materials, and energy it takes to produce an output.[15]

$$\frac{\text{Multifactor}}{\text{Productivity}} = \frac{\text{Outputs}}{(\text{Labor} + \text{Capital} + \text{Materials} + \text{Energy})}$$

Exhibit 18.1 shows the trends in multifactor productivity across a number of U.S. industries since 1987. With a 78 percent increase between 1997 (scaled at 100) and 2001 (when it reached a level of 178) and nearly a sixfold increase since 1987, the growth in multifactor productivity in the computers and electronic products industry far exceeded the productivity growth in retail stores, auto manufacturing, mining, utilities, finance and insurance, and air transporation as well as most other industries tracked by the U.S. government.

Should managers use multiple or partial productivity measures? In general, they should use both. Multifactor

Multitasking to Higher Productivity?

Think multitasking—or doing multiple tasks *at the same time*—is the answer to productivity increases? Think again. How effective can you be answering email, reviewing a report, and being attentive at a meeting—all at the same time? James C. Johnston, a research scientist at NASA, says, "Multitasking doesn't look to be one of the great strengths of human cognition. It's almost inevitable that each individual task will be slower and of lower quality." Anyone who's tried to hold a meaningful conversation and text message another person at the same time probably understands this painfully well. (Ever said "yes" when you meant "no," or clicked "send" at the wrong time?) The keys to productivity: focus and concentration, which lead to doing things right the first time. Could "multitasking" be code for not paying attention?

Source: J. Sandberg, "Yes, Sell All My Stocks. No, the 3:15 from JFK. And Get Me Mr. Sister," *Wall Street Journal*, 12 September 2006, B1.

©Photographer's Choice/Getty

productivity indicates a company's overall level of productivity relative to its competitors. In the end, that's what counts most. However, multifactor productivity measures don't indicate the specific contributions that labor, capital, materials, or energy make to overall productivity. To analyze the contributions of these individual components, managers need to use partial productivity measures.

2 Quality

With the average car costing more than $29,000, car buyers want to make sure that they're getting good quality for their money. Fortunately, as indicated by the number of problems per 100 cars (PP100), today's cars are of much higher quality than earlier models. In 1981, Japanese cars averaged 240 PP100. General Motors' cars averaged 670, Ford's averaged 740, and Chrysler's averaged 870 PP100! In other words, as measured by PP100, the quality of

Partial productivity a measure of performance that indicates how much of a particular kind of input it takes to produce an output

Multifactor productivity an overall measure of performance that indicates how much labor, capital, materials, and energy it takes to produce an output

Exhibit 18.1

Multifactor Productivity Growth across Industries

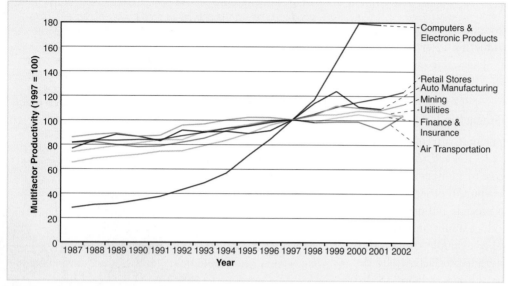

Multifactor Productivity (1997 = 100)

- Computers & Electronic Products
- Retail Stores
- Auto Manufacturing
- Mining
- Utilities
- Finance & Insurance
- Air Transportation

Year

1987 1988 1989 1990 1991 1992 1993 1994 1995 1996 1997 1998 1999 2000 2001 2002

Source: "Productivity and Costs," Bureau of Labor Statistics, [Online] available at http://data.bls.gov/cgi-bin/surveymost?ip, 1 July 2005.

American cars was two to three times worse than that of Japanese cars. In 2007, even the worst cars on the J.D. Power and Associates Survey of Initial Car quality beat the scores of the Japanese cars of decades ago. And high-quality cars like the Mercedes S-Class and Audi A8 even came in with scores under 100 (72 to be exact). That means, there's less than one problem per car![16]

The American Society for Quality gives two meanings for **quality**. It can mean a product or service free of deficiencies, such as the number of problems per 100 cars, or it can mean the characteristics of a product or service that satisfy customer needs.[17] In this sense, to-day's cars with their additional standard features (power brakes and steering, stereo/CD player, power windows and locks, air bags, cruise control, etc.) are of higher quality than those produced 20 years ago.

*In this part of the chapter, you will learn about **2.1 quality-related characteristics for products and services, 2.2 ISO 9000 and 14000, 2.3 the Baldrige National Quality Award,** and **2.4 total quality management.***

2.1 Quality-Related Characteristics for Products and Services

Quality a product or service free of deficiencies, or the characteristics of a product or service that satisfy customer needs

Quality products usually possess three characteristics: reliability, serviceability, and durability.[18] A breakdown occurs when a product quits working or doesn't do what it was designed to do.

The longer it takes for a product to break down, or the longer the time between breakdowns, the more reliable the product. Consequently, many companies define product reliability in terms of the average time between breakdowns.

Serviceability refers to how easy or difficult it is to fix a product. The easier it is to maintain a working product or fix a broken product, the more serviceable that product is. The Reva is an electric two-seater car, built in India, for city use. It goes 50 miles on a single battery charge (a recharge takes just five hours), and its operating costs per mile are one-third that of a typical gasoline-powered car. The Reva has high serviceability by virtue of a computerized diagnostic system that plugs into a portable electronic tool (PET) about the size of a personal digital assistant that assesses how well the car is running. Because the PET can be linked to a phone, customers can easily transmit their Reva's operational history to instantly find out if their car needs work and, if so, what kind.[19]

A product breakdown assumes that a product can be repaired. However, some products don't break down—they

A high-tech electric Reva cruising the streets of Bangalore on World Environment Day.

©AFP/Getty Images

fail. *Product failure* means products can't be repaired. They can only be replaced. Thus, durability is a quality characteristic that applies to products that can't be repaired. *Durability* is defined as the mean time to failure. Durability is crucial for products such as the defibrillation equipment used by emergency medical technicians, doctors, and nurses to restart patients' hearts. Imagine the lost lives (and lawsuits) that would occur if this equipment were prone to frequent failure. The mean time between failures for Physio-Control's defibrillation units is 55.6 to 69.4 years.[20]

While high-quality products are characterized by reliability, serviceability, and durability, services are different. With services, there's no point in assessing durability. Unlike products, services don't last. Services are consumed the minute they're performed. For example, once a lawn service has mowed your lawn, the job is done until the mowers come back next week to do it again. Likewise, services don't have serviceability. You can't maintain or fix a service. If a service wasn't performed correctly, all you can do is perform it again. Finally, the quality of service interactions often depends on how the service provider interacts with the customer. Was the service provider friendly, rude, or helpful? Five characteristics—reliability, tangibles, responsiveness, assurance, and empathy—typically distinguish a quality service.[21]

Service reliability is the ability to consistently perform a service well. Studies clearly show that reliability matters more to customers than anything else when buying services. When you take your clothes to the dry cleaner, you don't want them returned with cracked buttons or wrinkles down the front. If your dry cleaner gives you back perfectly clean and pressed clothes every time, it's providing a reliable service.

Also, although services themselves are not tangible (you can't see or touch them), services are provided in tangible places. Thus, *tangibles* refer to the appearance of the offices, equipment, and personnel involved with the delivery of a service. One of the best examples of the effect of tangibles on the perception of quality is the restroom. When you eat at a fancy restaurant, you expect clean, if not upscale, restrooms. How different is your perception of a business, say a gas station, if it has clean restrooms versus if it has filthy ones?

Responsiveness is the promptness and willingness with which service providers give good service (your dry cleaner returning your laundry perfectly clean and pressed in a day, in an hour). *Assurance* is the confidence that service providers are knowledgeable, courteous, and trustworthy. *Empathy* is the extent to which service providers give individual attention and care to customers' concerns and problems.

2.2 ISO 9000 and 14000

ISO, pronounced *ice-o,* comes from the Greek word *isos,* meaning *equal, similar, alike,* or *identical.* Thus, **ISO 9000** is a series of five international standards, from ISO 9000 to ISO 9004, for achieving consistency in quality management and quality assurance in companies throughout the world. **ISO 14000** is a series of international standards for managing, monitoring, and minimizing an organization's harmful effects on the environment.[22] (For more on environmental quality and issues, see Section 3.5 on controlling waste and pollution in Chapter 16.) The ISO 9000 and 14000 standards were created by the International Organization for Standardization, an international agency that helps set standards for 151 countries. The purpose of this agency is to develop and publish standards that facilitate the international exchange of goods and services.[23]

The ISO 9000 and 14000 standards publications, which are available from the American National Standards Institute, are general and can be used for manufacturing any kind of product or delivering any kind of service. Importantly, the ISO 9000 standards don't describe how to make a better-quality car, computer, or widget. Instead, they describe how companies can extensively document (and thus standardize) the steps they take to create and improve the quality of their products. ISO 9000 certification is increasingly becoming a requirement for doing business with many *Fortune* 500 companies.[24]

To become ISO certified, a process that can take months, a company must show that it is following its own procedures for improving production, updating design plans and specifications, keeping machinery in top condition, educating and training workers, and satisfactorily dealing with customer complaints.[25] Once a company has been certified as ISO 9000 compliant, an accredited third party will issue an ISO 9000 certificate that the company can use in its advertising and publications. This is the quality equivalent of the "*Good Housekeeping* Seal of Approval." Continued ISO 9000 certification is not guaranteed, however. Accredited third parties typically conduct periodic audits to make sure the company is still following quality procedures. If it is not, its certification is suspended or canceled.

ISO 9000 a series of five international standards, from ISO 9000 to ISO 9004, for achieving consistency in quality management and quality assurance in companies throughout the world

ISO 14000 a series of international standards for managing, monitoring, and minimizing an organization's harmful effects on the environment

See the American National Standards Institute (**http://www.ansi.org**; the ISO 9000 and ISO 14000 standards publications are available at this site for about $600 and $100, respectively), the American Society for Quality (**http://www.asq.org**), and the International Organization for Standardization (**http://www.iso.ch**) for additional information on ISO 9000 guidelines and procedures.

2.3 Baldrige National Quality Award

The Baldrige National Quality Award, which is administered by the U.S. government's National Institute for Standards and Technology, is given "to recognize U.S. companies for their achievements in quality and business performance and to raise awareness about the importance of quality and performance excellence as a competitive edge."[26] Each year, up to three awards may be given in these categories: manufacturing, service, small business, education, and health care.

The cost of applying for the Baldrige Award is $5,000 for manufacturing and service companies and $2,000 for small businesses.[27] At a minimum, each company that applies receives an extensive report based on 300 hours of assessment from at least eight business and quality experts. At $6.67 an hour for small businesses and about $16.67 an hour for manufacturing and service businesses, the *Journal for Quality and Participation* called the Baldrige feedback report "the best bargain in consulting in America."[28]

Businesses that apply for the Baldrige Award are judged on a 1,000-point scale based on the seven criteria in Exhibit 18.2.[29] With 450 out of 1,000 points, "results" are clearly the most important. In other words, in addition to the six other criteria, companies must show that they have achieved superior quality when it comes to products and services, customers, financial performance and market share, treatment of employees, organizational effectiveness, and leadership and social responsibility. This emphasis on "results" is what differentiates the Baldrige Award from the ISO 9000 standards. The Baldrige Award indicates the extent to which companies have actually achieved world-class quality. The ISO 9000 standards simply indicate whether a company is following the management system it put in place to improve quality. In fact, ISO 9000 certification covers less than 10 percent of the requirements for the Baldrige Award.[30]

Most companies that apply for the Baldrige Award do it to grow, prosper, and

Total quality management (TQM) an integrated, principle-based, organization-wide strategy for improving product and service quality

Exhibit 18.2

Criteria for the Baldrige National Quality Award

2007 CATEGORIES/ITEMS	POINT VALUES
1 LEADERSHIP	**120**
1.1 Senior Leadership	70
1.2 Governance and Social Responsibilities	50
2 STRATEGIC PLANNING	**85**
2.1 Strategy Development	40
2.2 Strategy Deployment	45
3 CUSTOMER AND MARKET FOCUS	**85**
3.1 Customer and Market Knowledge	40
3.2 Customer Relationships and Satisfaction	45
4 MEASUREMENT, ANALYSIS, AND KNOWLEDGE MANAGEMENT	**90**
4.1 Measurement, Analysis, and Improvement of Organizational Performance	45
4.2 Management of Information, Information Technology, and Knowledge	45
5 WORKFORCE FOCUS	**85**
5.1 Workforce Engagement	45
5.2 Workforce Environment	40
6 PROCESS MANAGEMENT	**85**
6.1 Work Systems Design	35
6.2 Work Process Management and Improvement	50
7 RESULTS	**450**
7.1 Product and Service Outcomes	100
7.2 Customer-Focused Outcomes	70
7.3 Financial and Market Outcomes	70
7.4 Workforce-Focused Outcomes	70
7.5 Process Effectiveness Outcomes	70
7.6 Leadership Outcomes	70
TOTAL POINTS 1,000	

Source: "Criteria for Performance Excellence," *Baldrige National Quality Program 2007*, [Online] available at http://www.quality.nist.gov/PDF_files/2007_Business_Nonprofit_Criteria.pdf, 7 April, 2007.

stay competitive.[31] Furthermore, the companies that have won the Baldrige Award have achieved superior financial returns. Since 1988, an investment in Baldrige Award winners would have outperformed the Standard & Poor's 500 stock index 80 percent of the time.[32]

2.4 Total Quality Management

Total quality management (TQM) is an integrated organization-wide strategy for improving product and service quality.[33] TQM is not a specific tool or technique.

Rather, TQM is a philosophy or overall approach to management that is characterized by three principles: customer focus and satisfaction, continuous improvement, and teamwork.[34]

Contrary to the arguments of most economists, accountants, and financiers that companies exist to earn profits for shareholders, TQM suggests that customer focus and customer satisfaction should be a company's primary goals. **Customer focus** means that the entire organization, from top to bottom, should be focused on meeting customers' needs. The result of that customer focus should be **customer satisfaction,** which occurs when the company's products or services meet or exceed customers' expectations. At companies where TQM is taken seriously, such as Enterprise Rent-a-Car, paychecks and promotions depend on keeping customers satisfied.[35] For example, Enterprise Rent-a-Car measures customer satisfaction with a detailed survey called the Enterprise Service Quality index. Enterprise not only ranks each branch office by operating profits and customer satisfaction, but it also makes promotions to higher-paying jobs contingent on above-average customer satisfaction scores.

Continuous improvement is an ongoing commitment to increase product and service quality by constantly assessing and improving the processes and procedures used to create those products and services. How do companies know whether they're achieving continuous improvement? Besides higher customer satisfaction, continuous improvement is usually associated with a reduction in variation. **Variation** is a deviation in the form, condition, or appearance of a product from the quality standard for that product. The less a product varies from the quality standard, or the more consistently a company's products meet a quality standard, the higher the quality. At Freudenberg-NOK, a manufacturer of seals and gaskets for the automotive industry, continuous improvement means shooting for a goal of "Six Sigma" quality, meaning just 3.4 defective or nonstandard parts per million (PPM). Achieving this goal would eliminate almost all product variation. In a recent year, Freudenberg-NOK made over 200 million seals and gaskets with a defect rate of 9 PPM, a rate that puts the company almost at its goal.[36] Furthermore, this represents a significant improvement from seven years ago when Freudenberg-NOK was averaging 650 defective PPM.[37]

The third principle of TQM is teamwork. **Teamwork** means collaboration between managers and nonmanagers, across business functions, and between the company and its customers and suppliers. In short, quality improves when everyone in the company is given the incentive to work together and the responsibility and authority to make improvements and solve problems. At Valassis, a printing company long famous for its use of teams, management turned to employees for additional suggestions when business fell during a recession. Teams offered so many ideas to cut costs and raise quality that the company was able to avoid layoffs.[38]

Together, customer focus and satisfaction, continuous improvement, and teamwork mutually reinforce each other to improve quality throughout a company. Customer-focused continuous improvement is necessary to increase customer satisfaction. At the same time, continuous improvement depends on teamwork from different functional and hierarchical parts of the company.

The goal of six sigma is to eliminate all product variation.

Customer focus an organizational goal to concentrate on meeting customers' needs at all levels of the organization

Customer satisfaction an organizational goal to provide products or services that meet or exceed customers' expectations

Continuous improvement an organization's ongoing commitment to constantly assess and improve the processes and procedures used to create products and services

Variation a deviation in the form, condition, or appearance of a product from the quality standard for that product

Teamwork collaboration between managers and nonmanagers, across business functions, and between companies, customers, and suppliers

Managing Operations

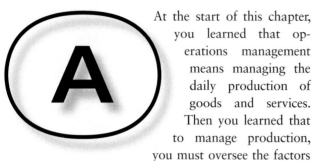

At the start of this chapter, you learned that operations management means managing the daily production of goods and services. Then you learned that to manage production, you must oversee the factors that affect productivity and quality. In this half of the chapter, you will learn about managing operations in service and manufacturing businesses. The chapter ends with a discussion of inventory management, a key factor in a company's profitability.

After reading the next three sections, you should be able to

3 explain the essentials of managing a service business.

4 describe the different kinds of manufacturing operations.

5 explain why and how companies should manage inventory levels.

3 Service Operations

Imagine that your trusty VCR breaks down as you try to record your favorite TV show. (You're still saving your money for a TiVo.) You've got two choices. You can run to Wal-Mart and spend $45 to $75 to pur-

chase a new VCR, or you can spend about the same amount (you hope) to have it fixed at a repair shop. Either way you end up with the same thing, a working VCR. However, the first choice, getting a new VCR, involves buying a physical product (a "good"), while the second, dealing with a repair shop, involves buying a service.

Services differ from goods in several ways. First, goods are produced or made, but services are performed. In other words, services are almost always labor-intensive: someone typically has to perform the service for you. A repair shop could give you the parts needed to repair your old VCR, but without the technician to perform the repairs, you're still going to have a broken VCR. Second, goods are tangible, but services are intangible. You can touch and see that new VCR, but you can't touch or see the service provided by the technician who fixed your old VCR. All you can "see" is that the VCR works. Third, services are perishable and unstorable. If you don't use them when they're available, they're wasted. For example, if your VCR repair shop is backlogged on repair jobs, then you'll just have to wait until next week to get your VCR repaired. You can't store an unused service and use it when you like. By contrast, you can purchase a good, such as motor oil, and store it until you're ready to use it. Finally, services account for 59.1 percent of gross national product whereas manufacturing accounts for only 30.9 percent.[39]

Because services are different from goods, managing a service operation is different from managing a manufacturing or production operation. Let's look at **3.1 the service-profit chain** *and* **3.2 service recovery and empowerment.**

3.1 The Service-Profit Chain

One of the key assumptions in the service business is that success depends on how well employees, that is, service providers, deliver their services to customers. However, the concept of the service-profit chain, depicted in Exhibit 18.3, suggests that in service businesses, success begins with how well management treats service employees.[40]

The first step in the service-profit chain is *internal service quality,* meaning the quality of treatment that employees receive from a company's internal service providers, such as management, payroll and benefits, human resources, and so forth. For example, Southwest Airlines is legendary for its positive culture and, to the surprise of many, its excellent customer service. According to Southwest's chairman Herb Kelleher, that's because "employees come first. If you treat them well, then they treat the customers well, and that means your customers come back and your shareholders are happy."[41]

SUCCESS BEGINS WITH HOW WELL MANAGEMENT TREATS SERVICE EMPLOYEES.

Exhibit 18.3

Service-Profit Chain

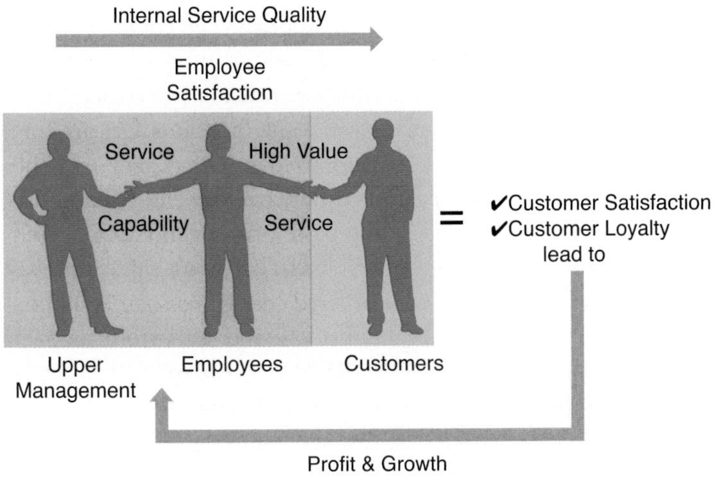

Internal Service Quality →

Employee Satisfaction

Upper Management → Employees → Customers

Service Capability / High Value Service

= ✔ Customer Satisfaction
✔ Customer Loyalty lead to

Profit & Growth →

Sources: R. Hallowell, L. A. Schlesinger, & J. Zornitsky, "Internal Service Quality, Customer and Job Satisfaction: Linkages and Implications for Management," *Human Resource Planning* 19 (1996): 20–31; J. L. Heskett, T. O. Jones, G. W. Loveman, W. E. Sasser, Jr., & L. A. Schlesinger, "Putting the Service-Profit Chain to Work," *Harvard Business Review*, March–April 1994, 164–174.

As depicted in Exhibit 18.3, good internal service leads to employee satisfaction and service capability. *Employee satisfaction* occurs when companies treat employees in a way that meets or exceeds their expectations. In other words, the better employees are treated, the more satisfied they are, and the more likely they are to give high-value service that satisfies customers.

Service capability is an employee's perception of his or her ability to serve customers well. When an organization serves its employees in ways that help them to do their jobs well, employees, in turn, are more likely to believe that they can and ought to provide high-value service to customers.

Finally, according to the service-profit chain shown in Exhibit 18.3, *high-value service* leads to *customer satisfaction* and *customer loyalty,* which, in turn, lead to *long-term profits and growth.* What's the link between customer satisfaction and loyalty and profits? To start, the average business keeps only 70 to 90 percent of its existing customers each year. No big deal, you say? Just replace leaving customers with new customers. Well, there's one significant problem with that solution. It costs ten times as much to find a new customer as it does to keep an existing customer. Also, new customers typically buy only 20 percent as much as established customers. In fact, keeping existing customers is so cost-effective that most businesses could double their profits by simply keeping 5 percent more customers per year![42]

3.2 Service Recovery and Empowerment

When mistakes are made, when problems occur, and when customers become dissatisfied with the service they've received, service businesses must switch from the process of service delivery to the process of **service recovery,** that is, restoring customer satisfaction to strongly dissatisfied customers.[43] Sometimes, service recovery requires service employees to not only fix whatever mistake was made, but also to perform heroic service acts that delight highly dissatisfied customers by far surpassing their expectations of fair treatment. When accountant Tom Taylor checked into a Hampton Inn in South Carolina, he wasn't happy. The company Web site had given him incorrect directions. The lights in his room weren't plugged in. The shower controls were backwards—"hot" was cold and "cold" was hot. And the air-conditioning was malfunctioning, so his room was freezing cold. When he complained, the employee at the front desk immediately offered him two free nights of lodging.[44]

Unfortunately, when mistakes occur, service employees often don't have the discretion to resolve customer complaints. Customers who want service employees to correct or make up for poor service are frequently told, "I'm not allowed to do that," "I'm just following company rules," or "I'm sorry, only managers are allowed to make changes of any kind." In other words, company rules prevent them from engaging in acts of service recovery meant to turn dissatisfied customers back into satisfied customers. The result is frustration for customers and service employees and lost customers for the company.

Now, however, many companies are empowering their service employees.[45] In Chapter 9, you learned that *empowering workers* means permanently passing decision-making authority and responsibility from managers to workers. With respect to service recovery, empowering workers means giving service employees the authority and responsibility to make decisions that immediately solve customer problems.[46] At Hampton Inn, all employees are empowered to solve customer problems. Senior vice president Phil Cordell says, "You don't have to call an 800 number. Just mention it at the front desk or to any employee—a housekeeper, maintenance person or breakfast hostess—and, on the spot, your stay is free."[47] Empowering service workers does entail some

Service recovery restoring customer satisfaction to strongly dissatisfied customers costs, although they are usually less than the company's savings from retaining customers.

4 Manufacturing Operations

DaimlerChrysler makes cars, and Dell does computers. Shell produces gasoline, whereas Sherwin-Williams makes paint. Boeing makes jet planes, but Budweiser makes beer. Maxtor makes hard drives, and Maytag makes appliances. The *manufacturing operations* of these companies all produce physical goods. But not all manufacturing operations, especially these, are the same. *Let's learn how various manufacturing operations differ in terms of 4.1 the amount of processing that is done to produce and assemble a product and 4.2 the flexibility to change the number, kind, and characteristics of products that are produced.*

4.1 Amount of Processing in Manufacturing Operations

Manufacturing operations can be classified according to the amount of processing or assembly that occurs after a customer order is received. The highest degree of processing occurs in **make-to-order operations**. A make-to-order operation does not start processing or assembling products until it receives a customer order. In fact, some make-to-order operations may not even order parts until a customer order is received. Not surprisingly, make-to-order operations produce or assemble highly specialized or customized products for customers.

For example, Dell has one of the most advanced make-to-order operations in the computer business. Because Dell has no finished goods inventory and no component parts inventory, its computers always have the latest, most advanced components, and Dell can pass on price cuts to customers. Plus, Dell can customize all of its orders, big and small. So whether you're ordering 5,000 personal computers for your company or just one personal computer for your home, Dell doesn't make the computers until you order them.

A moderate degree of processing occurs in **assemble-to-order operations**. A company using an assemble-to-order operation divides its manufacturing or assembly process into separate parts or modules. The company orders parts and assembles modules ahead of customer orders. Then, based on actual customer orders or on research forecasting what customers will want, those modules are combined to create semicustomized products. For example, when a customer orders a new car, General Motors may have already ordered the basic parts or modules it needs from suppliers. In other words, based on sales forecasts, GM may already have ordered enough tires, air-conditioning compressors, brake systems, and seats from suppliers to accommodate nearly all customer orders on a particular day. Special orders from customers and car dealers are then used to determine the final assembly checklist for particular cars as they move down the assembly line.

The lowest degree of processing occurs in **make-to-stock operations** (also called build-to-stock). Because the products are standardized, meaning each product is exactly the same as the next, a company using a make-to-stock operation starts ordering parts and assembling finished products before receiving customer orders. Customers then purchase these standardized products, such as Rubbermaid storage containers, microwave

Make-to-order operation a manufacturing operation that does not start processing or assembling products until a customer order is received

Assemble-to-order operation a manufacturing operation that divides manufacturing processes into separate parts or modules that are combined to create semicustomized products

Make-to-stock operation a manufacturing operation that orders parts and assembles standardized products before receiving customer orders

Is Anything Still Made in the USA?

Conventional wisdom is that all manufacturing will ultimately go to the country where labor is cheapest, which doesn't bode well for, say, the United States. In fact, however, much is still made here. High-end products, bulky products, and delicate products often continue to be produced in the U.S. and illustrate a key point for consideration in any discussion of globalization: there do exist physical and strategic limits. Some business will always be better accomplished close to the customer.

Source: M. Whitehouse, "For Some Manufacturers, There Are Benefits to Keeping Production at Home," *Wall Street Journal*, 22 January 2007, A2.

Sub-Zero makes high-end appliances in Madison, Wisconsin.

Bobcat makes, well, Bobcats in Fargo, North Dakota.

Sony makes hi-def TVs in Pittsburgh.

Courtesy of Sub-Zero   Courtesy of Bobcat, Inc.   Susan Van Etten

©Ablestock

ordering and final delivery of products. There is often a tradeoff between flexibility and cost, however, with the most flexible manufacturing operations frequently having higher costs per unit and the least flexible operations having lower costs per unit.[48] Some common manufacturing operations, arranged in order from the least flexible to the most flexible, are continuous-flow production, line-flow production, batch production, and job shops.

Most production processes generate finished products at a discrete rate. A product is completed, and then, perhaps a few seconds, minutes, or hours later, another is completed, and so on. By contrast, in **continuous-flow production,** products are produced continuously, rather than at a discrete rate. Like a water hose that is never turned off and just keeps on flowing, production of the final product never stops. Liquid chemicals and petroleum products are examples of continuous-flow production. Because of their complexity, continuous-flow production processes are the most standardized and least flexible manufacturing operations.

Line-flow production processes are preestablished, occur in a serial or linear manner, and are dedicated to making one type of product. Line-flow production processes are inflexible because they are typically dedicated to manufacturing one kind of product. For example, nearly every city has a local bottling plant for soft drinks or beer. The processes or steps in bottling plants are serial, meaning they must occur in a particular order: sterilize; fill with soft drinks or beer; crown or cap bottles; check for underfilling and missing caps; apply label; inspect a final time; and then place bottles in cases, cases on pallets, and pallets on delivery trucks.[49]

Batch production involves the manufacture of large batches of different products in standard lot sizes. This production method is finding increasing use among restaurant chains. To ensure consistency in the taste and quality of their products, many restaurants have central kitchens, or commissaries, that produce batches of food, such as

ovens, and vacuum cleaners, at retail stores or directly from the manufacturer. Because parts are ordered and products are assembled before customers order the products, make-to-stock operations are highly dependent on the accuracy of sales forecasts. If sales forecasts are incorrect, make-to-stock operations may end up building too many or too few products, or they may make products with the wrong features or without the features that customers want. These disadvantages are leading many companies to move from make-to-stock to build-to-order systems.

4.2 Flexibility of Manufacturing Operations

A second way to categorize manufacturing operations is by **manufacturing flexibility,** meaning the degree to which manufacturing operations can easily and quickly change the number, kind, and characteristics of products they produce. Flexibility allows companies to respond quickly to changes in the marketplace (i.e., competitors and customers) and to reduce the lead time between

Manufacturing flexibility the degree to which manufacturing operations can easily and quickly change the number, kind, and characteristics of products they produce

Continuous-flow production a manufacturing operation that produces goods at a continuous, rather than a discrete, rate

Line-flow production manufacturing processes that are preestablished, occur in a serial or linear manner, and are dedicated to making one type of product

Batch production a manufacturing operation that produces goods in large batches in standard lot sizes mashed potatoes, stuffing, macaroni and cheese, rice, quiche filling, and chili, in volumes ranging from 10 to 200 gallons. These batches are then delivered to restaurants, which serve the food to customers.

Finally, **job shops** are typically small manufacturing operations that handle special manufacturing processes or jobs. In contrast to batch production, which handles large batches of different products, job shops typically handle very small batches, some as small as one product or process per "batch." Basically, each "job" in a job shop is different, and once a job is done, the job shop moves on to a completely different job or manufacturing process for, most likely, a different customer. For example, Leggett & Platt Machine Products in Carthage, Missouri, is a job shop that makes coil springs, innerspring units, welded metal grids, and various other parts for mattress manufacturers around the world. Since its inception, its 225 employees have made over 25,000 *different* parts; in other words, they have completed 25,000 different jobs for customers.[50]

5 | Inventory

With SUVs and pickup trucks accounting for nearly 80 percent of its sales, Chrysler was reluctant to stop making them—even when consumer demand dried up. Despite a lack of orders for SUVs and pickups, Chrysler kept building cars—cars that people didn't want—and ended up with nearly a four-month supply of inventory. In addition to what was already on dealer lots, the automaker had 50,000 vehicles sitting on random storage lots around the midwestern United States.[51]

Inventory is the amount and number of raw materials, parts, and finished products that a company has in its possession. Like Chrysler, General Motors made the mistake of having too much inventory on hand; GM had to reduce production by over 10 percent at its plants to let existing sales draw down inventory levels to an acceptable and affordable level. Industry experts estimate Chrysler has some-

©Comstock/Jupiter Images

where between 80 and 126 days of inventory on hand, and it has more SUV inventory (82 days) than GM (77) and Ford (74) and almost three times as much as Toyota (28).[52] *In this section, you will learn about **5.1 the different types of inventory, 5.2 how to measure inventory levels, 5.3 the costs of maintaining an inventory,** and **5.4 the different systems for managing inventory.***

5.1 Types of Inventory

Exhibit 18.4 shows the four kinds of inventory a manufacturer stores: raw materials, component parts, work-in-process, and finished goods. The flow of inventory through a manufacturing plant begins when the purchasing department buys raw materials from vendors. **Raw material inventories** are the basic inputs in the manufacturing process. For example, to begin making a car, automobile manufacturers purchase raw materials like steel, iron, aluminum, copper, rubber, and unprocessed plastic.

Next, raw materials are fabricated or processed into **component parts inventories,** meaning the basic parts used in manufacturing a product. For example, in an automobile plant, steel is fabricated or processed into a car's body panels, and steel and iron are melted and shaped into engine parts like pistons or engine blocks. Some component parts are purchased from vendors rather than fabricated in-house.

The component parts are then assembled to make unfinished **work-in-process inventories,** which are also known as partially finished goods. This process is also called *initial assembly.* For example, steel body panels are welded to each other and to the frame of the car to make a "unibody," which comprises the unpainted interior frame and exterior structure of the car. Likewise, pistons, camshafts, and other engine parts are inserted into the engine block to create a working engine.

Next, all the work-in-process inventories are assembled to create **finished goods inventories,** which are the final outputs of the manufacturing process. This pro-

Job shops manufacturing operations that handle custom orders or small batch jobs

Inventory the amount and number of raw materials, parts, and finished products that a company has in its possession

Raw material inventories the basic inputs in a manufacturing process

Component parts inventories the basic parts used in manufacturing that are fabricated from raw materials

Work-in-process inventories partially finished goods consisting of assembled component parts

Finished goods inventories the final outputs of manufacturing operations

Exhibit 18.4

Types of Inventory

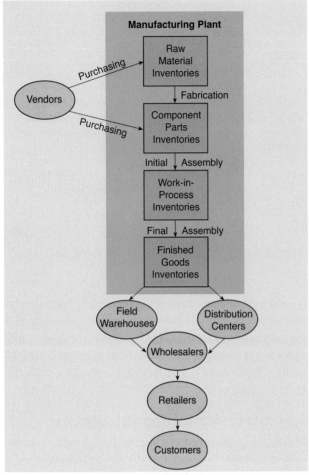

Source: R. E. Markland, S. K. Vickery, & R. A. Davis, *Operations Management*, 2nd ed. (Mason, OH: South-Western, 1998). Reprinted with permission.

cess is also called *final assembly*. For a car, the engine, wheels, brake system, suspension, interior, and electrical system are assembled into a car's painted unibody to make the working automobile, which is the factory's finished product. In the last step in the process, the finished goods are sent to field warehouses, distribution centers, or wholesalers, and then to retailers for final sale to customers.

5.2 Measuring Inventory

As you'll learn below, uncontrolled inventory can lead to huge costs for a manufacturing operation. Consequently, managers need good measures of inventory to prevent inventory costs from becoming too large. Three basic measures of inventory are average aggregate inventory, weeks of supply, and inventory turnover.

If you've ever worked in a retail store and had to "take inventory," you probably weren't too excited about the process of counting every item in the store and storeroom. It's an extensive task that's a bit easier today because of bar codes that mark items and computers that can count and track them. Nonetheless, inventories still differ from day to day depending on when in the month or week they're taken. Because of such differences, companies often measure **average aggregate inventory,** which is the average overall inventory during a particular time period. Average aggregate inventory for a month can be determined by simply averaging the inventory counts at the end of each business day for that month. One way companies know whether they're carrying too much or too little inventory is to compare their average aggregate inventory to the industry average for aggregate inventory. For example, 72 days of inventory is the average for the automobile industry.

Inventory is also measured in terms of *weeks of supply,* meaning the number of weeks it would take for a company to run out of its current supply of inventory. In general, there is an acceptable number of weeks of inventory for a particular kind of business. Too few weeks of inventory on hand, and a company risks a **stockout**—running out of inventory. During a recent holiday season, the busiest shopping time of the year, retail and online stores ran out of Apple Computer's fast-selling iPods.[53] Apple issued a statement saying, "To try to meet the high demand, we're making and shipping iPods as fast as we can. So, if one store has run out, you may find iPods in another authorized iPod reseller."[54] Nevertheless, iPods were in such short supply that the iPod mini was selling for $380 on eBay, $130 over the suggested retail price. On the other hand, a business that has too many weeks of inventory on hand incurs high costs (discussed below). Excess inventory can be reduced only by cutting prices or temporarily stopping production.

Average aggregate inventory average overall inventory during a particular time period

Stockout the situation when a company runs out of finished product

---

Uncontrolled inventory can lead to **huge costs** for a manufacturing operation.

Another common inventory measure, **inventory turnover,** is the number of times per year that a company sells or "turns over" its average inventory. For example, if a company keeps an average of 100 finished widgets in inventory each month, and it sold 1,000 widgets this year, then it "turned" its inventory 10 times this year.

In general, the higher the number of inventory "turns," the better. In practice, a high turnover means that a company can continue its daily operations with just a small amount of inventory on hand. For example, let's take two companies, A and B, which, over the course of a year, have identical inventory levels (520,000 widget parts and raw materials). If company A turns its inventories 26 times a year, it will completely replenish its inventory every two weeks and have an average inventory of 20,000 widget parts and raw materials. By contrast, if company B turns its inventories only two times a year, it will completely replenish its inventory every 26 weeks and have an average inventory of 260,000 widget parts and raw materials. So, by turning its inventory more often, company A has 92 percent less inventory on hand at any one time than company B.

Across all kinds of manufacturing plants, the average number of inventory turns is approximately eight per year, although the average can be higher or lower for different industries.[55] For example, whereas the average auto company turns its entire inventory 13 times per year, some of the best auto companies more than double that rate, turning their inventory 27.8 times per year, or once every two weeks.[56] For an auto company, turning inventory more frequently than the industry average can cut costs by several hundred million dollars per year. Finally, it should be pointed out that even make-to-order companies like Dell turn their inventory. In theory, make-to-order companies have no inventory. In fact, they've got inventory, but you have to measure it in hours. For example, in its factories, Dell turns its inventory 500 times a year, which means that on average it has 17 hours—that's hours and not days—of inventory on hand in its factories.[57]

5.3 Costs of Maintaining an Inventory

Maintaining an inventory incurs four kinds of costs: ordering, setup, holding, and stockout. **Ordering cost** is not the cost of the inventory itself, but the costs associated with ordering the inventory. It includes the costs of completing paperwork, manually entering data into a computer, making phone calls, getting competing bids, correcting mistakes, and simply determining when and how much new inventory should be reordered. For example, ordering costs are relatively high in the restaurant business because 80 percent of food service orders (in which restaurants reorder food supplies) are processed manually. It's estimated that the food industry could save $6.6 billion if all restaurants converted to electronic data interchange (see Chapter 17).[58]

Setup cost is the cost of changing or adjusting a machine so that it can produce a different kind of inventory.[59] For example, 3M uses the same production machinery to make several kinds of industrial tape, but it must adjust the machines whenever it switches from one kind of tape to another. There are two kinds of setup costs, downtime and lost efficiency. *Downtime* occurs whenever a machine is not being used to process inventory. So, if it takes five hours to switch a machine

Sharp Turns

If it takes an automaker 13 to 28 weeks to turn its inventory, what does that mean for the dealer? How long do cars stay on the dealers' lots? Surprisingly, the car that sells the fastest is the Mercedes-Benz G-Class (sticker $94,917), sitting on the lot only 8 days before being driven off by a happy owner—with a much lighter checkbook. The car that sells the second fastest is almost at the other end of the spectrum: The Honda Fit spends an average of 10 days on the lot and sells for only $16,372. The Honda CR-V, BMW X5, Saturn Sky, Lexus LS an ES series, Toyota Tundra, Nissan Versa, and BMW X3 and 5 Series all turn in less than three weeks. Anything else is just old.

Source: "Hot off the Lot," *Wall Street Journal*, 8 March 2007, D6. Data in article from Power Information Network, a division of J.D. Power & Associates.

Inventory turnover the number of times per year that a company sells or "turns over" its average inventory

Ordering cost the costs associated with ordering inventory, including the cost of data entry, phone calls, obtaining bids, correcting mistakes, and determining when and how much inventory to order

Setup cost the costs of downtime and lost efficiency that occur when a machine is changed or adjusted to produce a different kind of inventory

from processing one kind of inventory to another, then five hours of downtime have occurred. Downtime is costly because companies earn an economic return only when machines are actively turning raw materials into parts or parts into finished products. The second setup cost is *lost efficiency.* Typically, after a switchover, it takes some time to recalibrate a machine to its optimal settings. It may take several days of fine-tuning before a machine finally produces the number of high-quality parts that it is supposed to. So, each time a machine has to be changed to handle a different kind of inventory, setup costs (downtime and lost efficiency) rise.

Holding cost, also known as *carrying* or *storage cost,* is the cost of keeping inventory until it is used or sold. Holding cost includes the cost of storage facilities, insurance to protect inventory from damage or theft, inventory taxes, the cost of obsolescence (holding inventory that is no longer useful to the company), and the opportunity cost of spending money on inventory that could have been spent elsewhere in the company. For example, it's estimated that at any one time, U.S. airlines have a total of $60 billion worth of airplane parts in stock for maintenance, repair, and overhauling their planes. The holding cost for managing, storing, and purchasing these parts is nearly $12.5 billion—or roughly one-fifth of the cost of the parts themselves.[60]

Stockout costs are the costs incurred when a company runs out of a product, as happened to Apple when it failed to have enough iPods during the holiday shopping season. There are two basic kinds of stockout costs. First, the company incurs the transaction costs of overtime work, shipping, and the like in trying to quickly replace out-of-stock inventories with new inventories. The second and perhaps more damaging cost is the loss of customers' goodwill when a company cannot deliver the products that it promised.

5.4 Managing Inventory

Inventory management has two basic goals. The first is to avoid running out of stock and thus angering and dissatisfying customers. Consequently, this goal seeks to increase inventory levels to a "safe" level that won't risk stockouts. The second is to efficiently reduce inventory levels and costs as much as possible without impairing daily operations. Thus, this goal seeks a minimum level of inventory. The following inventory management techniques—economic order quantity (EOQ), just-in-time inventory (JIT), and materials requirement planning (MRP)—are different ways of balancing these competing goals.

Economic order quantity (EOQ) is a system of formulas that helps determine how much and how often inventory should be ordered. EOQ takes into account the overall demand (D) for a product while trying to minimize ordering costs (O) and holding costs (H). The formula for EOQ is

$$EOQ = \sqrt{\frac{2DO}{4}}$$

For example, if a factory uses 40,000 gallons of paint a year (D), ordering costs (O) are $75 per order, and holding costs (H) are $4 per gallon, then the optimal quantity to order is 1,225 gallons:

$$EOQ = \sqrt{\frac{2(40,000)\ (75)}{4}} = 1,225$$

And, with 40,000 gallons of paint being used per year, the factory uses approximately 110 gallons per day:

$$\frac{40,000\ gallons}{365\ days} = 110$$

Consequently, the factory would order 1,225 new gallons of paint approximately every 11 days:

$$\frac{1,225\ gallons}{110\ gallons\ per\ day} = 11.1\ days$$

While EOQ formulas try to minimize holding and ordering costs, the just-in-time (JIT) approach to inventory management attempts to eliminate holding costs by reducing inventory levels to near zero. With a **just-in-time (JIT) inventory system,** component parts arrive from suppliers just as they are needed at each stage of production. By having parts arrive "just in time," the manufacturer has little inventory on hand and thus avoids the costs associated with holding inventory.

To have just the right amount of inventory arrive at just the right time requires a tremendous amount of coordination between manufacturing operations and suppliers. One way to promote tight coordination under JIT is close proximity. Most parts suppliers for Toyota's JIT system at its Georgetown, Kentucky,

Holding cost the cost of keeping inventory until it is used or sold, including storage, insurance, taxes, obsolescence, and opportunity costs

Stockout costs the costs incurred when a company runs out of a product, including transaction costs to replace inventory and the loss of customers' goodwill

Economic order quantity (EOQ) a system of formulas that minimizes ordering and holding costs and helps determine how much and how often inventory should be ordered

Just-in-time (JIT) inventory system an inventory system in which component parts arrive from suppliers just as they are needed at each stage of production

plant are located within 200 miles of the plant. Furthermore, parts are picked up from suppliers and delivered to Toyota as often as 16 times a day.[61] A second way to promote close coordination under JIT is to have a shared information system that allows a manufacturer and its suppliers to know the quantity and kinds of parts inventory the other has in stock. Generally, factories and suppliers facilitate information sharing by using the same part numbers and names.

Manufacturing operations and their parts suppliers can also facilitate close coordination by using the Japanese system of kanban. **Kanban,** which is Japanese for "sign," is a simple ticket-based system that indicates when it is time to reorder inventory. Suppliers attach kanban cards to batches of parts. Then, when an assembly-line worker uses the first part out of a batch, the kanban card is removed. The cards are then collected, sorted, and quickly returned to the supplier, who begins resupplying the factory with parts that match the order information on the kanban cards. And, because prices and batch sizes are typically

Kanban a ticket-based JIT system that indicates when to reorder inventory

Materials requirement planning (MRP) a production and inventory system that determines the production schedule, production batch sizes, and inventory needed to complete final products

Independent demand system an inventory system in which the level of one kind of inventory does not depend on another

agreed to ahead of time, kanban tickets greatly reduce paperwork and ordering costs.[62]

A third method for managing inventory is **materials requirement planning (MRP).** MRP is a production and inventory system that, from beginning to end, precisely determines the production schedule, production batch sizes, and inventories needed to complete final products. The three key parts of MRP systems are the master production schedule, the bill of materials, and inventory records. The *master production schedule* is a detailed schedule that indicates the quantity of each item to be produced, the planned delivery dates for those items, and the time by which each step of the production process must be completed in order to meet those delivery dates. Based on the quantity and kind of products set forth in the master production schedule, the *bill of materials* identifies all the necessary parts and inventory, the quantity or volume of inventory to be ordered, and the order in which the parts and inventory should be assembled. *Inventory records* indicate the kind, quantity, and location of inventory that is on hand or that has been ordered. When inventory records are combined with the bill of materials, the resulting report indicates what to buy, when to buy it, and what it will cost to order. Today, nearly all MRP systems are available in the form of powerful, flexible computer software.[63]

Which inventory management system should you use? EOQ formulas are intended for use with **indepen-**

dent demand systems, in which the level of one kind of inventory does not depend on another. For example, because inventory levels for automobile tires are unrelated to the inventory levels of women's dresses, Sears could use EOQ formulas to calculate separate optimal order quantities for dresses and tires. By contrast, JIT and MRP are used with **dependent demand systems,** in which the level of inventory depends on the number of finished units to be produced. For example, if Yamaha makes 1,000 motorcycles a day, then it will need 1,000 seats, 1,000 gas tanks, and 2,000 wheels and tires each day. So, when optimal inventory levels depend on the number of products to be produced, use a JIT or MRP management system.

Dependent demand system an inventory system in which the level of inventory depends on the number of finished units to be produced

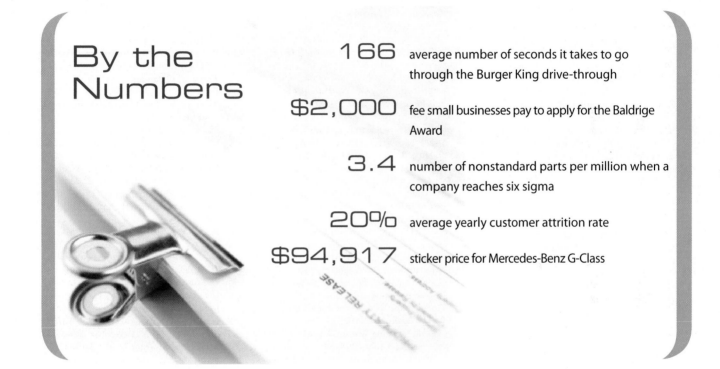

By the Numbers

166 average number of seconds it takes to go through the Burger King drive-through

$2,000 fee small businesses pay to apply for the Baldrige Award

3.4 number of nonstandard parts per million when a company reaches six sigma

20% average yearly customer attrition rate

$94,917 sticker price for Mercedes-Benz G-Class

Chapter 1

1. K. Voigt, "Top Dogs," *Wall Street Journal,* 15 March 2002, W1.
2. M. Herper & R. Langreth, "Dangerous Devices," *Forbes,* 27 November 2006, 94.
3. N. Byrnes & J. Merritt, "Professional Services: The Help Needs Help," *BusinessWeek,* 13 January 2003, 129.
4. T. Peters, "The Leadership Alliance" (Pat Carrigan excerpt), *In Search of Excellence* (Northbrook, IL: Video Arts distributor, 1985), videocassette.
5. K. Hickey, "Faster, Better, More," *Traffic World,* 6 October 2003, 24.
6. D. A. Wren, A. G. Bedeian, & J. D. Breeze, "The Foundations of Henri Fayol's Administrative Theory," *Management Decision* 40 (2002): 906–918.
7. H. Fayol, *General and Industrial Management* (London: Pittman & Sons, 1949).
8. K. Jaher, "Wal-Mart Seeks New Flexibility in Worker Shifts," *Wall Street Journal,* 3 January 2007, A1.
9. R. Stagner, "Corporate Decision Making," *Journal of Applied Psychology* 53 (1969): 1–13.
10. D. W. Bray, R. J. Campbell, & D. L. Grant, *Formative Years in Business: A Long-Term AT&T Study of Managerial Lives* (New York: Wiley, 1993).
11. N. Schwartzreporter & P. Neering, "The Biggest Company in America ... Is Also a Big Target," *Fortune,* 17 April 2006, 77.
12. A. Lashinsky, "Search and Enjoy," *Fortune,* 22 January 2007, 70.
13. "Yahoo! Re-Aligns Organization to More Effectively Focus on Key Customer Segments and Capture Future Growth Opportunities," Yahoo!, http://yhoo.client.shareholder.com/press/ReleaseDetail.cfm?ReleaseID=220987, 5 December 2006.
14. B. Morris, "The Accidental CEO," *Fortune,* 28 June 2003, 58.
15. Ibid.
16. "Xerox's Chief Copies Good Practice, Not Past Mistakes," *Irish Times,* 21 March 2003, 62.
17. "Xerox's 3Q Profits Jump on Product Sales," *eWeek,* 21 October 2004.
18. A. Warren, "The Small Stuff: It's the Little Things That Add Up—and Often Annoy," *Wall Street Journal,* 10 May 2004, R9.
19. H. S. Jonas III, R. E. Fry, & S. Srivastva, "The Office of the CEO: Understanding the Executive Experience," *Academy of Management Executive* 4 (1990): 36–47.
20. "Why Corporate Boardrooms Are in Turmoil," *Wall Street Journal,* 16 September 2006, A7.
21. M. Porter, J. Lorsch, & N. Nohria, "Seven Surprises for New CEOS," *Harvard Business Review,* October 2004, 62.
22. M. Murray, "As Huge Firms Keep Growing, CEOs Struggle to Keep Pace," *Wall Street Journal,* 8 February 2001, A1.
23. Q. Huy, "In Praise of Middle Managers," *Harvard Business Review,* September 2001, 72–79.
24. M. Arndt, "Creativity Overflowing," *Business Week,* 8 May 2006, 50.
25. Carol Hymowitz, "Middle Managers Are Unsung Heroes on Corporate Stage," *The Wall Street Journal,* September 19, 2005, p. B1.
26. "Management & Professional: Regional Manager," *Pharmacy Today,* 18 October 2006, 27.
27. T. Seideman, "Harnessing the Giant," *World Trade* 15 (2002): 28–29.
28. G. Will, "Waging War on Wal-Mart," *Newsweek,* 5 July 2004, 64.
29. J. Adamy, "A Menu of Options: Restaurants Have a Host of Ways to Motivate Employees to Provide Good Service," *Wall Street Journal,* 30 October 2006, R1–R6.
30. S. Tully, "What Team Leaders Need to Know," *Fortune,* 20 February 1995, 93.
31. B. Francella, "In a Day's Work," *Convenience Store News,* 25 September 2001, 7.
32. L. Liu & A. McMurray, "Frontline Leaders: The Entry Point for Leadership Development in the Manufacturing Industry," *Journal of European Industrial Training* 28, issue 2–4 (2004): 339–352.
33. Tully, "What Team Leaders Need to Know."
34. "What Makes Teams Work?" *Fast Company,* 1 November 2000, 109.
35. K. Hultman, "The 10 Commandments of Team Leadership," *Training & Development,* 1 February 1998, 12–13.
36. N. Steckler & N. Fondas, "Building Team Leader Effectiveness: A Diagnostic Tool," *Organizational Dynamics,* Winter 1995, 20–34.
37. H. Mintzberg, *The Nature of Managerial Work* (New York: Harper & Row, 1973).
38. P. Hales, "What Do Managers Do? A Critical Review of the Evidence," *Journal of Management Studies* 23, no. 1 (1986): 88–115.
39. J. Boorstin, "J. M. Smucker," *Fortune,* 12 January 2004, 58.
40. R. Levering & M. Moskowitz, "The 100 Best Companies to Work For," *Fortune,* 12 January 2004, 56.
41. Francella, "In a Day's Work."
42. Murray, "As Huge Firms Keep Growing."
43. "Industry Specific: News Segmented by Major Industries," *Businesswire,* http://www.businesswire.com/isn/index.html, 27 January 2003; "What Is FNS News Clips Online?" *FNS NewsClips,* http://www.news-clips.com/, 27 January 2003; "Media Monitoring," *CyberAlert,* http://www. cyberalert.com, 27 January 2003.
44. R. Guth, J. Delaney, & D. Clark, "Microsoft to Launch Challenge to Google, Yahoo," *Wall Street Journal,* 10 November 2004, A3.
45. C. Arnst, "The Best Medical Care in the U.S.: How Veterans Affairs Transformed Itself," *Business Week,* 17 July 2006, 50.
46. M. Langley, "Changing Gears," *Wall Street Journal,* 22 December 2006, A1.
47. M. Rieker, "E-Trade Raises Banking Sights for '07," *American Banker,* 8 January 2007, 1.
48. J. Welch & G. Khermouch, "Can GM Save an Icon?" *Business Week,* 8 April 2002, 60.
49. A. Sharma, "Poor Reception: After Sprint and Nextel Merge, Customers and Executives Leave," *Wall Street Journal,* 11 October 2006, A1.
50. L. A. Hill, *Becoming a Manager: Mastery of a New Identity* (Boston: Harvard Business School Press, 1992).
51. R. L. Katz, "Skills of an Effective Administrator," *Harvard Business Review,* September–October 1974, 90–102.
52. A. Bartlett & S. Ghoshal, "Changing the Role of Top Management: Beyond Systems to People," *Harvard Business Review,* May–June 1995, 132–142.
53. L. Schmidt & J. E. Hunter, "Development of a Causal Model of Process Determining Job Performance," *Current Directions in Psychological Science* 1 (1992): 89–92.
54. J. B. Miner, "Sentence Completion Measures in Personnel Research: The Development and Validation of the Miner Sentence Completion Scales," in *Personality*

Assessment in Organizations, ed. H. J. Bernardin & D. A. Bownas (New York: Praeger, 1986), 147–146.

55. M. W. McCall, Jr., & M. M. Lombardo, "What Makes a Top Executive?" *Psychology Today,* February 1983, 26–31; E. van Velsor & J. Brittain, "Why Executives Derail: Perspectives across Time and Cultures," *Academy of Management Executive,* November 1995, 62–72.

56. M.W. McCall, Jr., & M. M. Lombardo, "What Makes a Top Executive?"

57. K. Naj, "Corporate Therapy: The Latest Addition to Executive Suite Is Psychologist's Couch," *Wall Street Journal,* 29 August 1994, A1.

58. P. Wallington, "Management2 Toxic!" *Financial Mail,* 28 July 2006, 48.

59. J. Sandberg, "Overcontrolling Bosses Aren't Just Annoying; They're Also Inefficient," *Wall Street Journal,* 30 March 2005, B1.

60. J. Pfeffer, *The Human Equation: Building Profits by Putting People First* (Boston: Harvard Business School Press, 1996); *Competitive Advantage through People: Unleashing the Power of the Work Force* (Boston: Harvard Business School Press, 1994).

61. M. A. Huselid, "The Impact of Human Resource Management Practices on Turnover, Productivity, and Corporate Financial Performance," *Academy of Management Journal* 38 (1995): 635–672.

62. D. McDonald & A. Smith, "A Proven Connection: Performance Management and Business Results," *Compensation & Benefits Review* 27, no. 6 (1 January 1995): 59.

63. I. Fulmer, B. Gerhart, & K. Scott, "Are the 100 Best Better? An Empirical Investigation of the Relationship between Being a 'Great Place to Work' and Firm Performance," *Personnel Psychology* (Winter 2003): 965–993.

64. B. Schneider & D. E. Bowen, "Employee and Customer Perceptions of Service in Banks: Replication and Extension," *Journal of Applied Psychology* 70 (1985): 423–433; B. Schneider, J. J. Parkington, & V. M. Buxton, "Employee and Customer Perceptions of Service in Banks," *Administrative Science Quarterly* 25 (1980): 252–267.

Chapter 2

1. C. S. George, Jr., *The History of Management Thought* (Englewood Cliffs, NJ: Prentice Hall, 1972).

2. A. Erman, *Life in Ancient Egypt* (London: Macmillan & Co., 1984).

3. "History of the Organization of Work: Organization of Work in Preindustrial Times: Medieval Industry," *Britannica Online,* http://www.eb.com:180/cgi-bin/g? DocF=macro/5006/66/3.html, 15 January 1999.

4. "History of the Organization of Work: Organization of Work in Preindustrial Times: The Ancient World," *Britannica Online,* http://www.eb.com:180/cgi-bin/g? DocF=macro/5006/66/1.html, 15 January 1999.

5. J. B. White, "The Line Starts Here: Mass-Production Techniques Changed the Way People Work and Live throughout the World," *Wall Street Journal,* 11 January 1999, R25.

6. R. B. Reich, *The Next American Frontier* (New York: Times Books, 1983).

7. J. Mickelwait & A. Wooldridge, The Company: *A Short History of a Revolutionary Idea* (New York: Modern Library, 2003).

8. H. Kendall, "Unsystematized, Systematized, and Scientific Management," in *Scientific Management: A Collection of the More Significant Articles Describing the Taylor System of Management,* ed. C. Thompson (Easton, PA: Hive Publishing, 1972), 103–131.

9. United States Congress, House, Special Committee, *Hearings to Investigate the Taylor and Other Systems of Shop Management,* vol 3. (Washington D.C.: Government Printing Office, 1912).

10. Ibid.

11. Taylor, *The Principles of Scientific Management.*

12. A. Derickson, "Physiological Science and Scientific Management in the Progressive Era: Frederic S. Lee and the Committee on Industrial Fatigue," *Business History Review* 68 (1994): 483–514.

13. A. Scharf, "Scripted Talk: From 'Welcome to McDonald's' to 'Paper or Plastic?' Employers Control the Speech of Service Workers," *Dollars & Sense,* September–October 2003, 35; C. McCann, "Have a Nice Day and an Icy Stare," *Marketing Week,* 2 September 2004, 27.

14. United States Congress, House, Special Committee, 1912.

15. Taylor, *The Principles of Scientific Management.*

16. Wrege & Hodgetts, "Frederick W. Taylor's 1899 Pig Iron Observations"; Hough & White, "Using Stories to Create Change."

17. E. Locke, "The Ideas of Frederick W. Taylor: An Evaluation," *Academy of Management Review* 7 (1982): 14–24.

18. George, Jr., *The History of Management Thought.*

19. F. Gilbreth & L. Gilbreth, "Applied Motion Study," in *The Writings of the Gilbreths,* ed. W. R. Spriegel & C. E. Myers (1917; rpr. Homewood, IL: Richard D. Irwin, 1953), 207–274.

20. D. Ferguson, "Don't Call It 'Time and Motion Study,'" *IIE Solutions* 29, no. 5 (1997): 22–23.

21. Ibid.

22. P. Peterson, "Training and Development: The View of Henry L. Gantt (1861–1919)," *SAM Advanced Management Journal,* Winter 1987, 20–23.

23. H. Gantt, "Industrial Efficiency," *National Civic Federation Report of the 11th Annual Meeting,* New York, 12 January 1991, 103.

24. M. Weber, *The Theory of Economic and Social Organization,* trans. by A. Henderson & T. Parsons (New York: The Free Press, 1947).

25. D. Piller, "Enron's Watkins: Ethics Start Early," *Fort Worth Star-Telegram,* 3 May 2001, C1; "Instructions for Filing a Disclosure of Conflict of Interest Statement," Honolulu County, http://www.co.honolulu.hi.us/ethics/em-2.pdf, 3 May 2003; "FAQs: Ethics," Georgia Center for Nonprofits, http://www.nonprofitgeorgia.org/faq-ethics1.html, 1 May 2003.

26. M. Weber, *The Protestant Ethic and the Spirit of Capitalism* (New York: Scribner's, 1958).

27. D. Wren, "Henri Fayol As Strategist: A Nineteenth Century Corporate Turnaround," *Management Decision* 39 (2001): 475–487.

28. Ibid.

29. Ibid.

30. H. Verney, "Un grand ingénieur: Henri Fayol," *La fondateur de la doctrine administrative: Henri Fayol* (Paris: Dunod, 1925), as cited in Wren, "Henri Fayol As Strategist."

31. D. A. Wren, A. G. Bedeian, & J. D. Breeze, "The Foundations of Henri Fayol's Administrative Theory," *Management Decision* 40 (2002): 906–918.

32. Mary Parker Follett, *Mary Parker Follett—Prophet of Management: A Celebration of Writings from the 1920s,* ed. P. Graham (Boston: Harvard Business School Press, 1995).

33. Ibid.

34. M. Losey, "HR Comes of Age," *HRMagazine* 43, no. 3 (1998): 40–53.

35. J. H. Smith, "The Enduring Legacy of Elton Mayo," *Human Relations* 51, no. 3 (1998): 221–249.

36. E. Mayo, *The Human Problems of an Industrial Civilization* (New York: Macmillan, 1933).

37. Ibid.

38. "Hawthorne Revisited: The Legend and the Legacy," *Organizational Dynamics* (Winter 1975): 66–80.

39. D. Linden, "The Mother of Them All," *Forbes,* 16 January 1995, 75.

40. E. Mayo, *The Social Problems of an Industrial Civilization* (Boston: Harvard Graduate School of Business Administration, 1945) 65–67.

41. George, Jr., *The History of Management Thought.*

42. Ibid.

43. C. I. Barnard, *The Functions of the Executive* (Cambridge, MA: Harvard University Press, 1938), 4.

44. J. Fuller & A. Mansour, "Operations Management and Operations Research: A Historical and Relational Perspective," *Management Decision* 41 (2003): 422–426.

45. D. Ashmos & G. Huber, "The Systems Paradigm in Organization Theory: Correcting the Record and Suggesting

the Future," *Academy of Management Review* 12 (1987): 607–621; F. Kast & J. Rosenzweig, "General Systems Theory: Applications for Organizations and Management," *Academy of Management Journal* 15 (1972): 447–465; D. Katz & R. Kahn, *The Social Psychology of Organizations* (New York: Wiley, 1966).

46. R. Mockler, "The Systems Approach to Business Organization and Decision Making," *California Management Review* 11, issue 2 (1968): 53–58.

47. F. Luthans & T. Stewart, "A General Contingency Theory of Management," *Academy of Management Review* 2, issue 2 (1977): 181–195.

Chapter 3

1. Heller, Lorraine, "Health Could Boost Declining US Cookie Sales, Report," www.foodnavigator.com, 18 August 2006. http://www.foodnavigator-usa.com/news/ng.asp?id=69965-cookies-whole-grains-healthy-eating.

2. R. Guth, "Videogame Giant Links with Sony, Snubbing Microsoft," *Wall Street Journal*, 12 May 2003, A1; "Cost of Making Games Set to Soar," BBC News, 17 November 2005, http://news.bbc.co.uk/1/hi/technology/4442346.stm

3. E. Romanelli & M. L. Tushman, "Organizational Transformation as Punctuated Equilibrium: An Empirical Test," *Academy of Management Journal* 37 (1994): 1141–1166.

4. H. Banks, "A Sixties Industry in a Nineties Economy," *Forbes*, 9 May 1994, 107–112.

5. L. Cowan, "Cheap Fuel Should Carry Many Airlines to More Record Profits for 1st Quarter," *Wall Street Journal*, 4 April 1998, B17A.

6. "Airlines Still in Upheaval, 5 Years after 9/11," *CNNMoney.com*, 8 September 2006, http://money.cnn.com/2006/09/08/news/companies/airlines_sept11/?postversion=2006090812.

7. "New Product Review," *Dairy Foods*, http://www.dairyfoods.com/CDA/ArticleInformation/products/BNPProductItem/0,6783,141830,00.html, 15 January 2005; B. Jones, "The Changing Dairy Industry," Department of Agricultural & Applied Economics & Center for Dairy Profitability, http://www.aae.wisc.edu/jones/Presentations/Wisc&TotalDairyTrends.pdf, 15 January 2003.

8. S. Ghosemajumder, "Digital Music Distribution," *MIT Sloan School of Management*, http://shumans.com/digital-music/?p=1&p2=1.html; "30 Products for 30 Years," *MacWorld*, June 2006, 15-16; T. Mennecke, "CD Sales, Shipments Down in 2005," *Slyck News*, 31 March 2006, http://www.slyck.com/news.php?story=1143; P. Burrows, "Microsoft Singing Its Own iTune," *BusinessWeek* Online, 11

July 2006, 20; "Apple Presents iPod," 23 October 2001, http://www.apple.com/pr/library/2001/oct/23ipod.html, http://www.wikipedia.com.

9. "Samsung Invests $2.1B in LCD Line," *Electronic News*, 7 March 2005; "LG Philips LCD Develops 100-Inch LCD Panel, the Largest in the World," www.lgphilips-lcd.com/homeContain/jsp/eng/inv/inv101_j_e.jsp?BOARD_IDX=1054&languageSec=E ; "Samsung, LG. Philips Start New LCD Production," www.ciol.com/content/news/2006/106010202.asp; "Samsung Develops World's Largest (82″) Full HDTV TFT-LCD," http://www.samsung.com/Products/TFTLCD/News/category_TFTLCD_20050307_0000101494.htm, "Samsung and LG Philips Start New LCD Production," 1 January 2006, http://www.boston.com/business/articles/2006/01/01/samsung_and_lgphilips_start_new_lcd_production/; E. Ramstad, "I Want My Flat TV Now!" *Wall Street Journal*, 27 May 2004, B1.

10. "Consumer Products Brief—Kraft Foods Inc.: Price of Maxwell House Coffee to Rise 14% As Costs Increase," *Wall Street Journal*, 15 December 2004, A16.

11. "First, by the Numbers, the CFO Poll," *Fortune*, 17 February 2003, 30.

12. R. Sharpe, "Nannies on Speed Dial: There Is Growing Army of Domestic Help Out There, and More and More Families Are Picking Up the Phone," *BusinessWeek*, 18 September 2000, 108; N. Powell, "Going Above and Beyond," *The Hamilton Spectator*, 25 July 2006, http://www.circles.com/news/news_Jul06_article_Above_and_Beyond.htm.

13. "The Civil Rights Act of 1991," U.S. Equal Employment Opportunity Commission, http://www.eeoc.gov/policy/cra91.html, 16 January 2005.

14. "Compliance Assistance—Family and Medical Leave Act (FMLA)," U.S. Department of Labor: Employment Standards Administration Wage and Hour Division, http://www.dol.gov/esa/whd/fmla/, 16 January 2005.

15. R. J. Bies & T. R. Tyler, "The Litigation Mentality in Organizations: A Test of Alternative Psychological Explanations," *Organization Science* 4 (1993): 352–366.

16. D. Jones, "Fired Workers Fight Back . . . and Win," *USA Today*, 2 April 1998, B1.

17. S. Gardner, G. Gomes, & J. Morgan, "Wrongful Termination and the Expanding Public Policy Exception: Implications and Advice," *SAM Advanced Management Journal* 65 (2000): 38.

18. Jones, "Fired Workers Fight Back."

19. R. Johnston & S. Mehra, "Best-Practice Complaint Management," *Academy of Management Experience* 16 (November 2002): 145–154.

20. D. Smart & C. Martin, "Manufacturer Responsiveness to Consumer Correspondence: An Empirical Investigation of Consumer Perceptions," *Journal of Consumer Affairs* 26 (1992): 104.

21. S. Gray, "Trends (A Special Report)—On the Menu: Speed and Variety," *Wall Street Journal*, 22 November 2004, R4.

22. S. A. Zahra & S. S. Chaples, "Blind Spots in Competitive Analysis," *Academy of Management Executive* 7 (1993): 7–28.

23. M. Frazier, "You Suck: Dyson, Hoover and Oreck Trade Accusations in Court, on TV as Brit Upstart Leaves Rivals in Dust," *Advertising Age*, 25 July 2005, 1.

24. P. Grant, "Comcast Plans Major Rollout of Phone Service over Cable," *Wall Street Journal*, 10 January 2005, B1.

25. A. Squeo, "FCC Is Poised to Clarify Future of Internet Phone Calls," *Wall Street Journal*, 22 January 2004, B1.

26. K. G. Provan, "Embeddedness, Interdependence, and Opportunism in Organizational Supplier-Buyer Networks," *Journal of Management* 19 (1993): 841–856.

27. C. Unninayar & N. P. Sindt, "Diamonds an Industry in Transition: Sometimes the Speed of Change Is Alarming," *Couture International Jeweler*, August–Sept 2003, 68–75; N. Gaouette, "Israel's Diamond Dealers Tremble: Diamond Colossus DeBeers Today Launches Fundamental Changes to $56 Billion Retail Market," *Christian Science Monitor*, 1 June 2001, [Online].

28. N. Shirouzu, "Chain Reaction—Big Three's Outsourcing Plan: Make Parts Suppliers Do It," *Wall Street Journal*, 10 June 2004, A1.

29. D. Birch, "Staying on Good Terms," *Supply Management*, 12 April 2001, 36.

30. S. Parker & C. Axtell, "Seeing Another Viewpoint: Antecedents and Outcomes of Employee Perspective Taking," *Academy of Management Journal* 44 (2001): 1085–1100; B. K. Pilling, L. A. Crosby, & D. W. Jackson, "Relational Bonds in Industrial Exchange: An Experimental Test of the Transaction Cost Economic Framework," *Journal of Business Research* 30 (1994): 237–251.

31. "Carmakers Eye Economy with Unease," *USA Today*, 24 May 2004, B.06.

32. M. Horn, "Sinning in an SUV," *U.S. News & World Report*, 16 December 2002, 10; http://www.nhtsa.dot.gov/cars/rules/cafe/overview.htm

33. S. Dudley, "The Coming Shift in Regulation," *Regulation*, 1 October 2002.

34. S. Dudley, "Regulation and Small Business Competitive," *Federal Document Clearing House*, Congressional Testimony, Prepared Remarks for the House Committee on Small Business Subcommittee on Regulatory Reform and Oversight, 20 May 2004.

35. H. Morley, "Bush Orders Cut in Regulations—Change Will Cut Red Tape for Small Businesses," *Knight-Ridder Tribune*, 17 August 2002.

36. "EU's Aggressive Anti-Smoking Campaign," *Creative Bits*, http://iraszl.brinkster.net/cbforum/viewtopic.php?t=483, 17 January 2005.

37. M. Hudson, "PETA Doll Ruffles KFC's Feathers," *Roanoke Times*, http://www.

roanoke.com/extra%5C16581.html, 8 January 2005.

38. "Another Ford Trial: Steering around Activists," *Wall Street Journal,* 26 July 2006, A2.

39. N. E. Boudette & J. A. White, "At GM, Curbing Inventories Calls for Juggling Act," *Wall Street Journal,* 8 January 2007, A1; J. Ball, "Detroit Fears Some Consumers May Be Souring on Big SUVs," *Wall Street Journal Online,* http://online.wsj.com/ article/ 0,,SB1041979477724000464,00.html, 8 January 2003.

40. C. Hymowitz, "Top Marketing Officers Find Getting Together Helps Them Do the Job," *Wall Street Journal,* 11 January 2005, B1.

41. D. F. Jennings & J. R. Lumpkin, "Insights between Environmental Scanning Activities and Porter's Generic Strategies: An Empirical Analysis," *Journal of Management* 4 (1992): 791–803.

42. V. Vara, "Software Giants Seek Friends among Hackers," *Wall Street Journal,* 3 August 2006, B1.

43. S. E. Jackson & J. E. Dutton, "Discerning Threats and Opportunities," *Administrative Science Quarterly* 33 (1988): 370–387.

44. B. Thomas, S. M. Clark, & D. A. Gioia, "Strategic Sensemaking and Organizational Performance: Linkages among Scanning, Interpretation, Action, and Outcomes," *Academy of Management Journal* 36 (1993): 239–270.

45. R. Daft, J. Sormunen, & D. Parks, "Chief Executive Scanning, Environmental Characteristics, and Company Performance: An Empirical Study," *Strategic Management Journal* 9 (1988): 123–139; V. Garg, B. Walters, & R. Priem, "Chief Executive Scanning Emphases, Environmental Dynamism, and Manufacturing Firm Performance," *Strategic Management Journal* 24 (2003): 725–744; D. Miller & P. H. Friesen, "Strategy-Making and Environment: The Third Link," *Strategic Management Journal* 4 (1983): 221–235.

46. P. Grant, "Comcast Plans Major Rollout of Phone Service over Cable."

47. L. Yuan & C. Bryan-Low, "iPhone Hinges On the Likes of Mr. Digate: In High-End Realm, Handset Must Court the Affluent Tech-Set," *Wall Street Journal,* 11 January 2007, B4.

48. A. Harrington, N. Hira, & C. Tkaczyk, "Hall of Fame: If Making the 100 Best List Is an Enormous Accomplishment, Consider How Tough It Is to Repeat the Feat Every Single Year," *Fortune,* 24 January 2005, 94; "SAS Makes the *Fortune* 'Hall of Fame,'" SAS Web Site, http://www.sas.com/news/feature/16jan05/fortune.html, 20 January 2005.

49. P. Elmer-DeWitt, "Mine, All Mine; Bill Gates Wants a Piece of Everybody's Action, but Can He Get It?" *Time,* 5 June 1995.

50. D. M. Boje, "The Storytelling Organization: A Study of Story Performance in an Office-Supply Firm," *Administrative Science Quarterly* 36 (1991): 106–126.

51. S. Walton & J. Huey, *Sam Walton: Made in America* (New York: Doubleday, 1992).

52. M. Hayes, "Bowa Builders: NRS Excellence in Class, 50—Plus," *HousingZone.com,* http://www.housingzone.com/topics/pr/nrs/pr03ia009.asp, 19 January 2005.

53. D. R. Denison & A. K. Mishra, "Toward a Theory of Organizational Culture and Effectiveness," *Organization Science* 6 (1995): 204–223.

54. F. Haley, "Mutual Benefit: How Does Genencor Maintain Its Incredibly Loyal Workforce? By Involving Its Employees in Almost Everything," *Fast Company,* October 2004, 98–100.

55. "Company Profile," F. H. Faulding & Company, http://www.faulding.com.au/home/comp_profile/mission/mission.html, 21 June 2001.

56. S. Yearout, G. Miles, & R. Koonce, "Multi-Level Visioning," *Training & Development,* 1 March 2001, 31.

57. T. Brown, "A Vision from Scratch," *Across the Board,* 1 May 2001, 77.

58. "Hamburger University," McDonald's Media Site, http://www.media.mcdonalds.com/secured/company/training/, 18 January 2005.

59. J. Sorenson, "The Strength of Corporate Culture and the Reliability of Firm Performance," *Administrative Science Quarterly* 47 (2002): 70–91.

60. A. Zuckerman, "Strong Corporate Cultures and Firm Performance: Are There Tradeoffs?" *Academy of Management Executive,* November 2002, 158–160.

61. *McDonald's Summary Annual Report* 2005, 2-4; D. Stires, "McDonald's Keeps Right on Cooking," *Fortune,* 17 May 2004, 102.

62. E. Schein, *Organizational Culture and Leadership,* 2d ed. (San Francisco: Jossey-Bass, 1992).

63. E. Byron, "'Call Me Mike!' – To Attract and Keep Talent, JCPenney CEO Loosens Up Once-Formal Workplace," *Wall Street Journal,* 27 March 2006, B1.

64. Ibid.

65. C. Daniels, "Does This Man Need a Shrink? Companies Are Using Psychological Testing to Screen Candidates for Top Jobs," *Fortune,* 5 February 2001, 205.

Chapter 4

1. J. Schramm, "Perceptions on Ethics," *HR Magazine,* November 2004, online 18 January 2007, http://www.shrm.org/hrmagazine/articles/1104/1104futfocus.asp/

2. M. Jackson (Associated Press), "Workplace Cheating Rampant, Half of Employees Surveyed Admit They Take Unethical Actions," *Peoria Journal Star,* 5 April 1997.

3. C. Smith, "The Ethical Workplace," *Association Management* 52 (2000): 70–73.

4. K. Tyler, "Do the Right Thing: Ethics Training Programs Help Employees Deal with Ethical Dilemmas," *HR Magazine,* February 2005, online http://www.shrm.org/hrmagazine/articles/0205/0205tyler.asp.

5. R. K. Bennett, "How Honest Are We?" *Reader's Digest,* December 1995, 49–55; L. Callaway, "On the Wallet Watch—Honesty's Not Big Apple's Policy," *New York Post,* 31 July 2000, 41; A. Golab, "Results of Honesty Test: Mostly 'Finders, Keepers,'" *Chicago Sun-Times,* 12 March 1999, 3.

6. "2004 Report to the Nation on Occupational Fraud and Abuse," Association of Certified Fraud Examiners," http://www.cfenet.com/pdfs/2004RttN.pdf, 27 January 2005; K. Gibson, "Excuses, Excuses: Moral Slippage in the Workplace," *Business Horizons* 43, no. 6 (2000): 65; S. L. Robinson & R. J. Bennett, "A Typology of Deviant Workplace Behaviors: A Multidimensional Scaling Study," *Academy of Management Journal* 38 (1995): 555–572.

7. Ibid.

8. J. Norman, "Cultivating a Culture of Honesty," *The Orange County Register* (Santa Ana, CA), 23 October 2006.

9. S. Gaudin, "Computer Sabotage Case Back in Court," *Network World Fusion,* 19 April 2001, 12.

10. R. Hollinger & J. Davis, "2003 National Retail Security Final Report," Center for Studies in Criminology and Law, University of Florida, http://www.crim.ufl.edu/research/srp/srp.htm, 27 January 2005.

11. M. Pressler, "Cost and Robbers; Shoplifting and Employee Thievery Add Dollars to Price Tag," *Washington Post,* 16 February 2003, H05.

12. Lehr Middlebrooks & Vreeland, P.C. (byline), "Many U.S. Employers Aren't Doing Enough to Address Workplace Violence," *Alabama Employment Law Letter,* December 2006.

13. J. Merchant & J. Lundell, "Workplace Violence: A Report to the Nation," University of Iowa Injury Prevention Center, http://www.pmeh.uiowa.edu/iprc/NATION.PDF, 27 January 2005.

14. D. Palmer & A. Zakhem, "Bridging the Gap between Theory and Practice: Using the 1991 Federal Sentencing Guidelines as a Paradigm for Ethics Training," *Journal of Business Ethics* 29, no. 1/2 (2001): 77–84.

15. K. Tyler, "Do the Right Thing: Ethics Training Programs Help Employees Deal with Ethical Dilemmas."

16. D. R. Dalton, M. B. Metzger, & J. W. Hill, "The 'New' U.S. Sentencing Commission Guidelines: A Wake-Up Call for Corporate America," *Academy of Management Executive* 8 (1994): 7–16.

17. B. Ettore, "Crime and Punishment: A Hard Look at White-Collar Crime," *Management Review* 83 (1994): 10–16.

18. F. Robinson & C. C. Pauze, "What Is a Board's Liability for Not Adopting a Compliance Program?" *Healthcare Financial Management* 51, no. 9 (1997): 64.

19. D. Murphy, "The Federal Sentencing Guidelines for Organizations: A Decade of Promoting Compliance and Ethics," *Iowa Law Review* 87 (2002): 697–719.

20. Robinson & Pauze, "What Is a Board's Liability?"

21. B. Schwartz, "The Nuts and Bolts of an Effective Compliance Program," *HR Focus* 74, no. 8 (1997): 13–15.

22. L. A. Hays, "A Matter of Time: Widow Sues IBM over Death Benefits," *Wall Street Journal*, 6 July 1995.

23. T. M. Jones, "Ethical Decision Making by Individuals in Organizations: An Issue-Contingent Model," *Academy of Management Review* 16 (1991): 366–395.

24. S. Morris & R. McDonald, "The Role of Moral Intensity in Moral Judgments: An Empirical Investigation," *Journal of Business Ethics* 14 (1995): 715–726; B. Flannery & D. May, "Environmental Ethical Decision Making in the U.S. Metal-Finishing Industry," *Academy of Management Journal* 43 (2000): 642–662.

25. S. Sparks, "Federal Agents Seize Computers in 27 Cities as Part of Crackdown on Software Piracy," *Wall Street Journal*, 12 December 2001, B4.

26. L. Kohlberg, "Stage and Sequence: The Cognitive-Developmental Approach to Socialization," in *Handbook of Socialization Theory and Research*, ed. D. A. Goslin (Chicago: Rand McNally, 1969); L. Trevino, "Moral Reasoning and Business Ethics: Implications for Research, Education, and Management," *Journal of Business Ethics* 11 (1992): 445–459.

27. L. Trevino & M. Brown, "Managing to be Ethical: Debunking Five Business Ethics Myths," *Academy of Management Executive* 18 (May 2004): 69–81.

28. L. T. Hosmer, "Trust: The Connecting Link between Organizational Theory and Philosophical Ethics," *Academy of Management Review* 20 (1995): 379–403.

29. M. R. Cunningham, D. T. Wong, & A. P. Barbee, "Self-Presentation Dynamics on Overt Integrity Tests: Experimental Studies of the Reid Report," *Journal of Applied Psychology* 79 (1994): 643–658; J. Wanek, P. Sackett & D. Ones, "Toward an Understanding of Integrity Test Similarities and Differences: An Item-Level Analysis of Seven Tests," *Personnel Psychology* 56 (Winter 2003): 873–894.

30. H. J. Bernardin, "Validity of an Honesty Test in Predicting Theft among Convenience Store Employees," *Academy of Management Journal* 36 (1993): 1097–1108.

31. J. M. Collins & F. L. Schmidt, "Personality, Integrity, and White Collar Crime: A Construct Validity Study," *Personnel Psychology* (1993): 295–311.

32. W. C. Borman, M. A. Hanson, & J. W. Hedge, "Personnel Selection," *Annual Review of Psychology* 48 (1997).

33. P. E. Murphy, "Corporate Ethics Statements: Current Status and Future Prospects," *Journal of Business Ethics* 14 (1995): 727–740.

34. "Integrity Means ..." Nortel Networks, http://www.nortelnetworks.com/corporate/community/ethics/integrity1.html, 27 January 2005.

35. S. J. Harrington, "What Corporate America Is Teaching about Ethics," *Academy of Management Executive* 5 (1991): 21–30.

36. L. A. Berger, "Train All Employees to Solve Ethical Dilemmas," *Best's Review—Life-Health Insurance Edition* 95 (1995): 70–80.

37. L. Trevino, G. Weaver, D. Gibson, & B. Toffler, "Managing Ethics and Legal Compliance: What Works and What Hurts," *California Management Review* 41, no. 2 (1999): 131–151.

38. "Business Ethics Training: Teaching Right from Wrong," *Salt Lake Tribune*, 11 June 2000, E5.

39. Trevino, Weaver, Gibson, & Toffler, "Managing Ethics."

40. A. Countryman, "Leadership Key Ingredient in Ethics Recipe, Experts Say," *Chicago Tribune*, 1 December 2002, Business 1.

41. "2003 National Business Ethics Survey," Ethics Resource Center Research Department, http://www.ethics.org/nbes2003/2003nbes_summary.html, 27 January 2005.

42. G. Weaver & L. Trevino, "Integrated and Decoupled Corporate Social Performance: Management Commitments, External Pressures, and Corporate Ethics Practices," *Academy of Management Journal* 42 (1999): 539–552; G. Weaver, L. Trevino, & P. Cochran, "Corporate Ethics Programs as Control Systems: Influences of Executive Commitment and Environmental Factors," *Academy of Management Journal* 42 (1999): 41–57.

43. J. Salopek, "Do the Right Thing," *Training & Development* 55 (July 2001): 38–44.

44. M. Gundlach, S. Douglas, & M. Martinko, "The Decision to Blow the Whistle: A Social Information Processing Framework," *Academy of Management Executive* 17 (2003): 107–123.

45. M. Schwartz, "Business Ethics: Time to Blow the Whistle?" *Globe & Mail*, 5 March 1998, B2.

46. M. Jacobs, "The Legal Option: Employees Dreamed of Getting Rich from Stock Options; Now They're Heading to Court to Make Sure Those Dreams Come True," *Wall Street Journal*, 12 April 2001, R9.

47. "More Corporate Boards Involved in Ethics Programs; Ethics Training Becoming Standard Practice," *PR Newswire*, 16 October 2006, http://www.prnewswire.com.

48. M. P. Miceli & J. P. Near, "Whistleblowing: Reaping the Benefits," *Academy of Management Executive* 8 (1994): 65–72.

49. M. Master & E. Heresniak. "The Disconnect in Ethics Training," *Across the Board* 39 (September 2002): 51–52.

50. H. R. Bower, *Social Responsibilities of the Businessman* (New York: Harper & Row, 1953).

51. "Beyond the Green Corporation," *BusinessWeek*, 29 January 2007.

52. S. L. Wartick & P. L. Cochran, "The Evolution of the Corporate Social Performance Model," *Academy of Management Review* 10 (1985): 758–769.

53. J. Nocera, "The Paradox of Businesses as Do-Gooders," *New York Times*, 3 February 2007, C1.

54. S. Waddock, C. Bodwell, & S. Graves. "Responsibility: The New Business Imperative," *Academy of Management Executive* 16 (2002): 132–148.

55. T. Donaldson & L. E. Pr.eston, "The Stakeholder Theory of the Corporation: Concepts, Evidence, and Implications," *Academy of Management Review* 20 (1995): 65–91.

56. M. B. E. Clarkson, "A Stakeholder Framework for Analyzing and Evaluating Corporate Social Performance," *Academy of Management Review* 20 (1995): 92–117.

57. B. Agle, R. Mitchell, & J. Sonnenfeld, "Who Matters to CEOs? An Investigation of Stakeholder Attributes and Salience, Corporate Performance, and CEO Values," *Academy of Management Journal* 42 (1999): 507–525.

58. L. Etter, "Smithfield to Phase Out Crates: Big Pork Producer Yields to Activists, Customers on Animal-Welfare Issue," *Wall Street Journal*, 25 January 2007, A14.

59. E. W. Orts, "Beyond Shareholders: Interpreting Corporate Constituency Statutes," *George Washington Law Review* 61 (1992): 14–135.

60. A. B. Carroll, "A Three-Dimensional Conceptual Model of Corporate Performance," *Academy of Management Review* 4 (1979): 497–505.

61. Ibid.

62. J. Lublin & M. Murrary, "CEOs Leave Faster Than Ever Before as Boards, Investors Lose Patience," *Wall Street Journal Interactive*, 27 October 2000.

63. D. Woodruff, "Europe Shows More CEOs the Door," *Wall Street Journal*, 1 July 2002.

64. C. Bowman, "Success of Capital Area's War on Smog Challenged," *Sacramento Bee*, 7 February 1998, A1.

65. "Air Guide 31: Implementation of Part 201 and Part 212 Permitting and Reasonably Available Control Technology Requirements for Bakeries," New York State Department of Environmental Conservation, http://www.dec.state.ny.us/website/ogc/egm/airguide31.html, 5 February 2005.

66. T. Howard, "Low-Carb Message Not Popular, but Sales Are Up," *USA Today,* 8 December 2003, 10B.

67. "Results: How You're Helping," The Hunger Site, http://www.thehungersite.com/cgi-bin/WebObjects/CTDSites.woa/169/wo/8Y0000Bd300Sk100r3/

68. K. Scannell, "Witness Says Police-Vest Maker Ignored Safety Concerns," *Wall Street Journal,* 15 November 2004, C1.

69. S. Richardson, "No Time to Stop—Parsons Plant Gives Thanks," *The Pantagraph,* 14 July 2005, 1.

70. J. White, "Move by Honda Ups the Ante on Car Safety," *Wall Street Journal,* 30 October 2003, D1.

71. A. McWilliams & D. Siegel, "Corporate Social Responsibility: A Theory of the Firm Perspective," *Academy of Management Review* 26, no. 1 (2001): 117–127.

72. H. Haines, "Noah Joins Ranks of Socially Responsible Funds," *Dow Jones News Service,* 13 October 1995. A meta-analysis of 41 different studies also found no relationship between corporate social responsibility and profitability. Though not reported in the meta-analysis, when confidence intervals are placed around its average sample-weighted correlation of .06, the lower confidence interval includes zero, leading to the conclusion that there is no relationship between corporate social responsibility and profitability. See M. Orlitzky, "Does Firm Size Confound the Relationship between Corporate Social Responsibility and Firm Performance?" *Journal of Business Ethics* 33 (2001): 167–180.

73. J. Pereira, "Doing Good and Doing Well at Timberland," *Wall Street Journal,* 9 September 2003, B1.

74. T. Singer, "Can Business Still Save the World?" *Inc.,* 1 April 2001, 58.

Chapter 5

1. L. A. Hill, *Becoming a Manager: Master a New Identity* (Boston: Harvard Business School Press, 1992).

2. N. Shirouzu, "Low-Key Chief of Toyota's U.S. Unit Discloses Bold Goals," *Wall Street Journal,* 17 March 2004; A. Chozick, "Toyota Net Rises 39% As Auto Maker Deals with Growth Challenges," *Wall Street Journal,* 5 August 2006, A3.

3. E. A. Locke & G. P. Latham, *A Theory of Goal Setting & Task Performance* (Englewood Cliffs, NJ: Prentice Hall, 1990).

4. M. E. Tubbs, "Goal-Setting: A Meta-Analytic Examination of the Empirical Evidence," *Journal of Applied Psychology* 71 (1986): 474–483.

5. J. Bavelas & E. S. Lee, "Effect of Goal Level on Performance: A Trade-Off of Quantity and Quality," *Canadian Journal of Psychology* 32 (1978): 219–240.

6. D. Turner, "Ability, Aspirations Fine, but Persistence Is What Gets Results," *Seattle Times,* http://archives.seattletimes.nwsource.com/cgi-bin/texis.cgi/web/vortex/display?slug=dale15m&date=20030215, 13 February 2005.

7. Harvard Management Update, "Learn by 'Failing Forward,'" *The Globe & Mail,* 31 October 2000, B17.

8. C. C. Miller, "Strategic Planning and Firm Performance: A Synthesis of More Than Two Decades of Research," *Academy of Management Performance* 37 (1994): 1649–1665.

9. H. Mintzberg, "Rethinking Strategic Planning: Part I: Pitfalls and Fallacies," *Long Range Planning* 27 (1994): 12–21, and "Part II: New Roles for Planners," 22–30; H. Mintzberg, "The Pitfalls of Strategic Planning," *California Management Review* 36 (1993): 32–47.

10. P. Dvorak, "Sony TVs Take Sibling Tips—Latest Machines Borrow from Videogame and Audio Technology," *Wall Street Journal,* 20 August 2004, B3.

11. Mintzberg, "The Pitfalls of Strategic Planning."

12. Locke & Latham, *A Theory of Goal Setting & Task Performance.*

13. A. King, B. Oliver, B. Sloop, & K. Vaverek, *Planning & Goal Setting for Improved Performance: Participant's Guide* (Cincinnati, OH: Thomson Executive Press, 1995).

14. H. Klein & M. Wesson, "Goal and Commitment and the Goal-Setting Process: Conceptual Clarification and Empirical Synthesis," *Journal of Applied Psychology* 84 (1999): 885-886

15. Locke & Latham, *A Theory of Goal Setting & Task Performance.*

16. A. Pressman, "Ocean Spray's Creative Juices," *BusinessWeek,* 15 May 2006, 88–90.

17. A. Bandura & D. H. Schunk, "Cultivating Competence, Self-Efficacy, and Intrinsic Interest through Proximal Self-Motivation," *Journal of Personality & Social Psychology* 41 (1981): 586–598.

18. Locke & Latham, *A Theory of Goal Setting & Task Performance.*

19. M. J. Neubert, "The Value of Feedback and Goal Setting over Goal Setting Alone and Potential Moderators of This Effect: A Meta-Analysis," *Human Performance* 11 (1998): 321–335.

20. E. H. Bowman & D. Hurry, "Strategy through the Option Lens: An Integrated View of Resource Investments and the Incremental-Choice Process," *Academy of Management Review* 18 (1993): 760–782.

21. M. Lawson, "In Praise of Slack: Time Is of the Essence," *Academy of Management Executive* 15 (2000): 125–135.

22. J. C. Collins & J. I. Porras, "Organizational Vision and Visionary Organizations," *California Management Review* (Fall 1991): 30–52.

23. Ibid.

24. Ibid.

25. "President Bush Announces New Vision for Space Exploration Program," The White House, http://www.whitehouse.gov/news/releases/2004/01/20040114-1.html, 17 April 2005.

26. N. Gull, "Plan B (and C and D and . . .)," *Inc.,* March 2004, 40.

27. R. Richmond, "It's 10 a.m. Do You Know Where Your Workers Are?" *Wall Street Journal,* 12 January 2004, R1.

28. Adapted from quality procedure at G & G Manufacturing, Cincinnati, Ohio.

29. N. Humphrey, "References a Tricky Issue for Both Sides," *Nashville Business Journal* 11 (8 May 1995): 1A.

30. K. R. MacCrimmon, R. N. Taylor, & E. A. Locke, "Decision Making and Problem Solving," in *Handbook of Industrial & Organizational Psychology,* ed. M. D. Dunnette (Chicago: Rand McNally, 1976), 1397–1453.

31. "Airbus's 'Big Baby,' the A380 Airliner, Fights a Weight Problem," *JEC Composites,* http://www.globalcomposites.com/news/news_fiche.asp?id=1353&, 19 February 2005.

32. D. Michaels, "Jumbo Bet: At Airbus, Picturing Huge Jet Was Easy; Building It Is Hard," *Wall Street Journal,* 27 May 2004, A1.

33. MacCrimmon, Taylor, & Locke, "Decision Making and Problem Solving."

34. Michaels, "Jumbo Bet: At Airbus, Picturing Huge Jet Was Easy."

35. *Consumers Reports Buying Guide: 2006,* 129–131.

36. "New-Vehicle Ratings Comparison by Car Category," *ConsumerReports.org,* http://www.consumerreports.org/main/content/autos/ratingcompare.jsp, 19 February 2005.

37. P. Djang, "Selecting Personal Computers," *Journal of Research on Computing in Education* 25 (1993): 327.

38. "European Cities Monitor," Cushman & Wakefield Healy & Baker, 2005. Available online at http://www.cushmanwakefield.com/cwglobal/docviewer/European%20Cities%20Monitor.pdf?id=ca1500006&repositoryKey=CoreRepository&itemDesc=document.

39. B. Dumaine, "The Trouble with Teams," *Fortune,* 5 September 1994, 86–92.

40. L. Pelled, K. Eisenhardt, & K. Xin, "Exploring the Black Box: An Analysis of Work Group Diversity, Conflict, and Performance," *Administrative Science Quarterly* 44, no. 1 (March 1, 1999): 1.

41. I. L. Janis, *Groupthink* (Boston: Houghton Mifflin, 1983).

42. C. P. Neck & C. C. Manz, "From Groupthink to Teamthink: Toward the Creation

of Constructive Thought Patterns in Self-Managing Work Teams," *Human Relations* 47 (1994): 929–952; J. Schwartz & M. L. Wald, "'Groupthink' Is 30 Years Old, and Still Going Strong," *New York Times,* 9 March 2003, 5.

43. M. Bazerman & D. Chugh, "Decisions without Blinders," *Harvard Business Review,* January 2006, 84 (1): 88–97.

44. C. Gallo, "How to Run a Meeting Like Google," *Business Week Online,* 8 September 2006, 15.

45. A. Mason, W. A. Hochwarter, & K. R. Thompson, "Conflict: An Important Dimension in Successful Management Teams," *Organizational Dynamics* 24 (1995): 20.

46. C. Olofson, "So Many Decisions, So Little Time: What's Your Problem?" *Fast Company,* 1 October 1999, 62.

47. Ibid.

48. R. Cosier & C. R. Schwenk, "Agreement and Thinking Alike: Ingredients for Poor Decisions," *Academy of Management Executive* 4 (1990): 69–74.

49. K. Jenn & E. Mannix, "The Dynamic Nature of Conflict: A Longitudinal Study of Intragroup Conflict and Group Performance," *Academy of Management Journal* 44, no. 2 (2001): 238–251; R. L. Priem, D. A. Harrison, & N. K. Muir, "Structured Conflict and Consensus Outcomes in Group Decision Making," *Journal of Management* 21 (1995): 691–710.

50. A. Van De Ven & A. L. Delbecq, "Nominal versus Interacting Group Processes for Committee Decision Making Effectiveness," *Academy of Management Journal* 14 (1971): 203–212.

51. A. R. Dennis & J. S. Valicich, "Group, Sub-Group, and Nominal Group Idea Generation: New Rules for a New Media?" *Journal of Management* 20 (1994): 723–736.

52. R. B. Gallupe, W. H. Cooper, M. L. Grise, & L. M. Bastianutti, "Blocking Electronic Brainstorms," *Journal of Applied Psychology* 79 (1994): 77–86.

53. R. B. Gallupe & W. H. Cooper, "Brainstorming Electronically," *Sloan Management Review,* Fall 1993, 27–36.

54. Ibid.

55. G. Kay, "Effective Meetings through Electronic Brainstorming," *Management Quarterly* 35 (1995): 15.

Chapter 6

1. L. Kahney, "Inside Look at the Birth of the iPod," *Wired,* 21 July 2004, http://www.wired.com/news/culture/0,64286-0.html, http://www.apple-history.com/?page=gallery&model=ipod; K. Hall, "Sony's iPod Assault Is No Threat to Apple," *BusinessWeek,* 13 March 2006, 53; N. Wingfield, "SanDisk Raises Music-Player Stakes," *Wall Street Journal,* 21 August 2006, B4; "Growing Louder: Microsoft Plods after iPod Like a Giant—Powerful, Determined, Untiring,"

Winston-Salem Journal, 15 November 2006, D1-D2; A. Athavaley & R. A. Guth, "How the Zune Is Faring So Far with Consumers," *Wall Street Journal,* 12 December 2006, D1, D7.

2. J. Barney, "Firm Resources and Sustained Competitive Advantage," *Journal of Management* 17 (1991): 99–120; J. Barney, "Looking Inside for Competitive Advantage," *Academy of Management Executive* 9 (1995): 49–61.

3. J. Snell, "Apple's Home Run," *Macworld,* November 2006, 7.

4. J. D'Arcy, & T. Davies, "The Walkman at 20," *Maclean's,* 30 August 1999, 10; K. Hall, "Sony's iPod Assault Is No Threat to Apple," *BusinessWeek,* 13 March 2006, 53.

5. A. Athavaley & R.A. Guth, "How the Zune Is Faring So Far with Consumers," D7.

6. http://music.yahoo.com

7. J. Warren, "At New Web Store, Many Songs Sell for a Few Cents," *Wall Street Journal,* 14 October 2006, P2.

8. R. Levine, "Napster's Ghost Rises," *Fortune,* 6 March 2006, 30; "30 Products for 30 Years," *MacWorld,* June 2006, 15-16.

9. S. Hart & C. Banbury, "How Strategy-Making Processes Can Make a Difference," *Strategic Management Journal* 15 (1994): 251–269.

10. R. A. Burgelman, "Fading Memories: A Process Theory of Strategic Business Exit in Dynamic Environments," *Administrative Science Quarterly* 39 (1994): 24–56; R. A. Burgelman & A. S. Grove, "Strategic Dissonance," *California Management Review* 38 (1996): 8–28.

11. R. Burgelman & A. Grove, "Strategic Dissonance," *California Management Review* (Winter 1996): 8–28.

12. E. Smith & M. Peers, "Cost Cutting Is an Uphill Fight at Warner Music," *Wall Street Journal,* 24 May 2004, B1.

13. A. Fiegenbaum, S. Hart, & D. Schendel, "Strategic Reference Point Theory," *Strategic Management Journal* 17 (1996): 219–235.

14. "Reliability Histories: Detailed Histories for 1997 to 2004 Models," *Consumer Reports,* http://www.consumerreports.org/main/detailv4.jsp?CONTENT%3C%3Ecnt_id=394785&FOLDER%3C%3Efolder_id=113261&bmUID=1110081178754, 5 March 2005.

15. C. Metz, "19th Annual Reader Satisfaction Survey," *PC Magazine,* 21 August 2006, http://www.pcmag.com/article2/0,1895,2006502,00.asp.

16. D. J. Collis, "Research Note: How Valuable Are Organizational Capabilities?" *Strategic Management Journal* 15 (1994): 143–152.

17. L. Margonelli, "How Ikea Designs Its Sexy Price Tags," *Business 2.0,* http://www.business2.com/articles/mag/0,1640,43529,00.html, 1 October 2002.

18. A. Fiegenbaum & H. Thomas, "Strategic Groups as Reference Groups: Theory, Modeling and Empirical Examination of Industry and Competitive Strategy," *Strategic Management Journal* 16 (1995): 461–476.

19. R. K. Reger & A. S. Huff, "Strategic Groups: A Cognitive Perspective," *Strategic Management Journal* 14 (1993): 103–124.

20. http://homedepot.com; M. Hogan, "Big Box Battle: Home Depot vs. Lowes," *BusinessWeek Online;* 22 August 2006, 7; F. Miller, "Growing Pains," *Kitchen & Bath Business,* September 2006, 53.

21. http://ourcompany.acehardware.com/download/pdf_word/FACTFILE.PDF.

22. http://www.hardwarestore.com/about-aubuchon-hardware.aspx.

23. http://84lumber.com/About84/about.asp.

24. "Menards vs. Home Depot," WCCO Channel 4000, http://www.channel4000.com/news/dimension/news-dimension-19991117-205633.html, 25 September 2001.

25. S. Bucksot, C. Jensen, & D. Tratensek, "Where Are We Headed?" *2005 Market Measure: The Industry's Annual Report,* http://www.nrha.org/MM2004.pdf, 6 March 2005.

26. Ibid.

27. H. Murphy, "Menard's Tool in Retail Battle: Gigantic Stores," *Crain's Chicago Business,* 12 August 2002, 3.

28. M. Lubatkin, "Value-Creating Mergers: Fact or Folklore?" *Academy of Management Executive* 2 (1988): 295–302; M. Lubatkin & S. Chatterjee, "Extending Modern Portfolio Theory into the Domain of Corporate Diversification: Does It Apply?" *Academy of Management Journal* 37 (1994): 109–136; M. H. Lubatkin & P. J. Lane, "Psst . . . The Merger Mavens Still Have It Wrong!" *Academy of Management Executive* 10 (1996): 21–39.

29. "Who We Are," 3M, http://solutions.3m.com/wps/portal/_l/en_US/_s.155/116707/_s.155/116910, 6 March 2005.

30. "About Samsung," Samsung, http://www.samsung.com/AboutSAMSUNG/index.htm, 6 March 2005.

31. J. A. Pearce II, "Selecting among Alternative Grand Strategies," *California Management Review* (Spring 1982): 23–31.

32. "Financial and Other Numbers: Store Growth," *Walgreens.com,* http://www.walgreens.com/about/press/facts/fact1.jhtml, 8 May 2005; A. Tsao, "Why CVS May Be the Pick of the Pack; While Walgreen Is Considered the Drugstore Sector's Blue Chip, CVS Has a Much Cheaper P-E and Plenty of Upside Potential," *BusinessWeek Online,* http://www.businessweek.com/bwdaily/dnflash/may2003/nf20030512_9097_db014.htm, 13 May 2003.

33. S. Chandler, "Walgreen's Adding 500 Stores, Posts Record Profit," *Chicago Tribune,* 3 January 2001, 2.

34. "Subaru Archives Homepage," *Cars101.com*, http://www.cars101.com/subaru_archives.html, 8 March 2005.

35. J. A. Pearce II, "Retrenchment Remains the Foundation of Business Turnaround," *Strategic Management Journal* 15 (1994): 407–417.

36. http://www.walmartfacts.com/FactSheets/8252006_Merchandising.pdf; http://www.walmartfacts.com/content/default.aspx?id=3.

37. P. Wonacott, "Wal-Mart, Others Demand Lowest Prices, Managers Scramble to Slash Costs," *Wall Street Journal*, 13 November 2003, A1.

38. M. Veverka, "Bigger and Better: Costco's Costly Expansion Is About to Pay Off—For Shoppers and Shareholders," *Barron's*, 12 May 2003, 28.

39. L. Tischler, "The Price Is Right," *Fast Company*, 1 November 2003, 83.

40. http://www.containerstore.com

41. R. E. Miles & C. C. Snow, *Organizational Strategy, Structure, & Process* (New York: McGraw Hill, 1978); S. Zahra & J. A. Pearce, "Research Evidence on the Miles-Snow Typology," *Journal of Management* 16 (1990): 751–768; W. L. James & K. J. Hatten, "Further Evidence on the Validity of the Self Typing Paragraph Approach: Miles and Snow Strategic Archetypes in Banking," *Strategic Management Journal* 16 (1995): 161–168.

42. A. Deutschman, "The Fabric of Creativity," *Fast Company*, December, 2004, 54.

43. G. Harris & J. Slater, "Bitter Pills: Drug Makers See 'Branded Generics' Eating into Profits," *Wall Street Journal*, 17 April 2003, A1.

44. M. Chen, "Competitor Analysis and Interfirm Rivalry: Toward a Theoretical Integration," *Academy of Management Review* 21 (1996): 100–134; J. C. Baum & H. J. Korn, "Competitive Dynamics of Interfirm Rivalry," *Academy of Management Journal* 39 (1996): 255–291.

45. Ibid.

46. S. Leung, "Wendy's Sees Green in Salad Offerings—More Sophistication, Ethnic Flavors Appeal to Women, Crucial to Building Market Share," *Wall Street Journal*, 24 April 2003, B2.

47. M. Stopa, "Wendy's New-Fashioned Growth: Buy Hardee's," *Crain's Detroit Business*, 21 October 1996.

48. L. Lavelle, "The Chickens Come Home to Roost, and Boston Market Is Prepared to Expand," *The Record*, 6 October 1996.

49. "International Subway Locations," Subway, http://www.subway.com, 1 March 2007; "Investor Fact Sheet January 2004," McDonald's Corporation Annual Report 2005; N. Torres, "View from the Top: Subway Takes the Title of the #1 Franchise for the 13th Time," *Entrepreneur.com*, http://www.entrepreneur.com/franzone/article/ 0,5847,319045,00.html, 11 March 2005.

50. G. Marcial, "How Wendy's Stayed Out of the Fire," *Business Week*, 9 December 2002, 138.

51. D. Ketchen, Jr., C. Snow, & V. Street, "Improving Firm Performance by Matching Strategic Decision-Making Processes to Competitive Dynamics," *Academy of Management Executive* 18 (2004): 29–43.

52. S. Matthews, "Financial: Salads Help McD Post First U.S. Sales Gain in 14 Months," *Chicago Sun-Times*, 14 May 2003, 69.

Chapter 7

1. J. Adamy, "Pitching Tents That Go Up for Good: Chandeliers and Elevators," *Wall Street Journal*, 10 May 2004, A1.

2. T. M. Amabile, R. Conti, H. Coon, J. Lazenby, & M. Herron, "Assessing the Work Environment for Creativity," *Academy of Management Journal* 39 (1996): 1154–1184.

3. Ibid.

4. A. H. Van de Ven & M. S. Poole, "Explaining Development and Change in Organizations," *Academy of Management Review* 20 (1995): 510–540.

5. Amabile, et al., "Assessing the Work Environment for Creativity."

6. P. Anderson & M. L. Tushman, "Managing through Cycles of Technological Change," *Research/Technology Management*, May–June 1991, 26–31.

7. R. N. Foster, *Innovation: The Attacker's Advantage* (New York: Summit, 1986).

8. J. Burke, *The Day the Universe Changed* (Boston: Little, Brown, 1985).

9. http://www.kodak.com; "Industry Snapshot," *Time*, 5 December 2005, 110; W. Symonds, "Kodak: Is This the Darkest Hour?" *Business Week Online*, 8 August 2006, 3.

10. M. L. Tushman, P. C. Anderson, & C. O'Reilly, "Technology Cycles, Innovation Streams, and Ambidextrous Organizations: Organization Renewal through Innovation Streams and Strategic Change," in *Managing Strategic Innovation and Change*, ed. M. L. Tushman & P. Anderson (New York: Oxford Press, 1997), 3–23.

11. W. Abernathy & J. Utterback, "Patterns of Industrial Innovation," *Technology Review* 2 (1978): 40–47.

12. "Glossary," MP3.com, http://www.mp3.com/tech/glossary.php, 18 March 2005; B. Chaffin, "The Back Page: Music Format Wars," *Mac Observer*, http://www.macobserver.com/columns/thebackpage/2004/20040203.shtml, 18 March 2005; C. Goodwin, "Technology Insights: Online Music Stores," Ticker, http://www.ticker.com/story.htm?story_id=14766&t=r&s=&pn=Investment%20Research, 18 March 2005.

13. M. Schilling, "Technological Lockout: An Integrative Model of the Economic and Strategic Factors Driving Technology Success and Failure," *Academy of Management Review* 23 (1998): 267–284; M. Schilling, "Technology Success and Failure in Winner-Take-All Markets: The Impact of Learning Orientation, Timing, and Network Externalities," *Academy of Management Journal* 45 (2002): 387–398.

14. Amabile, et al., "Assessing the Work Environment for Creativity."

15. Ibid.

16. M. Csikszentmihalyi, *Flow: The Psychology of Optimal Experience* (New York: Harper & Row, 1990).

17. D. Garbato, "On the Beaten Track: Tractor Supply Co. Embraces Change but Stays Focused in All Areas of Its Business," *Retail Merchandiser*, January 2005, 30–31.

18. K. Capell, "Thinking Simple at Philips," 11 December 2006, *Business Week*, 50.

19. K. M. Eisenhardt, "Accelerating Adaptive Processes: Product Innovation in the Global Computer Industry," *Administrative Science Quarterly* 40 (1995): 84–110.

20. Ibid.

21. G. Bounds, "Sticky Fingers? How Avery Found an Office Problem to Solve," *Wall Street Journal*, 13 July 2004, B1.

22. C. Salter, "Ford's Escape Route," *Fast Company*, 1 October 2004, 106.

23. L. Kraar, "25 Who Help the U.S. Win: Innovators Everywhere Are Generating Ideas to Make America a Stronger Competitor. They Range from a Boss Who Demands the Impossible to a Mathematician with a Mop," *Fortune*, 22 March 1991.

24. M. W. Lawless & P. C. Anderson, "Generational Technological Change: Effects of Innovation and Local Rivalry on Performance," *Academy of Management Journal* 39 (1996): 1185–1217.

25. http://micro.gameboy.com.

26. P. Siekman, "The Snap-Together Business Jet," *Fortune*, 21 January 2002, 104[A].

27. http://movies.about.com/cs/upcomingreleases/a/harrypotter4dir.htm; http://www.wizardnews.com/; http://www.cinematical.com/2006/11/03/latest-harry-potter-director-michael-who/; K. Kelly, "Older Harry Rates a PG-13: The Awkward, Lovelorn Hero of 'Goblet of Fire' May Lose Kids, Gain Broader Audience," *Wall Street Journal*, 16 November 2005, B1.

28. B. Baumohl & W. Cole "The Perils of Having Way More than Enough," *Time*, 13 January 1997, 58; S. Forest, "Incredible Universe: Lost in Space," *Business Week*, 4 March 1996, http://www.businessweek.com/1996/10/b346580.htm.

29. P. Strebel, "Choosing the Right Change Path," *California Management Review*, Winter 1994, 29–51.

30. W. Weitzel & E. Jonsson, "Reversing the Downward Spiral: Lessons from W.T. Grant and Sears Roebuck," *Academy of Management Executive* 5 (1991): 7–22.

31. Ibid.

32. K. Lewin, *Field Theory in Social Science: Selected Theoretical Papers* (New York: Harper & Brothers, 1951).

33. A. Deutschman, "Making Change: Why Is It So Darn Hard to Change Our Ways?" *Fast Company,* May 2005, 52–62.

34. K. Lewin, *Field Theory in Social Science.*

35. A. B. Fisher, "Making Change Stick," *Fortune,* 17 April 1995, 121.

36. J. P. Kotter & L. A. Schlesinger, "Choosing Strategies for Change," *Harvard Business Review,* March–April 1979, 106–114.

37. M. Johne, "The Human Factor: Integrating People and Cultures after a Merger," *CMA Management,* 1 April 2000, 30.

38. K. Booker & J. Schlosser, "The Un-CEO," *Fortune,* 16 September 2002, 88.

39. Ibid.

40. B. Orwall, "Disney Decides It Must Draw Artists into Computer Age," *Wall Street Journal,* 23 October 2003, A1.

41. J. P. Kotter, "Leading Change: Why Transformation Efforts Fail," *Harvard Business Review* 73, no. 2 (March–April 1995): 59.

42. Booker & Schlosser, "The Un-CEO."

43. R. Berner, "At Sears, a Great Communicator," *Business Week,* 31 October 2005, 50-52.

44. "Sears Results Mixed," *MMR,* 18 September 2006, 5; "Sears Selects New Chief for Strategy: Former Best Buy Executive to Sharpen Focus on Customers," *Chicago Tribune,* 18 January 2007, online.

45. J. McCrackent & T. Kosdrosky, "Ford Plans to Offer Bonuses to Blue-Collar, Salaried Workers," *Wall Street Journal,* 9 March 2007, A10.

46. "Sears Results Mixed," *MMR,* 18 September 2006, 5; "Sears Selects New Chief for Strategy: Former Best Buy Executive to Sharpen Focus on Customers," *Chicago Tribune,* 18 January 2007, online.

47. S. Cramm, "A Change of Hearts," *CIO,* 1 April 2003, http://www.cio.com/archive/040103/hs_leadership.html, 20 May 2003.

48. M. Ihlwan, L. Armstrong, & M. Eidam, "Hyundai: Kissing Clunkers Goodbye," *Business Week,* 17 May 2004, 46.

49. Ibid.

50. R. N. Ashkenas & T. D. Jick, "From Dialogue to Action in GE WorkOut: Developmental Learning in a Change Process," in *Research in Organizational Change and Development,* vol. 6, ed. W. A. Pasmore & R. W. Woodman (Greenwich, CT: JAI Press, 1992), 267–287.

51. T. Stewart, "GE Keeps Those Ideas Coming," *Fortune,* 12 August 1991, 40.

52. W. J. Rothwell, R. Sullivan, & G. M. McLean, *Practicing Organizational Development: A Guide for Consultants* (San Diego, CA: Pfeiffer & Co., 1995).

53. Ibid.

Chapter 8

1. "World Investment Report, 2006," United Nations Conference on Trade & Development, http://www.unctad.org/en/docs/wir2006annexes_en.pdf, 30 January 2007.

2. G. Samor, "Steelmaker Girds for Growth—Gerdau of Brazil Looks to Bulk Up Further in United States Market," *Wall Street Journal,* 5 April 2005, B2.

3. C. Rong, "Chinese Assets Are Looking Pricey—How Much Is Too Much to Pay for Market Share? A Slew of Big-Profile Deals," *Wall Street Journal Europe,* 4 February 2005, M4.

4. J. Miller, "China's Low Fruit Prices Highlight EU's Vulnerabilities over Trade," *Wall Street Journal,* 26 December 2006, A4.

5. L. Etter, "Can Ethanol Get a Ticket to Ride?" *Wall Street Journal,* 1 February 2007, B1.

6. "Determination of Total Amounts and Quota Period for Tariff-Rate Quotas for Raw Cane Sugar and Certain Imported Sugars, Syrups, and Molasses," *Federal Register,* 15 April 2002, 18162.

7. J. Sparshott, "U.S. Sugar Growers Fear Losses from Free-Trade Push," *Washington Times,* 24 March 2005, C07.

8. "The Agreements: Anti-Dumping, Subsidies, Safeguards, Contingencies, etc.," *World Trade Organization,* http://www.wto.org/english/thewto_e/whatis_e/tif_e/agrm8_e.htm, 22 April 2005.

9. "USTR Lists Barriers to U.S. Trade, Focusing on Agriculture—Annual Report Also Emphasizes Intellectual Property, Transparency," U.S. Department Press Releases & Documents, 7 February 2007; J. Morgan, "Building Seeds of Case against OZ Apple Ban," *Dominion Post,* 18 January 2007, 7.

10. "USA Claims Airbus Drove Out Rivals," *Flight International,* 23 January 2007.

11. "Rocky Receives Customs Clarification on Imported Boots," *FN,* 31 March 2003.

12. H. Blodget, "How to Solve China's Piracy Problem: A Dozen Ideas. Maybe One Will Work," *Slate,* 12 April 2005, http://slate.msn.com/id/2116629/.

13. "The History of the European Union," *Europa—The European Union Online,* 7 February 2007, http://europa.eu.int/abc/history/index_en.htm; http://europa.eu/abc/european_countries/index_en.htm

14. Ibid.

15. D. Luhnow, "Crossover Success: How NAFTA Helped Wal-Mart Reshape the Mexican Market" *Wall Street Journal,* 31 August 2001, A1.

16. "Testimony of Under Secretary of Commerce for International Trade Grant D. Aldona: The Impact of NAFTA on the United States Economy," Senate Foreign Relations Committee, Subcommittee on International Economic Policy, Export & Trade Promotion, 7 February 2007, http://www.mac.doc.gov/nafta/Aldonas-Testimony.pdf.

17. Office of the United States Trade Representative, "The Case for CAFTA: Growth, Opportunity, and Democracy in Our Neighborhood," United States Department of Agriculture: Foreign Agricultural Service, http://www.ustr.gov/assets/Trade_Agreements/Bilateral/CAFTA/Briefing_Book/asset_upload_file235_7178.pdf, 10 February 2007.

18. "South American Community of Nations," Andean Community, http://www.comunidadandina.org/ingles/sudamerican.htm, 10 February 2007.

19. "Selected Basic ASEAN Indicators, 2005," Association of Southeast Nations, http://www.aseansec.org/stat/Table1.pdf, 10 February 2007; "Top Ten ASEAN Trade Partner Countries/Regions, 2005," Association of Southeast Nations, http://www.aseansec.org/Stat/Table20.pdf, 10 February 2007.

20. "ASEAN Free Trade Area (AFTA): An Update," Association of Southeast Nations, http://www.aseansec.org/view.asp?file=/general/publication/afta-upd.htm, 10 September 2001.

21. "Member Economies' Websites," Asia-Pacific Economic Cooperation, http://www.apecsec.org.sg/member/memb_websites.html, 10 September 2001.

22. "Frequently Asked Questions (FAQs): How Much of the World's Trade Takes Place in the APEC Region?" *Asia-Pacific Economic Cooperation,* http://www.apecsec.org.sg/apec/tools/faqs.html, 10 February 2007.

23. "The Big Mac Index," *Economist,* http://www.economist.com/markets/indicators/displaystory.cfm?story_id=8649005, 10 February 2007.

24. Ibid.

25. "Freer Trade Cuts the Cost of Living," *World Trade Organization,* http://www.wto.org/english/thewto_e/whatis_e/10ben_e/10b04_e.htm, 10 February 2007.

26. MTV Brasil, http://mtv.terra.com.br/mochilao, 30 January 2007; MTV China, http://mtvchina.com, 30 January 2007; MTV India, http:// http://www.mtvindia.com/sillypoint/sourav.php, 30 January 2007.

27. A. Sundaram & J. S. Black, "The Environment and Internal-Organization of Multinational Enterprises," *Academy of Management Review* 17 (1992): 729–757.

28. H. S. James, Jr., & M. Weidenbaum, *When Businesses Cross International Borders: Strategic Alliances & Their Alternatives* (Westport, CT: Praeger Publishers, 1993).

29. "Our Programmes: Idols," Fremantle-Media, http://www.fremantlemedia.com/our-programmes/view/Global+Hit+Formats/viewprogramme/Idols, 10 February 2007.

30. "Company Profile," Fuji Xerox, http://www.fujixerox.co.jp/eng/company/profile.html, 12 February 2007.

31. "Joint Venture Foundation of Giesecke & Devrient and Nokia Completed,"

Hugin Press Release, 20 December 2006.

32. B. R. Schlender, "How Toshiba Makes Alliances Work," *Fortune*, 4 October 1993, 116–120.

33. M. W. Hordes, J. A. Clancy, & J. Baddaley, "A Primer for Global Start-Ups." *Academy of Management Executive*, May 1995, 7–11.

34. D. Pavlos, J. Johnson, J. Slow, & S. Young, "Micromultinationals: New Types of Firms for the Global Competitive Landscape," *European Management Journal* 21, issue 2 (April 2003): 164; B. M. Oviatt & P. P. McDougall, "Toward a Theory of International New Ventures," *Journal of International Business Studies*, Spring 1994, 45–64; S. Zahra, "A Theory of International New Ventures: A Decade of Research," *Journal of International Business Studies*, January 2005, 20–28.

35. M. Copeland, "The Mighty Micro-Multinational," *Business 2.0*, 1 July 2006, 106.

36. "An Unofficial Price List of Everyday Items in Tokyo," *PriceCheckTokyo*, 10 February 2007, http://www.pricechecktokyo.com/.

37. D. Lynch, "Developing Nations Poised to Challenge USA as King of the Hill," *USA Today*, 8 February 2007, B.1; N. Srinivas, "Of Carats & Calories," *The Economic Times*, 29 December 2006.

38. "Operations Review: Selected Market Results: Estimated 2002 Volume by Operating Segment," *The Coca-Cola Company 2002 Annual Report*.

39. F. Vogelstein, "How Intel Got Inside," *Fortune*, 4 October 2004, 127.

40. "Customer Care in the Netherlands," The Netherlands Foreign Investment Agency, [Online] available at http://www.nfia.com/solutions.php?pageid=11, 13 February 2007; "Customer Care Centers," Netherlands Foreign Investment Agency Information Manual, 13 February 2007, [Online] available at http://www.nfia.com/downloads/customercare.htm.

41. J. Oetzel, R. Bettis, & M. Zenner, "How Risky Are They?" *Journal of World Business* 36, no. 2 (Summer 2001): 128–145.

42. K. D. Miller, "A Framework for Integrated Risk Management in International Business," *Journal of International Business Studies*, 2nd Quarter 1992, 311.

43. J. Schuman, "The Morning Brief: Shell, Partners Give In to Kremlin Oil Game . . . ," *Wall Street Journal*, 22 December 2006.

44. "Chapter 1: Political Outlook," *UAE Business Forecast Report*, 2007 1st Quarter, 5–10.

45. G. Hofstede, "The Cultural Relativity of the Quality of Life Concept," *Academy of Management Review* 9 (1984): 389–398; G. Hofstede, "The Cultural Relativity of Organizational Practices and Theories," *Journal of International Business Studies*, Fall 1983, 75–89; G. Hofstede, "The Interaction between National and Organizational Value Systems," *Journal of Management Studies*, July 1985, 347–357; M. Hoppe, "An Interview with Geert Hofstede," *Academy of Management Executive*, February 2004, 75–79.

46. R. Hodgetts, "A Conversation with Geert Hofstede," *Organizational Dynamics*, Spring 1993, 53–61.

47. T. Lenartowicz & K. Roth, "Does Subculture within a Country Matter? A Cross-Cultural Study of Motivational Domains and Business Performance in Brazil," *Journal of International Business Studies* 32 (2001): 305–325.

48. M. Janssens, J. M. Brett, & F. J. Smith, "Confirmatory Cross-Cultural Research: Testing the Viability of a Corporation-Wide Safety Policy," *Academy of Management Journal* 38 (1995): 364–382.

49. J. S. Black, M. Mendenhall, & G. Oddou, "Toward a Comprehensive Model of International Adjustment: An Integration of Multiple Theoretical Perspectives," *Academy of Management Review* 16 (1991): 291–317; R. L. Tung, "American Expatriates Abroad: From Neophytes to Cosmopolitans," *Columbia Journal of World Business*, 22 June 1998, 125; A. Harzing, "The Persistent Myth of High Expatriate Failure Rates," *International Journal of Human Resource Management* 6 (1995): 457–475; A. Harzing, "Are Our Referencing Errors Undermining Our Scholarship and Credibility? The Case of Expatriate Failure Rates," *Journal of Organizational Behavior* 23 (2002): 127–148; N. Forster, "The Persistent Myth of High Expatriate Failure Rates: A Reappraisal," *International Journal of Human Resource Management* 8 (1997): 414–433.

50. J. Black, "The Right Way to Manage Expats," *Harvard Business Review* 77 (March–April 1999): 52; C. Joinson, "No Returns," *HR Magazine*, 1 November 2002, 70.

51. C. Joinson, "No Returns," *HR Magazine*, November 2002, 70.

52. J. S. Black & M. Mendenhall, "Cross-Cultural Training Effectiveness: A Review and Theoretical Framework for Future Research," *Academy of Management Review* 15 (1990): 113–136.

53. K. Essick, "Executive Education: Transferees Prep for Life, Work in Far-Flung Lands," *Wall Street Journal*, 12 November 2004, A6.

54. P. W. Tam, "Culture Course—'Awareness Training' Helps U.S. Workers Better Know Their Counterparts in India," *Wall Street Journal*, 25 May 2004, B1.

55. W. Arthur, Jr., & W. Bennett, Jr., "The International Assignee: The Relative Importance of Factors Perceived to Contribute to Success," *Personnel Psychology* 48 (1995): 99–114; B. Cheng, "Home Truths about Foreign Postings; To Make an Overseas Assignment Work, Employers Need More Than an Eager Exec with a Suitcase. They Must Also Motivate the Staffer's Spouse," *BusinessWeek Online*, http://www.businessweek.com/careers/content/jul2002/ca20020715_9110.htm, 16 July 2002.

56. M. Netz, "It's Not Judging—It's Assessing: The Truth about Candidate Assessments," *NRRE Magazine*, March 2004, http://www.rismedia.com/index.php/article/articleview/5996/1/492/.

57. D. Eschbach, G. Parker, & P. Stoeberl, "American Repatriate Employees' Retrospective Assessments of the Effects of Cross-Cultural Training on Their Adaptation to International Assignments," *International Journal of Human Resource Management* 12 (2001): 270–287; "Culture Training: How to Prepare Your Expatriate Employees for Cross-Cultural Work Environments," *Managing Training & Development*, 1 February 2005.

58. J. Areddy, "Deep Inside China, American Family Struggles to Cope," *Wall Street Journal*, 2 August 2005, A1.

Chapter 9

1. B. Schlender, "Microsoft: The Beast Is Back," *Fortune*, 11 June 2001, 75.

2. Y. Noguchi, "Microsoft Remakes Corporate Structure," *Washington Post*, 21 September 2005, D5; "Microsoft Announces Plans for July 2008 Transition for Bill Gates," http://www.microsoft.com/presspass/press/2006/jun06/06-15CorpNewsPR.mspx.

3. M. Hammer & J. Champy, *Reengineering the Corporation: A Manifesto for Business Revolution* (New York: Harper & Row, 1993).

4. "Sara Lee Announces Transformation Plan; Brenda C. Barnes Appointed the Company's CEO, Effective Immediately," *Retail Merchandiser*, 10 February 2005; http://www.saralee.com/ourcompany/history_timeline.aspx.

5. J. G. March & H. A. Simon, *Organizations* (New York: John Wiley & Sons, 1958).

6. "Outline of Principal Operations," Sony Corporation, http://www.sony.com/SCA/outline.shtml, 30 April 2005.

7. "Our Companies," *United Technologies 2004 Annual Report*, http://www.utc.com/annual_reports/2004/html/page5.htm, 30 April 2005.

8. "Form 10-K, United Technologies Corporation: Segment Review," United States Securities and Exchange Commission, http://investors.utc.com/EdgarDetail.cfm?CompanyID=UTX&CIK=101829&FID=1193125-05-25271&SID=05-00&DocType=10-K#D10K_HTM_TX58532_10, 1 May 2005.

9. http://www2.sprint.com/mr/e.xListPrev.do?Span=20, 3 January 2007.

10. "Our Company: The Best Brands in the World," Coca-Cola Enterprises, http://www.cokecce.com/srclib/1.1.1.html, 21 May 2003.

11. http://www.pg.com/jobs/corporate_structure/four_pillars.jhtml; http://www.pg.com/news/management/bios_photos.jhtml.

12. L. R. Burns, "Adoption and Abandonment of Matrix Management Programs: Effects of Organizational Characteristics and Interorganizational Networks," *Academy of Management Journal* 36 (1993): 106–138.

13. H. Fayol, *General and Industrial Management*, trans. Constance Storrs (London: Pitman Publishing, 1949).

14. M. Weber, *The Theory of Social and Economic Organization*, trans. and ed. A. M. Henderson & T. Parsons (New York: Free Press, 1947).

15. Fayol, *General and Industrial Management*.

16. S. Holmes, "Inside the Coup at Nike," *BusinessWeek Online*, 26 January 2006.

17. S. Holmes, "Nike CEO Gets the Boot," *BusinessWeek Online*, 24 January 2006.

18. E. E. Lawler, S. A. Mohrman, & G. E. Ledford, *Creating High Performance Organizations: Practices and Results of Employee Involvement and Quality Management in Fortune 1000 Companies* (San Francisco: Jossey-Bass, 1995).

19. D. Welch, "Renault-Nissan: Say Hello to Bo," *BusinessWeek*, 31 July 2006, 56–57.

20. S. Curry, "Retention Getters," *Incentive*, 1 April 2005.

21. R. W. Griffin, *Task Design* (Glenview, IL: Scott, Foresman, 1982).

22. F. Herzberg, *Work and the Nature of Man* (Cleveland, OH: World Press, 1966).

23. J. R. Hackman & G. R. Oldham, *Work Redesign* (Reading, MA: Addison-Wesley, 1980).

24. T. Burns & G. M. Stalker, *The Management of Innovation* (London: Tavistock, 1961).

25. Hammer & Champy, *Reengineering the Corporation*.

26. Ibid.

27. J. D. Thompson, *Organizations in Action* (New York: McGraw-Hill, 1967).

28. J. B. White, "'Next Big Thing': Re-Engineering Gurus Take Steps to Remodel Their Stalling Vehicles," *Wall Street Journal Interactive Edition*, 26 November 1996.

29. Ibid.

30. G. M. Spreitzer, "Individual Empowerment in the Workplace: Dimensions, Measurement, and Validation," *Academy of Management Journal* 38 (1995): 1442–1465.

31. M. Schrage, "I Know What You Mean. And I Can't Do Anything about It," *Fortune*, 2 April 2001, 186.

32. K. W. Thomas & B. A. Velthouse, "Cognitive Elements of Empowerment," *Academy of Management Review* 15 (1990): 666–681.

33. G. Kahn, "Making Labels for Less—Supply-Chain City Transforms Far-Flung Apparel Industry; Help for 'The Button Guy,'" *Wall Street Journal*, 13 August 2004, B1.

34. G. G. Dess, A. M. A. Rasheed, K. J. McLaughlin, & R. L. Priem, "The New Corporate Architecture," *Academy of Management Executive* 9 (1995): 7–18.

35. G. McWilliams, "Apple Uses Software, Outsourcing to Gain Share As Sony Struggles to Grow," *Wall Street Journal*, 10 March 2005, A1; P. Cohen & J. Dalrymple, "Apple Updates iPod Line, Cuts Prices," *Computer World*, http://www.computerworld.com/softwaretopics/os/macos/story/0,10801,99956,00.html, 3 May 2005.

36. "Overview: Collaborative Business Network Solutions," *G5 Technologies: Agile Web*, http://www.agileweb.com/overview/index.html, 3 May 2005.

37. J. H. Sheridan, "The Agile Web: A Model for the Future?" *Industry Week*, 4 March 1996, 31.

38. C. C. Snow, R. E. Miles, & H. J. Coleman, Jr., "Managing 21st Century Network Organizations," *Organizational Dynamics*, Winter 1992, 5–20.

39. Sheridan, "The Agile Web: A Model for the Future?"

40. "Virtual Corporation Management System™ (VCMS™) Solution," *G5 Technologies: Agile Web*, http://www.agileweb.com/vcms/index.html, 3 May 2005.

Chapter 10

1. B. Dumaine, "The Trouble with Teams," *Fortune*, 5 September 1994, 86–92.

2. J. Hoerr, "The Payoff from Teamwork—The Gains in Quality Are Substantial—So Why Isn't It Spreading Faster?" *BusinessWeek*, 10 July 1989, 56.

3. J. R. Katzenback & D. K. Smith, *The Wisdom of Teams* (Boston: Harvard Business School Press, 1993).

4. S. E. Gross, *Compensation for Teams* (New York: American Management Association, 1995); B. L. Kirkman & B. Rosen, "Beyond Self-Management: Antecedents and Consequences of Team Empowerment," *Academy of Management Journal* 42 (1999): 58–74; G. Stalk & T. M. Hout, *Competing against Time: How Time-Based Competition Is Reshaping Global Markets* (New York: Free Press, 1990); S. C. Wheelwright & K. B. Clark, *Revolutionizing New Product Development* (New York: Free Press, 1992).

5. J. Marquez, "Hewitt-BP Split May Signal End of 'Lift and Shift' Deals," *Workforce Management*, 29 December 2006, 3.

6. R. D. Banker, J. M. Field, R. G. Schroeder, & K. K. Sinha, "Impact of Work Teams on Manufacturing Performance: A Longitudinal Field Study," *Academy of Management Journal* 39 (1996): 867–890.

7. C. Fishman, "The Anarchist's Cookbook: John Mackey's Approach to Management Is Equal Parts Star Trek and 1970s Flashback," *Fast Company*, 1 July 2004, 70.

8. J. L. Cordery, W. S. Mueller, & L. M. Smith, "Attitudinal and Behavioral Effects of Autonomous Group Working: A Longitudinal Field Study," *Academy of Management Journal* 34 (1991): 464–476; T. D. Wall, N. J. Kemp, P. R. Jackson, & C. W. Clegg, "Outcomes of Autonomous Workgroups: A Long-Term Field Experiment," *Academy of Management Journal* 29 (1986): 280–304.

9. "Declaration of Interdependence," Whole Foods Market, http://www.wholefoodsmarket.com/company/declaration.html, 15 January 2002.

10. A. Erez, J. Lepine, & H. Elms, "Effects of Rotated Leadership and Peer Evaluation on the Functioning and Effectiveness of Self-Managed Teams: A Quasi-Experiment," *Personnel Psychology* 55, issue 4 (2002): 929.

11. R. Liden, S. Wayne, R. Jaworski, & N. Bennett, "Social Loafing: A Field Investigation," *Journal of Management* 30 (2004): 285–304.

12. J. George, "Extrinsic and Intrinsic Origins of Perceived Social Loafing in Organizations," *Academy of Management Journal* 35 (1992): 191–202.

13. T. T. Baldwin, M. D. Bedell, & J. L. Johnson, "The Social Fabric of a Team-Based M.B.A. Program: Network Effects on Student Satisfaction and Performance," *Academy of Management Journal* 40 (1997): 1369–1397.

14. C. Joinson, "Teams at Work," *HRMagazine*, 1 May 1999, 30.

15. R. Wageman, "Critical Success Factors for Creating Superb Self-Managing Teams," *Organizational Dynamics* 26, no. 1 (1997): 49–61.

16. D. A. Harrison, S. Mohammed, J. E. McGrath, A. T. Florey & S. W. Vanderstoep, "Time Matters in Team Performance: Effects of Member Familiarity, Entrainment, and Task Discontinuity on Speed and Quality," *Personnel Psychology* 56(3) (2003, August): 633–669.

17. R. T. King, Jr., "Jeans Therapy: Levi's Factory Workers Are Assigned to Teams, and Morale Takes a Hit—Infighting Rises, Productivity Falls as Employees Miss the Piecework System," *Wall Street Journal*, 20 May 1998, A1.

18. Kirkman & Rosen, "Beyond Self-Management: Antecedents and Consequences of Team Empowerment."

19. S. Easton & G. Porter, "Selecting the Right Team Structure to Work in Your Organization," in *Handbook of Best*

Practices for Teams, vol. 1, ed. G. M. Parker (Amherst, MA: Irwin, 1996).

20. "Labor-Employee Participation Committees Receive NLRB's Approval," *Personnel Manager's Legal Letter,* 1 October 2001.

21. R. M. Yandrick, "A Team Effort: The Promise of Teams Isn't Achieved without Attention to Skills and Training," *HR Magazine* 46, no. 6 (June 2001).

22. A. Lashinsky, "RAZR's Edge: How a Team of Engineers and Designers Defied Motorola's Own Rules to Create the Cellphone that Revived Their Company," *Fortune,* 12 June 2006, 124–132.

23. R. J. Recardo, D. Wade, C. A. Mention, & J. Jolly, *Teams* (Houston: Gulf Publishing Co., 1996).

24. D. R. Denison, S. L. Hart, & J. A. Kahn, "From Chimneys to Cross-Functional Teams: Developing and Validating a Diagnostic Model," *Academy of Management Journal* 39, no. 4 (1996): 1005–1023.

25. J. Morgan, "Cessna Aims to Drive SCM to Its Very Core: Here Are 21 Steps and Tools It's Using to Make This Happen," *Purchasing,* 6 June 2002, 31.

26. A. M. Townsend, S. M. DeMarie, & A. R. Hendrickson, "Virtual Teams: Technology and the Workplace of the Future," *Academy of Management Executive* 13, no. 3 (1998): 17–29.

27. R. Karlgaard, "Flash Kid; Rich Karlgaard Meets a Teen Titan," *Forbes,* 17 March 2003, 39.

28. A. M. Townsend, S. M. DeMarie, & A. R. Hendrickson, "Are You Ready for Virtual Teams?" *HR Magazine* 41, no. 9 (1996): 122–126.

29. R. S. Wellins, W. C. Byham, & G. R. Dixon, *Inside Teams* (San Francisco: Jossey-Bass, 1994).

30. Townsend, DeMarie, & Hendrickson, "Virtual Teams."

31. W. F. Cascio, "Managing a Virtual Workplace," *Academy of Management Executive* 14 (2000): 81–90.

32. R. Katz, "The Effects of Group Longevity on Project Communication and Performance," *Administrative Science Quarterly* 27 (1982): 245–282.

33. D. Mankin, S. G. Cohen, & T. K. Bikson, *Teams and Technology: Fulfilling the Promise of the New Organization* (Boston: Harvard Business School Press, 1996).

34. A. P. Ammeter & J. M. Dukerich, "Leadership, Team Building, and Team Member Characteristics in High Performance Project Teams," *Engineering Management* 14, no. 4 (2002): 3–11.

35. K. Lovelace, D. Shapiro, & L. Weingart, "Maximizing Cross-Functional New Product Teams' Innovativeness and Constraint Adherence: A Conflict Communications Perspective," *Academy of Management Journal* 44 (2001): 779–793.

36. L. Holpp & H. P. Phillips, "When Is a Team Its Own Worst Enemy?" *Training,* 1 September 1995, 71.

37. S. Asche, "Opinions and Social Pressure," *Scientific American* 193 (1995): 31–35.

38. G. Smith, "How Nucor Steel Rewards Performance and Productivity," *Business Know How,* http://www.businessknowhow.com/manage/nucor.htm, 26 May 2003.

39. S. G. Cohen, G. E. Ledford, & G. M. Spreitzer, "A Predictive Model of Self-Managing Work Team Effectiveness," *Human Relations* 49, no. 5 (1996): 643–676.

40. K. Bettenhausen & J. K. Murnighan, "The Emergence of Norms in Competitive Decision-Making Groups," *Administrative Science Quarterly* 30 (1985): 350–372.

41. M. E. Shaw, *Group Dynamics* (New York: McGraw Hill, 1981).

42. S. E. Jackson, "The Consequences of Diversity in Multidisciplinary Work Teams," in *Handbook of Work Group Psychology,* ed. M. A. West (Chichester, UK: Wiley, 1996).

43. A. M. Isen & R. A. Baron, "Positive Affect as a Factor in Organizational Behavior," in *Research in Organizational Behavior* 13, ed. L. L. Cummings & B. M. Staw (Greenwich, CT: JAI Press, 1991), 1–53.

44. C. R. Evans & K. L. Dion, "Group Cohesion and Performance: A Meta Analysis," *Small Group Research* 22, no. 2 (1991): 175–186.

45. R. Stankiewicsz, "The Effectiveness of Research Groups in Six Countries," in *Scientific Productivity,* ed. F. M. Andrews (Cambridge: Cambridge University Press, 1979), 191–221.

46. F. Rees, *Teamwork from Start to Finish* (San Francisco: Jossey-Bass, 1997).

47. S. M. Gully, D. S. Devine, and D. J. Whitney, "A Meta-Analysis of Cohesion and Performance: Effects of Level of Analysis and Task Interdependence," *Small Group Research* 26, no. 4 (1995): 497–520.

48. E. Matson, "Four Rules for Fast Teams," *Fast Company,* August 1996, 87.

49. F. Tschan & M. V. Cranach, "Group Task Structure, Processes and Outcomes," in *Handbook of Work Group Psychology,* ed. M. A. West (Chichester, UK: Wiley, 1996).

50. D. E. Yeatts & C. Hyten, *High Performance Self Managed Teams* (Thousand Oaks, CA: Sage Publications, 1998); H. M. Guttman & R. S. Hawkes, "New Rules for Strategic Development," *The Journal of Business Strategy* 25, no. 1 (2004): 34–39.

51. Ibid; J. Colquitt, R. Noe, & C. Jackson, "Justice in Teams: Antecedents and Consequences of Procedural Justice Climate," *Personnel Psychology,* 1 April 2002, 83.

52. D. S. Kezsbom, "Re-Opening Pandora's Box: Sources of Project Team Conflict in the '90s," *Industrial Engineering* 24, no. 5 (1992): 54–59.

53. A. C. Amason, W. A. Hochwarter, & K. R. Thompson, "Conflict: An Important Dimension in Successful Management Teams," *Organizational Dynamics* 24 (1995): 20.

54. A. C. Amason, "Distinguishing the Effects of Functional and Dysfunctional Conflict on Strategic Decision Making: Resolving a Paradox for Top Management Teams," *Academy of Management Journal* 39, no. 1 (1996): 123–148.

55. K. M. Eisenhardt, J. L. Kahwajy, & L. J. Bourgeois III, "How Management Teams Can Have a Good Fight," *Harvard Business Review* 75, no. 4 (July–August 1997): 77–85.

56. Ibid.

57. C. Nemeth & P. Owens, "Making Work Groups More Effective: The Value of Minority Dissent," in *Handbook of Work Group Psychology,* ed. M. A. West (Chichester, UK: Wiley, 1996).

58. J. M. Levin & R. L. Moreland, "Progress in Small Group Research," *Annual Review of Psychology* 9 (1990): 72–78; S. E. Jackson, "Team Composition in Organizational Settings: Issues in Managing a Diverse Work Force," in *Group Processes and Productivity,* ed. S. Worchel, W. Wood, & J. Simpson (Beverly Hills, CA: Sage, 1992).

59. Eisenhardt, Kahwajy, & Bourgeois, "How Management Teams Can Have a Good Fight."

60. B. W. Tuckman, "Development Sequence in Small Groups," *Psychological Bulletin* 63, no. 6 (1965): 384–399.

61. Gross, *Compensation for Teams.*

62. J. F. McGrew, J. G. Bilotta, & J. M. Deeney, "Software Team Formation and Decay: Extending the Standard Model for Small Groups," *Small Group Research* 30, no. 2 (1999): 209–234.

63. Ibid.

64. J. Case, "What the Experts Forgot to Mention: Management Teams Create New Difficulties, But Succeed for XEL Communications," *Inc.,* 1 September 1993, 66.

65. J. R. Hackman, "The Psychology of Self-Management in Organizations," in *Psychology and Work: Productivity, Change, and Employment,* ed. M. S. Pallak & R. Perloff (Washington, DC: American Psychological Association, 1986), 85–136.

66. A. O'Leary-Kelly, J. J. Martocchio, & D. D. Frink, "A Review of the Influence of Group Goals on Group Performance," *Academy of Management Journal* 37, no. 5 (1994): 1285–1301.

67. Smith, "How Nucor Steel Rewards Performance and Productivity."

68. A. Zander, "The Origins and Consequences of Group Goals," in *Retrospections on Social Psychology,* ed. L. Festinger (New York: Oxford University Press, 1980), 205–235.

69. M. Erez & A. Somech, "Is Group Productivity Loss the Rule or the Exception? Effects of Culture and Group-Based Motivation," *Academy of Management Journal* 39, no. 6 (1996): 1513–1537.

70. S. Sherman, "Stretch Goals: The Dark Side of Asking for Miracles," *Fortune*, 13 November 1995, 231.

71. S. Kerr & S. Landauer, "Using Stretch Goals to Promote Organizational Effectiveness and Personal Growth: General Electric and Goldman Sachs," *Academy of Management Executive* (November 2004): 134–138.

72. K. R. Thompson, W. A. Hochwarter, & N. J. Mathys, "Stretch Targets: What Makes Them Effective?" *Academy of Management Executive* 11, no. 3 (1997): 48–60.

73. Sherman, "Stretch Goals."

74. Dumaine, "The Trouble with Teams."

75. G. A. Neuman, S. H. Wagner, & N. D. Christiansen, "The Relationship between Work-Team Personality Composition and the Job Performance of Teams," *Group & Organization Management* 24, no. 1 (1999): 28–45.

76. M. A. Campion, G. J. Medsker, & A. C. Higgs, "Relations between Work Group Characteristics and Effectiveness: Implications for Designing Effective Work Groups," *Personnel Psychology* 46, no. 4 (1993): 823–850.

77. B. L. Kirkman & D. L. Shapiro, "The Impact of Cultural Values on Employee Resistance to Teams: Toward a Model of Globalized Self-Managing Work Team Effectiveness," *Academy of Management Review* 22, no. 3 (1997): 730–757.

78. C. Fishman, "Engines of Democracy: The General Electric Plant in Durham, North Carolina Builds Some of the World's Most Powerful Jet Engines. But the Plant's Real Power Lies in the Lessons That It Teaches about the Future of Work and about Workplace Democracy," *Fast Company*, 1 October 1999, 174.

79. J. Bunderson & K. Sutcliffe, "Comparing Alternative Conceptualizations of Functional Diversity in Management Teams: Process and Performance Effects," *Academy of Management Journal* 45 (2002): 875–893.

80. J. Barbian, "Getting to Know You," *Training*, June 2001: 60–63.

81. J. Hackman, "New Rules for Team Building—The Times Are Changing—And So Are the Guidelines for Maximizing Team Performance," *Optimize*, 1 July 2002, 50.

82. Joinson, "Teams at Work."

83. K. Mollica, "Stay Above the Fray: Protect Your Time—and Your Sanity—by Coaching Employees to Deal with Interpersonal Conflicts on Their Own," *HRMagazine*, April 2005, 111.

84. S. Caudron, "Tie Individual Pay to Team Success," *Personnel Journal* 73, no. 10 (October 1994): 40.

85. Ibid.

86. Gross, *Compensation for Teams*.

87. G. Ledford, "Three Case Studies on Skill-Based Pay: An Overview," *Compensation & Benefits Review* 23, no. 2 (1991): 11–24.

88. J. R. Schuster & P. K. Zingheim, *The New Pay: Linking Employee and Organizational Performance* (New York: Lexington Books, 1992).

89. S. G. Cohen & D. E. Bailey, "What Makes Teams Work: Group Effectiveness Research from the Shop Floor to the Executive Suite," *Journal of Management* 23, no. 3 (1997): 239–290.

90. R. Allen & R. Kilmann, "Aligning Reward Practices in Support of Total Quality Management," *Business Horizons* 44 (May 2001): 77–85.

Chapter 11

1. S. Bing, "The Feds Make a Pass at Hooters," *Fortune*, 15 January 1996, 82.

2. J. Helyar, "Hooters: A Case Study," *Fortune*, 1 September 2003, 140.

3. A. Samuels, "Pushing Hot Buttons and Wings," *St. Petersburg Times*, 10 March 2003, 1A.

4. P. S. Greenlaw & J. P. Kohl, "Employer 'Business' and 'Job' Defenses in Civil Rights Actions," *Public Personnel Management* 23, no. 4 (1994): 573.

5. D. Lewis, "EEOC: Damage Awards Reach $420m in 2004," *Boston Globe*, 20 February 2005, D2.

6. J. L. Ledvinka, *Federal Regulation of Personnel and Human Resource Management* (Boston: Kent Publishing Co., 1982), 137–198.

7. Greenlaw & Kohl, "Employer 'Business' and 'Job' Defenses in Civil Rights Actions."

8. W. Peirce, C. A. Smolinski, & B. Rosen, "Why Sexual Harassment Complaints Fall on Deaf Ears," *Academy of Management Executive* 12, no. 3 (1998): 41–54.

9. B. Mims, "Suit Claims Costco Forced Woman to Quit After She Complained of Harassment," *Salt Lake Tribune*, 24 February 2005, C14.

10. Peirce, Smolinski, & Rosen, "Why Sexual Harassment Complaints Fall on Deaf Ears."

11. E. Larson, "The Economic Costs of Sexual Harassment," *Liberty Haven*, http://www.libertyhaven.com/personalfreedomissues/consensualcrimesorsexualissues/ecosexual.html, 18 May 2005.

12. G. Hyland-Savage, "General Management Perspective on Staffing: The Staffing Commandments," in N.C. Bukholder, P.J. Edwards, Jr., and L. Sartain (Eds.), *On Staffing* (Hoboken, NJ: Wiley), 280.

13. R. D. Gatewood & H. S. Field, *Human Resource Selection* (Fort Worth, TX: Dryden Press, 1998).

14. Ibid.

15. *Griggs v. Duke Power Co.*, 401 U.S. 424, 436 (1971); *Albemarle Paper Co. v. Moody*, 422 U.S. 405 (1975).

16. J. Breaugh & M. Starke, "Research on Employee Recruitment: So Many Studies, So Many Remaining Questions," *Journal of Management* 26 (2000): 405–434.

17. S. Gale, "Internet Recruiting: Better, Cheaper, Faster," *Personnel Journal*, 1 December 2000, 74.

18. K. Maher, "Corporations Cut Middlemen and Do Their Own Recruiting," *Wall Street Journal*, 14 January 2003, B10.

19. C. Camden & B. Wallace, "Job Application Forms: A Hazardous Employment Practice," *Personnel Administrator* 28 (1983): 31–32.

20. S. Adler, "Verifying a Job Candidate's Background: The State of Practice in a Vital Human Resources Activity," *Review of Business* 15, no. 2 (1993/1994): 3–8.

21. "More Than 70 Percent of HR Professionals Say Reference Checking Is Effective in Identifying Poor Performers," *Society for Human Resource Management*, http://www.shrm.org/press_published/CMS_011240.asp, 3 February 2005.

22. P. Babcock, "Spotting Lies: The High Cost of Careless Hiring," *HR Magazine* 48, no. 10 (October 2003).

23. M. Le, T. Nguyen, & B. Kleiner, "Legal Counsel: Don't Be Sued for Negligent Hiring," *Nonprofit World*, 1 May 2003, 14–15.

24. "Why It's Critical to Set a Policy on Background Checks for New Hires," *Managing Accounts Payable*, September 2004, 6; J. Schramm, "Future Focus: Background Checking," *HR Magazine*, January 2005.

25. C. Cohen, "Reference Checks," *CA Magazine*, November 2004, 41.

26. S. Marshall, "Spot Inflated Résumés with Simple Sleuthing," *Asian Wall Street Journal*, 7 April 2000, P3.

27. J. Hunter, "Cognitive Ability, Cognitive Aptitudes, Job Knowledge, and Job Performance," *Journal of Vocational Behavior* 29 (1986): 340–362.

28. F. L. Schmidt, "The Role of General Cognitive Ability and Job Performance: Why There Cannot Be a Debate," *Human Performance* 15 (2002): 187–210.

29. K. Murphy, "Can Conflicting Perspectives on the Role of *g* in Personnel Selection Be Resolved?" *Human Performance* 15 (2002): 173–186.

30. J. R. Glennon, L. E. Albright, & W. A. Owens, *A Catalog of Life History Items* (Greensboro, NC: The Richardson Foundation, 1966).

31. Gatewood & Field, *Human Resource Selection*.

32. I. Kotlyar & K. Ades, "HR Technology: Assessment Technology Can Help Match the Best Applicant to the Right Job," *HR Magazine*, 1 May 2002, 97.

33. M. S. Taylor & J. A. Sniezek, "The College Recruitment Interview: Topical Content and Applicant Reactions," *Journal of Occupational Psychology* 57 (1984): 157–168.

34. R. Burnett, C. Fan, S. J. Motowidlo, & T. DeGroot, "Interview Notes and Validity," *Personnel Psychology* 51, no. X (1998): 375–396; M. A. Campion,

D. K. Palmer, & J. E. Campion, "A Review of Structure in the Selection Interview," *Personnel Psychology* 50, no. 3 (1997): 655–702.

35. Campion et al., "A Review of Structure in the Selection Interview."

36. T. Judge, "The Employment Interview: A Review of Recent Research and Recommendations for Future Research," *Human Resource Management Review* 10, issue 4 (2000): 383–406.

37. J. Cortina, N. Goldstein, S. Payne, K. Davison, & S. Gilliland, "The Incremental Validity of Interview Scores Over and Above Cognitive Ability and Conscientiousness Scores," *Personnel Psychology* 53, issue 2 (2000): 325–351.

38. S. Livingston, T. W. Gerdel, M. Hill, B. Yerak, C. Melvin, & B. Lubinger, "Ohio's Strongest Companies All Agree That Training Is Vital to Their Success," *Cleveland Plain Dealer*, 21 May 1997, 30S.

39. S. Overby, "The World's Biggest Classroom," *CIO*, 1 February 2002, http://www.cio.com/archive/020102/dow_content.html, 31 May 2003.

40. M. Totty, "Better Training through Gaming," *Wall Street Journal*, 25 April 2005, R6.

41. J. Borzo, "Almost Human: Using Avatars for Corporate Training, Advocates Say, Can Combine the Best Parts of Face-to-Face Interaction and Computer-Based Learning," *Wall Street Journal*, 24 May 2004, R4.

42. D. L. Kirkpatrick, "Four Steps to Measuring Training Effectiveness," *Personnel Administrator* 28 (1983): 19–25.

43. L. Bassi, J. Ludwig, D. McMurrer, & M. Van Buren, "Profiting from Learning: Do Firms' Investments in Education and Training Pay Off?" *American Society for Training and Development*, http://www.astd.org/NR/rdonlyres/15C0E2AB-B16D-4E3C-A081-4205B865DA3F/0/PFLWhitePaper.pdf, 19 May 2005.

44. J. Stack, "The Curse of the Annual Performance Review," *Inc.*, 1 March 1997, 39.

45. D. Murphy, "Are Performance Appraisals Worse Than a Waste of Time? Book Derides Unintended Consequences," San Francisco *Chronicle*, 9 September 2001, W1.

46. U. J. Wiersma & G. P. Latham, "The Practicality of Behavioral Observation Scales, Behavioral Expectation Scales, and Trait Scales," *Personnel Psychology* 39 (1986): 619–628; U. J. Wiersma, P. T. Van Den Berg, & G. P. Latham, "Dutch Reactions to Behavioral Observation, Behavioral Expectation, and Trait Scales," *Group & Organization Management* 20 (1995): 297–309.

47. D. J. Schleicher, , D. V. Day, B. T. Mayes, R. E. Riggio, "A New Frame for Frame-of-Reference Training: Enhancing the Construct Validity of Assessment Centers," *Journal of Applied Psychology*, August 2002, 735–746.

48. H. H. Meyer, "A Solution to the Performance Appraisal Feedback Enigma," *Academy of Management Executive* 5, no. 1 (1991): 68–76; G. C. Thornton, "Psychometric Properties of Self-Appraisals of Job Performance," *Personnel Psychology* 33 (1980): 263–271.

49. D. A. Waldman, L. E. Atwater, & D. Antonioni, "Has 360 Feedback Gone Amok?" *Academy of Management Executive* 12, no. 2 (1998): 86–94.

50. J. Smither, M. London, R. Flautt, Y. Vargas, & I. Kucine, "Can Working with an Executive Coach Improve Multisource Feedback Ratings over Time? A Quasi-Experimental Field Study," *Personnel Psychology* (Spring 2003): 21–43.

51. A. Walker & J. Smither, "A Five-Year Study of Upward Feedback: What Managers Do with Their Results Matters," *Personnel Psychology* (Summer 1999): 393–422.

52. M. Fong, "Chinese Puzzle—Surprising Shortage of Workers Forces Factories to Add Perks; Pressure on Pay—and Prices," *Wall Street Journal*, 16 August 2004, B1.

53. G. T. Milkovich & J. M. Newman, *Compensation*, 4th ed. (Homewood, IL: Irwin,1993).

54. E. Rasmusson, "Ten Things Your Child Care Provider Won't Tell You," *SmartMoney*, 1 May 2003, 69.

55. S. Shellenbarger, "Tight Labor Market Is Putting Squeeze on Quality Day Care," *Wall Street Journal*, 21 October 1998, B1.

56. M. L. Williams & G. F. Dreher, "Compensation System Attributes and Applicant Pool Characteristics," *Academy of Management Journal* 35, no. 3 (1992): 571–595.

57. "Renault SAS to Pay EUR174.2M in Profit Sharing for 2006," *Dow Jones Newswires*, 8 February 2007, 8:11AM, http://online.wsj.com/article_print/BT-CO-20070208-708668.html.

58. M. Bloom, "The Performance Effects of Pay Dispersion on Individuals and Organizations," *Academy of Management Journal* 42, no. 1 (1999): 25–40.

59. L. Lavelle, F. Jespersen, S. Ante, & J. Kerstetter, "Executive Pay: The Days of the Fantasyland CEO Pay Package Appear to Be in the Past. A 33% Decline in Compensation Has Returned America's Bosses to the Year 1996," *BusinessWeek*, 21 April 2003, 86; L. Lavelle, "A Payday for Performance; Compensation Is Less Outrageous This Year, Except for CEOs Who Delivered," *BusinessWeek*, 18 April 2005, 78.

60. W. Grossman & R. E. Hoskisson, "CEO Pay at the Crossroads of Wall Street and Main: Toward the Strategic Design of Executive Compensation," *Academy of Management Executive* 12, no. 1 (1998): 43–57.

61. Bloom, "The Performance Effects of Pay Dispersion on Individuals and Organizations."

62. M. Bloom & J. Michel, "The Relationships among Organizational Context, Pay Dispersion, and Managerial Turnover," *Academy of Management Journal* 45 (2002): 33–42.

63. P. Michal-Johnson, *Saying Good-Bye: A Manager's Guide to Employee Dismissal* (Glenview, IL: Scott, Foresman & Co., 1985).

64. "Planned Layoffs May Top 1 Million for Fourth Year in a Row," U.S. Steel Workers of America, http://www.uswa.org/uswa/program/content/1733.php, 22 May 2005.

65. J. R. Morris, W. F. Cascio, & C. E. Young, "Downsizing after All These Years: Questions and Answers about Who Did It, How Many Did It, and Who Benefited from It," *Organizational Dynamics* 27, no. 3 (1999): 78–87.

66. K. E. Mishra, G. M. Spreitzer, & A. K. Mishra, "Preserving Employee Morale during Downsizing," *Sloan Management Review* 39, no. 2 (1998): 83–95.

67. J. Hilsenrath, "Adventures in Cost Cutting," *Wall Street Journal*, 10 May 2004, R1.

68. R. Mullins, "Early Retirement Programs Can End Up Being Costly," *Business Journal–Milwaukee*, 20 January 1996, Section 1, 25.

69. M. Willett, "Early Retirement and Phased Retirement Programs for the Public Sector," *Benefits & Compensation Digest*, April 2005, 31.

70. D. R. Dalton, W. D. Todor, & D. M. Krackhardt, "Turnover Overstated: The Functional Taxonomy," *Academy of Management Review* 7 (1982): 117–123.

71. J. R. Hollenbeck & C. R. Williams, "Turnover Functionality versus Turnover Frequency: A Note on Work Attitudes and Organizational Effectiveness," *Journal of Applied Psychology* 71 (1986): 606–611.

72. C. R. Williams, "Reward Contingency, Unemployment, and Functional Turnover," *Human Resource Management Review* 9 (1999): 549–576.

Chapter 12

1. J. H. Boyett & J. T. Boyett, *Beyond Workforce 2000* (New York: Dutton, 1995).

2. Ibid.

3. R. Stodghill, "The Coming Job Bottleneck," *BusinessWeek,* 24 March 1997, 183–185.

4. K. Wallsten, "Diversity Pays Off in Big Sales for Toyota Dealership," *Workforce*, September 1998, 91–92.

5. Equal Employment Opportunity Commission, "Affirmative Action Appropriate under Title VII of the Civil Rights Act of 1964, As Amended. Chapter XIV—Equal Employment Opportunity Commission, Part 1608," http://frwebgate.access.gpo.gov/cgi-bin/get-cfr.cgi?TITLE=29&PART= 1608&SECTION=1&TYPE=TEXT, 3 April 1999.

6. Equal Employment Opportunity Commission, "Federal Laws Prohibiting Job Discrimination: Questions and Answers," http://www.eeoc.gov/facts/qanda.html, 4 April 1999.

7. A. P. Carnevale & S. C. Stone, *The American Mosaic: An In-Depth Report on the Future of Diversity at Work* (New York: McGraw-Hill, 1995).

8. T. Roosevelt, "From Affirmative Action to Affirming Diversity," *Harvard Business Review* 68, no. 2 (1990): 107–117.

9. A. M. Konrad & F. Linnehan, "Formalized HRM Structures: Coordinating Equal Employment Opportunity or Concealing Organizational Practices?" *Academy of Management Journal* 38, no. 3 (1995): 787–820.

10. See, e.g., *Hopwood v. State of Texas*, 78 F.3d 932, 64 USLW 2591, 107 Ed. Law Rep. 552 (5th Cir. [Tex.], 18 March 1996) (No. 94-50569, 94-50664). The U.S. Supreme Court has upheld the principle of affirmative action but has struck down some specfic programs.

11. J. Madore, "Losing Historical Advantages: White Males Say They're Hurt, Too," *Newsday*, 9 April 2000, A45.

12. M. E. Heilman, C. J. Block, & P. Stathatos, "The Affirmative Action Stigma of Incompetence: Effects of Performance Information Ambiguity," *Academy of Management Journal* 40, no. 3 (1997): 603–625.

13. E. Orenstein, "The Business Case for Diversity," *Financial Executive*, May 2005, 22–25; G. Robinson & K. Dechant, "Building a Business Case for Diversity," *Academy of Management Executive* 11, no. 3 (1997): 21–31.

14. E. Esen, "2005 Workplace Diversity Practices: Survey Report," Survey conducted by the Society for Human Resource Management. SHRM Research Department, Alexandria, Virginia (www.shrm.org/research), October 2005.

15. E. Orenstein, "The Business Case for Diversity."

16. E. Esen, "2005 Workplace Diversity Practices: Survey Report."

17. E. Orenstein, "The Business Case for Diversity,"

18. M. Selmi, "The Price of Discrimination: The Nature of Class Action Employment Discrimination Litigation and Its Effects," *Texas Law Review*, 1 April 2003, 1249.

19. P. Wright & S. P. Ferris, "Competitiveness through Management of Diversity: Effects on Stock Price Valuation," *Academy of Management Journal* 38 (1995): 272–285.

20. Ibid.

21. E. Esen, "2005 Workplace Diversity Practices: Survey Report."; L. E. Wynter, "Business & Race: Advocates Try to Tie Diversity to Profit," *Wall Street Journal*, 7 February 1996, B1.

22. W. W. Watson, K. Kumar, & L. K. Michaelsen, "Cultural Diversity's Impact on Interaction Process and Performance: Comparing Homogeneous and Diverse Task Groups," *Academy of Management Journal* 36 (1993): 590–602; K. A. Jehn, G. B. Northcraft, & M. A. Neale, "Why Differences Make a Difference: A Field Study of Diversity, Conflict, and Performance in Workgroups," *Administrative Science Quarterly* 44 (1999): 741–763.

23. F. Rice, "How to Make Diversity Pay," *Fortune*, 8 August 1994, 78.

24. M. R. Carrell & E. E. Mann, "Defining Workplace Diversity Programs and Practices in Organizations," *Labor Law Journal* 44 (1993): 743–764.

25. D. A. Harrison, K. H. Price, & M. P. Bell, "Beyond Relational Demography: Time and the Effects of Surface- and Deep-Level Diversity on Work Group Cohesion," *Academy of Management Journal* 41 (1998): 96–107.

26. D. Harrison, K. Price, J. Gavin, & A. Florey, "Time, Teams, and Task Performance: Changing Effects of Surface- and Deep-Level Diversity on Group Functioning," *Academy of Management Journal* 45 (2002): 1029–1045.

27. Harrison, Price, & Bell, "Beyond Relational Demography."

28. Ibid.

29. J. Helyar & B. Cherry, "50 and Fired," *Fortune*, 16 May 2005, 78.

30. Ibid.

31. S. R. Rhodes, "Age-Related Differences in Work Attitudes and Behavior," *Psychological Bulletin* 92 (1983): 328–367.

32. A. Fisher, "Wanted: Aging Baby-Boomers," *Fortune*, 30 September 1996, 204.

33. G. M. McEvoy & W. F. Cascio, "Cumulative Evidence of the Relationship between Employee Age and Job Performance," *Journal of Applied Psychology* 74 (1989): 11–17.

34. S. E. Sullivan & E. A. Duplaga, "Recruiting and Retaining Older Workers for the Millennium," *Business Horizons* 40 (12 November 1997): 65.

35. T. Maurer & N. Rafuse, "Learning, Not Litigating: Managing Employee Development and Avoiding Claims of Age Discrimination," *Academy of Management Executive* 15, issue 4 (2001): 110–121.

36. B. L. Hassell & P. L. Perrewe, "An Examination of Beliefs about Older Workers: Do Stereotypes Still Exist?" *Journal of Organizational Behavior* 16 (1995): 457–468.

37. "Women in the Labor Force: A Databook (Updated and Available on the Internet)," Bureau of Labor Statistics, http://www.bls.gov/bls/databooknews2005.pdf, 25 May 2005.

38. "Top Facts about Women-Owned Businesses," Center for Women's Business Research, http://www.nfwbo.org/topfacts.html, 26 May 2005.

39. "Women Own 9 Million U.S. Businesses," U.S. Small Business Administration, http://www.sba.gov/advo/press/01-09.html, 23 May 2003.

40. "The 2005 *Fortune* 500: Women CEOs," *Fortune*, http://www.fortune.com/fortune/subs/article/ 0,15114,1046096,00.html, 26 May 2005.

41. "2003 Catalyst Census of Women Board Directors of the *Fortune* 1000," http://www.catalystwomen.org/knowledge/titles/title.php?page=cen_WBDO3, 26 May 2005.

42. M. Bertrand & K. Hallock, "The Gender Gap in Top Corporate Jobs," *Industrial & Labor Relations Review* 55 (2001): 3–21.

43. J. R. Hollenbeck, D. R. Ilgen, C. Ostroff, & J. B. Vancouver, "Sex Differences in Occupational Choice, Pay, and Worth: A Supply-Side Approach to Understanding the Male-Female Wage Gap," *Personnel Psychology* 40 (1987): 715–744.

44. A. Chaker & H. Stout, "Second Chances: After Years Off, Women Struggle to Revive Careers," *Wall Street Journal*, 6 May 2004, A1.

45. Korn-Ferry International, 1993.

46. Department of Industry, Labor and Human Relations, *Report of the Governor's Task Force on the Glass Ceiling Commission* (Madison, WI: State of Wisconsin, 1993).

47. M. Fix, G. C. Galster, & R. J. Struyk, "An Overview of Auditing for Discrimination," in *Clear and Convincing Evidence: Measurement of Discrimination in America*, ed. Michael Fix & Raymond Struyk (Washington, DC: Urban Institute Press, 1993), 1–68.

48. B. R. Ragins, B. Townsend, & M. Mattis, "Gender Gap in the Executive Suite: CEOs and Female Executives Report on Breaking the Glass Ceiling," *Academy of Management Executive* 12 (1998): 28–42.

49. N. Lockwood, "The Glass Ceiling: Domestic and International Perspectives," *HRMagazine* (2004 Research Quarterly): 2–10.

50. T. B. Foley, "Discrimination Lawsuits Are a Small-Business Nightmare: A Guide to Minimizing the Potential Damage," *Wall Street Journal*, 28 September 1998, 15.

51. J. Johnson, "Black CEOs Gaining in Corporate America," *San Francisco Chronicle*, http://www.sfgate.com/cgi-bin/article.cgi?file=/chronicle/archive/2005/02/10/BUGDRB8K781.DTL&type=business, 10 February 2005.

52. "Household Data: Annual Averages, Table 11. Employed Persons by Detailed Occupation, Sex, Race, and Hispanic or Latino Ethnicity," Bureau of Labor Statistics, ftp://ftp.bls.gov/pub/special.requests/lf/aat11.txt, 27 May 2005.

53. D. A. Neal & W. R. Johnson, "The Role of Premarket Factors in Black-White Wage Differences," *Journal of Political Economy* 104, no. 5 (1996): 869–895.

54. Fix, Galster, & Struyk, "An Overview of Auditing for Discrimination."

55. M. Bendick, Jr., C. W. Jackson, & V. A. Reinoso, "Measuring Employment Discrimination through Controlled Experiments," in *African-Americans and Post-Industrial Labor Markets*, ed. James B. Stewart (New Brunswick, NJ: Transaction Publishers, 1997), 77–100.

56. P. B. Riach & J. Rich, "Measuring Discrimination by Direct Experimental Methods: Seeking Gunsmoke," *Journal of PostKeynesian Economics* 14, no. 2 (Winter 1991–1992): 143–150.

57. A. P. Brief, R. T. Buttram, R. M. Reizenstein, & S. D. Pugh, "Beyond Good Intentions: The Next Steps toward Racial Equality in the American Workplace," *Academy of Management Executive* 11 (1997): 59–72.

58. L. E. Wynter, "Business & Race: Federal Agencies, Spurred on by Nonprofit Groups, Are Increasingly Embracing the Use of Undercover Investigators to Identify Discrimination in the Marketplace," *Wall Street Journal*, 1 July 1998, B1.

59. "The Americans with Disabilities Act: Questions and Answers," U.S. Department of Justice, http://www.usdoj.gov/crt/ada/ada.html, 27 May 2005.

60. "Frequently Asked Questions," *Disability Statistics: Online Resource for U.S. Disability Statistics*, http://www.ilr.cornell.edu/ped/disabilitystatistics/faq.cfm#Q2, 27 May 2005.

61. "Census Brief: Disabilities Affect One-Fifth of All Americans," U.S. Bureau of the Census, http://www.census.gov/prod/3/97pubs/cenbr975.pdf, 25 May 2003.

62. F. Bowe, "Adults with Disabilities: A Portrait," *President's Committee on Employment of People with Disabilities* (Washington, DC: GPO, 1992); D. Braddock & L. Bachelder, *The Glass Ceiling and Persons with Disabilities*, Glass Ceiling Commission, U.S. Department of Labor (Washington, DC: GPO, 1994). "Disability Status 2000," *Census Brief* 2000, March 2003, 11. Online at http://www.census.gov/prod/2003pubs/c2kbr-17.pdf.

63. Louis Harris & Associates, Inc., *Public Attitudes toward People with Disabilities* (Washington DC: National Organization on Disability, 1991); Louis Harris & Associates, Inc., *The ICD Survey II: Employing Disabled Americans* (New York: 1987).

64. R. Greenwood & V. A. Johnson, "Employer Perspectives on Workers with Disabilities," *Journal of Rehabilitation* 53 (1987): 37–45.

65. "Low Cost Accommodation Solutions," Office of Disability Employment Policy, http://www.jan.wvu.edu/media/LowCostSolutions.html, 27 May 2005.

66. "Study on the Financing of Assistive Technology Devices and Services for Individuals with Disabilities: A Report to the President and the Congress of the United States," National Council on Dis-ability, http://www.ncd.gov/newsroom/publications/assistive.html, 27 May 2005.

67. R. B. Cattell, "Personality Pinned Down," *Psychology Today* 7 (1973): 40–46; C. S. Carver & M. F. Scheier, *Perspectives on Personality* (Boston: Allyn & Bacon, 1992).

68. J. M. Digman, "Personality Structure: Emergence of the Five-Factor Model," *Annual Review of Psychology* 41 (1990): 417–440; M. R. Barrick & M. K. Mount, "The Big Five Personality Dimensions and Job Performance: A Meta-Analysis," *Personnel Psychology* 44 (1991): 1–26.

69. O. Behling, "Employee Selection: Will Intelligence and Conscientiousness Do the Job?" *Academy of Management Executive* 12 (1998): 77–86.

70. M. R. Barrick & M. K. Mount, "The Big Five Personality Dimensions and Job Performance," *Personnel Psychology* 44 (1991): 1–26. M. K. Mount & M. R. Barrick, "The Big Five Personality Dimensions: Implications for Research and Practice in Human Resource Management," *Research in Personnel & Human Resources Management* 13 (1995): 153–200; M. K. Mount & M. R. Barrick, "Five Reasons Why the 'Big Five' Article Has Been Frequently Cited," *Personnel Psychology* 51 (1998): 849–857; D. S. Ones, M. K. Mount, M. R. Barrick, & J. E. Hunter, "Personality and Job Performance: A Critique of the Tett, Jackson, and Rothstein (1991) Meta-Analysis," *Personnel Psychology* 47 (1994): 147–156.

71. Barrick & Mount, "The Big Five Personality Dimensions and Job Performance."

72. Mount & Barrick, "Five Reasons Why the 'Big Five' Article Has Been Frequently Cited."

73. Mount & Barrick, "Five Reasons Why the 'Big Five' Article Has Been Frequently Cited."

74. Staff, "The Diverse Work Force," *Inc.*, January 1993, 33.

75. D. A. Thomas & R. J. Ely, "Making Differences Matter: A New Paradigm for Managing Diversity," *Harvard Business Review* 74 (September–October 1996): 79–90.

76. E. Esen, "2005 Workplace Diversity Practices: Survey Report."

77. D. A. Thomas & S. Wetlaufer, "A Question of Color: A Debate on Race in the U.S. Workplace," *Harvard Business Review* 75 (September–October 1997), 118–132.

78. Thomas & Ely, "Making Differences Matter."

79. A. Fisher, "How You Can Do Better on Diversity," *Fortune*, 15 November 2004, 60.

80. Aetna – 2005 Diversity Annual Report (www.aetna.com) Obtained from SHRM Research Department.

81. J. R. Norton & R. E. Fox, *The Change Equation: Capitalizing on Diversity for Effective Organizational Change* (Washington, DC: American Psychological Association, 1997).

82. Ibid.

83. Thomas & Ely, "Making Differences Matter."

84. R. R. Thomas, Jr., *Beyond Race and Gender: Unleashing the Power of Your Total Workforce by Managing Diversity* (New York: AMACOM, 1991).

85. Ibid.

86. S. Lubove, "Damned If You Do, Damned If You Don't: Preference Programs Are on the Defensive in the Public Sector, but Plaintiffs' Attorneys and Bureaucrats Keep Diversity Inc. Thriving in Corporate America," *Forbes*, 15 December 1997, 122.

87. L. S. Gottfredson, "Dilemmas in Developing Diversity Programs," in *Diversity in the Workplace*, ed. S. E. Jackson & Associates (New York: Guildford Press, 1992).

88. R. Lieber, "Employers Offer New Pretax Perk: Debit Cards Allow Instant Access to Accounts for Medical Fees and Commuting Expenses," *Wall Street Journal*, 2 September 2003, D1.

89. "L'Oréal Receives Diversity Best Practices 2004 Global CEO Leadership Award," *PR Newswire*, 26 October 2004, 11:01.

90. A. Greenwald, B. Nosek, & M. Banaji, "Understanding and Using the Implicit Association Test: I. An Improved Scoring Algorithm," *Journal of Personality & Social Psychology* (August 2003): 197–206; S. Vedantam, "See No Bias; Many Americans Believe They Are Not Prejudiced," *Washington Post*, 23 January 2005, W12.

91. Carnevale & Stone, *The American Mosaic*.

92. D. Fenn, "Diversity: More Than Just Affirmative Action," *Inc.*, July 1995, 93.

93. J. R. Joplin & C. S. Daus, "Challenges of Leading a Diverse Workforce," *Academy of Management Executive* 11 (1997): 32–47.

94. Ibid.

95. Rice, "How to Make Diversity Pay."

Chapter 13

1. T. Daniel and G. Metcalf, "The Science of Motivation," *SHRM White Paper*, http://www.shrm.org/hrresources/whitepapers_published/CMS_012666.asp, May 2005.

2. J. P. Campbell & R. D. Pritchard, "Motivation Theory in Industrial and Organizational Psychology," in *Handbook of Industrial and Organizational Psychology*, ed. M. D. Dunnette (Chicago: Rand McNally, 1976).

3. P. Thomas, "Waitress Makes the Difference in Bringing Deaf to Pittsburgh," *Wall Street Journal Interactive Edition*, 2 March 1999.

4. E. A. Locke, "The Nature and Causes of Job Satisfaction," in *Handbook of Industrial and Organizational*

Psychology, ed. M. D. Dunnette (Chicago: Rand McNally, 1976).

5. A. H. Maslow, "A Theory of Human Motivation," *Psychological Review* 50 (1943): 370–396.

6. C. P. Alderfer, *Existence, Relatedness, and Growth: Human Needs in Organizational Settings* (New York: Free Press, 1972).

7. D. C. McClelland, "Toward a Theory of Motive Acquisition," *American Psychologist* 20 (1965): 321–333; D. C. McClelland & D. H. Burnham, "Power Is the Great Motivator," *Harvard Business Review* 54, no. 2 (1976): 100–110.

8. J. H. Turner, "Entrepreneurial Environments and the Emergence of Achievement Motivation in Adolescent Males," *Sociometry* 33 (1970): 147–165.

9. L. W. Porter, E. E. Lawler III, & J. R. Hackman, *Behavior in Organizations* (New York: McGraw-Hill, 1975).

10. C. Ajila, "Maslow's Hierarchy of Needs Theory: Applicability to the Nigerian Industrial Setting," *IFE Psychology* (1997): 162–174.

11. M. A. Wahba & L. B. Birdwell, "Maslow Reconsidered: A Review of Research on the Need Hierarchy Theory," *Organizational Behavior & Human Performance* 15 (1976): 212–240; J. Rauschenberger, N. Schmitt, & J. E. Hunter, "A Test of the Need Hierarchy Concept by a Markov Model of Change in Need Strength," *Administrative Science Quarterly* 25 (1980): 654–670.

12. E. E. Lawler III & L. W. Porter, "The Effect of Performance on Job Satisfaction," *Industrial Relations* 7 (1967): 20–28.

13. Porter, Lawler III, & Hackman, *Behavior in Organizations*.

14. K. Maher and K. Hudson, "Wal-Mart to Sweeten Bonus Plan for Staff," *Wall Street Journal*, 22 March 2007, A11.

15. Porter, Lawler III, & Hackman, *Behavior in Organizations*.

16. J. S. Lublin, "Creative Compensation: A CEO Talks about His Company's Innovative Pay Ideas. Free Ice Cream, Anyone?" *Wall Street Journal*, 10 April 2006, R6.

17. C. Caggiano, "What Do Workers Want?" *Inc.*, November 1992, 101–104; "National Study of the Changing Workforce," Families & Work Institute, http://www.familiesandwork.org/summary/nscw.pdf, 31 May 2005.

18. L. Buchanan, "Managing One-to-One," *Inc.*, 1 October 2001, 82.

19. "America@Work: A Focus on Benefits and Compensation," *Aon Consulting*, http://www.aon.com/pdf/ america/ awork2.pdf, 12 June 1999.

20. R. Kanfer & P. Ackerman, "Aging, Adult Development, and Work Motivation," *Academy of Management Review* (2004): 440–458.

21. "Staying Ahead of the Curve: The AARP Work and Career Study," *AARP*, http://assets.aarp.org/rgcenter/econ/ d17772_multiwork.pdf, 31 May 2005.

22. L. Lavelle, "A Payday for Performance; Compensation Is Less Outrageous This Year, Except for CEO Who Delivered," *BusinessWeek*, 18 April 2005, 78.

23. C. T. Kulik & M. L. Ambrose, "Personal and Situational Determinants of Referent Choice," *Academy of Management Review* 17 (1992): 212–237.

24. J. S. Adams, "Toward an Understanding of Inequity," *Journal of Abnormal Social Psychology* 67 (1963): 422–436.

25. R. A. Cosier & D. R. Dalton, "Equity Theory and Time: A Reformulation," *Academy of Management Review* 8 (1983): 311–319; M. R. Carrell & J. E. Dittrich, "Equity Theory: The Recent Literature, Methodological Considerations, and New Directions," *Academy of Management Review* 3 (1978): 202–209.

26. "Iberia Pilots' Strike Causes Cancellation of 30% of Flights—Airline Plans to Ask Union to Pay for Earlier Slowdown," *Wall Street Journal Europe*, 20 June 2001, 5; C. Vitzthum, "Chairman Voices Optimism after Airline Weathers Difficult Year—Spanish Carrier Overcomes Labor Strife, Industry Woes to Post Small Profit," *Wall Street Journal Europe*, 28 January 2002, 5.

27. C. Chen, J. Choi, & S. Chi, "Making Justice Sense of Local-Expatriate Compensation Disparity: Mitigation by Local Referents, Ideological Explanations, and Interpersonal Sensitivity in China-Foreign Joint Ventures," *Academy of Management Journal* (2002): 807–817.

28. K. Aquino, R. W. Griffeth, D. G. Allen, & P. W. Hom, "Integrating Justice Constructs into the Turnover Process: A Test of a Referent Cognitions Model," *Academy of Management Journal* 40, no. 5 (1997): 1208–1227.

29. S. Barr, "While the SEC Watches the Markets, the Job Market Is Draining the SEC," *Washington Post*, 10 March 2002, C3.

30. R. Folger & M. A. Konovsky, "Effects of Procedural and Distributive Justice on Reactions to Pay Raise Decisions," *Academy of Management Journal* 32 (1989): 115–130; M. A. Konovsky, "Understanding Procedural Justice and Its Impact on Business Organizations," *Journal of Management* 26 (2000): 489–512.

31. E. Barret-Howard & T. R. Tyler, "Procedural Justice as a Criterion in Allocation Decisions," *Journal of Personality & Social Psychology* 50 (1986): 296–305; Folger & Konovsky, "Effects of Procedural and Distributive Justice on Reactions to Pay Raise Decisions."

32. R. Folger & J. Greenberg, "Procedural Justice: An Interpretive Analysis of Personnel Systems," in *Research in Personnel and Human Resources Management*, Vol. 3, ed. K. Rowland & G. Ferris (Greenwich, CT: JAI Press, 1985); R. Folger, D. Rosenfield, J. Grove, & L. Corkran, "Effects of 'Voice' and

Peer Opinions on Responses to Inequity," *Journal of Personality & Social Psychology* 37 (1979): 2253–2261; E. A. Lind & T. R. Tyler, *The Social Psychology of Procedural Justice* (New York: Plenum Press, 1988); Konovsky, "Understanding Procedural Justice and Its Impact on Business Organizations."

33. V. H. Vroom, *Work and Motivation* (New York: John Wiley & Sons, 1964); L. W. Porter & E. E. Lawler III, *Managerial Attitudes and Performance* (Homewood, IL: Dorsey Press & Richard D. Irwin, 1968).

34. P. V. LeBlanc & P. W. Mulvey, "How American Workers See the Rewards of Work," *Compensation & Benefits Review* 30 (February 1998): 24–28.

35. A. Fox, "Companies Can Benefit When They Disclose Pay Processes to Employees," *HR Magazine* 47 (July 2002): 25.

36. K. W. Thomas & B. A. Velthouse, "Cognitive Elements of Empowerment," *Academy of Management Review* 15 (1990): 666–681.

37. E. L. Thorndike, *Animal Intelligence* (New York: Macmillan, 1911).

38. B. F. Skinner, *Science and Human Behavior* (New York: Macmillan, 1954); B. F. Skinner, *Beyond Freedom and Dignity* (New York: Bantam Books, 1971); B. F. Skinner, *A Matter of Consequences* (New York: New York University Press, 1984).

39. A. M. Dickinson & A. D. Poling, "Schedules of Monetary Reinforcement in Organizational Behavior Management: Latham and Huber Revisited," *Journal of Organizational Behavior Management* 16, no. 1 (1992): 71–91.

40. R. Ho, "Attending to Attendance," *Wall Street Journal Interactive*, 7 December 1998.

41. D. Grote, "Manager's Journal: Discipline without Punishment," *Wall Street Journal*, 23 May 1994, A14.

42. J. B. Miner, *Theories of Organizational Behavior* (Hinsdale, IL: Dryden, 1980).

43. Dickinson & Poling, "Schedules of Monetary Reinforcement in Organizational Behavior Management."

44. F. Luthans & A. D. Stajkovic, "Reinforce for Performance: The Need to Go beyond Pay and Even Rewards," *Academy of Management Executive* 13, no. 2 (1999): 49–57.

45. K. D. Butterfield, L. K. Trevino, & G. A. Ball, "Punishment from the Manager's Perspective: A Grounded Investigation and Inductive Model," *Academy of Management Journal* 39 (1996): 1479–1512.

46. R. D. Arvey & J. M. Ivancevich, "Punishment in Organizations: A Review, Propositions, and Research Suggestions," *Academy of Management Review* 5 (1980): 123–132.

47. R. D. Arvey, G. A. Davis, & S. M. Nelson, "Use of Discipline in an Organization: A Field Study," *Journal of Applied Psychology* 69 (1984): 448–460;

M. E. Schnake, "Vicarious Punishment in a Work Setting," *Journal of Applied Psychology* 71 (1986): 343–345.

48. E. A. Locke & G. P. Latham, *Goal Setting: A Motivational Technique That Works* (Englewood Cliffs, NJ: Prentice-Hall, 1984); E. A. Locke & G. P. Latham, *A Theory of Goal Setting and Task Performance* (Englewood Cliffs, NJ: Prentice-Hall, 1990).

49. G. P. Latham & E. A. Locke, "Goal Setting—A Motivational Technique That Works," *Organizational Dynamics* 8, no. 2 (1979): 68.

50. Ibid.

Chapter 14

1. S. Warren, "Remembrances: Lamar Muse (1920–2007) Steered Southwest Airlines' Take Off on Booze to Fliers and a Razor to Costs," *Wall Street Journal*, 10 February 2007, A4.

2. B. Gimbel, "Southwest's New Flight Plan," *Fortune*, 16 May 2005, 93.

3. J. Stancavage, "Southwest Has Fun, Profit," *Tulsa World*, 2 July 2006.

4. W. Bennis, "Why Leaders Can't Lead," *Training & Development Journal* 43, no. 4 (1989).

5. J. Adamy, "How Jim Skinner Flipped McDonald's," *Wall Street Journal*, 5 January 2007, B1.

6. A. Zaleznik, "Managers and Leaders: Are They Different?" *Harvard Business Review* 55 (1977): 76–78; A. Zaleznik, "The Leadership Gap," *The Washington Quarterly* 6 (1983): 32–39.

7. Bennis, "Why Leaders Can't Lead."

8. S. Berfield, "The Best of 2006: Leaders," *BusinessWeek*, 18 December 2006, 58.

9. D. Jones, "Not All Successful CEOs are Extroverts," *USA Today*, 7 June 2006, B.1.

10. Ibid.

11. M. Gladwell, "Why Do We Love Tall Men?" *Gladwell Dot Com*, http://www.gladwell.com/blink/blink_excerpt2.html, 24 February 2007.

12. R. J. House & R. M Aditya, "The Social Scientific Study of Leadership: Quo Vadis?" *Journal of Management* 23 (1997): 409–473; T. Judge, R. Illies, J. Bono, & M. Gerhardt, "Personality and Leadership: A Qualitative and Quantitative Review," *Journal of Applied Psychology* (August 2002): 765–782; S. A. Kirkpatrick & E. A. Locke, "Leadership: Do Traits Matter?" *Academy of Management Executive* 5, no. 2 (1991): 48–60.

13. House & Aditya, "The Social Scientific Study of Leadership"; Kirkpatrick & Locke, "Leadership: Do Traits Matter?"

14. D. Sacks, "The Accidental Guru," *Fast Company*, 1 January 2005, 64.

15. Kirkpatrick & Locke, "Leadership: Do Traits Matter?"

16. Elise Amendola, "P&G CEO Wields High Expectations, but No Whip," *USA Today*, 29 February 2007, http://www.usatoday.com/money/companies/management/2007-02-19-exec-pandg-usat_x.htm.

17. E. A. Fleishman, "The Description of Supervisory Behavior," *Journal of Applied Psychology* 37 (1953): 1–6; L. R. Katz, *New Patterns of Management* (New York: McGraw-Hill, 1961).

18. S. Tully & E. Levenson, "In This Corner! The Contender—Jamie Dimon—The New CEO of J.P. Morgan Chase," *Fortune*, 3 April 2006, 54.

19. L. Grant, "Retail Giant Wal-Mart Faces Challenges on Many Fronts; Protests, Allegations Are Price of Success, CEO Says," *USA Today*, 11 November 2003, B.01.

20. Ibid.

21. P. Weissenberg & M. H. Kavanagh, "The Independence of Initiating Structure and Consideration: A Review of the Evidence," *Personnel Psychology* 25 (1972): 119–130.

22. R. J. House & T. R. Mitchell, "Path-Goal Theory of Leadership," *Journal of Contemporary Business* 3 (1974): 81–97; F. E. Fiedler, "A Contingency Model of Leadership Effectiveness," in *Advances in Experimental Social Psychology*, ed. L. Berkowitz (New York: Academic Press, 1964); V. H. Vroom & P. W. Yetton, *Leadership and Decision Making* (Pittsburgh: University of Pittsburgh Press, 1973); P. Hersey & K. H. Blanchard, *The Management of Organizational Behavior*, 4th ed. (Englewood Cliffs, NJ: Prentice Hall, 1984); S. Kerr & J. M. Jermier, "Substitutes for Leadership: Their Meaning and Measurement," *Organizational Behavior & Human Performance* 22 (1978): 375–403.

23. F. E. Fiedler & M. M. Chemers, *Leadership and Effective Management* (Glenview, IL: Scott, Foresman, 1974); F. E. Fiedler & M. M. Chemers, *Improving Leadership Effectiveness: The Leader Match Concept*, 2d ed. (New York: John Wiley & Sons, 1984).

24. Fiedler & Chemers, *Improving Leadership Effectiveness*.

25. F. E. Fiedler, "The Effects of Leadership Training and Experience: A Contingency Model Interpretation," *Administrative Science Quarterly* 17, no. 4 (1972): 455; F. E. Fiedler, *A Theory of Leadership Effectiveness* (New York: McGraw-Hill, 1967).

26. L. S. Csoka & F. E. Fiedler, "The Effect of Military Leadership Training: A Test of the Contingency Model," *Organizational Behavior & Human Performance* 8 (1972): 395–407.

27. House & Mitchell, "Path-Goal Theory of Leadership."

28. Ibid.

29. B. M. Fisher & J. E. Edwards, "Consideration and Initiating Structure and Their Relationships with Leader Effectiveness: A Meta-Analysis," *Proceedings of the Academy of Management*, August 1988, 201–205.

30. M. Copeland, K. Crawford, J. Davis, S. Hamner, C. Hawn, R. Howe, P. Kaihla, M. Maier, O. Malik, D. McDonald, C. Null, E. Schonfeld, O. Thomas, and G. Zachary, "My Golden Rule," *Business 2.0*, 1 December 2005, 108.

31. J. C. Wofford & L. Z. Liska, "Path-Goal Theories of Leadership: A Meta-Analysis," *Journal of Management* 19 (1993): 857–876.

32. House & Aditya, "The Social Scientific Study of Leadership."

33. V. H. Vroom & A. G. Jago, *The New Leadership: Managing Participation in Organizations* (Englewood Cliffs, NJ: Prentice Hall, 1988).

34. C. Fishman, "How Teamwork Took Flight: This Team Built a Commercial Engine—and Self-Managing GE Plant—from Scratch," *Fast Company*, 1 October 1999, 188.

35. Ibid.

36. Ibid.

37. G. A. Yukl, *Leadership in Organizations*, 3d ed. (Englewood Cliffs, NJ: Prentice Hall, 1995).

38. B. M. Bass, *Bass & Stogdill's Handbook of Leadership: Theory, Research, and Managerial Applications* (New York: Free Press, 1990).

39. R. D. Ireland & M. A. Hitt, "Achieving and Maintaining Strategic Competitiveness in the 21st Century: The Role of Strategic Leadership," *Academy of Management Executive* 13, no. 1 (1999): 43–57.

40. P. Thoms & D. B. Greenberger, "Training Business Leaders to Create Positive Organizational Visions of the Future: Is It Successful?" *Academy of Management Journal* [Best Papers & Proceedings], 1995, 212–216.

41. M. Weber, *The Theory of Social and Economic Organizations*, trans. R. A. Henderson & T. Parsons (New York: Free Press, 1947).

42. C. Terhune, C. Mollenkamp, & A. Carrns, "Inside Alleged Fraud at HealthSouth, A 'Family' Plot—CEO Scrushy Cultivated Loyalties as Staffers Fixed Books, Played in His Band," *Wall Street Journal*, 3 April 2003, A1.

43. D. A. Waldman & F. J. Yammarino, "CEO Charismatic Leadership: Levels-of-Management and Levels-of-Analysis Effects," *Academy of Management Review* 24, no. 2 (1999): 266–285.

44. K. B. Lowe, K. G. Kroeck, & N. Sivasubramaniam, "Effectiveness Correlates of Transformational and Transactional Leadership: A Meta-Analytic Review of the MLQ Literature," *Leadership Quarterly* 7 (1996): 385–425.

45. J. M. Howell & B. J. Avolio, "The Ethics of Charismatic Leadership: Submission or Liberation?" *Academy of Management Executive* 6, no. 2 (1992): 43–54.

46. A. Deutschman, "Is Your Boss a Psychopath?" *Fast Company,* July 2005, 44.

47. Howell & Avolio, "The Ethics of Charismatic Leadership."

48. Ibid.

49. J. M. Burns, *Leadership* (New York: Harper & Row, 1978); B. M. Bass, "From Transactional to Transformational Leadership: Learning to Share the Vision," *Organizational Dynamics* 18 (1990): 19–36.

50. Bass, "From Transactional to Transformational Leadership."

51. B. M. Bass, *A New Paradigm of Leadership: An Inquiry into Transformational Leadership* (Alexandra, VA: U.S. Army Research Institute for the Behavioral and Social Sciences, 1996).

52. J. Byrne, "How to Lead Now: Getting Extraordinary Performance When You Can't Pay for It," *Fast Company,* 1 August 2003, 62.

53. Bass, "From Transactional to Transformational Leadership."

Chapter 15

1. E. E. Lawler III, L. W. Porter, & A. Tannenbaum, "Manager's Attitudes toward Interaction Episodes," *Journal of Applied Psychology* 52 (1968): 423–439; H. Mintzberg, T*he Nature of Managerial Work* (New York: Harper & Row, 1973).

2. J. D. Maes, T. G. Weldy, & M. L. Icenogle, "A Managerial Perspective: Oral Communication Competency Is Most Important for Business Students in the Workplace," *Journal of Business Communication* 34 (1997): 67–80.

3. R. Lepsinger & A. D. Lucia, *The Art and Science of 360 Degree Feedback* (San Francisco: Pfeiffer, 1997).

4. E. E. Jones & K. E. Davis, "From Acts to Dispositions: The Attribution Process in Person Perception," in *Advances in Experimental and Social Psychology,* vol. 2, ed. L. Berkowitz (New York: Academic Press, 1965), 219–266; R. G. Lord & J. E. Smith, "Theoretical, Information-Processing, and Situational Factors Affecting Attribution Theory Models of Organizational Behavior," *Academy of Management Review* 8 (1983): 50–60.

5. J. Zadney & H. B. Gerard, "Attributed Intentions and Informational Selectivity," *Journal of Experimental Social Psychology* 10 (1974): 34–52.

6. A. Taylor, "GM Gets Its Act Together. Finally," *Fortune,* 5 April 2004.

7. H. H. Kelly, *Attribution in Social Interaction* (Morristown, NJ: General Learning Press, 1971).

8. J. M. Burger, "Motivational Biases in the Attribution of Responsibility for an Accident: A Meta-Analysis of the Defensive-Attribution Hypothesis," *Psychological Bulletin* 90 (1981): 496–512.

9. D. A. Hofmann & A. Stetzer, "The Role of Safety Climate and Communication in Accident Interpretation: Implications for Learning from Negative Events," *Academy of Management Journal* 41, no. 6 (1998): 644–657.

10. C. Perrow, *Normal Accidents: Living with High-Risk Technologies* (New York: Basic Books, 1984).

11. A. G. Miller & T. Lawson, "The Effect of an Informational Opinion on the Fundamental Attribution Error," *Journal of Personality & Social Psychology* 47 (1989): 873–896; J. M. Burger, "Changes in Attribution Errors over Time: The Ephemeral Fundamental Attribution Error," *Social Cognition* 9 (1991): 182–193.

12. F. Heider, *The Psychology of Interpersonal Relations* (New York: Wiley, 1958); D. T. Miller & M. Ross, "Self-Serving Biases in Attribution of Causality: Fact or Fiction?" *Psychological Bulletin* 82 (1975): 213–225.

13. J. R. Larson, Jr., "The Dynamic Interplay between Employees' Feedback-Seeking Strategies and Supervisors' Delivery of Performance Feedback," *Academy of Management Review* 14, no. 3 (1989): 408–422.

14. C. Hymowitz, "Mind Your Language: To Do Business Today, Consider Delayering," *Wall Street Journal,* 27 March 2006, B1.

15. G. L. Kreps, *Organizational Communication: Theory and Practice* (New York: Longman, 1990).

16. Ibid.

17. K. Voight, "Office Intelligence," *Asian Wall Street Journal,* 21 January 2005, P1.

18. L. Landro, "The Informed Patient: Hospitals Combat Errors at the 'Hand-Off,'" *Wall Street Journal,* 28 June 2006, D1.

19. Kreps, *Organizational Communication: Theory and Practice.*

20. J. Sandberg, "Ruthless Rumors and the Managers Who Enable Them," *Wall Street Journal,* 29 October 2003, B1.

21. W. Davis & J. R. O'Connor, "Serial Transmission of Information: A Study of the Grapevine," *Journal of Applied Communication Research* 5 (1977): 61–72.

22. Sandberg, "Ruthless Rumors and the Managers Who Enable Them."

23. Source: J. Simons, "Stop Moaning about Gripe Sites and Log On," *Fortune,* 2 April 2001, 181.

24. K. Voight, "Office Intelligence," *Asian Wall Street Journal,* 21 January 2005, P1.

25. Davis & O'Connor, "Serial Transmission of Information: A Study of the Grapevine"; Hymowitz, "Managing: Spread the Word, Gossip Is Good."

26. W. C. Redding, *Communication within the Organization: An Interpretive View of Theory and Research* (New York: Industrial Communication Council, 1972).

27. D. T. Hall, K. L. Otazo, & G. P. Hollenbeck, "Behind Closed Doors: What Really Happens in Executive Coaching," *Organizational Dynamics* 27, no. 3 (1999): 39–53.

28. J. Kelly, "Blowing the Whistle on the Boss," *PR Newswire,* 15 November 2004.

29. R. McGarvey, "Lords of Discipline," *Entrepreneur Magazine,* 1 January 2000.

30. C. Hirschman, "Firm Ground: EAP Training for HR and Managers Improves Supervisor-Employee Communication and Helps Organizations Avoid Legal Quagmires," *Employee Benefit News,* http://www.benefitnews.com/education/detail.cfm?id=6452, 13 June 2005.

31. A. Mehrabian, "Communication without Words," *Psychology Today* 3 (1968): 53; A. Mehrabian, *Silent Messages* (Belmont, CA: Wadsworth, 1971); R. Harrison, *Beyond Words: An Introduction to Nonverbal Communication* (Upper Saddle River, NJ: Prentice Hall, 1974); A. Mehrabian, *Non-Verbal Communication* (Chicago: Aldine, 1972).

32. M. L. Knapp, *Nonverbal Communication in Human Interaction,* 2d ed. (New York: Holt, Rinehart & Winston, 1978).

33. H. M. Rosenfeld, "Instrumental Affiliative Functions of Facial and Gestural Expressions," *Journal of Personality & Social Psychology* 24 (1966): 65–72; P. Ekman, "Differential Communication of Affect by Head and Body Cues," *Journal of Personality & Social Psychology* 23 (1965): 726–735; A. Mehrabian, "Significance of Posture and Position in the Communication of Attitude and Status Relationships," *Psychological Bulletin* 71 (1969): 359–372.

34. J. Gottman & R. Levenson, "The Timing of Divorce: Predicting When a Couple Will Divorce over a 14-Year Period," *Journal of Marriage & the Family* 62 (August 2000): 737–745; J. Gottman, R. Levenson, & E. Woodin, "Facial Expressions during Marital Conflict," *Journal of Family Communication* 1, issue 1 (2001): 37–57.

35. T. Aeppel, "Career Journal: Nicknamed 'Nag,' She's Just Doing Her Job," *Wall Street Journal,* 14 May 2002, B1.

36. C. A. Bartlett & S. Ghoshal, "Changing the Role of Top Management: Beyond Systems to People," *Harvard Business Review,* May–June 1995, 132–142.

37. T. Andrews, "E-Mail Empowers, Voice-Mail Enslaves," *PC Week,* 10 April 1995, E11.

38. R. G. Nichols, "Do We Know How to Listen? Practical Helps in a Modern Age," in *Communication Concepts and Processes,* ed. J. DeVitor (Englewood Cliffs, NJ: Prentice Hall, 1971); P. V. Lewis, *Organizational Communication:*

The Essence of Effective Management (Columbus, OH: Grid Publishing Company, 1975).

39. E. Atwater, *I Hear You*, revised ed. (New York: Walker, 1992).

40. R. Adler & N. Towne, *Looking Out/Looking In* (San Francisco: Rinehart Press, 1975).

41. P. LaBaree, "Feargal Quinn: Ireland's 'Pope of Customer Service' Dominates His Market—and Continues to Beat Bigger and Better-Financed Rivals—with a Leadership Philosophy That Is at Once Folksy and Radical," *Fast Company*, 1 November 2001, 88.

42. B. D. Seyber, R. N. Bostrom, & J. H. Seibert, "Listening, Communication Abilities, and Success at Work," *Journal of Business Communication* 26 (1989): 293–303.

43. Atwater, *I Hear You*.

44. P. Sellers, A. Diba, & E. Florian, "Get Over Yourself—Your Ego Is Out Of Control. You're Screwing Up Your Career," *Fortune*, 30 April 2001, 76.

45. H. H. Meyer, "A Solution to the Performance Appraisal Feedback Enigma," *Academy of Management Executive* 5, no. 1 (1991): 68–76.

46. T. D. Schellhardt, "Annual Agony: It's Time to Evaluate Your Work, and All Involved Are Groaning," *Wall Street Journal*, 19 November 1996, A1.

47. C. Hymowitz, "How to Tell Employees All the Things They Don't Want to Hear," *Wall Street Journal*, 22 August 2000, B1.

48. C. Hymowitz, "Diebold's New Chief Shows How to Lead after a Sudden Rise," *Wall Street Journal*, 8 May 2006, B1.

49. A. Lashinsky, "Lights! Camera! Cue the CEO!" *Fortune*, 21 August 2006, 27.

50. M. Campanelli & N. Friedman, "Welcome to Voice Mail Hell: The New Technology Has Become a Barrier between Salespeople and Customers," *Sales & Marketing Management* 147 (May 1995): 98–101.

51. D. Harbrecht, "CEO Q&A: Baxter's Harry Kraemer: 'I Don't Golf,'" *BusinessWeek Online*, 28 March 2003, http://www.businessweek.com/bwdaily/dnflash/mar2002/nf20020328_0720.htm, 15 June 2003.

52. E. Florian & W. Henderson, "Class of '01: Ellen Florian Spotlights Four Retirees—Their Legacies, Their Plans, and What They've Learned That Can Help You Work Better," *Fortune*, 13 August 2001, 185.

53. K. Maher, "Global Companies Face Reality of Instituting Ethics Programs," *Wall Street Journal*, 9 November 2004, B8.

54. "HR, Anytime, Anywhere," *Human Resources*, http://www.humanresourcesmagazine.com.au/articles/83/0C03FC83.asp?Type=60&Category=875, 16 May 2006.

55. J. Bevan, "Leadership, Clarity, and a Very Thick Skin," *The Spectator*, 14 October 2006, 32.

56. D. Kirkpatrick & D. Roth, "Why There's No Escaping the Blog," *Fortune (Europe)*, 24 January 2005, 64.

57. S. Hargrave, "The Blog Busters," *Guardian*, http://www.guardian.co.uk/online/weblogs/story/0,14024,1279463,00.html, 9 August 2004.

58. W. Ross, Jr., "What Every Human Resource Manager Should Know about Web Logs," *SAM Advanced Management Journal*, 1 July 2005, 4.

Chapter 16

1. R. Leifer & P. K. Mills, "An Information Processing Approach for Deciding upon Control Strategies and Reducing Control Loss in Emerging Organizations," *Journal of Management* 22 (1996): 113–137.

2. D. Starkman, "Making 'Sick' Malls Better—Specialists Advise Landlords on Redesigns, Ejecting Stores; Step One: Fix the Food," *Wall Street Journal*, 21 January 2004, B1.

3. R. Rundle & P. Davies, "Hospitals Start to Seek Payment Upfront," *Wall Street Journal*, 2 June 2004, D1.

4. W. Mossberg & K. Swisher, "Using a Computer to Clean Up Spilled Milk," *Wall Street Journal*, 24 May 2005, D5.

5. B. Whitaker, "Yes, There Is a Job That Pays You to Shop," *New York Times*, 13 March 2005, 8.

6. M. Foley, "Blame Vista Delay on Quality?" *eWeek*, 3 April 2006, 33.

7. N. Wiener, *Cybernetics; Or Control and Communication in the Animal and the Machine* (New York: Wiley, 1948).

8. J. Dalrymple & M. Honan, "Nike to Add iPod Integration," *MacWorld*, August 2006, 22-23.

9. R. Guth, "The To-Do List: Make Software More Reliable," *Wall Street Journal*, 17 November 2003, R4.

10. Leifer & Mills, "An Information Processing Approach for Deciding upon Control Strategies and Reducing Control Loss in Emerging Organizations."

11. B. Wysocki, Jr., "The Lack of Vaccines Goes Beyond Flu Inoculations—Eight Shortages Since 2000," *Wall Street Journal*, 8 December 2003, A1.

12. Senator Bill Frist, "Letters to the Editor: Alarming Shortage of Eight Vaccines," *Wall Street Journal*, 30 August 2002, A9; Editorial, "A Needless Vaccine Shortage," *Wall Street Journal*, 21 May 2002, A18.

13. M. Higgins, "The Discounts You Aren't Meant to Have," *Wall Street Journal*, 3 December 2003, D1.

14. S. Greenhouse, "Workers Assail Night Lock-Ins by Wal-Mart," *New York Times*, 18 January 2004, 1.

15. Ibid.

16. Ibid.

17. S. Shellenbarger, "Is the Awful Behavior of Some Bad Bosses Rooted in Their Past?" *Wall Street Journal*, 17 May 2000, B1.

18. M. Weber, *The Protestant Ethic and the Spirit of Capitalism* (New York: Scribner's, 1958).

19. C. Forelle, "On the Road Again, but Now the Boss Is Sitting beside You," *Wall Street Journal*, 14 May 2004, A1.

20. J. Lublin, "CEO Bonuses Rose 46.4% at 100 Big Firms in 2004," *Wall Street Journal*, 25 February 2005, A1.

21. S. Williford, "Nordstrom Sets the Standard for Customer Service," *Memphis Business Journal*, 1 July 1996, 21.

22. A. DeFelice, "A Century of Customer Love: Nordstrom Is the Gold Standard for Customer Service Excellence," *CRM Magazine*, 1 June 2005, 42.

23. R. T. Pascale, "Nordstrom: Respond to Unreasonable Customer Requests!" *Planning Review* 2 (May–June 1994): 17.

24. Ibid.

25. Ibid.

26. J. R. Barker, "Tightening the Iron Cage: Concertive Control in Self-Managing Teams," *Administrative Science Quarterly* 38 (1993): 408–437.

27. N. Byrnes, "The Art of Motivation," *Business Week*, 1 May 2006, 56–62.

28. Barker, "Tightening the Iron Cage."

29. C. Manz & H. Sims, "Leading Workers to Lead Themselves: The External Leadership of Self-Managed Work Teams," *Administrative Science Quarterly* 32 (1987): 106–128.

30. J. Slocum & H. A. Sims, "Typology for Integrating Technology, Organization and Job Design," *Human Relations* 33 (1980): 193–212.

31. C. C. Manz & H. P. Sims, Jr., "Self-Management as a Substitute for Leadership: A Social Learning Perspective," *Academy of Management Review* 5 (1980): 361–367.

32. C. Manz & C. Neck, *Mastering Self-Leadership*, 3rd ed. (Upper Saddle River, NJ: Pearson, Prentice Hall, 2004).

33. R. S. Kaplan & D. P. Norton, "Using the Balanced Scorecard as a Strategic Management System," *Harvard Business Review*, January–February 1996, 75–85; R. S. Kaplan & D. P. Norton, "The Balanced Scorecard: Measures That Drive Performance," *Harvard Business Review*, January–February 1992, 71–79.

34. J. Meliones, "Saving Money, Saving Lives," *Harvard Business Review*, November–December 2000, 57–65.

35. M. H. Stocks & A. Harrell, "The Impact of an Increase in Accounting Information Level on the Judgment Quality of Individuals and Groups," *Accounting, Organizations & Society*, October–November 1995, 685–700.

36. B. Morris, "Roberto Goizueta and Jack Welch: The Wealth Builders," *Fortune*, 11 December 1995, 80–94.

37. G. Colvin, "America's Best & Worst Wealth Creators: The Real Champions Aren't Always Who You Think. Here's an Eye-Opening Look at Which Companies Produce and Destroy the Most

Money for Investors—Plus a New Tool for Spotting Future Winners," *Fortune*, 18 December 2000, 207.

38. E. Varon, "Implementation Is Not for the Meek," *CIO*, http://www.cio.com/archive/111502/meek_content.html, 20 June 2005.

39. "Welcome Complaints," Office of Consumer and Business Affairs, http://www.ocba.sa.gov.au/businessadvice/complaints/03_welcome.html, 20 June 2005.

40. C. B. Furlong, "12 Rules for Customer Retention," *Bank Marketing* 5 (January 1993): 14.

41. M. Raphel, "Vanished Customers Are Valuable Customers," *Art Business News*, June 2002, 46.

42. C. A. Reeves & D. A. Bednar, "Defining Quality: Alternatives and Implications," *Academy of Management Review* 19 (1994): 419–445.

43. "The 2002 Readers' Choice Awards: Top Travel Services, Condé Nast Traveler," Concierge.com, http://www.concierge.com/cntraveler/lists/readerschoice02/topservices, 20 June 2005.

44. "Singapore Airlines Presents Our Awards & Accolades," Singapore Airlines Web site, http://www.singaporeair.com/saa/app/saa/JSESSIONID_WLCS_PORTAL=C3fiOZQ2Bj5lXHqAcr3g1VqZm5uwENm2PSu24wqHAG2CtMDvHeG2!-1439203779!-1407778317!7501!7502?hidHeaderAction=onHeaderMenuClick&hidTopicArea=Awards$Accolades&currentSite=global, 20 June 2005.

45. S. Holmes, "Creature Comforts at 30,000 feet," *Business Week*, 18 December 2006, 138.

46. "ATW Daily News," *ATW*, http://www.atwonline.com/news/story.html?storyID=186, 20 June 2005.

47. K. Nirmalya, " Strategies to Fight Low-Cost Rivals," *Harvard Business Review* 84, no. 12 (2006): 104–112.

48. D. R. May & B. L. Flannery, "Cutting Waste with Employee Involvement Teams," *Business Horizons*, September–October 1995, 28–38.

49. F. Etherington, "Leak in City's Water Valve Angers Kitchener Man," *Kitchener-Waterloo Record*, 1 August 2002, B4.

50. B. Burlingham, "The Coolest Little Start-Up in America," *Inc.*, July 2006, 78–85.

51. M. Conlin & P. Raeburn, "Industrial Evolution: Bill McDonough Has the Wild Idea He Can Eliminate Waste. Surprise! Business Is Listening," *Business Week*, 8 April 2002, 70.

52. Ibid.

53. J. Sprovieri, "Environmental Management Affects Manufacturing Bottom Line," *Assembly*, 1 July 2001, 24.

54. B. Byrne, "EU Says Makers Must Destroy Their Own Brand End-of-Life Cars," *Irish Times*, 23 April 2003, 52.

55. S. Power, "Take It Back: Where Do Cars Go When They Die? In Europe, They Have Little Choice," *Wall Street Journal*, 17 April 2006, R6.

56. J. Szekely & G. Trapaga, "From Villain to Hero (Materials Industry's Waste Recovery Efforts)," *Technology Review*, 1 January 1995, 30.

57. "The End of the Road: Schools and Computer Recycling," Intel, http://www.intel.com/education/recycling_computers/recycling.htm, 20 June 2005.

58. B. Rose, "Where Old Computers Go: While Too Many Are Dumped Illegally, Sr. Center Salvages Thousands," *Press Democrat*, 18 June 2001, D1.

59. "Hardware Recycling Services—US," Hewlett-Packard, https://warp1.external.hp.com/recycle/, 6 May 2003.

Chapter 17

1. R. Lenzner, "The Reluctant Entrepreneur," *Forbes*, 11 September 1995, 162–166.

2. M. Totty, "Who's Going to Win the Living-Room Wars? The Battle to Control Home Entertainment Is Heating Up," *Wall Street Journal*, 25 April 2005, R1.

3. P. Grant & A. Schatz, "For Cable Giants, AT&T Deal Is One More Reason to Worry," *Wall Street Journal*, 7 March 2006, A1.

4. P. Grant, "Cable Firms Woo Business in Fight for Telecom Turf," *Wall Street Journal*, 17 January 2007, A1.

5. R. D. Buzzell & B. T. Gale, *The PIMS Principles: Linking Strategy to Performance* (New York: Free Press, 1987); M. Lambkin, "Order of Entry and Performance in New Markets," *Strategic Management Journal* 9 (1988): 127–140.

6. G. L. Urban, T. Carter, S. Gaskin, & Z. Mucha, "Market Share Rewards to Pioneering Brands: An Empirical Analysis and Strategic Implications," *Management Science* 32 (1986): 645–659.

7. N. Buckley & S. Voyle, "Can Wal-Mart Conquer Markets outside the US?" *Financial Times*, 8 January 2003.

8. M. Garry & S. Mulholland, "Master of Its Supply Chain: To Keep Its Inventory Costs Low and Its Shelves Fully Stocked, Wal-Mart Has Always Invested Extensively—and First—in Technology for the Supply Chain," *Supermarket News*, 2 December 2002, 55.

9. S. Rupley, "A Moveable Mesh," *PC Magazine*, 21 September 2004, 94.

10. L. Tischler, "Tech for Toques," *Fast Company*, 1 May 2006, 68.

11. R. Pastore, "Cruise Control," *CIO*, 1 February 2003, 60–66.

12. Ibid.

13. C. Quintanilla & L. Claman, "Acxiom Corporation—Chmn. & Pres. Interview," *CNBC/Dow Jones Business Video*, 21 November 2002.

14. P. Tam, "The Chief Information Officer's Job Isn't What It Used to Be; Just ask Hewlett-Packard's Randy Mott," *Wall Street Journal*, 16 April 2007, R5.

15. S. Mehta, "Behold the Server Farm!" *Fortune*, 7 August 2006, 68.

16. T. Knauss, "Niagara Mohawk Meters to Send Readings by Radio; $100 Million Project Will Eventually Eliminate Need for Door-to-Door Readers," *The Post-Standard Syracuse*, 17 September 2002, A1.

17. S. Lubar, *Infoculture: The Smithsonian Book of Information Age Inventions* (Boston: Houghton, Mifflin, 1993).

18. Ibid.

19. B. Worthen, "Bar Codes on Steroids," *CIO*, 15 December 2002, 53.

20. S. McCartney, "A New Way to Prevent Lost Luggage," *Wall Street Journal*, 27 February 2007, D1.

21. M. Stone, "Scanning for Business," *PC Magazine*, 10 May 2005, 117.

22. N. Rubenking, "Hidden Messages," *PC Magazine*, 22 May 2001, 86.

23. A. Carter & D. Beucke, "A Good Neighbor Gets Better," *Business Week*, 20 June 2005, 16.

24. Rubenking, "Hidden Messages."

25. G. Saitz, "Naked Truth—Data Miners, Who Taught Retailers to Stock Beer Near Diapers, Find Hidden Sales Trends, a Science That's Becoming Big Business," *The Star-Ledger*, 1 August 2002, 041.

26. M. Overfelt, "A Better Way to Sell Tickets," *Fortune Small Business*, 1 December 2006, 76.

27. B. Saporita, W. Boston, N. Gough, & R. Healy, "Can Wal-Mart Get Any Bigger? (Yes, a Lot Bigger . . . Here's How)," *Time*, 19 January 2003, 38.

28. B. Gottesman & K. Karagiannis, "A False Sense of Security," *PC Magazine*, 22 February 2005, 72.

29. F. J. Derfler, Jr., "Secure Your Network," *PC Magazine*, 27 June 2000, 183–200.

30. "Authentication," Webopedia.com, http://www.webopedia.com/TERM/a/authentication.html, 20 April 2003.

31. "Authorization," Webopedia.com, http://www.webopedia.com/TERM/a/authorization.html, 20 April 2003.

32. L. Seltzer, "Password Crackers," *PC Magazine*, 12 February 2002, 68.

33. B. Grimes, "Biometric Security," *PC Magazine*, 22 April 2003, 74.

34. M. McQueen, "Laptop Lockdown," *Wall Street Journal*, 28 June 2006, D1.

35. C. Metz, "Total Security," *PC Magazine*, 1 October 2003, 83.

36. J. van den Hoven, "Executive Support Systems & Decision Making," *Journal of Systems Management* 47, no. 8 (March–April 1996): 48.

37. "Business Objects Customers Take Off with Performance Management; Management Dashboards Help Organizations Gain Insight and Optimize Performance," *Business Wire*, 4 April 2005.

38. "Intranet," Webopedia.com, http://www.webopedia.com/TERM/i/intranet.html, 26 August 2001.

39. "IBM Dynamic Workplaces for Air," IBM, http://www.1.ibm.com/industries/

travel/doc/content/solution/185155106. html, 28 June 2005.

40. J. Ericson, "The Hillman Group Leverages Consolidated Reporting, Geographic Analysis to Support Its Hardware Manufacturing/Distribution Leadership," *Business Intelligence Review*, 1 March 2007, 12.

41. "Extranet," Webopedia.com, http://www.webopedia.com/TERM/E/extranet.html, 22 April 2003.

42. S. Hamm, D. Welch, W. Zellner, F. Keenan, & F. Engardio, "Down but Hardly Out: Downturn Be Damned, Companies Are Still Anxious to Expand Online," *BusinessWeek*, 26 March 2001, 126.

43. S. Nassauer, "Travel Watch: Eliminating the Human Element," *Wall Street Journal*, 14 November 2006, D7.

44. Hamm, Welch, Zellner, Keenan, & Engardio, "Down but Hardly Out."

45. K. C. Laudon & J. P. Laudon, *Management Information Systems: Organization and Technology* (Upper Saddle River, NJ: Prentice Hall, 1996).

46. J. Borzo, "Software for Symptoms," *Wall Street Journal*, 23 May 2005, R10.

47. Ibid.

48. R. Hernandez, "American Express Authorizer's Assistant," *Business Rules Journal*, http://www.bizrules.com/us/page/art_amexaa.htm, 28 June 2005.

Chapter 18

1. "Ryanair Celebrates 20 Years of Operations," Ryanair, http://www.ryanair.com/site/about/invest/docs/2005/q4_2005.pdf, 1 July 2005.

2. L. Tutor, "The Best Drive-Through in America,'06: Average Service Time Ranking," *Quick Service Restaurant*, http://www.qsrmagazine.com/reports/drive-thru_time_study/top25.phtml, 1 July 2006.

3. M. Richtel, "The Long-Distance Journey of a Fast-Food Order," *New York Times*, 11 April 2006, at http://www.nytimes.com/2006/04/11/technology/11fast.html?ei=5090&en=fba08317788e24.

4. "Employment Cost Index News Release Text," Bureau of Labor Statistics, http://www.bls.gov/news.release/eci.nr0.htm, 1 July 2005; "Productivity and Costs, First Quarter 2005, Revised," Bureau of Labor Statistics, http://www.bls.gov/news.release/prod2.nr0.htm, 1 July 2005.

5. "HINC-03. People in Households—Households, by Total Money Income in 2003, Age, Race, and Hispanic Origin of Householder," U.S. Census Bureau, http://pubdb3.census.gov/macro/032004/hhinc/new03_001.htm, 1 July 2005.

6. "Historical Income Tables—Families," U.S. Census Bureau, http://www.census.gov/hhes/income/histinc/f06.html, 1

July 2005; "Table H-6. Regions—All Races by Median and Mean Income: 1975 to 2003," U.S. Census Bureau, http://www.census.gov/hhes/www/income/histinc/h06ar.html, 1 July 2005.

7. "Productivity and Costs, First Quarter 2005, Revised," Bureau of Labor Statistics, ftp://ftp.bls.gov/pub/news.release/History/prod2.06022005.news, 1 July 2005; "Employment, Hours, and Earnings from the Current Employment Statistics Survey (National)," Bureau of Labor Statistics, http://data.bls.gov/cgi-bin/surveymost?ce, 1 July 2005; "Productivity and Costs, First Quarter 2006, Revised," Bureau of Labor Statistics, ftp://ftp.bls.gov/pub/news.release/History/prod2.06022005.news, 1 July 2006; "Employment, Hours, and Earnings from the Current Employment Statistics Survey (National)," Bureau of Labor Statistics, http://data.bls.gov/cgi-bin/surveymost?ce, 1 March 2007.

8. M. Ferguson. "It's the Right Time to Look for a New Job," *US News and World Report*, 9 April 2007, at http://cnn.usnews.com/pt/cpt?action=cpt&title=It%27s+the+right+time.

9. Joanne Fritz, "Giving USA Releases Report on Charitable Giving for 2005," http://www.nonprofit.about.com/od/trendsissuesstatistics/a/givingusa.htm, 5 April 2007.

10. "Cars' Affordability: Cheapest Since 1980," *CNN Money*, 13 November 2006, at http://cnnmoney.com/pt/cpt?action=cpt&title=cars%A0most+affordable; "Auto Affordability Shows a Record Deterioration; Comerica Bank Chief Economist Reports," http://www.theautochannel.com/news/2007/02/12/036903.html, 12 February 2007.

11. "Auto Affordability Slipped a Notch in Summer," *Comerica*, http://comerica.com/cma/cda/main/0,00,2_A_1299,00.html, 1 July 2005.

12. "Cars' Affordability: Cheapest Since 1980."

13. B. Clanton, "Asians Outpace Big Three Factory Efficiency," *Detroit News*, http://www.detnews.com/2005/autosinsider/0506/07/A01-202894.htm, 1 July 2005.

14. Ibid.

15. "Multifactor Productivity," Bureau of Labor Satistics, http://stats.bls.gov/bls/productivity.htm, 31 January 2007.

16. M. Rechtin "Porsche, Hyundai Score Big Gains in J.D. Power Quality Survey," *Auto Week*, 7 June 2006, online at http://www.autoweek.com/apps/pbcs.dll/article?AID=/20060608/FREE/60607007/1041&te.

17. "ASQ Glossary of Terms Search," American Society for Quality, http://www.asq.org/info/glossary/q.html, 3 June 2003.

18. R. E. Markland, S. K. Vickery, & R. A. Davis, "Managing Quality" (Chapter 7), *Operations Management: Concepts in*

Manufacturing and Services (Cincinnati, OH: South-Western College Publishing, 1998).

19. G. Rao, "Computers to Be at the Heart of a Car," *Economic Times*, 12 February 2004.

20. "The 'R' Word: Product Reliability Is Measured at Physio-Control," *InSync*, http://www.medtronic-ers.com/insync/archives/istfal97.htm, 2 June 2005.

21. L. L. Berry & A. Parasuraman, *Marketing Services* (New York: Free Press, 1991).

22. "ISO 9000 and ISO 14000 in Plain Language," International Organization for Standardization, http://www.iso.org/iso/en/iso9000-14000/understand/basics/general/basics_4.html.

23. "FAQs—General," International Organization for Standardization, http://www.iso.org/iso/en/faqs/faq-general.html, 2 July 2005.

24. J. Briscoe, S. Fawcett, & R. Todd, "The Implementation and Impact of ISO 9000 among Small Manufacturing Enterprises," *Journal of Small Business Management* 43 (1 July 2005): 309.

25. R. Henkoff, "The Not New Seal of Quality (ISO 9000 Standard of Quality Management)," *Fortune*, 28 June 1993, 116.

26. "Frequently Asked Questions about the Malcolm Baldrige National Quality Award," National Institute of Standards & Technology, http://www.nist.gov/public_affairs/factsheet/baldfaqs.htm, 2 June 2005.

27. "Baldrige Award Application Forms," National Institute of Standards & Technology, http://www.baldrige.nist.gov/PDF_files/2005_Award_Application_Forms.pdf, 2 July 2005.

28. "Frequently Asked Questions and Answers about the Malcolm Baldrige National Quality Award."

29. "Criteria for Performance Excellence," Baldrige National Quality Program 2003, http://www.quality.nist.gov/PDF_files/2005_Business_Criteria.pdf, 2 July 2005.

30. Ibid.

31. Ibid.

32. "NIST Stock Studies Show Quality Pays (Baldrige National Quality Award)," National Institute of Standards & Technology, http://www.quality.nist.gov/Stock_Studies.htm, 2 July 2005.

33. J. W. Dean, Jr., & J. Evans, *Total Quality: Management, Organization, and Strategy* (St. Paul, MN: West Publishing Co., 1994).

34. J. W. Dean, Jr., & D. E. Bowen, "Management Theory and Total Quality: Improving Research and Practice through Theory Development," *Academy of Management Review* 19 (1994): 392–418.

35. R. Allen & R. Kilmann, "Aligning Reward Practices in Support of Total Quality Management," *Business Horizons*, 1 May 2001, 77.

36. R. Carter, "Best Practices: Freudenberg-NOK/Cleveland, GA: Continuous Kaizens," *Industrial Maintenance & Plant Operations*, 1 June 2004, 10.
37. Ibid.
38. R. Levering, M. Moskowitz, L. Munoz, & P. Hjelt, "The 100 Best Companies to Work for," *Fortune*, 4 February 2002, 72.
39. "News Release: Gross Domestic Product and Corporate Profits," http://www.bea.gov/newsreleases/national/gdp/gdpnewsrelease.htm, 4 April 2007.
40. R. Hallowell, L. A. Schlesinger, & J. Zornitsky, "Internal Service Quality, Customer and Job Satisfaction: Linkages and Implications for Management," *Human Resource Planning* 19 (1996): 20–31; J. L. Heskett, T. O. Jones, G. W. Loveman, W. E. Sasser, Jr., & L. A. Schlesinger, "Putting the Service-Profit Chain to Work," *Harvard Business Review*, March–April 1994, 164–174.
41. J. Huey, G. Bethune, & H. Kelleher, "Two Texas Mavericks Rant about the Wreckage of the U.S. Aviation Industry—And Reveal How They've Managed to Keep Their Companies above the Miserable Average," *Fortune*, 13 November 2000, 237.
42. R. Eder, "Customer-Easy Doesn't Come Easy," *Drug Store News*, 21 October 2002, 52.
43. L. L. Berry & A. Parasuraman, "Listening to the Customer—The Concept of a Service-Quality Information System," *Sloan Management Review* 38, no. 3 (Spring 1997): 65; C. W. L. Hart,

J. L. Heskett, & W. E. Sasser, Jr., "The Profitable Art of Service Recovery," *Harvard Business Review*, July–August 1990, 148–156.
44. G. Stoller, "Companies Give Front-Line Employees More Power," *USA Today*, 27 June 2005, A.1.
45. D. E. Bowen & E. E. Lawler III, "The Empowerment of Service Workers: What, Why, How, and When," Sloan Management Review 33 (Spring 1992): 31–39; D. E. Bowen & E. E. Lawler III, "Empowering Service Employees," *Sloan Management Review* 36 (Summer 1995): 73–84.
46. Bowen & Lawler III, "The Empowerment of Service Workers: What, Why, How, and When."
47. Stoller, "Companies Give Front-Line Employees More Power."
48. G. V. Frazier & M. T. Spiggs, "Achieving Competitive Advantage through Group Technology," *Business Horizons* 39 (1996): 83–88.
49. "The Top 100 Beverage Companies: The List," *Beverage Industry*, July 2001, 30.
50. E. Gruber, "Cutting Time," *Modern Machine Shop*, March 2001, 102.
51. S. Silke Carty, "Chrysler Wrestles with High Levels of Inventory as Unsold Vehicles Sit on Lots," *USAToday*, 2 November 2006, at http://www.usatoday.com/money/autos/2006-11-02-chrysler-high-inventory_x.htm; J. D. Stoll, "Chrysler Maintains Plan to Cut Production as Inventory Rises," *Wall Street Journal*, 24 August 2006, online http://www.wsj.com.

52. Ibid.
53. N. Wingfield, "Out of Tune: iPod Shortage Rocks Apple," *Wall Street Journal*, 16 December 2004, B1.
54. Ibid.
55. D. Drickhamer, "Reality Check," *Industry Week*, November 2001, 29.
56. D. Drickhamer, "Zeroing In on World-Class," *Industry Week*, November 2001, 36.
57. J. Zeiler, "The Need for Speed," *Operations & Fulfillment*, 1 April 2004, 38.
58. "About EFR," *Efficient Foodservice Response*, http://www.efr-central.com/aboutefr.html, 3 July 2005.
59. J. R. Henry, "Minimized Setup Will Make Your Packaging Line S.M.I.L.E.," *Packaging Technology & Engineering*, 1 February 1998, 24.
60. J. Donoghue, "The Future Is Now," *Air Transport World*, 1 April 2001, 78.
61. N. Shirouzu, "Why Toyota Wins Such High Marks on Quality Surveys," *Wall Street Journal*, 15 March 2001, A1.
62. Ibid.
63. G. Gruman, "Supply on Demand; Manufacturers Need to Know What's Selling before They Can Produce and Deliver Their Wares in the Right Quantities," *Info World*, 18 April 2005.

Drive, 257
Drugstore.com, 319
DSS, 327
Duke's Children's Hospital, 301
Dunkin' Donuts, 104
DuPont, 124, 197
Durability, 333
Dynamic environment, 44
Dysfunctional turnover, 215
Dyson, 50

E

E-learning, 206
E-Trade Financial, 12
EA Sports, 44
EAP, 284
Early retirement incentive
    program (ERIP), 214
Eastman Kodak, 119
eBay, 4
Economic order quantity
    (EOQ), 343
Economic responsibility, 74
Economic value added (EVA),
    302–304
Economy, 46–47
EDI, 325
EEOC, 52, 194, 219
Effectiveness, 4
Efficiency, 3
Effort and performance, 236
Egyptians, 21
80 percent rule, 196
84 Lumber Company, 102
EIS, 324
Electronic brainstorming, 94
Electronic data interchange
    (EDI), 325
Electronic scanners, 317
Eli Lilly, 124
Elixir, 111
Email snooping, 320
Emotional stability, 227, 257
Empathetic listening, 287
Empathy, 333
Employee assistance program
    (EAP), 284
Employee-centered leadership,
    258
Employee involvement, 56
Employee involvement teams,
    180
Employee satisfaction, 337
Employee separation, 211
Employee shrinkage, 62
Employee stock ownership
    plan (ESOP), 212
Employee turnover, 215
Employment discrimination,
    193–196
Employment interview, 201,
    204, 205
Employment legislation,
    193–195
Employment references, 200
Employment security, 19
Empowering workers, 170,
    337
Empowerment, 170
Encoding, 279
Enterprise Rent-a-Car, 229, 335

Entrepreneur role, 11
Environment. See External
    environments; Internal
    environment
Environmental change, 43
Environmental complexity, 45
Environmental Protection
    Agency, 52
Environmental scanning, 53
EOQ, 343
Equal Employment
    Opportunity Commission
    (EEOC), 52, 194, 219
Equal Pay Act, 195
Equity, 33
Equity theory, 240–244
ERIP, 214
Esmond, Donald, 50
ESOP, 212
Esprit de corps, 33
Ethical behavior, 62
Ethical charismatics, 270, 272
Ethical climate, 71–72
Ethical decision making, 65–72
Ethical intensity, 66
Ethical responsibility, 75
Ethics, 60. See also Social
    responsibility
    codes of ethics, 70
    defined, 60
    ethical climate, 71–72
    ethical decision making,
        65–72
    ethics training, 70–71
    hiring practices, 70
    moral development, 67–68
    U.S. Sentencing
        Commission Guidelines for
        Organizations, 63–65
    whistleblowing, 72
    workplace deviance, 62
"Ethics Challenge, The," 70
Ethics training, 70–71
European Monitor, 89
European Union (EU), 308
EVA, 302–304
Evaluation apprehension, 94
Executive information system
    (EIS), 324
Expatriate, 152
Expectancy, 244
Expectancy theory, 244–246
Experiential approach to
    innovation, 123
Expert system, 327
Exporting, 143–144
External attribution, 277
External blogs, 291
External environments, 42–54
    changing environments,
        43–46
    defined, 42
    environmental scanning, 53
    general environment,
        46–48
    interpreting environmental
        factors, 54
    specific environment,
        48–52
    threats/opportunities, 54
External recruiting, 199
Externals, 264
Extinction, 248
Extranet, 325

Extraversion, 227
Extrinsic rewards, 238–239
Exxon, 5

F

Family and Medical Leave Act,
    48, 195
Fandray, Dayton, 71
Fannie Mae, 6
Fanning, Shawn, 99
Faulty action stage, 126
Fayol, Henri, 31–33
Federal Communications
    Commission, 52
Federal employment laws,
    194–195
Federal regulatory agencies, 52
Federal Reserve System, 52
Federal Trade Commission, 52
FedEx, 291
Feedback, 166, 287–288
Feedback control, 295
Feedback to sender, 280
Feedforward control, 295
Femininity, 150–151
Fiedler's contingency theory,
    260–262
Field simulation, 153
Figurehead role, 10
Films, 207
Financial ratios, 302
Financial Review Card, 302
Finished goods inventories,
    340
Firewall, 321
Firm-level strategies, 112–115
First-line managers, 8–9
First-mover advantage, 99, 312
Fixed ratio reinforcement
    schedules, 249
Flat-screen LCD, 45
Florist Network, 248
Flow, 122
FNS NewsClips Online, 11
Focus strategy, 111
Follett, Mary Parker, 32, 34
Food and Drug
    Administration, 52
Ford, Henry, 25, 35
Ford Motor Company, 12, 25,
    40, 49, 50, 153, 174, 291,
    319
Formal authority system, 265
Formal communication
    channel, 280–281
Forming, 186
Fortune Business Confidence
    Index, 47
Four-fifths rule, 196
Fox, 49
Franchise, 144
Franchisee, 144
Franchisor, 144
Freedom, 122
Fremantle-Media, 143
Frito-Lay, 220, 248
Fuji-Xerox, 145
Functional
    departmentalization, 156–157
Functional turnover, 215
Functions of the Executive,

The (Barnard), 36
Fundamental attribution error,
    278

G

Gainsharing, 191
Games, 207
Gantt, Henry, 28–30
Gantt chart, 28–30
Gap, 292, 296
Gates, Bill, 53, 55, 154
GATT, 138
Gazprom, 150
GE Aircraft Engines, 266
Gender, 222–224
Genencor, 56
Genentech, 283
General Agreement on Tariffs
    and Trade (GATT), 138
General Electric, 174, 188
General Electric workout, 132
General environment, 46–48
General Mills, 325–326
General Motors (GM), 12, 49,
    50, 126, 277, 331, 338
Generational change, 124
Genesco, 304
Geographic
    departmentalization, 158–159
Gerdau SA, 136
Germans, 143
*Getting to Yes: Negotiating
    Agreement without Giving
    In* (Fisher et al.), 32
Giannantonio, Frank, 324
Giesecke & Devrient, 145
Gilbreth, Frank and Lillian,
    27–28
Giuliano, Louis, 284
Giving of orders, 34
Glass ceiling, 222
Global business, 134–136
Global consistency, 142
Global joint ventures, 145
Global management, 134–153
    consistency vs. adaptation,
        142–143
    cooperative contracts, 144
    cultural differences,
        150–152
    exporting, 143–144
    global business, 134–136
    global new ventures,
        145–146
    political risk, 148–150
    preparing for international
        assignment, 152–153
    strategic alliances, 144–145
    trade agreements, 138–141
    trade barriers, 136–138
    where to go?, 146–153
    wholly owned affiliates,
        145
Global new ventures, 145–146
GM, 12, 49, 126, 277, 331,
    338
Goal acceptance, 251
Goal commitment, 81–82
Goal congruence rule, 267
Goal difficulty, 251
Goal setting, 81

Nucor Steel, 299

O

O/I ratio, 241
OAO Gazprom, 149
Objective control, 297
Objective performance
    measures, 208
Occupational Safety and
    Health Act, 195
Occupational Safety and Health
    Administration, 52, 195
Ocean Spray, 82
Office manager, 8
OJT, 207
Oldsmobile Motor Works, 37
Olive Garden, 40
On-the-job training (OJT), 207
One-on-one communication,
    283
*101 Mission Statements From
    Top Companies* (Abrahams),
    85
Online discussion forums, 289
Open system, 39
Openness to experience, 227
Operational plans, 85
Operations management, 36–37
Opportunistic behavior, 50
Opportunities, 54
Optical character recognition,
    317
Options-based planning, 83
Oral communication, 285
Order, 33
Ordering cost, 342
Oreck, 49
Organic organizations, 167
Organization, 36, 276
    departmentalization,
        156–161
    job design, 164–167
    modular, 170–171
    organizational authority,
        161–164
    organizational design,
        167–173
    structure, 154–161
    virtual, 171–173
Organization-wide
    communication, 288–291
Organizational authority,
    161–164
Organizational change,
    125–133
    change tools and techniques,
        131–133
    mistakes, 128–131
    organizational decline, 126
    resistance to change,
        127–128
Organizational culture, 55–59
Organizational decline, 126
Organizational design,
    167–173
Organizational development,
    132
Organizational
    encouragement, 122
Organizational heroes, 56
Organizational innovation,

116–125
    defined, 116
    discontinuous change,
        123–124
    incremental change,
        124–125
    innovation streams,
        119–121
    sources of innovation,
        121–122
    technology cycles, 117–119
Organizational mission, 84
Organizational plurality, 230
Organizational process, 154
Organizational silence, 290
Organizational stories, 55
Organizational strategy,
    96–115
    choosing strategic
        alternatives, 102–104
    corporate-level strategies,
        104–108
    firm-level strategies,
        112–115
    industry-level strategies,
        108–112
    need for strategic change,
        99–100
    situational analysis,
        100–102
    sustainable competitive
        advantage, 92–99
Organizational structure,
    154–161
Organizational vision, 84
Organizing, 5
Orr, Dominic, 92
Osborn, Alex, 95
Osco Drugs, 318
Oshman, Max, 181
Otis Elevators, 158
Outcome/input (O/I) ratio, 241
Outcomes, 241
Outplacement services, 214
Output control, 298
Overlapping steps, 125
Overreward, 241
Overt integrity tests, 70

P

P&G, 40, 124, 128, 159, 160,
    173, 174
Pacific Enterprises, 231
Papadellis, Randy, 82
Paralanguage, 284
Paraphrasing, 286, 287
Parsons, Bob, 76
Parsons Manufacturing, 76
Partial productivity, 331
Participative leadership, 263,
    265
Password cracking software,
    320
Path-goal theory, 262–265
Paulus, Paul, 93
Pay-level decisions, 211
Pay-structure decisions, 212–213
Pay-variability decisions, 212
Pelaez, Roy, 271
PepsiCo, 224
Perceived ability, 264

Perception, 275–279
Perception problems, 277
Perception process, 276
Perceptual filters, 276
Perez, William, 162
Performance appraisal,
    208–211
Performance feedback, 251
Performance tests, 203
Performing, 186
Perkins, David, 93
Personal aggression, 62
Personality, 226
Personality-based integrity
    tests, 70
PETA, 51
Pfeffer, Jeffrey, 18
Pfizer, 6
PGP, 323
Phased retirement, 215
Philip Morris, 85
Phishing, 320
Physical disability, 225–226
Piecework, 212
Pitney Bowes, 315
Planned readings, 207
Planning, 4, 78–86
    action plan, 82
    benefits, 80
    defined, 78
    flexibility, 83
    goal commitment, 81–82
    goal setting, 81
    pitfalls, 80–81
    top-down, 83–86
    tracking progress, 82–83
Plant manager, 7
PlantLove, 133
Policy, 85–86
Policy uncertainty, 149
Political deviance, 62
Political/legal component, 48
Political risk, 148–150
Political uncertainty, 148
Pollution, 306
Pooled interdependence, 169
Porter, Michael, 108, 110
Porter's five industry forces,
    108–110
Portfolio strategy, 105
Portsmouth, 313–314
Position power, 261
Positioning strategies, 110–111
Positive reinforcement, 248
Postconventional level of
    moral development, 67
Power, 34
Power distance, 150
Powerful leaders, 124
Pratt & Whitney, 158
Preconventional level of moral
    development, 67
Predictive patterns, 319
Pregnancy Discrimination Act,
    195
Pretty Good Privacy (PGP), 323
Primary stakeholders, 74
Primary work group, 265
Principle of distributive justice,
    69
Principle of government
    requirements, 69
Principle of individual rights,
    69

Principle of long-term self-
    interest, 68
Principle of personal virtue, 69
Principle of religious
    injunctions, 69
Principle of utilitarian benefits,
    69
Principles of management, 33
Proactive monitoring of
    customers, 49
Proactive strategy, 76
Probability of effect, 66
Problem-oriented feedback, 288
Problem structure rule, 267
Procedural justice, 243
Procedure, 86
Process modification, 308
Processing cost, 315
Processing information,
    318–319
Procter & Gamble (P&G), 40,
    124, 128, 159, 160, 173,
    174
Product boycott, 52
Product departmentalization,
    157–158
Product failure, 333
Product prototype, 123
Production blocking, 94
Production deviance, 62
Productivity, 329–331
Profit sharing, 212
"Project Big Green," 76
Project teams, 181
Property deviance, 62
Prospectors, 111
Protecting information,
    319–324
Protectionism, 137
Proximal goals, 82
Proximity of effect, 67
PRS Group, 149
Prudential Relocation
    Management, 153
Public communications, 51
Public key encryption, 323
Pulver, Jeff, 50
Punctuated equilibrium theory,
    44
Punishment, 248
Purchasing power, 146

Q

Quality, 305–306, 307,
    331–335
Quality rule, 267
Question marks, 106
Quid pro quo sexual
    harassment, 196
Quota, 137
QWERTY keyboard, 120

R

Racial and ethnic
    discrimination, 224–225
Radio frequency identification
    (RFID) tags, 317
Rainforest Action Network

REVIEW card/ CHAPTER 1

LEARNING OUTCOMES

Review 1: Management Is . . .

> Good management is working through others to accomplish tasks that help fulfill organizational objectives as efficiently as possible.

Review 2: Management Functions

> Henri Fayol's classic management functions are known today as planning, organizing, leading, and controlling. Planning is determining organizational goals and a means for achieving them. Organizing is deciding where decisions will be made, who will do what jobs and tasks, and who will work for whom. Leading is inspiring and motivating workers to work hard to achieve organizational goals. Controlling is monitoring progress toward goal achievement and taking corrective action when needed. Studies show that performing the management functions well leads to better managerial performance.

Review 3: Kinds of Managers

> There are four different kinds of managers. Top managers are responsible for creating a context for change, developing attitudes of commitment and ownership, creating a positive organizational culture through words and actions, and monitoring their company's business environments. Middle managers are responsible for planning and allocating resources, coordinating and linking groups and departments, monitoring and managing the performance of subunits and managers, and implementing the changes or strategies generated by top managers. First-line managers are responsible for managing the performance of nonmanagerial employees, teaching direct reports how to do their jobs, and making detailed schedules and operating plans based on middle management's intermediate-range plans. Team leaders are responsible for facilitating team performance, managing external relationships, and facilitating internal team relationships.

Review 4: Managerial Roles

> Managers perform interpersonal, informational, and decisional roles in their jobs. In fulfilling the interpersonal role, managers act as figureheads by performing ceremonial duties, as leaders by motivating and encouraging workers, and as liaisons by dealing with people outside their units. In performing their informational role, managers act as monitors by scanning their environment for information, as disseminators by sharing information with others in the company, and as spokespeople by sharing information with people outside their departments or companies. In fulfilling decisional roles, managers act as entrepreneurs by adapting their units to incremental change, as disturbance handlers by responding to larger problems that demand immediate action, as resource allocators by deciding resource recipients and amounts, and as negotiators by bargaining with others about schedules, projects, goals, outcomes, and resources.

KEY TERMS

Management getting work done through others

Efficiency getting work done with a minimum of effort, expense, or waste

Effectiveness accomplishing tasks that help fulfill organizational objectives

Planning (management functions) determining organizational goals and a means for achieving them

Organizing deciding where decisions will be made, who will do what jobs and tasks, and who will work for whom

Leading inspiring and motivating workers to work hard to achieve organizational goals

Controlling monitoring progress toward goal achievement and taking corrective action when needed

Top managers executives responsible for the overall direction of the organization

Middle managers managers responsible for setting objectives consistent with top management's goals and for planning and implementing subunit strategies for achieving these objectives

First-line managers managers who train and supervise the performance of nonmanagerial employees who are directly responsible for producing the company's products or services

Team leaders managers responsible for facilitating team activities toward goal accomplishment

Figurehead role the interpersonal role managers play when they perform ceremonial duties

Leader role the interpersonal role managers play when they motivate and encourage workers to accomplish organizational objectives

Liaison role the interpersonal role managers play when they deal with people outside their units

Monitor role the informational role managers play when they scan their environment for information

Disseminator role the informational role managers play when they share information with others in their departments or companies

Spokesperson role the informational role managers play when they share information with people outside their departments or companies

Entrepreneur role the decisional role managers play when they adapt themselves, their subordinates, and their units to change

Disturbance handler role the decisional role managers play when they respond to severe problems that demand immediate action

Resource allocator role the decisional role managers play when they decide who gets what resources

Negotiator role the decisional role managers play when they negotiate schedules, projects, goals, outcomes, resources, and employee raises

Technical skills the ability to apply the specialized procedures, techniques, and knowledge required to get the job done

Human skills the ability to work well with others

Conceptual skills the ability to see the organization as a whole, understand how the different parts affect each other, and recognize how the company fits into or is affected by its environment

Motivation to manage an assessment of how enthusiastic employees are about managing the work of others

How to Use the Card:

1. Look over the card to preview the new concepts you'll be introduced to in the chapter.

2. Read your chapter to fully understand the material.

3. Go to class (and pay attention).

4. Review the card one more time to make sure you've registered the key concepts.

5. Don't forget, this card is only one of many MGMT learning tools available to help you succeed in your management course.

Review 5: What Companies Look for in Managers

> Companies do not want one-dimensional managers. They want managers with a balance of skills. They want managers who know their stuff (technical skills), are equally comfortable working with blue-collar and white-collar employees (human skills), are able to assess the complexities of today's competitive marketplace and position their companies for success (conceptual skills), and want to assume positions of leadership and power (motivation to manage). Technical skills are most important for lower-level managers, human skills are equally important at all levels of management, and conceptual skills and motivation to manage increase in importance as managers rise through the managerial ranks.

Review 6: Mistakes Managers Make

> Another way to understand what it takes to be a manager is to look at the top mistakes managers make. Five of the most important mistakes made by managers are being abrasive and intimidating; being cold, aloof, or arrogant; betraying trust; being overly ambitious; and failing to build a team and then delegate to that team.

Review 7: The Transition to Management: The First Year

> Managers often begin their jobs by using more formal authority and less people management. However, most managers find that being a manager has little to do with "bossing" their subordinates. After six months on the job, the managers were surprised at the fast pace and heavy workload and that "helping" their subordinates was viewed as interference. After a year on the job, most of the managers had come to think of themselves not as doers but as managers who get things done through others. And, because they finally realized that people management was the most important part of their job, most of them had abandoned their authoritarian approach for one based on communication, listening, and positive reinforcement.

Review 8: Competitive Advantage through People

> Why does management matter? Well-managed companies are competitive because their workforces are smarter, better trained, more motivated, and more committed. Furthermore, companies that practice good management consistently have greater sales revenues, profits, and stock market performance than companies that don't. Finally, good management matters because good management leads to satisfied employees who, in turn, provide better service to customers. Because employees tend to treat customers the same way that their managers treat them, good management can improve customer satisfaction.

www.mgmt4me.com has great review tools: flash cards, quizzes, games, MP3 reviews, and self-assessments.

LEARNING OUTCOMES

Review 1: The Origins of Management

> Management as a field of study is just 125 years old, but management ideas and practices have actually been used since 6000 b.c. From the ancient Sumerians to sixteenth-century Europe, there are historical antecedents for each of the functions of management discussed in this textbook: planning, organizing, leading, and controlling. However, there was no compelling need for managers until systematic changes in the nature of work and organizations occurred during the last two centuries. As work shifted from families to factories, from skilled laborers to specialized, unskilled laborers, from small, self-organized groups to large factories employing thousands under one roof, and from unique, small batches of production to large standardized mass production, managers were needed to impose order and structure, to motivate and direct large groups of workers, and to plan and make decisions that optimized overall company performance by effectively coordinating the different parts of organizational systems.

Review 2: Scientific Management

> Scientific management recommended studying and testing different work methods to identify the best, most efficient ways to complete a job. According to Frederick W. Taylor, the "father of scientific management," managers should follow four scientific management principles. First, study each element of work to determine the "one best way" to do it. Second, scientifically select, train, teach, and develop workers to reach their full potential. Third, cooperate with employees to ensure implementation of the scientific principles. Fourth, divide the work and the responsibility equally between management and workers. Above all, Taylor felt these principles could be used to align managers and employees by determining a "fair day's work," what an average worker could produce at a reasonable pace, and "a fair day's pay," what management should pay workers for that effort. Taylor felt that incentives were one of the best ways to align management and employees.

Frank and Lillian Gilbreth are best known for their use of motion studies to simplify work. Whereas Taylor used time study to determine "a fair day's work," based on how long it took a "first-class man" to complete each part of his job, Frank Gilbreth used film cameras and micro chronometers to conduct motion studies to improve efficiency by eliminating unnecessary or repetitive motions. The Gilbreths also made significant contributions to the employment of workers with handicaps, encouraging the government to rehabilitate them, employers to identify jobs that they could perform, and engineers to adapt and design machines they could use. Henry Gantt is best known for the Gantt chart, which graphically indicates when a series of tasks must be completed to perform a job or project, but he also developed ideas regarding pay-for-performance plans (where workers were rewarded for producing more, but were not punished if they didn't) and worker training (all workers should be trained and their managers should be rewarded for training them).

Review 3: Bureaucratic and Administrative Management

> Today, we associate bureaucracy with inefficiency and "red tape." Yet, according to German sociologist Max Weber, bureaucracy, that is, running organizations on the basis of knowledge, fairness, and logical rules and procedures, would accomplish organizational goals much more efficiently than monarchies and patriarchies, where decisions were based on personal or family connections, personal gain, and arbitrary decision making. Bureaucracies are characterized by seven elements: qualification-based hiring; merit-based promotion; chain of command; division of labor; impartial application of rules and procedures; recording

KEY TERMS

Scientific management thoroughly studying and testing different work methods to identify the best, most efficient way to complete a job

Soldiering when workers deliberately slow their pace or restrict their work outputs

Rate buster a group member whose work pace is significantly faster than the normal pace in his or her group

Time study timing how long it takes good workers to complete each part of their jobs

Motion study breaking each task or job into its separate motions and then eliminating those that are unnecessary or repetitive

Gantt chart a graphical chart that shows which tasks must be completed at which times in order to complete a project or task

Bureaucracy the exercise of control on the basis of knowledge, expertise, or experience

Integrative conflict resolution an approach to dealing with conflict in which both parties deal with the conflict by indicating their preferences and then working together to find an alternative that meets the needs of both

Organization a system of consciously coordinated activities or forces created by two or more people

System a set of interrelated elements or parts that function as a whole

Subsystems smaller systems that operate within the context of a larger system

Synergy when two or more subsystems working together can produce more than they can working apart

Closed systems systems that can sustain themselves without interacting with their environments

Open systems systems that can sustain themselves only by interacting with their environments, on which they depend for their survival

Contingency approach holds that there are no universal management theories and that the most effective management theory or idea depends on the kinds of problems or situations that managers are facing at a particular time and place

rules, procedures, and decisions in writing; and separating managers from owners. Nonetheless, bureaucracies are often inefficient and can be highly resistant to change.

The Frenchman Henri Fayol, whose ideas were shaped by his 20-plus years of experience as a CEO, is best known for developing five management functions (planning, organizing, coordinating, commanding, and controlling) and 14 principles of management (division of work, authority and responsibility, discipline, unity of command, unity of direction, subordination of individual interests to the general interest, remuneration, centralization, scalar chain, order, equity, stability of tenure of personnel, initiative, and esprit de corps). He is also known for his belief that management could and should be taught to others.

Review 4: Human Relations Management

> Unlike most people who view conflict as bad, Mary Parker Follett believed that it should be embraced and not avoided, and that of the three ways of dealing with conflict—domination, compromise, and integration—the latter was the best because it focuses on developing creative methods for meeting conflicting parties' needs.

Elton Mayo is best known for his role in the Hawthorne Studies at the Western Electric Company. In the first stage of the Hawthorne Studies, production went up because the increased attention paid to the workers in the study and their development into a cohesive work group led to significantly higher levels of job satisfaction and productivity. In the second stage, productivity dropped because the workers had already developed strong negative norms. The Hawthorne Studies demonstrated that workers' feelings and attitudes affected their work, that financial incentives weren't necessarily the most important motivator for workers, and that group norms and behavior play a critical role in behavior at work.

Chester Barnard, president of New Jersey Bell Telephone, emphasized the critical importance of willing cooperation in organizations and said that managers could gain workers' willing cooperation through three executive functions: securing essential services from individuals (through material, nonmaterial, and associational incentives), unifying the people in the organization with a clear purpose, and providing a system of communication. Barnard maintains that it is better to induce cooperation through incentives, clearly formulated organizational objectives, and effective communication throughout the organization.

Review 5: Operations, Information, Systems, and Contingency Management

> Operations management uses a quantitative or mathematical approach to find ways to increase productivity, improve quality, and manage or reduce costly inventories. The manufacture of standardized, interchangeable parts, the graphical and computerized design of parts, and the accidental discovery of just-in-time management were some of the most important historical events in operations management.

Throughout history, organizations have pushed for and quickly adopted new information technologies that reduce the cost or increase the speed with which they can acquire, store, retrieve, or communicate information. Historically, some of the most important technologies that have revolutionized information management were the creation of paper and the printing press in the fourteenth and fifteenth centuries, the manual typewriter in 1850, cash registers in 1879, the telephone in the 1880s, time clocks in the 1890s, the personal computer in the 1980s, and the Internet in the 1990s.

A system is a set of interrelated elements or parts that function as a whole. Organizational systems obtain inputs from the general and specific environments. Managers and workers then use their management knowledge and manufacturing techniques to transform those inputs into outputs, which, in turn, provide feedback to the organization. Organizational systems must also address the issues of synergy, open versus closed systems, and entropy.

Finally, the contingency approach to management precisely states that there are no universal management theories. The most effective management theory or idea depends on the kinds of problems or situations that managers or organizations are facing at a particular time. This means that management is much harder than it looks.

LEARNING OUTCOMES

Review 1: Changing Environments

> Environmental change, complexity, and resource scarcity are the basic components of external environments. Environmental change is the rate at which conditions or events affecting a business change. Environmental complexity is the number of external factors in an external environment. Resource scarcity is the scarcity or abundance of resources available in the external environment. The greater the rate of environmental change, environmental complexity, and resource scarcity, the less confident managers are that they can understand, predict, and effectively react to the trends affecting their businesses. According to punctuated equilibrium theory, companies experience periods of stability followed by short periods of dynamic, fundamental change, followed by a return to periods of stability.

Review 2: General Environment

> The general environment consists of events and trends that affect all organizations. Because the economy influences basic business decisions, managers often use economic statistics and business confidence indices to predict future economic activity. Changes in technology, which transforms inputs into outputs, can be a benefit or a threat to a business. Sociocultural trends, like changing demographic characteristics, affect how companies run their businesses. Similarly, sociocultural changes in behavior, attitudes, and beliefs affect the demand for a business's products and services. Court decisions and new federal and state laws have imposed much greater political/legal responsibilities on companies. The best way to manage legal responsibilities is to educate managers and employees about laws and regulations and potential lawsuits that could affect a business.

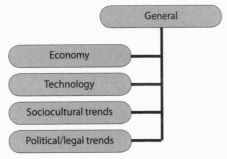

Review 3: Specific Environment

> The specific environment is made up of the five components shown here. Companies can monitor customers' needs by identifying customer problems after they occur or by anticipating problems before they occur. Because they tend to focus on well-known competitors, managers often underestimate their competition or do a poor job of identifying future competitors. Suppliers and buyers are very dependent on each other, and that dependence sometimes leads to opportunistic behavior, in which one benefits at the expense of the other. Regulatory agencies affect businesses by creating rules and then enforcing them. Advocacy groups cannot regulate organizations' practices. Nevertheless, through public communications, media advocacy, and product boycotts, they try to convince companies to change their practices.

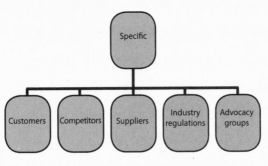

KEY TERMS

External environments all events outside a company that have the potential to influence or affect it

Environmental change the rate at which a company's general and specific environments change

Stable environment an environment in which the rate of change is slow

Dynamic environment an environment in which the rate of change is fast

Punctuated equilibrium theory a theory that holds that companies go through long, simple periods of stability (equilibrium), followed by short periods of dynamic, fundamental change (revolution), and ending with a return to stability (new equilibrium)

Environmental complexity the number of external factors in the environment that affect organizations

Simple environment an environment with few environmental factors

Complex environment an environment with many environmental factors

Resource scarcity the abundance or shortage of critical organizational resources in an organization's external environment

Uncertainty extent to which managers can understand or predict which environmental changes and trends will affect their businesses

General environment the economic, technological, sociocultural, and political trends that indirectly affect all organizations

Specific environment the customers, competitors, suppliers, industry regulations, and advocacy groups that are unique to an industry and directly affect how a company does business

Business confidence indices indices that show managers' level of confidence about future business growth

Technology the knowledge, tools, and techniques used to transform input into output

Competitors companies in the same industry that sell similar products or services to customers

Competitive analysis a process for monitoring the competition that involves identifying competition, anticipating their moves, and determining their strengths and weaknesses

Suppliers companies that provide material, human, financial, and informational resources to other companies

Supplier dependence the degree to which a company relies on a supplier because of the importance of the supplier's product to the company and the difficulty of finding other sources of that product

Buyer dependence the degree to which a supplier relies on a buyer because of the importance of that buyer to the supplier and the difficulty of finding other buyers for its products

Opportunistic behavior a transaction in which one party in the relationship benefits at the expense of the other

Relationship behavior mutually beneficial, long-term exchanges between buyers and suppliers

Industry regulation regulations and rules that govern the business practices and procedures of specific industries, businesses, and professions

Advocacy groups groups of concerned citizens who band together to try to influence the business practices of specific industries, businesses, and professions

Public communications an advocacy group tactic that relies on voluntary participation by the news media and the advertising industry to get the advocacy group's message out

Media advocacy an advocacy group tactic that involves framing issues as public issues; exposing questionable, exploitative, or unethical practices; and forcing media coverage by buying media time or creating controversy that is likely to receive extensive news coverage

Product boycott an advocacy group tactic that involves protesting a company's actions by convincing consumers not to purchase its product or service

Environmental scanning searching the environment for important events or issues that might affect an organization

Cognitive maps graphic depictions of how managers believe environmental factors relate to possible organizational actions

Internal environment the events and trends inside an organization that affect management, employees, and organizational culture

Organizational culture the values, beliefs, and attitudes shared by organizational members

Organizational stories stories told by organizational members to make sense of organizational events and changes and to emphasize culturally consistent assumptions, decisions, and actions

Organizational heroes people celebrated for their qualities and achievements within an organization

Company vision a business's purpose or reason for existing

Consistent organizational cultures when a company actively defines and teaches organizational values, beliefs, and attitudes

Behavioral addition the process of having managers and employees perform new behaviors that are central to and symbolic of the new organizational culture that a company wants to create

Behavioral substitution the process of having managers and employees perform new behaviors central to the "new" organizational culture in place of behaviors that were central to the "old" organizational culture

Visible artifacts visible signs of an organization's culture, such as the office design and layout, company dress code, and company benefits and perks, like stock options, personal parking spaces, or the private company dining room

Review 4: Making Sense of Changing Environments

> Managers use a three-step process to make sense of external environments: environmental scanning, interpreting information, and acting on it. Managers scan their environments based on their organizational strategies, their need for up-to-date information, and their need to reduce uncertainty. When managers identify environmental events as threats, they take steps to protect the company from harm. When managers identify environmental events as opportunities, they formulate alternatives for taking advantage of them to improve company performance. Using cognitive maps can help managers visually summarize the relationships between environmental factors and the actions they might take to deal with them.

Review 5: Organizational Cultures: Creation, Success, and Change

> Organizational culture is the set of key values, beliefs, and attitudes shared by organizational members. Organizational cultures are often created by company founders and then sustained through the telling of organizational stories and the celebration of organizational heroes. Adaptable cultures that promote employee involvement, make clear the organization's strategic purpose and direction, and actively define and teach organizational values and beliefs can help companies achieve higher sales growth, return on assets, profits, quality, and employee satisfaction. Organizational cultures exist on three levels: the surface level, where cultural artifacts and behaviors can be observed; just below the surface, where values and beliefs are expressed; and deep below the surface, where unconsciously held assumptions and beliefs exist. Managers can begin to change company cultures by focusing on the top two levels and by using behavioral substitution and behavioral addition, changing visible artifacts, and selecting job applicants with values and beliefs consistent with the desired company culture.

LEARNING OUTCOMES

Review 1: Workplace Deviance

> Ethics is the set of moral principles or values that define right and wrong. By contrast, workplace deviance is behavior that violates important organizational norms about right and wrong and harms the organization or its workers. Production deviance and property deviance harm the company, whereas political deviance and personal aggression harm individuals within the company.

Review 2: U.S. Sentencing Commission Guidelines

> Under the U.S. Sentencing Commission Guidelines, companies can be prosecuted and fined up to $300 million for employees' illegal actions. Fines are computed by multiplying the base fine by a culpability score. Companies that establish compliance programs to encourage ethical behavior can reduce their culpability scores and their fines.

Review 3: Influences on Ethical Decision Making

> Three factors influence ethical decisions: the ethical intensity of the decision, the moral development of the manager, and the ethical principles used to solve the problem. Ethical intensity is strong when decisions have large, certain, immediate consequences and when we are physically or psychologically close to those affected by the decision. There are three phases of moral maturity with two steps within each phase. At the preconventional level, decisions are made for selfish reasons. At the conventional level, decisions conform to societal expectations. At the postconventional level, internalized principles are used to make ethical decisions. Finally, managers can use a number of different principles when making ethical decisions: self-interest, personal virtue, religious injunctions, government requirements, utilitarian benefits, individual rights, and distributive justice.

Review 4: Practical Steps to Ethical Decision Making

> Employers can increase their chances of hiring ethical employees by testing all job applicants. Most large companies now have corporate codes of ethics. In addition to offering general rules, ethics codes must also provide specific, practical advice. Ethics training seeks to increase employees' awareness of ethical issues, make ethics a serious, credible factor in organizational decisions, and teach employees a practical model of ethical decision making. The most important factors in creating an ethical business climate are the personal examples set by company managers, involvement of management in the company ethics program, a reporting system that encourages whistleblowers to report potential ethics violations, and fair but consistent punishment of violators.

Review 5: To Whom Are Organizations Socially Responsible?

> Social responsibility is a business's obligation to benefit society. According to the shareholder model, a company's only social responsibility is to maximize shareholder wealth by maximizing company profits. According to the stakeholder model, companies must satisfy the needs and interests of multiple corporate stakeholders, not just shareholders. However, the needs of primary stakeholders, on which the organization relies for its existence, take precedence over those of secondary stakeholders.

Primary		Secondary
Governments	Suppliers	Media
Employees	Shareholders	Special Interest Groups
Customers	Local Communities	Trade Associations

KEY TERMS

Ethics the set of moral principles or values that defines right and wrong for a person or group

Ethical behavior behavior that conforms to a society's accepted principles of right and wrong

Workplace deviance unethical behavior that violates organizational norms about right and wrong

Production deviance unethical behavior that hurts the quality and quantity of work produced

Property deviance unethical behavior aimed at the organization's property or products

Employee shrinkage employee theft of company merchandise

Political deviance using one's influence to harm others in the company

Personal aggression hostile or aggressive behavior toward others

Ethical intensity the degree of concern people have about an ethical issue

Magnitude of consequences the total harm or benefit derived from an ethical decision

Social consensus agreement on whether behavior is bad or good

Probability of effect the chance that something will happen and then harm others

Temporal immediacy the time between an act and the consequences the act produces

Proximity of effect the social, psychological, cultural, or physical distance between a decision maker and those affected by his or her decisions

Concentration of effect the total harm or benefit that an act produces on the average person

Preconventional level of moral development the first level of moral development in which people make decisions based on selfish reasons

Conventional level of moral development the second level of moral development in which people make decisions that conform to societal expectations

Postconventional level of moral development the third level of moral development in which people make decisions based on internalized principles

Principle of long-term self-interest an ethical principle that holds that you should never take any action that is not in your or your organization's long-term self-interest

Principle of personal virtue an ethical principle that holds that you should never do anything that is not honest, open, and truthful and that you would not be glad to see reported in the newspapers or on TV

Principle of religious injunctions an ethical principle that holds that you should never take any action that is not kind and that does not build a sense of community

Principle of government requirements an ethical principle that holds that you should never take any action that violates the law, for the law represents the minimal moral standard

Principle of utilitarian benefits an ethical principle that holds that you should never take any action that does not result in greater good for society

Principle of individual rights an ethical principle that holds that you should never take any action that infringes on others' agreed-upon rights

Principle of distributive justice an ethical principle that holds that you should never take any action that harms the least fortunate among us: the poor, the uneducated, the unemployed

Overt integrity test a written test that estimates job applicants' honesty by directly asking them what they think or feel about theft or about punishment of unethical behaviors

Personality-based integrity test a written test that indirectly estimates job applicants' honesty by measuring psychological traits, such as dependability and conscientiousness

Whistleblowing reporting others' ethics violations to management or legal authorities

Social responsibility a business's obligation to pursue policies, make decisions, and take actions that benefit society

Shareholder model a view of social responsibility that holds that an organization's overriding goal should be profit maximization for the benefit of shareholders

Stakeholder model a theory of corporate responsibility that holds that management's most important responsibility, long-term survival, is achieved by satisfying the interests of multiple corporate stakeholders

Stakeholders persons or groups with a "stake" or legitimate interest in a company's actions

Primary stakeholder any group on which an organization relies for its long-term survival

Secondary stakeholder any group that can influence or be influenced by a company and can affect public perceptions about its socially responsible behavior

Economic responsibility the expectation that a company will make a profit by producing a valued product or service

Legal responsibility a company"s social responsibility to obey society's laws and regulations

Ethical responsibility a company's social responsibility not to violate accepted principles of right and wrong when conducting its business

Discretionary responsibility the expectation that a company will voluntarily serve a social role beyond its economic, legal, and ethical responsibilities

Social responsiveness refers to a company's strategy to respond to stakeholders' economic, legal, ethical, or discretionary expectations concerning social responsibility

Reactive strategy a social responsiveness strategy in which a company does less than society expects

Defensive strategy a social responsiveness strategy in which a company admits responsibility for a problem but does the least required to meet societal expectations

Accommodative strategy a social responsiveness strategy in which a company accepts responsibility for a problem and does all that society expects to solve that problem

Proactive strategy a social responsiveness strategy in which a company anticipates responsibility for a problem before it occurs and does more than society expects to address the problem

Review 6: For What Are Organizations Socially Responsible?

> Companies can best benefit their stakeholders by fulfilling their economic, legal, ethical, and discretionary responsibilities. Being profitable, or meeting one's economic responsibility, is a business's most basic social responsibility. Legal responsibility consists of following a society's laws and regulations. Ethical responsibility means not violating accepted principles of right and wrong when doing business. Discretionary responsibilities are social responsibilities beyond basic economic, legal, and ethical responsibilities.

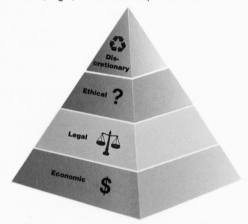

Review 7: Responses to Demands for Social Responsibility

> Social responsiveness is a company's response to stakeholders' demands for socially responsible behavior. There are four social responsiveness strategies. When a company uses a reactive strategy, it denies responsibility for a problem. When it uses a defensive strategy, it takes responsibility for a problem but does the minimum required to solve it. When a company uses an accommodative strategy, it accepts responsibility for problems and does all that society expects to solve them. Finally, when a company uses a proactive strategy, it does much more than expected to solve social responsibility problems.

Review 8: Social Responsibility and Economic Performance

> Does it pay to be socially responsible? Sometimes it costs, and sometimes it pays. Overall, there is no clear relationship between social responsibility and economic performance. Consequently, managers should not expect an economic return from socially responsible corporate activities. If your company chooses to practice a proactive or accommodative social responsibility strategy, it should do so to better society and not to improve its financial performance.

LEARNING OUTCOMES

Review 1: Benefits and Pitfalls of Planning

> Planning is choosing a goal and developing a method for achieving it. Planning is one of the best ways to improve organizational and individual performance. It encourages people to work harder (intensified effort), to work hard for extended periods (persistence), to engage in behaviors directly related to goal accomplishment (directed behavior), and to think of better ways to do their jobs (task strategies). However, planning also has three potential pitfalls. Companies that are overly committed to their plans may be slow to adapt to environmental changes. Planning is based on assumptions about the future, and when those assumptions are wrong, plans can fail. Finally, planning can fail when planners are detached from the implementation of plans.

Review 2: How to Make a Plan That Works

> There are five steps to making a plan that works: (1) Set S.M.A.R.T. goals—goals that are **S**pecific, **M**easurable, **A**ttainable, **R**ealistic, and **T**imely. (2) Develop commitment to the goals. Managers can increase workers' goal commitment by encouraging worker participation in goal setting, making goals public, and getting top management to show support for workers' goals. (3) Develop action plans for goal accomplishment. (4) Track progress toward goal achievement by setting both proximal and distal goals and by providing workers with regular performance feedback. (5) Maintain flexibility by keeping options open.

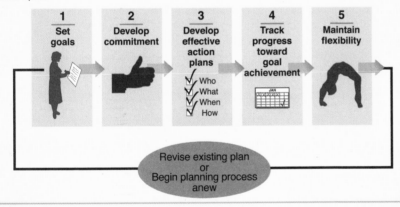

1	2	3	4	5
Set goals	Develop commitment	Develop effective action plans	Track progress toward goal achievement	Maintain flexibility
		✓ Who ✓ What ✓ When ✓ How		

Revise existing plan
or
Begin planning process
anew

Review 3: Planning from Top to Bottom

> Proper planning requires that the goals at the bottom and middle of the organization support the objectives at the top of the organization. Top management develops strategic plans, which start with the creation of an organizational vision and mission. Middle managers use techniques like management by objectives

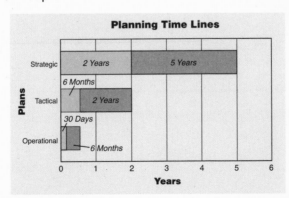

Planning Time Lines

Plans		
Strategic	2 Years	5 Years
Tactical	6 Months / 2 Years	
Operational	30 Days / 6 Months	

Years: 0 1 2 3 4 5 6

to develop tactical plans that direct behavior, efforts, and priorities. Finally, lower-level managers develop operational plans that guide daily activities in producing or delivering

KEY TERMS

Planning choosing a goal and developing a strategy to achieve that goal

S.M.A.R.T. goals goals that are specific, measurable, attainable, realistic, and timely

Goal commitment the determination to achieve a goal

Action plan the specific steps, people, and resources needed to accomplish a goal

Proximal goals short-term goals or subgoals

Distal goals long-term or primary goals

Options-based planning maintaining planning flexibility by making small, simultaneous investments in many alternative plans

Slack resources a cushion of extra resources that can be used with options-based planning to adapt to unanticipated change, problems, or opportunities

Strategic plans overall company plans that clarify how the company will serve customers and position itself against competitors over the next two to five years

Vision a statement of a company's purpose or reason for existing

Mission a statement of a company's overall goal that unifies company-wide efforts toward its vision, stretches and challenges the organization, and possesses a finish line and a time frame

Tactical plans plans created and implemented by middle managers that specify how the company will use resources, budgets, and people over the next six months to two years to accomplish specific goals within its mission

Management by objectives (MBO) a four-step process in which managers and employees discuss and select goals, develop tactical plans, and meet regularly to review progress toward goal accomplishment

Operational plans day-to-day plans, developed and implemented by lower-level managers, for producing or delivering the organization's products and services over a 30-day to six-month period

Single-use plans plans that cover unique, one-time-only events

Standing plans plans used repeatedly to handle frequently recurring events

Policy a standing plan that indicates the general course of action that should be taken in response to a particular event or situation

Procedure a standing plan that indicates the specific steps that should be taken in response to a particular event

Rules and regulations standing plans that describe how a particular action should be performed, or what must happen or not happen in response to a particular event

Budgeting quantitative planning through which managers decide how to allocate available money to best accomplish company goals

Decision making the process of choosing a solution from available alternatives

Rational decision making a systematic process of defining problems, evaluating alternatives, and choosing optimal solutions

Problem a gap between a desired state and an existing state

Decision criteria the standards used to guide judgments and decisions

Absolute comparisons a process in which each decision criterion is compared to a standard or ranked on its own merits

Relative comparisons a process in which each decision criterion is compared directly to every other criterion

Maximizing choosing the best alternative

Satisficing choosing a "good enough" alternative

Groupthink a barrier to good decision making caused by pressure within the group for members to agree with each other

C-type conflict (cognitive conflict) disagreement that focuses on problem- and issue-related differences of opinion

A-type conflict (affective conflict) disagreement that focuses on individuals or personal issues

Devil's advocacy a decision-making method in which an individual or a subgroup is assigned the role of a critic

Nominal group technique a decision-making method that begins and ends by having group members quietly write down and evaluate ideas to be shared with the group

Delphi technique a decision-making method in which members of a panel of experts respond to questions and to each other until reaching agreement on an issue

Brainstorming a decision-making method in which group members build on each others' ideas to generate as many alternative solutions as possible

Electronic brainstorming a decision-making method in which group members use computers to build on each others' ideas and generate many alternative solutions

Production blocking a disadvantage of face-to-face brainstorming in which a group member must wait to share an idea because another member is presenting an idea

Evaluation apprehension fear of what others will think of your ideas

an organization's products and services. There are three kinds of operational plans: single-use plans, standing plans (policies, procedures, and rules and regulations), and budgets.

Review 4: Steps and Limits to Rational Decision Making

> Rational decision making is a six-step process in which managers define problems, evaluate alternatives, and compute optimal solutions. The first step is identifying and defining the problem. Problems are gaps between desired and existing states. Managers won't begin the decision-making process unless they are aware of the gap, motivated to reduce it, and possess the necessary resources to fix it. Step 2 is defining the decision criteria used to judge alternatives. In Step 3, an absolute or relative comparison process is used to rate the importance of the decision criteria. Step 4 involves generating many alternative courses of action (i.e., solutions). Potential solutions are assessed in Step 5 by systematically gathering information and evaluating each alternative against each criterion. In Step 6, criterion ratings and weights are used to compute the optimal value for each alternative course of action. Rational managers then choose the alternative with the highest optimal value.

The rational decision-making model describes how decisions should be made in an ideal world without limits. However, bounded rationality recognizes that in the real world, managers' limited resources, incomplete and imperfect information, and limited decision-making capabilities restrict their decision-making processes.

Review 5: Using Groups to Improve Decision Making

> When groups view problems from multiple perspectives, use more information, have a diversity of knowledge and experience, and become committed to solutions they help choose, they can produce better solutions than individual decision makers. However, group decisions can suffer from these disadvantages: groupthink, slowness, discussions dominated by just a few individuals, and unfelt responsibility for decisions. Group decisions work best when group members encourage c-type conflict. However, group decisions don't work as well when groups become mired in a-type conflict. The devil's advocacy and dialectical inquiry approaches improve group decisions because they bring structured c-type (cognitive) conflict into the decision-making process. By contrast, the nominal group technique and the Delphi technique both improve decision making by reducing a-type (affective) conflict. The stepladder technique improves group decision making by adding each group member's independent contributions to the discussion one by one. Finally, because it overcomes the problems of production blocking and evaluation apprehension, electronic brainstorming is more effective than face-to-face brainstorming.

REVIEW card/

LEARNING OUTCOMES

Review 1: Sustainable Competitive Advantage

> Firms can use their resources to create and sustain a competitive advantage, that is, to provide greater value for customers than competitors can. A competitive advantage becomes sustainable when other companies cannot duplicate the benefits it provides and have, for now, stopped trying.

Review 2: Strategy-Making Process

> The first step in strategy making is determining whether a strategy needs to be changed to sustain a competitive advantage. The second step is to conduct a situational analysis that examines internal strengths and weaknesses, as well as external threats and opportunities. In the third step of strategy making, Strategic Reference Point Theory suggests that when companies are performing better than their strategic reference points, top management will typically choose a risk-averse strategy. When performance is below strategic reference points, risk-seeking strategies are more likely to be chosen.

KEY TERMS

Resources the assets, capabilities, processes, information, and knowledge that an organization uses to improve its effectiveness and efficiency, create and sustain competitive advantage, and fulfill a need or solve a problem

Competitive advantage providing greater value for customers than competitors can

Sustainable competitive advantage a competitive advantage that other companies have tried unsuccessfully to duplicate and have, for the moment, stopped trying to duplicate

Valuable resource a resource that allows companies to improve efficiency and effectiveness

Rare resources resources that are not controlled or possessed by many competing firms

Imperfectly imitable resources resources that are impossible or extremely costly or difficult for other firms to duplicate

Nonsubstitutable resource a resource that produces value or competitive advantage and has no equivalent substitutes or replacements

Competitive inertia a reluctance to change strategies or competitive practices that have been successful in the past

Strategic dissonance a discrepancy between a company's intended strategy and the strategic actions managers take when implementing that strategy

Situational (SWOT) analysis an assessment of the strengths and weaknesses in an organization's internal environment and the opportunities and threats in its external environment

Distinctive competence what a company can make, do, or perform better than its competitors

Core capabilities the internal decision-making routines, problem-solving processes, and organizational cultures that determine how efficiently inputs can be turned into outputs

Strategic group a group of companies within an industry that top managers choose to compare, evaluate, and benchmark strategic threats and opportunities

Core firms the central companies in a strategic group

Secondary firms the firms in a strategic group that follow strategies related to but somewhat different from those of the core firms

Strategic reference points the strategic targets managers use to measure whether a firm has developed the core competencies it needs to achieve a sustainable competitive advantage

Corporate-level strategy the overall organizational strategy that addresses the question "What business or businesses are we in or should we be in?"

Diversification a strategy for reducing risk by owning a variety of items (stocks or, in the case of a corporation, types of businesses) so that the failure of one stock or one business does not doom the entire portfolio

Portfolio strategy a corporate-level strategy that minimizes risk by diversifying investment among various businesses or product lines

Acquisition the purchase of a company by another company

Unrelated diversification creating or acquiring companies in completely unrelated businesses

BCG matrix a portfolio strategy, developed by the Boston Consulting Group, that categorizes a corporation's businesses by growth rate and relative market share, and helps managers decide how to invest corporate funds

Star a company with a large share of a fast-growing market

Question mark a company with a small share of a fast-growing market

Cash cow a company with a large share of a slow-growing market

Dog a company with a small share of a slow-growing market

Related diversification creating or acquiring companies that share similar products, manufacturing, marketing, technology, or cultures

Grand strategy a broad corporate-level strategic plan used to achieve strategic goals and guide the strategic alternatives that managers of individual businesses or subunits may use

Growth strategy a strategy that focuses on increasing profits, revenues, market share, or the number of places in which the company does business

Stability strategy a strategy that focuses on improving the way in which the company sells the same products or services to the same customers

Retrenchment strategy a strategy that focuses on turning around very poor company performance by shrinking the size or scope of the business

Recovery the strategic actions taken after retrenchment to return to a growth strategy

Industry-level strategy a corporate strategy that addresses the question "How should we compete in this industry?"

Character of the rivalry a measure of the intensity of competitive behavior between companies in an industry

Threat of new entrants a measure of the degree to which barriers to entry make it easy or difficult for new companies to get started in an industry

Threat of substitute products or services a measure of the ease with which customers can find substitutes for an industry's products or services

Bargaining power of suppliers a measure of the influence that suppliers of parts, materials, and services to firms in an industry have on the prices of these inputs

Bargaining power of buyers a measure of the influence that customers have on a firm's prices

Cost leadership the positioning strategy of producing a product or service of acceptable quality at consistently lower production costs than competitors can, so that the firm can offer the product or service at the lowest price in the industry

Differentiation the positioning strategy of providing a product or service that is sufficiently different from competitors' offerings that customers are willing to pay a premium price for it

Focus strategy the positioning strategy of using cost leadership or differentiation to produce a specialized product or service for a limited, specially targeted group of customers in a particular geographic region or market segment

Defenders an adaptive strategy aimed at defending strategic positions by seeking moderate, steady growth and by offering a limited range of high-quality products and services to a well-defined set of customers

Prospectors an adaptive strategy that seeks fast growth by searching for new market opportunities, encouraging risk taking, and being the first to bring innovative new products to market

Analyzers an adaptive strategy that seeks to minimize risk and maximize profits by following or imitating the proven successes of prospectors

Reactors an adaptive strategy of not following a consistent strategy, but instead reacting to changes in the external environment after they occur

Firm-level strategy a corporate strategy that addresses the question "How should we compete against a particular firm?"

Direct competition the rivalry between two companies that offer similar products and services, acknowledge each other as rivals, and act and react to each other's strategic actions

Market commonality the degree to which two companies have overlapping products, services, or customers in multiple markets

Resource similarity the extent to which a competitor has similar amounts and kinds of resources

Attack a competitive move designed to reduce a rival's market share or profits

Response a competitive countermove, prompted by a rival's attack, to defend or improve a company's market share or profit

> ## Review 3: Corporate-Level Strategies

Corporate-level strategies, such as portfolio strategy and grand strategies, help managers determine what businesses they should be in. Portfolio strategy focuses on lowering business risk by being in multiple, unrelated businesses and by investing the cash flows from slow-growth businesses into faster-growing businesses. One portfolio strategy is the BCG matrix. The most successful way to use the portfolio approach to corporate strategy is to reduce risk through related diversification.

The three kinds of grand strategies are growth, stability, and retrenchment/recovery. Companies can grow externally by merging with or acquiring other companies, or they can grow internally through direct expansion or creating new businesses. Companies choose a stability strategy when their external environment changes very little or after they have dealt with periods of explosive growth. Retrenchment strategy, shrinking the size or scope of a business, is used to turn around poor performance. If retrenchment works, it is often followed by a recovery strategy that focuses on growing the business again.

Review 4: Industry-Level Strategies

> Industry-level strategies focus on how companies choose to compete in their industry. Five industry forces determine an industry's overall attractiveness to corporate investors and its potential for long-term profitability. Together, a high level of these elements combine to increase competition and decrease profits. Positioning strategies (cost leadership, differentiation, focus) can help companies protect themselves from the negative effects of industry-wide competition. The four adaptive strategies help companies adapt to changes in the external environment. Defenders want to "defend" their current strategic positions. Prospectors look for new market opportunities by bringing innovative new products to market. Analyzers minimize risk by following the proven successes of prospectors. Reactors do not follow a consistent strategy, but instead react to changes in their external environment after they occur.

Industry-Level Strategies

Five Industry Forces	Positioning Strategies	Adaptive Strategies
Character of rivalry	Cost leadership	Defenders
Threat of new entrants	Differentiation	Analyzers
Threat of substitute products or services	Focus	Prospectors
Bargaining power of suppliers		Reactors
Bargaining power of buyers		

Review 5: Firm-Level Strategies

Firm-level strategies are concerned with direct competition between firms. Market commonality and resource similarity determine whether firms are in direct competition and thus likely to attack each other or respond to each other's attacks. In general, the more markets in which there is product, service, or customer overlap, and the greater the resource similarity between two firms, the more intense the direct competition between them. Market entries and exits are the most important kinds of attacks and responses.

Firm-Level Strategies
(Direct Competition)

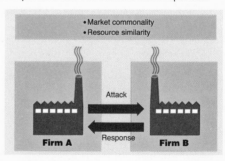

LEARNING OUTCOMES

Review 1: Why Innovation Matters

> Technology cycles typically follow an S-curve pattern of innovation. Early in the cycle, technological progress is slow, and improvements in technological performance are small. As a technology matures, however, performance improves quickly. Finally, as the limits of a technology are reached, only small improvements occur. At this point, significant improvements in performance must come from new technologies. The best way to protect a competitive advantage is to create a stream of innovative ideas and products. Innovation streams begin with technological discontinuities that create significant breakthroughs in performance or function. Technological discontinuities are followed by discontinuous change, in which customers purchase new technologies and companies compete to establish the new dominant design. Dominant designs emerge because of critical mass, because they solve a practical problem, or because of the negotiations of independent standards bodies. Because technological innovation is both competence enhancing and competence destroying, companies that bet on the wrong design often struggle, while companies that bet on the eventual dominant design usually prosper. Emergence of a dominant design leads to a focus on incremental change, lowering costs and making small, but steady improvements in the dominant design. This focus continues until the next technological discontinuity occurs.

Review 2: Managing Innovation

> To successfully manage innovation streams, companies must manage the sources of innovation and learn to manage innovation during both discontinuous and incremental change. Since innovation begins with creativity, companies can manage the sources of innovation by supporting a creative work environment in which creative thoughts and ideas are welcomed, valued, and encouraged. Creative work environments provide challenging work; offer organizational, supervisory, and work group encouragement; allow significant freedom; and remove organizational impediments to creativity.

Companies that succeed in periods of discontinuous change typically follow an experiential approach to innovation. The experiential approach assumes that intuition, flexible options, and hands-on experience can reduce uncertainty and accelerate learning and understanding.

A compression approach to innovation works best during periods of incremental change. This approach assumes that innovation can be planned using a series of steps and that compressing the time it takes to complete those steps can speed up innovation.

	Experiential Approach to Innovation: Managing Innovation During Discontinuous Change	Compression Approach to Innovation: Managing Innovation During Incremental Change

Environment	Highly uncertain
	    discontinuous change - technological
	        substitution and design competition
		Certain
		    incremental change - established
		        technology (i.e., dominant design)

Goals	Speed Significant improvements in performance Establishment of new dominant design	Speed Lower costs Incremental improvements in performance of dominant design
Approach	Build something new, different, and substantially better	Compress time and steps needed to bring about small improvements
Steps	Design iterations Testing Milestones Multifunctional teams Powerful leaders	Planning Supplier involvement Shortening the time of individual steps Overlapping steps Multifunctional teams

KEY TERMS

Organizational innovation the successful implementation of creative ideas in organizations

Creativity the production of novel and useful ideas

Technology cycle a cycle that begins with the "birth" of a new technology and ends when that technology reaches its limits and is replaced by a newer, substantially better technology

S-curve pattern of innovation a pattern of technological innovation characterized by slow initial progress, then rapid progress, and then slow progress again as a technology matures and reaches its limits

Innovation streams patterns of innovation over time that can create sustainable competitive advantage

Technological discontinuity a scientific advance or a unique combination of existing technologies creates a significant breakthrough in performance or function

Discontinuous change the phase of a technology cycle characterized by technological substitution and design competition

Technological substitution the purchase of new technologies to replace older ones

Design competition competition between old and new technologies to establish a new technological standard or dominant design

Dominant design a new technological design or process that becomes the accepted market standard

Technological lockout when a new dominant design (i.e., a significantly better technology) prevents a company from competitively selling its products or makes it difficult to do so

Incremental change the phase of a technology cycle in which companies innovate by lowering costs and improving the functioning and performance of the dominant technological design

Creative work environments workplace cultures in which workers perceive that new ideas are welcomed, valued, and encouraged

Flow a psychological state of effortlessness, in which you become completely absorbed in what you're doing and time seems to pass quickly

Experiential approach to innovation an approach to innovation that assumes a highly uncertain environment and uses intuition, flexible options, and hands-on experience to reduce uncertainty and accelerate learning and understanding

Design iteration a cycle of repetition in which a company tests a prototype of a new product or service, improves on that design, and then builds and tests the improved prototype

Product prototype a full-scale, working model that is being tested for design, function, and reliability

Testing the systematic comparison of different product designs or design iterations

Milestones formal project review points used to assess progress and performance

Multifunctional teams work teams composed of people from different departments

Compression approach to innovation an approach to innovation that assumes that incremental innovation can be planned using a series of steps and that compressing those steps can speed innovation

Generational change change based on incremental improvements to a dominant technological design such that the improved technology is fully backward compatible with the older technology

Organizational decline a large decrease in organizational performance that occurs when companies don't anticipate, recognize, neutralize, or adapt to the internal or external pressures that threaten their survival

Change forces forces that produce differences in the form, quality, or condition of an organization over time

Resistance forces forces that support the existing state of conditions in organizations

Resistance to change opposition to change resulting from self-interest, misunderstanding and distrust, or a general intolerance for change

Unfreezing getting the people affected by change to believe that change is needed

Change intervention the process used to get workers and managers to change their behavior and work practices

Refreezing supporting and reinforcing new changes so that they "stick"

Review 3: Organizational Decline: The Risk of Not Changing

> The five-stage process of organizational decline begins when organizations don't recognize the need for change. In the blinded stage, managers fail to recognize the changes that threaten their organization's survival. In the inaction stage, management recognizes the need to change, but doesn't act, hoping that the problems will correct themselves. In the faulty action stage, management focuses on cost cutting and efficiency rather than facing up to the fundamental changes needed to ensure survival. In the crisis stage, failure is likely unless fundamental reorganization occurs. Finally, in the dissolution stage, the company is dissolved through bankruptcy proceedings, by selling assets to pay creditors, or through the closing of stores, offices, and facilities. If companies recognize the need to change early enough, however, dissolution may be avoided.

Review 4: Managing Change

> The basic change process is unfreezing, change, and refreezing. Resistance to change, which stems from self-interest, misunderstanding and distrust, and a general intolerance for change, can be managed through education and communication, participation, negotiation, top management support, and coercion. Knowing what not to do is as important as knowing what to do to achieve successful change. Managers should avoid these errors when leading change: not establishing urgency, not creating a guiding coalition, lacking a vision, undercommunicating the vision, not removing obstacles to the vision, not creating short-term wins, declaring victory too soon, and not anchoring changes in the corporation's culture. Finally, managers can use a number of change techniques. Results-driven change and the GE workout reduce resistance to change by getting change efforts off to a fast start. Organizational development is a collection of planned change interventions (large system, small group, person-focused), guided by a change agent, that are designed to improve an organization's long-term health and performance.

Different Kinds of Organizational Development Interventions

LARGE SYSTEM INTERVENTIONS	
Sociotechnical systems	An intervention designed to improve how well employees use and adjust to the work technology used in an organization.
Survey feedback	An intervention that uses surveys to collect information from the members, reports the results of that survey to the members, and then uses those results to develop action plans for improvement.
SMALL GROUP INTERVENTIONS	
Team building	An intervention designed to increase the cohesion and cooperation of work group members.
Unit goal setting	An intervention designed to help a work group establish short- and long-term goals.
PERSON-FOCUSED INTERVENTIONS	
Counseling/coaching	An intervention designed so that a formal helper or coach listens to managers or employees and advises them on how to deal with work or interpersonal problems.
Training	An intervention designed to provide individuals with the knowledge, skills, or attitudes they need to become more effective at their jobs.

Source: W. J. Rothwell, R. Sullivan, & G. M. McLean, *Practicing Organizational Development: A Guide for Consultants* (San Diego: Pfeiffer & Co., 1995).

Coercion using formal power and authority to force others to change

Results-driven change change created quickly by focusing on the measurement and improvement of results

General Electric workout a three-day meeting in which managers and employees from different levels and parts of an organization quickly generate and act on solutions to specific business problems

Organizational development a philosophy and collection of planned change interventions designed to improve an organization's long-term health and performance

Change agent the person formally in charge of guiding a change effort

LEARNING OUTCOMES

Review 1: Global Business, Trade Rules, and Trade Agreements

> Today, there are more than 77,000 multinational corporations worldwide; just 3.1 percent are based in the United States. Global business affects the United States in two ways: through direct foreign investment in the United States by foreign companies, and through U.S. companies' investment in business in other countries. U.S. direct foreign investment throughout the world typically amounts to about $2 trillion per year, whereas direct foreign investment by foreign companies in the U.S. amounts to $1.6 trillion per year. Historically, tariffs and nontariff trade barriers, such as quotas, voluntary export restraints, government import standards, government subsidies, and customs classifications, have made buying foreign goods much harder or more expensive than buying domestically produced products. In recent years, however, worldwide trade agreements, such as GATT, along with regional trading agreements, like the Maastricht Treaty of Europe, NAFTA, CAFTA-DR, Mercosur, SACN, ASEAN, and APEC, have substantially reduced tariff and nontariff barriers to international trade. Companies have responded by investing in growing markets in Asia, Eastern Europe, and Latin America. Consumers have responded by purchasing products based on value, rather than geography.

Review 2: Consistency or Adaptation?

> Global business requires a balance between global consistency and local adaptation. Global consistency means using the same rules, guidelines, policies, and procedures in each location. Managers at company headquarters like global consistency because it simplifies decisions. Local adaptation means adapting standard procedures to differences in markets. Local managers prefer a policy of local adaptation because it gives them more control. Not all businesses need the same combinations of global consistency and local adaptation. Some thrive by emphasizing global consistency and ignoring local adaptation. Others succeed by ignoring global consistency and emphasizing local adaptation.

Regional trading zones areas in which tariff and nontariff barriers on trade between countries are reduced or eliminated

Maastricht Treaty of Europe a regional trade agreement between most European countries

North American Free Trade Agreement (NAFTA) a regional trade agreement between the United States, Canada, and Mexico

Central America Free Trade Agreement (CAFTA) a regional trade agreement between Costa Rica, the Dominican Republic, El Salvador, Guatemala, Honduras, Nicaragua, and the United States

Association of Southeast Asian Nations (ASEAN) a regional trade agreement between Brunei Darussalam, Cambodia, Indonesia, Lao PDR, Malaysia, Myanmar, the Philippines, Singapore, Thailand, and Vietnam

Asia-Pacific Economic Cooperation (APEC) a regional trade agreement between Australia, Canada, Chile, the People's Republic of China, Hong Kong, Japan, Mexico, New Zealand, Papua New Guinea, Peru, Russia, South Korea, Taiwan, the United States, and all members of ASEAN, except Cambodia, Lao PDR, and Myanmar

Global consistency when a multinational company has offices, manufacturing plants, and distribution facilities in different countries and runs them all using the same rules, guidelines, policies, and procedures

Local adaptation when a multinational company modifies its rules, guidelines, policies, and procedures to adapt to differences in foreign customers, governments, and regulatory agencies

KEY TERMS

Global business the buying and selling of goods and services by people from different countries

Multinational corporation a corporation that owns businesses in two or more countries

Direct foreign investment a method of investment in which a company builds a new business or buys an existing business in a foreign country

Trade barriers government-imposed regulations that increase the cost and restrict the number of imported goods

Protectionism a government's use of trade barriers to shield domestic companies and their workers from foreign competition

Tariff a direct tax on imported goods

Nontariff barriers nontax methods of increasing the cost or reducing the volume of imported goods

Quota a limit on the number or volume of imported products

Voluntary export restraints voluntarily imposed limits on the number or volume of products exported to a particular country

Government import standard a standard ostensibly established to protect the health and safety of citizens but, in reality, often used to restrict imports

Subsidies government loans, grants, and tax deferments given to domestic companies to protect them from foreign competition

Customs classification a classification assigned to imported products by government officials that affects the size of the tariff and imposition of import quotas

General Agreement on Tariffs and Trade (GATT) a worldwide trade agreement that reduced and eliminated tariffs, limited government subsidies, and established protections for intellectual property

World Trade Organization (WTO) as the successor to GATT, the only international organization dealing with the global rules of trade between nations. Its main function is to ensure that trade flows as smoothly, predictably, and freely as possible.

Exporting selling domestically produced products to customers in foreign countries

Cooperative contract an agreement in which a foreign business owner pays a company a fee for the right to conduct that business in his or her country

Licensing an agreement in which a domestic company, the licensor, receives royalty payments for allowing another company, the licensee, to produce the licensor's product, sell its service, or use its brand name in a specified foreign market

Franchise a collection of networked firms in which the manufacturer or marketer of a product or service, the franchisor, licenses the entire business to another person or organization, the franchisee

Strategic alliance an agreement in which companies combine key resources, costs, risk, technology, and people

Joint venture a strategic alliance in which two existing companies collaborate to form a third, independent company

Wholly owned affiliates foreign offices, facilities, and manufacturing plants that are 100 percent owned by the parent company

Global new ventures new companies that are founded with an active global strategy and have sales, employees, and financing in different countries

Purchasing power a comparison of the relative cost of a standard set of goods and services in different countries

Political uncertainty the risk of major changes in political regimes that can result from war, revolution, death of political leaders, social unrest, or other influential events

Policy uncertainty the risk associated with changes in laws and government policies that directly affect the way foreign companies conduct business

National culture the set of shared values and beliefs that affects the perceptions, decisions, and behavior of the people from a particular country

Expatriate someone who lives and works outside his or her native country

Review 3: Forms for Global Business

❯ The phase model of globalization says that as companies move from a domestic to a global orientation, they use these organizational forms in sequence: exporting, cooperative contracts (licensing and franchising), strategic alliances, and wholly owned affiliates. Yet not all companies follow the phase model. For example, global new ventures are global from their inception.

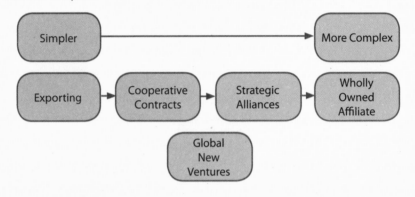

Review 4: Finding the Best Business Climate

❯ The first step in deciding where to take your company global is finding an attractive business climate. Be sure to look for a growing market where consumers have strong purchasing power and foreign competitors are weak. When locating an office or manufacturing facility, consider both qualitative and quantitative factors. In assessing political risk, be sure to examine political uncertainty and policy uncertainty. If the location you choose has considerable political risk, you can avoid it, try to control the risk, or use a cooperation strategy.

Review 5: Becoming Aware of Cultural Differences

❯ National culture is the set of shared values and beliefs that affects the perceptions, decisions, and behavior of the people from a particular country. The first step in dealing with culture is to recognize meaningful differences, such as power distance, individualism, masculinity, uncertainty avoidance, and short-term/long-term orientation. Cultural differences should be carefully interpreted because they are based on averages, not individuals. Adapting managerial practices to cultural differences is difficult because policies and practices can be perceived differently in different cultures. Another difficulty is that cultural values may be changing in many parts of the world. Consequently, when companies try to adapt management practices to cultural differences, they need to be sure that they are not using outdated assumptions about a country's culture.

Review 6: Preparing for an International Assignment

❯ Many expatriates return prematurely from international assignments because of poor performance. However, this is much less likely to happen if employees receive language and cross-cultural training, such as documentary training, cultural simulations, or field experiences, before going on assignment. Adjustment of expatriates' spouses and families, which is the most important determinant of success in international assignments, can be improved through adaptability screening and intercultural training.

LEARNING OUTCOMES

Review 1: Departmentalization

> There are five traditional departmental structures: functional, product, customer, geographic, and matrix. Functional departmentalization is based on the different business functions or expertise used to run a business. Product departmentalization is organized according to the different products or services a company sells. Customer departmentalization focuses its divisions on the different kinds of customers a company has. Geographic departmentalization is based on the different geographic areas or markets in which the company does business. Matrix departmentalization is a hybrid form that combines two or more forms of departmentalization, the most common being the product and functional forms. There is no "best" departmental structure. Each structure has advantages and disadvantages.

Review 2: Organizational Authority

> Organizational authority is determined by the chain of command, line versus staff authority, delegation, and the degree of centralization in a company. The chain of command vertically connects every job in the company to higher levels of management and makes clear who reports to whom. Managers have line authority to command employees below them in the chain of command, but have only staff, or advisory, authority over employees not below them in the chain of command. Managers delegate authority by transferring to subordinates the authority and responsibility needed to do a task; in exchange, subordinates become accountable for task completion. In centralized companies, most authority to make decisions lies with managers in the upper levels of the company. In decentralized companies, much of the authority is delegated to the workers closest to problems, who can then make the decisions necessary for solving the problems themselves.

Delegation: Responsibility, Authority, and Accountability

Manager — Subordinate

Responsibility →
Authority →
← Accountability

Source: C. D. Pringle, D. F. Jennings, & J. G. Longenecker, *Managing Organizations: Functions and Behaviors* © 1990. Adapted by permission of Pearson Education, Inc., Upper Saddle River, NJ.

Review 3: Job Design

> Companies use specialized jobs because they are economical and easy to learn and don't require highly paid workers. However, specialized jobs aren't motivating or particularly satisfying for employees. Companies have used job rotation, job enlargement, job enrichment, and the job characteristics model to make specialized jobs more interesting and motivating. The goal of the job characteristics model is to make jobs intrinsically motivating. For this to happen, jobs must be strong on five core job characteristics (skill variety, task identity, task significance, autonomy, and feedback), and workers must experience three critical psychological states (knowledge of results, responsibility for work outcomes, and meaningful work). If jobs aren't internally motivating, they can be redesigned by combining tasks, forming natural work units, establishing client relationships, vertical loading, and opening feedback channels.

KEY TERMS

Organizational structure the vertical and horizontal configuration of departments, authority, and jobs within a company

Organizational process the collection of activities that transform inputs into outputs that customers value

Departmentalization subdividing work and workers into separate organizational units responsible for completing particular tasks

Functional departmentalization organizing work and workers into separate units responsible for particular business functions or areas of expertise

Product departmentalization organizing work and workers into separate units responsible for producing particular products or services

Customer departmentalization organizing work and workers into separate units responsible for particular kinds of customers

Geographic departmentalization organizing work and workers into separate units responsible for doing business in particular geographic areas

Matrix departmentalization a hybrid organizational structure in which two or more forms of departmentalization, most often product and functional, are used together

Simple matrix a form of matrix departmentalization in which managers in different parts of the matrix negotiate conflicts and resources

Complex matrix a form of matrix departmentalization in which managers in different parts of the matrix report to matrix managers, who help them sort out conflicts and problems

Authority the right to give commands, take action, and make decisions to achieve organizational objectives

Chain of command the vertical line of authority that clarifies who reports to whom throughout the organization

Unity of command a management principle that workers should report to just one boss

Line authority the right to command immediate subordinates in the chain of command

Staff authority the right to advise, but not command, others who are not subordinates in the chain of command

Line function an activity that contributes directly to creating or selling the company's products

Staff function an activity that does not contribute directly to creating or selling the company's products, but instead supports line activities

Delegation of authority the assignment of direct authority and responsibility to a subordinate to complete tasks for which the manager is normally responsible

Centralization of authority the location of most authority at the upper levels of the organization

Decentralization the location of a significant amount of authority in the lower levels of the organization

Standardization solving problems by consistently applying the same rules, procedures, and processes

Job design the number, kind, and variety of tasks that individual workers perform in doing their jobs

Job specialization a job composed of a small part of a larger task or process

Job rotation periodically moving workers from one specialized job to another to give them more variety and the opportunity to use different skills

Job enlargement increasing the number of different tasks that a worker performs within one particular job

Job enrichment increasing the number of tasks in a particular job and giving workers the authority and control to make meaningful decisions about their work

Job characteristics model (JCM) an approach to job redesign that seeks to formulate jobs in ways that motivate workers and lead to positive work outcomes

Internal motivation motivation that comes from the job itself rather than from outside rewards

Skill variety the number of different activities performed in a job

Task identity the degree to which a job, from beginning to end, requires the completion of a whole and identifiable piece of work

Task significance the degree to which a job is perceived to have a substantial impact on others inside or outside the organization

Autonomy the degree to which a job gives workers the discretion, freedom, and independence to decide how and when to accomplish the job

Feedback the amount of information the job provides to workers about their work performance

Mechanistic organization an organization characterized by specialized jobs and responsibilities; precisely defined, unchanging roles; and a rigid chain of command based on centralized authority and vertical communication

Organic organization an organization characterized by broadly defined jobs and responsibility; loosely defined, frequently changing roles; and decentralized authority and horizontal communication based on task knowledge

Intraorganizational process the collection of activities that take place within an organization to transform inputs into outputs that customers value

Reengineering fundamental rethinking and radical redesign of business processes to achieve dramatic improvements in critical measures of performance, such as cost, quality, service, and speed

Task interdependence the extent to which collective action is required to complete an entire piece of work

Pooled interdependence work completed by having each job or department independently contribute to the whole

Sequential interdependence work completed in succession, with one group's or job's outputs becoming the inputs for the next group or job

Reciprocal interdependence work completed by different jobs or groups working together in a back-and-forth manner

Empowering workers permanently passing decision-making authority and responsibility from managers to workers by giving them the information and resources they need to make and carry out good decisions

Empowerment feelings of intrinsic motivation, in which workers perceive their work to have impact and meaning and perceive themselves to be competent and capable of self-determination

Interorganizational process a collection of activities that take place among companies to transform inputs into outputs that customers value

Modular organization an organization that outsources noncore business activities to outside companies, suppliers, specialists, or consultants

Virtual organization an organization that is part of a network in which many companies share skills, costs, capabilities, markets, and customers to collectively solve customer problems or provide specific products or services

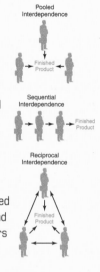

Review 4: Intraorganizational Processes

> Today, companies are using reengineering and empowerment to change their intraorganizational processes. Reengineering changes an organization's orientation from vertical to horizontal and its work processes by decreasing sequential and pooled interdependence and by increasing reciprocal interdependence. Reengineering promises dramatic increases in productivity and customer satisfaction, but it has been criticized as simply an excuse to cut costs and lay off workers. Empowering workers means taking decision-making authority and responsibility from managers and giving it to workers. Empowered workers develop feelings of competence and self-determination and believe that their work has meaning and impact.

Review 5: Interorganizational Processes

> Organizations are using modular and virtual organizations to change interorganizational processes. Because modular organizations outsource all noncore activities to other businesses, they are less expensive to run than traditional companies. However, modular organizations require extremely close relationships with suppliers, may result in a loss of control, and could create new competitors if the wrong business activities are outsourced. Virtual organizations participate in a network in which they share skills, costs, capabilities, markets, and customers. Virtual organizations can reduce costs, respond quickly, and, if they can successfully coordinate their efforts, produce outstanding products and service.

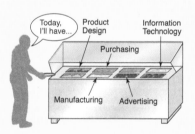

Trivia answer: The original Mechanical Turk was an 18th-century chess playing automaton that purportedly could beat anyone at chess. The Turk was a mannequin, but the machine concealed a human chess master who would actuate the Turk with mechanical controls. The Turk beat many statesmen and luminaries, including Napoleon Bonaparte and Benjamin Franklin. Read more in Tom Standage's book *The Mechanical Turk*.

LEARNING OUTCOMES

Review 1: The Good and Bad of Using Teams

> In many industries, teams are growing in importance because they help organizations respond to specific problems and challenges. Teams have been shown to increase customer satisfaction (specific customer teams), product and service quality (direct responsibility), and employee job satisfaction (cross training, unique opportunities, and leadership responsibilities). Although teams can produce significant improvements in these areas, using teams does not guarantee these positive outcomes. Teams and teamwork have the disadvantages of initially high turnover and social loafing (especially in large groups). Teams also share many of the advantages (multiple perspectives, generation of more alternatives, and more commitment) and disadvantages (groupthink, time, poorly run meetings, domination by a few team members, and weak accountability) of group decision making. Finally, teams should be used for a clear purpose, when the work requires that people work together, when rewards can be provided for both teamwork and team performance, when ample resources can be provided, and when teams can be given clear authority over their work.

ADVANTAGES AND DISADVANTAGES OF TEAMS

ADVANTAGES 👍	DISADVANTAGES 👎
☺ Customer satisfaction	☹ Initially high employee turnover
☺ Product and service quality	☹ Social loafing
☺ Speed and efficiency in product development	☹ Disadvantages of group decision making (groupthink, inefficient meetings, domination by a minority, lack of accountability)
☺ Employee job satisfaction	
☺ Better decision making and problem solving (multiple perspectives, more alternative solutions, increased commitment to decisions)	

Review 2: Kinds of Teams

> Companies use different kinds of teams to make themselves more competitive. Autonomy is the key dimension that makes teams different. Traditional work groups (which execute tasks) and employee involvement groups (which make suggestions) have the lowest levels of autonomy. Semi-autonomous work groups (which control major, direct tasks) have more autonomy, while self-managing teams (which control all direct tasks) and self-designing teams (which control membership and how tasks are done) have the highest levels of autonomy. Cross-functional, virtual, and project teams are common, but are not easily categorized in terms of autonomy. Cross-functional teams combine employees from different functional areas to help teams attack problems from multiple perspectives and generate more ideas and solutions. Virtual teams use telecommunications and information technologies to bring coworkers "together," regardless of physical location or time zone. Virtual teams reduce travel and work time, but communication may suffer since team members don't work face-to-face. Finally, project teams are used for specific, one-time projects or tasks that must be completed within a limited time. Project teams reduce communication barriers and promote flexibility; teams and team members are reassigned to their departments or new projects as old projects are completed.

KEY TERMS

Work team a small number of people with complementary skills who hold themselves mutually accountable for pursuing a common purpose, achieving performance goals, and improving interdependent work processes

Cross-training training team members to do all or most of the jobs performed by the other team members

Social loafing behavior in which team members withhold their efforts and fail to perform their share of the work

Traditional work group a group composed of two or more people who work together to achieve a shared goal

Employee involvement team team that provides advice or makes suggestions to management concerning specific issues

Semi-autonomous work group a group that has the authority to make decisions and solve problems related to the major tasks of producing a product or service

Self-managing team a team that manages and controls all of the major tasks of producing a product or service

Self-designing team a team that has the characteristics of self-managing teams but also controls team design, work tasks, and team membership

Cross-functional team a team composed of employees from different functional areas of the organization

Virtual team a team composed of geographically and/or organizationally dispersed coworkers who use telecommunication and information technologies to accomplish an organizational task

Project team a team created to complete specific, one-time projects or tasks within a limited time

Norms informally agreed-on standards that regulate team behavior

Cohesiveness the extent to which team members are attracted to a team and motivated to remain in it

Forming the first stage of team development, in which team members meet each other, form initial impressions, and begin to establish team norms

Storming the second stage of development, characterized by conflict and disagreement, in which team members disagree over what the team should do and how it should do it

Norming the third stage of team development, in which team members begin to settle into their roles, group cohesion grows, and positive team norms develop

Performing the fourth and final stage of team development, in which performance improves because the team has matured into an effective, fully functioning team

Structural accommodation the ability to change organizational structures, policies, and practices in order to meet stretch goals

Bureaucratic immunity the ability to make changes without first getting approval from managers or other parts of an organization

Individualism-collectivism the degree to which a person believes that people should be self-sufficient and that loyalty to one's self is more important than loyalty to team or company

Team level the average level of ability, experience, personality, or any other factor on a team

Team diversity the variances or differences in ability, experience, personality, or any other factor on a team

Interpersonal skills skills, such as listening, communicating, questioning, and providing feedback, that enable people to have effective working relationships with others

Skill-based pay compensation system that pays employees for learning additional skills or knowledge

Gainsharing a compensation system in which companies share the financial value of performance gains, such as productivity, cost savings, or quality, with their workers

---

Work Team Characteristics

> The most important characteristics of work teams are team norms, cohesiveness, size, conflict, and development. Norms let team members know what is expected of them and can influence team behavior in positive and negative ways. Positive team norms are associated with organizational commitment, trust, and job satisfaction. Team cohesiveness helps teams retain members, promotes cooperative behavior, increases motivation, and facilitates team performance. Attending team meetings and activities, creating opportunities to work together, and engaging in nonwork activities can increase cohesiveness. Team size has a curvilinear relationship with team performance: teams that are very small or very large do not perform as well as moderate-sized teams of six to nine members. Teams of this size are cohesive and small enough for team members to get to know each other and contribute in a meaningful way, but are large enough to take advantage of team members' diverse skills, knowledge, and perspectives. Conflict and disagreement are inevitable in most teams. The key to dealing with team conflict is to maximize cognitive conflict, which focuses on issue-related differences, and minimize affective conflict, the emotional reactions that occur when disagreements become personal rather than professional. As teams develop and grow, they pass through four stages of development: forming, storming, norming, and performing. After a period of time, however, if a team is not managed well, its performance may decline as the team regresses through the stages of de-norming, de-storming, and de-forming.

HOW TEAMS CAN HAVE A GOOD FIGHT

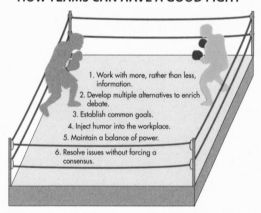

1. Work with more, rather than less, information.
2. Develop multiple alternatives to enrich debate.
3. Establish common goals.
4. Inject humor into the workplace.
5. Maintain a balance of power.
6. Resolve issues without forcing a consensus.

Source: K. M. Eisenhardt, J. L. Kahwajy, & L. J. Bourgeois III, "How Management Teams Can Have a Good Fight," *Harvard Business Review* 75, no. 4 (July-August 1997): 77–85.

Enhancing Work Team Effectiveness

> Companies can make teams more effective by setting team goals and managing how team members are selected, trained, and compensated. Team goals provide a clear focus and purpose, reduce the incidence of social loafing, and lead to higher team performance 93 percent of the time. Extremely difficult stretch goals can be used to motivate teams as long as teams have autonomy, control over resources, structural accommodation, and bureaucratic immunity. Not everyone is suited for teamwork. When selecting team members, companies should select people who have a preference for teamwork (individualism-collectivism) and should consider team level (average ability on a team) and team diversity (different abilities on a team). Organizations that successfully use teams provide thousands of hours of training to make sure that teams work. The most common types of team training are for interpersonal skills, decision-making and problem-solving skills, conflict resolution, technical training to help team members learn multiple jobs (i.e., cross training), and training for team leaders. Employees can be compensated for team participation and accomplishments in three ways: skill-based pay, gainsharing, and nonfinancial rewards.

LEARNING OUTCOMES

Review 1: Employment Legislation

> Human resource management is subject to numerous major federal employment laws and subject to review by several federal agencies. In general, these laws indicate that sex, age, religion, color, national origin, race, disability, and pregnancy may not be considered in employment decisions unless these factors reasonably qualify as BFOQs. Two important criteria, disparate treatment (intentional discrimination) and adverse impact (unintentional discrimination), are used to decide whether companies have wrongly discriminated against someone. The two kinds of sexual harassment are quid pro quo and hostile work environment.

Review 2: Recruiting

> Recruiting is the process of finding qualified job applicants. The first step in recruiting is to conduct a job analysis, which is used to write a job description of basic tasks, duties, and responsibilities and to write job specifications indicating the knowledge, skills, and abilities needed to perform the job. Whereas internal recruiting involves finding qualified job applicants from inside the company, external recruiting involves finding qualified job applicants from outside the company.

Importance of Job Analysis to Human Resource Management

HR Decisions
Recruiting
Selection
Training
Performance
Appraisal
Separation

HR Subsystems
• Job Description
• Job Specification

← Job Analysis →

Review 3: Selection

> Selection is the process of gathering information about job applicants to decide who should be offered a job. Accurate selection procedures are valid, are legally defendable, and improve organizational performance. Application forms and résumés are the most common selection devices. Managers should check references and conduct background checks even though previous employers are reluctant to provide such information for fear of being sued for defamation. Unfortunately, without this information, other employers are at risk of negligent hiring lawsuits. Selection tests generally do the best job of predicting applicants' future job performance. The three kinds of job interviews are unstructured, structured, and semistructured interviews.

Review 4: Training

> Training is used to give employees the job-specific skills, experience, and knowledge they need to do their jobs or improve their job performance. To make sure training dollars are well spent, companies need to determine specific training needs, select appropriate training methods, and then evaluate the training.

Training objectives

Impart information and knowledge | Develop analytic and problem-solving skills | Practice, learn, or change behaviors

Review 5: Performance Appraisal

> The keys to successful performance appraisal are accurately measuring job performance and effectively sharing performance feedback with employees. Organizations should develop good performance appraisal scales; train raters how to accurately evaluate performance; and impress upon managers the value of providing feedback in a clear, consistent, and fair manner, and setting goals and monitoring progress toward those goals.

Review 6: Compensation and Employee Separation

> Compensation includes both the financial and the nonfinancial rewards that organizations give employees in exchange for their work. There are three basic kinds of compensation decisions: pay level, pay variability, and pay structure. Employee separation is the loss of an employee, which can occur voluntarily or involuntarily. Companies use downsizing and early retirement incentive programs to reduce the number of employees in the organization and lower costs, but companies generally try to keep the rate of employee turnover low to reduce costs associated with finding and developing new employees. Functional turnover can be good for organizations, however.

Kinds of Compensation Decisions

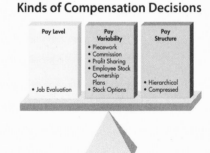

Pay Level
• Job Evaluation

Pay Variability
• Piecework
• Commission
• Profit Sharing
• Employee Stock Ownership Plans
• Stock Options

Pay Structure
• Hierarchical
• Compressed

KEY TERMS

Human resource management (HRM) the process of finding, developing, and keeping the right people to form a qualified work force

Bona fide occupational qualification (BFOQ) an exception in employment law that permits sex, age, religion, and the like to be used when making employment decisions, but only if they are "reasonably necessary to the normal operation of that particular business." BFOQs are strictly monitored by the Equal Employment Opportunity Commission.

Disparate treatment intentional discrimination that occurs when people are purposely not given the same hiring, promotion, or membership opportunities because of their race, color, sex, age, ethnic group, national origin, or religious beliefs

Adverse impact unintentional discrimination that occurs when members of a particular race, sex, or ethnic group are unintentionally harmed or disadvantaged because they are hired, promoted, or trained (or any other employment decision) at substantially lower rates than others

Four-fifths (or 80 percent) rule a rule of thumb used by the courts and the EEOC to determine whether there is evidence of adverse impact. A violation of this rule occurs when the selection rate for a protected group is less than 80 percent or four-fifths of the selection rate for a nonprotected group.

Sexual harassment a form of discrimination in which unwelcome sexual advances, requests for sexual favors, or other verbal or physical conduct of a sexual nature occurs while performing one's job

Quid pro quo sexual harassment a form of sexual harassment in which employment outcomes, such as hiring, promotion, or simply keeping one's job, depend on whether an individual submits to sexual harassment

Hostile work environment a form of sexual harassment in which unwelcome and demeaning sexually related behavior creates an intimidating and offensive work environment

Recruiting the process of developing a pool of qualified job applicants

Job analysis a purposeful, systematic process for collecting information on the important work-related aspects of a job

Job description a written description of the basic tasks, duties, and responsibilities required of an employee holding a particular job

Job specifications a written summary of the qualifications needed to successfully perform a particular job

Internal recruiting the process of developing a pool of qualified job applicants from people who already work in the company

External recruiting the process of developing a pool of qualified job applicants from outside the company

Selection the process of gathering information about job applicants to decide who should be offered a job

Validation the process of determining how well a selection test or procedure predicts future job performance. The better or more accurate the prediction of future job performance, the more valid a test is said to be.

Employment references sources such as previous employers or coworkers who can provide job-related information about job candidates

Background checks procedures used to verify the truthfulness and accuracy of information that applicants provide about themselves and to uncover negative, job-related background information not provided by applicants

Specific ability tests (aptitude tests) tests that measure the extent to which an applicant possesses the particular kind of ability needed to do a job well

Cognitive ability tests tests that measure the extent to which applicants have abilities in perceptual speed, verbal comprehension, numerical aptitude, general reasoning, and spatial aptitude

Biographical data (bio-data) extensive surveys that ask applicants questions about their personal backgrounds and life experiences

Work sample tests tests that require applicants to perform tasks that are actually done on the job

Assessment centers a series of managerial simulations, graded by trained observers, that are used to determine applicants' capability for managerial work

Interviews a selection tool in which company representatives ask job applicants job-related questions to determine whether they are qualified for the job

Unstructured interviews interviews in which interviewers are free to ask the applicants anything they want

Structured interviews interviews in which all applicants are asked the same set of standardized questions, usually including situational, behavioral, background, and job-knowledge questions

Training developing the skills, experience, and knowledge employees need to perform their jobs or improve their performance

Needs assessment the process of identifying and prioritizing the learning needs of employees

Performance appraisal the process of assessing how well employees are doing their jobs

Objective performance measures measures of job performance that are easily and directly counted or quantified

Behavioral observation scales (BOSs) rating scales that indicate the frequency with which workers perform specific behaviors that are representative of the job dimensions critical to successful job performance

Rater training training performance appraisal raters in how to avoid rating errors and increase rating accuracy

360-degree feedback a performance appraisal process in which feedback is obtained from the boss, subordinates, peers and coworkers, and the employees themselves

Compensation the financial and nonfinancial rewards that organizations give employees in exchange for their work

Employee separation the voluntary or involuntary loss of an employee

Job evaluation a process that determines the worth of each job in a company by evaluating the market value of the knowledge, skills, and requirements needed to perform it

Piecework a compensation system in which employees are paid a set rate for each item they produce

Commission a compensation system in which employees earn a percentage of each sale they make

Profit sharing a compensation system in which a company pays a percentage of its profits to employees in addition to their regular compensation

Employee stock ownership plan (ESOP) a compensation system that awards employees shares of company stock in addition to their regular compensation

Stock options a compensation system that gives employees the right to purchase shares of stock at a set price, even if the value of the stock increases above that price

Wrongful discharge a legal doctrine that requires employers to have a job-related reason to terminate employees

Downsizing the planned elimination of jobs in a company

Outplacement services employment-counseling services offered to employees who are losing their jobs because of downsizing

Early retirement incentive programs (ERIPs) programs that offer financial benefits to employees to encourage them to retire early

Phased retirement employees transition to retirement by working reduced hours over a period of time before completely retiring

Employee turnover loss of employees who voluntarily choose to leave the company

Functional turnover loss of poor-performing employees who voluntarily choose to leave a company

Dysfunctional turnover loss of high-performing employees who voluntarily choose to leave a company

LEARNING OUTCOMES

Review 1: Diversity: Differences That Matter

> Diversity exists in organizations when there is a variety of demographic, cultural, and personal differences among the people who work there and the customers who do business there. A common misconception is that workplace diversity and affirmative action are the same. However, affirmative action is more narrowly focused on demographics, is required by law, and is used to punish companies that discriminate on the basis of race, color, religion, sex, or national origin. By contrast, diversity is broader in focus (going beyond demographics), voluntary, more positive in that it encourages companies to value all kinds of differences, and, at this time, substantially less controversial than affirmative action. Thus, affirmative action and diversity differ in purpose, practice, and the reactions they produce. Diversity also makes good business sense in terms of cost savings (reducing turnover, decreasing absenteeism, and avoiding lawsuits), attracting and retaining talent, and driving business growth (improving marketplace understanding and promoting higher-quality problem solving).

General Purpose of Diversity Programs

To create a positive work environment where

- no one is advantaged or disadvantaged.
- "we" is everyone.
- everyone can do his or her best work.
- differences are respected and not ignored.
- everyone feels comfortable.

Source: T. Roosevelt, "From Affirmative Action to Affirming Diversity," *Harvard Business Review* 68, no. 2 (1990): 107–117.

Review 2: Surface-Level Diversity

> Age, sex, race/ethnicity, and physical and mental disabilities are dimensions of surface-level diversity. Because those dimensions are (usually) easily observed, managers and workers tend to rely on them to form initial impressions and stereotypes. Sometimes this can lead to age, sex, racial/ethnic, or disability discrimination (i.e., treating people differently) in the workplace. In general, older workers, women, people of color or different national origins, and people with disabilities are much less likely to be hired or promoted than white males. This disparity is often due to incorrect beliefs or stereotypes, such as "job performance declines with age," or "women aren't willing to travel on business," or "workers with disabilities aren't as competent as able workers." To reduce discrimination, companies can determine the hiring and promotion rates for different groups, train managers to make hiring and promotion decisions on the basis of specific criteria, and make sure that everyone has equal access to training, mentors, reasonable work accommodations, and assistive technology. Finally, companies need to designate a "go-to person" that employees can talk to if they believe they have suffered discrimination.

KEY TERMS

Diversity a variety of demographic, cultural, and personal differences among an organization's employees and customers

Affirmative action purposeful steps taken by an organization to create employment opportunities for minorities and women

Surface-level diversity differences such as age, sex, race/ethnicity, and physical disabilities that are observable, typically unchangeable, and easy to measure

Deep-level diversity differences such as personality and attitudes that are communicated through verbal and nonverbal behaviors and are learned only through extended interaction with others

Social integration the degree to which group members are psychologically attracted to working with each other to accomplish a common objective

Age discrimination treating people differently (e.g., in hiring and firing, promotion, and compensation decisions) because of their age

Sex discrimination treating people differently because of their sex

Glass ceiling the invisible barrier that prevents women and minorities from advancing to the top jobs in organizations

Racial and ethnic discrimination treating people differently because of their race or ethnicity

Disability a mental or physical impairment that substantially limits one or more major life activities

Disability discrimination treating people differently because of their disabilities

Disposition the tendency to respond to situations and events in a predetermined manner

Personality the relatively stable set of behaviors, attitudes, and emotions displayed over time that makes people different from each other

Extraversion the degree to which someone is active, assertive, gregarious, sociable, talkative, and energized by others

Emotional stability the degree to which someone is not angry, depressed, anxious, emotional, insecure, and excitable

Agreeableness the degree to which someone is cooperative, polite, flexible, forgiving, good-natured, tolerant, and trusting

Conscientiousness the degree to which someone is organized, hardworking, responsible, persevering, thorough, and achievement oriented

Openness to experience the degree to which someone is curious, broad-minded, and open to new ideas, things, and experiences; is spontaneous; and has a high tolerance for ambiguity

Organizational plurality a work environment where (1) all members are empowered to contribute in a way that maximizes the benefits to the organization, customers, and themselves, and (2) the individuality of each member is respected by not segmenting or polarizing people on the basis of their membership in a particular group

Awareness training training that is designed to raise employees' awareness of diversity issues and to challenge the underlying assumptions or stereotypes they may have about others

Skills-based diversity training training that teaches employees the practical skills they need for managing a diverse work force, such as flexibility and adaptability, negotiation, problem solving, and conflict resolution

Diversity audits formal assessments that measure employee and management attitudes, investigate the extent to which people are advantaged or disadvantaged with respect to hiring and promotions, and review companies' diversity-related policies and procedures

Diversity pairing a mentoring program in which people of different cultural backgrounds, sexes, or races/ethnicities are paired together to get to know each other and change stereotypical beliefs and attitudes

Review 3: Deep-Level Diversity

> Deep-level diversity matters because it can reduce prejudice, discrimination, and conflict while increasing social integration. It consists of dispositional and personality differences that can be learned only through extended interaction with others. Research conducted in different cultures, settings, and languages indicates that there are five basic dimensions of personality: extraversion, emotional stability, agreeableness, conscientiousness, and openness to experience. Of these, conscientiousness is perhaps the most important because conscientious workers tend to be better performers on virtually any job. Extraversion is also related to performance in jobs that require significant interaction with others.

Review 4: Managing Diversity

> The three paradigms for managing diversity are the discrimination and fairness paradigm (equal opportunity, fair treatment, strict compliance with the law), the access and legitimacy paradigm (matching internal diversity to external diversity), and the learning and effectiveness paradigm (achieving organizational plurality by integrating deep-level diversity into the work of the organization). Unlike the other paradigms that focus on surface-level differences, the learning and effectiveness program values common ground, distinguishes between individual and group differences, minimizes conflict and divisiveness, and focuses on bringing different talents and perspectives together. What principles can companies use when managing diversity? Follow and enforce federal and state laws regarding equal employment opportunity. Treat group differences as important, but not special. Find the common ground. Tailor opportunities to individuals, not groups. Reexamine, but maintain, high standards. Solicit negative as well as positive feedback. Set high but realistic goals. The two types of diversity training are awareness training and skills-based diversity training. Companies also manage diversity through diversity audits and diversity pairing and by having top executives experience what it is like to be in the minority.

Paradigms for Managing Diversity

DIVERSITY PARADIGM	FOCUS	SUCCESS MEASURED BY	BENEFITS	LIMITATIONS
Discrimination & Fairness	Equal opportunity Fair treatment Recruitment of minorities Strict compliance with laws	Recruitment, promotion, and retention goals for underrepresented group	Fairer treatment Increased demographic diversity	Focus on surface-level diversity
Access & Legitimacy	Acceptance and celebration of differences	Diversity in company matches diversity of primary stakeholders	Establishes a clear business reason for diversity	Focus on surface-level diversity
Learning & Effectiveness	Integrating deep-level differences into organization	Valuing people on the basis of individual knowledge, skills, and abilities	Values common ground Distinction between individual and group differences Less conflict, backlash, and divisiveness Bringing different talents and perspectives together	Focus on deep-level diversity is more difficult to measure and quantify

LEARNING OUTCOMES

Review 1: Basics of Motivation

> *Motivation* is the set of forces that initiates, directs, and makes people persist in their efforts over time to accomplish a goal. Managers often confuse motivation and performance, but job performance is a multiplicative function of motivation times ability times situational constraints. Needs are the physical or psychological requirements that must be met to ensure survival and well-being. Different motivational theories (Maslow's Hierarchy of Needs, Alderfer's ERG Theory, and McClelland's Learned Needs Theory) specify a number of different needs. However, studies show that there are only two general kinds of needs, lower-order needs and higher-order needs. Both extrinsic and intrinsic rewards motivate people.

MOTIVATING TO INCREASE EFFORT

- **Start by asking people what their needs are.**
- **Satisfy lower-order needs first.**
- **Expect people's needs to change.**
- **As needs change and lower-order needs are satisfied, satisfy higher-order needs by looking for ways to allow employees to experience intrinsic rewards.**

Review 2: Equity Theory

> The basic components of equity theory are inputs, outcomes, and referents. After an internal comparison in which employees compare their outcomes to their inputs, they then make an external comparison in which they compare their O/I ratio with the O/I ratio of a referent, a person who works in a similar job or is otherwise similar. When the O/I ratio is equal to the referent's O/I ratio, employees per... when their O/I ratio is different... treated inequitably or unfairly. Th... Underreward, which occurs when... leads to anger or frustration. Ove... than the employee's O/I ratio, can...

MOTIVA...

- **Look for and correct major i...**
- **Reduce employees' inputs.**
- **Make sure decision-making p...**

Review 3: Expectancy The...

> Expectancy theory holds that three... about their motivation: valence, expec... holds that for people to be highly motivated, ...three fac... ...me of these factors declines, overall motivation will decline, too.

MOTIVATING WITH EXPECTAN... THEORY

- **Systematically gather information to find out what employees want from their jobs.**
- **Take specific steps to link rewards to individual performance in a way that is clear and understandable to employees.**
- **Empower employees to make decisions if management really wants them to believe that their hard work and effort will lead to good performance.**

(handwritten note overlapping text): Environmental complexity — the number + the intensity of external factors in the @ environment that affect organizations. Simple — few, complex — many

KEY TERMS

Motivation the set of forces that initiates, directs, and makes people persist in their efforts to accomplish a goal

Needs the physical or psychological requirements that must be met to ensure survival and well-being

Extrinsic reward a reward that is tangible, visible to others, and given to employees contingent on the performance of specific tasks or behaviors

Intrinsic reward a natural reward associated with performing a task or activity for its own sake

Equity theory a theory that states that people will be motivated when they perceive that they are being treated fairly

Inputs in equity theory, the contributions employees make to the organization

Outcomes in equity theory, the rewards employees receive for their contributions to the organization

Referents in equity theory, others with whom people compare themselves to determine if they have been treated fairly

Outcome/input (O/I) ratio in equity theory, an employee's perception of how the rewards received from an organization compare with the employee's contributions to that organization

Underreward a form of inequity in which you are getting fewer outcomes relative to inputs than your referent is getting

Overreward a form of inequity in which you are getting more outcomes relative to inputs than your referent

Distributive justice the perceived degree to which outcomes and rewards are fairly distributed or allocated

Procedural justice the perceived fairness of the process used to make reward allocation decisions

Expectancy theory a theory that states that people will be motivated to the extent to which they believe that their efforts will lead to good performance, that good performance will be rewarded, and that they will be offered attractive rewards

Valence the attractiveness or desirability of a reward or outcome

Expectancy the perceived relationship between effort and preformance

Instrumentality the perceived relationship between performance and rewards

Reinforcement theory a theory that states that behavior is a function of its consequences, that behaviors followed by positive consequences will occur more frequently, and that behaviors followed by negative consequences, or not followed by positive consequences, will occur less frequently

Reinforcement the process of changing behavior by changing the consequences that follow behavior

Reinforcement contingencies cause-and-effect relationships between the performance of specific behaviors and specific consequences

Schedule of reinforcement rules that specify which behaviors will be reinforced, which consequences will follow those behaviors, and the schedule by which those consequences will be delivered

Positive reinforcement reinforcement that strengthens behavior by following behaviors with desirable consequences

Negative reinforcement reinforcement that strengthens behavior by withholding an unpleasant consequence when employees perform a specific behavior

Punishment reinforcement that weakens behavior by following behaviors with undesirable consequences

Extinction reinforcement in which a positive consequence is no longer allowed to follow a previously reinforced behavior, thus weakening the behavior

Continuous reinforcement schedule a schedule that requires a consequence to be administered following every instance of a behavior

Intermittent reinforcement schedule a schedule in which consequences are delivered after a specified or average time has elapsed or after a specified or average number of behaviors has occurred

Fixed interval reinforcement schedule an intermittent schedule in which consequences follow a behavior only after a fixed time has elapsed

Variable interval reinforcement schedule an intermittent schedule in which the time between a behavior and the following consequences varies around a specified average

Fixed ratio reinforcement schedule an intermittent schedule in which consequences are delivered following a specific number of behaviors

Review 4: Reinforcement Theory

> Reinforcement theory says that behavior is a function of its consequences. Reinforcement has two parts: reinforcement contingencies and schedules of reinforcement. The four kinds of reinforcement contingencies are positive reinforcement and negative reinforcement, which strengthen behavior, and punishment and extinction, which weaken behavior. There are two kinds of reinforcement schedules, continuous and intermittent; intermittent schedules, in turn, can be divided into fixed and variable interval schedules and fixed and variable ratio schedules.

Review 5: Goal-Setting Theory

> A goal is a target, objective, or result that someone tries to accomplish. Goal-setting theory says that people will be motivated to the extent to which they accept specific, challenging goals and receive feedback that indicates their progress toward goal achievement. The basic components of goal-setting theory are goal specificity, goal difficulty, goal acceptance, and performance feedback. Goal specificity is the extent to which goals are detailed, exact, and unambiguous. Goal difficulty is the extent to which a goal is hard or challenging to accomplish. Goal acceptance is the extent to which people consciously understand and agree to goals. Performance feedback is information about the quality or quantity of past performance and indicates whether progress is being made toward the accomplishment of a goal.

Motivating with the Integrated Model

MOTIVATING WITH	MANAGERS SHOULD . . .
THE BASICS	• Ask people what their needs are. • Satisfy lower-order needs first. • Expect people's needs to change. • As needs change and lower-order needs are satisfied, satisfy higher-order needs by looking for ways to allow employees to experience intrinsic rewards.
EQUITY THEORY	• Look for and correct major inequities. • Reduce employees' inputs. • Make sure decision-making processes are fair.
EXPECTANCY THEORY	• Systematically gather information to find out what employees want from their jobs. • Take specific steps to link rewards to individual performance in a way that is clear and understandable to employees. • Empower employees to make decisions if management really wants them to believe that their hard work and efforts will lead to good performance.
REINFORCEMENT THEORY	• Identify, measure, analyze, intervene, and evaluate critical performance-related behaviors. • Don't reinforce the wrong behaviors. • Correctly administer punishment at the appropriate time. • Choose the simplest and most effective schedules of reinforcement.
GOAL-SETTING THEORY	• Assign specific, challenging goals. • Make sure workers truly accept organizational goals. • Provide frequent, specific, performance-related feedback.

Variable ratio reinforcement schedule an intermittent schedule in which consequences are delivered following a different number of behaviors, sometimes more and sometimes less, that vary around a specified average number of behaviors

Goal a target, objective, or result that someone tries to accomplish

Goal-setting theory a theory that states that people will be motivated to the extent to which they accept specific, challenging goals and receive feedback that indicates their progress toward goal achievement

Goal specificity the extent to which goals are detailed, exact, and unambiguous

Goal difficulty the extent to which a goal is hard or challenging to accomplish

Goal acceptance the extent to which people consciously understand and agree to goals

Performance feedback information about the quality or quantity of past performance that indicates whether progress is being made toward the accomplishment of a goal

LEARNING OUTCOMES

Review 1: Leaders Versus Managers

> Management is getting work done through others; leadership is the process of influencing others to achieve group or organizational goals. Leaders are different from managers. The primary difference is that leaders are concerned with doing the right thing, while managers are concerned with doing things right. Organizations need both managers and leaders. But, in general, companies are overmanaged and underled.

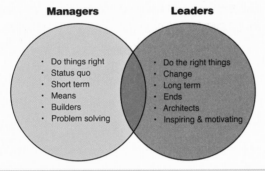

Managers
- Do things right
- Status quo
- Short term
- Means
- Builders
- Problem solving

Leaders
- Do the right things
- Change
- Long term
- Ends
- Architects
- Inspiring & motivating

Review 2: Who Leaders Are and What Leaders Do

> Trait theory says that effective leaders possess traits or characteristics that differentiate them from nonleaders. Those traits are drive, the desire to lead, honesty/integrity, self-confidence, emotional stability, cognitive ability, and knowledge of the business. Traits alone aren't enough for successful leadership; however, leaders who have these traits (or many of them) must also behave in ways that encourage people to achieve group or organizational goals. Two key leader behaviors are initiating structure, which improves subordinate performance, and consideration, which improves subordinate satisfaction. There is no "best" combination of these behaviors. The "best" leadership style depends on the situation.

Review 3: Putting Leaders in the Right Situation: Fiedler's Contingency Theory

> Fiedler's theory assumes that leaders are effective when their work groups perform well, that leaders are unable to change their leadership styles, that leadership styles must be matched to the proper situation, and that favorable situations permit leaders to influence group members. According to the Least Preferred Coworker (LPC) scale, there are two basic leadership styles. People who describe their LPC in a positive way have relationship-oriented leadership styles. By contrast, people who describe their LPC in a negative way have task-oriented leadership styles. Situational favorableness, which occurs when leaders can influence followers, is determined by leader-member relations, task structure, and position power. In general, relationship-oriented leaders with high LPC scores are better leaders under moderately favorable situations, while task-oriented leaders with low LPC scores are better leaders in highly favorable and unfavorable situations. Since Fiedler assumes that leaders are incapable of changing their leadership styles, the key is to accurately measure and match leaders to situations or to teach leaders how to change situational factors. Though matching or placing leaders in appropriate situations works well, "reengineering situations" to fit leadership styles doesn't because of the complexity of the model, which makes it difficult for people to understand.

KEY TERMS

Leadership the process of influencing others to achieve group or organizational goals

Trait theory a leadership theory that holds that effective leaders possess a similar set of traits or characteristics

Traits relatively stable characteristics, such as abilities, psychological motives, or consistent patterns of behavior

Initiating structure the degree to which a leader structures the roles of followers by setting goals, giving directions, setting deadlines, and assigning tasks

Consideration the extent to which a leader is friendly, approachable, and supportive and shows concern for employees

Leadership style the way a leader generally behaves toward followers

Contingency theory a leadership theory that states that in order to maximize work group performance, leaders must be matched to the situation that best fits their leadership style

Situational favorableness the degree to which a particular situation either permits or denies a leader the chance to influence the behavior of group members

Leader-member relations the degree to which followers respect, trust, and like their leaders

Task structure the degree to which the requirements of a subordinate's tasks are clearly specified

Position power the degree to which leaders are able to hire, fire, reward, and punish workers

Path-goal theory a leadership theory that states that leaders can increase subordinate satisfaction and performance by clarifying and clearing the paths to goals and by increasing the number and kinds of rewards available for goal attainment

Directive leadership a leadership style in which the leader lets employees know precisely what is expected of them, gives them specific guidelines for performing tasks, schedules work, sets standards of performance, and makes sure that people follow standard rules and regulations

Supportive leadership a leadership style in which the leader is friendly and approachable, shows concern for employees and their welfare and treats them as equals, and creates a friendly climate

Participative leadership a leadership style in which the leader consults employees for their suggestions and input before making decisions

Achievement-oriented leadership a leadership style in which the leader sets challenging goals, has high expectations of employees, and displays confidence that employees will assume responsibility and put forth extraordinary effort

Normative decision theory a theory that suggests how leaders can determine an appropriate amount of employee participation when making decisions

Strategic leadership the ability to anticipate, envision, maintain flexibility, think strategically, and work with others to initiate changes that will create a positive future for an organization

Visionary leadership leadership that creates a positive image of the future that motivates organizational members and provides direction for future planning and goal setting

Charismatic leadership the behavioral tendencies and personal characteristics of leaders that create an exceptionally strong relationship between them and their followers

Ethical charismatics charismatic leaders who provide developmental opportunities for followers, are open to positive and negative feedback, recognize others' contributions, share information, and have moral standards that emphasize the larger interests of the group, organization, or society

Unethical charismatics charismatic leaders who control and manipulate followers, do what is best for themselves instead of their organizations, want to hear only positive feedback, share only information that is beneficial to themselves, and have moral standards that put their interests before everyone else's

Transformational leadership leadership that generates awareness and acceptance of a group's purpose and mission and gets employees to see beyond their own needs and self-interests for the good of the group

Transactional leadership leadership based on an exchange process, in which followers are rewarded for good performance and punished for poor performance

Review 4: Adapting Leader Behavior: Path-Goal Theory

> Path-goal theory states that leaders can increase subordinate satisfaction and performance by clarifying and clearing the paths to goals and by increasing the number and kinds of rewards available for goal attainment. For this to work, however, leader behavior must be a source of immediate or future satisfaction for followers and must complement and not duplicate the characteristics of followers' work environments. In contrast to Fiedler's contingency theory, path-goal theory assumes that leaders can and do change and adapt their leadership styles (directive, supportive, participative, and achievement oriented), depending on their subordinates (experience, perceived ability and internal or external locus of control) and the environment in which those subordinates work (task structure, formal authority system, and primary work group).

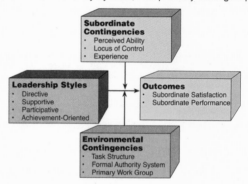

Review 5: Adapting Leader Behavior: Normative Decision Theory

> The normative decision theory helps leaders decide how much employee participation should be used when making decisions. Using the right degree of employee participation improves the quality of decisions and the extent to which employees accept and are committed to decisions. The theory specifies five different decision styles or ways of making decisions: autocratic decisions (AI or AII), consultative decisions (CI or CII), and group decisions (GII). The theory improves decision quality via the quality, leader information, subordinate information, goal congruence, and problem structure decision rules. The theory improves employee commitment and acceptance via the commitment probability, subordinate conflict, and commitment requirement decision rules. These decision rules help leaders improve decision quality and follower acceptance and commitment by eliminating decision styles that don't fit the decision or situation they're facing. Normative decision theory then operationalizes these decision rules in the form of yes/no questions, as shown in the decision tree displayed in Exhibit 14.8.

Review 6: Visionary Leadership

> Strategic leadership requires visionary, charismatic, and transformational leadership. Visionary leadership creates a positive image of the future that motivates organizational members and provides direction for future planning and goal setting. Charismatic leaders have strong, confident, dynamic personalities that attract followers, enable the leader to create strong bonds, and inspire followers to accomplish the leader's vision. Followers of ethical charismatic leaders work harder, are more committed and satisfied, are better performers, and are more likely to trust their leaders. Followers can be just as supportive and committed to unethical charismatics, but these leaders can pose a tremendous risk for companies. Unethical charismatics control and manipulate followers and do what is best for themselves instead of their organizations. Transformational leadership goes beyond charismatic leadership by generating awareness and acceptance of a group's purpose and mission and by getting employees to see beyond their own needs and self-interests for the good of the group. The four components of transformational leadership are charisma or idealized influence, inspirational motivation, intellectual stimulation, and individualized consideration.

LEARNING OUTCOMES

Review 1: Perception and Communication Problems

> Perception is the process by which people attend to, organize, interpret, and retain information from their environments. Perception is not a straightforward process, however. Because of perceptual filters, such as selective perception and closure, people exposed to the same information stimuli often end up with very different perceptions and understandings. Perception-based differences can also lead to differences in the attributions (internal or external) that managers and workers make when explaining workplace behavior. In general, workers are more likely to explain behavior from a defensive bias, in which they attribute problems to external causes (i.e., the situation). Managers, on the other hand, tend to commit the fundamental attribution error, attributing problems to internal causes (i.e., the worker associated with a mistake or error). Consequently, when things go wrong, it's common for managers to blame workers and for workers to blame the situation or context in which they do their jobs. Finally, this problem is compounded by a self-serving bias that leads people to attribute successes to internal causes and failures to external causes. So, when workers receive negative feedback from managers, they may become defensive and emotional and not hear what their managers have to say. In short, perceptions and attributions represent a significant challenge to effective communication and understanding in organizations.

BASIC PERCEPTION PROCESS

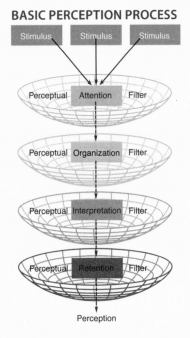

Review 2: Kinds of Communication

> Organizational communication depends on the communication process, formal and informal communication channels, one-on-one communication, and nonverbal communication. The major components of the communication process are the sender, the receiver, noise, and feedback. Senders often mistakenly assume that they can pipe their intended messages directly into receivers' heads with perfect clarity. Formal communication channels, such as downward, upward, and horizontal communication, carry organizationally approved messages and information. By contrast, the informal communication channel, called the "grapevine," arises out of curiosity and is carried out through gossip or cluster chains. There are two kinds of one-on-one communication. Coaching is used to improve on-the-job performance while counseling is used to communicate about non-job-related issues affecting job performance. Nonverbal communication, such as kinesics and paralanguage, accounts for as much as 93 percent of a message's content and understanding.

THE INTERPERSONAL COMMUNICATION PROCESS

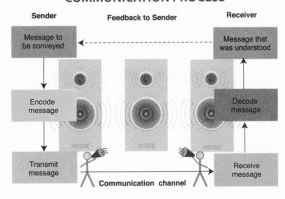

KEY TERMS

Communication the process of transmitting information from one person or place to another

Perception the process by which individuals attend to, organize, interpret, and retain information from their environments

Perceptual filters the personality-, psychology-, or experience-based differences that influence people to ignore or pay attention to particular stimuli

Selective perception the tendency to notice and accept objects and information consistent with our values, beliefs, and expectations, while ignoring or screening out or not accepting inconsistent information

Closure the tendency to fill in gaps of missing information by assuming that what we don't know is consistent with what we already know

Attribution theory a theory that states that we all have a basic need to understand and explain the causes of other people's behavior

Defensive bias the tendency for people to perceive themselves as personally and situationally similar to someone who is having difficulty or trouble

Fundamental attribution error the tendency to ignore external causes of behavior and to attribute other people's actions to internal causes

Self-serving bias the tendency to overestimate our value by attributing successes to ourselves (internal causes) and attributing failures to others or the environment (external causes)

Encoding putting a message into a written, verbal, or symbolic form that can be recognized and understood by the receiver

Decoding the process by which the receiver translates the written, verbal, or symbolic form of a message into an understood message

Feedback to sender in the communication process, a return message to the sender that indicates the receiver's understanding of the message

Noise anything that interferes with the transmission of the intended message

Jargon vocabulary particular to a profession or group

Formal communication channel the system of official channels that carry organizationally approved messages and information

Downward communication communication that flows from higher to lower levels in an organization

Upward communication communication that flows from lower to higher levels in an organization

Horizontal communication communication that flows among managers and workers who are at the same organizational level

Informal communication channel ("grapevine") the transmission of messages from employee to employee outside of formal communication channels

Coaching communicating with someone for the direct purpose of improving the person's on-the-job performance or behavior

Counseling communicating with someone about non-job-related issues that may be affecting or interfering with the person's performance

Nonverbal communication any communication that doesn't involve words

Kinesics movements of the body and face

Paralanguage the pitch, rate, tone, volume, and speaking pattern (i.e., use of silences, pauses, or hesitations) of one's voice

Communication medium the method used to deliver an oral or written message

Hearing the act or process of perceiving sounds

Listening making a conscious effort to hear

Active listening assuming half the responsibility for successful communication by actively giving the speaker nonjudgmental feedback that shows you've accurately heard what he or she said

Empathetic listening understanding the speaker's perspective and personal frame of reference and giving feedback that conveys that understanding to the speaker

Destructive feedback feedback that disapproves without any intention of being helpful and almost always causes a negative or defensive reaction in the recipient

Constructive feedback feedback intended to be helpful, corrective, and/or encouraging

Online discussion forums the in-house equivalent of Internet newsgroups. By using Web- or software-based discussion tools that are available across the company, employees can easily ask questions and share knowledge with each other.

Televised/videotaped speeches and meetings speeches and meetings originally made to a smaller audience that are either simultaneously broadcast to other locations in the company or videotaped for subsequent distribution and viewing

Organizational silence when employees withhold information about organizational problems or issues

Company hotlines phone numbers that anyone in the company can call anonymously to leave information for upper management

Survey feedback information that is collected by surveys from organizational members and then compiled, disseminated, and used to develop action plans for improvement

Blog a personal Web site that provides personal opinions or recommendations, news summaries, and reader comments

---

Review 3: Managing One-on-One Communication

> One-on-one communication can be managed by choosing the right communication medium, being a good listener, and giving effective feedback. Managers generally prefer oral communication because it provides the opportunity to ask questions and assess nonverbal communication. Oral communication is best suited to complex, ambiguous, or emotionally laden topics. Written communication is best suited for delivering straightforward messages and information. Listening is important for managerial success, but most people are terrible listeners. To improve your listening skills, choose to be an active listener (clarify responses, paraphrase, and summarize) and an empathetic listener (show your desire to understand, reflect feelings). Feedback can be constructive or destructive. To be constructive, feedback must be immediate, focused on specific behaviors, and problem oriented.

Review 4: Managing Organization-Wide Communication

> Managers need methods for managing organization-wide communication and for making themselves accessible so that they can hear what employees throughout their organizations are feeling and thinking. Email, online discussion forums, televised/videotaped speeches and conferences, and broadcast voice mail make it much easier for managers to improve message transmission and "get the message out." By contrast, anonymous company hotlines, survey feedback, frequent informal meetings, and surprise visits help managers avoid organizational silence and improve reception by hearing what others in the organization feel and think. Monitoring internal and external blogs is another way to find out what people are saying and thinking about your organization.

LEARNING OUTCOMES

Review 1: The Control Process

> The control process begins by setting standards, measuring performance, and then comparing performance to the standards. The better a company's information and measurement systems, the easier it is to make these comparisons. The control process continues by identifying and analyzing performance deviations, and then developing and implementing programs for corrective action. However, control is a continuous, dynamic, cybernetic process, not a onetime achievement or result. Control requires frequent managerial attention. The three basic control methods are feedback control (after-the-fact performance information), concurrent control (simultaneous performance information), and feedforward control (preventive performance information). Control, however, has regulation costs and unanticipated consequences and therefore isn't always worthwhile or possible.

Cybernetic Control Process

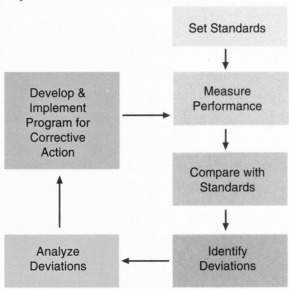

Source: H. Koontz & R. W. Bradspies, "Managing through Feedforward Control: A Future-Directed View," *Business Horizons*, June 1972, 25–36. Reprinted with permission from *Business Horizons*, © 1972 by the Trustees at Indiana University, Kelley School of Business.

Review 2: Control Methods

> There are five methods of control: bureaucratic, objective, normative, concertive, and self-control (self-management). Bureaucratic and objective controls are top-down, management-based, and measurement-based. Normative and concertive controls represent shared forms of control because they evolve from company-wide or team-based beliefs and values. Self-control, or self-management, is a control system in which managers turn much, but not all, control over to the individuals themselves.

Bureaucratic control is based on organizational policies, rules, and procedures. Objective controls are based on reliable measures of behavior or outputs. Normative control is based on strong corporate beliefs and careful hiring practices. Concertive control is based on the development of values, beliefs, and rules in autonomous work groups. Self-control is based on individuals' setting their own goals, monitoring themselves, and rewarding or punishing themselves with respect to goal achievement.

We end this section (flip over card) by noting that each of these control methods may be more or less appropriate depending on the circumstances.

KEY TERMS

Control a regulatory process of establishing standards to achieve organizational goals, comparing actual performance against the standards, and taking corrective action when necessary

Standards a basis of comparison for measuring the extent to which various kinds of organizational performance are satisfactory or unsatisfactory

Benchmarking the process of identifying outstanding practices, processes, and standards in other companies and adapting them to your company

Cybernetic the process of steering or keeping on course

Feedback control a mechanism for gathering information about performance deficiencies after they occur

Concurrent control a mechanism for gathering information about performance deficiencies as they occur, thereby eliminating or shortening the delay between performance and feedback

Feedforward control a mechanism for monitoring performance inputs rather than outputs to prevent or minimize performance deficiencies before they occur

Control loss the situation in which behavior and work procedures do not conform to standards

Regulation costs the costs associated with implementing or maintaining control

Cybernetic feasibility the extent to which it is possible to implement each step in the control process

Bureaucratic control the use of hierarchical authority to influence employee behavior by rewarding or punishing employees for compliance or noncompliance with organizational policies, rules, and procedures

Objective control the use of observable measures of worker behavior or outputs to assess performance and influence behavior

Behavior control the regulation of the behaviors and actions that workers perform on the job

Output control the regulation of workers' results or outputs through rewards and incentives

Normative control the regulation of workers' behavior and decisions through widely shared organizational values and beliefs

Concertive control the regulation of workers' behavior and decisions through work group values and beliefs

Self-control (self-management) a control system in which managers and workers control their own behavior by setting their own goals, monitoring their own progress, and rewarding themselves for goal achievement

Balanced scorecard measurement of organizational performance in four equally important areas: finances, customers, internal operations, and innovation and learning

Suboptimization performance improvement in one part of an organization but at the expense of decreased performance in another part

Cash flow analysis a type of analysis that predicts how changes in a business will affect its ability to take in more cash than it pays out

Balance sheets accounting statements that provide a snapshot of a company's financial position at a particular time

Income statements accounting statements, also called "profit and loss statements," that show what has happened to an organization's income, expenses, and net profit over a period of time

Financial ratios calculations typically used to track a business's liquidity (cash), efficiency, and profitability over time compared to other businesses in its industry

Budgets quantitative plans through which managers decide how to allocate available money to best accomplish company goals

Economic value added (EVA) the amount by which company profits (revenues, minus expenses, minus taxes) exceed the cost of capital in a given year

Customer defections a performance assessment in which companies identify which customers are leaving and measure the rate at which they are leaving

Value customer perception that the product quality is excellent for the price offered

When to Use Different Methods of Control

BUREAUCRATIC CONTROL	• When it is necessary to standardize operating procedures • When it is necessary to establish limits
BEHAVIOR CONTROL	• When it is easier to measure what workers do on the job than what they accomplish on the job • When "cause-effect" relationships are clear, that is, when companies know which behaviors will lead to success and which won't • When good measures of worker behavior can be created
OUTPUT CONTROL	• When it is easier to measure what workers accomplish on the job than what they do on the job • When good measures of worker output can be created • When it is possible to set clear goals and standards for worker output • When "cause-effect" relationships are unclear
NORMATIVE CONTROL	• When organizational culture, values, and beliefs are strong • When it is difficult to create good measures of worker behavior • When it is difficult to create good measures of worker output
CONCERTIVE CONTROL	• When responsibility for task accomplishment is given to autonomous work groups • When management wants workers to take "ownership" of their behavior and outputs • When management desires a strong form of worker-based control
SELF-CONTROL	• When workers are intrinsically motivated to do their jobs well • When it is difficult to create good measures of worker behavior • When it is difficult to create good measures of worker output • When workers have or are taught self-control and self-leadership skills

Sources: L. J. Kirsch, "The Management of Complex Tasks in Organizations: Controlling the Systems Development Process," *Organization Science* 7 (1996): 1–21; S. A. Snell, "Control Theory in Strategic Human Resource Management: The Mediating Effect of Administrative Information," *Academy of Management Journal* 35 (1992): 292–327.

Review 3: What to Control?

> Deciding what to control is just as important as deciding whether to control or how to control. In most companies, performance is measured using financial measures alone. However, the balanced scorecard encourages managers to measure and control company performance from four perspectives: financial, customers, internal operations, and innovation and learning. Traditionally, financial control has been achieved through cash flow analysis, balance sheets, income statements, financial ratios, and budgets. (For a refresher on these traditional financial control tools, see the next card, which is a Financial Review Card.) Another way to measure and control financial performance, however, is through economic value added (EVA). Unlike traditional financial measures, EVA helps managers assess whether they are performing well enough to pay the cost of the capital needed to run the business. Instead of using customer satisfaction surveys to measure performance, companies should pay attention to customer defectors, who are more likely to speak up about what the company is doing wrong. Performance of internal operations is often measured in terms of quality, which is defined in three ways: excellence, value, and conformance to expectations. Minimization of waste has become an important part of innovation and learning in companies. The four levels of waste minimization are waste prevention and reduction, recycling and reuse, waste treatment, and waste disposal.

Calculating Economic Value Added (EVA)

1.	Calculate net operating profit after taxes (NOPAT).	$3,500,000
2.	Identify how much capital the company has invested (i.e., spent).	$16,800,000
3.	Determine the cost (i.e., rate) paid for capital (usually between 5 percent and 13 percent).	10%
4.	Multiply capital used (Step 2) times cost of capital (Step 3).	(10% × $16,800,000) = $1,680,000
5.	Subtract the total dollar cost of capital from net profit after taxes.	$3,500,000 OPTA −$1,680,000 Total cost of capital $1,820,000 Economic value added

Basic Accounting Tools for Controlling Financial Performance

STEPS FOR A BASIC CASH FLOW ANALYSIS

1. Forecast sales (steady, up, or down).
2. Project changes in anticipated cash inflows (as a result of changes).
3. Project anticipated cash outflows (as a result of changes).
4. Project net cash flows by combining anticipated cash inflows and outflows.

PARTS OF A BASIC BALANCE SHEET (ASSETS = LIABILITIES + OWNER'S EQUITY)

1. Assets
   a. Current Assets (cash, short-term investment, marketable securities, accounts receivable, etc.)
   b. Fixed Assets (land, buildings, machinery, equipment, etc.)

2. Liabilities
   a. Current Liabilities (accounts payable, notes payable, taxes payable, etc.)
   b. Long-Term Liabilities (long-term debt, deferred income taxes, etc.)

3. Owner's Equity
   a. Preferred stock and common stock
   b. Additional paid-in capital
   c. Retained earnings

BASIC INCOME STATEMENT

```
   SALES REVENUE
−  sales returns and allowances
+  other income
=  NET REVENUE
−  cost of goods sold (beginning inventory, costs of goods purchased, ending inventory)
=  GROSS PROFIT
−  total operating expenses (selling, general, and administrative expenses)
=  INCOME FROM OPERATIONS
−  interest expense
=  PRETAX INCOME
−  income taxes
=  NET INCOME
```

Common Kinds of Budgets

Revenue Budgets—used to project or forecast future sales.	• Accuracy of projection depends on economy, competitors, sales force estimates, etc. • Determined by estimating future sales volume and sales prices for all products and services.
Expense Budgets—used within departments and divisions to determine how much will be spent on various supplies, projects, or activities.	• One of the first places that companies look for cuts when trying to lower expenses.
Profit Budgets—used by profit centers, which have "profit and loss" responsibility.	• Profit budgets combine revenue and expense budgets into one budget. • Typically used in large businesses with multiple plants and divisions.
Cash Budgets—used to forecast how much cash a company will have on hand to meet expenses.	• Similar to cash flow analyses. • Used to identify cash shortfalls, which must be covered to pay bills, or cash excesses, which should be invested for a higher return.
Capital Expenditure Budgets—used to forecast large, long-lasting investments in equipment, buildings, and property.	• Help managers identify funding that will be needed to pay for future expansion or strategic moves designed to increase competitive advantage.
Variable Budgets—used to project costs across varying levels of sales and revenues.	• Important because it is difficult to accurately predict sales revenue and volume. • Lead to more accurate budgeting with respect to labor, materials, and administrative expenses, which vary with sales volume and revenues. • Build flexibility into the budgeting process.

Common Financial Ratios

RATIOS	FORMULA	WHAT IT MEANS	WHEN TO USE
LIQUIDITY RATIOS			
Current Ratio	$\dfrac{\text{Current Assets}}{\text{Current Liabilities}}$	• Whether you have enough assets on hand to pay for short-term bills and obligations. • Higher is better. • Recommended level is two times as many current assets as current liabilities.	• Track monthly and quarterly. • Basic measure of your company's health.
Quick (Acid Test) Ratio	$\dfrac{\text{(Current Assets} - \text{Inventories)}}{\text{Current Liabilities}}$	• Stricter than current ratio. • Whether you have enough (i.e., cash) to pay short-term bills and obligations. • Higher is better. • Recommended level is one or higher.	• Track monthly. • Also calculate quick ratio with potential customers to evaluate whether they're likely to pay you in a timely manner.
LEVERAGE RATIOS			
Debt to Equity	$\dfrac{\text{Total Liabilities}}{\text{Total Equity}}$	• Indicates how much the company is leveraged (in debt) by comparing what is owed (liabilities) to what is owned (equity). • Lower is better. A high debt-to-equity ratio could indicate that the company has too much debt. • Recommended level depends on industry.	• Track monthly. • Lenders often use this to determine the creditworthiness of a business (i.e., whether to approve additional loans).
Debt Coverage	$\dfrac{\text{(Net Profit} + \text{Noncash Expense)}}{\text{Debt}}$	• Indicates how well cash flow covers debt payments. • Higher is better.	• Track monthly. • Lenders look at this ratio to determine if there is adequate cash to make loan payments.
EFFICIENCY RATIOS			
Inventory Turnover	$\dfrac{\text{Cost of Goods Sold}}{\text{Average Value of Inventory}}$	• Whether you're making efficient use of inventory. • Higher is better, indicating that inventory (dollars) isn't purchased (spent) until needed. • Recommended level depends on industry.	• Track monthly by using a 12-month rolling average.
Average Collections Period	$\dfrac{\text{Accounts Receivable}}{\text{(Annual Net Credit Sales Divided by 365)}}$	• Shows on average how quickly your customers are paying their bills. • Recommended level is no more than 15 days longer than credit terms. If credit is net 30 days, then average should not be longer than 45 days.	• Track monthly. • Use to determine how long company's money is being tied up in customer credit.
PROFITABILITY RATIOS			
Gross Profit Margin	$\dfrac{\text{Gross Profit}}{\text{Total Sales}}$	• Shows how efficiently a business is using its materials and labor in the production process. • Higher is better, indicating that a profit can be made if fixed costs are controlled.	• Track monthly. • Analyze when unsure about product or service pricing. • Low margin compared to competitors means you're underpricing.
Return on Equity	$\dfrac{\text{Net Income}}{\text{Owner's Equity}}$	• Shows what was earned on your investment in the business during a particular period. Often called "return on investment." • Higher is better.	• Track quarterly and annually. • Use to compare to what you might have earned on the stock market, bonds, or government Treasury bills during the same period.

LEARNING OUTCOMES

Review 1: Strategic Importance of Information

> The first company to use new information technology to substantially lower costs or differentiate products or services often gains first-mover advantage, higher profits, and larger market share. Creating a first-mover advantage can be difficult, expensive, and risky, however. According to the resource-based view of information technology, sustainable competitive advantage occurs when information technology adds value, is different across firms, and is difficult to create or acquire.

Using Information Technology to Sustain a Competitive Advantage

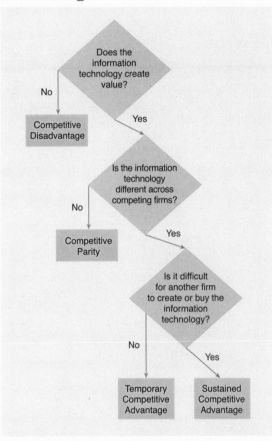

Source: Adapted from F. J. Mata, W. L. Fuerst, & J. B. Barney, "Information Technology and Sustained Competitive Advantage: A Resource-Based Analysis," *MIS Quarterly* 19, no. 4 (December 1995): 487–505. Reprinted by special permission by the Society for Information Management and the Management Information Systems Research Center at the University of Minnesota.

Review 2: Characteristics and Costs of Useful Information

> Raw data are facts and figures. Raw data do not become information until they are in a form that can affect decisions and behavior. For information to be useful, it has to be reliable and valid (accurate), of sufficient quantity (complete), pertinent to the problems you're facing (relevant), and available when you need it (timely). Useful information does not come cheaply. The five costs of obtaining good information are the costs of acquiring, processing, storing, retrieving, and communicating information.

Review 3: Capturing, Processing, and Protecting Information

> Electronic data capture (bar codes, radio frequency identification [RFID] tags, scanners, and optical character recognition) is much faster, easier, and cheaper than manual data

KEY TERMS

Moore's law the prediction that every 18 months, the cost of computing will drop by 50 percent as computer-processing power doubles

Raw data facts and figures

Information useful data that can influence people's choices and behavior

First-mover advantage the strategic advantage that companies earn by being the first to use new information technology to substantially lower costs or to make a product or service different from that of competitors

Acquisition cost the cost of obtaining data that you don't have

Processing cost the cost of turning raw data into usable information

Storage cost the cost of physically or electronically archiving information for later use and retrieval

Retrieval cost the cost of accessing already-stored and processed information

Communication cost the cost of transmitting information from one place to another

Bar code a visual pattern that represents numerical data by varying the thickness and pattern of vertical bars

Radio frequency identification (RFID) tags tags containing minuscule microchips that transmit information via radio waves and can be used to track the number and location of the objects into which the tags have been inserted

Electronic scanners an electronic device that converts printed text and pictures into digital images

Optical character recognition the ability of software to convert digitized documents into ASCII (American Standard Code for Information Interchange) text that can be searched, read, and edited by word processing and other kinds of software

Processing information transforming raw data into meaningful information

Data mining the process of discovering patterns and relationships in large amounts of data

Data warehouse stores huge amounts of data that have been prepared for data mining analysis by being cleaned of errors and redundancy

Supervised data mining the process when the user tells the data mining software to look and test for specific patterns and relationships in a data set

Unsupervised data mining the process when the user simply tells the data mining software to uncover whatever patterns and relationships it can find in a data set

Association or affinity patterns when two or more database elements tend to occur together in a significant way

Sequence patterns when two or more database elements occur together in a significant pattern, but one of the elements precedes the other

Predictive patterns patterns that help identify database elements that are different

Data clusters when three or more database elements occur together (i.e., cluster) in a significant way

Protecting information the process of ensuring that data are reliably and consistently retrievable in a usable format for authorized users, but no one else

Authentication making sure potential users are who they claim to be

Authorization granting authenticated users approved access to data, software, and systems

Two-factor authentication authentication based on what users know, such as a password, and what they have in their possession, such as a secure ID card or key

Biometrics identifying users by unique, measurable body features, such as fingerprint recognition or iris scanning

Firewall a protective hardware or software device that sits between the computers in an internal organizational network and outside networks, such as the Internet

Virus a program or piece of code that, against your wishes, attaches itself to other programs on your computer and can trigger anything from a harmless flashing message to the reformatting of your hard drive to a systemwide network shutdown

Data encryption the transformation of data into complex, scrambled digital codes that can be unencrypted only by authorized users who possess unique decryption keys

Virtual private network (VPN) software that securely encrypts data sent by employees outside the company network, decrypts the data when they arrive within the company computer network, and does the same when data are sent back to employees outside the network

capture. Processing information means transforming raw data into meaningful information that can be applied to business decision making. Data mining helps managers with this transformation by discovering unknown patterns and relationships in data. Supervised data mining looks for patterns specified by managers, while unsupervised data mining looks for four general kinds of data patterns: association/affinity patterns, sequence patterns, predictive patterns, and data clusters. Protecting information ensures that data are reliably and consistently retrievable in a usable format by authorized users, but no one else. Authentication and authorization, firewalls, antivirus software for PCs and corporate email and network servers, data encryption, virtual private networks, and Web-based secure sockets layer (SSL) encryption are some of the best ways to protect information. Be careful with wireless networks, which are easily compromised even when security and encryption protocols are in place.

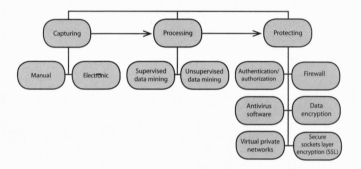

Review 4: Accessing and Sharing Information and Knowledge

> Executive information systems, intranets, and corporate portals facilitate internal sharing and access to company information and transactions. Electronic data interchange and the Internet allow external groups, like suppliers and customers, to easily access company information. Both decrease costs by reducing or eliminating data entry, data errors, and paperwork and by speeding up communication. Organizations use decision support systems and expert systems to capture and share specialized knowledge with nonexpert employees.

Secure sockets layer (SSL) encryption Internet browser–based encryption that provides secure off-site Web access to some data and programs

Executive information system (EIS) a data processing system that uses internal and external data sources to provide the information needed to monitor and analyze organizational performance

Intranets private company networks that allow employees to easily access, share, and publish information using Internet software

Corporate portal a hybrid of executive information systems and intranets that allows managers and employees to use a Web browser to gain access to customized company information and to complete specialized transactions

Electronic data interchange (EDI) when two companies convert their purchase and ordering information to a standardized format to enable the direct electronic transmission of that information from one company's computer system to the other company's computer system

Extranets networks thatallow companies to exchange information and conduct transactions with outsiders by providing them direct, Web-based access to authorized parts of a company's intranet or information system

Knowledge the understanding that one gains from information

Decision support system (DSS) an information system that helps managers understand specific kinds of problems and potential solutions and analyze the impact of different decision options using "what if" scenarios

Expert system an information system that contains the specialized knowledge and decision rules used by experts and experienced decision makers so that nonexperts can draw on this knowledge base to make decisions

REVIEW card/

LEARNING OUTCOMES

Review 1: Productivity

> Productivity is a measure of how many inputs it takes to produce or create an output. The greater the output from one input, or the fewer inputs it takes to create an output, the higher the productivity. Partial productivity measures how much of a single kind of input, such as labor, is needed to produce an output. Multifactor productivity is an overall measure of productivity that indicates how much labor, capital, materials, and energy are needed to produce an output.

$$\text{Partial Productivity} = \frac{\text{Outputs}}{\text{Single Kind of Input}}$$

$$\frac{\text{Multifactor}}{\text{Productivity}} = \frac{\text{Outputs}}{(\text{Labor} + \text{Capital} + \text{Materials} + \text{Energy})}$$

Review 2: Quality

> Quality can mean a product or service free of deficiencies or the characteristics of a product or service that satisfy customer needs. Quality products usually possess three characteristics: reliability, serviceability, and durability. Quality service means reliability, tangibles, responsiveness, assurance, and empathy. ISO 9000 is a series of five international standards for achieving consistency in quality management and quality assurance, while ISO 14000 is a set of standards for minimizing an organization's harmful effects on the environment. The Baldrige National Quality Award recognizes U.S. companies for their achievements in quality and business performance. Each year, three Baldrige Awards may be given for manufacturing, service, small business, education, and health care. Total quality management (TQM) is an integrated organization-wide strategy for improving product and service quality. TQM is based on three mutually reinforcing principles: customer focus and satisfaction, continuous improvement, and teamwork.

Review 3: Service Operations

> Services are different from goods. Goods are produced, tangible, and storable. Services are performed, intangible, and perishable. Likewise, managing service operations is different from managing production operations. The service-profit chain indicates that success begins with internal service quality, meaning how well management treats service employees. Internal service quality leads to employee satisfaction and service capability, which, in turn, lead to high-value service to customers, customer satisfaction, customer loyalty, and long-term profits and growth. Keeping existing customers is far more cost-effective than finding new ones. Consequently, to prevent disgruntled customers from leaving, some companies are empowering service employees to perform service recovery—restoring customer satisfaction to strongly

Service-Profit Chain

Internal Service Quality →

Employee Satisfaction

Service Capability — High Value Service

= ✔Customer Satisfaction ✔Customer Loyalty lead to

Upper Management — Employees — Customers

Profit & Growth

Sources: R. Hallowell, L. A. Schlesinger, & J. Zornitsky, "Internal Service Quality, Customer and Job Satisfaction: Linkages and Implications for Management," *Human Resource Planning* 19 (1996): 20–31; J. L. Heskett, T. O. Jones, G. W. Loveman, W. E. Sasser, Jr., & L. A. Schlesinger, "Putting the Service-Profit Chain to Work," *Harvard Business Review*, March–April 1994, 164–174.

KEY TERMS

Productivity a measure of performance that indicates how many inputs it takes to produce or create an output

Partial productivity a measure of performance that indicates how much of a particular kind of input it takes to produce an output

Multifactor productivity an overall measure of performance that indicates how much labor, capital, materials, and energy it takes to produce an output

Quality a product or service free of deficiencies, or the characteristics of a product or service that satisfy customer needs

ISO 9000 a series of five international standards, from ISO 9000 to ISO 9004, for achieving consistency in quality management and quality assurance in companies throughout the world

ISO 14000 a series of international standards for managing, monitoring, and minimizing an organization's harmful effects on the environment

Total quality management (TQM) an integrated, principle-based, organization-wide strategy for improving product and service quality

Customer focus an organizational goal to concentrate on meeting customers' needs at all levels of the organization

Customer satisfaction an organizational goal to provide products or services that meet or exceed customers' expectations

Continuous improvement an organization's ongoing commitment to constantly assess and improve the processes and procedures used to create products and services

Variation a deviation in the form, condition, or appearance of a product from the quality standard for that product

Teamwork collaboration between managers and nonmanagers, across business functions, and between companies, customers, and suppliers

Service recovery restoring customer satisfaction to strongly dissatisfied customers

Make-to-order operation a manufacturing operation that does not start processing or assembling products until a customer order is received

Assemble-to-order operation a manufacturing operation that divides manufacturing processes into separate parts or modules that are combined to create semicustomized products

Make-to-stock operation a manufacturing operation that orders parts and assembles standardized products before receiving customer orders

Manufacturing flexibility the degree to which manufacturing operations can easily and quickly change the number, kind, and characteristics of products they produce

Continuous-flow production a manufacturing operation that produces goods at a continuous, rather than a discrete, rate

Line-flow production manufacturing processes that are preestablished, occur in a serial or linear manner, and are dedicated to making one type of product

Batch production a manufacturing operation that produces goods in large batches in standard lot sizes

Job shops manufacturing operations that handle custom orders or small batch jobs

Inventory the amount and number of raw materials, parts, and finished products that a company has in its possession

Raw material inventories the basic inputs in a manufacturing process

Component parts inventories the basic parts used in manufacturing that are fabricated from raw materials

Work-in-process inventories partially finished goods consisting of assembled component parts

Finished goods inventories the final outputs of manufacturing operations

Average aggregate inventory average overall inventory during a particular time period

Stockout the situation when a company runs out of finished product

Inventory turnover the number of times per year that a company sells or "turns over" its average inventory

Ordering cost the costs associated with ordering inventory, including the cost of data entry, phone calls, obtaining bids, correcting mistakes, and determining when and how much inventory to order

Setup cost the costs of downtime and lost efficiency that occur when a machine is changed or adjusted to produce a different kind of inventory

Holding cost the cost of keeping inventory until it is used or sold, including storage, insurance, taxes, obsolescence, and opportunity costs

Stockout costs the costs incurred when a company runs out of a product, including transaction costs to replace inventory and the loss of customers' goodwill

Economic order quantity (EOQ) a system of formulas that minimizes ordering and holding costs and helps determine how much and how often inventory should be ordered

Just-in-time (JIT) inventory system an inventory system in which component parts arrive from suppliers just as they are needed at each stage of production

Kanban a ticket-based JIT system that indicates when to reorder inventory

Materials requirement planning (MRP) a production and inventory system that determines the production schedule, production batch sizes, and inventory needed to complete final products

Independent demand system an inventory system in which the level of one kind of inventory does not depend on another

Dependent demand system an inventory system in which the level of inventory depends on the number of finished units to be produced

dissatisfied customers—by giving them the authority and responsibility to immediately solve customer problems. The hope is that empowered service recovery will prevent customer defections.

Review 4: Manufacturing Operations

> Manufacturing operations produce physical goods. Manufacturing operations can be classified according to the amount of processing or assembly that occurs after receiving an order from a customer.

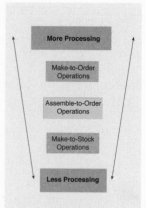

Manufacturing operations can also be classified in terms of flexibility, the degree to which the number, kind, and characteristics of products can easily and quickly be changed. Flexibility allows companies to respond quickly to competitors and customers and to reduce order lead times, but it can also lead to higher unit costs.

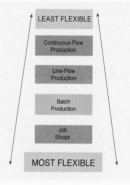

Review 5: Inventory

> There are four kinds of inventory: raw materials, component parts, work-in-process, and finished goods. Because companies incur ordering, setup, holding, and stockout costs when handling inventory, inventory costs can be enormous. To control those costs, companies measure and track inventory in three ways: average aggregate inventory, weeks of supply, and turnover. Companies meet the basic goals of inventory management (avoiding stockouts and reducing inventory without hurting daily operations) through economic order quantity (EOQ) formulas, just-in-time (JIT) inventory systems, and materials requirement planning (MRP).

$$EOQ = \sqrt{\frac{2DO}{4}}$$

Use EOQ formulas when inventory levels are independent, and use JIT and MRP when inventory levels are dependent on the number of products to be produced.